CONSTRUCTION MANAGEMENT and REAL ESTATE DEVELOPMENT

The textbook in two parts

Under the general scientific editorship of Professor P.G. Graboviy

Part I
CONSTRUCTION MANAGEMENT

4th edition revised and expanded

Russian Academy of Architecture and Construction Sciences recommended the book as textbook for students of educational institutions of higher education

08.03.01 “Construction” (bachelor’s level),
08.04.01 “Construction” (master’s level),
08.05.01 “Construction of unique buildings and structures” (engineer’s level),
08.06.01 “Engineering and construction technologies” (lecturer-researcher’s level)

ASV Construction

Stockholm, Sweden

2020

UDC 69.003: 005 (075.8)
BBK 65.31ya73-1

Publishing of the book was supported by LLC "Centr nezavisimoy ekspertizy sobstvennosti" (Center for Independent Expertise of Property, CIEP)

Under the General scientific editorship of Doctor of economy science, Professor P.G. Graboviy

Reviewers:

Department of construction management of the St. Petersburg State University of Architecture and Civil Engineering (head of the department, Candidate of economy science, docent, Drozdov A.D.);

Department of expertise and management of real estate of Kazan State State University of Architecture and Civil Engineering (head of the department, Doctor of economy science, docent, Sirazetdinov R.M.);

Academician of RAACS, Doctor of economy science, Professor Panibratov Yu.P.

Construction management and real estate development. Part I: Construction management. *4-th edition revised and expanded / under the general scientific editorship of Professor P.G. Graboviy.* **ASV Construction,** *2020. – 672 p.*

ISBN 978-91-982223-8-8

The textbook "Construction management and real estate development" is devoted to the problems of modern efficient and harmonious real estate management based on the life cycles of buildings and on the use a two-pronged scientific and practical concept, both management and development in the investment and construction sector.

The book shows the significant role of construction as a branch of material production in the national economy. This one presents modern relations between participants of investment and construction process as well as methods of construction management, pricing, conducting of tenders and contracts for the implementation of investment construction projects.

The issues presented in the first part such as construction control, acceptance, enter the completed real estate, fixed assets, infrastructure objects and modeling of construction production and construction management were described very well. The second part describes the problem of the foundations of real estate development.

The issues of investment resources and information technologies in construction, environmental expertise and protection of environment and organization of a recreational cluster with regard to timely control of changes are in the sphere of constant attention and control of specialists.

The questions of the construction management for erection of unique objects, "green" and low-rise cottage construction, as well as topics presented in the textbook of modern directions of improvement of the construction management based on an innovative platform are widely demanded in practice.

Systematic application of the author's organizational and development approach in relation to the structure of the educational material allows forming modern professional competences focused on complex and multilateral perception of construction management and real estate problems linked with life cycle of reproduction of various estate objects.

The textbook is intended for managers and specialists of firms, companies and enterprises, as well as for researchers, postgraduates and students interested in and studying practical issues of modern construction management and real estate development.

ISBN 978-91-982223-8-8

Authors

Part I:

Benuzh A.A., Candidate of Tech. Sciences, Associate Professor — sections 11.5–11.7, Chapter 11;

Bizhanov A. H., Doctor of Economics, Associate Professor — sections 8.1, 8.2, Chapter 8;

Bolotin S. A., Doctor of Technical Sciences, Professor, **Dadar A. H.,** Candidate of Technical Sciences, associate Professor — sections 9.5–9.9, Chapter 9;

Butyrin A. Yu., Doctor of law, Senior Researcher — sections 5.1, 5.2, Chapter 5;

Verstina N. G., Doctor of Economics, Professor, **Evseev E. G.,** Candidate of Physical and Mathematical Sciences, Associate Professor – Chapter 7

Volkov A. A., Doctor of Technical Sciences, Professor 9.3, 9.4, Chapter 9;

Volkov R. V., Candidate of Economics, Associate Professor — sections 3.5, 3.9, Chapter 3;

Ginzburg A.V., Doctor of Technical Sciences, Professor — 9.1, 9.2, Chapter 9;

Graboviy K. P., Doctor of Economics, Professor — sections 3.6–3.8, Chapter 3;

Graboviy P. G., Doctor of Economics, Professor — Introduction, General edition, sections 1.4–1.8, Chapter 1;

Grebenshchikov V. S., Candidate of Economics, Associate Professor — sections 10.4, Chapter 10;

Gusakova E. A., Doctor of Technical Sciences, Professor — sections 2.1–2.6, Chapter 2

Doan Zuong Hai, Candidate of Tech. Sciences, Associate Professor — sections 4.9, Chapter 4;

Ivanov A.V., Engineer — sections 2.7, 2.8, Chapter 2; sections 3.1–3.4, Chapter 3;

Kazarnovsky V. A., Candidate of Tech. Sciences, Associate Professor — sections 6.1–6.4, Chapter 6;

Korol E. A., Doctor of Technical Sciences, Professor, **Korol O. A.,** Candidate of Tech. Sciences, Associate Professor — section 6.5, Chapter 6;

Kulakov K. Yu., Doctor of Economics, Professor — sections 12.1-12.3, Chapter 12;

Lukinov V. A., Doctor of Economics, Professor — section. 5.8, Chapter 5;

Lunyakov M. A., Doctor of Economics, Professor — section 5.3–5.7, Chapter 5;

Mishchenko V. Ya., Doctor of Technical Sciences, Professor — section 12.4, Chapter 12;

Ovsyannikova T. Yu., Doctor of Economics, Professor — sections 1.1–1.4, Chapter 1; sections 4.1–4.8, Chapter 4;

Orlov A. K., Candidate of Economics, Associate Professor — section 8.3, Chapter 8;

Panchev A. V., Engineer — section 10.5, Chapter 10;

Simeonova N. E., Doctor of Economics, Professor — sections 8.4, 8.5, Chapter 8;

Telichenko V. I., Doctor of Technical Sciences, Professor 10.1–10.3, Chapter 10;

Khrustalev B. B., Doctor of Economics, Professor — sections 12.5–12.8, Chapter 12;

Sheina S. G., Doctor of Technical Sciences, Professor, **Vinogradov A. V.,** Candidate of Tech. Sciences, Associate Professor — sections 11.1-11.4, Chapter 11;

Part II:

Avilova I. P., Candidate of Economics, Associate Professor, **Naumov A. E.**, Candidate of Tech. Sciences, Associate Professor, **Le Van Thuong, Doctor of** Architecture, Associate Professor – sections 2.4–2.13, Chapter 2;

Baronin S. A., Doctor of Economics, Professor, **Grebenshchikov V. S.**, Candidate of Economics, Associate Professor — sections 10.3, Chapter 10;

Belyakov S. I., Candidate of Economics, Associate Professor — sections 11.3, 11.4, Chapter 11;

Bolotin S. A., Doctor of Tech. Sciences, Professor — section 11.2, Chapter 11;

Butyrin A. Yu. Doctor of law, Senior Researcher — section 5.2, Chapter 5;

Godovnikov S. V., Econ. — section 11.1, Chapter 11;

Graboviy K. P., Doctor of Economics, Professor, **Pavlov V. V.,** Candidate of Economics — sections 9.1–9.5, Chapter 9;

Graboviy P. G., Doctor of Economics, Professor — section 4.7, Chapter 4;

Kirillova A. N., Doctor of Economics, Professor – section 5.4, Chapter 5;

Kuzina O. N., Candidate of Tech. Sciences, Associate Professor — section 10.2, Chapter 10;

Kulakov K. Yu., Doctor of Economics, Professor — Chapter 6;

Lukmanova I. G., Doctor of Economics, Professor — section 4.6, Chapter 4;

Mishlanova M. Yu., Candidate of Tech. Sciences, Associate Professor — section 9.6, Chapter 9;

Narezhnaya T. K., Candidate of Economics, Associate Professor — section 10.1, Chapter 10;

Prykin B.V., Doctor of Tech. Sciences, Professor, **Prykina L.V.,** Doctor of Economics, Professor — section 1.8, Chapter 1;

Silka D. N., Doctor of Economics, Associate Professor — section 5.1, Chapter 5;

Sternik S. G., Doctor of Economics, Professor, **Fedotova M. A.,** Doctor of Economics, Professor — Chapter 7, Chapter 8;

Timofeev K. P., Econ. — section 5.3, Chapter 5;

Fedorovskaya A. A., Candidate of Tech. Sciences, Associate Professor — sections 1.1-1.7, Chapter 1;

Sheina S. G., Doctor of Tech. Sciences, Professor, **Girya L. V.,** Doctor of Economics, Professor — sections 2.1-2.3, Chapter 2

Yaskova N. Yu., Doctor of Economics, Professor — Chapter 3; sections 4.1–4.5, 4.7, 4.8, Chapter 4;

Under the General editorship of Doctor of Economics, Professor **P. G. Graboviy**

Contents

Contents of Part II

"REAL ESTATE DEVELOPMENT"

To the reader!

Construction, as the main branch of the national economy producing fixed assets, largely determines the possibility of functioning and development of all sectors of the national economy.

Even in times of recession and uncertainty in the external environment, the construction industry continues to perform two major tasks of life support of the population: production and economic and social.

This book reveals the purpose, objectives and content of the two main areas of construction activity: construction management and real estate development.

The material of both parts of the book allows readers to form modern professional competencies focused on a comprehensive, multifaceted perception of organizational, managerial, production and technological problems, taking into account the entire life cycle of real estate.

The book covers the issues of systemic interaction and relationships of participants of investment and construction projects, highlights the main methods of organization, planning, pricing, use of fixed assets, analysis and decision-making, legal support of the full construction cycle.

In the sphere of constant attention of the specialist there should be processes of control of expenditure of resources, management of the personnel, application of modern information technologies, ensuring quality and ecology of construction production, environmental protection and safety of production.

All these problems are duly reflected in the textbook. The issues of construction of unique "green" objects, development of territories of advanced social and economic development are not forgotten.

I believe that the novelty and timeliness of the author's approach, which combined in one textbook the two main functional areas of construction as well as a modern and advanced analysis of the problems will make the book very popular.

I am sure that the book will be a good assistant to students and professionals who have connected their lives with the construction industry, not only during studying, but also in their future professional activities.

Chairman of the Committee on entrepreneurship
in the field of construction of the CCI of Russia,
President of the Association "self-regulatory organization
"Interregional Association of builders"
Basin E. V.

PREFACE

This edition of the book is the fourth after the publication in 1999 of the book “Organization of construction production” under the general editorship of Doctor of Technical Science, Professor Tsay T.N. and Doctor of Economics, Professor Graboviy P.G. That book for a long time served as the basis for studying of civil engineers in higher educational institutions of the country and it is still in demand by students and lecturers.

In the second edition (2006) of the book, main attention was paid to the methods of planning and management of construction production, which until recently were considered, unfortunately, as auxiliary tools or means of achieving production goals, i.e. goals set for construction organizations. When assessing the factors affecting the increase in labor productivity in construction, the management factor got no more than 10–15%, which were calculated, as a rule, on the residual principle after the limit of “weight” was exhausted as applied to other factors, including organizational ones, technological, production etc. In contrast to this approach, foreign practice, especially in management practices in the US and other developed countries, management factor attracts increased attention.

The third edition (2013) of the book included sections related to the modern concept of project management, including the concept of development and its varieties, features of the organization of low-rise residential cottage building. If the project related to the construction process, then it is necessary to consider the possible risk of incomplete construction. Therefore, its participant and developers (investors) must come to agreement regarding guarantees of construction completion before one begins.

The value of using foreign experience in organizing, planning and management of construction production, as well as modern domestic practice of such activities, comes down not only to understanding the problems of evolution of organizational and managerial structures in the field of construction activities, but also to the possibility of using economic instruments relevant to the market conditions of the economic environment, especially during crises and the unstable state of economies.

The key task facing the team of authors preparing this book was to ensure continuity with respect to basic postulates underlying previous editions, taking into account their actualization and rethinking in the context of the modern realities of the construction industry and the strategic directions of its development. Methodological basis for integrity and integrated nature of the consideration of various aspects of the organization, planning and construction management, is the concept of the real estate life cycle, which includes the stages of design, construction, operation, taking into account further development (development).

In the proposed fourth edition of the book, an attempt was made to consider construction not only as an analysis of the statics of objects, but also patterns the dynamics of their development. That is, the reproduction cycles of any object in time divided into phases — design, construction (creation) and operation, taking into account organizational forms and internal company management structures, organization of management decision-making processes and management methods, application of BIM-technologies in construction management, management of innovations in construction, organization of a quality system in construction and others.

Authors' team includes collectives from the National Research Moscow State University of Civil Engineering, Belgorod State Technological University named after V.G. Shukhov, Financial University under the Government of the Russian Federation, Voronezh State Technical University, St. Petersburg State University of Architecture and Civil Engineering, Penza State University of Architecture and Civil Engineering, Don State Technical University, Hanoi University of Civil Engineering (Vietnam), Ho Chi Minh University of Architecture (Vietnam), JSC "Stroytransgaz" as well as other scientists and practitioners whose activities are related to the organization, construction planning and management.

The authors and editors of the book tried to answer for all possible questions of students of various levels of studying and professional retraining who learn the course "Construction management and real estate development".

The development of the country's economy leads to significant changes in various aspects of the construction and functioning of organizational and production systems, including investment and construction sector. The forms of ownership of enterprises are changing, some business entities are being restructured or liquidated, areas of activity (industry and subject specialization) are adjusted, production and technological potential is updated to ensure the competitiveness of construction companies in the domestic and foreign markets. The enterprises of the investment and construction complex seek to increase mobility and flexibility to adapt to the new environment, to new territorial and regional markets. At the same time, the basic laws inherent in production systems in general and in construction production in particular are preserved.

Organization, planning and construction management have its own characteristics, due to the specifics of construction production. Among these features, it is worth noting the peculiar arrhythmia of production, its discrete nature, mobility, the multiplicity of participants in the construction process, the production cycle that is longer than the industry, the stationary nature of the use of construction products, exposure to random factors, including weather, geographic conditions, etc. For these objective reasons, the area of improving construction management has historically always lagged behind the area of improving management of industrial production. The mutual penetration of these two most important areas of activity, the modern trends of integration, internationalization and industrialization of construction processes bring them together to a large extent, "pulling" the organization, planning and construction management sphere to the forefront. Positive trends are already emerging. A number of achievements in the field of construction management are becoming the subject of analysis for the sphere of industry. This is especially related to development activities. Therefore, the book is divided into two parts: the first part, "Theoretical foundations of the organization of construction and its main forms," and the second part, "Real estate development." The developer becomes the most important participant in the construction project, is interested in its implementation and achieving the goal, as it is the future owner and users of the project results.

Considering a construction company as a complex dynamic system, it is necessary to evaluate its organizational and technological reliability and sustainability to study its composition in order to identify elements that can collapse and thereby affect the entire system. In this regard, there are many researches, various opinions and definitions, which characterize enterprises as some kind of integral systems.

For example, an investment and construction complex can be considered as a system consisting of a number of elements — construction enterprises, design organizations, production and technological equipment departments, logistics divisions, construction industry enterprises, etc., subordinated to a common goal — commissioning of finished construction products. Planned tasks (information), material, financial, fuel and energy and technical resources (substance and energy) are placed on input to this system receives, and at the output there are finished objects (substance and energy) and information about the performance of work and the cost of resources (information).

At first, the organization of building systems is the construction of the organizational structure and the adoption of a certain form of management. The structure of the system is a combination of elements and their interconnections, ensuring its integrity and stability under various external and internal changes. Thus, the concept of sustainability is associated primarily with the structure of the building system.

The scale and pace of development of material production is largely determined by the ability to accelerate investment processes, in the practical implementation of which the decisive role belongs to capital construction. The improvement of the market economic mechanism in the country caused a radical change in the structure, mechanism and methods of organization, planning and management in the investment and construction complex.

The greatest emphasis in the book is placed on those issues and their features, which, subject to a constructive critical approach to the generalized results of existing domestic experience, can either be of practical interest or serve the further development of the search in this important direction.

Each chapter of the textbook concludes with questions for self-monitoring, discussion and independent solution of the problem, which are mostly practical and aimed at consolidating the material covered.

The sequence of presentation of the textbook material should contribute effective transfer of necessary knowledge to students. In the first part of the textbook in chapter I “Construction and its role in the socio-economic development of society”, the role of construction as an industry of material production in the national economy. The structure of the construction complex is considered, modern trends in the development of its development are analyzed.

The organizational forms of construction production, the methods of construction, and the main directions of reducing labor costs are described.

Chapter II “Organizational and contractual relations” describes the basic concepts of project management, considers the life cycle of project management in real estate, analyzes the structure, management functions, as well as the main participants in the projects. The general provisions for tendering and concluding contracts in construction are outlined. The practical aspects of the implementation of large investment and construction projects are considered.

Chapter III, "Methods of organization of construction production," discusses the preparations for construction and the organization of construction production, the development and design of a construction organization project and a project for the production of works. The chapter sets out the main recommendations for the organization of construction and works with the use of lifting machines. The methods of organization of construction production are analyzed. The key aspects of the design of the flow organization of construction, network modeling of construction production and scheduling are disclosed.

In chapter IV "Pricing and estimate in construction. Contract strategies" examined the theoretical foundations of market pricing, types of prices and pricing features in construction. Issues of formation of estimated cost and cost of construction products are revealed. The chapter reflects the approaches and methods for determining the estimated cost of construction and installation works, gives an estimated and normative base for determining the estimated cost of construction, and considers the composition and procedure for the development of budget documentation.

The issues of the contract strategy for managing the implementation of the investment and construction project are also disclosed.

Chapter V, "Construction Control, Acceptance, and Commissioning of Real Estate Completed", is devoted to topical issues in the examination of design documentation and engineering survey results, construction control and state construction supervision. The chapter also discusses the issues of issuing permits for putting an object into operation and conducting construction, technical and cost studies. The methodological foundations of the research conducted during the audit, as well as important aspects of the acceptance and commissioning of the completed construction of real estate, are disclosed.

Chapter VI, "Fixed Assets of Construction and its Resource Support", outlines the place of fixed assets in the structure of production, analyzes the composition of the means of labor, and reveals issues in the production of fixed assets and their renewal. In addition, special attention in the chapter is paid to the topic of resource support for construction production.

Chapter VII "Construction of objects of engineering infrastructure" contains general information about engineering networks as infrastructure facilities for the development of the territory and prospects for their development, analyzes certain types of infrastructure facilities, including engineering networks for heat supply, gas supply, water supply and sanitation. The chapter also discusses the organization of the construction of infrastructure facilities — engineering networks.

Chapter VIII "Planning of construction production and management of the construction organization" is devoted to the operational planning of construction production, monitoring the implementation of operational plans and business planning of the activities of the construction organization. The actual topic of business management of construction organizations is considered, methods for their rating are analyzed.

Chapter IX, "Information Technologies in Construction," analyzes the main prerequisites for the introduction of information modeling technologies in construction, gives the basic concepts and terminology of information modeling in construction, and touches on the informational interaction of participants in the life cycle of a construction object. The tasks that are solved using information modeling at different stages of the life cycle of an investment construction project are disclosed, and the practical aspects of applying BIM technology are analyzed (using Autodesk as an example).

The chapter also discusses modern methods for predicting the duration of construction.

In chapter X "Organization of construction of unique objects. The effectiveness of territorial concentration and the specialization of industrial construction" reveals the main features and organization of the construction of unique facilities, provides a classification of industrial, civil and residential buildings by design solutions and features of the technology of construction and installation works. The issues of technological design of unique objects are considered. The chapter analyzes the effectiveness of the concentration and specialization of single-industry industrial production, as well as the efficiency of the construction of launching territorial single- industry complexes.

Chapter XI "Green Building" discusses current issues of stimulating and developing green building in Russia and abroad.

The international certification systems for green building are analyzed. The basic terms and definitions of "green" technologies of the living environment are disclosed, the classification of "green" technologies is given.

Chapter XII "Low-Rise Cottage Construction" reveals the modern structure of building materials and low-rise housing construction. The chapter gives a classification of the main organizational and technological schemes of wooden low-rise housing construction; the optimal conditions for assessing the choice of site for construction are indicated.

The issues of mobility of construction production at low-rise housing construction and the formation of rational forms of organization, management of the process of construction of low-rise residential real estate objects are considered.

In addition, the chapter focuses on the main features of the scientific organization of the construction of low-rise residential real estate.

The textbook is equipped with diagrams, figures, and tables illustrating the main provisions of the relevant sections of the book and allowing readers to become more familiar with the basics of organizing the construction and real estate development.

Chapter 1

CONSTRUCTION AND ITS ROLE IN THE SOCIO-ECONOMIC DEVELOPMENT OF SOCIETY

1.1 Construction as a branch of material production and its role in the national economy

The modern economy is a complex diversified industrial and economic complex, consisting of many sectors, organizations, and productions. A special role in this complex is played by the construction industry, which is one of the basic branches of material production. In the process of construction, not only material goods are created that directly satisfy the needs of individuals and society as a whole (for example, housing that meets the housing needs of a person; schools and hospitals that satisfy the educational and health needs of the population; roads that provide mobility needs, etc.). However the material basis for the functioning of all other sectors of the economy is being formed — production buildings and structures, roads, public buildings are being created. These objects constitute the material basis of any production — its fixed assets.

The role of the construction industry in the national economy is also determined by the fact that construction products are the basis of the economic growth of the country and regions. Economic growth is the main goal of the economic policy of any state. The condition for economic growth is expanded reproduction, which is impossible without additional investments and the construction of new production facilities and facilities. Each year, the construction complex ensures the construction and commissioning of two hundred to three hundred thousand new buildings for various purposes. For example, in 2016, 278.3 thousand industrial and non-industrial buildings were

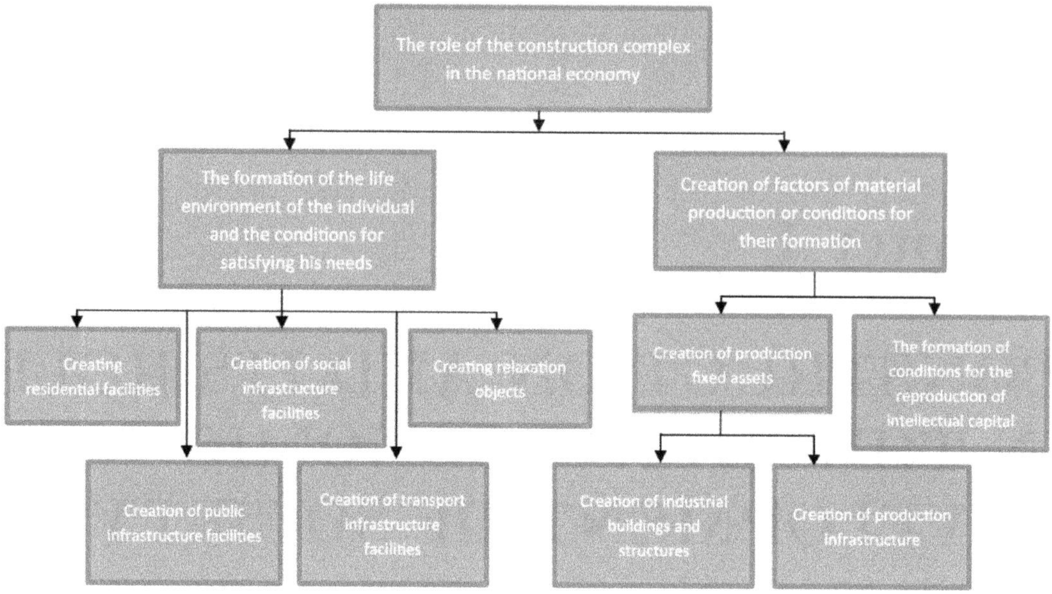

Figure 1.1: The role of the construction complex in the national economy

commissioned, and the total cost of the fixed assets exceeded 13 trillion. rub.[1] The construction industry provides the country's economy with automobile and railway and highways, power transmission lines, water and heating networks, oil and gas pipelines and others with weapons. In practice, not a single branch of the national economy can function without construction products.

The construction complex not only provides other industries with fixed capital, it creates the conditions for the formation and reproduction of human capital, which in the conditions of the postindustrial economy based on knowledge, becomes the main production factor. The result of construction activity is that urban environment in which a person lives and functions, in which he forms and realizes his intellectual potential. This environment largely determines the attractiveness of the region, the country for people and businesses, and, consequently, the competitiveness of the territory in the global markets of intellectual and investment capital. All this determines the huge role of the construction complex in the national economy (Fig. 1.1).

1.2 The structure of the construction complex

Construction products are created as a result of a complex technological process, in which enterprises of various types of activity participate: construction, industry, research, design, etc. Such production interaction allows us to combine all these enterprises into a single intersectoral complex. The construction

[1] Investments in Russia. 2017 : Stat. Sat / Rosstat. —M ., 2017 — 188 p.

complex is an organized system of cooperating enterprises and manufactures, united by stable production, technological, economic and economic ties. The backbone factor is the common goal of all subsystems of the construction complex — the creation of finished construction products that can satisfy the needs of the individual and society as a whole. The subsystems (elements) of the construction complex are various enterprises and organizations involved in the process of creating new facilities and production capacities.

All business entities included in the construction complex can be divided into several groups (Fig. 1.2).

1. Construction organizations. The core of the construction complex is the construction and installation organizations that perform various types of construction and installation works in the construction of buildings and structures and ensure the creation of finished construction products.

According to Rosstat, in the construction complex, as of 2016, 271.6 thousand construction organizations were functioning that performed various types of work. Over the past 15 years, their number has almost doubled, mainly due to the disintegration of large companies and the formation of small businesses. More than 6.2 million people work in these organizations, and the amount of work performed by the type of activity "Construction" exceeded 7 trillion rubles.[2]

All construction organizations can be classified according to a number of signs:

a) by type of work performed:

- general construction, performing the main types of construction work on the construction of buildings and structures;
- specialized, performing certain special types of work (installation of electrical equipment, installation of elevators, etc.);
- repair and construction, performing work on the repair of buildings and structures;

b) by type of facilities being built or types of construction:

- housing construction;
- industrial engineering;
- road construction;
- construction of transport facilities;
- construction and arrangement of oil and gas facilities, etc.

c) the size of the organization:

---

[2]Russian Statistical Yearbook. 2017 Stat. Sat / Rosstat. — M., 2017 — 686 p.

- large;
- medium;
- small ones.

More than 90% of construction organizations are small enterprises with less than 100 employees. The bulk of the work is carried out by large construction companies, which are vertically integrated production structures. Large companies with diversified production are more stable in unstable economic conditions and have significant competitive advantages in the construction market, as they have more powerful production potential, are able to introduce new technologies, and have access to significant and sufficient financial resources. At the same time, large companies, unlike small ones, are less adaptive to changes in the market situation and respond more slowly to changes in the volumes and structure of demand.

This allows small enterprises to compete with large companies to perform specialized individual types of construction work.

2. Enterprises for the production of building materials, products and designs. Construction is a rather resource-intensive type of activity — construction resources account for more than 60% of the cost of final construc-

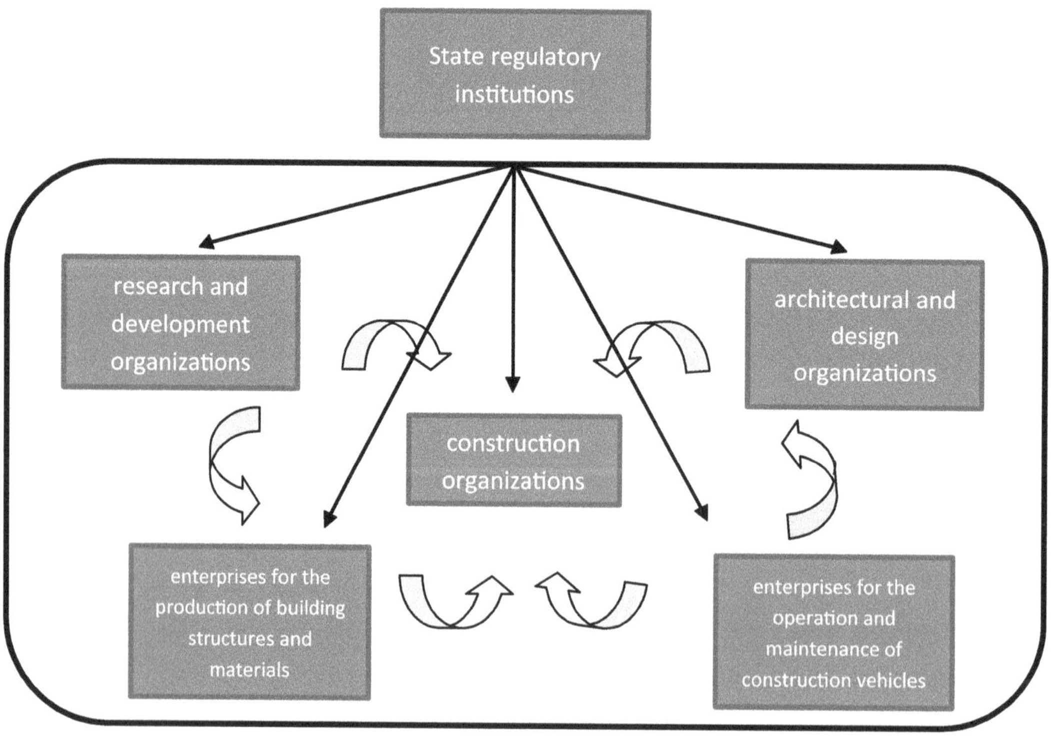

Figure 1.2: The structure of the construction complex

tion products. Enterprises producing construction materials, structures and products form the basis of the material and technical basis of Article swarms stances. And although they are still referred to the building materials industry (or the construction industry), and the cost of work by the type of activity "Construction" does not take into account the cost of the products they produce, these enterprises are, of course, part of the construction complex.

According to the types of products manufactured, these enterprises can be divided into several groups:

- enterprises for the production of reinforced concrete products and structures (factories of reinforced concrete products, reinforced concrete products, plants of large-panel housing construction);
- enterprises for the production of ceramic products (factories for the production of bricks, expanded clay, ceramic tiles);
- enterprises for the production of building concrete and mortar;
- enterprises for the production of pilots for wood, wood products and constructions;
- enterprises for the extraction of non-metallic building materials (sand, gravel), etc.

Many enterprises for the production of building materials are part of large construction companies, being subsidiaries or production divisions of these companies. In connection with the improvement of technologies for building production, new enterprises are being created to produce new building materials, products, and structures that were previously imported from abroad. Along with enterprises with a long history, new facilities provide the material base for construction. For example, in recent years, new enterprises have appeared for the production of windows and doors made of polyvinyl chloride (PVC) and aluminum profiles, for the production of new heaters, metal-plastic pipes, new facade systems, etc. have been developed.

3. Architectural and design and design and survey organizations. Any construction begins with a project containing architectural, planning, structural and engineering solutions that will be embodied in a future project. The project determines the resource intensity and cost of the future facility, the costs and effectiveness of its operation, its operational characteristics and the durability of use. A huge number of architectural, design and survey organizations carry out engineering surveys and develop design estimates for construction. Such organizations, as a rule, specialize in the design of certain objects — civil, industrial or transport construction.

In recent times, large design institutes carried out the bulk of design work for construction. However, at present, the vast majority of organizations performing design and survey works for construction are small architectural workshops or design bureaus. Large construction corporations may also include design and engineering units. Engineering includes the provision of consulting services for technical expertise in the field of civil engineering, architecture, land allocation, urban planning, project planning and management, pricing and budgeting, determining the estimated cost of construction, construction equipment, patents, computing operations and systems and etc.

4. Research and development organizations that develop new engineering and technical solutions, new materials and structures, new technologies for the production of building materials, structures and construction and installation works, new construction machines and mechanisms. Most of the scientific and research organizations of the construction complex operate in the structure of higher educational institutions of architectural and construction education. Once large scientific research institutes working in construction, now, due to limited financial resources, have either been liquidated or forced to provide engineering services. Large corporations engaged in the design and construction of technically sophisticated facilities, as a rule, have research and development or technical-innovative units in their composition.

5. Enterprises for the operation and maintenance of construction machinery and equipment. These are enterprises specializing in the provision of motor transport services and mechanization services (motor transport enterprises, mechanization directorates), which provide construction machinery and equipment for rent (leasing), as well as repair and maintenance of equipment. Large construction companies are, as a rule, own construction vehicles and relevant units that serve it. However, a small construction business cannot afford to have all the necessary construction machinery and equipment; therefore, it uses the services of specialized organizations for the operation and maintenance of construction equipment.

All organizations included in the construction complex may have various forms of ownership. These may be enterprises:

- state;
- municipal;
- private
- mixed ownership.

The main part of organizations is private ownership — 99% of the volume of construction and installation works is carried out by private companies.

Organizations of the construction complex may also differ in organizational and legal forms of ownership: enterprises as commercial organizations (with the exception of research organizations, which are mostly institutions); non-profit organizations, but with the right to carry out commercial activities:

- business partnerships (full partnership, limited partnership);
- Business Entities (OOO- of societies with limited liability, PAO- public joint stock companies, AO non-public stock of societies);
- production cooperatives;
- unitary enterprises (state unitary and municipal unitary enterprises).

As noted above, the bulk of the work by type of activity "Construction" is carried out by large companies. Such companies operate on the principle of large corporations (holdings), combining several subsidiaries in their structure, ensuring a closed production cycle. At the same time, the parent company manages the activities of subsidiaries by virtue of the predominant participation in their authorized capital. Vertically integrated structures in construction include, as a rule, the architectural and design organizations, enterprises for the production of building materials and construction, construction companies, specialized installation companies, mechanization management, and others. In addition, large companies are actually performing functions of Developers which perform independent searching, formation and preparation of land development projects of planning and development, the development of investment projects and urban planning etc. placing, search for financial sources and financing facilities provide the process of creating a real estate and its implementation. Many development companies take on the functions of the subsequent management of real estate. For example, for developers whom implement building of residual objects, the closure is characteristically in a single technological cycle of not only industrial activity, but also the production — such companies create in the structure housing the operating unit (management company), which is provided management constructed real estate (fig. 1.3).

In fact, such large developer companies combine in their structure all the functions of the main subjects of investment and construction activities: investor, customer-developer, designer, contractor, resource provider and management function.

As already mentioned above, the bulk of the building complex organizations are private companies that independently determine the goals of their activities, types and scale of production. However, in a market economy, business activity is subject to state regulation; therefore, the *state exercises regulatory and oversight functions.* The regulation of the construction complex is to create a regulatory field for such companies, implement a unified architectural and construction policy, issue permits for the construction and commissioning

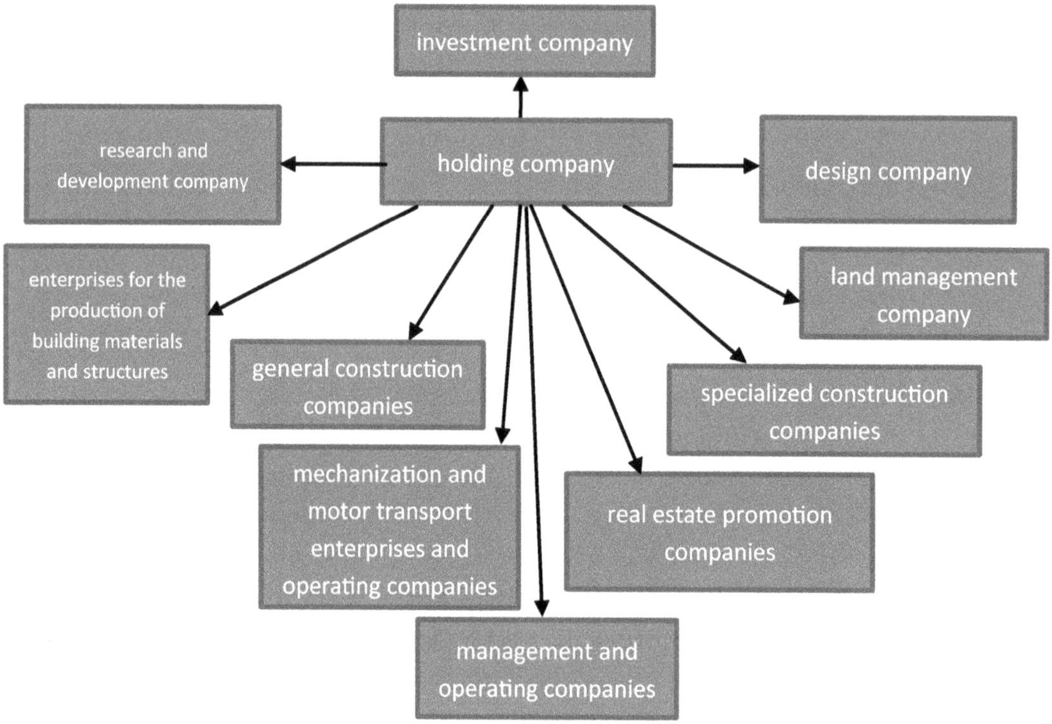

Figure 1.3: Approximate structure of a large vertically integrated developer company

of facilities, monitor compliance with the requirements of building codes, examination of design estimates and certification of building materials. The powers and functions of state regulatory institutions are determined by the Town Planning Code of the Russian Federation[3] and include:

- preparation of technical regulation in the field of urban development;
- information and scientific and methodological support of urban development activities;
- organization and conduct of state examination of design documentation;
- implementation of federal state construction supervision;
- regulation of pricing and budgeting in construction;
- and approval of territorial planning documents and others.

The state regulatory institution, the main federal executive institute that manages the industry, is the Ministry of Construction and Housing and Utilities — the Ministry of Construction of Russia.

[3]Urban Planning Code of the Russian Federation / Consultant Plus. — Reference legal system

The Ministry carries out the development and implementation of state policy and legal regulation in the field of construction, architecture, urban planning and housing and communal services. In the Public Declaration of the goals and objectives of the Ministry of Construction of the Russian Federation[4] identified six key objectives:

1. Providing affordable and comfortable housing for citizens of the Russian Federation.
2. Improving legislation in the field of shared construction.
3. Reform of urban development.
4. Improving the system of self-regulation in construction.
5. Modernization of the housing stock in the Russian Federation and improvement of its management system.
6. The development of public-private partnership mechanisms in housing and communal services.

You can see that five of the above goals relate directly to the construction complex and reflect the main problems of its functioning.

The system of state regulation of the construction complex has a vertical structure corresponding to the federal structure of the Russian Federation: regulatory functions are transferred from the federal institution to regional institutions created in the executive power system of the constituent entities of the Federation (regional ministries of construction or departments), from them to municipal institutions that include services architectural and construction regulation.

Due to the special importance of the construction complex and its impact on human life safety and the functioning of production, an important role is played by institutions that carry out supervisory functions. Since 2006, by a Decree of the Government of the Russian Federation, the authority to carry out *state construction supervision is* vested in the Federal Service for Ecological, Technological and Nuclear Supervision (Rostekhnadzor)[5].

The purpose of the activities of the state construction supervision institutions is the prevention, detection and suppression of violations of legislation in the field of urban development. The functions of construction supervision are defined in Art. 54 of the Town Planning Code of the Russian Federation

---

[4]The public declaration of goals and tasks of the Ministry of construction and housing — communal economy at 2016 / Ministry of Construction of the Russian Federation. The official site. [Electronic resource] : URL: http://www.minstroyrf.ru/upload/iblock/7ef/publichnaya-deklaratsiya-26.04.pdf

[5]Federal Service for Ecological, Technological and Nuclear Supervision (Rostekhnadzor) : official site. — [Electronic resource] : URL http://www.gosnadzor.ru

and provide for monitoring the compliance of work performed during the construction or reconstruction of capital construction projects, as well as the applied building materials and the results of such work with the requirements of technical regulations and design documentation, checking for a building permit and complying with the requirements of the Town Planning Code of the Russian Federation. As part of the executive institutions of the constituent entities of the Federation, regional construction supervision institutions are created — inspections of state construction supervision, which exercise their powers at the territorial level.

An important role in ensuring safe construction and compliance of building products with regulatory requirements is played by *state expert institutions of design and estimate documentation.* The functions of the state examination of project documentation, examination results of engineering studies, validation of determining the estimated cost of construction, reconstruction, modernization and overhaul assigned to the Federal Autonomous Institution "Main State Expertise" (FAI "Glavgosexpertiza Rossii")[6], which is a government agency subordinate to the Ministry of Construction and Housing and Communal Services of the Russian Federation. The Main State Expertise of Russia has several territorial branches, between which powers are allocated for state examination of projects and estimates of objects at the regional level. Article 49 of the Town Planning Code of the Russian Federation also allows for non-state examination of projects and estimates. The developer or technical customer of his choice may send the design documentation and the results of engineering surveys to the state or non-state examination, with the exception of cases stipulated by law.

Land plots on which construction is carried out, completed construction and commissioned buildings and structures become objects of property rights of economic entities. These rights are subject to *state registration, which is carried out by the territorial institutions of the Federal Service for State Registration, Cadaster and Cartography (Rosreestr)*, which is entrusted with the responsibility for maintaining the cadaster, registration of rights, compiling maps, and land management. The same institutions carry out state land supervision, cadastral work and cadastral valuation of real estate, geodetic and cartographic support of investment and construction activities, etc.

In addition to the construction complex, enterprises and manufactures of other sectors of the economy take part in the creation of final construction products. For example, a significant part of building materials is produced at enterprises of other sectors of the economy that are not part of the construction sector: paint and varnish products, various sealants are produced at chemical

---

[6]Main State Expertise: Official site — [Electronic resource]: URL https://gge.ru

enterprises, paper wallpapers at pulp and paper enterprises, lumber and wooden structures at wood processing enterprises etc. The energy complex provides construction production with energy resources, the mining industry — non-metallic materials, the engineering complex — construction machines, vehicles and equipment.

In the modern market economy, an important role is played by organizations that perform the functions of *market infrastructure* — financial organizations (banks), insurance organizations, market intermediaries (realtors), and others. The organizations of the construction complex in their production activities closely interact with the organizations of market infrastructure that provide the process of creating a construction financial resources, insure risks and compensate for losses, promote finished objects on the market and ensure their implementation, etc.

Thus, the construction complex as an intersectoral association of many industries that ensure the creation of finished construction products is a complex hierarchical open type system that closely interacts with other industry systems that are part of the national macroeconomic system.

1.3 Modern trends in the development of the construction complex

In order to develop a development strategy for the construction complex, determine the main areas of activity and make managerial decisions, it is necessary to understand the main trends in economic development, the correspondence of the pace and scale of development of the industry to these trends. For this, it is necessary to carry out a statistical analysis of the main indicators of the construction industry on the basis of official statistics and the results of sample observations.

The functioning of the construction complex is characterized by a system of technical and economic indicators, which can be divided into three groups:

1. Quantitative indicators characterizing the growth rate of the industry, the role of the construction complex in the national economy (share in gross domestic income), the volume of construction and installation works, the amount of investment in fixed assets, the number of facilities under construction and commissioning, the number of functioning organizations, the number working in the industry and their share in the working-age population, etc.

2. Structural indicators characterizing the structure of investments, construction and installation works, the structure of organizations, the cost structure of construction and installation works, etc.
3. Qualitative indicators characterizing the development of patterns of ownership in the construction industry, changes in investment sources, level of competitiveness, level of entrepreneurial confidence, etc.

The analysis of these indicators in dynamics allows us to judge the state and development trends of the construction complex, helps to identify key industry problems and ways to improve the efficiency of construction activities.

The peculiarity of construction is such that this industry is most sensitive to changes in the economic situation in the country. This is due to the fact that the volume of construction directly depends on investment activity, since it is investments that determine the demand for construction products.

On the eve of the crisis, the investment activity of economic entities is sharply reduced, as investment risks increase, and investors refrain from implementing new projects. This can be clearly seen in the graph shown in Fig. 1.4.

In the graphs shown in Fig. 1.4, it can be seen that the dynamics of investment indicators and the volume of work by type of activity "Construction" is much more pronounced than the dynamics of the main indicator of the country's economic development — in the scarlet domestic product. In the upward phase, the growth rate of investments and construction is higher than the growth rate of GDP; in the downward phase, investment and the volume of construction and installation works are reduced much more.

This is clearly visible both during the crisis of 2008–009 and during the crisis of 2014–015. A similar relationship is confirmed by a retrospective analysis of economic dynamics. This relationship can be represented in the form of a certain model, which shows that the amplitude of fluctuations in the indicators of investment activity at different phases of the economic cycle is greater than in the economy as a whole (Fig. 1.5).

Outstripping the growth rate (recession) of investments, the growth rate (recession) of the economy as a whole indicates not only the sensitivity of the investment sector to the overall economic dynamics, but also that in order to overcome the crisis and economic growth, it is necessary to significantly ensure faster growth of investments and construction volumes.

An assessment of the role of the construction complex in the national economy can be made on the basis of an analysis of the industry's share in the country's gross domestic product (GDP). In 2014–2015 there was a slight decrease in the contribution of the industry compared to previous years, due to the protracted crisis, to which, as we have shown above, the industry is more

Figure 1.4: Dynamics of changes in the main indicators of the construction complex[8]

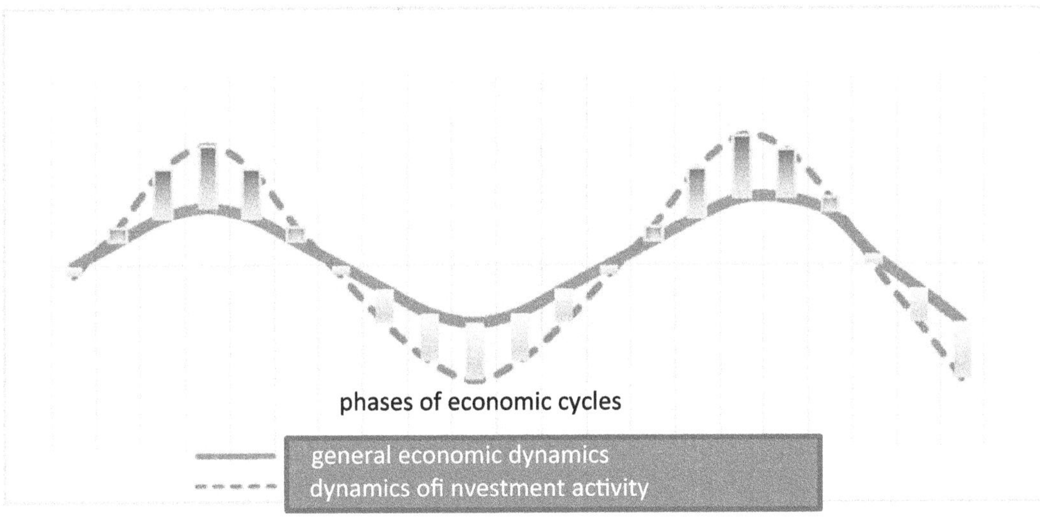

Figure 1.5: Correlation of general economic dynamics and investment dynamics by phases of economic development (economic cycles)

[8]Here and further used data of Rosstat : Key socio-economic characteristics of the Russian Federation. Russian statistical yearbook. 2016 : Stat. Sat. / Federal State Statistics Service — M., 2016. — 725 p.; Socio-economic indicators of the Russian Federation in 1991–2015 years. / Federal State Statistics Service : [Electronic resource] : URL http://www.gks.ru/wps/wcm/connectrosstat_main/rosstat/ru/statistics/publications/catalog/doc_1270707126016; Socio-economic situation in Russia. Report / Federal State Statistics Service. — M., 2017. — 371 p.;. Construction in Russia. 2016: Stat. Sat. / Rosstat. — M., 2016. — 111 p.

sensitive than others. But in 2017, according to the Federal State Statistics Service, the share of construction in GDP increased slightly and amounted to 6.3%. However, the system of national accounts adopted in Russia for statistical monitoring takes into account only the volumes of work carried out directly by construction organizations by the type of activity "Construction". But, as we already know, the construction complex is not only construction organizations. Production of building materials is accounted for by type of activity "Manufacturing". For example, the production of basic building materials -n about the activity "Manufacture of other non-metallic mineral products" Timber and structures of wood — by activity "Processing of wood and of products of wood and cork, except furniture, manufacture of articles of straw and plaiting materials" etc. The scope of design and exploration work for construction is accounted for as "Activities in the field of architecture and engineering design; technical tests, research and analysis "as part of the scope of work by the type of activity "Professional, scientific and technical activities", a separate section "Activities in real estate operations" includes operations for the sale of construction products, etc.[9] Thus, when taking into account the share in GDP for the above types of activities, we will see that in reality the contribution of the construction industry to the country's economy is much larger and amounts to 9-12%, which once again confirms the important role of the construction industry in the economic development of Russia.

Due to the above features of statistical accounting, we will consider in dynamics the main technical and economic indicators of the industry by the type of activity "Construction" (Table 1.1).

By analyzing statistics, one can judge the problems and development trends of the construction organizations that make up the core of the construction industry.

1.4 Features of the construction industry

As a branch of material production, construction has a number of features that distinguish it from other industries. Features of the industry are explained by the nature of its final products, specific working conditions, and a number of specifics of the applied equipment, technology, organization of production, financing, management and logistics. These features are divided into *general,* inherent in the entire industry, regardless of the facilities being constructed and their purpose, and *special,* characteristic for certain types of construction.

[9]OKVED 2. The All-Russian Classifier of Types of Economic Activities / Ministry of Economic Development of the Russian Federation. Federal Agency for Technical Regulation and Metrology / Federal State Statistics Service : [Electronic resource]: URL http : // www . gks . com / metod / classifiers . html

Table 1.1 Main economic indicators for the type of activity "Construction"

Indicators	2005	2010	2011	2012	2013	2014	2015	2016*	2017*
Volume of work performed by type of activity "Construction" billion rubles (at actual prices)	1754.4	454.2	5140.3	5714.1	6019.5	6125.2	7010.4	7204.2	
— as a percentage of the previous year (at constant prices)	113.2	105.0	105.1	102.5	100.1	97.72	95.2	95.7	
The average annual number of people employed in construction, thousand people	4986.1	5399.1	5473.6	5641.9	5711.9	5664.1	5651.9		
— as a percentage of the previous year	105.1	100.9	101.8	103.1	101.2	99.2	98.42		
The proportion of people employed in construction in the total number of employees, percent	7.5	8.0	8.1	8.3	8.4	8.4	8.3		
— of which are employed in the construction of buildings and structures	2286.3	2520.4			2123.1	2057.1	1964.7		
The average monthly nominal accrued wages of construction workers: rub.	9043	21172	23682	25951	27701	29354	29960		
— as a percentage of the previous year	123.8	116.8	111.9	109.6	106.7	106.0	102.32		
— as a percentage of the average level in the economy	105.7	101.0	101.3	97.5	93.0	90.3	88.0		
Investments in fixed assets, billion rubles		9152.1	11035.7	12586.1	13450.2	13902.6	13897.2	14639.8	
— per capita, thousand rubles		64.1	77.2	87.9	93.7	95.2	94.9	99.8	
— as a percentage of the previous year (in comparable prices)		106.3	110.8	106.8	100.8	98.54	89.9	99.1	
— as a percentage of gross domestic product			20.7	20.9	21.2	20.5	19.6	20.4	
Development investments in fixed assets construction, billion rubles (at actual prices)	129.5	342.1	336.8	348.6	438.1	469.3	448.7	852.2	
— the proportion of investment in construction in the total volume of investment in fixed assets, percent	3.6	3.7	3.1	2.8	3.3	3.4	3.1	7.8	
The presence of fixed assets in construction, billion rubles (by full accounting value; at the end of the year)	604.9	1499.9	1553.0	1581.9	1676.9	1774.7	2047.9		
Gross value added of construction, billion rubles (in current basic prices)	989.9	2587.8	3517.5	4010.2	4301.0	4396.4	4264.2		
— the proportion of construction in gross domestic product, percent	5.3	6.5	7.4	7.6	7.0	6.5	5.9	6.2	
— change in gross value added of construction (in constant prices), as a percentage of the previous year	110.2	104.4	107.6	102.6	100.1	97.2	92.6		
The cost of construction organizations to perform work on the elements, as a percentage of the total cost:			57.4	55.2					
— material costs	57.4	56.3	19.1	18.8	56.1	58.3	60.0		
— labor costs	21.1	20.2	92	90	18.9	20.1	18.2		

Table 1.1 continuation

Indicators	2005	2010	2011	2012	2013	2014	2015	2016*	2017*
The cost of one ruble of work performed by construction organizations, cop.	88	90	106.9	176.2	95	90	88		
Balanced financial result in construction (profit minus loss, billion rubles)	39.0	87.0	7139.5	7824.5	601.3	-75.1	-54.3		135.6
— reference: on the economy as a whole, billion rubles.	3225.9	6330.6	4.3	5.0	6853.8	4346.8	7502.7		10320
Profitability level in construction, percent	3.9	4.5	9.6	8.6	8.3	3.4	3.8		
— reference: for the economy as a whole, percent	13.5	10.0	71.0	72.3	7.0	7.3	8.1		
The proportion of profitable organizations in the total number of organizations, percent	66.0	70.8	70.0	70.9	70.6	68.1	67.2		75.1
— reference: for the economy as a whole, percent	63.6	70.1	57.4	55.2	69.0	67.0	67.4		73.7
Commissioning of buildings:			227.2	241.3					
— the number of buildings, thousand	141.6	216.5	423.2	485.1	258.1	304.2	306.4	278.3	
— total construction volume of buildings, million cubic meters m	265.4	397.4	99.0	110.1	526.7	617.8	622.8	608.5	
— total area of buildings, mln. Sq. m	66.3	91.5	227.2	241.3	117.8	138.6	139.4	135.8	
The number of buildings, structures under construction, thousand	128.5	103.1	108.1	104.8	103.4	101.6	98.0		
The number of operating construction organizations, thousand, total	112.8	196.2	209.2	205.1	218.0	226.8	235.3	497.8	
— including small businesses (including micro)	102162	186195	200643	195836	208993	217968	227452		
From the number of operating organizations by ownership as a percentage of the total:	100	100	100	100	100	100	100	100	
— state	1.7	0.6			0.4	0.4	0.4	0.4	
— municipal	0.6	0.3			0.2	0.2	0.2	0.2	
— private	96.4	97.9			98.2	98.3	99.1	96.3	
— mixed Russian	1.8	0.4			0.2	0.2	0.1	0.2	
— other	1.3	0.8			1.0	0.9	0.2	2.9	
The volume of work performed by type of economic activity "Construction", billion rubles	1754.4	4454.2	5140.3	5714.1	6019.5	6125.2	6148.4		
— as a percentage of the previous year (at constant prices)	113.2	105.0	105.1	102.5	100.1	97.7	95.2		

Sources: Construction in Russia. 2014.: Stat. Sat / Rosstat; Construction in Russia. 2016: Stat. Sat / Rosstat. — M., 2016*; Russia in numbers. 2017: Brief stat. Sat / Rosstat. — M., 2017; Investments in Russia. 2017: Stat. Sat / Rosstat. — M., 2017.

* This collection is published once every two years, so some data for 2016 and 2017 will appear in the collection for 2018.

A. General construction features:

1. The non-stationarity, temporary nature, heterogeneity of the construction industry and the nature of the final product. With the commissioning of the facilities, construction and installation works are interrupted at the habitable place, and the means of production are moved to a new place. In construction, technical and human resources moving in the production process are mobile, and products are stationary. In industry, as a rule, products are mobile in nature, and jobs are spatially fixed. The final construction products are created for a long time and are used in the same place where they are geographically fixed. Products from the construction industry are durable and have served the community for tens and hundreds of years.

2. The technological relationship of all operations that are part of the construction process. In industry, before the start of production, the production technology is being worked out. In construction, prior to the start of construction and installation works, temporary industrial and domestic and administrative buildings are created, laying and relocation of utilities, roads, power lines, etc. All these features require peculiar organizational forms and additional costs. Along with this, long construction periods cause the diversion of funds from economic turnover to construction in progress. Further improvement of technological progress leads to a review of previously adopted decisions on the progress of construction, taking into account the use of new equipment and technology. The technology of construction production requires a strict sequence in the implementation of its individual processes: the completion of one work process precedes the beginning of another. No construction process can begin without ending the previous one; under these conditions, the products of one's labor cannot be accumulated in intermediate warehouses. In this regard, construction processes cannot be spatially arranged; difficulties arise in the simultaneous use of workers in accordance with their specialty and qualifications.

3. The instability of the ratio of construction and installation works by their complexity and types during the month, which complicates the calculation of the numerical and vocational qualifications of workers.

4. The participation of various construction organizations in the production of final products. In industrial production, at any degree of cooperation, the final product is released by one contractor who implements these products. Several construction organizations (general contractor, subcontractors) that create separate structural elements of the building simultaneously participate in the construction of facilities. Each of these business entities sells (hands over) the manufactured part of its products.

As noted in section 1.1, construction is closely related to all sectors of the economy and especially to industry. On the one hand, the increase in construction volumes depends on the development of industries that provide its technical equipment, on the other hand, performing construction and installation work for other sectors of the economy, construction organizations are inextricably linked with the activities of customers acting in relation to construction, as suppliers, and as consumers of construction products. Construction is the most material-intensive industry: in order to obtain final products, construction materials are supplied to it by more than 80% of the country's economy sectors.

5. The role of climatic and local conditions in construction and installation works. Despite the elimination of seasonality in construction, negative temperatures require the implementation of measures to ensure the construction of facilities in winter conditions. The construction of buildings of the same type in different regions of the country requires different costs of material and technical and labor resources. Construction conditions are largely determined by seismicity, topography, geological structure of the soil, the presence of groundwater, the method of delivery of structures and materials to the construction site.

   Construction workers are more exposed to climatic conditions than workers in other industries. This feature requires the concentration of large forces in the most favorable period of the year. In this regard, in the estimated calculations for the main construction, installation and repair-construction works, correction factors are introduced that allow taking into account deviations from standard working conditions.

B. Special construction features are caused by a wide variety of facilities under construction and the process of updating the existing buildings. These include: industrial, housing, civil, social, transport, agricultural facilities, as well as land reclamation and water facilities, trunk pipelines, power lines, etc.

The construction of *industrial facilities is* characterized by their concentration in the allotted territory and the complexity of the facilities under construction. Work in one place has been ongoing for over a year. On the construction companies engaged in the armament of a relatively long-term facilities, less affected by the relocation means of production. In such construction organizations, as a rule, a stable composition of personnel.

The construction and reconstruction of *housing and civil and social facilities is* characterized by strict adherence to the sequence and sequence of work. Renovation of the existing housing development involves the development of the housing segment, expressed in qualitative and quantitative changes, both of the individual elements and the housing stock as a whole, the transformation of its structure and composition in accordance with modern requirements. In this regard, along with the construction of multifunctional complexes, roads, water supply, energy supply systems, heating systems, schools, nurseries and kindergartens, objects of trade, culture and consumer services should be built. Failure to comply with the requirements for the construction of these facilities leads to a violation of sanitary and urban planning norms and rules.

The construction *of transport facilities, trunk pipelines, land reclamation and water management, agricultural facilities and power lines* are characteristic: a small amount of work in one place, the need to work at different facilities, remote from each other, as well as the mobility of jobs as the construction of one or another facility and their construction in uninhabited places.

The products of the construction industry are both individual objects and multifunctional complexes completed by construction and commissioned, including industrial real estate objects, railways and roads, power plants, irrigation and shipping channels, ports, residential buildings (residential real estate objects) and other objects forming fixed assets of the national economy.

C. Construction as a branch of the economy is involved in the creation of fixed assets for all sectors of the economy. Capital construction products are the commissioned and adopted in the established manner production facilities and non-production facilities. As they become operational, they become fixed assets. Buildings and structures equipped with technological, energy and other equipment and machinery constitute the natural-material content of fixed assets.

Thus, *capital construction creates the material conditions, providing the ability to operate means of production for the entire national economy.*

Construction organizations include legal entities of all forms of ownership that perform work under construction contracts or contracts. Developers (customers) and developers manage capital investments, the sources of which are own, borrowed funds of credit organizations, as well as funds of the state and municipal budgets.

The development of construction, increasing its effectiveness is based on its industrialization and innovations, the main directions of which are: transferring part of technological processes from construction sites to plants to stationary production conditions in order to increase the assembly of buildings and structures being constructed; improvement of technological design solutions of buildings and structures, their further typification and unification; automated line production for the manufacture of structures, products, parts and materials in factories with a high degree of their building readiness; mechanized in-line execution of technological operations and construction processes of monolithic frame buildings and structures; installation of building materials and structures from wheels in order to ensure continuous production of construction works, etc.

In addition to the creation of fixed assets, the functions of capital construction include the expansion, reconstruction and technical re-equipment of existing fixed assets, i.e. the main task of capital construction is the expanded reproduction and high-quality renewal of fixed assets of all sectors of the country's economy through capital investments. The concepts of "capital investments" and "investments" have the following differences.

Under *capital investments* are understood the costs of reproduction of fixed assets or "financial resources spent on the construction of new ones, reconstruction and technical re-equipment of existing enterprises (production capital investments), as well as on housing, communal and cultural construction (non-production capital investments).

At the same time, *investment* (from the English. *Investments* - a synonym for capital investments) is understood as a *long-term investment of capital* in order to increase it, generate income or achieve other beneficial effect. Investments include investments in fixed assets (actual capital investments in the creation or acquisition of new fixed assets, renovation of existing ones), investments in initial working capital (inventories, financial reserves) and investments in intangible assets (intellectual property costs, promotion costs new product to the market, etc.).

Economic relations of the construction industry with other sectors of the national economy in the production and distribution of various products (services) are called *intersectoral.*

In construction, 50% of the products of the building materials industry are used, about 18% of metal, 40% of lumber, more than 10% of the products of the engineering industry. Almost all types of transport are used to transport building materials, building structures and construction equipment: automobile, railway, river, sea and air. The value of transport costs in the cost of construction reaches 20%.

In terms of output and workforce of human resources on the construction industry accounts for about a tenth of the B VI page Ana.

In the process of creating fixed assets representing construction products, working personnel are employed, means of labor (equipment) and objects of labor (materials) are used. Interacting with each other, the basic elements of the construction process create the final construction products, which are buildings and structures in physical and monetary terms.

The reproduction cycles of any object (life cycle) can be divided into the following phases (formula 1.1):

$$\tau = t_{des} + t_{constr} + t_{dev} + t_{n.u} + t_{decay}; \quad \text{years} \tag{1.1}$$

where τ — duration of the production cycle, which reflects the actual sequence of the design phases, respectively (t_{des}), construction (t_{constr}) and capacity development (t_{dev}) enterprise (industry average);

$t_{n.o}$ — the duration of the normal operation period, sufficient to evaluate the effectiveness ($t_{n.o} = t_n$, where t_n is the payback period);

t_{decay} — the length of the period of extinction (liquidation) of the object.

Each phase has its own tasks. Therefore, for example, in the process of feasibility studies, the main technical and economic indicators of the future facility are determined and the economic feasibility of its construction is assessed. At the design stage, constructive and layout solutions of the object, methods for organizing its construction and the technology of work are developed, estimated cost of construction is determined.

In the construction phase, three stages can be distinguished:

1) preparation for construction (pre-investment stage);

2) construction (investment stage);

3) sales of construction products — commissioning of the finished construction project (implementation stage).

At the construction stage, at the construction site, all technological elements of the construction process are combined, as a result of which construction products are created, the total actual costs of construction production, material and material elements of buildings and structures, their architectural and construction expressiveness and quality are formed. The completion of the facility occurs with the start of sales of construction products — the commissioning of completed facilities and their transfer to the customer as fixed assets.

The results of the calculation of the optimal service life of the facility depend (see formula 1.1) on which of the three phases (initial development t_{dev}, normal operation $t_{n.o.}$ or extinction t_{decay}) reduces or lengthens t_{sl} (the moment the end of the service life of the object). "Limit" operation phase t_{dev} and $t_{n.o.}$ unfavorable economically. The theory of economic static when establishing rational t_{sl} made the main emphasis on the extinction phase t_{decay}, the presence of which creates the prerequisite for the cessation of operation of the object.

Less attention when establishing economically sound t_{sl} was given to the phase of the initial "development" t_{dev}. In reality, the role of this phase in these estimates is increased, because it falls on the nearest part of the considered time period. And all the damages and costs associated with it, from the perspective of a time factor, are most significant.

The innovation process constantly occurring in the industry and the national economy leads to an increasing pressure of external factors on any long-functioning facilities. The phenomenon of obsolescence of an object associated with this can accelerate the completion of its service life.

1.5 Organizational forms of construction production and the main directions of reducing labor costs in construction

The basic concept of the development of the construction industry includes the tasks of radical improvement in the construction sector, a fundamental change in the functioning of the construction complex, due to its sources of financing and the responsibility of developers and developers, which objectively decides the role in the reproduction of the public product, which determines the impact on the structure, pace and proportion of the development of farms.

The implementation of these tasks will give the construction industry integrating and system-forming functions, provide deep multifunctional ties with other industries and the socio-economic sphere.

In this regard, the most important strategic direction of the development of the construction industry is the formation of the basic principles and foundations of the organization of construction as a system of interrelated organizational, economic, technological, technical and managerial measures for the preparation of construction production, the implementation of construction with the projected cost, timely commissioning of facilities and high quality.

The transition to a qualitatively new organizational level is achieved primarily through the formation of investment, construction and development processes for the construction of facilities; selection of rational organizational forms of project management; effective distribution of liability risks among contractors; selection of contracts for risk sharing by costs and terms of contract management of the entire life cycle.

Technical progress in construction changes the construction site and turns it into an installation site, primarily due to:

- aggregation of material and technical resources and maximum transfer of work with the specifics of industrial production;
- development of mobile forms of concentration of capacities of construction organizations with widespread use of expeditionary, shift and expeditionary-shift organization of labor.

The final products of capital construction as a branch of material production are finished construction products, i.e. commissioned capacities and areas of enterprises, buildings and structures. To create these products, labor resources and means of production (objects of labor and means of labor) are needed, as well as corresponding resource support — labor, material, financial, information, natural and energy resources. More detailed resource support for construction will be discussed in Chapter 6.

Manpower, acting via means of labor on the objects of labor, produce construction products, using an effective combination of *forms of organization of building production* — specialization, cooperation, concentration, combination.

A. Specialization reflects the level of the social division of labor and includes four main forms or directions of development - industry, object (subject), technological and detail. *Industry* specialization, orienting construction organizations to the construction of dissimilar objects and the implementation of diverse works, allows you to:

at the stage of construction of production determine the rational structure of the labor force and the composition means of labor, and provide measures to increase the intensity (strength) of labor and reduce labor intensity;

at the stage of construction, the efficient use of labor resources and the full use of labor with the widespread use of industrial methods of work.

Form of manifestation *of the objective* of division of labor are *submicro-branch,* specializing in the construction of technologically homogeneous objects, the production of certain items, goods and services by type of construction (housing and civil, industrial, energy, etc.). This specialization is called *object* (subject). In construction, the overwhelming mass of production, due to the various technologies for the construction of a particular group of objects, now appears in the form of submicroindustries of the subject division of labor, through the creation of multifunctional shopping and hotel complexes, technology parks, industrial (industrial) parks, free economic zones of an industrial orientation, etc. including:

in housing and communal construction:

- residential buildings and arrays;
- multifunctional complexes (hotels, office buildings, commercial buildings, etc.).
- individual trade institutions and complexes;
- buildings for cultural purposes;
- roads, bridges and embankments;
- construction of city water supply networks, sewerage, heating, gasification, etc.;

in industrial construction:

- objects of heavy and metallurgical industries;
- enterprises of the oil industry;

- engineering enterprises;
- coal and mining enterprises;
- pulp and paper industry enterprises;
- food industry facilities;
- light industry enterprises;
- enterprises of the building materials industry, etc.;
- communication facilities;

in energy construction:

- hydraulic engineering power plants;
- thermal power plants;
- nuclear power plants;
- facilities and devices for the transportation of electricity;

in transport and oil and gas pipeline construction:

- railways;
- roads;
- bridge structures;
- airfields;
- tunnels and subways;
- sea and river port facilities;
- trunk oil and gas pipelines;

in agricultural construction:

- livestock, poultry facilities and other industrial buildings;
- elevators, warehouses and storages;
- water facilities;
- rural electrification facilities;
- drill wells and rural water supply;
- rural roads.

This form is constantly being complicated and updated with new varieties of objects, because the needs of people are constantly increasing and the production process itself and its technology are being improved. With the acceleration of scientific and technological progress, the leading branches of production receive significant development, new tools, BIM technologies, materials, goods and services appear, and new productions arise with them. Over the past decade alone, such industries as the petrochemical, microbiological, plastic products, fiberglass and stone casting industries, enterprises for the production of porous aggregates: expanded clay, agloporite, expanded perlite, termite, etc. have been rapidly developed.

Within the object (subject) specialization, a further division of labor into technological and detail is manifested.

Technological specialization by type of work: excavation, installation of foundations and foundations, installation of reinforced concrete and steel structures, stone work, finishing work, installation of technological, energy and mechanical equipment, installation of sanitary and electrical systems and installations, etc.

Detailed specialization is divided by the types of production of individual parts, structures, units at the construction industry enterprises - DSC, reinforced concrete plants, reinforcement and carpentry shops, etc.

The continuous development of construction production, the concentration of capital investments at start-up facilities, constantly require accelerating the pace of construction. In order to accelerate construction at the first stage of the *separation of* technological processes, the number of performers is increasing due to the *operational division of labor.* A complex technological process that allows for technological interruptions is divided into simpler processes and operations. Concrete work, for example, can be divided into technologically interconnected but technologically interruptible processes: formwork, reinforcement of structures, concrete mix laying. In this set of technological processes, such a division of labor between the links of carpenters, reinforcers and concrete workers is dictated by the conditions of the concrete work technology.

B. Cooperation is an organizational form of interaction between participants in the construction of buildings and structures. In construction, both external and internal cooperation has developed. In the first direction, production relations are established between the general contracting and subcontracting organizations with the enterprises of the construction industry. With internal cooperation, such relations are spread within units, teams, and sections. Therefore, the development of cooperation makes it possible:

- at the stage of preparation for construction production, determine the maximum combination of periods of construction, establish appropriate terms for opening the front of work and organize a complete supply of materials, structures and technological equipment;
- at the construction stage, to carry out a significant amount of work at an early stage (as a rule, in the first year of construction), create continuous

long-term flows and ensure timely complete supply of materials, structures and technological equipment.

C. Concentration characterizes the capacity building of construction organizations and industrial enterprises. As a result, the necessary conditions are created for the introduction of new technology, the efficient allocation of resources in time and over construction projects. Thus, the development of concentration allows you to:

- at the stage of preparation for construction production, determine the required capacity of construction organizations through the amount of necessary labor resources and means of labor, as well as to create normal production and sanitary conditions for workers in advance;
- the implementation phase of construction to ensure not only the efficient allocation of labor resources in time and means of labor, but also their interaction during the entire construction period, and is also widely used for the construction of the mobile systems of inventory of buildings and permanent buildings.

D. Combination is a special organizational form of combining a construction company and an industrial enterprise. In this form of organization in a company concentrated closed technological cycle of construction production — from manufacturing materials, structures, components and transporting them to the site to construction and commissioning of the object (e.g., housing factory — (DSC)).

Consequently, the applicable form of organization of building production, constantly interacting, expressed in terms of its characteristics workforce communication rules, means of labor and objects of labor, which is an estimate of the productivity of labor.

Labor productivity is the ratio between the result of the production process (for example, m^3, units, m^2) and the number of production factors used (for example, working time, machine operating time).

The level of labor productivity in construction is determined by two main indicators: *production* — the ratio of revenue (gross income) to the average headcount (for example, m^3 / person, m^2 / person) or *labor intensity* (reciprocal of the output — the time spent on production units products (for example, people. days.)).

The state of the production process between the initial and final conditions is evaluated by the indicators of rhythm, uniformity, continuity and intensity of work. Such indicators, on the one hand, reflect the rate of materialization of labor at a given construction site, and on the other hand, characterize the effectiveness of the construction organization.

And since the growth of labor productivity allows you to get additional volume of construction products, then, therefore, the *intensity of labor*, as the effective consumption of labor by qualifications and time resources, is the most important factor in the influence of the organization of construction production on the growth of labor productivity and the rate of output of finished construction products. Naturally, labor costs should include losses in labor productivity due to various interruptions and downtime, as well as uneven workload of workers, etc.

The main directions of reducing labor costs in the construction industry are reducing the complexity of work, increasing the intensity of labor, the formation of a rational composition of workers and improving working and leisure conditions.

The first area contains mainly technical and technological factors for reducing labor intensity and is considered as a necessary, initial condition for the development of organizational solutions.

The second direction basically provides for the maximum use of labor resources in time and qualifications. In addition, this area includes measures for the full use of mechanization, improving the quality of work, eliminating all types of losses, strengthening labor discipline, etc., i.e. measures that are directly aimed at the maximum use of labor resources and, therefore, most fully reflect the effectiveness of organizational decisions.

The third and fourth directions, being mainly organizational in content, are usually solved at the stage of preparation for construction production and are implemented in a relatively long period of time.

In the context of mechanized and automated production within each organization, a *technical division of labor* is required, caused by the technical conditions of production. For mechanized production in construction can be attributed, for example, the laying of asphalt mixes using an asphalt paver; various methods of excavation using a bulldozer, scraper, grab or excavator; pile foundation device; drilling and blasting and mechanized sinking and other works using means of mechanization; Automated production may include, for example, the manufacture of finished products and structures at the construction industry enterprises from lightweight porous concrete, plastic products for engineering infrastructure, enclosing wall structures, etc.

In the production of these types of work, due to the division of labor, various categories of workers are distinguished: workers who *operate machines,* with a few assistants; workers who *provide* car *care* or simply *feed* labor material into the machine. In addition to them, there is a category of workers who are not directly involved in the technological process. Such workers carry out the necessary *repairs of machines.* And, finally, special staff stands out, as a rule, having extensive practical experience or special education. It includes, for example, engineers, managers, economists, technicians, mechanics engaged in *coordinating the* actions of these workers, *arranging control* of all machines, *taking into account* labor and manufactured products, *organizing* internal and external production relations, and also performing other functions of economic activity.

The entire mass of living labor in modern mechanized production can be divided into the following groups:

- *main labor* directly involved in the technological process of modifying objects of labor through machines (for example, labor of an excavator driver);
- *auxiliary labor,* providing power and car care (for example, labor as an assistant excavator operator) or supplying materials to the machine (for example, auxiliary workers in the construction of pile foundations, workers in supply and transport organizations);
- *maintenance work,* not directly involved in the technological process, but only maintaining the machine in working condition by making the necessary repairs (for example, labor of workers at bases and mechanization departments);
- *economic labor,* performing one of the most important functions of the "total worker", not only in organizing and managing production processes, but also in economic calculation.

The technical division of labor into basic, auxiliary, servicing and economic labor indicates the qualification ratio or the proportion of these varieties in the total mass of labor. There are examples in construction when auxiliary work is no less complicated and skilled than the main one. For example, the work of a tower crane driver is auxiliary to the main work of a bricklayer, but he is of no less qualification, and relative to the link of installers, he becomes the main labor.

In the process of mechanization of production auxiliary labor becomes more complex and skilled. The same can be said about the labor serving. With the development of technology, its specific gravity, qualification and cultural level are constantly increasing, since the machine itself is the subject of labor (for example, BIM-technologies).

1.6 Construction Methods

The methods that determine the various *methods of organizing construction,* taking into account the remoteness of the facilities being built from the locations of construction organizations are divided into:

A. Construction of individual facilities. Any sufficiently large construction, as a rule, consists of a complex of separate objects on which work cycles are performed (zero-cycle work, work on the construction of the aerial part, internal work, etc.). Thus, in spatial terms, construction is divided into objects (object specialization), and in technology — into types of work (technological specialization). If construction is carried out according to start-up complexes or lines, some of the facilities may represent finished construction products. At the same time, *finished construction products* are usually understood to mean a separate construction company, start-up industrial complexes, urban development complexes, and also separate housing and communal facilities that are ready either to produce products (production facilities) or to satisfy goods (residential buildings) that are completely completed by construction, or to the provision of services (hotels, shops, etc.). Another part of the objects, in a certain sense, may not be finished construction products, since they have an auxiliary value. These objects may include engineering infrastructure.

However, in all cases, both spatially distinguished groups are immovable objects, and their construction requires the movement of all necessary types of resources: tangible (cash, construction machines and mechanisms, building materials, etc.) and intangible (licenses, patents, technologies, etc.).

B. Construction of a complex of facilities in a nodal way. As a rule, as part of any major construction, it is possible to distinguish technically separate units, for example, an administrative and household building, a complex of water treatment facilities, workshops for the main production, etc. Within the boundaries of the allocated units, construction and installation processes are carried out to ensure their readiness for commissioning and commissioning. This isolation is the essence of the nodal method of organizing construction, which allows you to combine construction and installation processes as much as possible and organize their implementation by the flow method (for example, the construction of industrial (industrial) parks, nuclear power plants, thermal power plants, hydroelectric power plants, etc.). When dividing the construction into nodes, the following requirements must be considered:

- constructive completeness of the construction part allocated to the unit and ensuring its spatial stability;
- completeness of a separate technological cycle provided by this unit in the general technological process of the facility under construction; the possibility of autonomous testing and commissioning of individual production lines and plants;

- the possibility of creating conditions for stream construction and the accelerated opening of subsequent work fronts for related construction and installation organizations;
- the desirability of securing on the node of the lead (head) contractor with a predominant volume of construction and installation works;
- the need for the complete completion of construction and installation work on a specific site by the relevant contracting units before moving them to other sites.

C. Construction in a complete block way provides for the separation of individual objects under construction into volumetric modules. In this way of organization of construction, a building or structure is erected from separate spatial structures — prefabricated blocks. As a rule, the manufacture and testing of structural blocks and equipment takes place at manufacturing enterprises, and construction and technological blocks, blocks of engineering networks and technological pipelines at assembly plants and bases of the construction industry of construction and installation organizations. The order of delivery of blocks from manufacturers, assembly and assembly bases to the place of their installation in the design position is determined by the technological sequence of the construction of the facility, provided for in the project for the organization of construction (POC) and the project for work (PW).

The following buildings and structures are recommended for construction in complete block construction: boiler houses, boiler rooms, heating units, transformer substations, diesel power plants, compressor stations, warehouses, temporary buildings and structures located at the construction site, etc.

In the general case, both the order of construction of the facilities and the technological sequence of the work allow either sequential, parallel, or continuous (combined) construction, which may also include their rational combinations.

By the *method of remoteness of constructed objects* from the location of construction organizations:

A. Expeditionary method of construction of facilities by mobile units. It is carried out at a considerable distance from the construction sites from the locations of construction organizations. With this method, the construction is carried out by mobile units, which are sent to the place of work, usually for one season or quarter. Mobile units are located in expeditionary mobile villages deployed at stationary settlements and as close to the work object as possible. The cycle of trips to the place of work and returns to the base settlement is repeated in a pre-planned sequence. The organization of social services in the expeditionary settlement is calculated on the basis of meeting the daily and periodic needs of workers living without family members, and includes limited trade and consumer services, organization of leisure outside working hours and on rest days.

B. Shift way of organizing construction. This method is used when the construction sites are far from the locations of construction companies (more than three months), that is, large compared to the expeditionary method. Therefore, with this method, the working personnel changes at relatively small fixed intervals of time (week and decade).

Construction and installation works are carried out by shift personnel, who during their stay at the construction site live in specially created shift camps and systematically return to the location of the construction organization and permanent residence. The condition for applying the rotational method is the presence or organization of an interconnected system of housing production bases. Housing and industrial complexes of the base camp include a developed social infrastructure for permanent residence, cultural and social services for workers and a shift camp, designed for temporary residence of workers without family members, but with the satisfaction of their daily needs. The nearest border of the shift construction zone is determined within the duration of transport traffic of 1–1.5 hours.

C. Expeditionary rotational method of organizing construction. The combination of shift and expeditionary methods is defined as expeditionary-rotational method. For expeditionary and rotational methods of organizing construction, the use of mobile buildings and structures, which are classified according to the following criteria, is of great importance:

- by type of mobility — for container ones, consisting of one block container of full factory readiness, and collapsible, consisting of separate block containers, connected to a single system at the place of operation;
- for execution in accordance with climatic influences — on the northern, ordinary and southern;
- according to the functional purpose — to production, storage, auxiliary, residential, public and their varieties.

1.7 Parties to the construction and their functions

General Provisions The main efforts of the participants in the investment process are aimed at improving the effective management of investment construction projects (hereinafter, ICP) or programs implemented through capital investments, taking into account the functioning of the construction complex.

According to the Federal Laws "On investment activity in the Russian Federation carried out in the form of capital investments" (Federal Law No. 39 of February 25, 1999, as amended of December 18, 2006), taking into account the following additions and changes, "On participation in shared construction of apartment buildings and other real estate objects and on amendments to some legislative acts of the Russian Federation" (Federal Law No. 214 of December 30, 04), the subjects of investment activity in construction are customers, developers, developers, developers, investors, designers, contractors, consultants, users Ateliers-operators, users of capital investment objects and other persons. Any subject of investment activity has the right to combine the functions of the above management entities, unless otherwise provided by agreements or contracts concluded between them.

The state in accordance with federal laws, laws of the constituent entities of the Russian Federation and other regulatory and legal acts of the Russian Federation (and its constituent entities) guarantees to all parties to investment and construction activities, regardless of ownership, the following:

- ensuring equal rights in the implementation of investment activities;
- publicity in the discussion of investment projects;
- the right to appeal in court decisions and actions (inaction) of state authorities, local authorities and their officials;
- protection of capital investments.

The subjects and objects of management can be various management institutions, interconnected according to a hierarchical principle and regulated in their activities by the charters of organizations, regulations on structural units and job descriptions. The subject of construction management can be any individual or legal entity, for example, a construction organization, its structural divisions and officials performing specific functions in the design, construction and operation process. The grassroots (primary) object of management in construction is construction production, since it is through its implementation that finished construction products are created. The specific composition of management entities listed below may vary (vary) depending on the combination of functions. So, for example, the developer, customer and investor can be represented by one legal entity if the developer has its own investment resource and structural unit in the form of a capital construction department, through which the function of the customer-developer is realized. In Fig. 1.6. shows an approximate scheme of interaction of the main subjects of management, and their distribution by the main stages of implementation is shown in table. 1.2. Consider the tasks and functions of the main participants in the investment and construction process.

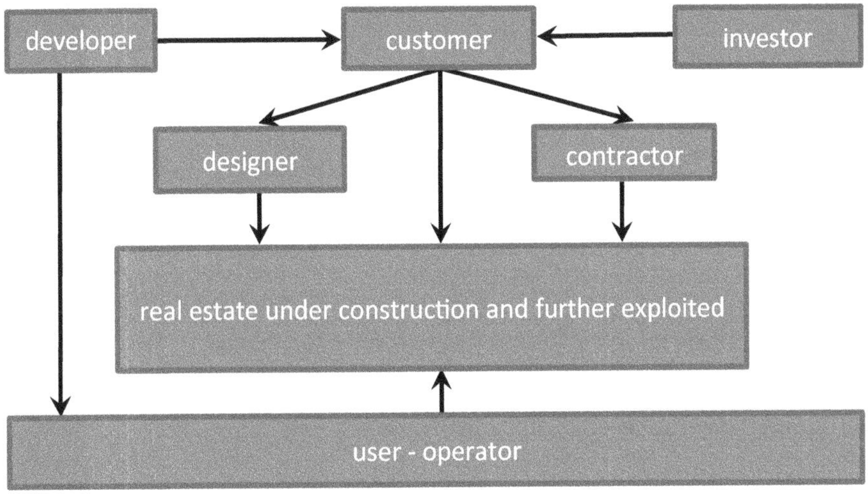

Figure 1.6: The interaction of the main subjects of management in the organization of construction and management of ICP

A. The developer is an individual or legal entity in whose interests the construction is carried out. The builder, in principle, may not be a specialist in the field of construction, and therefore, the implementation of the functions of the customer assigned to him, in particular related to the technical supervision of construction, requires the involvement of appropriate, usually licensed or certified specialists (builders). Moreover, the specific form certifying the professionalism of a specialist is determined by law, for example, legislation on self-regulatory organizations.

The developer provides:

- uninterrupted transfer of "financial resources" to the "customer" to pay for design and survey work and to finance construction within the allocated volumes of capital investments according to the agreed schedule attached to annual agreements;
- coordinates the volumes of construction production to be carried out and their compliance with the volumes of materials and structures necessary for construction;
- assists the "customer" in its interaction with organizations involved in the investment process in the implementation of the relevant investment program.

The cost of construction assigned to the "customer" under the contracts concluded with him and annual contracts is determined in the manner established by the governments of the constituent entities of the Russian Federation. The volume of construction, the timing of commissioning, financing schedules,

Table 1.2 Example stages of the implementation of the investment construction project and management entities

<table>
<tr><th>No</th><th>The name of the implementation phase of ICP</th><th>The main document being developed</th><th>The main stage performer</th><th colspan="3">Belonging to the studied discipline</th></tr>
<tr><td>1</td><td>Technical and economic rationale</td><td>ICP business plan</td><td>Developer</td><td rowspan="5"></td><td rowspan="3"></td><td rowspan="10">Investment project management</td></tr>
<tr><td>2</td><td>Predesign stage</td><td>Urban Plan.
Design assignment</td><td>Developer, customer, developer</td></tr>
<tr><td>3</td><td>Design and survey work</td><td>Projects, estimates, project of construction organization (POC)</td><td>Designer, customer, developer</td></tr>
<tr><td>4</td><td>Organizational preparation</td><td>Organization of bidding</td><td>Customer, developer, applicants</td><td rowspan="7">Construction management</td></tr>
<tr><td>5</td><td>Contract bidding</td><td>Work agreement</td><td>Customer, developer, contractor</td></tr>
<tr><td>6</td><td>Obtaining a building permit</td><td>Work permit</td><td>Customer, contractor</td><td rowspan="5">Organization of construction production</td></tr>
<tr><td>7</td><td>Technical preparation</td><td>Project of work production (PWP)</td><td>Contractor</td></tr>
<tr><td>8</td><td>Construction, control, accounting and reporting</td><td>General journal of works, technical supervision, field supervision</td><td>Contractor, customer, designer</td></tr>
<tr><td>9</td><td>Commissioning</td><td>Permission to put an object into operation</td><td>All management entities</td></tr>
<tr><td>10</td><td>Operation of the property by the developer</td><td>Object passport, technical documentation, registration</td><td>Bodies of operation and registration</td></tr>
</table>

the rights and obligations of the "builder" and "customer", as well as their property liability are determined by the general agreement (contract).

B. A customer is a management entity whose main function is the organization of construction and implementation of ICP as a whole (for example, in the interests of the Government of Moscow), at the expense of funds transferred to it by the respective developer, or on his behalf by the Department of Finance and other institutions (for example, the Government Of the Russian Federation or the Government of Moscow), as well as through equity transfers and other means, carries out at its own risk the construction of its own and attracted funds and the commissioning of facilities on time and in volumes determined by the developer. In some cases, the customer assumes the fulfillment of complex responsibilities for the implementation of the functions of the customer-developer in the design and construction of facilities (for example, according to the program and title list approved by the Office for the Prospective Development of the city on the conditions established by the Moscow Government).

In this case, the customer-developer agrees to provide integrated development (renovation), the allocated territory of the city in accordance with the master plan for the integrated economic and social development of the city and planning plans, urban planning plans and the terms of the contract, in compliance with technical regulations, building norms and rules, technical conditions and delivery of finished immovable objects. Placement of orders for the execution of contracting work on the design and construction of objects of investment programs of the Government of Moscow is carried out by customers-developers based on a competitive selection of a general contractor and organizations of contractors who have proposed the most favorable conditions for fulfilling orders.

The cost of construction of the facilities entrusted to the customer is determined by contractual prices agreed by the customer with contracting organizations drawn up in accordance with the procedure (for example, established by the Moscow Government on the basis of declared and registered selling prices for building materials, parts and structures, and coefficients for increasing the estimated cost of construction and installation works approved by the interdepartmental commission under the Government of Moscow).

The customer provides an increase in the efficiency of capital investments and a reduction in the duration of the investment cycle and carries out the construction of urban facilities in established volumes. He places on a competitive basis orders for the implementation of the municipal program among contracting organizations that have the appropriate licenses and certificates (the necessary form is determined by current legislation). The customer submits to the developer accounting and statistical reports, reports on the use of financial resources, as well as operational information on the placement and implementation of fulfilled orders and the state of their construction, various certificates on the development of allocated funds and the need for financial resources for the next month, etc.

The customer cannot spend funds transferred by the developer to the customer for financing contractual facilities for other purposes. Therefore, the parties periodically reconcile transfers and expenditures of funds for the purposes specified in the agreement concluded between them.

C. Developer — being the main participant in the investment and construction project, he is interested in implementing the project and achieving its goal. Unlike the customer, the main activities in the developer's activities are financial and economic aspects (choosing the commercial viability of the project, attracting investments, ensuring the financial and economic sustainability of the project, etc.). He can become the future owner and user of the project results.

Most often, they try to identify the concept of "developer" with the well-known Russian concept of "builder". However, this concept is absent in the fundamental legislative acts, and in the Law of the Russian Federation of July 14, 1998 No. 3295-1 "On the Basics of Urban Planning in the Russian Federation". It is used as an analogue of the word "customer". An attempt is made to replace the term "development with the term "organizer". As you can see, so far, attempts to replace the foreign word "development" with the original Russian have not yet succeeded.

Developer — an entrepreneur (legal entity or individual), who received his profit from the creation, development and promotion of usually technically complex real estate.

Developers are usually divided into three types:

1) a *developer of the "Western" type* — is only the organizer of the process, preferring to attract third-party organizations to solvc onc or another part of the project. A significant drawback of this type of development can be considered its great dependence on the external environment;

2) a *developer,* which is a *vertically integrated holding* , which includes all the necessary capacities for the construction of construction projects (complexes) and a large staff. Despite the universality of such a structure, its drawback is organizational rigidity;

3) a *developer* in the form of a *horizontally integrated holding,* which is a development business unit of large financial and industrial groups, which is the result of structural changes within these groups in connection with the development of new attractive types of business. Such development companies build relations with other business units of their group on a purely market basis. They are the most stable on the market and quickly adapt to adverse fluctuations in supply and demand (Fig. 1.7).

The second part of this textbook "Real Estate Development" is devoted in more detail to development.

D. An investor is a management entity whose main function is to finance a project or investment program with the goal of generating a profit determined by the percentage (investor's profit) on invested capital.

Investors can be both individuals and legal entities, created based on an agreement on joint activities, not having the status of a legal entity, associations of legal entities, state institutions, local governments, as well as foreign business entities (foreign investors).

For municipal projects, it is possible to attract non-municipal investors for fully or partially finance the construction (renovation) of objects of invest-

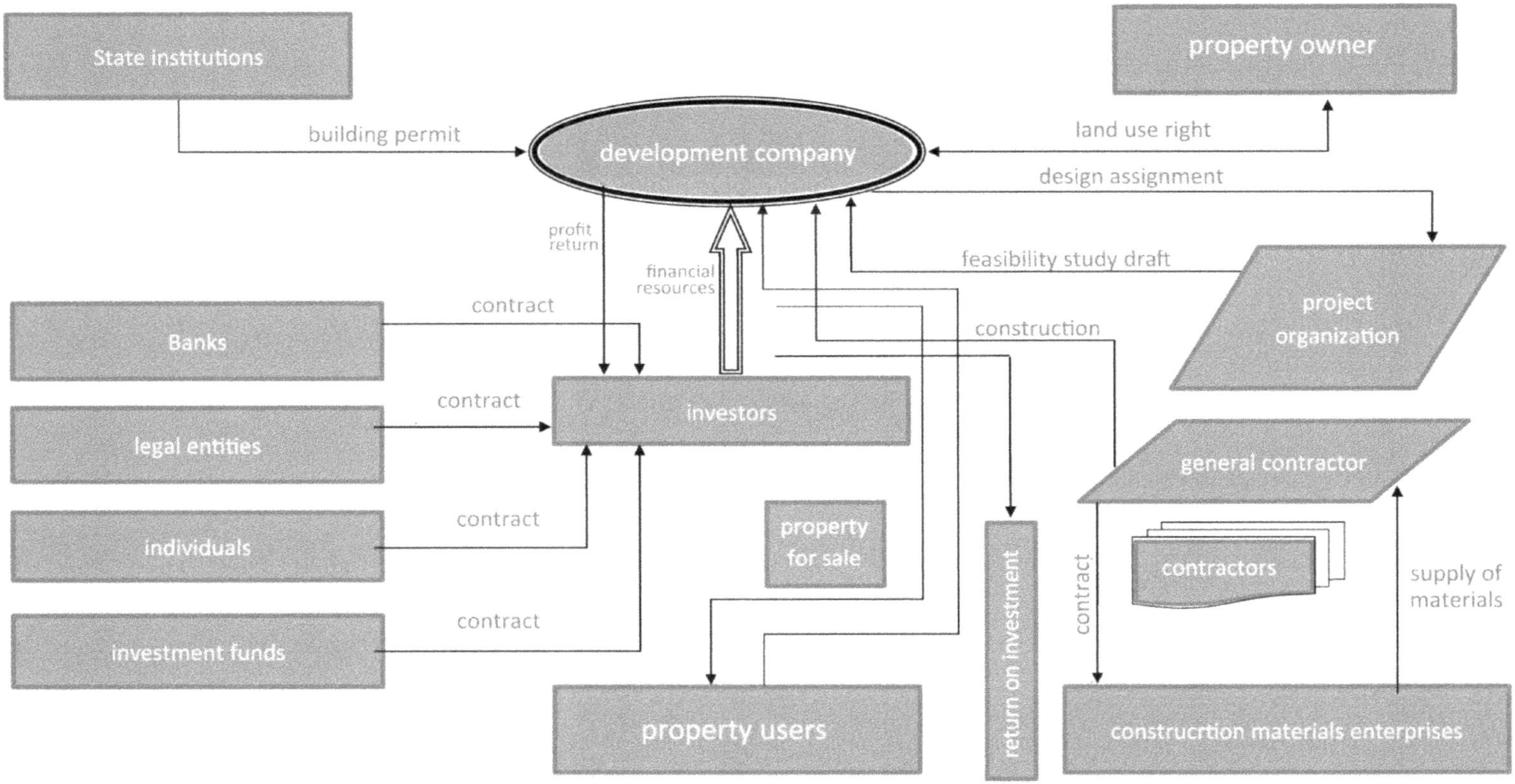

Figure 1.7: Interaction of participants in an investment construction project

ment programs of the governments of the constituent entities of the Russian Federation. However, it should be carried out solely based on competitions.

The purpose of the competition is to select the investors who proposed the most favorable conditions (in particular, at a lower rate of return on invested capital) to participate in financing the design and (or) construction of the investment object in accordance with the requirements established in the tender documentation. Any investment activity in the field of capital construction (reconstruction) of objects on the territory of the constituent entities of the Russian Federation that are not part of the approved investment programs of the governments of the constituent entities of the Russian Federation is also carried out on the basis of contracts.

E. A designer is a management entity whose main function is to carry out design and survey work necessary to create design estimates and field supervision of construction (carried out under a separate agreement with the customer).

Design and survey contractors involved in the preparation of the construction of facilities under the general contract are also involved on a competitive basis. A designer who has concluded a general contract for design and exploration work with a customer is defined as a general designer, and designers who have concluded subcontracts with a general designer are called subprojectors. A design and engineering firm can act as a designer.

F. Consultant. The main activities of consulting management companies are issues of strategies and policies of development companies, finance, the human factor, information and management systems, marketing, project management.

The system of consulting services in construction management has a relatively small history. Having appeared in the mid-90s, management-consulting firms in construction are now widely developed. Management consulting firms are small organizations; more than 90% of their total number consists of 3 to 25 consultants.

The main reasons for accessing consulting services in management are the following: the need to diagnose the state of affairs and business, to develop an organizational structure, strategy, information systems, the purpose of which is to improve the quality and effectiveness of management. Due to the high dynamism of the external environment, which is characteristic of the current stage of development, even large construction organizations are not able to conduct a professional analysis of current situations and develop proposals for an appropriate reorganization. Leading specialists of a construction organization, as a rule, do not have such an opportunity due to lack of time. In addition, they cannot always look at the problem with the systemic position: acting effect "habituation". Contacting consultants provides the customer with additional knowledge and information, i.e. The counseling process is also a learning process.

Among the consulting services are distinguished such as jurisprudence, accounting and reporting, engineering (see section 1.2). Legal ***services*** include advice on legal relationships, labor disputes. ***Services in field of accounting*** include advice in matters of accounting, finance, financial and accounting reports.

G. Contractor. Its main function is $\ll$ physical $\gg$ construction of facilities in accordance with the developed design and estimate documentation. The contractor who has entered into a general contract with the customer is defined as the general contractor, and the contractors who have entered into subcontracts with the general contractor are called subcontractors. Contractors are individuals and legal entities that perform work under a contract and (or) a state contract concluded in accordance with the Civil Code of the Russian Federation. Contractors are required to have a license to carry out those types of special activities that are subject to licensing, or to have appropriate certificates, the issuance of which and their form is determined in accordance with federal laws.

As a contractor, any legal entity capable of bearing property responsibility for non-fulfillment or improper fulfillment of obligations under a contract with the customer can participate in the implementation of investment orders (see Section 1.2).

H. User. Its main function is the use and operation of a construction site, including the operation of its production facilities. Users of capital investment objects are individuals and legal entities, including foreign, as well as state institutions, local self-government institutions, foreign states, international associations and organizations for which these objects are created.

An important element in the initial operation of the facility is to ensure for the user his right to provide warranty service for the facility.

The warranty period for the normal operation of the facility and its engineering systems, equipment, materials and work is established starting from the date of signing the permission to put the finished facility into operation by the state construction supervision and state examination institution. If during the period of warranty operation of the facility defects are found that impede its normal operation, the customer is obliged to arrange for their elimination at his own expense and within the agreed time. The warranty period in this case is extended accordingly for the period of elimination of defects. It should be borne in mind that the above guarantees do not apply to cases of intentional damage to an object by third parties.

1.8 The main problems of construction management

The current stage of development of the world building system is characterized by increased competition for new construction markets, the outcome of which in the conditions of the scientific and technological revolution largely depends on the comprehensive improvement of production and its management. Competition, commercial goals and interests serve as a decisive impulse for the search for new solutions for the organization of production and management, the rapid implementation of science in practice.

Improving management is one of the most important areas of increasing the efficiency of construction production, growth of labor productivity. Foreign construction companies pay significant, sometimes even excessive attention to these issues, seeing in management the reason for the majority of their successes and failures and explaining the miscalculations in management as objective flaws and imperfections in the external environment. It is worth noting that the underestimation of the importance of thc management factor, inherent, in particular, to our capital construction, is associated with large losses, the non-use of a powerful reserve to increase the efficiency of construction production.

For the first time, the question of the need to separate management activity itself into a special object of research and an independent type of production activity was proposed by the French researcher A. Fayole (1841-1925), who, in particular, belongs to the first most successful classification of management functions that later became classical, subdivided into the functions of forecasting, planning, organization, coordination and control. Fayole proposed 14 principles of management that are universal in nature and applicable to almost all areas of administrative (managerial) activity: 1) division of labor; 2) power; 3) discipline; 4) unity of command; 5) unity of leadership; 6) submission of individual interests to the common interest; 7) remuneration; 8) centralization; 9) the line of power; 10) order; 11) equality; 12) the stability of the personnel hierarchy; 13) initiative; 14) corporate spirit.

It was Fayole's work that served as the initial impetus in the development of the so-called "classical" management theory, which became the basis of the modern theory of internal management. Among the largest works in this direction, the works of the German sociologist M. Weber, who developed the model of an "ideal" administrative organization, which was called "bureaucracy" and is characterized by the following features, should be highlighted:

1) The structuring of goals and objectives; 2) standardization; 3) impartiality in evaluating the actions of subordinates; 4) compliance with the qualifications of the post.

Research in the field of management theory in the West goes in two main directions: model (theoretical) and heuristic (practical).

In accordance with the first direction, model constructions and hypotheses are built, which are then verified by the results of practical activities of a significant number of organizations. Therefore, research is being conducted on hypotheses about the relationship between the internal structure and production technology, the existence of universal principles for constructing organizational management structures, the hypotheses of M. Weber mentioned above about specialization and standardization in management.

Such studies allow us to outline the general, main ways of improving management. The second direction is heuristic, based on the synthesis of experimental data and the development of practical recommendations on the implementation of advanced achievements in the field of management.

Factor management models that establish the dependence of management effectiveness on factors influencing it are widely used. Among the main factors that have a decisive influence on the duration of construction, as one of the three main criteria for the effectiveness of construction production (time, cost, quality), the factor of management organization, the use of organizational forms of management, traditional (general contracting system) and non-traditional (management the construction of the facility by the customer, the combination of the design and construction stages in time, professional construction management, etc.). As the analysis showed, in most cases, non-traditional methods of organization of management provide earlier completion dates; as studies have shown, at least one third of the facilities whose construction was carried out as part of traditional forms of management organization had a duration below the average.

The key factor influencing the reduction of construction time was recognized as the "continuity of management" factor, the essence of which is the need to control the progress of the project, starting from the earliest stages of the investment process (for example, deciding on the construction of an object). If in traditional systems this function is assigned to the customer, then in non-traditional control systems it is transferred either to a project-building company or to a specialized management company. Analysis of time losses at various stages of the project allowed us to identify the main causes of the delay. At the design stage, these reasons are the lack of information necessary for the development of design solutions or its insufficient accuracy; at the construction stage — difficulties in interacting with subcontractors, lack of proper coordination, unjustified complexity of design decisions, lack of financial and labor resources during certain periods of construction, etc.

The management factor is considered by the overwhelming majority of specialists as the most important from the point of view of influence on increasing labor productivity in construction and its effectiveness.

Under *effectiveness* generally means the volume of products made from a unit volume of resources per unit of time, and in relation to the construction — the time it takes to complete a full range of works on the construction of the facility. Construction products are distinguished by the following five system-wide characteristics: high stationarity; great difficulty; long duration; high price; high level of social responsibility.

The indicated characteristics are in varying degrees inherent in any construction project and vary depending on its type and size.

The seasonality factor also plays a large role in construction, influencing the cost and duration of the construction of facilities. Attempts to develop and implement the so-called "off — season" construction technologies, which are independent of the climatic conditions, result in a sharp rise in the cost of construction. Therefore, a more promising are efforts to find construction technologies that provide rapid assembly of structures and units directly to the construction site.

For the current stage of development of construction and construction management systems, two characteristics are characteristic. The first is an attempt to approach the problem of improving management on a systemic basis i.e. by simultaneously reviewing all the basic elements of a management system, including organizational forms and management structures, management functions and decision-making methods, management tools (communication and data processing tools). The second is in the structural and organizational separation of management improvement issues, which are becoming more and more specialized, into an independent management function, called the "development" function.

Questions for self-control

1. What is the construction complex, what is its role in the national economy?
2. What organizations are included in the construction complex? What unites the branches of the economy into a single intersectoral system?
3. What organizations are the core of the construction complex? Why?
4. On what grounds are construction organizations classified?
5. What industries and complexes does the construction complex closely interact with?
6. How is the regulation of the construction complex on a national and regional scale?
7. What organizations carry out supervisory functions over the activities of the construction complex?

8. List the features of construction.
9. What signs determine how to organize construction?
10. What are the general and excellent signs of shift and expeditionary ways of organizing construction?
11. The main participants in the construction.
12. What tasks are the responsibilities of the builder, developer?
13. Can a developer and investor be a contractor?
14. What are the challenges of managing construction?

Questions for discussion

1. What are the state and development trends of the construction complex in Russia?
2. How does the construction complex respond to crisis phenomena in the economy?
3. Is state regulation of the construction complex necessary? Should government influence be strengthened in a crisis?

Questions to solve the problem yourself

1. Review the statistics presented in table

   Present the main indicators characterizing the activity by type "Construction" graphically. What conclusions can you draw about the state and dynamics of the construction industry?
2. What are the main problems of building complex management?
3. Check out statistics on the activities of the construction complex in your area. Make a table according to statistics.

   Present the dynamics of indicators graphically. Make a conclusion about the dynamics of the main indicators and the trends you identified. Do your trends coincide with the all-Russian? What other indicators can be used to judge industry development trends?

Indicators	2010	2011	2012	2013	2014	2015	2016	2017	2018	***
Investments in fixed assets, billion rubles, in% by 1990										
The volume of contract work, billion rubles										
The number of people employed in construction, million people										
The number of organizations operating in the construction complex										
The share of investment in fixed assets in GDP,%										
Sources of investment in fixed assets, in% of the total:										
Total Including: budget resources including: federal budget budgets of constituent entities of the Federation and local budgets extrabudgetary funds of them: own funds of enterprises										
Distribution of organizations by ownership, in% to the total Total state municipal private mixed										
Distribution of organizations by the number of employees, in% of the total number Total up to 100 people 101-200 people over 200 people										
The commissioning of residential buildings, million sq.m.										

Chapter 2

ORGANIZATIONAL AND CONTRACTUAL RELATIONS

Organizational and contract relations are formed based on direct production management methods. In the extractive industries, energy, water supply, taking into account the specifics of the processes, continuous management methods are used. In serial industrial production, trade, transport — continuous cyclic methods. State and municipal activities are characterized by a program-targeted management method. In construction and other industries whose products are individual and large-scale objects, the project management method is used. Organizational and contractual relations are also based on the project management method in shipbuilding, aviation and space industries. This method is applied and in other areas when developing new unique products, computer programs or equipment.

2.1 Project Management Concepts

In Russian-language professional terminology, there are two concepts:

1. A project, as a set of project documentation necessary for the construction or reconstruction of an object (for example, "a project for the construction of a sports and recreation complex");

2. A project, as the process of achieving the goal of creating or improving a large system (for example, "investment project", "national project").

In other languages, different terms are used for these concepts: in English - "design" and "project", in German — and "Entwurf" and "Project", in French — "dessin" and "projet".

The project is determined uniquely by the statement of the problem, by setting the goal (solving the problem) and the means to achieve it. The American Institute for Project Management (PMI) defines the *project* as a temporary enterprise, carried out to create a unique product [142]. The construction of a real estate property certainly fits this definition.

A project in construction is a complex of interrelated activities with clearly defined goals for creating buildings or structures.

Project management is a way of organizing production aimed at the timely achievement of a one-time, non-repeating goal with the optimal use of available resources.

In modern economic conditions, project management in construction and real estate, solving the problems of reproduction of fixed assets is carried out as part of investment and construction activities.

Investment and construction project (ICP) - the justification of economic feasibility, volume and timing of capital investments, including the necessary design estimates, developed in accordance with the laws of the Russian Federation and standards (norms and rules) approved in the established manner, as well as a description of practical action on the implementation of investments (business plan). Construction is onc of the main stages of the implementation of ICP. Construction projects require significant and long-term investments, the sources of which are financial institutions: commercial banks, credit and insurance companies, various kinds of investment funds. Management of ICP involves providing it not only with investment resources, but also with all other necessary types of resources: labor, information, organizational, material, and legal.

As noted in Section 1.7, Chapter 1, one of the modern concepts that goes beyond the traditional understanding of the project is *development,* which implies a significant expansion of the scope of project management.

It is not limited only to the creation of a real estate object — whether from the position of a general contractor, customer-developer or investor. The role of the developer is special at all stages of the investment and construction project and is different from the role of all other participants.

Most often, he is not a general contractor, he may not be an investor, and his functions in the design and construction of a building are not completely reduced to those of a customer-developer. The main difference between development and other forms of organization of construction activities is to expand the scope of active participation until the full commissioning and further development of the property. It is important for the developer that the building was designed based on the needs of potential customers identified by him and taking into account all architectural and building codes. It is equally important that the building was built in accordance with the project, on time and within the approved budget. However, perhaps the most important thing for the developer is the effective use of the resulting construction products — real estate, since it is at this stage that all income is received.

At the same time, the developer can solve the problems of not only selling real estate and industrial facilities to individuals or legal entities engaged in direct operation, but also transferring the object for rent in completely or in part. The developer is actively interested in the fact that the created object brings as long and as much profit as possible. Therefore, he actively develops this object based on his own knowledge of the market and the need to meet its requirements during the operation period. Thus, development as a new form of investment and construction activity does not fit into the traditional understanding of the terminal project.

Moreover, a common understanding of development can be reduced to increase the efficiency of use of any real estate object, and, of course, the primary real estate object — land. Currently, organizational approaches are being developed within which the concept of project management is not applied to the construction or creation of a real estate object, but to the beneficial acquisition of such an object and a further increase in its cost in a variety of ways (not necessarily by carrying out construction, installation, repair and restoration works or reconstruction of buildings and structures).

Within the framework of the development project, not only there is an object created (an industrial or civil building, an engineering structure, for example, a gas pipeline), but there is a constant organizational development of the object and its management system, a constant search for more and more conformity of the object and requirements to it from the market, constant increase the effectiveness of its use. Thus, a development project is an example of a so-called developing project — a modern concept that has been actively developed in many subject areas of application of project management, such as the development and development of information systems and technologies, the development and continuous improvement of complex technical goods and systems (cars, aircraft etc.).

The experience gained so far in the joint and effective application of planning methods, information support, organizational and economic models and interaction schemes of participants in the process of project implementation is the basis of a system of generally applicable international management standards — project management methodologies.

The project management methodology is a system of methods for planning, organizing, controlling the costs of human and material resources, as well as regulating changes during the project life cycle that allow achieving the project goal at a given time and budget.

The project management system and its development are dealt with by the International Project Management Association[1], German Project Manage-

[1]International Project Management Association, IPMA

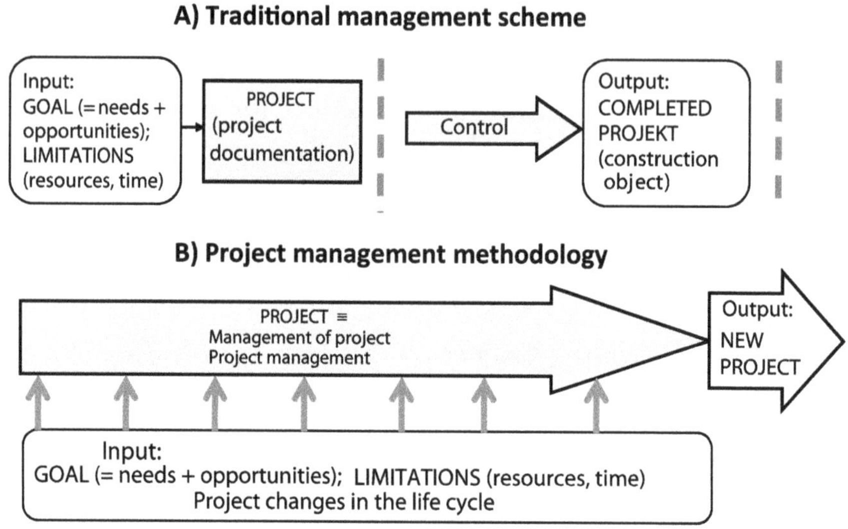

Figure 2.1: Unlike conventional control circuit and control methodology projects

ment Society[2], American Project Management Institute[3], American Project Management Society[4], Japan Project Management Association[5] and others. In the Russian Federation, the Eurasian Project Management Center, the Project Management Association (SOVNET), the Russian branch of the International Association for the Development of Cost Engineering (MARSI) and others are engaged in scientific and applied research in this area.

The concept of project management is based on an understanding of the project in the unity of the management object and the process of managing this object. In project management, the project acts both as a management object that has specific industry features (for example, a construction object, real estate, property complex), and as a process to achieve the goal, taking into account industry specifics (Fig. 2.1). Based on this, in project management it is methodologically justified to understand the terms "project", "project management" and "project management" as almost identical terms and focus on the relationship between the concepts of the project and its management. Based on this, project management in construction and real estate suggests that the building project and the processes of its construction and operation are planned and implemented as a single system.

Modern project management has developed into a scientific direction and a separate methodology due to the combination and consolidation of practical

[2]Deutsche Gesellschaft fur Projektmanagement e.V., GPM

[3]Project Management Institute

[4]American Society for the Advancement of Project Management

[5]Project Management Association of Japan, PMAJ

experience, methods and concepts into a single system. This system is open — it constantly incorporates new developments that have proven effectiveness in practice. Currently, the components of the system of project management methods include:

1. Systemic project planning;
2. Modeling the project life cycle;
3. Methods of structuring and restructuring the project;
4. The process approach;
5. Network planning;
6. Logistics;
7. Risk management;
8. System management of project functions;
9. Object-oriented management structures;
10. Methods of forming project teams;
11. Special software systems and information support for project life cycle;
12. The philosophy of project management.

The project management methodology and its individual elements and methods are widely used in IPP management. Project management methods and tools reflect the specifics of construction. The necessity and relevance of the project management methodology in construction and real estate is determined by many factors. In and x the following factors should be highlighted:

- An increase in the number of management entities and the related complication of construction complex management models. The criteria for optimizing the goals, resources and timing of the implementation of projects by management entities may differ and be contradictory;
- An increase in the number of owners and forms of ownership of real estate.
- The economic and other interests of owners are often multidirectional, which requires the use of special methods for substantiating organizational and economic schemes and models of project management;
- A massive and significant increase in the scope and cost of projects and, as a result of this, an increase in the importance of the criteria for the success of an individual project;
- Economic globalization and the related dissemination of international management standards in Russia, which are based on project management methodology;

- Increasing the dynamics of the market and the structure of demand for real estate. This necessitates the most versatile pre — investment and pre-project substantiation of decisions;
- Growth in aggregate risks and uncertainty in the conditions for the implementation of investment construction and development projects. They require accounting and analysis, which can be carried out by project management methods;
- Tougher competition, in which the application of the project management methodology becomes a factor in increasing the competitiveness of the project.

In the project management methodology, the project subject is the project as a whole, the subject of management is the person or organizational structure that initiates and implements the project. Four approaches to management can be high: system, policy-making, situational and process.

The systematic approach becomes the leading one in management when for the subject of management the strategic goal is a rigid dominant for the sake of which the project is initiated. The signs of a systematic approach are functionality (integrity) and subjectivity. Functionality or integrity in project management means that the whole dominates the component parts, that the goal is always more important than the processes to achieve it. The subjectivity in project management suggests that the subject of management selectively engages the participants and the project subsystem in relations of assistance in order to obtain the most useful results for itself, and controls the elements of the system that contribute most to the achievement of the goal. Since there are many participants involved in the implementation of ICP, the goals of which are different, from the point of view of a systematic approach to managing a project (a real estate object, a building, a property complex) is at the same time many systems, both during the life cycle and at any given time.

At the same time, for each participant the project is its own (subjective) system, with its own key and system-forming elements and relations of assistance.

A directive approach to management is based on strict regulation of functions, rights, obligations, standards, plans and tasks. The policy approach as the dominant of project management is typical for large organizational structures (concerns, holdings, alliance of organizations, consortia, etc.).

The situational approach to management is characterized by the absence of a rigid goal and strategy, the change of project concepts under the influence of external influence factors, the use of monitoring data, operational response, etc. as the basis for decision-making. In a situational approach, the goal and the ways to achieve it are modeled flexible, to quickly adapt to changes in the external environment. Situational management in its pure form is used for small projects or for the management of real estate at the operational stage. Elements of the situational approach are also present in the management of large projects, which is inevitable in the conditions of the dynamics of economic changes and the long term of operation of real estate.

The process approach to management is based on structuring the project into separate, most standardized processes, control and coordination of these processes. The process (production, business process), as a sequence of elementary operations to create or transform products, is an integral part of each production and management.

Project management also consists of processes — a certain set of functionally interrelated tasks, work that use resources, and require management. The need to develop a process approach is based on the following idea: if the production process is performed correctly (i.e., in the best, standard, standard, licensed way), then the result is guaranteed to be of high quality, and process control will be cheaper than a poor-quality result. International experience has shown that in the context of increasing scale and complexity of projects, the variability of development priorities, it is easier to manage the project and ensure its quality by presenting the project as a sequence of interconnected and standard processes. The process approach is increasingly used in the world practice of managing various projects and business lines, including in the field of construction and real estate. In the construction of an integrated system for process about process is not developed. The process approach is reflected in separate industry and regional documents, as well as documents of the National Association of Builders (NOSTROY). Despite the fact that the specifics of construction and development projects is a significant proportion of individualized and unique processes, the processes of construction and development of real estate, like other business processes, can be structured and largely standardized.

An international system of quality standards and activity certification (ISO 9001) is based on a process approach. In the national system of standards GOST R ISO distinguish generalized groups of processes that make up the project.

When developing processes, the Plan-Do-Check-Act (PDCA) cycle is usually used, consisting of the following operations:

1. Planning (development of goals and processes) to achieve the goals;
2. Implementation of these plans — implementation of the developed processes;
3. Control of processes for compliance with the goals of the company;
4. Activities for the continuous improvement of process indicators.

Based on the four generalized groups of processes listed above, the main management functions can be distinguished: planning; execution of plans (organization), control and regulation of changes.

The methods of project management in real estate are based on the general and inter- sectoral laws of projects and the specific laws of the functioning of the construction and real estate sectors.

Each project is uniquely characterized by three main parameters: the purpose or scope of the project, the cost and time of the project. If we interpret this graphically, then we can say that any project is implemented in a 3-dimensional space "scale-cost-time". For each project, there is a combination of three parameters (three coordinates) that provide regulatory quality. These coordinates are often called the project triangle (Fig. 2.2).

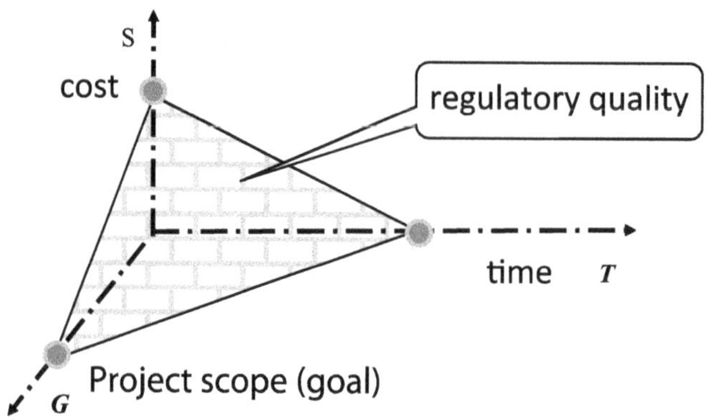

Figure 2.2: The general pattern of project management

The general regularity of all projects is the interdependence of the three main parameters of the project: the scale of the project, its cost and lead-time.

A change in one of the parameters causes a change in the others. In practice, accurately calculating and predicting specific changes in interrelated parameters is an extremely complex and difficult to formalize task, accessible to professionals, developers, top managers of the highest class.

The specific patterns of real estate project management are determined by three groups of factors:

- land properties, as the basis of real estate,
- features of the organization and technology of construction works,
- features of the operation of buildings and structures.

To date, the requirements of project management tasks are very significantly affected by the requirements of technology and the organization of construction work.

The complexity and quality of many construction works (excavation, installation, roofing, etc.) directly depends on atmospheric, climatic, hydrogeological, soil, and other cycles of the development region. In large- scale investment construction and development projects, it takes a large number of participants, which from the point of view of project management requires special elaboration of organizational schemes and coordination of their activities. High consumer qualities of modern buildings and structures from the point of view of operation are provided by a large number of technological and engineering subsystems, each of which has its own cycle of functioning, taking into account physical and moral wear and tear. This requires accounting and integration of the multi- sectoral subsystems of the project, as well as the selection of technologically advanced structural and engineering solutions adapted to the objectively inevitable repair, modernization and reconstruction.

A real estate project is fundamentally different from other ambiguity management facilities. The building, depending on the priorities of the owner or other management entity, can be an *object of consumption* (i.e., satisfy the needs for housing, a place of work, production, leisure), a *resource* (i.e., be a long-term investment involved in the production of over many cycles, it is the initial possibility of production — fixed assets), as well as an *asset* (i.e., one of the main factors affecting indicators of the financial condition of an organization). At the same time, one and the same real estate object can act simultaneously in several roles, and the significance of each of the three components (consumer, resource and financial) can change over the course of its life cycle depending on the market situation.

The classification of many ICP is carried out according to certain criteria that are significant for the choice of control methods. The purpose of the classification is to systematize projects into relatively homogeneous groups and develop on this basis management methods that are most effective for a particular class of projects.

There are various classifications of projects. The generally accepted classification characteristics of projects: type, class, scale, duration, complexity, field of activity and level of the project (Table 2.1).

According to the type of projects, technical, organizational, economic, social, and mixed projects are distinguished. The classification basis here is the focus of the project results. Project classes vary in organizational complexity. Therefore, for the implementation of the mono-project, one gene of the contractor is enough; for the implementation of the multi-project, several general contracting organizations will be required. Multi-projects are closely related to the concept of a project portfolio.

The project portfolio is a group of projects united by a strategic goal.

Table 2.1 Classification of projects according to various characteristics of management

1	Type of project	Technical, organizational, economic, social, mixed
2	Proect class	MONOPROJECTS (one general contractor); MULTIPROJECTS (several general contracting organizations); MEGAPROJECTS (target programs, national projects)
3	Project scope	SMALL (contract with a fixed price); AVERAGE (a contract with a fixed price, a contract for a time, a contract with payment of costs and additional remuneration); LARGE (contract for a time, contract with payment of costs and additional remuneration); ESPECIALLY BIG (life cycle contract)
4	Project duration	SHORT-TERM (oriented up to 3 years); MEDIUM-TERM (oriented from 3 to 5 years); LONG-TERM (oriented over 5 years)
5	Project complexity	Simple, complex, unique (very complex)
6	Field of activity	Investment; research; innovative; venture capital; social; educational; combined
7	Project level	Local, regional, state, international

Portfolio projects can be independent, and common resources can be used in them. As a rule, a project portfolio is created in the interests of and within the framework of one organization (holding, group of companies). With respect to its portfolio of projects, the company has a difficult task of creating a balanced (optimal) set of projects (customs) in the portfolio. The competitive enterprises collect projects on the criterion of maximum profitability, taking into account the different risks and the stage of the project, as well as the prospects of its development.

Megaprojects can include several multi-projects that are executed coordinated in a common implementation schedule. Megaprojects include targeted programs and national projects.

Program (target program) — a set of interconnected projects managed in a coordinated (joint) manner. Projects included in the program have a common strategic goal, a single implementation schedule, and, as a rule, unified financing and resources. Project projects may not be located in the same development area or in the same region. A single coordinating body manages the program; at the same time, a single project management program may be absent.

2.2 Real Estate Project Management Life Cycle

Modern processes of globalization reinforce the mutual influence of all significant economic and innovation-technological factors and lead to the fact that the acceleration of changes becomes a long-term characteristic and basic pattern of development of the investment and construction complex and society as a whole. In real estate, acceleration processes are manifested by a combination of problems:

- socio-economic problems associated with the rapid change in perceptions about the necessary parameters of buildings and structures projects, consumer requirements for various types of real estate, the emergence and formation of new socio-economic needs among consumers;
- urban development problems caused by the exacerbation of contradictions between the real estate form of buildings and structures and the growth of the dynamics of the surrounding buildings and infrastructure;
- production related to the increase in the variability and level of uncertainty of the conditions for the implementation of ICP, the situational nature of the external and internal parameters of construction production.
- The solution of socio-economic, urban planning and production problems requires a targeted change and optimization of the existing construction, development and implementation of new projects, i.e. — real estate development.

Real estate development is the deliberate transformation of an object (land, buildings, structures, territorial property complex) caused by socio-economic needs. Activities for the *management of real estate development* correspond to the term "development", which came from Western practice (from the English. *Development* — creation, evolution). The concept of real estate development in modern conditions constitutes the theoretical basis for development and the analytical basis for decision making by developers, investors, designers, and other professional participants in the real estate market.

Real estate development is an objective and constantly operating factor from the current global economy. For megacities and large cities, such development is a continuous process.

A fundamental question arises: is it possible, under conditions of accelerated changes, to ensure that the decisions on the project that are being taken now become not the cause of problems, but the source of additional opportunities for social, social, and economic development? This is answered by the concept of real estate development, the installation priorities of which are as follows:

- Real estate object transformations are inevitable and objectively necessary in the conditions of accelerated changes, market dynamics and demand structure;
- development needs may arise at any stage of the life cycle of a property;
- it is advisable to forecast, plan and take into account the prospects, directions and intensity of development of the property in the initial stages of project development;
- the higher the potential for the development of real estate (that is, the more opportunities for the development of a real estate property are incorporated in the project), the more effectively its life cycle can be realized.

The diverse work on real estate development can be divided into two types: construction work at the facility and changing the functional purpose of the facility. In the first case, it is assumed that the development of the property can be carried out without changing its functions. For example, the construction of a new production and warehouse building in industrial buildings, an increase in the area of a building due to its superstructure, etc. In the case of the development of real estate by changing its functional purpose, most often it also requires the implementation of construction work at the facility associated with the reconstruction, expansion or new construction. For example, when re- profiling a building of an obsolete factory into a loft apartment or a shopping center, it is necessary to reorganize the facility's engineering systems, new zoning of premises, finishing work, landscaping, modernization of the parking space, etc.

Real estate project management, including analysis and calculation methods, organizational and technological models and management functions, covers the project life cycle.

The life cycle of the ICP is a set of interrelated tasks and activities that form a complete development process from the emergence of a project plan to the completion of a project.

The cyclic pattern of development is universal and characteristic of many systems of various nature, not only biological, but also social, and technical. The cycle is inherent in the existence of a real estate project. It is expressed in the repeating stages of project development, the accumulation and transfer of experience about the results from previous cycles to subsequent ones. Unlike natural cycles, man-made cycles are focused, which means that they require management throughout their entire length.

The life cycle of COI and the life of a property are different.

The life cycle of ICP is limited to the stages of pre-design work and the design, construction and commissioning of an object. The tasks and activities that make up the ICP life cycle include design and construction, and organizational and managerial work. At the same time, the ICP life cycle is part of the

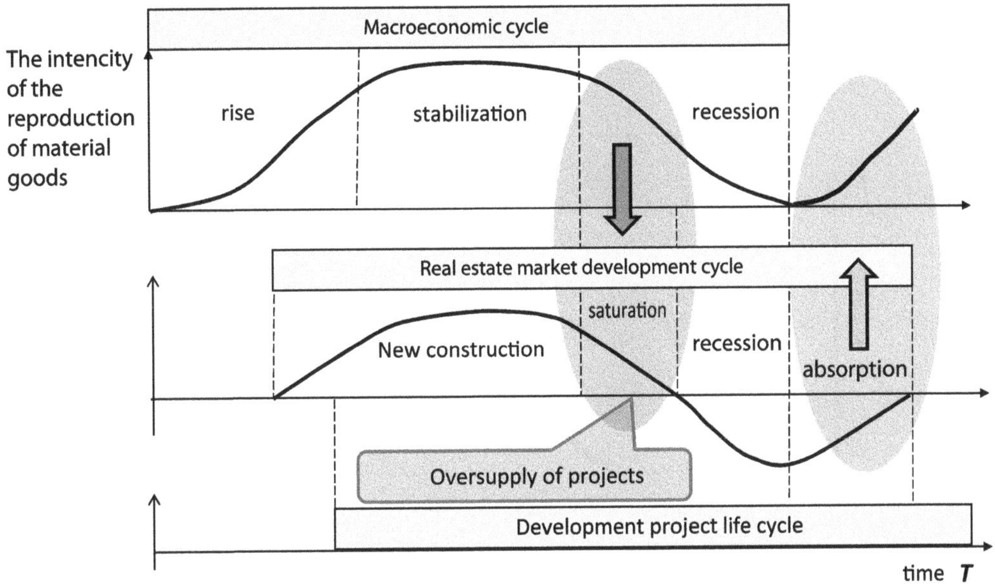

Figure 2.3: Patterns of mutual influence of development cycles

project for the development of real estate, industry and regional development cycles, the development cycle of the real estate market. In turn, the life cycle of a real estate development project is an integral part of cycles of a higher hierarchical level, such as the cycle of development of the real estate market as a whole and the macroeconomic cycle of development of the territory and region.

By presenting hierarchical development cycles in the coordinate axes "Reproduction Intensity — Time", we can analyze how the cycle of a real estate development project, projecting onto a built-up territory and region, affects the real estate market and investment and construction activity in general (Fig. 2.3). The life cycles of business activity, built-up environment and real estate will be discussed in more detail in Part II "Real Estate Development" of this textbook (chapter 4).

There is no universal approach to the structure of the project life cycle. Classical projects distinguish between the conceptual stage, the development and implementation stage, and the final stage. In the full life cycle of an investment construction project, the following sequence of stages is considered (Fig. 2.4):

1. concept;
2. development;
3. implementation;
4. operation;
5. liquidation.

At the same time, the total costs and effects of the project during the entire life cycle include the costs of pre-project surveys, design and construction (S_1), income from the operation of the constructed facility (S_2), and expenses for

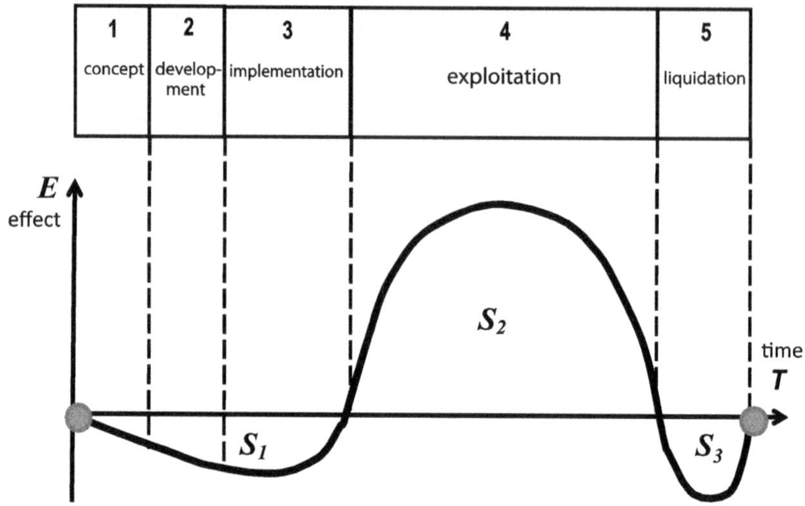

Figure 2.4: Real estate project life cycle stages and effects distribution scheme

exit from the project and liquidation (S_3). The development strategy, which consists in the targeted development of the territory in time by improving it, is based on the full life cycle and forecasting the corresponding costs and effects.

The conceptual stage (initial) of ICP, as a rule, consists of formulating a project idea with defining the goals and objectives of the project, marketing market research, conducting a project analysis and evaluating possible alternative of the project, business planning and on the limitation of the viability of the project, the rationale for investments and the feasibility study. From the point of view of project management, it is advisable to distinguish the pre-investment and pre-project phases as part of the conceptual (or initial) stage of the ICP. This is due to the fact that many construction issues are considered before the appearance of the customer and even before the appearance of the investor. The pre-design phase requires the presence of a technical customer for the construction.

At *the development stage, the* necessary input data are collected; design and survey work are being conducted; project structure is being developed; planning and documenting the design are being performed; terms of implementation and resource requirements are being formed; main performers are being determined; project expertise is being carried out.

At the *stage of the* project *implementation,* the construction is ensured with the necessary types of resources, all types of construction, installation and commissioning work are carried out, the functions of control, operational management and coordination are performed. The implementation stage includes the short-term phase of putting the facility into operation (or the final phase of construction). At the final phase of the construction project, final or warranty tests are carried out, the object is displayed on the calculated parameters, the constructed object is transferred to the user (investor), and final construction documents are drawn up. At the construction completion phase, an analysis of the results of the construction project is carried out, which is necessary for future projects and the accumulation of experience by project participants.

The facility operation phase is the target and longest stage of the project life cycle. During this stage, with the necessary frequency, not only routine maintenance, technical and other maintenance work is carried out at the real estate object, but its updating and development — ongoing, scheduled and major repairs, modernization, reconstruction and re-profiling of the object.

The liquidation stage in real estate projects includes work packages for dismantling and demolishing a building, removal and disposal of waste, and land reclamation. The liquidation stage is becoming increasingly important in the life cycle of a real estate project, which is caused by the high cost, laboriousness and engineering and technological complexity of the above construction works.

From an engineering and construction point of view, the life cycle of a project is realized through analysis, design, manufacturing, transportation, installation, operation, repair, and many other tasks (Fig. 2.5).

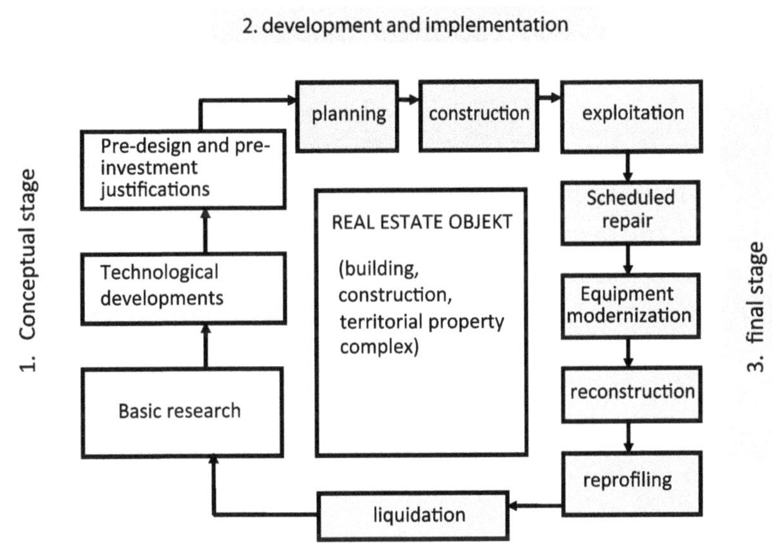

Figure 2.5: The contents of the stages of the life cycle of a real estate project

The duration of the stages of the life cycle for different types of buildings is different. The specific time for the implementation of the stages is determined by the technological, organizational, and economic opportunities and limitations of the project participants. In general, the life cycle of construction projects tends to decrease, which is caused by a number of objective trends:

1. improvement of technologies for the implementation and combination of design and construction works;
2. acceleration of obsolescence of structures associated with the emergence of new progressive technological and structural solutions;
3. acceleration of the physical deterioration of structures due to increased aggressiveness of the environment and the complication of operating conditions of objects.

There are various ideas about the beginning and end of the project life cycle. These concepts are interpreted differently and determined by the project participants depending on their role in the project, experience and the specific purpose of the project. Theoretically, there can be as many different points of view on the content of the full life cycle of real estate as there are participants in project management. For example,

for the owner (project initiator (owner)), the full life cycle covers the period from the acquisition to the sale of the object. Moreover, the full life cycle of a physical object (building) includes many of the changing owners of the object;

for the general contractor, the full life cycle covers the period from the start of construction to the commissioning of the facility. A speculative developer will include in the project life cycle a part of the operation stage before the sale of the object's space, and a strategic developer will be included in the full life cycle and operation and liquidation of the object;

for the Federal Registration Service, the legal sign of the beginning and end of the life cycle is official state registration procedures (registration of rights, registration of termination of rights), etc.

For the applied purposes of real estate project management and substantiation on this basis of management methods and tools, three main approaches to the full life cycle of a real estate project can be distinguished (Fig. 2.6). Firstly, a real estate project can be analyzed as a construction project and, in this case, the full life cycle covers the period from the development of a concept and allocation of a plot to the liquidation of a building. At the same time, the criterion for the completion of the life cycle is the physical and moral deterioration of the building. Secondly, a real estate project can be analyzed as a financial asset — the full life cycle is considered from acquisition to exit from the project. The criterion for completing the full life cycle in the second case is a decrease in the dynamics of project profitability. Thirdly, a real estate project can be analyzed as an object of consumption. Moreover, the full life cycle is considered from creation to sale, and the criterion for completing the full life cycle is the dynamics of consumer utility.

In practice, very few companies and other participants in the real estate market are systematically involved in the analysis of the full life cycle of the

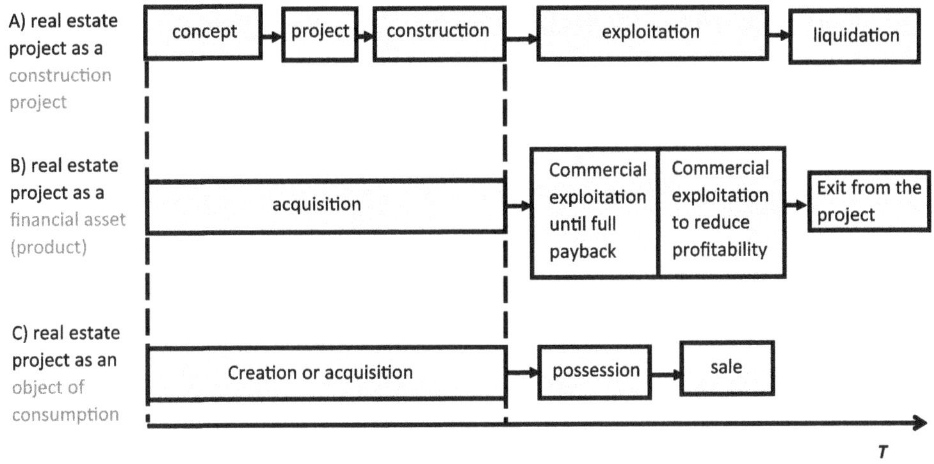

Figure 2.6: Three approaches to the full life cycle of a real estate project

project and the formation of a strategic vision for the development prospects of the project. Prediction of the future of promoted projects and the market is carried out, as a rule, sporadically and fragmentarily.

2.3 Project Management Conceptual Stage

The conceptual stage is considered the beginning of the life cycle of the project. It can also be called the initial stage, the commercial or the initiation stage, and includes the pre-investment and pre-project phases.

At the conceptual stage, a fundamental question is solved: is the project idea viable? This is a big and difficult job. Any initial data related to the future project and all types of analysis of this data are fundamentally important for the initiator of the project, the investor and all who are going to participate in the project. The cost of research and project justification at the initial stage can reach 3-5% of the cost of future construction.

Nevertheless, spending money on pre-investment research is objectively more profitable than investing in an insolvent project. This primarily refers to large-scale construction.

The conceptual stage, as a rule, is distinguished by the lack of accurate and complete information about the project. This may be a general idea and concept of a project, approximate terms of its implementation, preliminary generalized parameters of a project's resource requirements. For integrated evaluations, indicators of similar implemented projects are used.

Pre-investment research begins in the uncertain conditions of the project idea, and ends with quite extensive information, data and knowledge about the future project. To form these data, direct and indirect information related to the project is considered from different points of view. The methods of pre-investment research, analysis and justification of the project, practiced in practice, are applied. The methods of analysis and justification of the project are divided into 2 groups: quantitative (or numerical) and qualitative (or motivational). For *quantitative methods* include:

- methods of expert evaluations that allow, based on the ordering (ranking) of potentially possible alternative project options, choose the best option. They are used in cases where the conditions of the analytical problem are difficult to clearly formalize;
- methods of probabilistic estimates, which are used with a high level of uncertainty in the conditions of the project;
- methods of discounting or accounting for the time factor, which make it possible to compare the project costs at different times in the calculations.
- *Qualitative* or *motivational methods of* analysis and justification of the project differ in the motivation of certain decisions and include:
- the method of production necessity, in which the most significant factor in the need for new construction is the maintenance of existing production;
- method of competitive necessity — this method is used when it is necessary to increase the competitiveness of products and modernize production;
- priority method ("sacred cow") — in this method, decisions on the priority of the project and the corresponding motivation are determined by higher levels of management and leadership.

Different types of studies of the conceptual stage are based on common initial data and information related to the future project.

However, they are carried out for different purposes, therefore, they have different decision-making criteria, consider the initial data from various points of view and take them into account with a different degree of detail and significance level. At the conceptual stage, 4 main areas of research can be distinguished: project concept, project analysis, feasibility study and business plan of the project (Fig. 2.7).

The project concept considers starting expectations from the project and the feasibility of the project idea, and parties interested in the project are identified. The concept is developed in two stages:

1. A preliminary expert analysis of the feasibility of the project is carried out, in the framework of which unpromising ideas are screened out;
2. A declaration of intent is formulated reflecting the investor's intent.

Declaration of intent — a document describing initial expectations from the project. It contains:

- information about the investor;
- estimated location of the development site;
- purpose and engineering and technological data of the construction object;
- justification of the socio-economic need for this construction project;
- resource needs of the project and sources of their satisfaction (manpower, raw materials, water supply, energy, transport, etc.);
- analysis of the impact of the construction project on the environment;
- prospective sources of financing;
- planned distribution of finished products.

Project analysis is the second direction of conceptual research, in which the future project is considered as a direction and area of investment. The purpose of the project analysis is to evaluate the value of the future results of the project, its feasibility and viability. To do this, compare the benefits of the project with the costs of it. There are 7 types of project analysis, which cover all aspects of the project: technical; organizational; commercial; social; ecological; financial; economic. Work on the implementation of certain types of analysis can be combined in time.

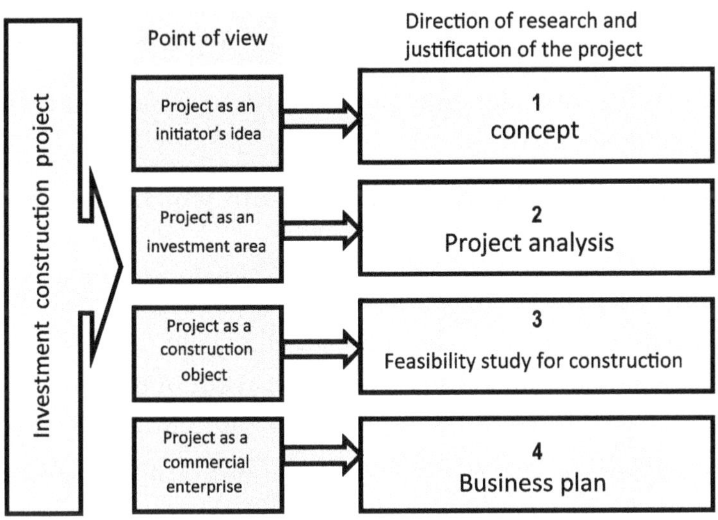

Figure 2.7: The conceptual stage of the project: areas of research and justification

The *technical analysis* examines the *technical* capabilities of the project: location, project scale, project timing, future production technology, the possibility of providing material and technical resources and equipment. As part of the technical analysis, a preliminary cost estimate is determined and an enlarged project implementation schedule is drawn up. All tasks and work repeatedly refined, they are an increasing degree of accuracy are also performed as part of a feasibility study and the development of working documentation.

The *organizational analysis* assesses the conditions for the implementation of the project in two areas:

- stage of construction, for which appropriate methods of organizing and coordinating the relationships of project participants are selected;
- stage of operation, for which a production structure is developed that is expedient at the stage of operation of the facility.

All aspects of the organizational and administrative environment in which the project will be implemented are evaluated. As a result of this, recommendations are made on organizational structures, management, planning, staffing, and coordination of activities.

In a *commercial analysis, the* project is evaluated from the point of view of the end users of the products and services offered by the project:

- the demand for products is studied, the price of products;
- The market of resources and raw materials for the future enterprise is being studied.

Social analysis evaluates the socio- territorial aspects of the project, for this:

- the socio-cultural and demographic characteristics that fall under the project are being studied;
- The production potential of the region in which the project is being implemented is considered.

The *environmental analysis* establishes and assesses the potential environmental damage caused by the project lifecycle, as well as to develop methods and conservation activities and restoration of environment. Detection and prevention of the possible negative environmental effects of production processes, including the investment and construction projects, is based on the ISO 14000 standard "Environmental management".

Financial analysis determines the financial possibilities of the project and includes the following sections:

- analysis of the financial profitability of the project;
- determination of the required amount of investment in the project;
- analysis of cost recovery for output;
- financial analysis of the organization operating the project.

An economic analysis evaluates the economic or budget efficiency of a project from the point of view of the investor and the state. This is a socially significant part of project analysis. When calculating the effectiveness of the project, external costs are taken into account, i.e. environmental, social and other consequences of the project.

The feasibility study of construction (feasibility study) is the third line of research of the conceptual stage, in which the project is studied as a construction object and the feasibility of construction is justified.

The feasibility study includes the development of design documentation for the main parameters of the construction object: space-planning, structural, technological, operational, economic, social, environmental. The feasibility study is developed, as a rule, by specialized engineering firms (design institutes) authorized to carry out the appropriate types of design work on the basis of an agreement with the customer. As part of the feasibility study, options for achieving the project goal should be considered; financing options; balance of investment and public interests and the estimated period of economic indicators. In preparing the feasibility study, the following documentation is used: general plan, access roads, infrastructure; architectural and planning decisions; engineering equipment, networks and building systems; technological solutions; manufacturing control; construction organization; environmental protection; engineering solutions for the safe operation of the building; estimate documentation; return on investment.

In the fourth direction of conceptual research, the project is considered as a commercial enterprise, for which a business plan for the investment construction project is being developed.

The project's business plan is a document describing the main aspects of the project as a future commercial enterprise: problems that the project may encounter and ways to solve them. The business plan is intended for three categories of project participants:

1. for investors and future owners, it is a tool to attract partners and justify the prospects of the project;
2. for lenders and partners — a business plan is a confirmation of the commercial attractiveness of the project;
3. for project management who benefit from the competent organization of the planning process.

In modern conditions, business planning is a generally accepted form of presenting a project to potential investors, partners, creditors and the main document that technically and financially agrees on the commercial attractiveness of the project in a competitive environment. The basis for the development of business plans is the results of project analysis. A business plan is a forecast document; it is drawn up 3-5 (sometimes 10) years in advance to see how the funds invested in the construction will behave after the construction of the facility. The business plan is developed by the project initiator with the involvement of professional consultants: experts, consulting firms and firms specializing in the field of marketing. The composition of the business plan is presented in table. 2.2.

Table 2.2 the composition of the business plan

	section	content
1	summary	Essence of the project proposal and conclusions with the assessment
2	Market conditions	The state and forecast of processes in the investment and construction sector as a whole and in the development region
3	Marketing strategy	Factor of demand, purchasing power, pricing policy
4	Organization of work and financing	Work flowchart, funding by project implementation period
5	Cost determination	One-time and current costs, discounting and inflation forecast
6	Income determination	Volumes of production (services), their cost, pricing and taxation conditions
7	Cash flow generation	Balance of financial expenses and income
8	Efficiency mark	Calculation of indicators: payback period, return on investment, break-even point of the project, etc.
9	Commercial risk insurance	Types of probable risks, conditions for their occurrence, prevention mechanism, insurance forms

Initial information for drawing up a business plan:

1. Demand Information:
   - product advantages (characteristics, price, promotion of demand, place of sale) — marketing complex;
   - market requirements for products;
   - identification of potential buyers of products;
   - expected demand.
2. production information:
   - manufacturing, processes and operations;
   - raw materials;
   - equipment;

- labor resources;
- premises;
- overhead costs.

3. financial information:
    - analysis of funds that can be invested in the project;
    - prices of competitors;
    - government regulation measures and pricing principles.

The structure of a business plan is similar to project analysis. The difference is in the analysis of the source information: in contrast to the project analysis, the business plan refers to a commercial enterprise.

2.4 Project structure and participants

The structure of the construction project is complex and multifaceted; it integrates the content of a specific project, the features of the external environment of the project, and the internal organizational relations of the project participants. Structuring is the most important project management method. For the convenience of management, the project is divided into separate, smaller elements (sections, floors, building spans; types of work, organizational subsystems) that are easier to manage, the cost of which is easier to calculate. Structuring the project consistently includes:

- project breakdown into manageable elements or decomposition project
- element-wise assessment of the costs of funds, time, resources;
- distribution of responsibility between project participants;

Creation of a unified information base for planning, control and regulation of changes in the project.

Investment and construction project structured by subject areas of management — subsystems, types of management activity — a function of the control wells and relations between them. Such an approach makes it possible to reveal the content of the subject and management functions.

Project subsystems are relatively autonomous subject areas, among which the main ones are distinguished: work; resources; risks; quality; information. In development, all project subsystems are considered as resources necessary for the implementation of the project.

Project management functions (PM) is a species management activity, which are carried out at all stages s of the project lifecycle. In regard with international system standards of quality and certification activity ISO 9000, including PM functions distinguished: planning, organization, control and regulation changes.

Subsystems and functions of the unitary enterprise are combined into a single structure that makes up the project, by interconnections and with the ultimate goal of the project.

The links in the structure of the unitary enterprise are divided into vertical links — administrative decision-making processes and horizontal links — technological sequences of work.

In the knowledge base on PM (PMBK Guide, *Project Management Body of Knowledge, PMI)*, project structuring is represented regardless of its type (construction, engineering, software, etc.) as a set of processes and areas of knowledge, representing the sum of professional knowledge of PM. PMBoK defines 5 main groups of processes and 9 areas of knowledge typical of almost all projects. Five main groups of processes: initiation, planning, execution, monitoring and control, completion and closure. PMBK includes nine areas of knowledge: project integration management, project scope, timelines, costs, quality, human resources, communication channels, risks and procurement. Each area of knowledge contains all or some of the processes of UP (Fig. 2.8.)

The project structure is formed from two points of view:

substantial structure of the project, the task of which is to answer the question "what are we doing?" " And reflect the organizational and technological sequence of work on the project;

the organizational structure of the project, the task of which is to answer the question "who does it?" And reflect the totality of actions of project participants, structural units and positions, relations between them.

The content structure of the project in management is reflected by the methods of calendaring and network planning (see chapter 3).

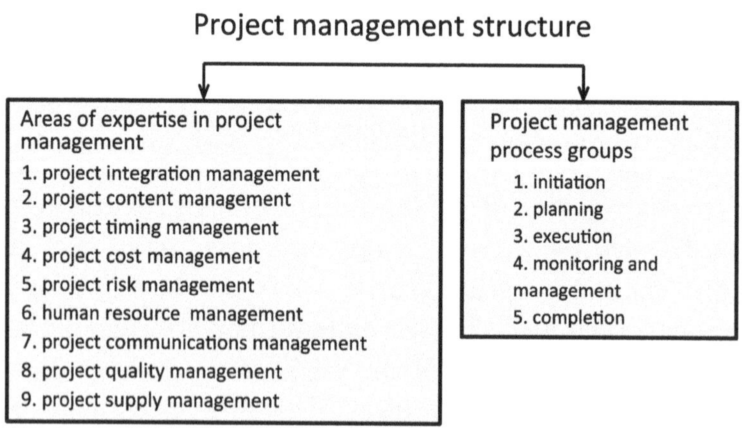

Figure 2.8: Project Management Framework by PMI PMBoK Guide

The organizational structures of the project in management theory are classified according to the principles of their construction:

1. on the internal content of the project;
2. according to the external environment;
3. according to the system of relations of project participants.

Several main types of organizational structures are distinguished — functional, matrix, design-target, divisional, and a number of their varieties.

In practice, these control structures function, as a rule, in a mixed form; they are adapted to the particularities and conditions of a particular project.

The content of the project imposes restrictions on possible solutions for the division of labor of employees and a combination of vertical and horizontal ties (Fig. 2.9).

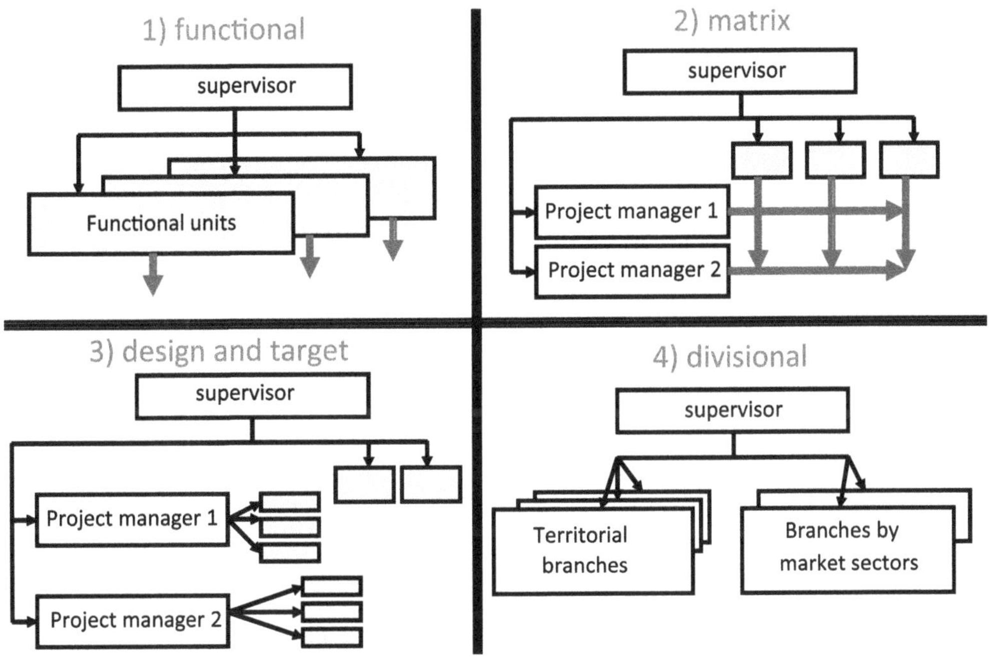

Figure 2.9: Organizational Classification

The classic version of the division of labor into vertical management processes (planning service, production, financial, marketing and commerce, etc.) are *functional organizational structures.* In a functional structure, managers have the right to give orders directly to performers. Employees of one profile are united in functional departments. Functional organizational structures are formed in construction and installation departments, firms and medium-sized organizations.

A simplified version of the functional structure for managing small units (department, sector, team) is a linear or linear-staff structure.

Matrix organizational structures implement various forms of dual subordination to functional and project managers. The advantages of matrix structures are strengthening interaction with the functionality of the business, a clear separation of management functions, elimination of intermediate Pts GOVERNMENTAL structural units, the rapid introduction of new technologies in construction.

Matrix structures are more flexible and allow maneuvering with common resources while simultaneously implementing several projects. Depending on the role of construction managers in the total set of managerial relations, firms distinguish weak, balanced and strong matrix structures. In the matrix management structure, the general director (or president) directs the activities of company directors. The functions of the executive director are optimization of the control mechanism, coordination of the provision of construction, installation, commissioning or design work. Thc technical director is responsible for the technology and safety of production, staff development, and the quality of construction products. The commercial director controls the cost of the work, ensures their uninterrupted financing.

The marketing director monitors and analyzes the contract market, selects potential customers, participates in tenders, and conducts contract work. Project managers are in direct contact with customers, organize the work of construction and installation units at the construction site.

The heads of functional departments (sections) provide technical guidance and support for the work of subordinate specialists and workers at various construction sites. The problem area of ??the matrix management structure is the double subordination of performers, which can cause executive problems and delays, bureaucratic conflicts of interest. The matrix structure is mainly used in large engineering firms and design organizations, where it is easier to ensure clear work planning for a long period.

Design and target (project) organizational structures provide autonomy of management to concentrate on the implementation of a specific project. This type of structures, as far as possible, corresponds to the organizational relations of the project management methodology. In design-target structures, in comparison with matrix structures, the focus of management responsibility moves to the management of projects (construction projects), in which a coordination group is created for the entire period of the project. There are no permanent production divisions in the *design and target* structure of the company, and temporary groups of performers like divisions are organizationally little dependent on each other. The head of each project plans work and the distribution of financial resources, mobilizes resources for the project, and motivates timely and high-quality execution of work. The project office on behalf of the head of the company provides methodological guidance to project managers. Functional departments work with projects as independent units. After the completion of the project, the organizational structure is reorganized. The advantage of the project with a targeted structure is the provision of high management flexibility with a relatively small number of management (managerial personnel). At the same time, the simultaneous implementation of several projects and the optimal allocation of material and technical and labor resources between them is an extremely difficult management task. In the investment and construction sector, such a temporary structure is used forcibly, preference is given to a functionally constant personnel and a stable organizational structure.

Divisional organizational structures allow you to specialize within the organization to fulfill certain goals, for example, in different geographical regions, in different market sectors, in different types of customers or consumers of products. Division structures are formed in holdings, large production companies, industrial and financial groups. The company has divisions — production associations of structural divisions resembling independent branches of companies. The divisions functionally specialize in the type of projects being implemented, in the covered development area or region. In addition to construction divisions, a number of divisions of a different profile can be formed in parallel with the development of a company. The central organization reserves the tasks of strategic planning, a single personnel and financial policy, the implementation of research and development, the development of a common brand, advertising, etc. The division structure is convenient in managing large multidisciplinary organizations, it allows you to diversify capital and provides higher sustainability of the company. At the same time, the management structure becomes more cumbersome, more links and levels of management appear, horizontal connections and interactions between divisions are poorly organized, more often duplication of managerial and production functions occurs.

Almost all organizational structures are hierarchical, i.e. provide for the subordination of the performer to the immediate superior, from the chief to the supervisor of a higher level, etc. Functional divisions, as a rule, deal not with executors, but with heads of divisions. Such organizational relationships partially eliminate the possibility of inconsistent decisions. However, at the same time, the process of making and coordinating decisions requires significantly more time. The workload of lower and middle managers is also growing. The hierarchy levels in organizational structures of management are used for large construction organizations, trusts, administrations, firms in the form of joint-stock companies and holdings.

The need for the formation of new organizational structures in construction arises frequently, with almost every new project. The general sequence of development of organizational structures includes a careful choice of the type of structure, detailed design of the vertical and horizontal division of labor, communication systems, development of job descriptions, and the formation of the proper structure with the selection and training of personnel (Fig. 2.10).

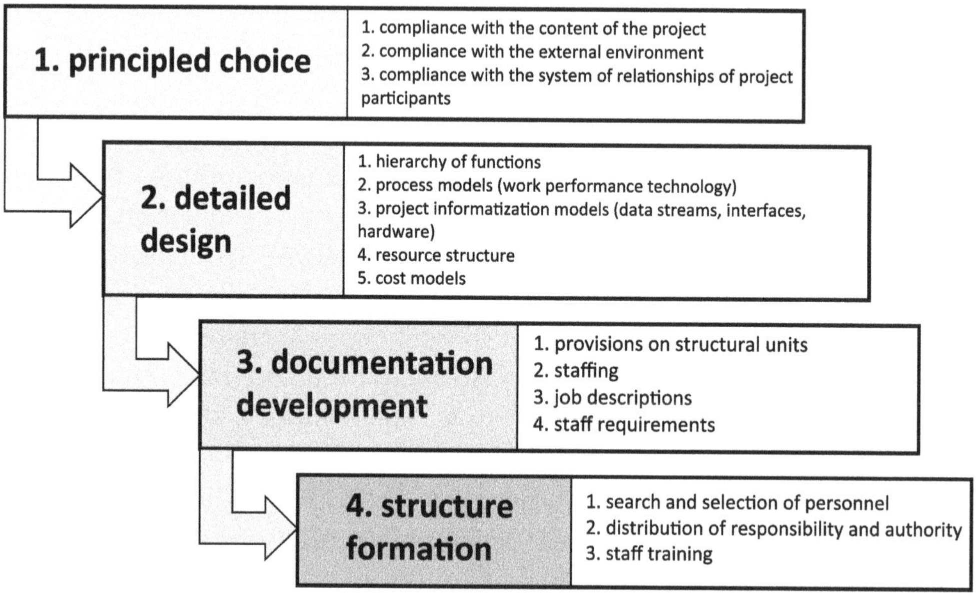

Figure 2.10: Organizational structure development sequence

The formation of organizational management structures should be based on an analysis of the goals of the organization's production activities, the need for management functions, and taking into account external and internal factors of the organization and projects. When developing structures, they are based on the experience of using similar structures; model the functional system of relationships between departments and divisions, and various options for organizing production.

Depending on the scale, from one to several dozen organizations can participate in the project.

Project participants — groups and categories of organizations that ensure the implementation of the project. As noted in Section 1.7 (Chapter 1), the main participants of the ICP are: customers, developers, developers, investors, designers, contractors, suppliers, the project manager, government agencies, professional consultants and other participants.

A characteristic feature of the project management method is the appointment of a project manager. The project manager is a legal entity to which the client and the investor have delegated authority to manage the project. In construction, this role is usually performed by a representative of the technical customer service or developer. The main tasks of the project manager are (see section 1.4, chapter 1):

1. the formation of the project team;
2. selection of designers, contractors and suppliers;
3. preparation of documentation for the conclusion of contracts;
4. conclusion of contracts for the supply of materials and equipment; project planning;
5. control of the cost, time and quality of work and the project as a whole;
6. planning, coordination and control and motivation of the activities of all project participants.

Participants have their own economic and economic interests, subjective goals and expectations, which are likely to conflict with the interests of other project participants. Therefore, one of the problem areas and complex tasks of the project manager is the integration of the economic interests of the participants.

For the period of the project, the project manager creates a special organizational unit, the project team. Unlike other project participants, the essence of the team is a single obligation for the team members (appointment or mission). This requires that all members of the project team have complementary professional and managerial skills. The project team includes specialists responsible for the design, construction, procurement and supply, contracts, project costs, communications. The project manager assembles a team of specialists either from his organization, or, in a more complicated case, involving representatives from other participating organizations. When the project manager is an employee of the technical customer, the project team should include representatives of the designer, general contractor, main subcontracting organizations and suppliers, investor or state customer, financing bank, supervisory authorities and local government.

The organizational forms of project management determine the relationship of the project manager with the customer and other project participants. Among them, the main form and the form of advanced management are distinguished. The main form of management — the project manager is responsible for the progress of the project, does not bear financial responsibility for the relations adopted, and enters into contractual relations only with the customer. At the same time, the risks associated with the project lie with the customer, which allows the project manager to make more decisions that are objective during the implementation of the project. Advanced management form — the project manager is responsible for the implementation of the project within a fixed price and enters into contractual relations not only with the customer, but also with other project participants. At the same time, the project risks lie with the project manager.

2.5 Project Management Features

Project management functions are the types of management activities that are carried out at all stages of the project life cycle. There are different approaches to their classification. Based on the PDCA (Plan — Do — Check — Act) cycle, which is used in the development and development of licensing processes according to the international system of quality standards and activity certification ISO 9001, the following project management functions are distinguished: project planning, organization (execution or implementation of the project), control over the implementation and regulation of changes to the project (Fig. 2.11).

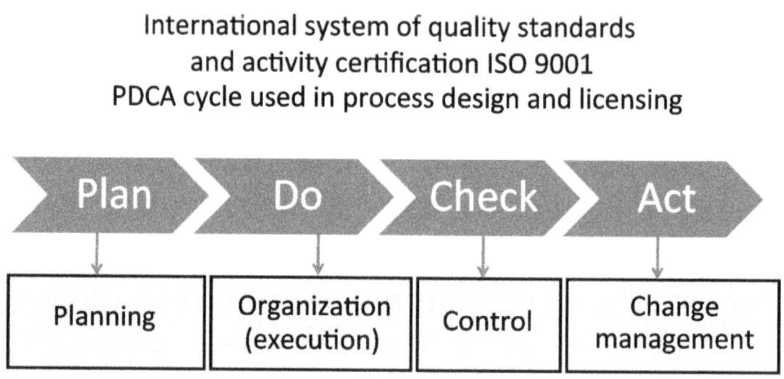

Figure 2.11: Project Management Features

Planning is the definition of the project goal and approach to achieve it in a timely manner and at a certain cost. In any economy, planning is an essential management task. Planning in the investment and construction sector is the most important and complex management function, since the parameters and many planning processes are unique here, they are developed and implemented one- time for each project. Planning of construction occurs in the framework of their enterprises organizations, and within the ICP. In planning, the best model for achieving the goal (goals) of the project is developed, its strategy and life cycle are predicted based on real opportunities and means available by the time the decision is made.

In the planning process, the main parameters of the project are calculated: the volume of work, indicators of the need for material and technical and labor resources, duration of work, cost of work, organizational and technological dependencies of the work. All plan parameters are interconnected. For example, the volume of work determines the need for material, technical, labor, and financial resources; The adopted technology of work determines their duration, delivery time, needs, volumes and terms of attracting subcontracting organizations. A plan with an accessible degree of accuracy should take into account many laws, conditions and limitations of the project, among which there are uncertain and random factors of influence.

Planning consists of a number of processes, which in importance divide the main and auxiliary processes. The main planning processes relate to the content of the project, methods and means of their implementation include:

1. Determination of the necessary work:
    - project content planning;
    - identification of the main stages and subprojects;
    - formation of a list of works in accordance with the chosen technology and organization of construction;
2. Definition of work performance methods:
    - determination of technological dependencies of work;
    - organizational planning (justification and choice of methods for performing work and distribution of responsibility);
3. Determining the means of work:
    - assessment of labor costs and duration of work;
    - planning of material and human resources;
    - budgeting.

Supporting planning processes include:

1. quality planning (determination of quality standards relevant to the project and design of methods for their achievement);
2. supply planning and suppliers;
3. identification and risk assessment;
4. modeling of information flows of the project (from the sets of documentation accompanying the execution of the project, to the creation of the program-communication environment of the project, which enables the information management of the project and continuous information support of the project life cycle).

Planning follows the established hierarchical levels of management, in accordance with which, as a rule, three levels of planning and a system of *general* (target), strategic, tactical and operational plans of the project are formed (Fig. 2.12).

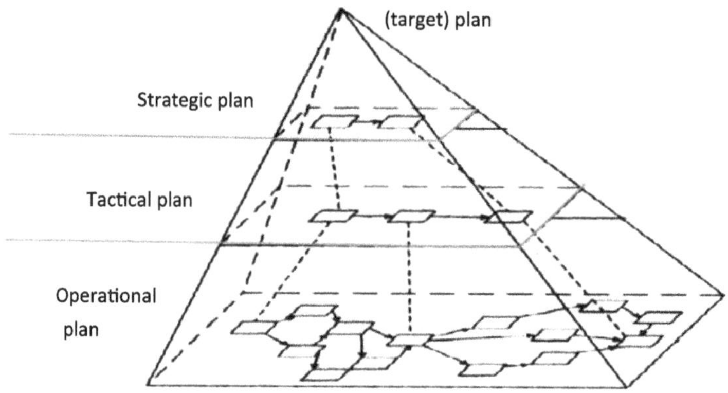

Figure 2.12: Levels (hierarchy) of planning

The general (target) plan is an enlarged plan for the entire life cycle, reflecting the place and goals of the project in the general plan for the development of the territory, region, city. In the process of developing a general (target) plan based on a diverse factor analysis of the territory, the state of the real estate market and the economic situation as a whole, the overall content of the project is determined: goals, possible alternative options for achieving the goal, main directions of the project (subject areas, enlarged structure works, preliminary estimates the duration and cost of the project). The master plan is the basis for the next level of planning — the development of a strategic plan.

A strategic plan is a long-term *plan* for the entire project life cycle, dividing the project goals into meaningful and technologically completed stages. This is the life cycle level of an individual project, where key stages, subprojects, milestones are analyzed, as well as for each stage, the terms of preparation of the front of work, their implementation and completion, delivery time of equipment, cash flows for the periods of the work are determined.

A tactical plan is a medium-term plan drawn up for a period of 1 to 3 years. Since planning is necessary for all project participants, tactical plans are varied and numerous.

An operational plan is a short-term plan drawn up for a period of up to 1 year.

These include work plans of individual project participants, types of work, stages of the project life cycle, etc. The operational plans include:

- current plans, which plan the activities of individual project participants' responsible executors) within one year;
- operational plans, in which, based on current plans, tasks for a month, decade or week are specified;

- master plans, where all the work of the project of the planned year is coordinated;
- detailed plans for stages and types of work, developed for a month or a year.

Planning levels are connected into the system by direct and feedback.

Direct communications consist in transferring down targets, constraints, and granularity of data from level to level. At each level, the planned data and indicators are reflected with varying degrees of generalization and specification. General targets are used in the master plan, they are structured by subprojects, stages and work packages in the strategic plan of the project and, at the level of tactical plans, are detailed down to operational plans of work and activities.

Feedbacks indicate information processes of transferring the actual data and refinements to the upper levels of management, as well as their aggregation into the most significant indicators at key stages. Feedback allows you to not only compare planned indicators with actual data and clarify the real state of affairs on the project. Aggregating data makes it possible to analyze and regulate changes in the future life cycle of the project, to compile statistics for government purposes and the next round of strategic planning. It also helps to make more informed decisions on subsequent similar projects.

In the planning of ICP, their substantive structure, and the organizational and technological sequence of work, the most widely used methods of calendar-network planning (see chapter 3).

Calendar and network planning project a is a complex of methods for modeling and graphical display of project activities and dependencies between them.

The calendar-network plan is developed in stages:

1. The list of project activities is determined. The ultimate goal of the project is divided into sub-goals, groups of work and individual work;

2. technological dependencies between the works are established, which are presented in the form of a network diagram;

3. The parameters of work are estimated (volumes, labor costs; duration; the need for material and technical and labor resources; cost);

4. The start time of the project is determined.

As a result, a meaningful model of the project is formed, which reflects the totality of all the work necessary for the implementation of the project and their organizational and technological dependencies in the form of a calendar and network schedule.

An effective tool for managing complex and large-scale projects is aggregated calendar-network schedules, which reflect and coordinate the longest durations (critical paths) of work packages or subprojects for higher levels of management.

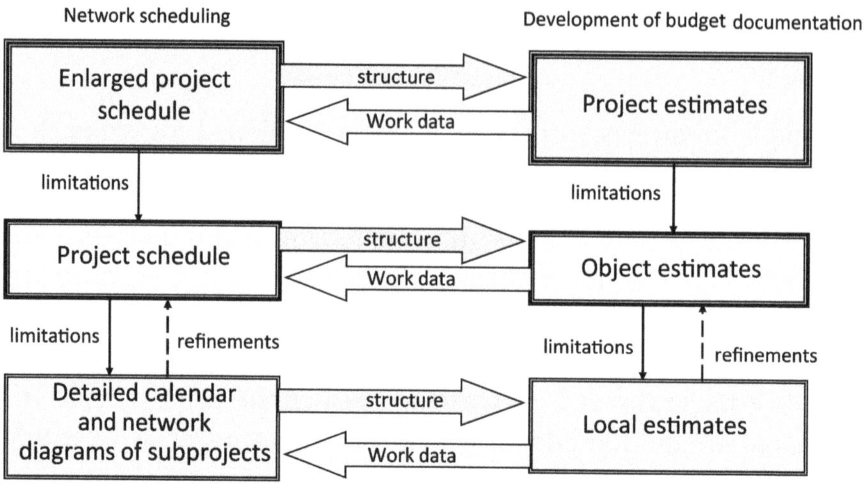

Figure 2.13: The relationship of network and budget planning

Parallel scheduling is carried out *estimates for plans* that is calculation of the project cost based on the volume of work database, requiring by direct resources and prices (Figure 2.13.).

Under modern management conditions, planning becomes a continuous function that covers all stages of the project life cycle.

The development of project plans is synchronous with the stages of the project life cycle (table. 2.3).

ICP planning is almost always an iterative activity, all planning processes can be repeated, and the parameters of the plan are refined and changed. Several times during the life cycle, the analysis of resources, cost, terms, expert decision making, etc. is repeated. At the same time, the plan is not a dogma; it is believed that it is necessary to start revising plans every time as soon as significant discrepancies with the actual state of affairs are revealed.

The main functions of IPP management include the organization of construction (execution, project implementation). *Organization of construction* is

Table 2.3 Planning at the stages of the project life cycle

#	stage	Planning stages
1	Conceptual (initial, commercial, initiation, pre-investment, pre-project)	Development of a general (conceptual) plan
2	design	Strategic plan development
3	construction	Development of a tactical plan
4	exploitation	Development of a tactical plan
5	liquidation	Development of a tactical plan; Development of a conceptual plan for a new project

a system of economic and engineering methods to ensure the implementation of the project at the planned pace. The construction organization will be discussed in more detail in chapters 3, 10, 12.

The control function in project management is to identify deviations of project parameters from planned values and analysis of the reasons for these deviations. The control makes it possible to determine whether plans should be reviewed if certain parameters deviate from acceptable values. The control function is part of the project management method. The control system for the project implementation includes: determining the purpose of the control, the parameters being monitored, the timing of the monitoring activities and those responsible for their implementation.

The function of regulating changes during the project life cycle is the replacement of decisions in the process of project implementation. The project changes are distinguished as forced (as a result of control and uncontrolled) and desirable, which are initiated by project participants. For example, initiated by the customer in order to improve the technical and economic indicators of the project, by the designer to improve the initial version of the project documentation, by the contractor (for example, to optimize the technology for the production of construction and installation works, the structure of the division of work and the sequence of their implementation).

Project changes may be required at any stage of its life cycle. The implementation of changes almost always requires analysis, special technologies for replacing solutions, and additional costs. Forced changes must be identified in a timely manner and implemented with the least damage to the project. Therefore, the sooner and faster changes are made, the less their negative impact on the final result of the project. The most difficult to implement changes are the need for which arises in the final phase.

2.6 Bidding and contracts. General Provisions

The project requires a variety of resources. These include not only material and labor resources, but also project implementation services (engineering, consulting, logistics, legal, audit, information support, etc.). All types of resources are mobilized and accumulated for the project through procurement. As experience shows, the selection of those wishing to receive an order to perform work or the services necessary for the project is expediently carried out at tenders on a competitive basis. Competitive bidding in most cases allows for the optimal selection of the contractor with the best technical and economic indicators. In COI, the executors are determined during the bidding process.

Contract tendering in construction is such a way of purchasing materials and equipment, placing orders and issuing contracts for specific types of work and services, in which the selection of a supplier and contractor is made on a competitive basis. The term "contracting" is old Russian, used traditionally, emphasizing that the subject of bidding is work or service, in contrast to auction bidding, where a competitive sale is held.

Trades should provide contracting construction companies equal condition for competition and the customer can choose the most beneficial proposal of costs, technical and other conditions. The basic principles of contract bidding were laid down by Peter I and remain relevant to this day. It includes: competitiveness and competition; savings; equal rights and integrity of participants; publicity of conduct. Relations between bidders are legislatively, normatively and methodically provided by the Civil Code of the Russian Federation (Article 447 "Conclusion of an Agreement at Tenders"); Regulation on contract bidding in the Russian Federation, (Gosstroy of the Russian Federation, 1993); Federal law (dated December 30, 2015 No. 44-FZ "On the contract system in the field of procurement, goods, work, services to ensure state and municipal needs"); a number of methodological recommendations on the development of tender documentation by customers and offers by bidders and their individual parts, according to the preliminary qualification of bidders, on the selection of a winner based on the results of tenders, on the development of sections of a construction contract, etc.

Tendering for the performance of work and the provision of services for federal state needs is mandatory. In other cases, the customer independently determines the need for them.

By the method of bidding, there are:

- open bidding, in which all interested applicants for the performance of work and services can participate;
- open bidding with prequalification of bidders, in which bidders can submit prequalification requirements to bidders. Such tenders are held, as a rule, for technologically complex and highly specialized works;
- closed tenders, which are held at the invitation of the organizer with companies in which the tendering customer is interested. Closed tenders are held if the subject of the tender is high technology, expensive equipment;
- technologically complex construction and installation works requiring high qualifications;
- single tenders — held with one organization selected by the customer (for example, the patent holder).

Open bidding means the possibility of participation in them all wishing their organizations. They are also called "public" because of their announcement published on the official website and in press: Ministry of Economic Development published bulletin "Competitive bidding"; The EBRD Procurement opportunities bulletin is issued by the European Bank for Reconstruction and Development on projects financed by its loans, credits and guarantees; The World Bank issued bulletin Development Forum Business and etc.

Five groups of organizations participate in the bidding (Fig. 2.14):

- customer — the person for whom the object is being built;
- organizer of tenders — the person to whom the customer instructed them to conduct;
- tender committee — a permanent or temporary body created by the organizer of tenders to organize their conduct. It is formed from the representatives of the auction organizer, customer, investor, as well as experts and government organizations;
- applicants — organizations that have decided to participate in tenders and have submitted applications;
- Bidders — bidders who sent tenders (offers), secured by a bank guarantee. The bidder acquires the status of the provider from the moment of registration of the offer.

Tender documentation is a set of documents containing initial information on the technical, commercial and organizational characteristics of the subject of bidding, as well as on the conditions and procedure for bidding.

Tender documentation includes:

1. Invitation to bid;
2. General information about the object and subject of bidding (built-up area, building dimensions, scope of work, etc.);
3. Design documentation (technical part);
4. Instructions to providers;
5. The bidder's application form;
6. Terms and conditions of tendering;
7. Draft contract indicating the starting price of the subject of the contract.

The tender committee sells tender documentation to bidders. Due to this, the tender organizer reimburses the costs of preparing tender documents and cuts off low-powered companies from participating in tenders.

An offer or tender proposal is a set of documents confirming in writing the bidders intention to bid and conclude a contract regarding the subject of bidding on the conditions specified in the tender documentation. In accordance with the Civil Code of the Russian Federation, the offer is irrevocable, information about the organization is included in its composition; work schedule; list of subcontracting organizations; commercial part containing the price and proposed forms of payment.

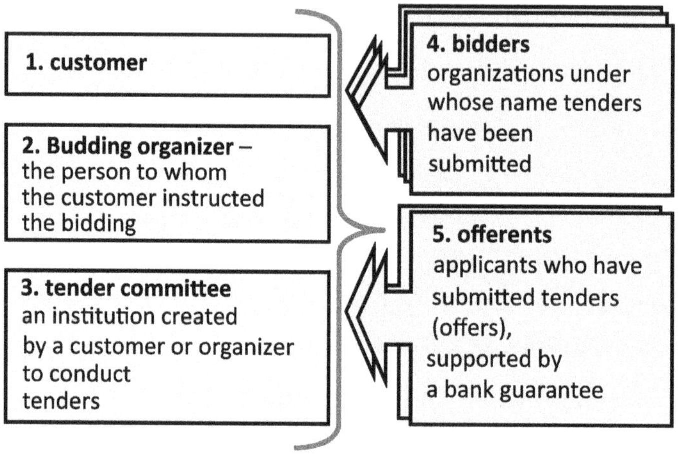

Figure 2.14: Bidders

The tender committee determines the time and place of opening of offers, the closing date of tenders, carries out the examination of offers. Tendering includes:

1. Preparation of tenders;
2. Submission of proposals by bidders;
3. Examination and evaluation of proposals by the tender committee and selection of the winner of the tender. The examination period depends on the complexity of the subject and the object of bidding, but should not exceed 6 months;
4. Signing a contract with the winner of the tender.

The general organizational chart of the bidding is presented in Fig. 2.15.

Contract (agreement) — a bilateral silt and multilateral legal agreement between the parties on the establishment, amendment or termination of their civil rights, in accordance with the law.

A construction contract is a contract (contract) under which one party (*contractor*) undertakes to perform the established work and hand it over to the customer, and the customer agrees to accept the result of the work and pay for it.

Delivery contract — the supplier agrees to transfer the goods (materials, equipment) to the buyer within a certain time, and the buyer agrees to accept the goods and pay the agreed amount for it. The basis for concluding a supply contract for project management are: specification; technical conditions characterizing the quantity and quality of equipment, structures, materials, etc.; schedules of equipment and materials needs, developed on the basis of their coordination with the general project plan.

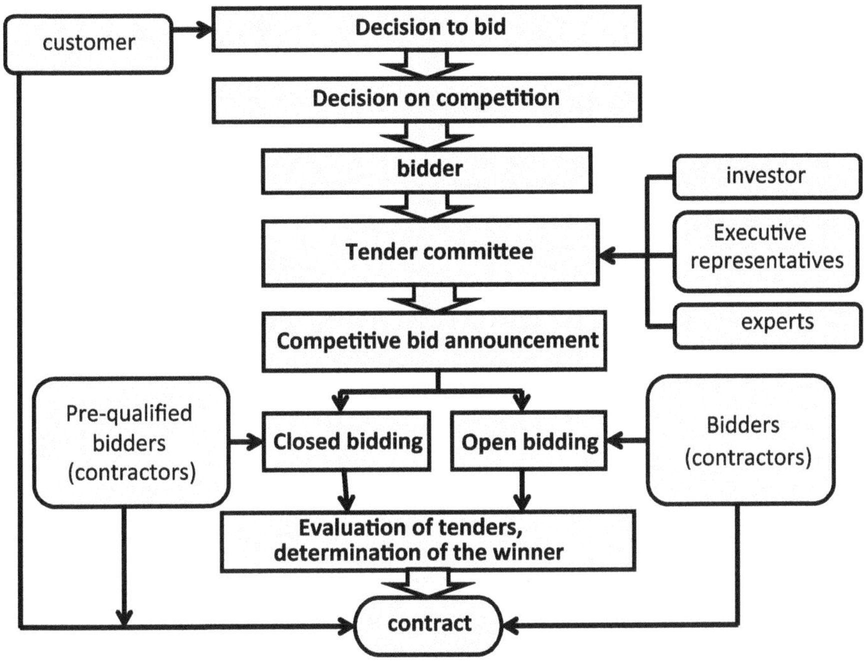

Figure 2.15: General organizational chart of tendering

The types of agreements (contracts) in the investment ion-construction sphere are extremely diverse, which is associated with the individual parameters of each construction object and organizational and economic schemes for their implementation. The classification of contracts for different classification criteria is used:

- on the subject of the contract;
- by the method of setting the contract price;
- by the nature of the relationship between the participants and the division of responsibility between them.

Depending on the subject of the contract, the types of contracts in construction are divided into: contracts for goods, contracts for work, contracts for services or their combinations (Fig. 2.16).

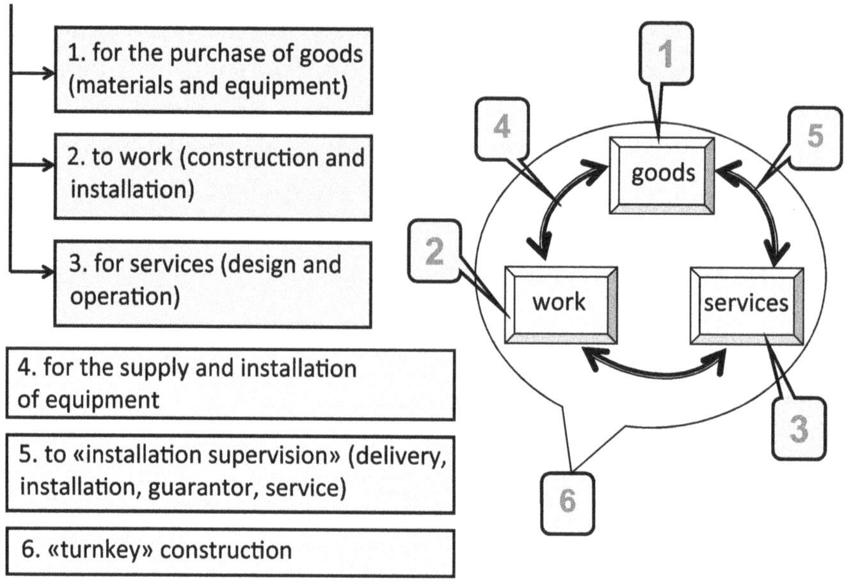

Figure 2.16: Types of contracts depending on the subject of the contract

Allocate contracts for the purchase of material s; to work; for services; on delivery and installation; on "installation supervision" and "turnkey". Contracts are also applied, including various combinations of the listed types of contracts.

According to the method of pricing, the contracts are divided into:

1. Contracts with a fixed price (the price cannot be changed in case of changes in costs, while the risks lie with the contractor);
2. Contracts with reimbursement of expenses, which are divided into:

2.1 Fixed price contracts;

2.2 Contracts with a fixed amount and incentive payment (the contractor can receive an additional amount if it provides additional quality and productivity);

2.3 Contracts with a fixed price and a range of possible price revisions;

2.4 Mark-up contracts (which provide for the possibility of increasing the cost of the project in exchange for greater project control and management rights);

2.5 Contracts with payment of costs plus a fixed fee;

2.6 Contract with payment of costs plus a percentage of the costs.

By the nature of the relationship between the participants and the division of responsibility between them, the following types of contracts are distinguished:

1. Traditional (agreement between the customer and the general contractor (for design and construction; for construction according to completed project documentation);
2. The contract for the construction of "turnkey" with full responsibility of general contractor snip for the facility to operate;
3. Contracts such as EPC and EPCM.

Contracts of the type EPC and EPCM relate to development contractual models and are characterized by a number of features. The appearance of the abbreviation and the corresponding contractual models is associated with the entry into the 90s of the mountains on the Russian market of foreign companies using their usual terminology and contractual schemes:

1. EPC agreement (*Engineering, Procurement, Construction* — engineering, supply, construction); EPC-contractor is a company engaged in design, procurement, supply, construction and installation.
2. EPCM agreement (*Engineering, Procurement, Construction, Management* — management of engineering, supplies, construction); EPCM-contractor is a company that manages on behalf of the customer design, procurement, supply, construction and installation.

Typical EPC Terms:

1. Fixed price (all excesses on the contractor);
2. The liability of the contractor is either limited by the price of the contract or unlimited;
3. All contractual risks lie with the contractor.

The areas of rational application of this type of contract are projects where an experienced contractor can very accurately assess the amount of expenses and the degree of risk, i.e. construction project of a typical, standard medium — sized facility. Moreover, low economic and other risks, as well as a developed market of local subcontractors should characterize the conditions for the implementation of the project.

Typical EPCM contract terms:

1. The fixed price for managing an EPCM contractor; contracts are concluded by the order on its own behalf, the risks lie with the customer;
2. The price "costs + remuneration", as a result of which part of the responsibility within the remuneration is transferred to the contractor;
3. The price "costs + remuneration + marginal (indicative) amount of expenses", while the risk of exceeding is shared by the customer and the contractor.

The analysis of typical conditions of development contractual models of the EPC / EPCM type shows that in terms of organizational and technological content they do not carry anything new in comparison with the Russian model "turnkey construction". There are also no fundamental organizational and technological differences between EPC and EPCM contracts, since project management is built into the EPC contract — without management, this model cannot obviously be implemented. The difference between EPC and EPCM contracts is not in the organization of construction, but in the distribution of risks and obligations of the customer and the contractor.

At present, in the world practice, the whole variety of contracts and contracts are referred to three main alternative schemes:

1. Scheme of direct contract (there is no general contractor, the customer-developer concludes all contracts for the project directly with the executing companies);
2. Project management scheme — project implementation through a management company;
3. Development scheme — the full responsibility of the developer company for the results of the project as a whole.

2.7 Practical implementation of large investment and construction projects

2.7.1 Project implementation sequence

For large building and construction projects (see Table 2.1 earlier), detailed and careful planning and organization of early project work is a key factor in minimizing possible risks in the implementation of ICP and the operation of a property.

In order to ensure a systematic approach to the preparation of construction works, several key actions of importance are carried out, which, in order to improve the assimilation of the material, are conventionally outlined in 20 steps to the working project plan:

1. Describe the goals and boundaries of the project (including an explicit indication of what is being done and is NOT being done within the framework of the project), to indicate the key requirements of the Customer's Terms of Reference and commercial parameters of the project.
2. Briefly describe the current stage of the project, the degree of knowledge of the project, form a review of the sources of source data and their variability,

including the degree to which these data can be trusted, describe the premises and assumptions adopted during project planning.

3. Describe the composition and scope of key project work, information on the target project implementation schedule (in accordance with the General Contract).
4. Describe the region (district) of construction with conclusions on the conditions of work, including a description of climatic features, transport accessibility, the provision of collected information about regional (district) freight turnover, logistics capabilities for the delivery of material and technical resources and equipment (MTRE), the movement of people resources, possible living conditions for working personnel and engineers, project management staff.
5. Indicate known limitations and burdens of the project.
6. Describe key issues, risks, open-ended questions on the project, including prospective risk tracking tools and proposed risk management strategies.
7. Provide general information about the selection of the General Designer, designers and performers, including work experience, size and qualifications of the Design Group, its organizational structure, Personal data on the project manager, GUIs, key specialists, information on the instrumental (technical) base of the institute, etc.:
   - the main results of engineering, geological, hydrogeological and other types of research;
   - Provision of design (working) documentation, including information:
     - on the availability of design and estimate documentation (DED), its legitimacy (state examination (GGE), approval by the Customer), completeness (quantitative composition of sets of taxiways),
     - on the readiness of sets of working documentation (WD) for the issuance of work,
     - About the schedule for the delivery of sets of taxiways by the design institute;
   - information on the proposed / agreed upon scheme of interaction with the general designer to ensure the construction of relevant documents and management of changes in it,
   - information on the scheme of organization of field supervision by a design institute,
   - information about the specialists of the design institute who, in order to optimize change management, will carry out operational design at the construction site,

- availability of budget documentation, including information about its availability, completeness, compliance with the drawings of working documentation on the types and volumes of planned work,
- provision of approvals and permits, separately for the areas of responsibility of the Customer and the General Contractor, including, but not limited to:
  - land allotment for construction, availability of a building permit, availability and sufficiency of technical conditions (TU) for connections to utilities, etc.,
  - permits for the transportation of goods on public roads,
  - a description of the conditions of storage / removal / disposal of construction waste, soil, solid waste, conditions for ensuring the sewage of household and rainwater, information about regional organizations involved in waste disposal;
- description of the management scheme for project documentation, including the procedure for interaction with contractors, collection of documentation, its accumulation, verification, analysis, version control, transfer of work to production;
- a description of the change management scheme in the project documentation (including a scheme for organizing "field" design).

8. Provide a list of available documents for the planning of construction and installation works, including: Construction general plan, Title list of objects, PIC, Documents PD / WD, Estimated calculations and estimates, etc.
9. Indicate the situational plan of the site, describing the main construction sites.
10. Provide a description of the structure of the allocated construction sites (construction zones) for the organization of construction management (each of the sites includes a set of objects in the construction / systems / types of work, etc.). If the division of the site is not performed, describe the principles of future separation.
11. Description of the general schedule (sequence) of construction and installation works at the facilities (construction and installation schedule of the 2nd level of detail), including:
    - applicable principles of site management (construction and installation sites and subcontractors), procedures for monitoring the implementation of construction and installation works in terms of volume and quality;
    - description of tools for monitoring the timing of work, including those reflected in construction contracts;

- description of the procedure for collecting executive documentation on completed construction and installation work and transferring it to the Customer;
- a schedule of the main key events (milestones) of the project, a description of the requirements for the results of work and activities associated with each of the planned milestones;
- target project implementation schedule (in the form of a Gantt chart), including:
  - providing design documentation,
  - coordination and permission,
  - MTRE of the project, with the allocation of supplies in the area of responsibility of the Customer, General Contractor and Subcontractors,
  - selection and contracting of suppliers,
  - Construction and installation work of the project, within the framework of the allocated construction and installation sites with the division into work on individual construction objects,
  - commissioning (commissioning) of the project with the allocation of individual and comprehensive tests for facilities, systems, the whole project,
  - Selection and contracting of contractors (performers).

12. Develop a detailed (work schedule) for the next 3-6 months of project implementation. Describe the procedure for the development and updating of the project schedule, including:
    - the need for the project in the workforce — a monthly schedule of the need for workforce (in the context of the groups "main workers", "machine operators", auxiliary workers);
    - project need for machines and mechanisms — monthly demand for machines and mechanisms — by main equipment groups: Earthmoving equipment, Drilling and pile driving equipment, Loaders, Rollers, Graders, Road milling machines, lifting equipment, Aerial platforms, Pipe layers, Tipper, Cargo, welding equipment (positions), shift the vehicle, means of mechanization, other.
13. Provide a description of the contracting strategy of construction and installation work, MTRE of the project, including a description of the scope of work in Lots, a description of the policy in attracting contractors to perform work within the lots (or groups of lots):
    - composition and brief characteristics of potential project counterparties performing construction and installation works and commissioning;

- a description of the selection and engagement of counterparties for construction and installation work and commissioning, including a description of the procedure for redistributing the volume of work between contractors within the framework of the project — to expedite the implementation of the project;
- justification of the feasibility of engaging in the m project own forces with an assessment of the optimal "volume" of their participation by type of work;
- schedule of contracting construction and installation and commissioning;
- a description of the types of materials and equipment for the project, a description of the most difficult delivery items (bulky goods, long-term production, requiring special means of transportation and / or special storage conditions;
- a description of the key principles for the separation of responsibilities for procurement and rates (Customer-General Contractor-Subcontractor and), listing information on the separate sheet "Customer-General Contractor" — if any;
- substantiation of the policy of transferring goods and materials to contractors ("tolling" scheme or implementation);
- description of the procedure for the Directorate for the implementation of the project to control the ordered, received and used MTO;
- supplier contracting schedule;
- material requirements plan and turnover satisfaction (enlarged rate schedule);
- the need for materials and equipment required to complete before the release respectively sets of wok documentation, description of the company picking / order lane during regular materials / equipment;
- A brief description of the planning process for the need for materials and equipment based on the issued sets of taxiways.

14. Describe the logistics scheme for the delivery of goods, including:
    - location of warehouses on a situational plan, composition of warehouses, their brief description;
    - a description of the procedure for acceptance into the warehouse of materials and equipment received, organization of incoming control;
    - organization of export (disposal, temporary storage) of containers and other containers;

- organization of accounting for received, issued and used materials and equipment;
- organization of intra-logistics unit of time "on-site" warehouses.

15. Justify the choice of a strategy for providing the project with construction equipment, machines and mechanisms — in the options: purchase (investment costs), rent, contracting "with equipment".
16. To plan an approach to ensuring labor protection (LP), industrial safety (IS), and environmental protection (EP):
    - indicate the list of types of work that pose the greatest danger to the life and health of personnel affecting industrial safety and the environment;
    - list of violations of LP, hazardous substances and environmental protection, representing an increased danger;
    - a description of the requirements for documenting actions aimed at ensuring health, safety and environmental protection;
    - a description of the organization of control over the implementation of requirements and standards of LP, IS and EP;
    - a plan for providing employees of the project management with overalls and personal protective equipment.
17. To plan an approach to project management at the level of the project team:
    - the organizational structure of the Project team, which includes employees of the Project Management Directorate who are 100% engaged in the project, and Head Office employees who are partly involved in the project and provide functional support for the project;
    - organizational structure, staff and number of the Directorate for the implementation of the project, the current status of filling out the structure with personnel, sources of personnel attraction to the Project Directorate, customers and those responsible for staff recruitment;
    - a schedule for the staff of the Project Directorate, a schedule for the search and selection of staff for vacant positions;
    - information on current (actual) appointments to positions in the Directorate for Project Implementation;
    - Information about the appointed or potential employees of the project management senior management;
    - description of the functionality and distribution of responsibility between the key participants of the Project team (responsibility matrix);
    - motivation plan of the Directorate for the implementation of the project.

18. Formulate a project cost management plan:
    - contract price, principles of its formation;
    - The need for bank guarantees and insurance. Assessment of expenses for BG and insurance;
    - sources of input data for estimating costs and the accuracy of evaluating budget indicators;
    - main indicators of the Construction Project Budget (with the appendix of the CPB schedule);
    - cash flow budget (CF chart) and an assessment of the need for additional funds.
19. Generate a description of special aspects of the project:
    - the composition of household and office facilities, project life support facilities, including: change houses, toilets, dining room, laundry, first-aid post, rooms for storing work clothes, personal protective equipment, household equipment, fire — fighting facilities, heat supply devices / electricity, office premises, temporary accommodation, etc.;
    - location scheme of the indicated facilities on the site and their brief characteristics (situational plan);
    - special requirements for providing the construction staff and other office premises, including equipping common areas with visual aids and means of visualizing production information;
    - organization of accommodation for the staff of the Project Directorate (outside the construction site). Adopted "in- project" standards for compensation for the cost of rental housing;
    - organization of medical services on site;
    - the need for space (capacity) of the construction camp in accordance with the schedule of mobilization of labor for the project;
    - requirements for the organization of workplaces, a system of information technology (IT) and communications, software, network infrastructure, an IT security system, and equipment for workstations;
    - a schedule for the deployment of IT and communications systems; an estimate of the costs of IT and communications.
20. Provide a plan for the deployment of infrastructure supporting the implementation of the project (plan early work" project):
    - a list of information materials posted on the walls of office premises and requirements for their updating, including: materials about the project,

about the project schedule and its implementation, work progress, Company policies and specific requirements in the field of health, safety and environmental protection, etc.;

- location of the paper information archive, measures to ensure its safety, deployment plan, access restriction;
- Organization of an electronic archive of information on the project, the structure of the folders for storing information responsible for functional administration;
- a plan for deploying a perimeter security system and restricting access to the site;
- organization of checkpoints for working personnel (with an assessment of the time to ensure access to the site);
- a plan for the preparation of the construction site and mobilization, including a description and schedule of preparatory work at the site, priority organizational and technical activities, mobilization activities (machines / mechanisms, personnel);
- budget costs for preparatory and mobilization activities.

Note: The indicated sequence of actions, of course, is not exhaustive and, all the more, a guarantee of the absence of risks during the implementation of a real project. However, this sequence — the essence of the experience of JSC "Stroytransgaz", which may be useful as a practical experience for avoiding many of the pitfalls and problems encountered in the implementation of projects in the national reality. In the course of sections of the textbook, which include the present material, each of the described steps is revealed, detailed, and saturated with practical examples of practical application.

2.7.2 Life cycle monitoring of a major investment and construction project

A. Organization and holding of tenders

The organization and holding of contracted tenders (contests) can be considered as a certain project, the purpose of which is to choose the best proposal for the successful completion of work and the provision of services (Table 2.4).

The presented phases of the bidding project correspond to the procedure and sequence of performance of certain works by bidders.

The composition and volume of the phases are general in nature and can be changed and supplemented in each case. At each step of the bidding project, bidders act within the framework of their rights, functions and responsibilities.

Table 2.4 the Organizational process of contract bidding

Bidding phases	Bidding process procedures
Initial phase	Bidding initiation Appointment of the organization of bidding Determination of the volume and subject of bidding Bid announcement
Bidding project development phase: preparation and bidding	Formation of a tender committee Prequalification Development of tender documentation Calculation of investor and offeror estimates Preparation of the offers Meetings and negotiations Visiting the construction site Verification of documents Making a deposit
Bidding project implementation phase: bidding	Approval of regulations and evaluation criteria Bid opening procedure Evaluation of proposals and their analysis Justification of the tender committee Selection of a general contractor Subcontractor selection Control and verification of documents
Completion phase: contracting	Preparation of the contract Conclusion of contracts and subcontracts Control of documents, procedures, analysis and data bank
	Winner and contract information

There are a number of guidelines, standards and methods (methods) have been developed to achieve compliance with the requirements of regulatory documents that are applied at each of the phases of the bidding project, and the process of conducting bidding should be considered as a stage in the life cycle of the investment project.

Prior to the decision to conduct nuclear bidding, the customer must receive the necessary investment resources (or the right to dispose of them at the time interval required for the creation of the object), confirmed with the relevant financial documents, for example, a loan agreement, bank statement, resolution of the executive body of state power, for full or partial financing of facilities for federal state needs.

The next set of problems that must be resolved to the customer to call for tenders is to develop a concept of the future contract relations of between the customer and the winning bidder. The essence of the concept is expressed in the degree of responsibility of all entities and investment activities. The degree of responsibility is determined by the organization of the relationship between the customer and the contractor.

The most developed form of relations between the customer and the contractor is the selection of the general contractor (general contractor). The degree of responsibility for the performance of work is determined on the basis of a contract concluded between the customer and the general contractor. Based on these contractual relations, the general contractor chooses subcontractors to perform special types of work.

After the above conditions are met, one of the first problems that the customer should solve is the determination and appointment of the organizer of the auction.

The customer can delegate the functions of the bidding organizer to one of the specialized firms licensed for this type of activity, or by the order of the head of the administration of a subject of the Russian Federation, the firm is determined to be entrusted with work throughout the territory of this subject of the Russian Federation.

The tender organizer performs the following functions: it forms and approves the composition of the tender committee, prepares documents for the tender announcement, publishes an announcement or sends out proposals, organizes the development and distribution of tender and other necessary documentation, approves the tender results, and liquidates the tender committee.

The authority of the organizer of the tender is confirmed by the administrative document of the customer or the corresponding agreement. The organizer has the right to delegate part of his authority to the tender committee.

After the bidding organizer has been appointed, the ordering person or bidding organizer determines the object and subject of the bidding.

Before the announcement of the auction, the organizer of the auction, realizing the conditions of the customer, decides on the type of auction: open auction or closed, with or without prequalification.

At *closed tenders, the* customer invites several firms already known to him to participate in tenders. At *open bidding, the* customer, by announcing in an *open* press, invites everyone to take part in the bidding. A tender announcement published in the press is compiled in any form, all interested foreign and local companies can participate in open tenders.

A notice of prequalification must be contained in the announcement of the tender. When conducting closed tenders, a message on the preliminary qualifications is contained in the invitation.

Depending on the object and subject of bidding, the customer (or the organizer of the bidding) independently forms a tender committee, attracting its own specialists, representatives of research, design, engineering and consulting and other organizations, individual consultants and experts on the basis of agreements concluded with them in accordance with applicable law.

The tender committee may include representatives of the Russian Ministry of Construction and the Interdepartmental Commission for Contracting Tenders under the Russian Ministry of Construction.

The tender committee, together with the organizer of tenders and the customer, are fully responsible for the correct preparation, conduct and objectivity of the results of tenders, compliance with laws and other regulatory acts of the Russian Federation, international agreements. The tender committee has the right to delegate part of its functional responsibilities for the development, distribution and examination of tender documents, evaluation of competitive proposals to engineering and consulting organizations that have the appropriate license.

If the customer decides to conduct tenders with the preliminary qualifications of the bidders, the procedure for determining technical, economic, organizational, and other potential opportunities of the applicant for the execution of the tender submitted for bidding. Prequalification provides certain guarantees for the selection of potential applicants.

As noted in Section 2.6., after this, the tender committee develops tender documents (tender), consisting of technical and commercial parts.

At the final stage of bidding (identifying the winner and signing the contract), the final contract price of the contracted work is determined. Although the price is not always the most important criterion in the composition of the indicators of the offer when assessing the potential capabilities of the applicant, nevertheless, it occupies one of the leading places, and its determination is perhaps the most difficult, laborious and responsible task. Moreover, if other private indicators (criteria) are at the time of their submission and determined conditionally constant values (construction experience, indicators of the financial condition of contractors, the qualifications of specialists, the level of technical equipment, etc.), then the offer price is such a particular indicator, the value of which cannot be unambiguous.

To determine the value during the preparation of proposals free (contractual) prices for construction products, the following are inserted:

- when developing the investment grounds and design estimates for the investor's order, investor estimates;
- in the preparation of the contract, when the tender documentation has been developed, the calculations of the contractor.

It should be borne in mind that the values determined by investor estimates and calculations of the contractor may not coincide.

The investor and contractor estimates can be made by various methods, the choice of which is carried out in each case, depending on contractual conditions and the general economic situation.

Guidelines for determining the value of the subject of contract bidding in construction include two options:

1) determination of the value of the subject of contract bidding (C_t) in the presence of pre-design and design estimates, when:

$$C_t = A_t + K_n + K_{VAT} \; ; \tag{2.1}$$

where A_t is the estimated value at the current price level for the period of contract bidding,

K_n is inflation coefficient to the value of the subject of bidding until the moment of payment under the contract,

K_{VAT} is the coefficient of VAT.

2) Determination of the value of the subject of contracted tenders in the absence of pre- design and design estimates for aggregated indicators and similar objects with several options, bearing in mind that it is necessary to consider the main design decisions and deadlines for the execution of work.

In market relations, the contractor needs to calculate the cost of contract work according to the cost structure, which does not comply with the recommendations of the Ministry of Construction of the Russian Federation. This is due to the fact that in a comparative analysis of the cost of construction for all tenders of the customer is not interested in the cost structure of the contractor. The tenderer for whom the price determined by him, as well as other parameters to be most acceptable for the customer, will win the bidding process. He will receive the right to conclude a contract for the performance of contract work.

Thus, the proposed new approach to the pricing system and determination of the construction cost allows one to streamline the determination of contract prices for construction products taking into account the coordination of the interests of customers and contractors.

When submitting documents to the tender committee to confirm the seriousness of their intentions, each applicant makes a deposit, as a rule, on average 2% of the amount of the proposal. If offers are rejected, then the security deposit is returned to the applicant.

As noted in Section 2.6., for the success of suppliers' performance at tender great importance is the strict observance of all provisions and requirements specified in the bidding conditions, as well as the preparation of bids for a strictly defined form. Without observance of these requirements, the possibility of winning a bid is practically unrealistic, since their organizers have the right not only to reject, but also not to consider at all those proposals that do not meet the agreed conditions. In addition to compliance with all the above formalities, offers bidders shall be duly signed, stamped and sent to the tenderer organizers of trading in the taped, and sometimes (as — is required in some countries) — in double envelopes. In this case, only the address of the organization conducting the bidding (or the address of the accepting offer) is written on the external one, and on the internal — the bid number, the name of the object and the date.

After holding meetings and negotiations, visiting the construction site, checking documents, the bidder is determined in accordance with the approved regulations, drawn up by the protocol of the tender committee, which is not an act of legal binding of the transaction.

Envelopes with offers are opened on the appointed day and hour, but because the offers contain a large amount of information, an announcement is made on all bidders and on applicants who are admitted for further consideration. Decision-making and order awarding usually takes place a few months after studying proposals, the creditworthiness of applicants, and their production capabilities.

The final stage in the event of the successful completion of the final auction ends with the signing of the contract.

Regulatory documents presuppose a long chain of legal actions, starting from the development of tender documentation and the placement of a tender announcement in the media and ending with the determination of the tender winner and the conclusion of a contract with him.

A contract to make it binding must be legally executed.

In the markets of capital construction projects, a significant number of contract models are used, differing in the ways of assessing the cost of the work performed by the contractor and the degree of responsibility involved in the work. Details of contractual relations in construction will be discussed in section 2.8.

B. Rules for placing government orders

The importance of the state order for the development of the economy, social, cultural and other spheres of the country's life cannot be overestimated. Through the system of state procurement, goods, works, and services are purchased for the needs of healthcare, education, road construction, public utilities, and other sectors of the economy financed from budgets of all levels: federal, regional, and local.

Placement of a state order in the country is carried out in accordance with the requirements of Federal Law 44-FZ "On the Contract System in the Sphere of Procurement of Goods, Works, and Services for Ensuring State and Municipal Needs" (94-FZ was in effect until 31.12.2013). It spells out all possible ways by which it is possible to place state and municipal orders, as well as clearly formulated algorithms of actions as organizers bidding, and other participants in these processes, their rights and obligations.

B.1. the main amendments to the Law No. 44-FZ from January 1, 2016

From January 1, 2016, the provisions of Law No. 44-FZ are in force that regulate certain areas of activity of customers and procurement participants (part 2 of article 114 of this Law).

The main changes are as follows.

1. Responsibilities for planning, including drawing up and approving procurement plans, and justifying purchases are introduced (Art. Art. 16, 17, 18 of the Law 44-FZ).

   Customers are required to draw up procurement plans (Article 17 of Law No. 44-FZ).

   In procurement plans, it is necessary to indicate the purpose of the procurement, on the names of the procurement objects, the timing (frequency) of the procurement, the amount of financial support, some other information (part 2 of article 17 of Law No. 44-FZ). A procurement plan is formed in the process of drafting and reviewing draft budgets of the budget system of the Russian Federation and is approved within 10 business days after bringing to the state or municipal customer the amount of rights in monetary terms to accept and (or) fulfillment of obligations in accordance with budget legislation (h. 7, article 17 of the Law of the Law No. 44-FZ).

   Budget institutions must approve procurement plans within 10 days after the approval of their financial and economic activity plan (part 8 of article 17 of Law No. 44-FZ).

   Customers are required to justify all purchases that are included in the procurement plan, schedule (part 1 of article 18 of Law No. 44-FZ). Customers must prove the compliance of planned purchases with the goals specified in Art. 13 of the Law No. 44-FZ:

   - implementation of state and municipal, international programs;
   - Fulfillment of international obligations of the Russian Federation;
   - performance of the functions and powers of customers as state and municipal bodies, bodies of management of extra-budgetary funds.

2. The requirements established by Law No. 44-FZ apply to the content and form of the schedule, the procedure for their formation, approval and amendment.

   Customers are required to formulate schedules in accordance with procurement plans (part 2 of article 21 of Law No. 44-FZ). The basic requirements for the content, the procedure for the formation, approval and amendment, as well as for the form of schedules, are provided for in

Part 1 - 10, 12 - 15 Art. 21, paragraph 2, part 4 of article 38 of the Law No. 44-FZ.

3. The need has been introduced to include information on the prices of goods (works, services) that develop on product markets and requests for prices placed by customers when determining the initial (maximum) contract price (clause 16, part 3) in a single information system (hereinafter referred to as UIS) Article 4 of Law No. 44-FZ).

   Such information is included in the UIS in order to assist customers in determining and justifying the initial (maximum) contract prices using the method of comparable market prices (market analysis).

4. The need is introduced to indicate in the documents provided for by Law No. 44-FZ (for example, in an agreement on holding a joint tender or auction) the identification code of the procurement (part 1 of article 23, paragraph 1.1 of part 2 of article 25 of the said Law)

5. Provisioning regulation applies.

   Procurement regulation refers to the establishment of requirements for goods (works, services) purchased by the customer and (or) standard costs for the functions of state bodies, governing bodies of state extra-budgetary funds, municipal bodies (including territorial bodies and subordinate state institutions, respectively) (Part 1 of Article 19 of the Law No. 44-FZ).

   These requirements include requirements for the quantity, consumer properties and other characteristics (in particular, the marginal price) of goods (works, services) (parts 1 and 2 of article 19 of Law No. 44-FZ).

6. The obligation of the executive authorities, local authorities to make a decision on the exercise by them and their subordinate entities of the authority of the customer on their own or with the involvement of authorized bodies and institutions is introduced (part 5 of article 26 of Law No. 44-FZ).

If a decision is made on the implementation and procurement involving authorized bodies and institutions, they may be delegated functions only to identify suppliers or plan and carry out procurements in general (including identifying suppliers, concluding and executing contracts).

B.2. The main amendments to Law No. 44-FZ.

Starting January 1, 2017, the procurement procedure was changed as follows:

1. The stipulated h. 11 Article. 21 of the Law No. 44-FZ prohibition of procurement, which are not included in the schedule.
2. The functions of the EIS are expanding (paragraph 2 of Part 1 of Article 4 of Law No. 44-FZ).

In the future, the EIS will also perform the functions of ensuring compliance control:

- information on the amount of financial support in accordance with the procurement plans; information on the amount of financial support brought to the customer;
- information included in the schedule, information contained in the procurement plans;
- information in procurement notices, information on procurement of information in schedules;
- information in the protocols for determining suppliers of information in the procurement documentation;
- terms of the draft contract sent in the form of an electronic document to the procurement participant, information in the protocol for determining the supplier;
- information about the contract included in the register of contracts, the terms of the contract.

3. The entry into force of Art. 20 of Law No. 44-FZ, establishing the need for public discussion of certain types of procurement.

   Cases in which a public discussion of procurement is mandatory, as well as the procedure for such discussion are determined by the Government of the Russian Federation (part 1 of article 20 of Law No. 44-FZ).

   Based on the results of mandatory public discussion, changes to procurement plans, schedules, procurement documents, or procurement can be made (part 3 of article 20 of Law No. 44-FZ).

4. The obligation is introduced to indicate in the procurement notice, the registry of contracts and the registry of unscrupulous suppliers an identification code for procurement (paragraph 3 of article 42, paragraph 12 of paragraph 2 of article 103, paragraph 5 of paragraph 3 of article 104 of Law No. 44-Federal Law).
5. The customer will have an obligation to indicate the name of the procurement object during its planning and implementation in accordance with the catalog of goods, works, services for state and municipal needs (part 4 of article 23 of Law No. 44-FZ).
6. The mechanism for determining procurement monitoring (part 1 of article 97 of the Law of the Law No. 44-FZ) has entered into force.

   Under the *monitoring of the procurement* will be understood by observing the system in the field of procurement, which will be carried out on an ongoing basis through the collection, generalization, systematization and evaluation of information on the implementation of the procurement, including the implementation of procurement plans and schedules.

7. The powers of the executive authorities, carrying out functions of cash servicing of budget execution and control in the field of procurement, were specified (part 5 of article 99 of Law No. 44-FZ).

   Note: If, with respect to the period until January 1, 2017, Law No. 44-FZ stipulates only that the Treasury of Russia, the financial bodies of the constituent entities of the Russian Federation and municipalities, the governing bodies of state non- budget funds, exercise control over the procurement within their authority, then from January 1, 2017, the specific powers of such bodies in this area will be fixed at the legislative level. These will include compliance control:

   - information on the amount of financial support in accordance with the procurement plans; information on the amount of financial support brought to the customer;
   - information on identification codes x of procurements and on the volume of financing of procurements presented in various documents, for example, in the schedule and in the procurement plan.

It is assumed that these powers will be exercised by these authorities through the operation of the EIS (the corresponding functions of the EIS are secured by clause 2 of Part 1 of Article 4 of Law No. 44-FZ). In this case, the introduction of this form of control will not require customers to submit additional documents to the regulatory authorities.

C. Types of public procurement

At present, state and municipal orders can be placed by the methods presented in Fig. 2.17.

Open competition

The most common method of competitive procurement is an open tender, in which any supplier can participate. A notice of an open competition is published in specialized publications, on the ordering website, and in the media. The open tender procedure lasts at least a month and requires large resources (preparation of tender documentation, evaluation of applications, etc.).

The competition is held by the customer or completely soaked. All requirements for the subject of procurement and suppliers, as well as selection criteria for the winner and the tender procedure, are set out in the tender documentation. Competition participants submit applications drawn up in accordance with the requirements. If only one application has been submitted for the competition, it shall be considered invalid.

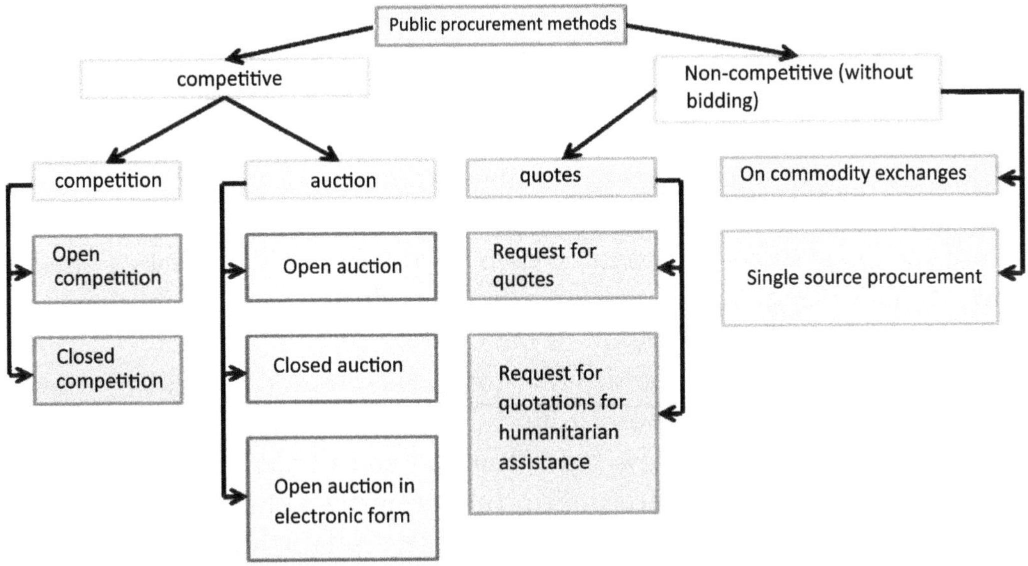

Figure 2.17: Ways to place state and municipal orders

At the public bid opening procedure, bidders and their price offers are announced. The tender commission evaluates all applications and determines the winner — the participant who submitted the most advantageous offer. He is negotiating a contract.

If negotiations come to a standstill, the contest organizer conducts them with delivery for the person who made the next most profitable offer.

Closed competition

The rules of the closed competition are the same as in the open competition. The difference is in the choice of participants. If any eligible supplier can participate in an open tender, then an invitation to participate in a closed tender must not be published. Only those suppliers whom the customer has invited can participate in it. Information on the results of a closed tender is also not published.

Closed competition is held in the following cases:

- only a limited number of suppliers have products or a limited number of suppliers have qualifications that suit the customer;
- products are purchased for safety needs or the purchase is confidential;
- the time and costs that will be required to consider and evaluate a large number of competitive applications are incommensurable with the cost of purchased products.

Open auction an open auction allows you to implement a government order by submitting an application online. A contract for a state order providing for the provision of goods, work or services is called a lot. The main criterion for determining the winner of any auction is the price. Therefore, the winner of the auction is the person who has offered the lowest price of a state or municipal contract.

The notice of an open auction is published in the official print media and posted on the official website at least twenty days before the deadline for submitting applications for participation in the auction. In cases specified by law, a notice of a public auction may be reduced to seven business days before the deadline for submission of bids.

Bids at the auction can be discrete (with a certain step) and continuous. An auction can consist of several rounds, at each of which participants have the opportunity to make a new bid. If at the end of the round no new bids are made, the auction ends. To confirm the seriousness of the intentions of the auction participants, they usually take a non-refundable contribution, pledge or other security for bids.

Closed auction

Like contests, auctions are open and closed. However, if in closed tenders, the rules are the same as in open tenders, but a limited circle of suppliers is allowed to participate, then there are no such restrictions in closed auctions. The difference between closed auctions is that auctioneers do not know the applications of other participants, since they are submitted in sealed envelopes, whereas in open auctions all participants know each application.

Notice of a closed auction, auction documentation, amendments made to it, as well as clarifications of auction documentation shall not be published in the media and posted on the Internet. Customer, authorized body, no later than twenty days before the deadline for filing applications for participation in the auction, send in writing invitations to participate in a closed auction to persons who satisfy the requirements of the law, have access to information that is a state secret, and are able to carry out the supply of goods, performance of work, rendering of services that are subject of auction.

Closed auctions are most often used to reduce the risks of the customer, primarily associated with possible collusion of participants. However, the cost for this is reduced efficiency.

Electronic auction

An open auction in electronic form (OAEF) is an auction in electronic form on the site of electronic trading platforms accredited by the Ministry of Economic Development of the Russian Federation. Its order is regulated by Art. 59 of the Federal Law dated 05.04.2013 No. 44-FZ (as amended on 12.30.2015) "On the contract system in the field of procurement of goods, work, services for the state and municipal needs" and government decrees.

Notification of the auction, as well as other information on the progress and results of the auction, is posted directly on electronic platforms.

Fig. 2.18 shows the total prices of electronic auctions and the total amount of contracts concluded in 2014–2015.

1. **Accredited electronic trading platforms (ETP) for government orders**

   According to the decision of the Ministry of Economic Development of Russia, by January 1, 2010, five electronic trading platforms were selected:

   - CJSC "Sberbank-AST";
   - OJSC "Unified Electronic Trading Platform";
   - State Unitary Enterprise "Agency for the state order of the Republic of Tatarstan";
   - Joint-Stock Company "Moscow Interbank Currency Exchange";
   - OOO "RTS-tender".

2. **Differences between electronic auctions and other types of bidding**

   A comparative analysis of electronic auctions from other types of bidding is given in table. 2.5.

3. **The benefits of electronic auctions**

   In addition to saving budget funds and reducing the risk of corruption, the OAEF provides broad access to government procurement for small and medium — sized enterprises, expanding sales markets for their goods and services. Among the advantages of electronic auctions, compared with conventional auctions and competitions, are the following:

   - short terms;
   - saving budgetary funds for organizing and conducting tenders;
   - transparency and openness of the procurement process;
   - fair competition, excluding non-price methods of warfare;
   - equal rights of all suppliers of goods, works and services;
   - participation in tenders is possible from anywhere in the world without leaving your office;
   - high level of security and protection, the use of electronic digital signature;
   - accessibility for representatives of medium and small businesses that used to be
   - could not enter the area of public procurement.

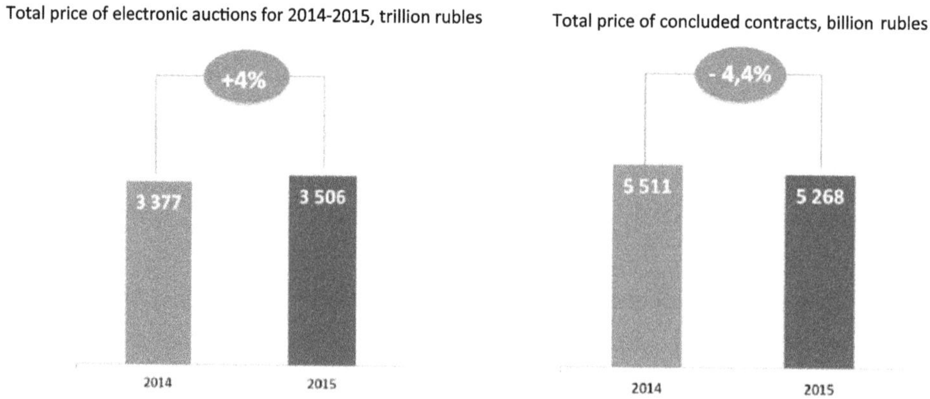

Figure 2.18: The total price of electronic auctions for 2014–2015. (Trillion rubles) and the total price of concluded contracts (billion rubles).

Table 2.5 Differences between electronic auctions and other types of bidding.

Parameters	Electronic auction	Request for quotes	Open competition
Submission of proposals	Multiple/ electronic	Single/ paper	Single/ paper
Obligations of the customer and the winning bidder	Legally fixed (based on electronic digital signature)	absent	Legally fixed
Relative volume of workflow	Minimal, served once	small	Significant, submitted separately for each competition

4. **The rules for conducting open auctions in electronic form.**

To participate in the auction, you need to register on the electronic trading platform and on the day of the auction go to the auction website using identification tools or electronic digital signature (EDS). An electronic digital signature in an electronic document is equivalent to a handwritten signature in a document on paper. Everything you need to know about electronic digital signatures is contained in the Federal Law of 04/06/2011

No. 63-FZ (as amended on December 30, 2015) "On electronic signature".

The auction is held to lower prices. If the price drops to zero — then increase.

At the beginning of the auction, the participant can make a price offer within the current auction step, not exceeding the initial (maximum) price of the contract, using the special form on the site.

The participant can repeatedly submit price offers.

Bidding is considered completed if, after 10 minutes from the start of bidding or the last price offer, the bidder has not received a proposal providing a lower price.

The winner is the participant who has offered the lowest contract price.

A participant is also identified who has made the next best price offer after the winner.

The system automatically creates a protocol with the results of the auction within a few minutes.

Request for quotes

A quotation request is a way of placing an order in which information on the needs for goods, work, services for state or municipal needs is communicated to an unlimited number of persons by posting a notice on the conduct of a quotation request on the official website. The order of the request for quotations is regulated by Chapter 3 of the Federal Law of 04/05/2013

No. 44-FZ (as amended on December 30, 2015) "On the contract system in the field of procurement of goods, work, services to meet state and municipal needs".

This method is usually used in those cases when it comes to serial, standard products, for example, computers, office supplies, fuels and lubricants, some types of construction work, rental of premises, etc. A participant is recognized as the winner the lowest bidder for the contract.

The border for placing an order by requesting quotations at the maximum price of the contract should not exceed 500,000 rubles.

The way to request quotes is the simplest and fastest of the competitive procedures. In this case, it is not necessary to develop competitive documentation and criteria for evaluating applications, and since serial production is most often purchased, the evaluation of quotation applications, taking into account all approvals, takes about 1–7 days.

Comparison of the main characteristics of an open auction and request for quotations are given in table. 2.6.

The disadvantage of the method of requesting quotes is the ability of interested parties to influence the outcome of the purchase, because all offered the organizers know prices before the deadline for applications.

Placing an order with a single supplier

Placing an order with a single supplier is the purchase of goods, work or services for an amount not exceeding one hundred thousand rubles. At the same time, the annual volume of purchases that the customer is entitled to carry out on the basis of this paragraph should not exceed two million rubles or should not exceed five percent of the total annual purchases of the customer and should not exceed more than fifty million rubles The contract is concluded only after the winning participant has provided it to ensure fulfillment of contractual obligations:

- an irrevocable bank guarantee issued by a bank or other credit institution;

- transferring money to the customer as a pledge, including in the form of a deposit (deposit) in the amount of security for the execution of the contract.

Table 2.6 Comparison of the main characteristics of an open auction and request for quotations

Parameters	Request for quotes	Open auction
Notice placement	Posted on the official website	Published in the official print media and posted on the official website
Initial contract price	Does not exceed 500 thousand rubles	No limits
Additional conditions for	Auction was declared invalid, and the initial price of the contract does not exceed 500 thousand rubles	Goods, work, services can only be compared at a price
Order placement restrictions	The customer has the right to make purchases by conducting a quotation request, provided that the initial (maximum) contract price does not exceed 500 thousand rubles. At the same time, the annual volume of purchases carried out by conducting a request for quotations should not exceed 10% of the total annual volume of purchases of the customer and should not be more than 100 million rubles	The government establishes a list of goods, works, services carried out by auction

The amount of security for the execution of the contract should be from 5% to 30% of the initial (maximum) price of the contract. In the event that if the contract provides for the payment of an advance, the amount of security for the execution of the contract increases by the amount of the advance.

Authorized executive bodies carry out control in the field of placing state and municipal orders. Such bodies are the Federal Antimonopoly Service of the Russian Federation and the Federal Service for Defense Orders.

When purchasing from a single source, the customer submits an offer to conclude a contract and negotiates with only one supplier.

Purchasing from one supplier is used in the following cases:

- when the products are provided only one supplier or equipment of patented and can only be acquired from a single source, but no equivalent replacement;
- when extending a contract, if it provided for such an opportunity;
- if the contractor needs to purchase the key positions from individual supplier as a guarantee of performance of the contract;
- in emergency situations (liquidation of consequences of natural disasters);

- if there were no suitable offers during the procurement using the competitive method.

It is advisable to purchase products from one supplier with insignificant amounts of purchases, when the costs of the customer for the search and selection of suppliers are much higher than the price of the purchased products.

2.8 Contractual relationship

In accordance with the Civil Code of the Russian Federation (part two) dated 01/26/1996 No. 14-FZ (as amended on 12/05/20 17), a construction contract is a contract by which the contractor undertakes to build a specific facility by the order of the customer or to perform other construction work, and the customer agrees to create the necessary conditions for the contractor to perform the work, accept their result and pay the stipulated price.

Requirements of Federal Law 44-FZ 5/4/2013 (as amended on 12.31.2017) "About contract system in the procurement of goods, works and services for the maintenance of the state and municipal needs" within the organization of construction and development for state and municipal needs identified conclusion of government contracts.

Within the framework of this textbook, a unified concept of the construction contract is adopted as the main document regulating the relationship between the participants in the process of organizing the construction and real estate development and defining the legal rights and obligations of all parties at various stages of the life cycle of an object.

The types of construction contracts have a direct impact on such vital issues of the functioning of construction and development companies as the choice of objects (projects) for inclusion in the portfolio of orders, ensuring a stable financial position of the company, the choice of a rational organizational form of management and organizational structure of an internal company management, selection and development of personnel, etc. A specific type of contract makes special demands on each of the participants, accounting of which leads to the appropriateness of the restructuring of the strategy for the functioning and development of the construction (development) company. Therefore, when choosing objects (projects), the company takes into account such factors as its own production capabilities, the level of equipment with construction equipment, the availability of qualified personnel, and the need in attracting resources "from the side", etc.

The construction contract briefly describes the work to be performed, stipulates the amount of payment, the term of the contract and the amount of the penalty for violation of the deadlines, in practice, the contracts can be supplemented with a number of annexes defining the rights and obligations of the parties:

1. Terms of reference, determining the technical and organizational procedure for achieving the required results. Under the terms of the contract, the general contractor is obliged to draw up a written guarantee to the customer that the qualifications of the workers, the quality of the materials and the work performed will meet the requirements of the contract. It requires the same guarantees, in turn, from manufacturers and subcontractors who perform work and supply finished products;
2. Technological maps describing the structural components of the object and the sequence of their assembly. The cards must indicate the physical and chemical properties of the materials, the dimensions of each element of the fixing devices and the distance between them, the exact relative position of the moving parts, the assembly sequence, etc. The contractor is responsible for the work in accordance with these instructions.

   The author of the project (design organization) is fully responsible for the exact correspondence of the project to its purpose;
3. Technical conditions that establish the technical requirements for the work performed within the framework of integration into the general network life support systems issued by energy supplying organizations, local self-government bodies and other authorized structures;
4. Sheets of materials and finished products, equipment specifications that stipulate the use of certain types of materials, equipment and finished products, which are not similar in all respects. The author of the project is responsible to the customer for the compliance of their performance with the data given in the descriptions;
5. The schedule for the production of work drawn up in accordance with the technological conditions and regulatory terms of construction.

A supplier offering materials or equipment must prepare their quotation proposals. The availability of specifications for the main applications ensures the best quality control of materials and equipment.

Currently, three types of construction contracts (contracts) are most often used in Russia. The most common of them is a contract of the type "Fixed *Contract Price*", or a contract with a fixed price, which is an agreement to carry out a project at a fixed price, regardless of the actual cost of the construction contractor. The contract (agreement) presupposes the availability of full project documentation for the building under construction, it guarantees the customer the project to be completed on time within the specified (estimated) cost, but is characterized by a high degree of risk for the contractor, which must provide for all possible deviations at the stage of concluding the contract and difficulties that may arise during the implementation of the project. This situation naturally affects the growth of the contract price, the proposed by contractor. The key disadvantage of this type of contract is the obsolescence factor of design decisions, which manifests itself with particular force in the construction of large facilities and caused by the requirement to have a complete set of design estimates before construction begins. A fixed-price contract is attractive primarily for those customers who do not have sufficient construction experience and do not have qualified specialists in the field of construction and its management who are able effectively manage a construction contract.

Contract "with the price determined RESOURCES waist method -by actually under the evidence supporting the charges", or can be designated contract "price-plus" is an agreement on the implementation of the project within the framework of the agreed price, based on current prices. In accordance with the contract, the customer pays all the confirmed additional costs of the contractor during the construction of the facility.

At the same time, the contractor's fee is set either at a mark predetermined by the contract, or as a percentage of the project's estimated cost. Under the conditions of a contract of this type, all risk associated with the possibility of exceeding the price established by the contract is passed on to the customer. Construction within the framework of this type of contract can be started before all design estimates have been prepared, in which it is allowed to introduce changes arising during construction, which are caused, inter alia, by the development of scientific and technological progress.

Despite the nature of the contract that is clearly costly for the customer, these contracts are nevertheless concluded, since in the absence of a complete set of design estimates for the customer, there is simply no other alternative.

Under the terms of the contract "with the price determined by the resource method — in fact, confirmed expenses" more active involvement of customer representatives in the design and construction processes is required than, for example, in a contract with a fixed price. And above all, builders in the design process, which makes it possible to take into account the requirements of building technological adaptability of design solutions and thereby helps to reduce the number of conflict situations that arise during construction due to design errors. According to experts, the participation of builders in the design process provides savings of up to 20% of the project cost.

When the contract *"Turnkey"* (the contract "design -construction") the customer enters into an agreement with one m the general contractor, which provides guidance to both the main phases of construction process: design and construction. To carry out certain stages and works, the general contractor engages specialized companies, the relations with which he maintains based on independent contracts, which in their type may differ from the type of the head contract. The construction can be started before the completion of design estimates, and the success of the construction under this type of contract depends entirely on the capabilities and practical experience of the general contractor or the company taking on the role of general contractor. In particular, this remark concerns the tasks of monitoring the design process.

In a sense, the development of contract-type "design — construction" can be considered as a contract *"construction management"*. As part of this type of contract, a special group is created for the management of the contract or project, consisting of representatives of the customer, construction manager, project author, who jointly resolves all issues related to the cost of the project as a whole and its individual stages, and the queues, the choice of the construction site, and the development of instructive materials, etc. As practice shows, this form of organizing the interaction of participants in the construction contract provides both significant time savings in the process of making managerial decisions and, to the best extent, concentration of responsibility in a single governing body.

In the countries of the European Union and the United States, the above types of contracts are used, so are the types of contracts that are not typical for our country:

A contract of type *"Guaranteed maximum or upset price control"* (the contract with guaranteed maximum price) of the relationship between the Customer and the contractor remains practically the same as with the contract of the "price-plus" type, however, the contractor already guarantees to the customer that it agrees the so-called maximum project price associated with it will not be exceeded.

Otherwise, if the contractor nevertheless exceeds this price, the costs will fall entirely on his shoulders. If the actual cost of the project turns out to be less than the agreed price, then the difference of these values, under the conditions stipulated by the specific contract, is transferred to the contractor, taking into account the contractor's fees for the project.

A contract of type *"Construction bonding"* (CB) is one of the common forms of contracts aimed at reducing risk in the process of project implementation and increasing the financial stability of its main participants (customer and contractor). Its essence consists in attracting a company acting as a guarantor to participate in the construction contract. Unlike the insurance system that is widespread in construction, in accordance with which the insurance company assumes financial responsibility (in the proportion stipulated by the insurance contract) for possible breach of the contract regarding the cost, terms and quality of construction, a contract of type CB guarantees the customer project implementation in full accordance with the contract. If the contractor, for one reason or another, cannot fulfill the contractual obligations, the guarantor company itself fulfills them or involves other contracting firms for this.

In other words, a contract of type CB does not guarantee reimbursement of the possible costs to the customer, but the construction of the facility in full compliance with the contractual conditions. The formal basis for this type of contract is a tripartite agreement between the customer, the contractor and the guarantor. The contractor company, acting as the project manager, pays a fee to the guaranteeing company (guaranteeing company), the size of which substantially depends on the scale of the project and its participants. In most cases, it ranges from 0.3 to 1.5% of the total contract value. It is in this amount that the contractor's gain is estimated by reducing the risk during the implementation of the project under a CB type contract.

This type of contract is the most popular among contractors in the public sector and, to a lesser extent, in the private sector. Its main drawback is the increase in the value of the contract due to the additional payment of the fee to the firm- guarantor. The main advantage is the increase in the stability of the financial situation of contracting construction companies, especially those that are simultaneously involved in the implementation of a small number of projects.

There are varieties of contracts of type CB, among which the following three are of most interest: *"Bid Bond"* (BB), *"Payment Bond"* (PB), *"Performance Bond"* (PB) The form of the contract type BB is intended to protect the customer regarding the total cost of the contract. Its essence lies in the fact that the guarantor company assumes responsibility for the execution of the contract within the framework of the price stipulated by the agreement between it and the customer if the contractor refuses to fulfill the contract for one reason or another.

The contract type *RV is* intended to protect the interests of the customer in terms of remuneration of contract participants, including workers and employees, as part of the general contractor and subcontracting firms, as well as hired workers and employees of supplier firms.

The contract form of the P*B* type is the most effective from the point of view of the customer, since it guarantees him during the construction process the exact observance of design decisions and contract terms by the contractor.

In cases where the contractor does not comply with the terms of the tripartite agreement, the guarantor firm, as a rule, completes the contract at a price that exceeds the originally stipulated contract.

The conclusion of a *CB* type contract can be considered as a measure of the struggle of contracting firms and, to a lesser extent, contracting firms for increasing the stability of their financial situation in the conditions of a long-term decline in the economy and the construction industry as well.

The possibility of choosing this type of construction contract, which is most suitable for the particularities and conditions of specific contracting firms, is one way to increase the efficiency of the construction process. Naturally, the choice of an adequate form of a construction contract is not always possible, if only for the reason that there is one more party in the contract — the customer, whose interests in choosing the form of the contract may differ from the interests of the contractor.

According to experts, the contract "with the price defined with the resource method using actual support expenses" may be the effectively implemented in the event of a major project, subject to availability of completely finished project documentation and system of separation of the contract between the plurality of sub-contracting of construction companies, which in this acquires the status of the so called main (as opposed to general) contracting firms subordinate directly to the management group representing the interests of the customer.

Experience has shown that a contract "with the pricc dctermined by the resource method — at actually confirmed costs" can be successfully applied in smaller projects, due to the reduction of construction time, cost reduction and improvement of construction quality. As noted, construction under a contract "with a price determined by the resource method — based on actually confirmed costs" can begin long before the completion of design work.

In fig. 2.19 a comparative analysis of the duration of construction is carried out under the contracts, respectively, "with a fixed contract price" and "with the price determined by the resource method — based on actually confirmed expenses".

Under the terms of the contract "with the price determined by the resource method — based on actually confirmed expenses", the customer is much more actively involved in control and management than in the contract with a fixed price. Due to the ability to conduct construction in the absence of full design documentation, it is possible to minimize or eliminate time losses. A prerequisite for reducing the cost of construction in the contract "with the price determined by the resource method — based on the actually confirmed costs" is the availability of qualified personnel at the customer who is able to carry out reliable cost control.

The contract "with the price determined by the resource method — at virtually fixed costs" minimizes the number of claims, each of which costs the customer a very specific amount. Unlike fixed-price contracts, all changes associated with design errors, as well as the customer's desire to amend the project, forced downtime increase the amount of unforeseen costs paid by the customer.

Under the terms of the contract "with the price determined by the resource method — based on the actually confirmed expenses", the joint work of designers and builders at the design stage ensures an increase in the quality of the project by taking into account the requirements of building manufacturability, elaborating multivariate design solutions and choosing the most rational of them. At the same time, under a contract with a firm contract price, the builder is not directly interested in increasing the quality of construction, in any case, higher than the level formulated in the contract documentation and specifications. Contract "with the price determined by the resource -by actually confirmed expenses" only effective when the Contract Management System is effective, in which employs highly skilled workers, specialists in marketing, purchasing, procurement of equipment, etc.

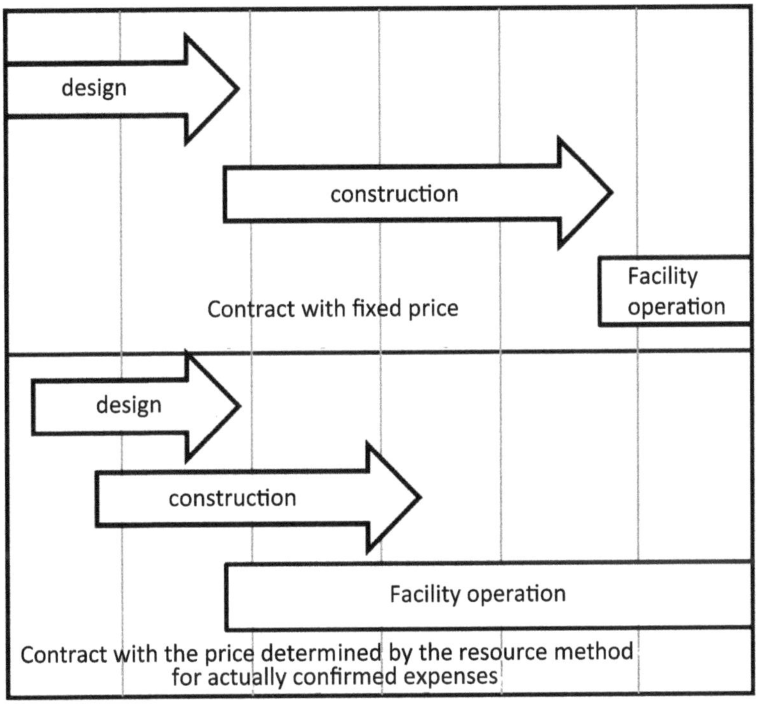

Figure 2.19: A comparative analysis of the duration of construction of facilities under contracts with a firm contract price and with a price determined by the resource method — based on actually confirmed expenses.

An important reserve for the effectiveness of the contract "with the price determined by the resource method — based on the actually confirmed costs" is the prerequisites created by its internal economic mechanism for the active involvement of all participants in the construction contract and primarily the contractor in the design process, and if possible at earlier stages of design, particularly at the stage of conceptual design, since solutions adopted at these stages, not in spite of relatively small part required for them complements costs have a significant impact on the key performance indicators of construction production (Fig. 2.20).

A significant reserve for the effectiveness of the contract "with the price determined by the resource method — at actually confirmed costs" is the minimization of changes and alterations in the project and in the course of construction work. To solve this problem, a joint council (commission) is created from the representatives of the customer and the contractor who are looking for solutions acceptable to both parties.

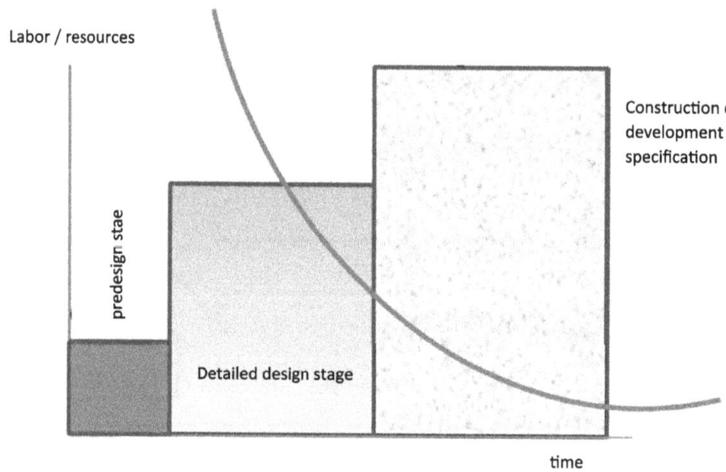

Figure 2.20: The impact of decisions made at various stages of the design of buildings and structures on the costs of resources and labor

The contract "with the price determined by the resource method — at virtually confirmed costs" requires the development of a joint system and procedure for monitoring labor productivity and productivity indicators. The basic scheme of such a procedure is shown in Fig. 2.21. There is an opinion that a contract "with a price determined by the resource method — practically at a fixed cost" is characterized by low productivity compared to, for example, a contract with a firm contract price. Experience shows that with a well-organized system of contract management and an integrated approach to organizing planning and managing a contract "with the price determined by the resource method — for actually confirmed costs", this indicator is not inferior to a contract with a firm contract price.

The effectiveness of project implementation in contractual relationships consists in achieving several criteria simultaneously: minimizing cost, minimizing deviations from the work schedule, maximizing the achievement of a given level of construction quality and labor safety in the workplace, and maximally satisfying the interests of the customer and the contractor.

In general, all types of contracts can be conditionally divided into two groups: "compensation" and "fixed price contracts".

Compensation contracts to a greater extent lead to a reduction in the severity of contradictions between the customer and the contractor than fixed-price contracts. This is manifested in a smaller number of controversial and conflict situations.

Fixed price contracts require a significantly greater effort from the customer in terms of preparing pre-design and project documentation at the stages prior to the start of construction itself. This naturally leads to an increase in labor costs, finances, and an increase in the duration of the preparatory period. Compensation contracts in this sense look preferable to the customer.

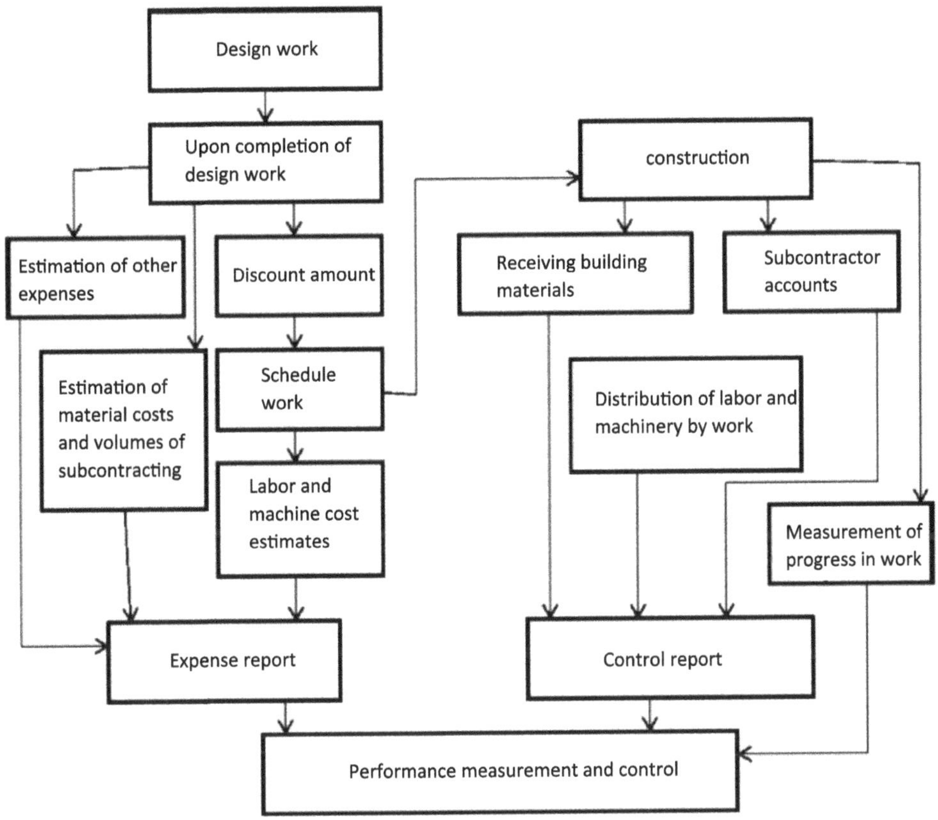

Figure 2.21: Schematic diagram of the procedure for monitoring the effectiveness of construction production under a contract "with the price determined by the resource method – at actually confirmed expenses."

Since each type of contract is characterized by a different combination of values of the main criteria for construction efficiency, the choice of the most suitable contract is a very difficult task, especially since there are no quantitative data reflecting the degree of preference of one type of contract over others due to the fact that the customer stops in specific projects one's choice is based on one type of contract; therefore, when conducting a comparative analysis, it is advisable to resort to the use of expert estimates.

As the contract forms developed, the role of civil engineers and designers, the nature of their relationship with the customer, and representatives of local authorities changed.

The latest forms of contracts have demonstrated that the management of the design process, including the stages of conceptual and detailed design, is not necessarily the function of the project's chief engineer or project's chief architect, as was traditionally thought. The project manager, who, in addition, supervises the construction of the facility, successfully carried out this function. Depending on the type of contract, the degree of risk that the developer assumes varies.

Consider the most common ways to implement development activities in the performance of construction contracts.

The first, traditional, according to which such stages of the investment construction process as design, bidding, construction, are carried out sequentially in time. Initially, design work is carried out, then, if there is a lot of work on local objects or stages of work compiled in accordance with the developer's method of calculating estimates, a suitable contractor company is able to carry out construction according to the specified design drawings. This type of contract has many varieties, depending on the nature of the use of the principle of combining during the individual stages of the construction process, i.e. when one stage can begin before the previous one has ended. The contract between the Customer and the contractor stipulates the role of the author of the project, and the project manager works directly under the leadership of the customer: his role and tasks, duties and responsibilities are defined in a separate contract concluded between him and the customer.

The second method involves a detailed distribution of responsibility and requires the direct participation of the customer in the implementation of the contract by permanent representation at the facility. Within the framework of this contract, high resolution of conflict situations is achieved, a good microclimate is created within the project group, the possibility of an alternative approach to the selection of project solutions, the search for ways to implement the project, and forms of organization of the design process management is allowed. So, in accordance with one of the varieties, the design responsibility is assigned to the design engineer (project author), in accordance with another, the responsibility for the design stage is shared between the design engineer (the preliminary design stage is assigned to it) and contractor (assigned to him the function of working, detailed design). At the same time, the contractor can resort to the services of the same project team or seek help from its own project team. This method involves a high level of training and the era of the customer or his representative.

The *third method* involves development activities of the type of "project management", the main purpose of which is to centralize the functions and responsibilities for managing and the progress of the project in a single body. The project manager in this type of development activity acts as the representative of the customer. An alternative to this solution may be the role of the project manager as the coordinator of the work of the design engineer and contractor.

This method is most widely used for managing large and complex projects that require a large amount of coordination work.

Project teams are formed by the customer, but taking into account the proposals and recommendations of the project manager.

The fourth type of activity is "contract management", which is focused on the implementation, as a rule, of very large and complex projects.

The task is to involve the contractor in the investment process, if possible at an earlier stage of design. The purpose of such involvement is to expand the participation of the contractor in the formation of design decisions, the formulation of the requirements for the construction technology of design solutions, which requires additional effort and time from the contractor. In the strictest form, this type assumes fixing the full responsibility for the final construction results to the contractor. In a more general case, the contract allows for the step-by-step distribution of responsibility.

At the same time, the main stages are separated in time: construction begins only when the detailed design is completed. The contract manager acts in a role similar to the project manager: its main task is the distribution and coordination of work between subcontractors.

Historically, the most common organizational form of management in construction is the *general contracting* system. However, the experience of its operation over many decades shows that customers have to deal with facts such as exceeding the estimated cost of construction, deviation from the timing of putting the facility into operation. In addition, in the framework of the organizational form of general contracting, the customer has to perform many additional functions, firstly, not peculiar to the profile of its main activity, and secondly, associated with risk. In the modern history of Russia over the past 15–0 years, fundamental changes have taken place in the construction industry, which are caused not so much by technological innovations, how much organizational change. Performance degradation labor in construction, characteristic of recent years, including largely due to the slowdown in the growth of construction management efficiency.

In this chapter, the functions of the construction manager are structured, which are reduced to three main, in addition to general management, functions: cost control, timing control and quality control.

Cost control involves preparing the project budget and ensuring that the project documentation for the cost fit into the framework of the project budget. The construction manager analyzes the budget line items, participates in the design work, monitors the costs of the construction process, makes monthly settlements with contractors, evaluates the changes made to the project, settles claims and claims, and participates in determining the final cost of the project and construction.

The second function of the manager is to control the timing. Its task is to identify deviations from the planned dates and develop proposals for their elimination. Quality control is carried out by analyzing project documentation with the aim of identifying and eliminating possible conflicts, checking compliance with the standards and requirements of the contract; at the construction stage, control is carried out directly at the construction site, while the construction manager signals possible deviations to the author of the project. The construction manager organizes tests and inspections during construction and installation works.

Effective work of the construction manager is a prerequisite for the successful functioning of the organizational form of "construction management". An important prerequisite for success is the choice of that particular modification of the organized form of implementation of the construction project, which most closely meets the specifics and requirements of the participants. When choosing a particular modification, it is necessary to take into account such factors as the characteristics of the construction object itself, customer requirements, experience, nature and extent of risk distribution between participants in the construction process.

Effective organization of the "construction management" system requires a clear separation of functions and responsibilities of the project author and construction manager based on relevant contracts. The concept of a "divided contract" between them demonstrates high efficiency in practice, allowing solving the problem of the dual role of the construction manager, which was mentioned above.

Questions for self-control

1. What are the meanings of the term "project"?
2. What is project management?

3. What is the object of management in the project management methodology?
4. What is the essence of the process approach to management?
5. What factors determine the specifics of project management in real estate?
6. How are many investment construction projects classified?
7. What is a portfolio of projects and a targeted program?
8. What includes the life cycle of a classic design and construction project?
9. What approaches are used to analyze the full life cycle of a project?
10. What are the main studies of the project carried out at the conceptual stage?
11. What is the purpose and content of the structuring of the project?
12. List the main types of organizational structures of management.
13. What are the challenges facing the project manager and the project team?
14. What are the features of project management?
15. What types of plans do you know of what processes project planning consists of?
16. What methods of bidding do you know?
17. What types of contracts are used in investment and construction projects?
18. Explain the essence of the construction contract, what applications can it be supplemented at the conclusion? What are the main types of contracts in the construction industry, what is their essence?
19. Explain the main reasons for concluding contracts with a firm contract price and with a price determined by a resource method — in fact, at proven costs that affect the duration of construction and the cost of real estate.
20. What are the most common ways to implement development activities in the performance of construction contracts? What is their essence?
21. List the main organizational forms of construction management and briefly describe them.
22. What are the main functions of the construction manager in the implementation of construction projects?

Questions for discussion

1. Describe the features and specifics of project management in construction.
2. Analyze different points of view on the content and division at the stage (phase) of the full life cycle of the project.

3. Should the pre-investment phase and pre-project phases requiring the presence of a technical customer be distinguished in the conceptual stage of the project?
4. Describe the structure of project management by process groups applied by the Project Management Institute (PMI). Does it require adaptation to the specifics of construction projects?
5. Analyze the integration methods of the temporary organizational unit — the project manager and the temporary organizational structure — the project team with permanent structures.
6. According to what classification criteria can contractual relations be divided into the implementation of construction and real estate development?
7. Describe the role of the organization of construction management in creating effective construction products at various stages of the life cycle of a property.
8. In your opinion, "compensation contracts" or "contracts with a fixed price" is more efficient in the implementation of use of construction projects in the domestic economy.

Questions to solve the problem yourself

1. Analyze the problem of formation of optimal portfolio investment and construction company, and the approach to its solution.
2. Consider the example of a specific development project, the impact of its life cycle on the business and activity of a built-up area and the real estate market.
3. Justify the most significant strategic factors of influence on the project, which should be taken into account at the conceptual stage of design.
4. Analyze and highlight the organizational advantages and problems of forming a project team related to the specifics of the investment and construction sector.
5. Consider the features and benefits of EPC and EPCM contracts from a customer and contractor perspective.
6. Consider ways of pricing a construction contract for a real estate object.

Expand the requirements for organizational and contractual relations, the implementation of which will increase the efficiency of construction according to the main characteristics — price, time and quality of construction.

Chapter 3

METHODS OF ORGANIZATION OF CONSTRUCTION PRODUCTION

3.1 Preparation for construction and organization of construction production

3.1.1 Stages and content of organizational and technical preparation for construction

The construction of new facilities is allowed to begin only after all the necessary preparations for the construction are carried out. *Under the preparation of construction production is understood a set of organizational and technical measures that facilitate the deployment and implementation of construction within the time frame established by the project.* Preparation for construction is carried out before the start of construction works. Preparations for the construction of large facilities include three stages:

1st — organizational preparatory measures;

2nd — off-site work;

3rd — on-site preparatory work.

At the *first stage of* preparation for construction, a number of organizational measures should be carried out before starting work on the construction site. Organizational preparatory measures are carried out by the organization-builder in accordance with SNiP 12-01-2004 "Organization of construction", and only if necessary, design organizations and contracting construction organizations are involved in the work.

During the construction of large enterprises, the developer creates the directorate of the enterprise under construction and invites a specialized management company on trust. Organizational preparatory measures carried out before the start of work at the construction site include:

- obtaining a building permit, which is issued on the basis of certified rights to the land;
- ensuring the construction of design estimates. Such collateral is the responsibility of the customer (developer). The construction of new enterprises, buildings, structures is allowed to begin only with the availability of design documentation, and above all approved technical (techno-working) project;
- selection of a construction site and obtaining a land plot for the construction of an object. The choice of a site for construction is carried out in accordance with the requirements of the Land Code of the Russian Federation and taking into account the development and placement of enterprises in the region's industry. The construction site is also determined taking into account project documentation, the development of appropriate communications and networks, railways and roads, energy systems;
- placing orders for building materials, the necessary structures provided for in the project;
- placing orders for priority deliveries of equipment for the enterprise under construction;
- solving the issue of the procedure for using local building materials (sand, gravel, crushed stone, etc.);
- determination of the construction organization and conclusion of a contract with it;
- registration with a bank of financing for construction.

Second stage : off-site preparatory work.
Off-site preparatory work includes the following main types of work:

- construction of access roads to the construction site;
- construction of communication lines, power transmission, water supply, sewage facilities; connection to sources of water and gas, steam; laying a quarry for the extraction of sand, gravel, stone.

On-site preparatory work (third stage) includes: creating a geodetic alignment base for construction (installation of high-rise benchmarks, laying of the main axes of buildings, (red lines);

- clearing the territory of the construction site, demolition of structures not used during the construction process, replanting trees, cutting and storing the vegetative soil layer;

- territory planning;
- creation of a warehouse for building materials and structures; device fire extinguishing, communications and signaling.

At construction sites with a relatively small number of objects, the second and third stages of preparation are usually combined. Off-site and on-site preparatory work is called ***technical (engineering) training.*** The time for off-site and on-site preparatory work is called the ***preparatory period.***

3.1.2 Selection and allocation of land for the construction of facilities

Land relations in Russia in order to ensure the rational use and protection of land, create conditions for the equitable development of various forms of land management are regulated by the Land Code of the Russian Federation and other regulatory acts. The Land Code of the Russian Federation establishes the procedure for the seizure, submission and transfer of land to property and rental. According to the Land Code of the Russian Federation, for the construction of industrial enterprises and other non-agricultural needs, land plots of non-agricultural use or land unsuitable for agriculture or agricultural land of the worst quality are provided, by agreement with the owner of the land (landowner, land user) according to cadastral valuation. For the construction of power lines, communications, roads, trunk pipelines and other linear structures, it is allowed to provide land of higher quality. These objects are located mainly along roads, existing routes and crop rotation boundaries. Provision of land plots on the areas of occurrence of minerals is carried out in agreement with the bodies of state mining supervision.

Enterprises, institutions, organizations interested in the construction of an object, apply to the local administration of the district (city) with a request for preliminary approval of the place of its location, justifying the approximate sizes of land plots and terms of land use. The administration of the district (city) or, on its instructions, the local committee on land reform and land resources ensures the selection of the land plot in kind (on the ground). When choosing a site, rural (settlement) administrations, land owners (tenants, representatives of relevant public services and representatives of organizations interested in land allotment) take part. The results of the work are drawn up by the act of choosing the land for the placement of the object. Cartographic materials, calculations of losses of land owners, landowners (tenants) and losses of agricultural production associated with the seizure of land are attached to the act. Applications for preliminary approval of the location of new and expansion of existing industrial enterprises, designed to meet federal and republican needs or having inter-regional significance, are examined with the consent of the authorities of the republics that are part of the Russian Federation, and for the construction of enterprises designed to provide regional, regional needs, — the consent of the administration of the region, region. Local district administrations inform the population about the possible (upcoming) provision of land for the placement of objects whose activities affect their interests, and find out the opinion of citizens through local referenda, meetings, gatherings of citizens, and other forms of direct information.

Citizens, public organizations and bodies of territorial public self-government have the right to participate in the consideration of issues related to the seizure and provision of land affecting the interests of the population. The materials of the preliminary approval of the location of the facility are approved by the district administration and the decision of the representative body, which are the basis for design and survey work and the decision to seize and provide land.

The right of ownership of the land and the right to use the land plot are certified by a state act, which is issued and registered by the relevant local administration of the district (city, settlement).

The use of land is allowed after the establishment of the boundaries of these sites in kind (on the ground). Losses caused by the seizure of land for the construction of facilities are subject to compensation in full (including lost profits in the calculation for the coming period). Compensation for losses, including lost profits, is made by enterprises, organizations to which allotted land plots are allocated. Prior approval of the location of the facility is not required in cases of the provision of land for agricultural production, construction of facilities in settlements in accordance with their master plans and projects of district planning and development. All the lands of cities, towns, rural settlements are used in accordance with their master plans and planning and development projects. Permits for the construction of facilities on the land on which the urban planning regulation is established or the urban planning regulation applies are issued by the local government. In other cases, permission is issued by the federal executive body, the executive authority of the constituent entity of the Russian Federation, or the local government in accordance with their competence. To obtain permission, the developer sends an application to the appropriate authority with the following documents:

- title documents for the land;
- urban development plan of the land;
- materials contained in the design documentation and other documents provided for by Art. 51 of the Town Planning Code of the Russian Federation (approved by the Federal Law of July 3, 2016 No. 373-FZ).

3.2 Development and design of a project for the organization of construction and a project for the production of works

The project of the organization of construction (POC) and the project for production of work (PPW) are the main organizational and technological documents in the construction of housing and civil and industrial facilities. These documents contain measures for the most efficient construction organization. These documents include the most advanced technologies of construction production, which contribute to improving the quality, reducing the time and cost of work. POC and PPW provide not only high quality and on time, but, most importantly, safe performance of work, because they contain measures to fulfill the requirements of the Technical Regulations in construction.

In accordance with the regulatory documents of the Russian Federation, it is prohibited to carry out construction and installation works without an approved construction organization project (POC, PPW). The construction organization project is a binding document for the customer, contractors, as well as organizations that provide financing and material and technical support for construction.

Carrying out construction and installation works without the approved POC and PPW by Russian standards is prohibited, and all deviations from POC and PPW should be coordinated with the organizations that developed and approved them.

The presence and use of construction organization projects and construction projects in construction production largely determine the competitiveness of the construction organization.

POC and PPW are used when licensing a construction organization as documents confirming the organization's readiness for work, and in certification of quality systems and construction products — in the status of regulatory documents of the enterprise.

POC is usually developed by the general designer or, on his instructions, some other (subcontracting) design organization. In a two-stage design, the POC is developed at the first stage of the "Project". PPW is usually developed by a general contractor or a specialized organization involved by him. In any case, the PPW is approved by the head of the general contracting organization. In the two-stage design, the design and construction documentation is compiled at the "Working Documentation" stage (in time this usually coincides with the organizational preparation of the construction). The composition of POC and PPW is regulated by the norms of SNiP 12-01-2004 "Organization of construction".

This section contains the rules, the procedure for the preparation and execution of POC and PPW.

A. General provisions

The construction of enterprises, buildings and structures is carried out in accordance with the design documentation — the project (working draft), POC and PPW.

POC is part of the project for the construction of the facility. If POC is not developed as part of a working draft, then the list and procedure of control procedures for assessing the quality of construction and the compliance of construction with safety requirements are established by the terms of the contract between the construction participants.

POC is developed, as a rule, for the entire volume of construction provided for by the project (working draft).

During the construction of the facility in turn, the POC is developed additionally, first of all, taking into account the project for the entire construction volume.

POC is compiled according to the working drawings on the basis of POC for the work of the preparatory period for construction, for the implementation of certain types of construction and installation works (construction and installation works), as well as for the construction of the facility as a whole and (or) its component parts.

POC is developed with the aim of putting the facility into operation on a planned schedule by ensuring the appropriate organizational and technical level of construction. POC serves as the basis for the distribution of capital investments and construction and installation works by stages and periods of construction.

PPW is developed with the aim of choosing the most effective construction and installation work, which helps to reduce construction and improve the quality of work. POC and PPW are developed taking into account:

- application of advanced methods of organization and management of construction in order to ensure the shortest possible duration of construction; development of the projected capacity of the facility in a given time frame;
- application of technological processes providing a given level of construction quality;
- use of modern technical means of dispatch communication and automated systems for managing construction production;
- complete delivery for the construction of structures, products and materials based on removable gripper (per section, tier, floor, etc.);

- maximum use of the front of work, combining construction processes with ensuring their continuity and flow, equal use of resources and production capacities;
- the use of progressive building structures, products and materials; mechanization of work with the maximum use of productive
- tires in two or three shifts;
- installation of building structures directly from vehicles;
- supply and installation of technological equipment in enlarged units;
- compliance with safety and environmental requirements established in the Technical Regulations.

When developing a project for the organization of construction and a project for the production of works, the climatic features of the construction area should be taken into account.

When developing POC and PPW for adverse climatic zones, the following should be considered:

- physical and geographical conditions (the duration of the cold period with low air temperatures, strong winds and snow drifts, the permafrost state of soils, polar day and night, etc.);
- territorial fragmentation of construction and the need for a complete supply of building structures and materials;
- seasonality in the delivery of building structures, products and materials;
- the need to use special modes of transport;
- the need to develop special measures for safety and labor protection.

POC and PPW for mountain and high mountain areas should be developed taking into account:

- low barometric pressure, requiring compliance with the special operating conditions of builders and machines;
- the use of machines adapted to work on steep slopes;
- avalanche, mudflow and landslide phenomena.

The development of POC and PPW is based on a technical and economic comparison of solution options. The options are compared in terms of terms of construction, quality of construction products and the cost of construction works.

When developing POC and PPW, one should use standard organizational and technological documentation: standards (standard projects) for the organization of construction and work, technological maps for the production of certain types of work; teaching aids.

Development and POC and PPW are carried out according to the standard forms of documents below. These forms can be specified in accordance with the specifics of the construction and local conditions, as well as the requirements for the electronic documentation system.

B. Composition and content of the construction organization project

The composition of the project depends on the complexity of the construction project. When assessing complexity and determining the composition of the project, the following should be considered:

- composition of the object and its space-planning parameters;
- complexity of design solutions;
- construction conditions and applicable processes;
- number of contractors involved in construction.

The starting materials for the preparation of the construction organization project are:

- project (detailed design) of a building (structure);
- results of topographic, geological and hydrogeological surveys;
- decisions on the application of methods for organizing construction, building structures, products and materials, means of mechanization of construction and installation works, data on sources and procedures for providing construction with water, electricity, steam, etc.;
- information on the possibility of providing construction with workers, residential and domestic premises;
- data on the capacity of general construction and specialized construction organizations, the availability of a production base and the possibilities for its use.

POC is developed, as a rule, simultaneously with the development of construction and other parts of the project (working) project. Space-planning, structural and technological solutions are coordinated with the conditions of the organization of construction and work.

As part of the POC (Fig. 3.1), the following are developed: situational plan; construction master plan; construction schedule; organizational and technological schemes for the construction of a building (structure) with a description of the sequence and content of the main technological processes; statement of volumes of construction, installation and special works; a schedule of the

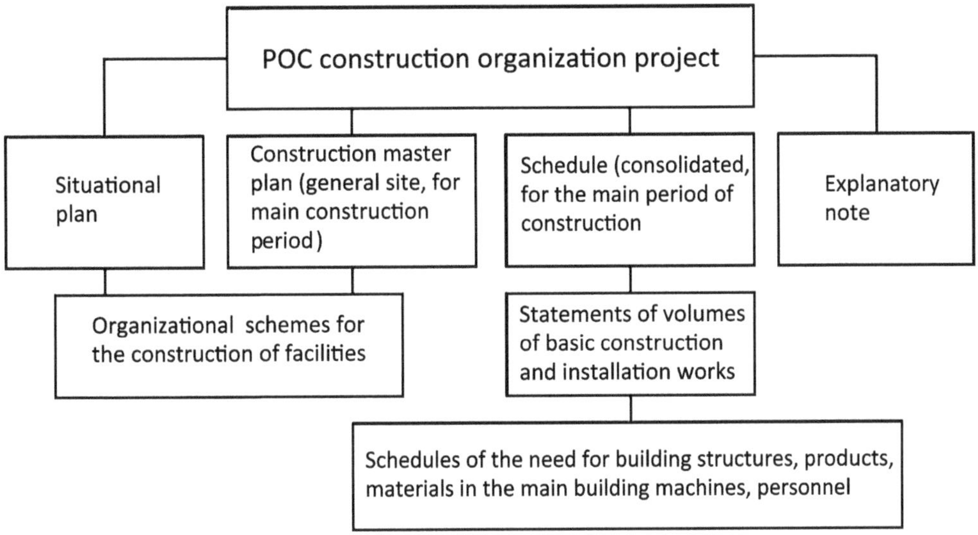

Figure 3.1: The composition of the construction organization project (POC)

need for building structures, products and materials; schedule requirements for major construction vehicles; a schedule of the need for workforce; explanatory note.

The construction schedule contains the sequence and timelines for the construction of the main and auxiliary buildings and structures, start-up complexes and preparatory work with the distribution of investments and the volume of construction and installation work by construction stage and time. The schedule is compiled in the form shown in table 3.1.

Based on the construction schedule, a general schedule of construction and installation works at the facility is compiled, in development and refinement to which the schedules for the year and quarter are attached.

A calendar plan for the preparatory period with monthly work planning can be drawn up separately.

Table 3.1 Construction schedule

Names of objects and works (preparatory period, main, start-up, etc.)	Full estimated cost, thousand rubles	The cost of construction and installation work, thousand rubles	Distribution of work volumes by periods (by months, quarters, years), thousand rubles	
			First	Second, etc.

The construction master plan is compiled separately for the preparatory and main periods of construction, indicating the location of buildings and structures under construction, sites for the placement of temporary inventory buildings and structures, permanent and temporary railways and highways, basic engineering communications, warehouses, installation cranes, production facilities (with allocation of facilities under construction during the preparatory period), as well as existing and demolished buildings.

The list of volumes of construction, installation and special works (including the installation of technological equipment) with the allocation of work for individual facilities, start-up complexes and construction periods is compiled in the form shown in table 3.2.

Table 3.2 Statement of volumes of construction, installation and special works

Name of works	unit of measurement	Scope of work	Distribution of work volumes by periods (by months, quarters, years), thousand rubles	
			First	Second, etc.

The schedule for the need for building structures, products and materials with a distribution by objects, start-up complexes and construction periods is compiled in the form shown in table 3.3.

Table 3.3 Schedule of need for building structures, products and materials

Name	unit of measurement	Total construction	Including the main facilities	Distribution by periods (by months, quarters)
			No. 1 No. 2	First Second, etc.

The explanatory note contains:

- description of construction conditions;
- substantiation of the choice of methods for the production of construction, installation and special works;
- justification of the need for basic construction vehicles;
- justification of the need for vehicles, loading and unloading machines, storage facilities;
- justification of the need for housing and consumer services;
- calculations of the need for electricity, water, steam, compressed air, as well as inventory buildings and temporary structures for construction and installation works;
- measures for labor protection and the environment;
- basic technical and economic indicators.

For complex objects, the construction organization project includes, in addition to the above:

- an enlarged network schedule, which indicates the duration of the main stages of the construction of the facility, the sequence of construction of individual buildings and structures, the delivery time of technological equipment;
- measures for the development of the design capacity of the enterprise, including commissioning;
- situational construction plan with drawing the boundaries of the facility, with the location of the production base, external roads and roads, communication lines and power lines.

POC for small projects (see earlier, Table 2.1, Section 2.1, Chapter 1) is compiled in an abridged form and consists of: a construction schedule; construction master plan; statements of volumes of construction and installation works, schedules of the need for materials, construction machines; brief explanatory note.

In the complex development of a residential area (quarter), the construction organization project provides for the simultaneous commissioning of both residential and cultural facilities, as well as the timely completion of landscaping and landscaping of the built-up territory.

In the calendar plan, the stages of work should be distinguished:

- engineering preparation of the territory;
- erection of a building (structure).

In the project of organizing the construction of an agricultural facility, the priority of construction — the main production, utility and service purposes, energy, transport and communications, external water supply, sewage, heat and gas supply networks, landscaping — is established depending on the technological scheme of agricultural production.

The project for the organization of construction (reconstruction) of an industrial facility should additionally:

- establish the sequence and procedure for the combined construction and installation work with the indication of the sections and workshops in which the technological processes of the main production are stopped or changed during the construction and installation works;
- indicate on the construction master plan the current, dismantled and redeployed utilities, places for connecting temporary utilities, thoroughfares throughout the territory, etc.;
- determine the procedure for protecting existing equipment during the replacement of wall fences, ceilings and coatings;

- determine the scope of work of the preparatory period so that the lead time for basic work related to complete or partial shutdown of the production process is the smallest;
- establish a list, volumes and determine methods of work in cramped conditions.

The sections of the POC (in order to comply with the mandatory safety requirements during the construction process) should contain:

- measures to ensure during the construction process the strength and stability of the constructed and existing buildings and structures;
- programs of necessary research, testing and operational observations for complex and unique objects, including the organization of stations, polygons, measuring posts, etc.;
- decisions on the construction of facilities in difficult climatic conditions, as well as in cramped conditions;
- measures to temporarily close streets, to restrict traffic, change routes of transport;
- situational construction plan with the location of junctions to the railways, river and sea berths, temporary settlements, etc.;
- a list of works and structures whose quality indicators affect the safety of the facility and during the construction process are subject to special control and assessment of compliance with regulatory requirements;
- methods and means of monitoring and testing;
- safety measures, staff training and education.

C. Composition and content of the project work

The starting materials for the development of PPW are: POC; working drawings for the construction of a building or structure.

PPW are developed for the construction of the facility as a whole and (or) its components, for the work of the preparatory period for construction, as well as for the implementation of certain types of construction and installation works.

As part of the PPW for the construction of the object as a whole and (or) its components are developed:

- a schedule of work on the facility;
- construction master plan;
- schedule of receipt of building structures at the facility, products and materials; a schedule of the need for workforce;

- demand schedule for basic construction vehicles; technological maps for certain types of work;
- cards (schemes) for quality control of work; measures for labor protection and safety;
- explanatory note.

The schedule of work sets the sequence and timing of work, depending on the complexity of the facility, the volume and technology of work. According to the schedule, the need for machines, in workers, the delivery time of building structures, products and materials, technological equipment are determined, the work schedule is compiled in units: workload — time (days, weeks, months).

The schedule of work is compiled in the form shown in table 3.4.

Table 3.4 Schedule work

Name of works	Volume of work, units rev.	Labor input, person-shift	Number of shifts	Number of workers per shift	Machine, number of machine shifts

The construction master plan is being developed in the part necessary for the production of works at the facility. The plan indicates the location of permanent and temporary transport routes, water supply, sewage, electricity, heat supply, administrative and dispatch communications, assembly cranes, warehouses, temporary inventory buildings, structures and devices used to ensure construction.

The schedule of receipt at the facility for the production of this type of work of building structures, products and materials is compiled in the form shown in table 3.5.

Table 3.5 Schedule of receipt of building structures, products and materials

Name	unit of measurement	number	Schedule of receipt by days, weeks, months

The schedule of the need for working personnel for the production of this type of work at the facility is compiled in the form shown in table 3.6.

The schedule for the need for basic construction vehicles for work at the facility is compiled in the form shown in table 3.7.

Technological maps are developed for separate (complex) types of work and for work performed using new technologies.

For other works, standard technological maps are applied, which are adjusted taking into account the characteristics of the given facility and local conditions. Technological maps are developed and executed according to MDS 12-29.2006.

Table 3.6 Workforce Demand Schedule

Name of workers	professions	Number of workers	The average daily number of workers by month, week, day
			1 2 etc.

Table 3.7 Schedule the need for construction vehicles

Name of machines	Number of cars	The average daily number of cars by day, week, month
		1 2 etc.

Cards (schemes) for quality control of works are developed for monitoring and evaluating the quality of technological processes and operations. The map is compiled in the form shown in table 3.8.

Table 3.8 Quality control

Name of technological processes and operations	Controlled process parameter (operation)	Allowed parameter values	Control method, applied devices (tool)

This section of the PPW should contain schemes for operational control of work performed; list of required certificates of examination of hidden works; instructions on the timing of quality control of work with laboratory tests of materials, structural elements, temperature and humidity conditions, as well as on the procedure for testing individual units and systems of engineering equipment.

Occupational health and safety measures are indicated by standard (standard, for example, protective fences and visors) and requiring design work (for example, fastening earthen slopes, temporary strengthening of structures).

The explanatory note should contain:

- description and justification of decisions made in the draft;
- calculations of the need for electricity, water, steam, oxygen, compressed air, working drawings of a temporary lighting device for a construction site and workplaces, supplying networks to the object from power sources;
- a list of mobile (inventory) buildings and structures with the calculation of their needs;
- technical and economic indicators of the project work.

PPW for the preparatory period for construction should contain:

- work schedule;
- schedule of receipt for construction of building structures, products and materials necessary for this period;
- the construction master plan for the construction site, indicating the locations of inventory buildings and temporary structures, off-site and on-site communications and networks built during the preparatory period;
- layout of signs for performing geodetic constructions and geodetic control of the position of the structures of the object and communications, as well as instructions on the accuracy of geodetic measurements and a list of necessary technical means;
- a brief explanatory note.

For a complex object as part of the PPW, an integrated network schedule should be developed.

PPW for small projects may consist of a work schedule, a construction master plan, a basic work flow chart, and a brief explanatory note.

In PPW, as a rule, the following technical and economic indicators are given: labor input, duration and cost of construction and installation works. For a number of works, specific indicators can be given, for example, for 1 m, 1 m2, 1 m3, etc.

PPW is approved by the chief engineer of the general contracting construction organization, and sections of the installation and special construction works project are approved by the chief engineers of the respective subcontracting organizations.

The approved project is transferred to the construction site before the start of work.

3.3 Development of projects for the production of work with cranes (PPWc)

The operation of hoisting machines (hoisting cranes, cranes, manipulators, construction hoists, hoists (towers)) controlled by the Federal Environmental, Industrial and Nuclear Supervision Service (hereinafter referred to as the Service) is carried out in accordance with Federal Law No. 184-FZ of December 27, 2002, "n technical regulation" in accordance with the requirements of technical regulations, standards and RD-11-06-2007" Methodological recommendations on the procedure for the development of projects for the production of work by lifting machines and technological maps of loading and unloading"(approved by Order of Rostekhnadzor dated 10.05.2007 No. 317).

The installation of hoisting machines, the organization and execution of construction and installation works with their application are carried out in accordance with the project for the production of work by hoisting cranes (PPWc), specially developed for these purposes.

Loading and unloading and warehousing of cargoes by cranes and crane manipulators at bases, warehouses, sites are carried out according to the technological maps of loading and unloading (TM l / u works).

As noted in Section 3.2, construction organization (POC) projects are developed by design organizations with the involvement of specialized design organizations licensed for this type of activity. Projects for the production of work and flow charts for construction, installation and handling operations using lifting machines are developed by specialists with experience in construction, trained and certified in the field of industrial safety of hazardous production facilities in the manner established by thc Scrvicc. Training and certification is carried out in accordance with the Regulation on the procedure for training and certification of employees of organizations operating in the field of industrial safety of hazardous production facilities controlled by the Service (RD 03-444-02), approved by Resolution No. 21 of the Gosgortekhnadzor of Russia registered by the Ministry Justice of Russia 05/31/2002, reg. No. 3489, for programs and tickets agreed with the Service. The protocol and the certificate of the specialist engaged in the development of PPWc and TM l / u work, makes a note on the certification of knowledge of industrial safety requirements for specific Rules for the design and safe operation of cranes, cranes, cranes, hoists (towers) with the right to develop PPWc TM l /ur works, as well as the development of projects on crane tracks.

The developed PPWc is agreed with the owner of the load-lifting machine supervising the head of the organization that developed the PPWc and approved by the head of the general contracting construction and installation organization (customer).

Persons who approve and approve PPWc are certified in the field of industrial safety of hazardous production facilities and in the amount of requirements of the relevant rules.

Based on Art. 13 of the Federal Law of July 21, 1997 No. 116-FZ "On Industrial Safety of Hazardous Production Facilities" and Clause 3.2.1 "Provisions for the Expertise of Industrial Safety of Hazardous Production Facilities that Use Lifting Facilities" RD 10-528-03 approved By the resolution of the Gosgortekhnadzor of Russia dated 04.03.2003 No. 5, registered by the Ministry of Justice of Russia on March 28, 2003 No. 4345, "crane work projects are subject to industrial safety expertise".

Examination of projects can be carried out by organizations that meet the requirements of the legislation of the Russian Federation imposed on organizations performing industrial safety expertise, licensed by the Industrial Safety Expertise for design documentation for the construction, expansion, reconstruction, technical re-equipment, conservation and liquidation of hazardous production facilities, where stationary mounted hoisting mechanisms are used.

Certification of experts is carried out in accordance with the Rules of certification of experts adopted by the Supervisory Board, decision No. 2/42 of 04.25.2006, and "Recommendations for the preparation and certification of experts and experts performing industrial safety reviews of lifting structures", approved by the Lifting Commission of the System of industrial safety (from 25.04.2006 — technical Commission of the Unified system of conformity assessment on facilities controlled by the Federal service for ecological, technological and Nuclear Supervision) from 16.04.2003, Protocol 7.

Prior to commencement of work, the conclusion of the PPWc examination is registered with the territorial authority of Rostekhnadzor along with the PPWc.

Complex construction and installation and loading and unloading operations (lifting and moving goods with two cranes, etc.) are carried out according to PPWc developed in accordance with the approved by Montazhspetsstroy Corporation 06.25.99 Methodological guidelines for the preparation of projects for the production of complex construction and loading and unloading operations with cranes agreed with the Russian State Technical Supervision Service by Letter No. 12-07 / 569 dated 06/18/1999 on 06/18/1999.

When carrying out work by cranes near power lines (closer than 30 m), it is necessary to coordinate PPWc with the owner of power lines.

Depending on the scope of work and technological capabilities, PPWc is developed for the construction of the entire building as a whole (aboveground and underground parts) or in stages, depending on the cranes involved, the sequence of work and the timing.

During construction, the author of the PPWC checks the work on the project developed by him, and in case of gross deviations from the project that could lead to an accident or accident, he immediately informs the department for supervision of lifting structures of the territorial authority of Rostekhnadzor (federal subjects).

Changes to the PPWC are entitled to be made by the developer of the PPWC with the consent of the expert organization with the signature of the developer and expert.

Prior to the start of work with the PPWc, the executors of the work at the construction site (responsible persons, slingers (installers), and crane operators) are familiarized with the signature.

Binding of the crane is carried out in strict accordance with the land plot allocated for construction, drawn up in accordance with the procedure established by law (title document for the land plot).

Design decisions and activities reflected in the POC and work projects using lifting machines are determined by the rules for the construction and safe operation of the respective machines, approved by the Russian State Technical Supervision Authority, and are also set out in Section 2 of RD-11-06-2007 "Methodological Recommendations on the Procedure for Project Development works by hoisting machines and technological maps of loading and unloading operations "(approved by Order of Rostekhnadzor dated May 10, 2007 No. 317).

According to the Decree of the Government of the Russian Federation dated 01.02.2006 No. 54 "On State Construction Supervision in the Russian Federation", drawings for special equipment, fixtures and accessories are being developed for the construction of capital construction projects of hazardous, technically complex and unique facilities as part of POC.

The criteria for particularly dangerous, technically complex and unique include capital construction projects, the design documentation of which provides at least one of the following characteristics:

a) height of more than 75 meters or with spans of 100 meters, as well as departures consoles over 20 meters;

b) the presence of more than 1 underground floor;

c) the use of structures and constructive systems that require the use of non-standard methods of calculation taking into account physical or geometric nonlinearity or the development of special calculation methods, as well as those used in territories whose seismicity exceeds 9 points.

The project for the production of works is approved by the head of the general contracting construction and installation organization, and for the production of installation and special works, it is approved by the head of the relevant subcontracting organization in agreement with the general contracting construction and installation organization. Persons approving PPWc are certified in the field of industrial safety of hazardous production facilities in the amount of requirements of the relevant rules. Projects for the production of reconstruction, expansion and technical re-equipment of an existing enterprise (buildings, structures) are also agreed with the head or responsible representative of this enterprise.

Projects for the production of work using lifting machines are agreed with the owners of these machines.

When developing design solutions for the organization of construction and production sites, work sites, it is necessary to identify areas dangerous to people. The areas of hazardous and harmful production factors associated with the technology and conditions of work when using lifting machines are determined in accordance with SNiP 12-03-2001 in POS, and the rest in PPWc. Deviations from decisions made in the POC during the development of the PPWC are not allowed without agreement with the organization that developed the POC.

Drawings of construction organization projects and construction projects by cranes are recommended to be carried out at a scale of 1: 50–1: 200, and individual parts — at a scale of 1: 10–1: 20, a construction plan — at a scale of 1: 500.

The project for the production of work by cranes is transferred to the construction site 5 days before the start of the execution of the work for which it was developed.

Before starting construction and installation work with the use of lifting machines in the territory of the organization, the general contractor (subcontractor) and the administration of the organization operating (constructing) this object draw up an admission certificate.

To work with the use of lifting machines in areas of hazardous or harmful production factors, the occurrence of which is not related to the nature of the work performed, an admission order is issued.

In order to ensure that the hoisting machines are in good condition and safe working conditions at the construction site, the owner of the hoisting machines, as well as the head of the organization operating the hoisting machines, depending on the existing fleet of vehicles, appoint:

- an engineer and technician to oversee the safe operation of hoisting cranes, lifting devices and containers, cranes, construction hoists, hoists (towers);
- an engineer and technical worker responsible for the maintenance of hoisting cranes, cranes, manipulators, construction hoists, hoists (towers) in good condition;
- by order, the person responsible for the safe execution of work by cranes, cranes, construction hoists, hoists (towers) in each workshop, on a construction site or other work site in each shift;
- by order of slingers.

The person responsible for the safe performance of work by lifting machines can be appointed from among the foremen, foremen, shop managers, sections, and during the operation of lifts (towers) and cranes, in addition, from among the foremen.

All nominated persons with the appropriate qualifications pass a knowledge test of their device rules and the safe operation of the corresponding hoisting machines with the receipt of a certificate of the established form.

Managers and specialists in the development of PPWC, crane ways, experts bear the statutory responsibility for the compliance of the developed solutions with the requirements of industrial safety and labor protection. The construction organization is responsible for the compliance of the construction site with the project for the construction of cranes (PPWc), industrial safety and labor protection requirements.

3.4 The main recommendations for the projects of the organization of construction and work with the use of lifting machines

In the POC with the use of hoisting cranes, the following are provided:

- Correspondence of the installed cranes to the conditions of construction and installation work in terms of load capacity, lifting height and reach (crane load characteristic);
- ensuring a safe distance from networks and overhead power lines, places of movement of public transport and pedestrians, as well as safe distances of approaching cranes to buildings and storage areas for building parts and materials;
- conditions for the installation and operation of cranes near the slopes of pits;
- conditions for the safe operation of several cranes and other mechanisms located at the construction site;
- storage areas.

If technical decisions are made to reduce hazardous areas near the building under construction in the form of protective shields or other protective structures, the working documentation for them is developed at the design stage.

According to Art. 9.5.18 PB 10-382-00 "Rules for the Construction and Safe Operation of Hoisting Cranes" construction and installation works using hoisting cranes should be carried out according to the project for the production of cranes (PPWc), which should provide for:

- compliance of the installed cranes with the conditions of construction and installation work on load capacity, lifting height and reach (cargo characteristic of the crane);
- ensuring safe distances from networks and overhead power lines, places of movement of public transport and pedestrians, as well as safe distances of the proximity of cranes to buildings and storage areas for building parts and materials;

- conditions for the installation and operation of cranes near the slopes of pits;
- conditions for the safe operation of several cranes on one track and on parallel tracks using appropriate safety devices and devices;
- a list of used gripping devices and a graphic image (diagram) of cargo sling;
- places and dimensions of cargo storage, access roads, etc.;
- measures for the safe performance of work, taking into account specific conditions in the area where the crane is installed (fencing of the construction site, installation area, etc.);
- location of premises for sanitary services for builders, drinking installations and recreation facilities;
- a section of the building to full height, with the position of the crane jib above the building (maximum and minimum reach) and a dashed line — protruding metal structures of the crane when turning 180?;
- elevator, parapet and engine room elevators;
- safe distances from the bottom of the transported cargo to the most vertically protruding parts of the building or structure (must be at least 0.5 m, and to floors and platforms where people can be, at least 2.3 m), as well as the height of the slings (traverses);
- safe distances from parts of the boom, counterweight console, taking into account the dimensions of the counterweight ballast blocks to the most vertically protruding parts of the building or structure;
- the dimensions of the most protruding elements in the horizontal plane of the building or structure (cornices, balconies, fences, bay windows, peaks and entrances).

According to Art. 5.5.10 10-257-98 "Rules for the design and safe operation of hoisting cranes-manipulators" construction and installation work using cranes-manipulators should be carried out according to the project of work with cranes-manipulators, which provides for:

- compliance of the installed cranes-manipulators with the conditions construction and installation work on carrying capacity, lifting height and reach;
- ensuring safe distances from the network and overhead power lines, places of public transport and pedestrians, as well as safe distances of the proximity of cranes to buildings and storage areas for building parts and materials;
- conditions for installation and operation of cranes-manipulators near the slopes of pits (ditch);

- a list of used gripping devices and a graphic image (diagram) of cargo sling;
- places and dimensions of cargo storage, access roads, etc.

According to Art. 4.5.12 PB 10-518-02 "Rules for the Construction and Safe Operation of Construction Hoists" work with the use of hoists should be carried out according to the project for the production of works, which in particular should include:

- compliance of the installed lifts with the conditions for carrying capacity and lifting height;
- installation conditions of the elevator on the site;
- conditions for safe operation of several lifts, including joint work of freight and passenger-and-freight lifts together with the work of front elevators, as well as joint work of the said lifts and tower cranes;
- measures for the safe performance of work, taking into account specific conditions in the area where the lift is installed (fencing of the site, installation area, etc.).

According to Art. 4.5.9 10-611-03 "Rules for the design and safe operation of elevators (towers)" construction and installation works using elevators (towers) are carried out according to the project of work with elevators, which should include:

- compliance of the installed lifts with the conditions of construction and installation work in terms of load capacity, lifting height;
- ensuring safe distances from networks and overhead power lines, places of public transport and pedestrians, as well as safe distances of elevators to buildings and storage areas for building parts and materials;
- conditions for the installation and operation of elevators near the slopes of pits or ditches;
- conditions for the safe operation of several lifts;
- a list of used gripping devices and a graphic image (diagram) of a cargo line for hoists equipped with a hook;
- places and dimensions of cargo storage, access roads, etc.;
- measures for the safe performance of work, taking into account specific conditions in the area where the lift is installed (fencing of the construction site, installation zone or work zone), the level of lighting in the dark at least 20 lux, etc.

Technological maps for loading and unloading and warehousing of goods with hoisting cranes and cranes-manipulators at bases, warehouses and sites are developed taking into account the requirements of GOST 12.3.009-76.

Projects for the production of work using lifting machines, technological maps for loading and unloading, and other technological regulations are approved by the head of the organization performing the work, and are given to the construction site 2 months before the start of the work provided there.

Persons responsible for the safe performance of work by hoisting machines, crane operators, operators (operators), cradles and slingers should be familiarized with the design for the execution of works for painting before the start of work.

3.5 Construction Organization Methods

Organization of construction production is a functional system that includes construction objects, resources for their construction (temporary, labor, material, technical, financial, etc.) and their interaction, to achieve a given result — the release of finished construction products in the form of finished for the operation of buildings and structures.

In construction, the following methods of organization of construction production are used:

- consistent;
- parallel;
- in- line (combined);

To determine the characteristic features of each of the above methods, we consider a conditional example.

Example 3.1 Suppose that it is necessary to build N identical buildings divided into n technological processes, namely, the zero-cycle device, the construction of the aerial parts and finishing work, with the same duration (tp) for each individual building.

The construction of these buildings can be organized in a sequential, parallel or in-line method.

Option 1. With a *consistent* construction *method,* each building is erected after the previous one (Fig. 3.2a).

The total duration of construction with this method is determined by the total duration of construction of N buildings:

$$T_1 = N * t_i; \tag{3.1}$$

where t_i — the duration of the construction of one building; T_1 — the duration of the construction of N buildings.

The intensity of resource consumption per unit time is equal to:

$$J_1 = \frac{\sum_{i=1}^{N} Q_i}{T_1} = \frac{\sum_{i=1}^{N} Q_i}{t_i \cdot N}; \tag{3.2}$$

where Q_i — the cost of resources for the construction of the i-th building.

With this method, the level of resource consumption per unit time (J_1) will be minimal, and the duration of their consumption (T_1) will be maximum. Also, each of the types of resources (workers, material and technical) performing the nth technological process on the building is involved periodically (t_n), which will undoubtedly lead to downtime of workers, machines and mechanisms or losses for their additional relocation.

Option 2. A parallel method of organizing construction significantly reduces the duration of construction of all buildings, since the construction of buildings is carried out simultaneously (Fig. 3.1b). Moreover, the total duration of the construction of all N buildings is equal to the duration of the erection of one building, and the intensity of resource consumption per unit time will be:

$$J_2 == \frac{\sum_{i=1}^{N} Q_i}{t_i}; \tag{3.3}$$

In the parallel method, the same type of construction processes (n) are carried out simultaneously on all buildings, the intensity of resource consumption becomes maximum, the duration of construction is minimum. Consequently, this method requires the simultaneous attraction of a large number of resources (labor, material, technical, financial, etc.), which is only possible for large construction enterprises.

Option 3. The stream method combines serial and parallel:

The in-line method of organizing construction (Fig. 3.2c) provides for the consistent implementation of homogeneous technological processes of work on all N buildings and parallel — for heterogeneous processes, while preserving the advantages of consistent and parallel methods.

The duration of construction with the in-line method is determined by the duration of construction of one building $t\ i$ and the sum of one of the same type of construction processes at all other objects:

$$T_3 = t_i + t_n(N-1); \tag{3.4}$$

and the average intensity of consumption per unit time is equal to:

$$J_3 = \frac{\sum_{i=1}^{N} Q_i}{T_3} = \frac{\sum_{i=1}^{N} Q_i}{t_i + t_n(N-1)}; \tag{3.5}$$

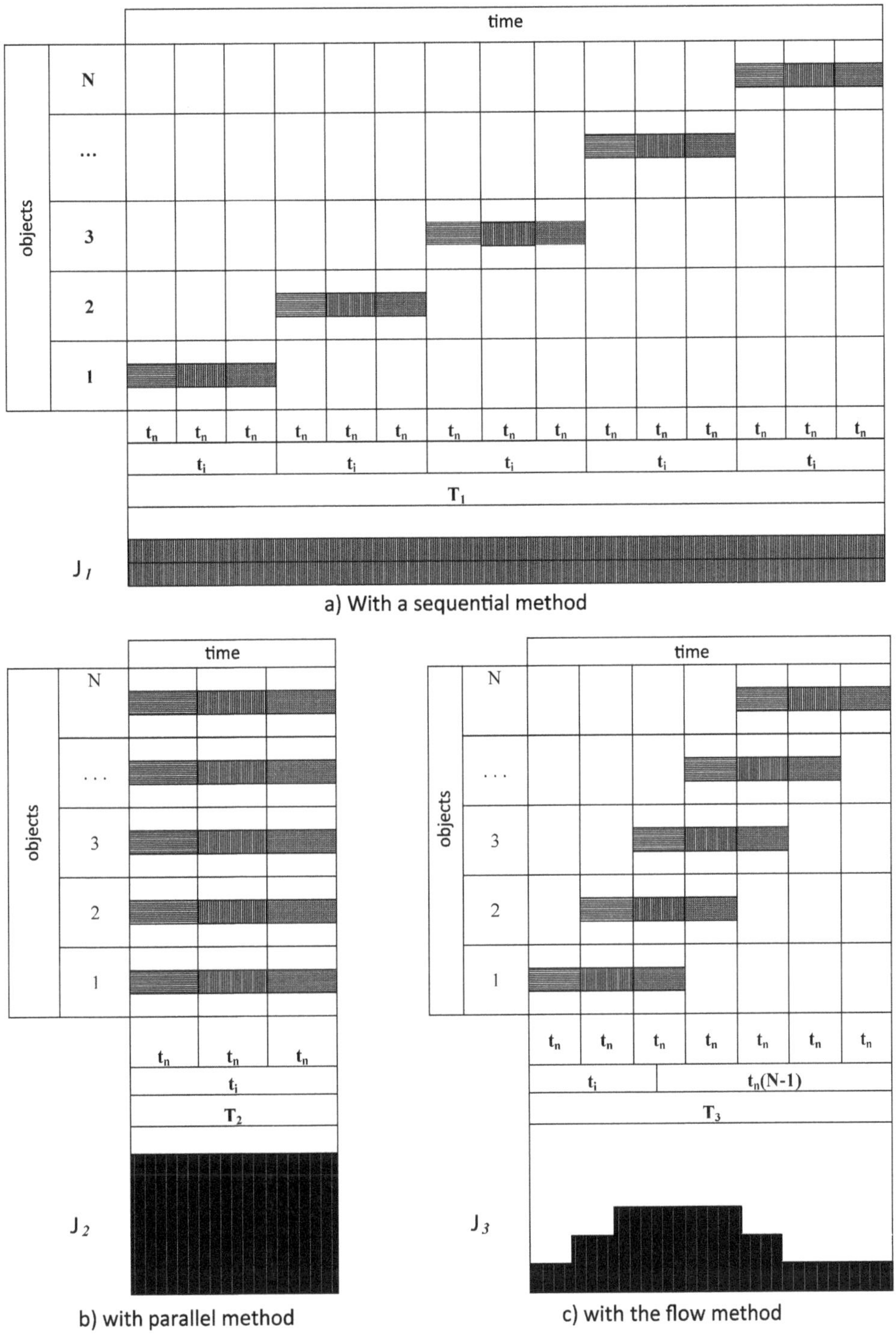

Figure 3.2: Construction and resource schedules

The in-line method takes less time to build N buildings than in the sequential one, and the maximum intensity of resource consumption is less than in parallel.

3.6 Design of the flow organization of construction

3.6.1 Basic principles of construction flow design

Stream is called such a method of organizing construction, which provides a systematic and rhythmic production of finished construction products based on the continuous and uniform work of teams (units) of constant composition, provided timely and complete delivery with all necessary material and technical resources.

The main task of designing the flow is to reduce the duration of construction, which would ensure the most productive use of workers and mechanisms by saturating the front of the work with the optimal amount of resources. Moreover, all calculations should be based on the real amount of resources that can be allocated by the relevant construction organizations to carry out the volume of work on the stream.

Using the basic principles of flow organization, widely used in industrial production, and taking into account the peculiarities of construction production, the following principles and sequence of designing a stream for the construction of homogeneous construction objects have been developed:

- we determine the objects to be constructed by the flow method, ie close to each other in design, layout, number of storeys and technology;
- we divide the designed object into processes, preferably equal to or multiple in labor intensity;
- we establish an appropriate sequence of processes for the construction of an object and combine interconnected processes into a common aggregate process, such a division and synchronization of processes serves as a prerequisite for the continuity of one of the important factors in the advanced organization of production;
- we establish the sequence of inclusion of individual objects in the construction stream, we assign processes to certain teams of workers, we establish the movement of teams at individual objects in the course of the technological process and from object to object, according to the adopted sequence with minimal (idle) transitions;
- we equip the brigades of workers with construction machines, tools, fixtures, thereby ensuring high-performance execution of processes assigned to the brigades;
- calculate the main indicators (parameters) of the flow;
- we design relocation from object to object in the established sequence, taking into account the observance of the given rhythm of work of the brigades and the construction machines, tools and devices attached to them.

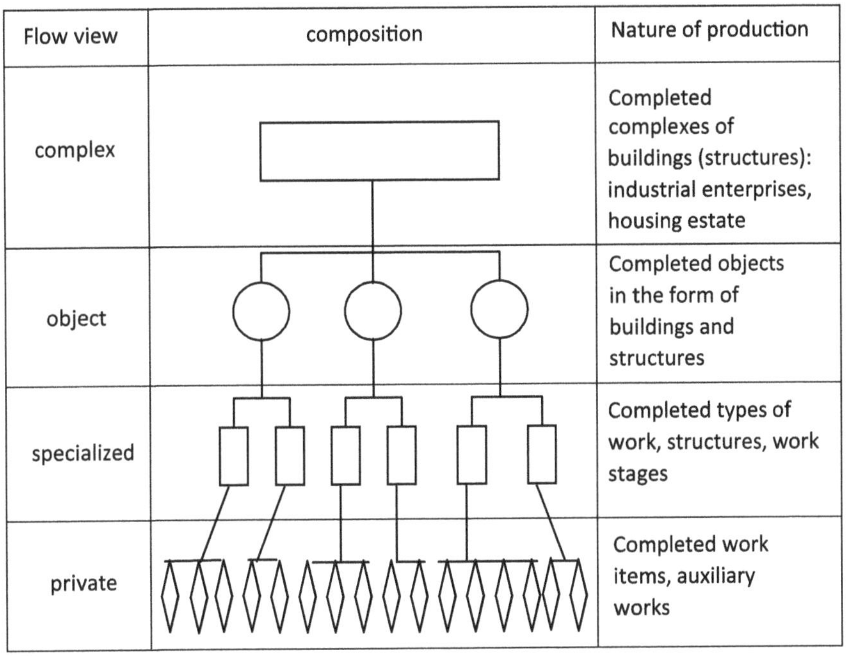

Figure 3.3: Technological structure diagram and resource flow levels

3.6.2 Varieties and types of construction flows

Construction flows are classified according to the following general characteristics:

1) According to the structure and type of product: **private, specialized, object and integrated** (Fig. 3.3).

Private stream — an elementary stream, which is one or several processes performed by one team (team or unit) on the private fronts of work m (trench, project, section, floor, etc.).

Private stream products may include earthworks, foundation work, wall masonry, plastering, etc. (Fig. 3.4 a).

Specialized stream — a set of technologically connected private flows, united by a single system of parameters and flow scheme. Its products are a finished type of work, a structural element or part of a building (structure) (Fig. 3.4 b).

Private and specialized flows can have different directions of development. The directions of the flow development depend on the space-planning and structural solution of the building, the types of work performed and their stages, the construction machines and mechanisms used. They can develop in a horizontal or vertical pattern.

At the same time, flows of one-story industrial buildings, as well as flows of the zero cycle and roofing devices have a horizontal direction (Fig. 3.5 a),

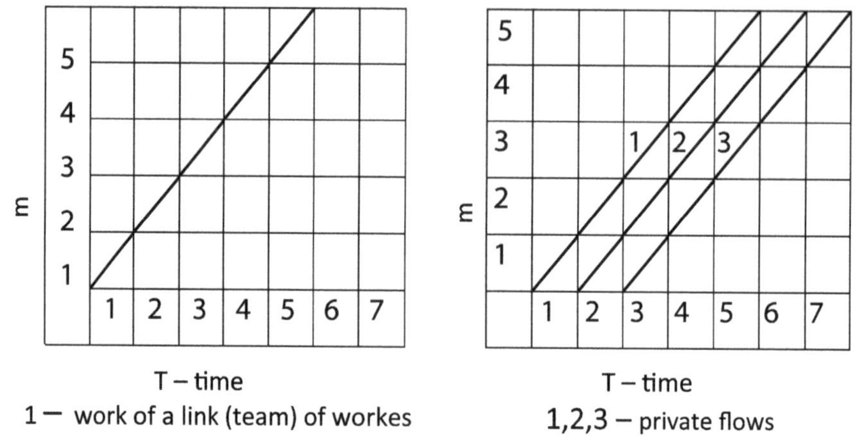

Figure 3.4: Cyclograms of private (a) and specialized (b) flows

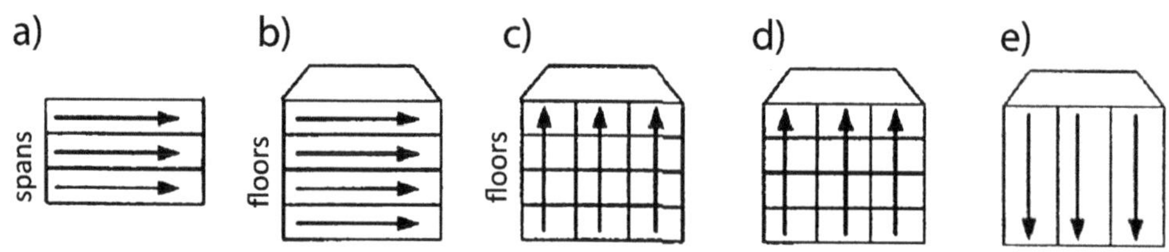

Figure 3.5: Flow Development Schemes

flows for the construction of a box of a multi-storey building have a horizontal-upward or vertical direction (Fig. 3.5 b, c), flows of specialized finishing works — vertically ascending or vertically descending direction (Fig. 3.5 g, d).

Object stream — a set of technologically and organizationally related specialized flows, the joint products of which are built separate buildings (structures).

Integrated flow — a set of organizationally related object flows, the joint products of which are an industrial enterprise, housing estate, etc.

2) By the nature of rhythm: **rhythmic, different rhythmic and non-rhythmic flows.**

In the rhythmic flow, the rhythm of the work of the brigade is constant, i.e. the same duration of work is observed by each individual brigade on private work fronts.

The rhythmic flow is organized during the construction of homogeneous or identical objects, when all elements of the flow have a single pace for the development of all component flows.

Rhythmic flows can be rhythmic, multiple rhythmic and different rhythmic.

In equally rhythmic flows, the rhythms of all teams on all fronts of work are equal to each other (Fig. 3.6 a).

In the rhythmic rhythm of one flow, it is a multiple of the rhythm of another (Fig. 3.6 b), therefore it is possible to attract two, three or several teams to a longer flow in accordance with the multiplicity of the rhythm of neighboring processes.

In fig. 3.6 b rhythm of the 2nd stream is twice the rhythm of the previous one, therefore two teams are involved in the 2nd stream — 2a and 2b.

In different rhythmic flows, the rhythms of teams remain constant, but are not equal to each other and are not multiple to each other (Fig. 3.6 c).

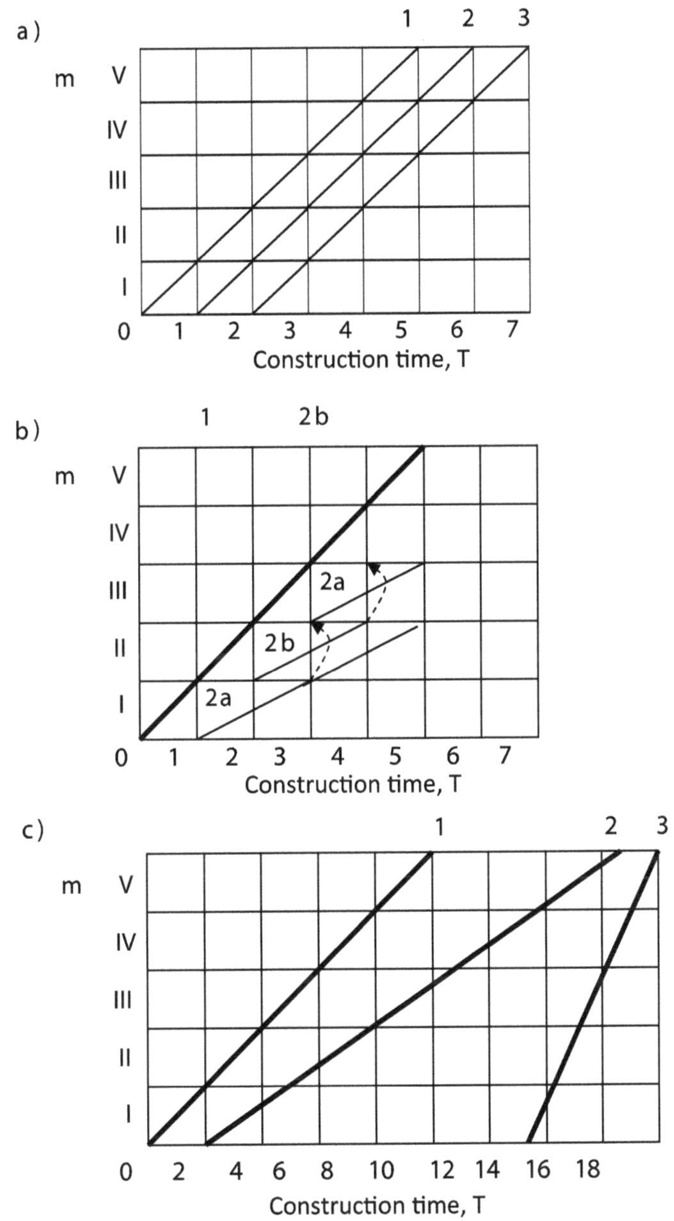

Figure 3.6: Rhythmic flows

A different flow is characteristic for the construction of heterogeneous and unequal buildings and structures that differ in size, number of storeys and other volumetric indicators.

Irregular is a stream in which the rhythm of the work of the brigade is variable, i.e. the duration of each individual brigade of work on private fronts varies.

Irregular flows are designed for the construction of objects with a complex configuration in plan, at different heights of their rooms and uneven distribution of the volume of work in space. Such objects are difficult to divide into bays (sections), equal in complexity. Therefore, the duration of the work on the grips by individual teams of constant strength is different.

Irregular flows can be with a uniform change in rhythm (Fig. 3.7 a) and with a non-uniform change in rhythm (Fig. 3.7 b).

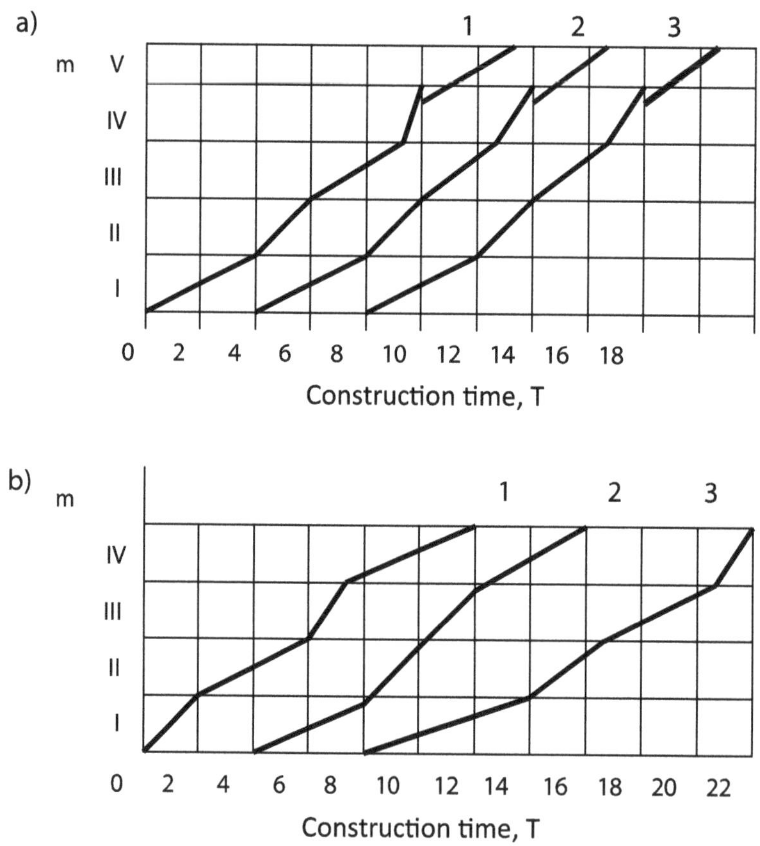

Figure 3.7: Irregular flows

The rhythm of work of teams in such flows is variable, i.e. unequal on different fronts of work, but in the first case, it changes the same for all brigades, repeating itself on the same fronts of work, and in the second case, the rhythms of the brigades change differently.

3) By the duration of operation: **short-term and long-term flows.**

Short-term flow is organized during the construction of individual buildings (structures) or groups of buildings, the duration of construction of which does not exceed one year.

A long-term flow is organized during the construction of buildings or complexes of objects, the construction duration of which exceeds one year.

The organization of long-term continuous construction is carried out with the aim of achieving for a long period (one year, two or more) continuous loading of construction (installation and commissioning) organizations, the coordinated work of customers, design organizations, manufacturers and suppliers of materials, structures and equipment during the construction of homogeneous objects in sectors of the economy and heterogeneous objects, the construction of which is carried out by territorial construction and installation organizations, as well as providing input into the day Your production capacity on time.

Long-term flows contribute to the rhythmic work of construction organizations, make fuller use of construction machinery, labor and material resources.

In addition, such flows create conditions for the rhythmic work of transport and manufacturing enterprises in the construction industry, and contribute to a reduction in the volume of construction in progress.

3.6.3 Construction Flow Parameters

The organization of continuous construction of enterprises, buildings and structures provides for the determination of spatial, technological and temporal parameters and dependencies between them.

The spatial parameters of the flow include: bay, site, object (building or structure).

Bay (m) — a part of a building or its structural element, within which private streams that are part of a specialized stream develop and are linked together. The dimensions of the grips are set based on their planning, volumetric and structural solutions of the building and the directions of development of the main processes for its construction. Repeated spans, sections, floors, etc. are taken as bays.

The breakdown of the building is carried out taking into account the necessary stability and spatial rigidity of the supporting structures.

The boundaries of the grips are often combined with the structural division of the building by temperature and sedimentary seams, which makes it possible to stop and resume work without violating technical conditions.

During the construction of multi-story buildings, the breakdown of buildings into grips, as mentioned above, is carried out not only horizontally, but also vertically, while the grips obtained will be called **tiers.** A tier may include a floor or a group of floors.

Analysis of the design features of any multi-storey building allows us to establish the presence of:

- a technical floor (floors), which has significant planning differences from other floors;
- typical floors with a repeating layout characteristic of the purpose of the building in question;
- foundation structures located below the zero mark, which can be combined as a technical underground;
- a roof that can be made in a flat, tent or other design.

Obviously, due to technological conditions, the size of the tier in height cannot be less than the size of the column in height. It must be borne in mind that there are column designs for two and three floors.

A site is a part of a building under construction, within which interconnected specialized flows are included in the structure of the object stream. The site is a spatial structural and technological part of the building, the construction of which repeats the entire complex of construction, installation and special works.

The technological parameters of the flow include: the number of private, specialized or object flows (n), the volume and complexity of the work, the intensity (power) of the stream.

The intensity (power) of the flow — the number of products (in physical terms) produced by the construction stream per unit time, for example, the number of square meters of total housing area per day.

The temporary parameters of the flow include: T_0 — the total duration of work on the stream as a whole; t — flow step — this is the period of time through which

finished products (building, construction, finished parts, etc.) are produced; k — the rhythm of the work of the team — the duration of the work assigned to her

Noah bay (site);

T is the duration of the construction;

T_{rav} (T_1) — the period of the deployment of the flow — the time interval between the beginning of the first and the end of the final processes, i.e. the time during which all teams participating in a specialized or object stream are gradually included in the construction stream;

T_{ol} (T_2) — the period of production of finished products — the time equal to the duration of the work of the final team (private, specialized or object stream);

$T_{St.}$ — the period of coagulation of the stream — the period during which all teams consistently go out of the stream with an interval equal to its rhythm;

T_{mouth} — the period of steady flow — the period to which corresponds to a constant and maximum number of workers, that is, the time of simultaneous work of all teams.

When organizing the in-line method of construction, two main types of brigades were formed: **specialized and integrated.**

Specialized brigades can be ordinary and complex-specialized. An ordinary team performs one type of specialized work (plastering, painting, sanitary, electrical, etc.).

An integrated team performs a range of technologically related civil works. For example, an integrated team for the construction of an object performs bricklaying of walls, installation of reinforced concrete floors and staircases, installation of window and door blocks, etc. A complex- specialized team performs two or more specialized types of technologically related work (painting, wallpaper and flooring from linoleum or plastering and facing work, etc.).

3.6.4 Technological coordination and calculation of parameters of construction flows

Technological linking of flows is performed on the basis of the following assumptions:

- work on each subsequent bay begins with an interval equal to a step flow;
- one brigade (link) or several brigades with the same rhythm can work on one grab;
- the size of each bay remains unchanged for each type of work performed on the bay;
- after completing the whole complex of works on one bay, the work on each of the subsequent bays is completed no later than at an interval equal to the step of the flow.

A. Calculation of the parameters of equal and short rhythmic flows

Using the above concepts and notation, the duration of the eurhythmics and short rhythmic flows can be expressed by the following formulas (Fig. 3.8):

$$T = T_1 + T_2, \tag{3.6}$$

Where

$$T_1 = (n-1) * t, T_2 = m * k, \tag{3.7}$$

in the rhythmic flow $t = k$.

Then:

$$T = (n-1) * t + m * t = (m + n - 1) * t, \tag{3.8}$$

Depending on the nature of the initial data, various flow parameters can be calculated using formula (3.3).

So, for a given total duration of construction (T) and a known number of crews (n) and grips (m), the step size of the stream

$$t = T/(m + n - 1); \tag{3.9}$$

the number of teams n for a given T and accepted t and m

$$n = \frac{T}{l} + 1 - m; \tag{3.10}$$

number of bays

$$m = \frac{T}{t} + 1 - n; \tag{3.11}$$

When designing flows, possible technological (t_{tech}) and organizational (t_{org}) breaks.

If the subsequent work on the bay can only be performed after a certain break due to the technology of work, for example, exposure concrete structure before the start of its demolition, drying of the plaster before the start of painting work, etc., then there is a need for technological breaks.

Organizational breaks occur in a number of cases under labor protection conditions, etc.

If these breaks are not taken into account in the duration of the flow step, then their values are included in the calculation formula of the total flow duration, i.e.

$$T_0 = (m + n - 1)\, t + \sum t_{tech} + \sum t_{org}. \tag{3.12}$$

Construction flows can be graphically represented in the form of a linear calendar chart by G.L. Gant (Fig.3.9a) or cyclogram of M.S. Budnikov (Fig.3.7b). On the line graph, for each specialized flow brigade, a horizontal strip is highlighted, and the period of operation of such a brigade on different grips is shown by segments shifted relative to each other.

In the cyclogram, the calendar scale of the line graph is saved. But the horizontal strip is allocated for bays in the order of their numbers from the bottom up. Therefore, the work of each brigade is depicted by an inclined line,

a) rhythmic flow — a linear graph of Gant G.L. (1890)

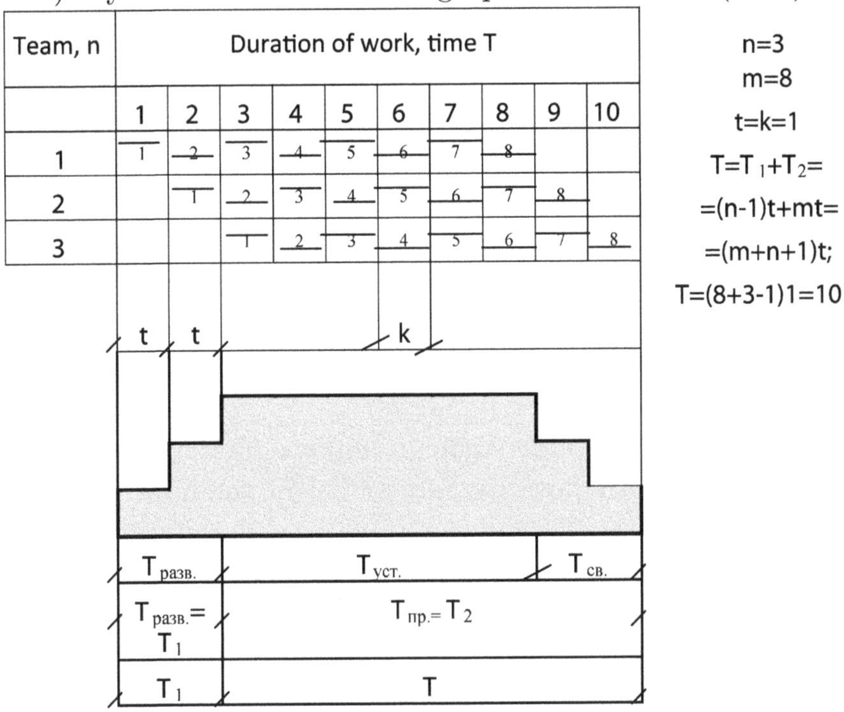

b) cyclogram of the objects stream M.S. Budnikov 1935)

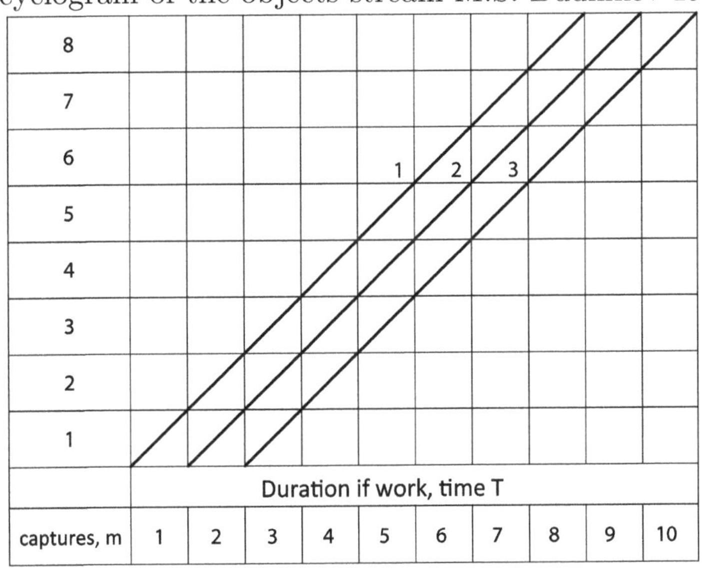

Figure 3.8: Technological coordination of rhythmic flow

which, as it were, symbolizes the movement of each brigade along the front of the work of one bay and the transition of the teams from one bay to another.

In the development of each construction stream within the framework of an object or complex, three periods can be distinguished:

- The period of deployment of the stream (T_{ra});
- The period of steady flow (T_{mouth});
- The period of coagulation of the flow ($T_{St.}$);
- The period of production of finished products (T_{ol}).

In a stable flow there is also a **period of steady flow** (T_{mouth}).

The more stable the flow, the longer the period T_{mouth}. The flow stability index is determined by the formula:

$$\alpha = \frac{T_{mouth}}{T} \tag{3.13}$$

The shorter the periods of deployment and coagulation of the flow and the longer the period of steady flow, the more efficient the flow.

B. Calculation of parameters of different rhythmic flows

In different rhythmic flows, the same rhythm of work of teams, equal to a certain number of days, can be adopted for the execution of some processes, and for others, due to the increased complexity of the work, the rhythms must be taken several times larger.

For example, in fig. 3.9a shows the cyclogram of a specialized stream for the construction of the underground part of the building. The rhythm of the work of the first team for excavation of the excavation pit and the third — of waterproofing the foundation walls and backfilling the foundation sinuses with soil is 2 days, and the rhythm of the second brigade for concreting the foundation is 4 days.

Technological coordination of the work of teams in the considered different rhythmic flow is as follows.

The second brigade, since the rhythm of its work is greater than the rhythm of the previous brigade, is included in the work immediately after the first brigade releases the first bay.

The third brigade, since the rhythm of its work is less than the rhythm of the previous brigade is included in the work only after the release of the last bay of the second brigade (see the right part of Fig. 3.9a). This is because only in this case the third team will not stand idle in anticipation of the front of work. The number of brigades $n = 3$ (the rhythm of the first brigade $k_1 = 2$ days, the second brigade $k_2 = 4$ days, the third brigade $k_3 = 2$ days); number of bays $m = 4$.

During the functioning of different rhythmic flows, in order to prevent bays from being idle, they strive to increase the number of workers in the brigade who have the highest rhythm, and thereby equalize the rhythms to the smallest

a) Option at $t = k_j = 4$ days; number of bays m = 4

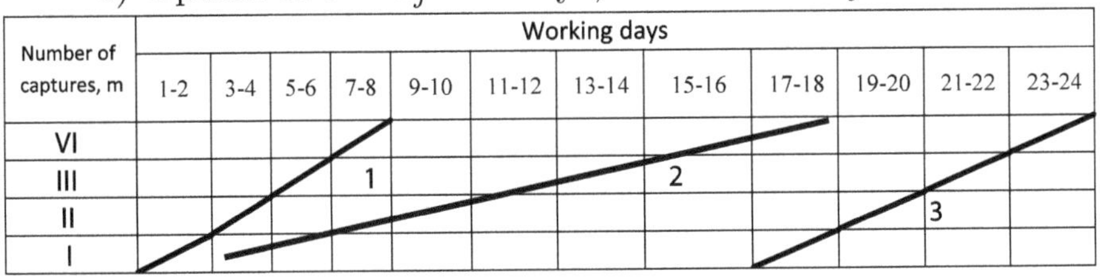

a) Option at $t = k_j = 2$ days; number of captures m = 4

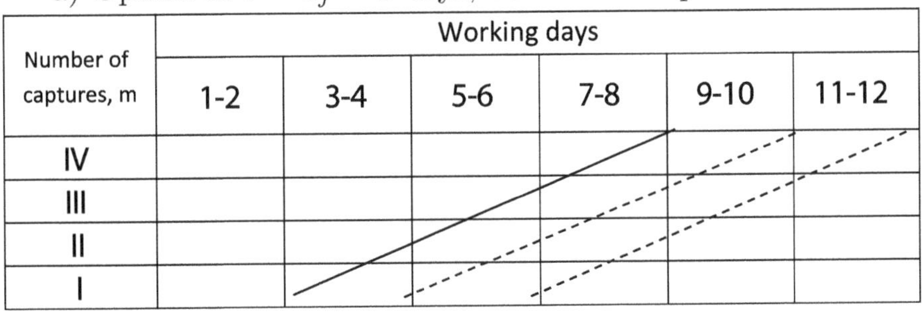

a) Option at $t = k_j = 5$ days; number of bays m = 4

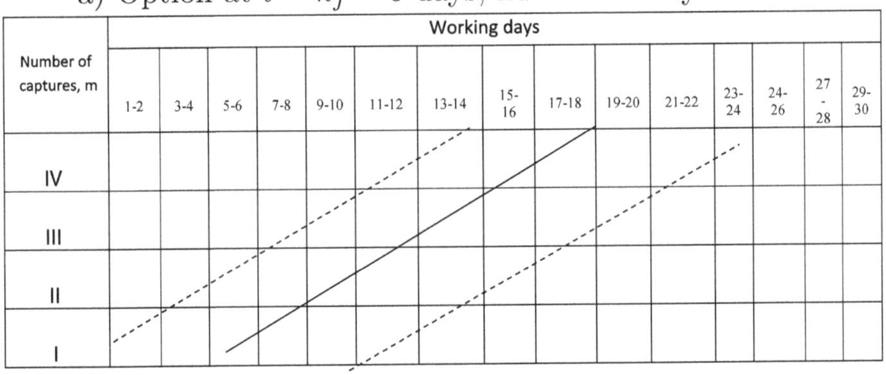

Figure 3.9: Cyclogram of a different rhythmic flow and options for converting it into rhythmic flows

(in Fig. 3.9, *b* — 2 days). However, this is not always possible for various reasons: the scope of work is small, the productivity of the crane is limited, etc.

In order to avoid empty bay, one can organize the stream with the same rhythms teams, taking as a basis the highest rate (Figure 3.9. *In* 5 days). But at the same time, one of the drawbacks of such flows remains — the unreasonably long duration of work.

It is possible to avoid these shortcomings in the design of flows by striving for the values of the rhythms of the work of teams to be multiples of each other.

After that, the execution of processes with lengthening rhythms is entrusted to several teams. For example, when the multiplicity of rhythms is equal to two, two teams are appointed to perform one production process; with a multiplicity of rhythms equal to three, three brigades, etc.

In fig. 3.10 a stream is presented, the rhythm of which is a multiple of two.

a) The number of brigades $n = 3$ (the rhythm of the first and third brigades $k_i = k_3 = 2$ days, the second brigade $k_2 = 4$ days; the number of bays $m = 4$.

In a specialized stream (Fig. 3.10, b), the first and third teams work with a rhythm of 2 days, and the second team works with a rhythm of 4 days, i.e. a multiple of 2 days. Then we organize two parallel private flows — 2a and 2b, performing the same processes, one of which (2a) develops on odd grips, and the other (2b) — on even ones.

Technological coordination of such flows is also quite simple — brigades are switched on as the corresponding bays are released by the previous brigade.

C. Calculation of non-rhythmic flow parameters

The technological linking of non-rhythmic flows has some features due to the uneven duration of their functioning on private fronts of work.

Irregular flows can be:

a) with the same change in the rhythms of the work of brigades on private fronts (Fig. 3.10);

b) with an uneven change in the rhythms of the work of brigades on private fronts (Fig. 3.11).

Technological coordination of irregular flows is carried out graphically and by calculation methods or using matrices.

We will analyze the essence of the graphical linking method using the example of a non-rhythmic specialized flow with the same rhythm of work of teams on private fronts (Fig. 3.11). To do this, we build a cyclogram. First, we apply the first private stream to the sequence diagram, then the second, and the second is turned on when the first stream releases the first grip.

In this example, this occurs on the 2nd day (dashed line). After that, the development of the second private flow along the grips is analyzed. Provided that two brigades cannot work at the same grab at the same time, the second brigade will stand idle on the 3rd day.

On the second bay, it will be idle during the 3rd and 4th days of operation, on the third bay — during the 6th day, etc. On the cyclogram, these time intervals are shown by segments a1, a2, a3, and a4 (Fig. 3.11).

In order to ensure the uninterrupted development of the second private stream along bays, it is necessary to postpone the beginning of its functioning by the number of days equal to the largest value of the segments “a”. In this case

$$t_0 = t_3 = a_3 = 3 \text{ days}, \tag{3.14}$$

If the duration of the work of the brigade on the first grab is denoted by $t_{1.1}$, then the start of the second brigade should be designed through an interval equal to $t_{1.1} + t_o$.

For this flow, all other teams should be included in the work also after $t_{and} + t_o = l + 3 = 4$ days.

As can be seen from the cyclogram, the uninterrupted operation of all brigades will be ensured: the second private stream passes to the fourth bay the next day after the first private stream has finished work on it. At this point, the second private stream is **as close as possible** to the first stream (occupies the so-called **critical position).**

The total flow duration in this case can be expressed by the following formula:

$$T = (t_u + t_O)(n - l) + T_{ol} \tag{3.15}$$

We will consider the calculation method of technological linking of flows using an example of an irregular flow with an uneven rhythm of work of teams on private fronts, shown in Fig. 3.10.

a)The number of brigades n=3 (the rhythm of the first and third brigades $k_1 = k_3 = 2$ days,the second brigade $2 = 4$ days; the number of bays $m = 4$

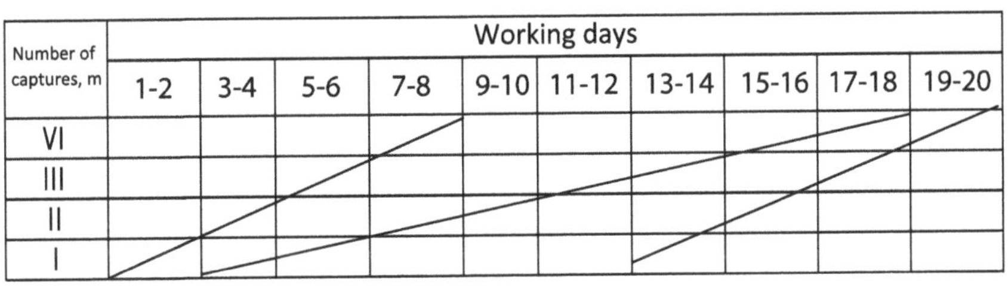

T=20

b) the number of brigades $n = 4$ (the rhythm of the first and third brigades is $k_1 = k_3 = 2$ days; brigades $2a = 2$ days; brigades $2 = 2$ days); number of bays $m = 4$

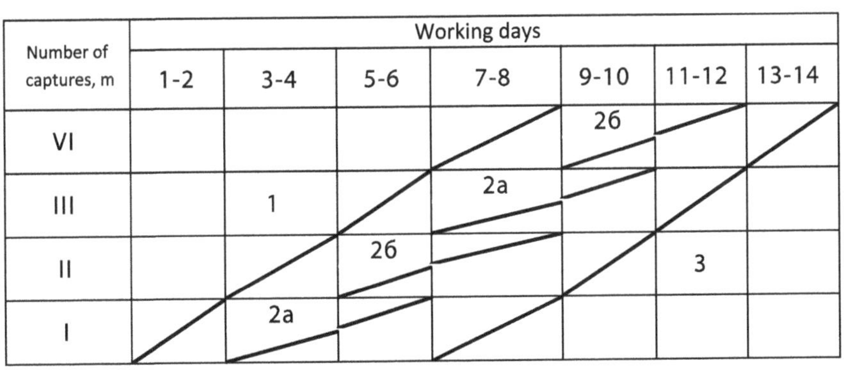

T - (4+4-1) 2 = 14 days

Figure 3.10: Cyclogram of a different rhythmic flow and its transformation into a multi-rhythmic flow

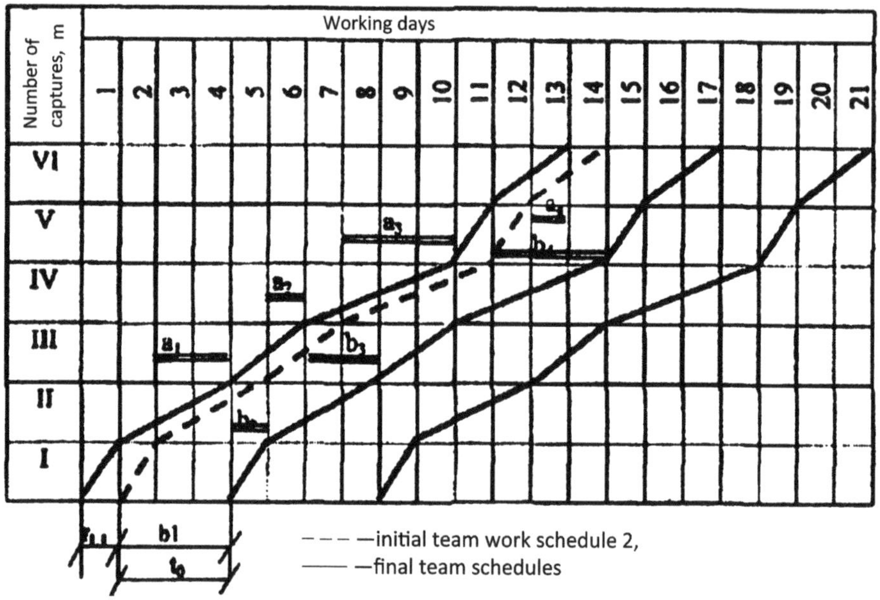

Figure 3.11: Cyclogram of irregular flow with the same duration of work of teams on private fronts

The irregular flow is presented with the following rhythm of work of the teams on six private fronts (in days): — along the first team, $k_{1,1} = 1$, $k_{1,2} = 1$, $k_{1,3} = 1$, $k_{1,4} = 3$, $k_{1,5} = 3$, $k_{1,6} = 3$;

— according to the second team, $k_{2,1} = 2$, $k_{2,2} = 1$, $k_{2,3} = 3$, $k_{2,4} = 1$, $k_{2,5} = 2$, $k_{2,6} = 1$;

— according to the third brigade, $k_{3,1} = 1$, $k_{3,2} = 1$, $k_{3,3} - 2$, $k_{3,4} - 1$, $k_{3,5} = 2$, $k_{3,6} = 1$.

Having shown in fig. 3.12 source data, we put the sequence diagram of the first team.

In order for the second team (i = 2) not to stand idle waiting for the front of work on the first bay (j = 1), it must be included in the flow when on this bay the first (i = l) brigade (k 1 , 1) will finish the work. Period for inclusion in the work the second stream of the conditions of t 2 , 1 = k 1 / 1.

In the flow shown in Fig. 3.12, t 2 , 1 = 1.

In order for the second team (i = 2) not to stand idle waiting for the front of work on the second bay (j = 2), it should be included in the work when the first team finishes work on the second bay. The period of inclusion in the work of the second stream, taking into account this condition, can be expressed by the following dependence:

$$t_{2,2} = k_{1,1} + k_{1,2} - k_{2,1} \quad , \tag{3.16}$$

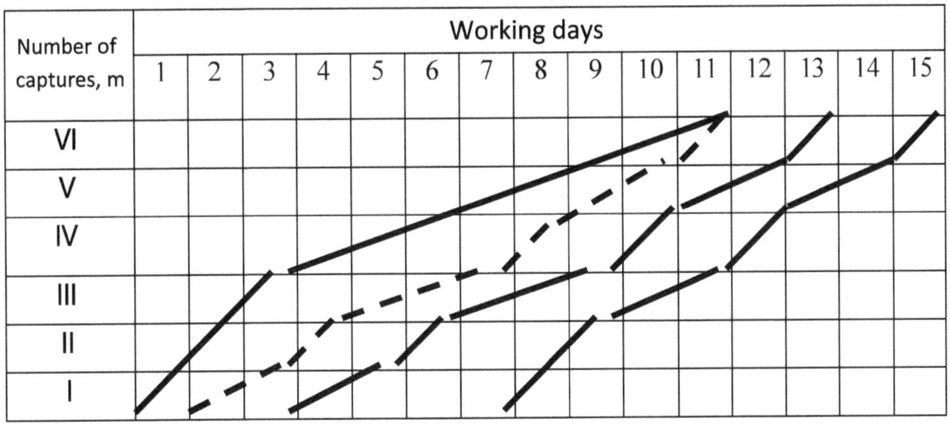

Figure 3.12: A cyclogram of an irregular flow with an uneven rhythm of work of brigades on private fronts

Where $k_{2,1}$ is the working time of the second brigade at the first bay.
In the flow shown in Fig. 3.12.

$$t_{2,2} = 1 + 1 - 2 = 0.$$

The period of switching on the second stream, taking into account the fact that the team will not stand idle on the j-th bay, by analogy with the previous one, is:

$$t_{2,j} = \sum_{j=1}^{m} k_{1,j} - \sum_{j-1}^{m} k_{2,(j-1)} \quad , \tag{3.17}$$

In order for the i-th team not to stand idle waiting for the previous team to release the front of work, the period of inclusion in the work of the stream should be accepted as the maximum of the calculated values:

$$t_1 = \max \left| \sum_{i=1}^{m} k_{i,j} - \sum k_{(i+1)(j-1)} \right| \quad , \tag{3.18}$$

The total duration of the work is calculated according to the following formula:

$$T = \sum_{i=2}^{n} t_i + \sum_{j=1}^{m} t_{n,j} \quad , \tag{3.19}$$

where: $\sum_{i=2}^{n} t_i$ — the period of the deployment of the stream, equal to the sum of the periods of inclusion in the work of all private flows;
$\sum_{j=1}^{m} t_{n,j}$ — production period, i.e. period of work of the last team on all m fronts of work.

As an example, we calculate the inclusion period of the second and third private non-rhythmic specialized flows shown in Fig. 3.12.

To do this, we write in accordance with (3.18) by cumulative totals of the durations of the first and second, and then the second and third flows, as well as the difference of these durations (Table 3.9 and Table 3.10).

Table 3.9 Calculation of the period of inclusion of the second private non-rhythmic specialized flow

Rooms	Estimated figures	Bay numbers, j = 1, m					
		I	II	III	IV	V	VI
1		1	2	3	6	10	12
2		0	2	3	6	7	
3	t2	1	0	0	0	3	

Table 3.10 Calculation of the period of inclusion of the 3rd private non-rhythmic specialized flow

Rooms	Estimated figures	Bay numbers, j = 1, m					
		I	II	III	IV	V	VI
1		2	3	6	7	9	10
2		0	1	2	4	5	
3	T3	2	2	4	3	4	

According to the calculation, the largest difference is 3 days, i.e. the period of inclusion of the second private non-rhythmic specialized flow $t_2 = 3$ days.

According to the calculation, the largest difference is 4 days, i.e. the period of inclusion of the third private non-rhythmic specialized flow $t_3 = 4$ days.

3.7 Network modeling of building production

The main method for solving planned and managerial tasks in construction is the method of network planning and management (NPM). The NPM method includes the construction, calculation, analysis and optimization of network models and is used to solve problems associated with the planning and management of construction.

The NPM method combines automated accounting and control, selection and management decisions. The results of the calculation of the network model contain an assessment of the fulfillment by contractors of work to achieve the goal. This allows managers to focus on issues on which the time frame for achieving the goal depends on the moment. Based on information on time, volume and resource parameters, variants of regulatory influences are modeled, the most rational of which is used. A network model is used as a model of the production process.

A network model is a directed graph (a graph is a geometric figure consisting of many points and lines connecting these points. If they have a direction, they are called arcs, and the graph is oriented), which displays the sequence and organizational and technological relationships between the jobs that are necessary for achieving the goal.

A network model presented graphically on a plane with calculated time and resource parameters is called a network graph. Network charts are used to calculate time parameters and optimize calendar plans.

A network model with the required degree of detail displays the relationship of individual works on the construction of an object (complex) and makes it possible to carry out mathematical analysis of the calendar plan, predict its future state, and evaluate the effectiveness of decisions made.

3.7.1 Networking Rules

To build a network schedule, it is necessary to identify the sequence and relationship of the work: to establish what work needs to be done and what conditions to ensure that this work can be started, what work can and should be done in parallel with it, what work should be started after its completion. These questions allow us to identify the technological relationship between individual works, provide a logical construction of the network schedule and its compliance with the simulated work package.

The level of detail of the network schedule depends on the complexity of the facility under construction, the amount of resources used, the amount of work and the duration of the construction.

There are two types of network diagrams:

- peaks — work;
- peaks — events.

A. Networks of the type "peaks — work"

Elements of such a schedule are work and dependencies.

The work is a certain production process, requiring time and resources for its implementation and leading to the achievement of certain results. It is represented by a rectangle. **Dependence** (fictitious work) shows the organizational and technological relationship between the work that does not require time and resources, is shown by an arrow. If there is an organizational or technological break between jobs, then the duration of this break is indicated

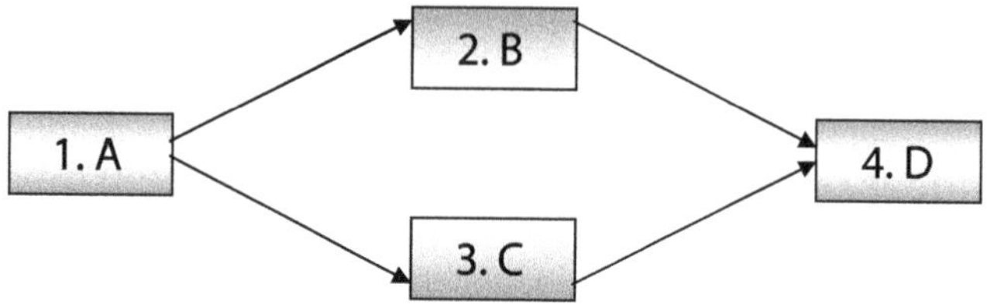

Figure 3.13: Peer-to-peer network diagram

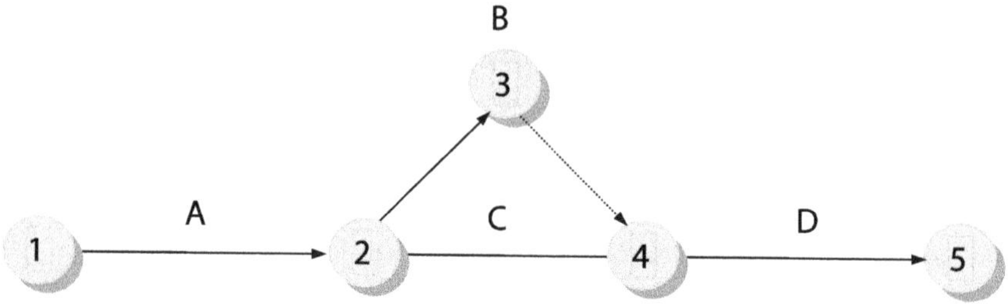

Figure 3.14: Top-Event Network Diagram

on the dependency. An example of a network diagram of "peaks — work" is shown in Fig. 3.13.

If the work of the "top-work" network schedule does not have previous jobs, then it is the original work of this schedule. If the work has no subsequent work, then it is the final work of the network.

The work of the network diagram is numbered in a technological sequence from left to right by numbers of the natural series, which should not be repeated. The serial number of the work is its code. The code for the subsequent work should be larger than the code for the previous one.

B. Networks of the "peak – event" type

Elements of this type of graph are work, dependencies, and events. The work is represented by a solid arrow, the dependence is dashed. An event is the result of one or more work, necessary and sufficient to start one or more subsequent work, and is indicated by a circle.

In the network diagrams of this type, each work is between two events: the initial one from which it exits and the final one into which it enters. Network events are numbered, so each work has a code consisting of the numbers of its start and end events. In this case, the number of the initial event of operation is less than the number of its final event. For example, in fig. 3.14, works are encoded as (1,2); (2,3); (2.4); (4,5).

If the event of the "vertex – event" network graph does not have previous works, then it is the initial event of this graph. The works immediately

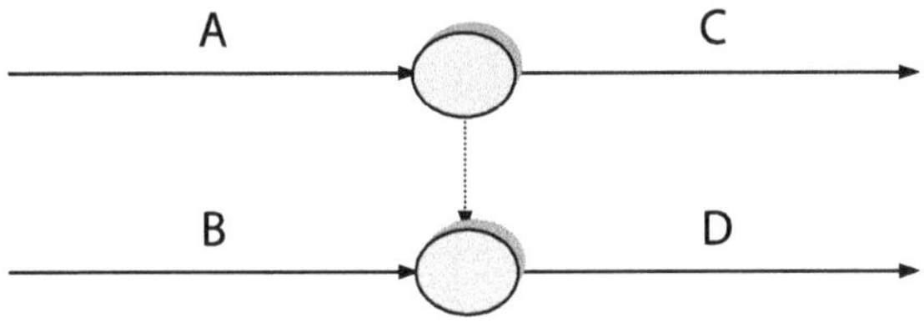

Figure 3.15: Image of the relationship between differentially dependent jobs

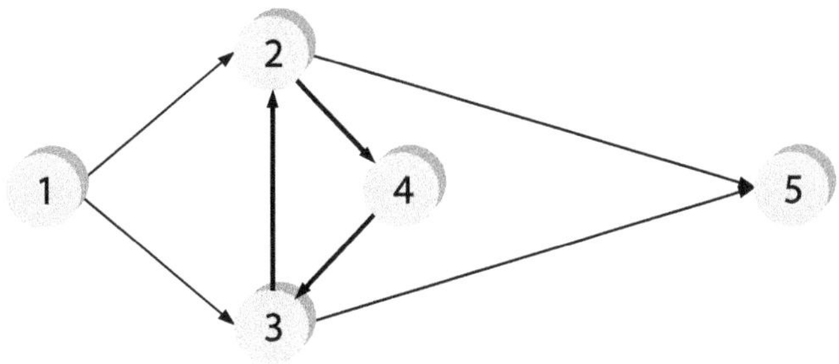

Figure 3.16: Closed Loop Example (2,4,3,2)

following him are called the source ones. If the event has no subsequent work, then it is the final event.

The work included in it is called the final work of the network.

In order to correctly display the interconnections between the work, the following basic rules for constructing a network "peaks — events" must be observed:

- When depicting simultaneously or simultaneously performed work (for example, works "B" and "C" in Fig. 4.13), dependence (3.4) and an additional event (3) are introduced, otherwise different works will have the same code, which is unacceptable.
- If, to start work "D", it is necessary to perform work "A" and "B", and to start work "C" — only work "A" (differentially dependent work), then a dependency and an additional event are introduced (Fig. 3.15).
- In the network diagram there should not be closed loops (cycles), that is, a chain of work returning to the event from which they left (Fig. 3.16).
- In the network diagram with the flow organization of construction, additional events and dependencies are introduced (Fig. 3.17).

C. Comparison of network diagrams such as "work-tops" and "event tops"

Networks of the "peak-event" type have a longer history, they have been used since the 50s of the twentieth century. And only at the end of the

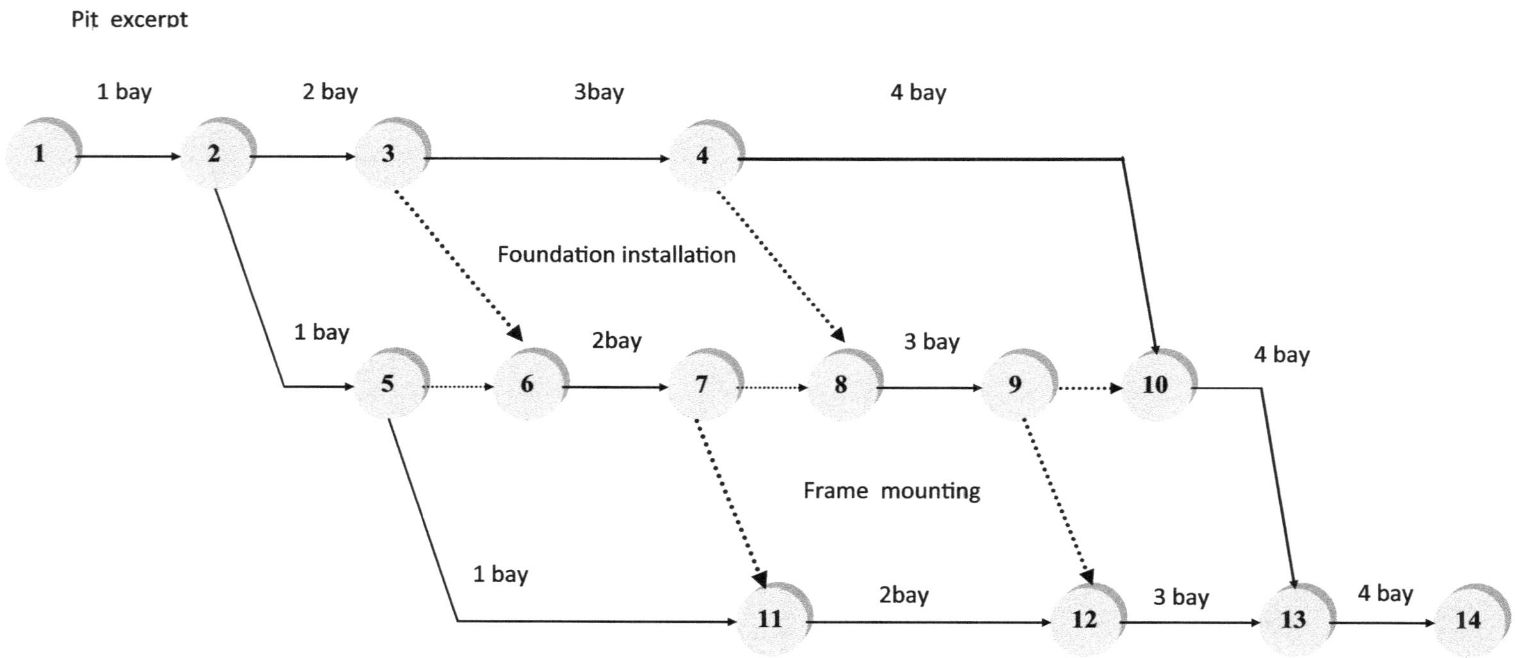

Figure 3.17: An example of the image of flows of homogeneous work

60s appeared network diagrams such as "top-work". Currently, peaks-work network graphics are becoming more widely used for the following reasons:

1. The absence of events and dotted dependencies allows you to determine the relationship of work before building a network schedule from the source data table. Each work is assigned a permanent number **(code) that** does not depend on changes and additions in the network schedule. The separate position of each work allows you to enter special codes for all performers.
2. It is more convenient to build a network diagram of this type. All rectangles can be drawn on a sheet, and then organizational and technological dependencies are placed between them. The introduction of new works and relationships, as well as the exclusion of previously existing ones, is carried out without changing its topology. For network diagrams of the "peak-event" type, this cannot be done, since each work is between two events, which implies a different logic.
3. Writing applications for building and calculating peaks-work networks is the easiest thing, so most modern applications are only applicable to such networks.
4. Networks of the "peak-work" type are adapted to management standards and are used in specialized planning and operational management software packages.

3.7.2 Parameters of network diagrams and algorithms for their calculation. Time Settings of Network

Each work of the network schedule has a temporary assessment — duration. The duration (t) of the work is measured in units of time: hours, days, weeks, etc.

Any continuous workflow in a network is called a path. The path from the initial to the final work (event) is the full path of the network schedule **a.** If the duration of each work is known, then the duration of the journey can be determined. Duration of any path is equal to the sum of the durations of its constituent works. The full path with the longest duration is called critical.

The duration of the critical path (T_{cr}) determines the total duration of the construction. Therefore, in order to reduce the duration of construction, it is necessary to reduce the duration of critical works, that is, works that are on a critical path. One of the main tasks of construction managers is to carefully monitor compliance with the established durations of these works, find ways to reduce them and take operational measures to prevent their breakdown.

To determine the duration of the critical path and the timing of each work, the following time parameters of the network model are determined:

- early onset — t^{pn};
- early ending — t^{po};
- late start — t^{mon};
- late completion — t^{po};
- full reserve of time — R;
- free time reserve — r.

An early start is the earliest start time. The early start of the initial work of the network is zero. The early start of any other work is equal to the maximum early end of previous work.

Early completion of work is the earliest moment of completion of this work. It is equal to the sum of its early start and duration.

Late completion of work — the latest moment of completion of work at which the duration of the critical path does not change. The late completion of the final work is equal to the duration of the critical path. Late completion of any work is equal to the minimum late start of subsequent work.

Late start of work — the latest moment of the start of work at which the duration of the critical path does not change. It is equal to the difference between the late end of this work and its duration.

The work of the critical path, the early and late start and end dates are equal to each other, so they do not have time reserves. Work that does not lie on a critical path (non-critical work) has time reserves.

The full reserve of working time is the maximum time by which you can increase the duration of work or move its beginning without increasing the duration of the critical path. It is equal to the difference between a late start and an early start or a late end and an early end to work.

Free reserve of working time — the time by which you can increase the duration of the work or postpone its beginning, without changing the early start of subsequent work. It is equal to the difference between the early start of subsequent work and the early end of this work.

D. Calculation of the network diagram of "top-work"

To calculate the network diagram of the "vertex – work", the rectangle depicting the work is divided into 7 parts (Fig. 3.18). In the upper three parts of the rectangle, the early beginning, duration and early end of the work are recorded, in the three lower parts — its late start, time reserves and late end. The central part contains the code (number) and the name of the work.

An example of calculating the network diagram of the "top – work" is shown in Fig. 3.19.

t^{pn}	t	t^{po}
code and name of work		
t^{pn}	R/r	t^{po}

Figure 3.18: The image of the work in the network diagram of the "top-work"

The calculation of the network begins with the definition of early dates. Early beginnings and endings are calculated sequentially from the original to the final work. The early start of the initial work is 0, the early end is the sum of the early start and the duration of the work:

$$t^{po} = t^{pn} + t \tag{3.20}$$

For example, for (1) $t_1^{po} = t_1^{pn} + t_1 = 0 + 2 = 2$.

The early start of subsequent work is equal to the early end of previous work. If several works directly precede this work, then its early beginning will be equal to the maximum of the early endings of previous works:

$$t^{pn} = \max\{t^{po}_{previous}\}. \tag{3.21}$$

For example, for (5) $t^{pn} = \max\{t_2^{po}; t_3^{po}\} = \max\{7; 5\} = 7$.

Thus, the early dates of all network work are determined and entered in the upper left and right sectors.

The early completion of final work (10) determines the duration of the critical path ($T_{cr} = 20$).

Late dates are calculated in the reverse order from final to initial work. The late completion of the final work is equal to its early completion, that is, the duration of the critical path: $t_{cr} = 20$.

Late onset is calculated as the difference between late end and duration:

$$t_{pn} = t_{no} - t. \tag{3.22}$$

For example, for work (10): $t_{10}^{pn} = t_{10}^{po} - t_{10} = 20 - 1 = 19$.

The late commencement of subsequent work determines the late completion of previous work. If several works directly follow this work, then its late completion will be equal to the minimum of the late beginnings of subsequent works:

$$t^{no} = \min t^{pn}_{series}. \tag{3.23}$$

For example, for work (5): $t_5^{no} = \min\{t^{pn}7; t_8^{pn}; t_9^{pn}\} = \min\{17; 15; 12\} = 12$.

In a similar way, the late dates of all network work are determined and recorded in the lower left and right sectors.

The full reserve of time, equal to the difference between late and early dates, is entered in the numerator of the middle of the lower part:

$$R = t^{pn} - t^{rn} = t^{po} - t^{ro}. \qquad (3.24)$$

For example, for (3) $R_3 = t_3^{pn} - t_3^{rn} = 4 - 2 = 2 = t_3^{po} - t_3^{ro} = 7 - 5 = 2$.

The free time reserve equal to the difference between the minimum early start of subsequent work and the early end of this work is recorded in the denominator of the middle of the lower sector:

$$r = t^{no} = \min t^{pn}_{series} - t. \qquad (3.25)$$

For example, for work (3): $r_3 = \min\{t_5^{pn};\ t_6^{pn}\} - t_3^{po} = \min\{7;\ 5\} - 5 = 5 - 5 = 0$

Free reserve is always less than or equal to the full reserve of work.

The sequence of work with zero time reserves is a critical way to network. In this example, jobs 1, 2, 5, 9, 10 are on a critical path.

E. Calculation of the network diagram of "peaks – events"

Figure 3.20 shows the network diagram of the "peak – event" including the same works as the graph of the "peak – work" (Fig. 3.19).

There are several algorithms for calculating such a graph. The most common of them is the calculation of the network diagram in tabular form and directly on the graph (sector method).

Example 3.2. The algorithm for calculating the network in tabular form

The initial data for the calculation are entered from the network in columns 1, 2 and 3 of the table (see table. 3.11). All three of these columns are filled in simultaneously.

Column 1 contains the numbers of the initial events of previous works. For example, for the work (7,9), the previous ones are the work (3,7) and the dependence (6,7), therefore, in column 1, the numbers of the initial events of these works 3 and 6 are entered.

In group 2, the codes of work and dependencies are entered in the order of increasing initial numbers of events, that is, first the work coming out of event 1, then from event 2, etc.

In column 3, the durations of work and dependencies are affixed.

Similarly, the early beginnings and endings of all work are determined and are entered in columns 4 and 5 of the table. 3.11.

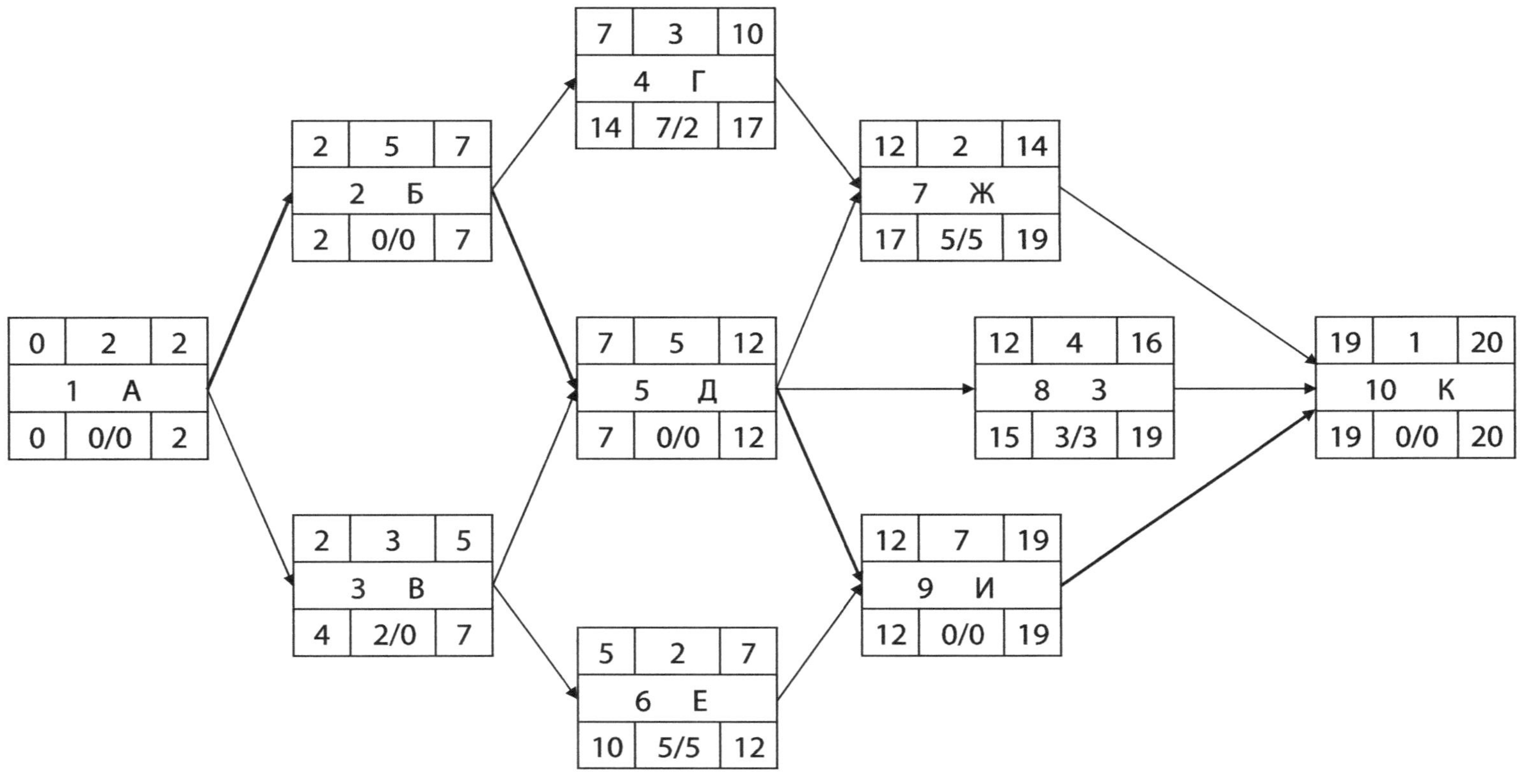

Figure 3.19: An example of calculating the network diagram “peaks — work”

Table 3.11 the calculation of the network in the table

Number of initial events for previous work	Code of work (i,j)	Duration of work (i,j)	Early start of work $t^{ro}(i,j)$	early completion (i,j)	late start of work (i,j)	Late completion (i,j)	full reserve of work time $R(i,j)$	free time reserve $r(i,j)$
1	2	3	4	5	6	**7**	8	9
-	(1.2)	2	0	2	0	2	0	0
1	(2.3)	5	2	7	2	7	0	0
1	(2.4)	3	2	5	4	7	2	0
2	(3.5)	0	7	7	7	7	0	0
2	(3.7)	3	7	10	14	17	7	2
2	(4.5)	0	5	5	7	7	2	2
2	(4.8)	2	5	7	10	12	5	5
3,4	(5.6)	5	7	12	7	12	0	0
5	(6.7)	0	12	12	17	17	5	0
5	(6.8)	0	12	12	12	12	0	0
5	(6.9)	4	12	16	15	19	3	3
3.6	(7.9)	2	12	14	17	19	5	5
4.6	(8.9)	7	12	19	12	19	0	0
6,7,8	(9.10)	1	19	20	19	20	0	0

Early start and end dates are calculated according to the table from top to bottom. The early start of work emerging from the first event is zero. The early end of any network work is equal to the sum of the early start and duration:

$$t^{ro}_{(i,j)} = t^{pn}_{(i,j)} + t_{(i,j)} \tag{3.26}$$

For example, for work (1,2): $t^{ro}_{(1,2)} = t^{pn}_{(1,2)} + t_{(1,2)} = 0 + 2 = 2$.

Early initiation of subsequent work equal to the maximum of the early endings of previous works: $t^{pn}_{(j,k)} = \max t^{ro}_{(i,j)}$.

For example, for work (5,6) $t^{rn}_{(1,2)} = \max\{t^{po}_{(3,5)}; t^{po}_{(3,4)}\} = \max\{7; 5\} = 7$.

The maximum value from the early end of work included in the final event determines the duration of the critical path. In this example $T_{cr} = t^{po}_{(9,10)} = 20$.

Late start and end dates are recorded in columns 6 and 7 of the table. 3.4. Their calculation is carried out in the table from the bottom up.

For the works included in the final event, the later end of the duration of the critical path are: $t^{po}_{(9,10)} = 20$.

The late start of any work is determined by the difference between its late end and duration:

$$t^{pn}_{(i,j)} = t^{po}_{(i,j)} - t_{(i,j)}. \tag{3.27}$$

For example, for (9,10) $t^{pn}_{(9,10)} = t^{po}_{(9,10)} - t_{(9,10)} = 20 - 1 = 19$.

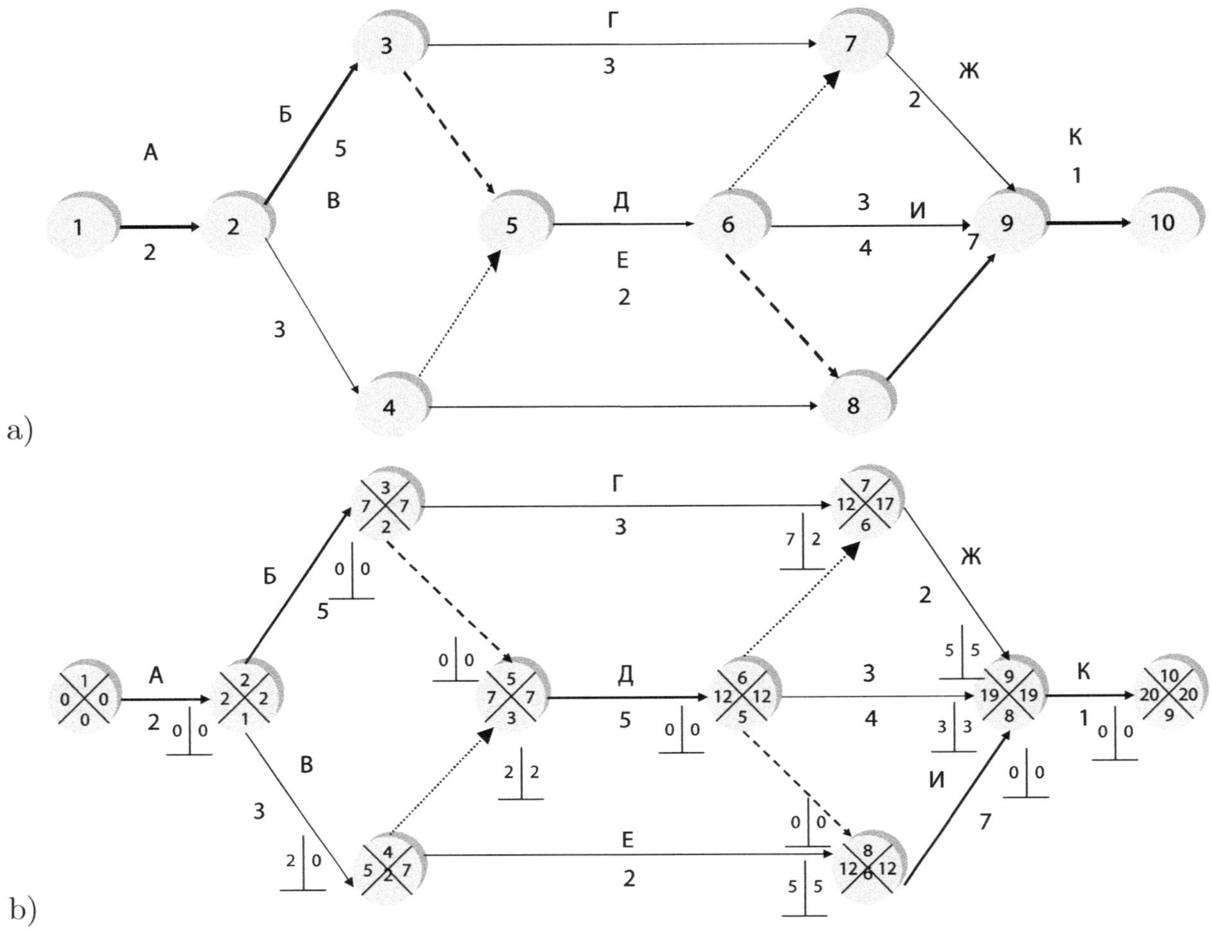

Figure 3.20: a) An example of a network diagram of “peaks — events”, b) An example of a calculation on a network diagram of “peaks — events”

Late completion of any work is equal to the smallest value from the late beginnings of subsequent work:

$$t^{pn}_{(i,j)} = \min t^{po}_{(i,j)}. \tag{3.28}$$

For example, for work (2,4): $t^{by}(2,4) = \min t^{mon}(4,5); t^{mon}(4,8) = \min\{7;10\} = 7$.

In this way, the late dates of all network work are determined.

The full reserve of time for each work and dependence is equal to the difference between late and early dates:

$$R_{(i,j)} = t^{po}_{(i,j)} - t^{ro}_{(i,j)} = t^{pn}_{(i,j)} - t^{po}_{(i,j)}. \tag{3.29}$$

For example, for work (2,4): $R_{(i.j)} = t^{po}_{(2,4)} - t^{ro}_{(2,4)} = 7 - 5 = 2 = t^{pn}_{(2,4)} - t^{rn}_{(2,4)} = 4 - 2 = 2$.

The full reserve of time is recorded in column 8 of the table. 3.4.

The free time reserve is entered in column 9 and is determined by the difference between the early start of subsequent work and the early end of this work

$$r_{(i,j)} = t^{rn}_{(i,k)} - t^{ro}_{(i,j)}. \tag{3.30}$$

For example, for work (3,7): $r_{(3,7)} = t^{pn}_{(7,9)} - t^{po}_{(3,7)} = 12 - 10 = 2$.

The free reserve of working time is always less than or equal to its full reserve:

$$r_{(i,j)} \le R_{(i,k)} - t^{po}_{(i,j)}. \tag{3.31}$$

For critical path jobs, the total and free time reserves are zero. Define critical work, this is (1,2); (2,3); (3,5); (5.6); (6.8); (8.9); (9.10). The critical path of the network in question will be (1, 2, 3, 5, 6, 8, 9, 10).

Example 3.3. Calculation algorithm directly on the network diagram (sector method)

For calculation directly on the network diagram, each event is divided into 4 sectors (Fig. 3.21).

Initially, the early beginnings of the network are determined. The calculation is carried out from left to right from the source to the final event. To the left sector of the initial event (1) we write "0", since the early start of work leaving this event is zero. The initial work of the network has no previous work, so in the lower sector we also write "0".

The early start of subsequent work is equal to the maximum early end of previous work, that is, the maximum sum of the early start and duration of previous work:

$$r_{(j,k)} = \max\{t^{pn}_{(i,j)} - t^{po}_{(i,j)}\}. \tag{3.32}$$

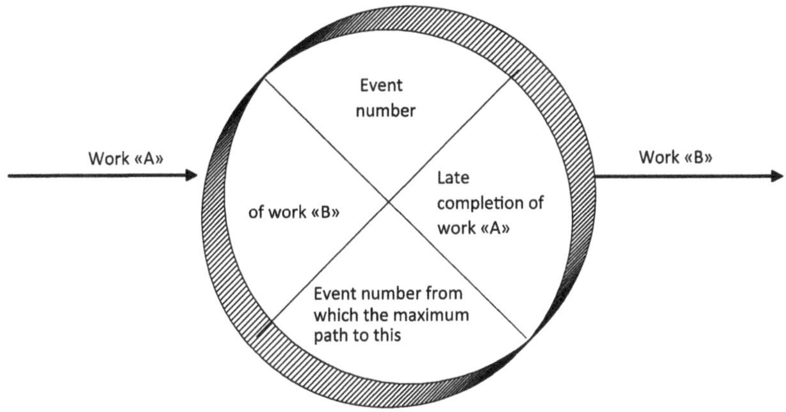

Figure 3.21: Event sectors content

For example, for work (7,9):
$t^{pn}_{(7,9)} = \max\{(t^{pn}_{(3,7)} + t_{(3,7)}); (t^{pn}_{(6,7)} + t_{(6,7)}0\} = \max\{(7+3); (12+0)\} = 12.$
In the left sector of the event (7), write 12 — the early start of work (7.9), in the bottom we write 6 — the number of the event, from which the maximum path goes to this one. Similarly, the early beginnings of all work are determined. Works emerging from a single event have the same early beginnings.

The maximum value from the sums of the early beginnings and the durations of the final works is entered into the left sector of the final event (10) — this will be the *duration of the critical path.* For the considered example: $T_{cr} = t^{rn}_{(9,10)} + t_{(9,10)} = 19 + 1 = 20.$

Enter 20 in the left sector of the event (10), and event (9) in the lower sector.

The following are critical jobs. The critical path ends event (10), in the lower sector of which 9 is recorded. Therefore, event (9) is also on the critical path, 8 is recorded in its lower sector, that is, the critical path passes through event (8), in the lower sector of which figure 6, which means that event (6) lies on the critical path, etc. before the starting event. The critical path in this example passes through events (1,2,3,5,6,8,9,10), critical works: (1,2); (2,3); (3,5); (5.6); (6.8); (8.9); (9.10).

The late completion of work is determined by a reverse move from right to left, from the final to the initial event.

The late completion of the final work is equal to the duration of the critical path, so 20 is placed in the right sector of event (10).

Late completion of previous work is equal to the minimum difference of late endings and duration of subsequent work:

$$t^{po}_{(i,j)} = \min\{t^{po}_{(j,k)} - t_{(j,k)}\} \tag{3.33}$$

For example, for work (2,4): $t^{po}_{(2,4)} = \min\{(t^{po}_{(4,5)} - t_{(4,5)}), (t^{po}_{(4,8)} - t_{(4,8)})\} = \min\{(7-0);(12-2)\} = 7$.

In the right sector of event (4) we write 7. All works included in one event have the same late endings.

After calculating the early and late dates, time reserves are determined.

The full reserve of work time is the difference between the late end and the sum of the early start and the duration of this work:

$$R_{(i,j)} = t^{po}_{(i,j)} - (t^{pn)}_{(i,j)} + t_{(i,j)}) \tag{3.34}$$

For example, for work (3,7) $R_{(3,7)} = t^{po}_{(3,7)} - (t^{pn)}_{(3,7)} + t_{(3,7)}) = 17-(7+3) = 7$.

The free reserve of work time is equal to the difference between the early start of subsequent work and the sum of the early start and duration of this work:

$$r_{(i,j)} = t^{pn}_{(i,k)} - (t^{pn)}_{(i,j)} + t_{(i,j)}). \tag{3.35}$$

For example, for work (3,7) : $r_{(3,7)} = t^{pn}_{(3,9)} - (t^{pn)}_{(3,7)} + t_{(3,7)}) = 12-(7+3) = 2$.

Reserves of work time and dependencies are recorded on the graph under the arrow: full reserve on the left, free reserve on the right.

3.7.3 Software

The most important component of construction management based on network schedules are computer software packages. These packages are designed for compiling network schedules, calendar plans, solving operational management problems, monitoring and controlling time and cost.

Currently, the following foreign software tools are used: Artemis, Primavera, CA-Super Project, Microsoft Project and domestic: Spider Project.

Each software package, solving the problems of network optimization and resource allocation, has certain limitations. So, in the Microsoft Project package, priority is given to work with a minimum reserve. The Artemis and Primavera packages offer enumeration of direct heuristics to find the best work schedules.

The Russian Spider Project package provides the most rational calendar plans due to new optimization algorithms based on the interchangeability of resources.

When choosing a software package, the following should be considered:

1. Computer base, which has a construction organization;
2. The availability of Russified software and documentation for it;
3. The possibility of technical support for the package and training.

3.8 Object planning scheduling

3.8.1 Assignment of the construction schedule of the facility

The schedule is intended to determine the sequence of deadlines for the implementation of general construction, special and installation works carried out during the construction of the facility.

The purpose of scheduling is to describe the proposed method of construction of the facility and to ensure that the facility is built within the time period specified by the contract with the help of available resources.

The schedule is developed before the start of construction, covers the construction period of the facility and is the main document for the development of schedules for the types of work — for civil works, electrical, plumbing and other types of low-level work.

In addition, the calendar plan is designed to provide information to all participants in the construction of the facility and act as a binding document after its approval.

According to the method of providing, calendar plans can be either time charts (Gantt chart, Budnikov cyclogram) or in the form of a network chart.

On the basis of the calendar plan, the need for workforce, material and technical resources and funds for temporary periods is determined.

The schedule for the construction of the facility is developed by the General Contracting Construction Organization or an enterprise specializing in the development of organizational and technological documentation for the order of the general contracting organization.

3.8.2 The procedure for preparing the source data for the development of the schedule

The initial data for leaving the calendar plan are:

- regulatory terms of construction or terms established by the contract;
- design estimates;
- list of construction participants;
- data on the composition of the teams;
- production rates;
- availability of construction vehicles;
- routings for construction, installation and special work for the construction of this facility.

Table 3.12 statement of volumes of work

No.	Name of works	Scope of work		Cost thousand rubles	Executor
		Unit.	Quantity		
1	2	3	4	5	6

A. Compilation of the statement of work

Based on the design and estimate documentation, a list of works performed during the construction of the facility is left, their volume in physical units of measurement and cost is determined, and the contractor is also indicated.

The volume of construction work is calculated according to the working drawings and estimates. You can also use the statement of volumes compiled during the preparation of the estimate, but it cannot always be used, since it usually does not take into account the requirements of production planning when grouping activities.

The statement of volumes of work is compiled according to the form given in Table 3.12.

The list of works (column 2 of Table 3.12) is filled in the technological sequence of execution with a grouping of them by type of work. When grouping, it should be possible to combine, enlarge the work so that the schedule is convenient for use.

When enlarging the work, the following restrictions must be taken into account: it is impossible to combine the work performed by different performers, and in the complex of work performed by one performer, it is necessary to separate separately that part of the work that opens the front for the next performer.

Thus, the enlargement of the list of works depends on the sequence of processes and the distribution of work among performers. At the same time, the work of subcontracting organizations is planned in less detail — only their relationship with the work of the general contractor and with each other is reflected.

At the same time, when organizing the execution of works on bays (sections), it is necessary to separate the execution of works on each bay in the list of works.

The volume of work is determined in units adopted in production standards or ENiR (column 4, table. 3.12). The cost of work (column 5) is determined by estimates.

B. The choice of methods of work

The choice of work production methods largely depends on the specifics of the object, available resources and general conditions. The choice of method of production is largely influenced by the volume of construction and installation works.

Technological documentation containing construction and installation work methods is developed as part of technological maps and labor process maps. This takes into account the performance of work by progressive methods.

Technological maps determine the order of performance of work by complex or specialized teams. Cards of labor processes determine the order of the work of links or individual workers.

The head of the site (foreman) checks the technological maps and maps of labor processes in accordance with the specific conditions of work at the facility. New technological maps are developed for complex work and work performed by new methods that are not widely used. For the rest of the work, for which there are technological maps, schemes of work organization are developed with a description of the sequence and methods of work organization. For particularly difficult types of work to perform, instead of technological maps and workflow schemes, separate sections of the design documentation for types of work can be compiled.

Cards of labor processes are developed for certain types of processes, containing measures for the preparation of the process, technology and organization of the process, the composition of the performers, the list of objects and tools, the organization of jobs, as well as labor techniques and methods.

When developing a calendar plan, it is necessary to choose the most rational way of performing work on the basis of analysis of technological maps and labor process maps. The most rational way will be to ensure that the work is completed on time at the lowest ore cost and cost of work.

Methods for the production of works at the facility are determined in accordance with existing or newly developed technological maps.

When choosing a method of production, the presence of certain machines and mechanisms, as well as the possibility and expediency of renting or acquiring new ones, should be taken into account.

For the rhythmic execution of work at the facility, it is necessary to choose a set of machines that ensures the performance of basic and auxiliary operations in a mechanized way. Due to the fact that the processes and operations during the construction of objects are carried out in a certain sequence, it is necessary to balance the machines in terms of performance. In this case, the uniformity of technological processes is achieved, which creates the prerequisites for the maximum use of equipment and labor of workers.

C. Determination of the composition of the teams

When the methods of work are defined, you can set the number of workers needed to complete each job. The composition and number of teams depend on a number of factors, including the volume of work and the size of the front of work, the possibility of simultaneously performing different operations on a separate front of work. Consequently, the composition and size of the brigade are related to the nature and size of the front of work. The composition of the brigade and the number of brigades are limited by the smallest front of work. The smallest size of the front of work is determined by the shift output of the team. The transfer of the team from one front to another during the shift is unacceptable, as it is associated with unjustified loss of time.

Work fronts should be formed in such a way as to ensure normal conditions for the production of work, to exclude unnecessary transitions of workers and the movement of machines. The front should correspond to the scope of work for at least one shift of any brigade.

The composition of the brigades is calculated taking into account the complex of work assigned to the brigade, the experience and qualifications of workers, the combination of professions and achieved production standards.

The quantitative composition of the brigade is determined on the basis of the volume of work assigned to the brigade, and shift standards for the development of the brigade:

$$N_{br} = \frac{V}{B}, \tag{3.36}$$

where N_{br} — the total number of teams;

V — The volume of work performed by the team in physical units or in monetary terms;

B — shift production of the brigade in physical units or in monetary terms;

When performing mechanized work, the time required by the host machine to perform the intended complex of work is taken into account.

The complex of tasks assigned to the team includes all technologically related or dependent works, as well as those necessary for the smooth operation of the driving machine.

The professional and qualification composition of the teams for each type of work is determined on the basis of the EniR, labor process cards or production estimates. With a small amount of work that does not ensure full load of the brigade, provide for the combination of professions.

D. Determination of the technological sequence of work

The technological sequence of work depends on design decisions and is determined taking into account the need to provide a front for the implementation of subsequent work as soon as possible. The preparedness period for the front of work in some cases can be increased due to the need to observe technological breaks between two consecutive works, technological breaks are not constant and, if necessary, can be shortened by using more intensive methods (for example, methods for accelerating concrete hardening).

The technological sequence of a number of works is affected by the period of the year and the construction area. Therefore, when determining the technological sequence, it is necessary to take into account what kind of work is advisable to perform in the autumn-winter period. Work that is not interconnected should be carried out independently of each other. And interconnected — continuously. Work, technologically related, and within a common front are carried out combined. In this case, the rules of labor protection must be taken into account.

When determining the technological sequence of work, it is necessary to provide for the transition of work crews from one section to another without downtime to wait for the front of work. When developing organizational and technological solutions, it should additionally be taken into account: the design of load-bearing structures; material of constructions; number of storeys; length and configuration in plan; seasonal conditions for the production of work, the current level of technology and organization of work.

E. Establishing shift work

The shift of work depends on the construction machines used and the availability of workers.

When using the main machines (mounting cranes, etc.), the number of shifts is at least 2, work without the use of machines, as a rule, should be carried out in one shift.

The shift of work performed manually using a mechanized tool depends on the available front of work and the availability of working personnel. As a rule, with a sufficient front, it is advisable to plan these works only in the first shift, in which the working conditions improve, the possibility of a more precise organization and management of work is increased, more precise organization and management of work, and higher productivity are provided. In addition, some work, such as finishing, is preferable to perform on a day shift. The production of certain types of work in the second shift, especially in the autumn-winter period, requires additional measures, such as lighting of workplaces, walkways, additional safety measures, etc. However, the implementation of these measures will not completely eliminate the inconvenience of the second shift. Manual work is assigned to the second shift in rare cases when the front of work is sharply limited and the team is forced to split up for shift work.

F. Determination of the duration of work.

The duration of the work is calculated based on data on the work teams and the amount of work.

The duration of the work is determined by dividing the volume of work in physical units of measurement by the work achieved in teams in physical terms:

$$T = \frac{V}{B_{br} * n}, \tag{3.37}$$

where T is the duration of the work;

V — the volume of work in physical units or in monetary terms;

B_{br} — shift production brigade in kind or in money terms; n is the number of shifts per day.

The duration of mechanized work is determined based on the performance of the machine:

$$T_{mech} = \frac{V}{P_{mach} * k * n} \tag{3.38}$$

where T_{mech} — the duration of the mechanized work;

V — the volume of work performed by a mechanized method in physical units or in monetary terms;

P_{mach} — the productivity of one machine per shift in physical terms or in monetary terms; k is the number of cars; n is the number of shifts of machines in knocking.

The duration of work depends on the size of the front of work, the availability of workers and the technology of work.

3.8.3 Development of a schedule of work on the facility

When all the works included in the object's schedule are defined, their duration is calculated, and the sequence of work is determined, a schedule can be drawn up.

The schedule is the basis of production and technological documentation, i.e. documentation developed during the construction of the facility. When developing a calendar plan, work is coordinated in time and space, and the volume of supply and expenditure of resources is also determined. To compile a schedule, the standard form is used.

The schedule of work on the object consists of two parts: left — estimated, right — graphic.

The left part is filled in the following sequence. The name, amount and cost of work (gr. 2-5) are taken from the statement of volumes of work. In this case, the accepted method of organization of construction (in-line, sequential, parallel) and the technological sequence of work are taken into account. The required number of construction vehicles, work crews and the number of shifts per day are determined by the above algorithm.

The duration of work (column 12 of Table 3.13) is determined by the formulas (3.37, 3.38).

The right part of the schedule is a schedule of work, which clearly reflects the progress of work in time, the sequence and coordination of work among themselves.

The scheduling should begin with the leading work or process, on which the overall duration of the construction of the facility depends to a decisive extent.

Comparing with a given construction duration, it is possible, if necessary, to reduce the duration of the lead process, increasing the shift and the number of mechanisms in mechanized work or the number of performers in manual jobs. Depending on the period for which the schedule is designed, and the complexity of the object, there may be several leading processes.

The terms of the remaining processes are tied to the lead. All non-ignorant processes can be divided into two groups: 1) performed in-line (as a rule, in equal or multiple rhythm with the leading stream) or 2) performed outside the stream.

The duration of the processes carried out off-stream is assigned within the limits of the technologically determined periods of work, taking into account the general terms for the construction of the facility.

Obtained on the basis of the schedule of works, the duration of the construction of the object is compared with the terms established in the contract. If the received duration exceeds the terms established by the contract, then it is necessary to change the parameters of the left side of the calendar plan.

Therefore, when developing a schedule and constructing a schedule of work (table 3.8) — such parameters as the number of machines (column 8), the number of workers (column 9), shift (column 12) and the duration of work (column 13) can alternately act as an argument or functions depending on the accepted source data and assumptions.

A fragment of the schedule of work on the facility is shown in Fig. 3.22.

3.8.4 Resource Demand Plotting

Based on the schedule, resource utilization graphs are plotted in the form of diagrams.

Resource plots clearly show the level of need, expense, availability of each type of resources (workforce, construction machinery, materials and cash). On the basis of the diagrams of resources, their lack in one or another period of time is revealed, and also the uniformity of resource consumption is determined.

Resource schedules are built on the basis of a calendar plan in the coordinate axes, where the amount of resources is plotted on the vertical axis, and the flow (receipt) time on the horizontal axis.

Resource graphs can be differential and integral. Differential graphs reflect resource requirements over time intervals. The area of the plot in this case cor-

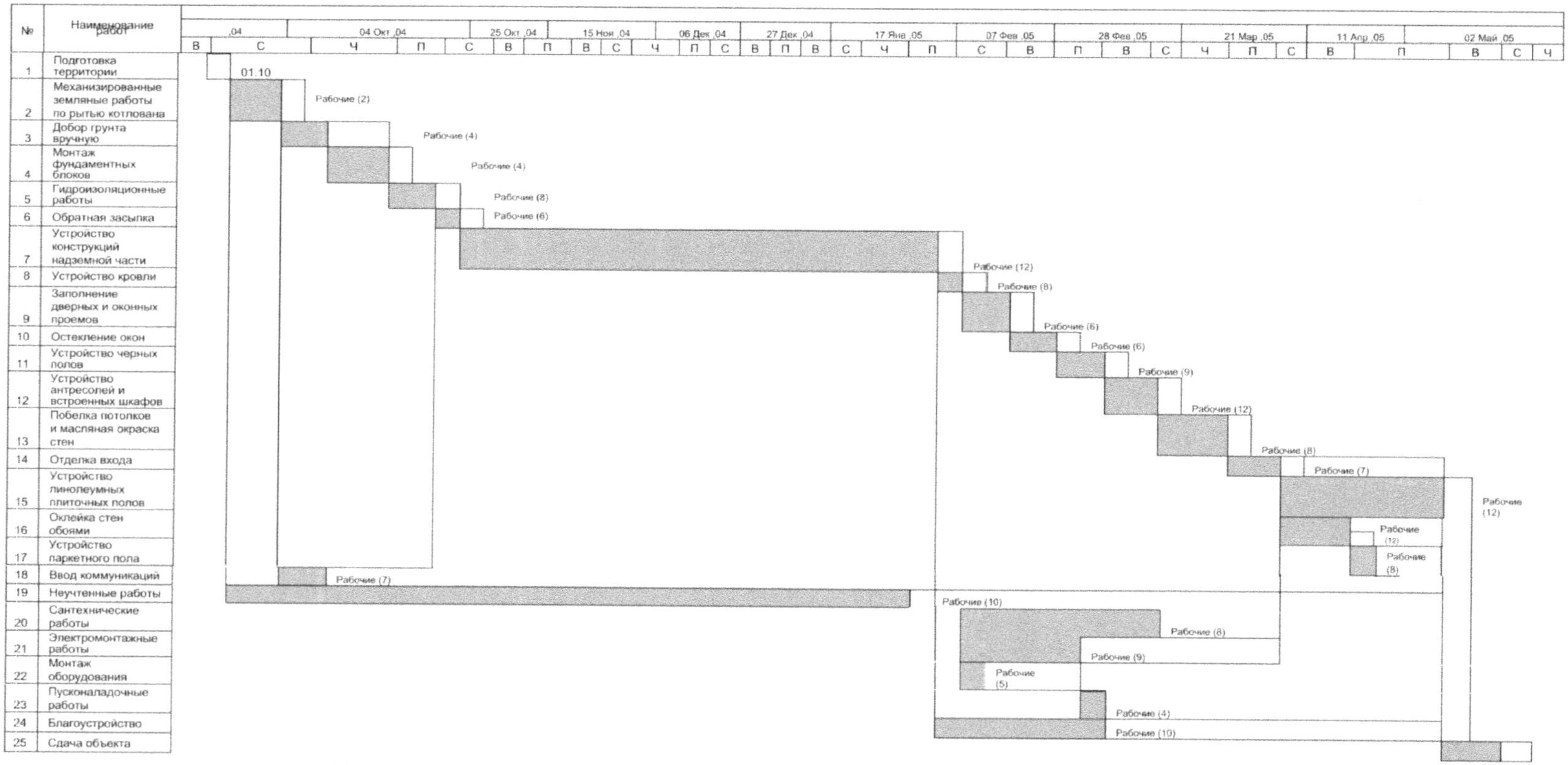

Figure 3.22: A schedule of work on the facility (Gantt line chart)

Table 3.13. A schedule of work on the facility

No	Name of works	scope of work		Price, mln. rubles	Required machines			need for workforce			Number of shifts	Duration, days	Shedule, work days				
		units	quan-tity		Kind of mach.	perfor-mance	quan-tity	number of workers per shift	team composition	Team performance per work shift			1	2	3	4	5
1	2	3	4	5	6	7	8	9	10	11	12	13	14	15	16	17	18

responds to the total volume of this type of resources. Integrated (cumulative) graphs show the total demand resource availability from the beginning of the planning period. The tangent of the angle between the integrated line and the horizontal axis is determined by the intensity of resource consumption.

The need for workers, machines and materials is determined on the basis of differential graphs.

Based on the schedule for the need for construction vehicles, a schedule of construction vehicles for the facility can be built.

The movement schedule of the main machines makes it possible to distribute in time the use of machines at the construction site in such a way that the construction can be carried out in accordance with the schedule.

After plotting the distribution of resources, it is necessary to check the uniformity of consumption of basic resources, primarily labor. The uniform need for workers by profession is ensured by the consistent and uninterrupted transition of work crews from one job site to another in accordance with the principles of stream construction. Alignment of the need for workforce for the facility as a whole is achieved by reallocating the start and end dates of the work in the calendar plan. This alignment must be performed only within the rational technological sequence of work. The total duration of the construction should not exceed that established in the contract.

3.9 Calendar-network schedule of the construction project

The calendar and network schedule of the construction project (Schedule) is a universal tool for operational planning, organization of work, monitoring and forecasting the timing of completion of the project. The schedule can be used (in the presence of the corresponding budget documentation and other initial data) as a tool for developing a plan of direct costs of the project, which is achieved by assigning a schedule of resources (work personnel, machines and mechanisms, materials and equipment) and their costs.

A. Purpose, types and structure of schedules, general requirements for schedules

A schedule is a collection of all project schedules of varying degrees of detail that are interconnected through work codes and dependencies.

The schedule should allow:

- describe the scope of the project in a structured and detailed manner:
- fix the sequence of work;

- get reasonable start and finish dates for the work, taking into account their technological relationships, the influence of external factors, the availability of resources, the mode of work;
- receive reasonable information about the plan and the current fact of spending resources, as well as the plan and current fact of direct costs during the implementation of the project;
- use the parameters of the schedule to organize the operational weekly and monthly and daily planning, evaluate the impact on the construction and commissioning work of the timing of the working documentation for the selection of suppliers / contractors, conclusion of contracts, delivery of equipment and materials;
- analyze the progress of work at different levels of management, taking into account actual and forecast deviations.

The schedule is compiled to monitor the progress of the following main work packages:

- design and development work, development of design and working documentation (if this type of activity is included in the area of responsibility of the Company);
- obtaining approvals and permits;
- receipt and analysis of PD / WD sets;
- planning the need for supplies of materials and equipment;
- supply of equipment and materials;
- conducting FFP and competitive procedures, concluding contracts with subcontractors, suppliers and other counterparties;
- mobilization and other organizational activities;
- construction and installation works;
- commissioning;
- acceptance and transfer of work performed;
- organizational work on the commissioning of the facility;
- other works and activities, the control of which is necessary due to the individual characteristics of ongoing projects.

B. General Schedule Requirements:

1. For development of schedules, Oracle Primavera EPPM software version no lower than 7.0 should be used, the recommended version is 8.2.

2. When developing schedules, it is necessary to be guided by the following basic rules (principles):
   - The hierarchical structure of work (WBS) is the basis for drawing up a calendar-network schedule for project implementation and monitoring the progress of work on the project.
   - When developing a schedule, it is necessary to use unified (for this particular project) structured guides, including the coding structure, resource guides, calendars;
   - The schedule should contain key events (milestones) of the project, including milestones of the beginning and end of the project;
   - The schedule should be developed using the critical path method.
   - It is unacceptable to use time limits for the performance of work as a tool to reduce the time reserve, because they contradict the purpose of the critical path method. Time limits are acceptable only if they reflect an agreed or contracted key event or it is not possible to display the logic of the work performed by technological dependencies.
   - Each work schedule must have a predecessor (except for the milestone of the start of the project) and a follower (except for the milestone of the completion of the project); It is recommended to avoid delays between jobs with different calendars, due to different ways of calculating the schedule — based on the calendar of the predecessor or follower;
   - When developing a schedule, it is necessary to use the principle of "inheritance", ie ensure that the WBS of the project is repeated from level to level with constant detail;
   - The cost of work stipulated by the schedule is indicated without VAT;
   - For any work of value, a cost item must be defined.
   - The network schedule should allow you to evaluate the status of the work on the project, analyze deviations and automatically prepare project reports.
3. The schedule is a tool for analyzing relevant project information. Therefore, factual information on the implementation of the project should be regularly entered into the schedule. All planned parameters of the schedule (in particular, the volume of work, duration of work, key milestones, costs) should be updated.
4. Participation in making changes to the calendar-network schedule of the project is the responsibility of all employees of the Directorate. Significant deviations from the plan should be drawn up in accordance with the

regulation "Procedure for managing changes in the implementation of the construction project". The deviation is considered significant, which affects the date of the key event (milestone) of the project.

5. The completion date of the project is the main guideline and determines the timing of commissioning, construction, procurement and design. The deadlines for the implementation of individual stages, key events in the Schedule must correspond to the deadlines established in the Agreement.
6. The schedule should describe in a structured way the full scope of work under the Agreement, and contain in the form of external dependencies events that are the responsibility of other project participants that have a direct impact on the timing of the work by the Contractor.
7. The schedule is developed on the basis of the information available at the time of development, design, working documentation (to the extent available at the time of development), as well as on the basis of experience in implementing similar projects (for the amount of work for which there was no documentation at the time of development of the schedule). In the absence of the necessary initial data, the schedule is developed in a large-scale and is further systematically (at least once a month) updated by the "incident wave" method with an increase in the level of detail so that:
   - explicitly record the fact of work;
   - build a more detailed (than earlier) schedule for the horizon for at least the next 3 months of operation.

C. General information about the structure of the decomposition of the work of the network calendar (Work Breakdown Structure — WBS)

Each work package of the network calendar should contain more detailed work packages, individual work, or both. Each work package should be characterized by an objective and measurable result, as well as responsible for achieving this result (for example, by a subcontracting organization).

WBS should define the entire scope of the project as a hierarchical structure of work that can be accounted for and measured. WBS provides control over schedule implementation, resource utilization and disbursement, as the cost of both resources and work is consolidated in accordance with WBS.

Responsible persons should be assigned to the WBS levels and, in accordance with the level of responsibility, the access rights of system users to the project and its individual parts are distributed.

The basic principle of the formation of WBS is the structure of the decomposition of work should describe 100% of the content of the project. The approach to building WBS should be universal for all projects.

For specific projects, WBS may differ from the typical WBS (to take into account the individual characteristics of the project). So, if the project does not provide for the implementation of one or more project disciplines, then these WBS levels are deleted or hidden by display settings. If, within the framework of one project, for example, more than one technological installation is built (or there are several subprojects), then the second level (the level next to the "Project" level) will be determined by the name of these installations (subprojects).

D. General information about resource planning and work management on the "critical path".

Planning for attracting and loading resources is the distribution of the estimated number of working hours for a certain amount of work, taking into account the deadline for this amount of work indicated in the Schedule.

The purpose of resource planning is to forecast the necessary labor costs, as well as to develop a plan for attracting and demobilizing personnel in accordance with all types of work and with the necessary results included in the Schedule. A plan for attracting and loading resources is developed for each of the disciplines of the project (in accordance with WBS) and is the basis for assessing performance indicators throughout the project.

The inclusion of quantitative indicators of resources (equipment, materials, machines and mechanisms, personnel) in the Schedule allows for alignment of resources — to optimize their use throughout the project. The alignment of resources should include an increase or decrease in the number of personnel (equipment) to perform specific work while maximizing the use of available resources. Resource equalization techniques are embedded in software-implemented algorithms that are executed when appropriate restrictions are imposed on resources. These tools, already included in Primavera software, help to create a real project schedule taking into account resource needs, on the one hand, and with virtually limited access to resources, on the other hand.

Partial transfer of resources from works that are not included in the critical path to the works of the critical path will reduce the duration of the critical path and thereby ensure the most likely project to be completed on time and without increasing resources.

The duration of the critical path determines the shortest total duration of work on the project as a whole. The duration of the entire project can be reduced by reducing the duration of work lying on a critical path. Accordingly, any delay in completing the tasks of the critical path will entail an increase in the duration of the project. The critical path concept provides the manager with a focus on critical work. However, the main advantage of the critical path method is the ability to manipulate the timing of tasks that do not lie on the critical path.

To reduce the duration of the critical path works:

- use the possibility of applying the scheme of irregular working hours, going to work on weekends or in several shifts.
- increase the productivity of resources by changing the technology of work and their mechanization.

When developing the Schedule, the balance of estimated resources (costs, hours, unit prices) assigned to the work of the Schedule should be observed, taking into account the agreed base cost of the project. As changes are approved in the cost management system, they must be made to the Schedule resource plan.

E. Responsible for the development of the Schedule and its users

Responsibility for the development, content, relevance of the Schedule and its compliance with these requirements lies with the Project Director (if one is appointed) and the Head of the project planning and control function of the Business Unit. The functional divisions of the Company (project documentation management, resource supply, cost estimation and estimated rationing, construction management, construction and construction management quality control) should provide the Project Director with the information necessary for developing the schedule.

The development of the schedule is carried out directly by the PCB specialist, who is subordinate to the Project Director. The PCB specialist brings the calendar-network schedule to the employees of the Directorate, monitors its implementation, analyzes the progress of work and reports on the progress of work to the employees of the Directorate. The results of the planning are consistent with all project managers of the project disciplines of the Directorate, as well as with the Project Curator.

Main users of Graphics (in general):

- Director for evaluation and control of projects;
- Director for the implementation of projects of business units of the Company;
- Director for planning and monitoring the implementation of projects of the Company's business units;
- heads of the units of calendar and network planning of the business units of the Company;
- project directors (project directors);

- specialists in calendar and network planning of Project Directorates.

F. Requirements for the organization of the development of a calendar-network schedule

For the initial preparation of the calendar-network schedule, it is necessary to regularly hold meetings with the participation of managers of all project disciplines. The organization of these meetings is the responsibility of the Project Director.

The agendas of the meetings (posed issues) for planning are:

- The purpose of the project, concept, objectives, main results.
- The scope of the project and the basis for constructing the schedule — a general summary of the content;
- Issues of forming a land plot and registration of rights to a land plot for construction (if relevant);
- Conducting design and research, development of design and working documentation (in conjunction with subobjects);
- Contracting of works and services in accordance with the standards of the Company: preliminary competitive selection, tender commission, conclusion of contracts with subcontractors, suppliers;
- Organizational work necessary for the timely execution of production work (transfer of source data, obtaining permits, etc.);
- Ordering, manufacturing, supplying and installing equipment (in relation to subobjects), materials;
- Schedules of mobilization and demobilization of labor, machines and mechanisms;
- WBS (Hierarchical Structure of Jobs);
- OBS (Organizational Structure);
- Design numbering systems, including the numbering of drawings, equipment and instructions;
- The structure of the assessment of project (direct) costs and the level of detail;
- The structure of the calendar and network schedule of the project and its level of detail;
- The structure of the coding of the project for control purposes;
- Contract strategy, Contract package / boundaries of responsibility and principles for its separation;

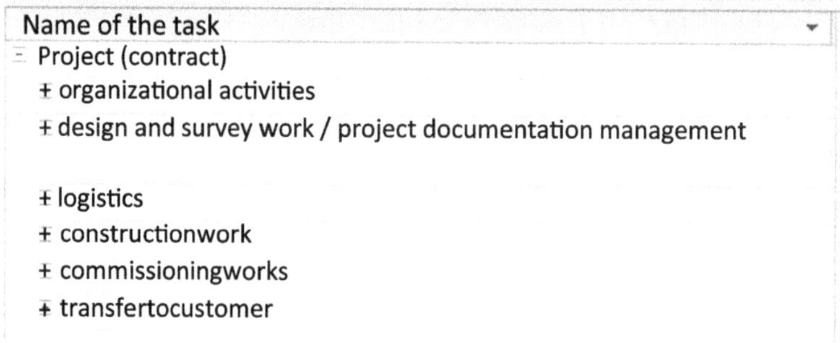

Figure 3.23: Level 1 Graphics Template

- Risk identification, quantification and mitigation strategy;
- Structure, principles and requirements for project reporting.

During the implementation of the project, it is necessary to conduct separate workshops within each project discipline. If necessary, specialists from related disciplines should be invited to workshops to discuss interdisciplinary communications and the timing of tasks. Procurement / contract specialists must be ready to attend all meetings, and construction management specialists must be present at all meetings without fail. Decisions made following the results of each meeting are reflected in the Schedule before the next meeting.

G. Requirements for detailing the information contained in the calendar network schedule

In the system of calendar and network planning, schedules of different levels should be applied, differing in the goals of their creation, in the stage of the project at which they are created and applied, in the level of detail of information, solved production tasks, and in the level of control and management. To manage the project at all stages of the project, a four-level model of the project's calendar and network schedules should be universally used, including:

The chart of the 1st level of detail describes the duration of the main stages of the project without indicating the relationship between them. Due to its low information content, the Schedule of the 1st level of detail can be used in the development of various kinds of presentations, with the exception of those whose purpose is to demonstrate the status of the project. The Graphic Template of the 1st level of detail, as an example, is presented in Figure 3.23.

The 2nd level schedule is intended for planning and monitoring the timing of achievement of key events (milestones) of the project, coordination of the project and implementation of organizational measures, as well as for reflecting contractual activities within the project. The 2nd level schedule allows at the

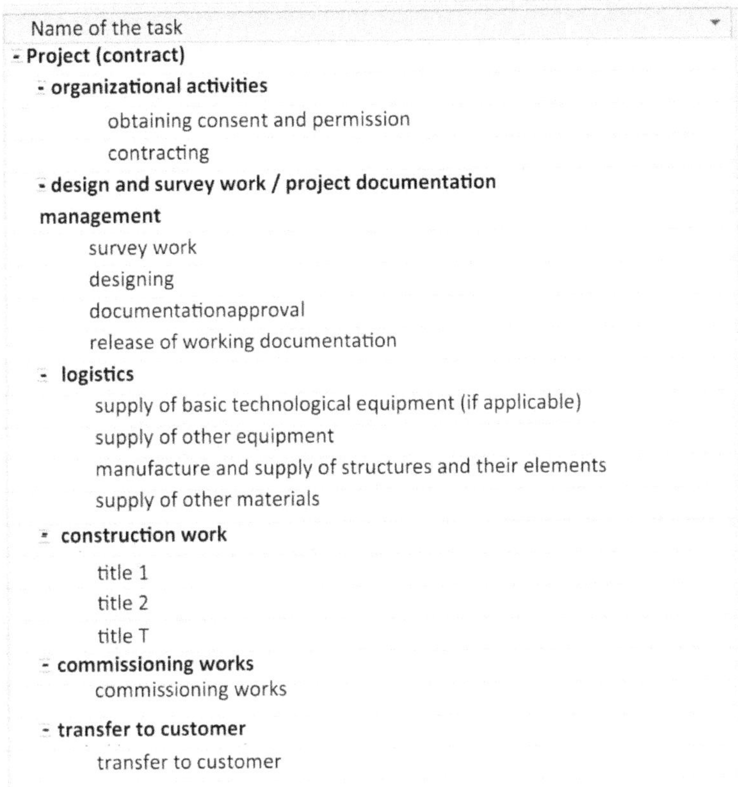

Figure 3.24: Level 2 Graphics Template

initial stage of the project to approximately describe the types of work on the project based on the information available at the time of the development of the Schedule. As more accurate and detailed information becomes available, each work in Level 2 Graphics should be detailed in Level 3 Graphics. The 2nd level schedule is formed at the time of signing the Agreement with the Customer and, as a rule, is an appendix to this Agreement. The source of information for determining the cost of work reflected in the Schedule of the 2nd level (for budgeting of direct costs) is the developed summary estimated calculations or, in their absence, summary estimated calculations for similar facilities. The Graphic Template of the 2nd level of detail, as an example, is presented in Figure 3.24.

The Level 3 Schedule is a detail of the Level 2 Schedule and is a calendar-network schedule that describes for each title list object not only the types of work on the project, but also the complex processes that correspond to the sets of working drawings, individual types of equipment / materials supplied, groups of organizational events, etc. The schedule for the 3rd level of detail should also reflect the distribution of complex processes by subcontracting organizations (that is, reflect "contracted" and "non-contracted" types of work). The source of information for determining the cost of work reflected

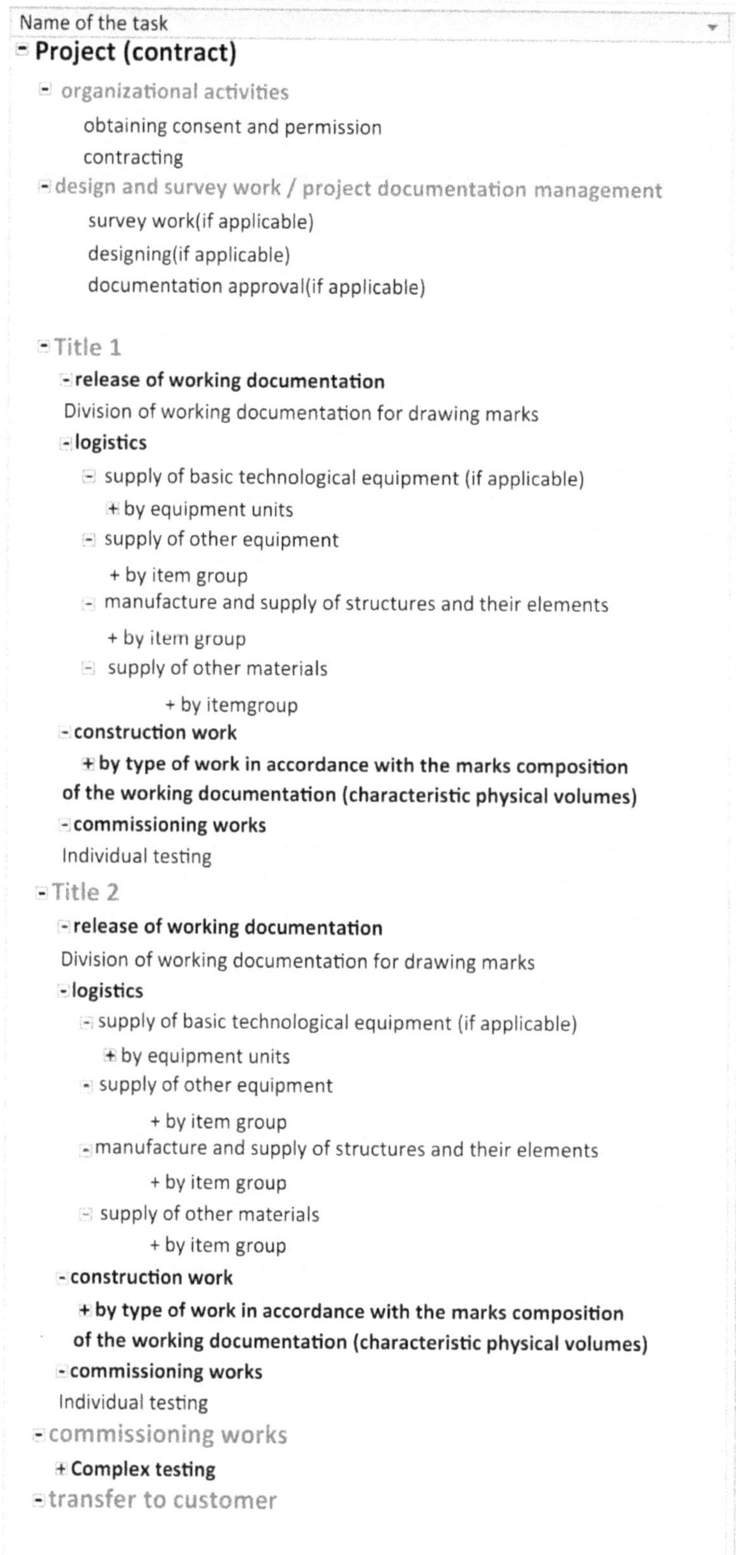

Figure 3.25: Level 3 Graphics Template

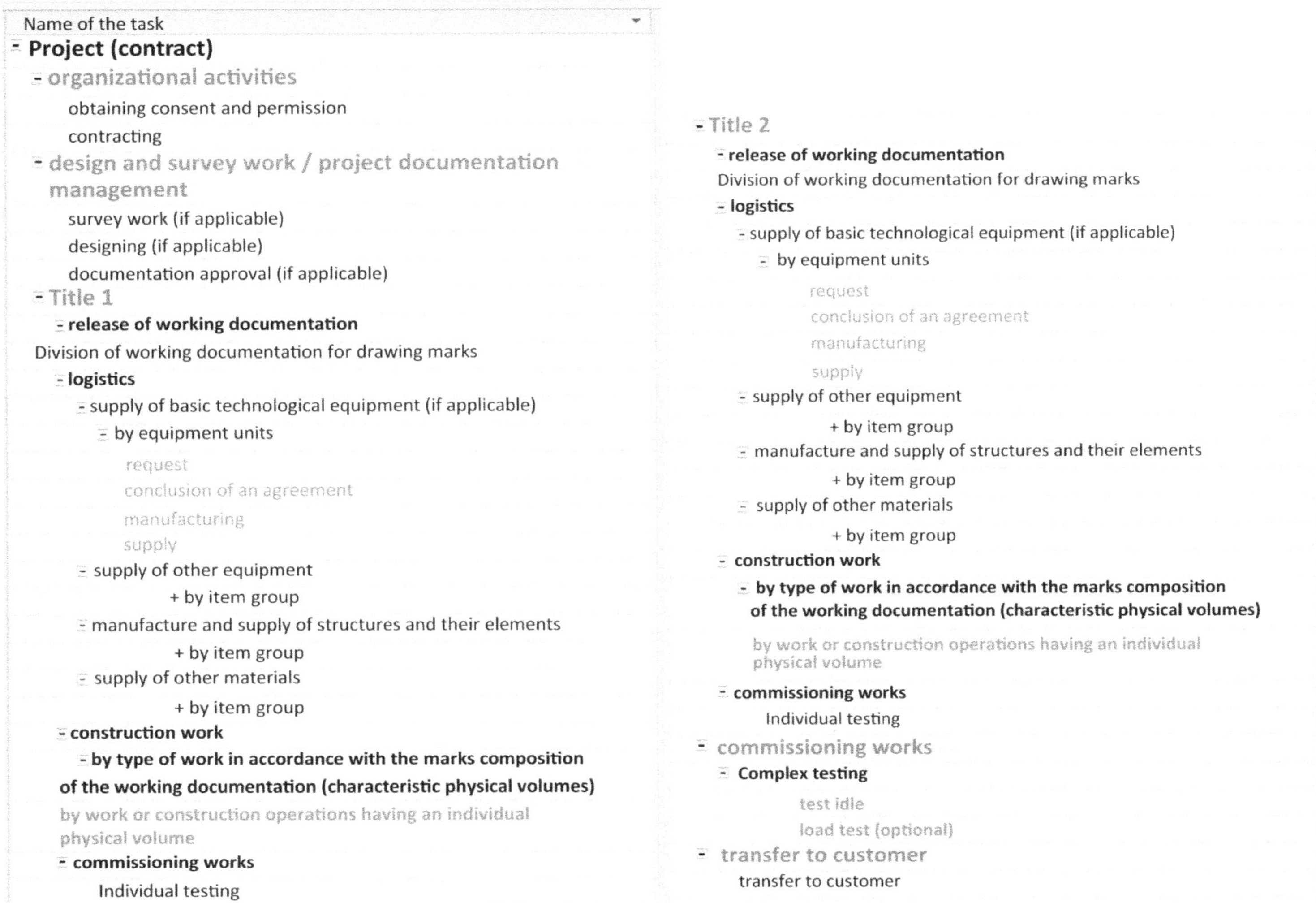

Figure 3.26: Level 4 Graphics Template (differences from graph 3 are highlighted in red)

in the Schedule of the 3rd level (for budgeting direct costs) is the developed object estimates (or, in their absence, object estimates of analogous objects), as well as information on the concluded subcontracting and supply of materials and equipment. The graphic template of the 3rd level of detail, as an example, is shown in Figure 3.25.

The 4th level chart is a detail of the 3rd level chart and is a calendar-network chart describing for each object of the title list not only the types of work on the project and complex processes, but also work operations that have individual physical volumes that can be individually plan and control implementation. The schedule for the 4th level of detail should also reflect the distribution of work operations by subcontracting organizations (that is, reflect "contracted" and "non-contracted" types of work). The source of information for determining the cost of work reflected in the Level 4 Schedule (for budgeting direct costs) is the developed local estimates (or, in their absence, local estimates of analogous objects), as well as information about the concluded subcontracting and supply of materials and equipment. The Graphic Template of the 4th level of detail, as an example, is shown in Figure 3.26.

As a tool for operational planning and control of work, it is necessary to use a daily-monthly schedule (if necessary, a Weekly monthly schedule), which is formed by "unloading" data from a level 4 schedule in a given format. The daily-monthly (weekly-monthly) schedule should be an official document prescribing to the subcontracting organization the composition and scope of work that it should perform in the planning month in the physical volumes of work in relation to titles, objects, systems, grips, zones, axes, etc. P. On the basis of the daily-monthly (weekly-monthly) schedule, the subcontracting organization draws up its own planned tasks issued to the direct manufacturers of work (plots, teams) for a day, a week, a month.

To control deviations from the set deadlines, a network-planning model should be applied that includes two types of schedules: a basic plan, the key events of which must always comply with the terms of the general contract;

current (operational) schedule, reflecting the real situation in the project, reliable status and forecast of the implementation of work within the project. The basic plan, once developed at the start of the project, should be adjusted only if the contractual conditions with the Customer are amended. The current project schedule should be updated regularly, at least once a week.

H. Requirements for working with basic (target) schedules

To maintain agreed and / or approved versions of project schedules of various levels for the purpose of subsequent analysis of the "plan / fact", the standard mechanism of target plans available in Oracle Primavera software is used:

- target plans should be created for all levels of project schedules;
- coding of target plans similar to the schedules for which they are created;

The process of planning and control of work, using the network calendar schedules of the project, cannot be determined solely by the scope of decisions made on the project and contracts for the performance of any work on the project. Those. the creation of targeted plans based on the decisions taken on the project and contracts is a necessary minimum for fulfilling the functions of planning and control.

In turn, the management decisions of the project team, as well as decisions of the management of the Company, may contradict the terms dictated by the contractual relationship, and the creation of new target schedules, constrained not only by the scope of contracts, but also by the framework of management decisions.

During the course of the project, the composition of some of the design data may change. For example, a job has been added or removed, resource assignments have changed. However, a comparison of the current project with the initial target plan will not allow to effectively evaluate its implementation. In this case, you need to update the target plan.

I. Requirements for the schedule and network schedule in order to generate reports on the project

The schedule and network schedule should allow monitoring and control of the project to provide interested parties (Leaders, Curators, Project Director, etc.) with reliable and up-to-date information on the actual state of the project — to make the necessary management decisions.

Project monitoring and control processes should be carried out at all levels of project management. Accordingly, an integrated analysis of project performance indicators is used on the schedules of the 1st and 2nd levels, and a detailed analysis on the schedules of the 3rd and 4th levels.

Reporting is divided into daily, weekly and monthly.

K. Reporting requirements

Daily reporting

Daily reporting is used only at the "Implementation" stage for the discipline "Construction and Installation Work" and "NDP" (in the most critical cases, the release of taxiway and MTO may be included). The main reporting document is the daily-monthly schedule (hereinafter referred to as SMG). The report is generated from the current project implementation schedule.

Weekly Reporting

The following reports should be included in the weekly reporting package:

- An updated project implementation schedule, formed by Primavera software. The level of detail of the schedule — depending on the stage of the project in accordance with the requirements of this STP.
- detailed and summary reports on progress — on the implementation of physical volumes and the number of staff.

Monthly reporting

Monthly reports are presented in the form of a progress report on the project in Power Point format. The content and methodology for generating the monthly report are given in the document "Procedure for preparing reports on the progress of the project." The source of information for the preparation of the monthly report (status of achievement of the project milestones, information on the progress of the project, its components and individual works) is unloaded from Primavera software.

L. Requirements for maintaining the knowledge base of completed projects After the completion of the project, the specialist in network planning conducts the procedure for maintaining the accumulated experience of the project in the knowledge base, in which the following should be stored:

- templates of calendar and network diagrams from the 1st to 4th levels;
- standards for production and time for work;
- the amount of resources assigned to work;
- cost of work;

After the completion of the project, the specialist in network planning should analyze the execution of the schedule in order to identify:

- typical (typical) structures of decomposition of works in the schedule;
- deviations from the base (target) schedule in terms of duration — preparation and adoption of a decision on changing the internal corporate standard for the performance of work;
- the ability to use packages and chains of work (with arranged sequences, duration, assigned resources) as Templates — for further use in the development of schedules on other projects.

The templates developed as a result of the analysis of the schedule of the completed project, after their approval, are saved in the Primavera system for future use.

M. Requirements for setting up Oracle Primavera software and data dictionaries.

Setting up the Primavera application and data dictionaries should be done at the same time before starting the development of the project schedule. Primavera application setup requirements consist of:

- Requirements for configuring the parameters of the application itself
- Currency setting requirements
- Requirements for setting up a project structure (Enterprise Project Structure — EPS)
- Requirements for setting up a liability structure (Organization Breakdown Structure — OBS)
- Requirements for setting up the resource structure
- Requirements for setting up a directory of typical units
- Requirements for setting up the structure of cost items
- Requirements for customizing custom fields
- Calendaring requirements
- Requirements for setting global user access profiles
- Requirements for setting up design user access profiles
- Requirements for project settings
- Requirements for user settings
- Requirements for schedule calculation settings

Requirements for coding projects, works and resources

Requirements for coding projects, works and resources consist of requirements:

- to the structure of project codes;
- to the structure of global work codes;
- to global work codes "Type of work (progress)";
- to the global work codes "Type of work (physics)";
- to the structure of design work codes;
- to the structure of resource codes;
- to build a WBS project.

Questions for self-control:

1. What is the essence of the flow organization of construction production?
2. What are the basic principles of designing threads?
3. Give a classification of construction flows.
4. What are the parameters of construction flows?
5. What are the main patterns and technological linkage of construction flows?
6. Give an example of calculating the parameters of the rhythmic flow.
7. Give an example of calculating the parameters of different rhythmic flows.
8. What is the maximum approximation or critical position of the work of two adjacent teams on the sequence diagram?
9. Give an example of calculating flow parameters using matrices.
10. What is a network diagram?
11. Give the elements of the network diagram.
12. State the rules for building network diagrams.
13. Specify the time parameters of the network and the formula for their calculation.
14. The procedure for adjusting the network schedule in accordance with the specified restrictions.
15. What is the "critical path" of ICP?

Questions for discussion:

1. Are the concepts "network model" and "network diagram" the same?
2. What does the parameter "event potential" mean on the network diagram?
3. Consider during the discussion and analyze the advantages and disadvantages of network models using tabular and sectoral methods in the context of complex investment and construction projects?
4. In what cases are changes in the plot of resources (workers, construction machines, materials and cash resources) possible on the calendar schedule for the construction of complex facilities?

Questions and tasks for self-solving problems

Task 1

Given the dependences of the start of some work on the full or partial completion of others, and provided that work A and B begin at the same time, build a fragment of the network diagram with a minimum number of fictitious links and encode it.

Ending	Start	Ending	Start
-	A	B, G (Part)	D
-	B	B, G (part)	E
A, B (part)	IN	B, G	F
A, B (part)	G	D, E, F	3

Task 2

Using the given job codes (ij) and their duration t, construct a fragment of the network diagram, avoiding intersections, and calculate it using the fraction method with determining the total and partial time reserves (R/r), finding the critical and subcritical paths. Initial data.

ij	t	ij	t	ij	t	ij	t
1-2	1	2-6	6	5-7	2	7-9	3
1-3	3	3-5	5	5-8	3	8-10	8
2-3	4	4-5	0	5-9	2	9-10	9
2-4	2	4-7	8	6-7	5		

Task 3.

Build a network diagram for the codes of work and their duration in terms of a unit of time t_i and calculate it in a tabular manner. Critical work highlight on the graph and in the table. Initial data.

Task 4.

Based on the given work codes and their duration t, build a network diagram, calculate it in a sector-wide way, and tie it to the calendar according to the early beginnings by constructing a timeline with a start date of 10 / VI. Enter all dates in the lower sector of the network diagram.

Initial data.

ij	t	ij	t	ij	t	ij	t
1-2	5	2-4	0	5-6	3	6-8	2
1-3	2	3-4	2	5-7	2	7-8	1
1-4	4	4-5	6	6-7	4		

ij	t	ij	t	ij	t	ij	t
1-2	6	2-3	0	5-8	5	7-11	6
1-3	7	2-4	5	6-9	0	8-9	0
1-6	8	3-5	8	6-11	9	8-10	4
1-7	10	4-9	4	7-9	0	9-10	7
						10-11	3

Task 5.

Based on the given codes of work and from the duration, construct two network diagrams: 1 — scale-free with the calculation of all its parameters by the potential method, 2 — on a time scale from the earliest beginnings with the allocation of private time reserves on it.

Initial data.

ij	t	ij	t	ij	t	ij	t
0-1	1	1-4	8	3-4	0	5-6	6
0-2	10	2-3	4	3-5	8		
1-2	2	2-4	8	4-5	5		
1-3	7	2-6	10	4-6	2		

Task 6.

For 9 processes of a certain duration, build and calculate a combined generalized network model under the following communication conditions: 1) process 2 begins after the end of process 1; 2) process 3 begins after 50% of process 5 is completed, and ends 28% after it; 3) process 4 begins after the end of process 3; 4) process 5 begins after 75% of the implementation of process 4, and ends 25% later; 5) process 6 begins 1 day after the end of process 5; 6) process 7 depends on process 5, but begins immediately after its completion; 7) process 8 depends on process 6 and begins after its completion; 8) process 9 depends on processes 7 and 7, but can only begin 1 day after the end of process 7.

The duration of the work is: $t_1 = 8$, $t_2 = 10$, $t_3 = 7$, $t_4 = 12$, $t_5 = 4$, $t_6 = 2$, $t_7 = 4$, $t_8 = 1$, $t_9 = 2$.

Task 7.

Build and calculate a network diagram using the potential method, analyze the progress of work after taking information on the 25th day after the start of construction with the following data: work 1-2, 1-3, 2-4 completed; 7 days left before the end of work 1-5; up to 4-5 -5; up to 4-6 -6 (work started); up to 2-6-10; up to 3-7 -12; up to 3-8 -14 (time estimate has changed from 14 to 17 days). Create a table of analysis of the progress of work with the identification of reserves and lags.

Initial data.

The code	t ij	The code	t ij	The code	t ij
1-2	8	3-7	14	6-7	8
1-3	16	3-8	14	6-9	12
1-5	18	4-5	9	7-9	10
2-4	10	4-6	6	8-9	7
2-6	20	5-9	6		

Task 8.

Determine the size of the reserve by the total area and capital investments at the beginning of the planned year for the construction of three groups of residential buildings to be put into operation during the planned year with the distribution by quarters (in% of the total area of all houses of each group): I - 22; II - 26; III - 28; IV - 24 (table). Build a schedule.

Property Description				Number of houses introduced during a year	Duration construction standards, months
types of houses	number of floors	common area one house, thousand m^2	estimated cost, million rubles		
Large panel	16	12.5	2.25	4	15
	9	9	1.53	12	10
Brick	9	7.5	1.35	8	12

Chapter 4

PRICING AND ESTIMATE IN CONSTRUCTION. CONTRACT STRATEGIES

4.1 Theoretical Foundations of Market Pricing

Pricing is one of the most important economic mechanisms of a market economy and to a large extent determines the effectiveness of any economic activity, including investment.

The basis of market pricing is the interaction of the laws of *supply and demand.*

Demand in the product market is the aggregate social needs for a particular product, provided by the purchasing power of consumers. Demand is a rather dynamic characteristic of the market. Demand in a particular product market depends on a number of factors, the main of which are:

- level of socio-economic development of the country, region;
- income level of potential consumers;
- climatic conditions, season;
- national traditions and customs, religious principles;
- inflationary expectations of consumers;
- public opinion, fashion;
- possibilities of alternative consumption, availability of substitute goods;
- government policy, regulatory mechanisms (support or containment) of demand, etc.

An offer on the product market is the total amount of goods offered by sellers on the market for sale. The offer is also not a permanent characteristic of the product market, it depends on many factors, including:

- the pace of scientific and technological progress;
- the level of social and individual production costs;
- development of a competitive environment, the presence of entry and exit barriers in a particular product market;
- economic conditions of entrepreneurial activity (tax legislation, credit and financial system, risks);
- national traditions and customs, religious principles;
- seasonality, fashion;
- state policy, regulatory mechanisms (support or containment) of the proposal, etc.

But the main factor determining the level of supply and demand in a particular product market is the price of the product. It is this dependence of supply and demand on price that is described by the laws of supply and demand. The mechanism of this interaction is described by Alfred Marshall[1] in his *theory of equilibrium price.*

The law of demand establishes a relationship between the price of a product and the demand for this product (sales): the lower the price of the product, the higher the demand for the product, since the low price makes the product more accessible and attractive to consumers[2].

The law of supply establishes the relationship between offer and price: the higher the price, the greater the offer on the market, since the high price allows manufacturers to get a higher rate of return, and capital, as you know, tends to where the maximum rate of return is provided.

The state of sustainable economic equilibrium in the commodity market is characterized by the equality of demand and supply ($C = P$), and this state corresponds to the equilibrium price (Fig. 4.1).

Using the A. Marshall model, one can easily demonstrate the mechanism of action of the equilibrium price. Suppose, in some product market, due to external factors, there was a decrease in demand for the product (Fig. 4.2, a). This violated the equilibrium existing in the market when, at the price Pe,

[1]Alfred Marshall (1842–1924) is an English economist, one of the founders of the neoclassical trend in economic science.

[2]The effect of the law of demand is not unconditional. The so-called "Giffen phenomenon" is known — when the increase in prices for essential goods does not cause a decrease in demand for them, but rather its growth. One of the reasons for this phenomenon is that consumers, fearing a further increase in prices for this product, seek to buy this product for future use. For example, in the housing market in Russia, on the eve of each crisis, there is a sharp jump in property prices, which, however, does not reduce demand, but, on the contrary, generates consumer excitement, which, in turn, leads to a new jump in prices. So it was after the default of 1998, at the beginning of the crises of 2009, 2014.

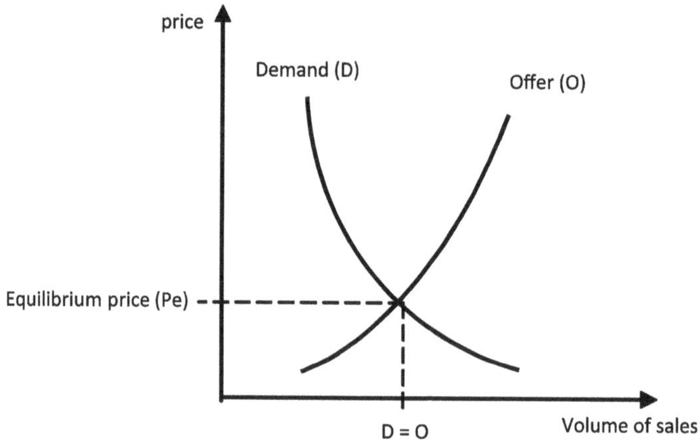

Figure 4.1: Laws of supply and demand and equilibrium price

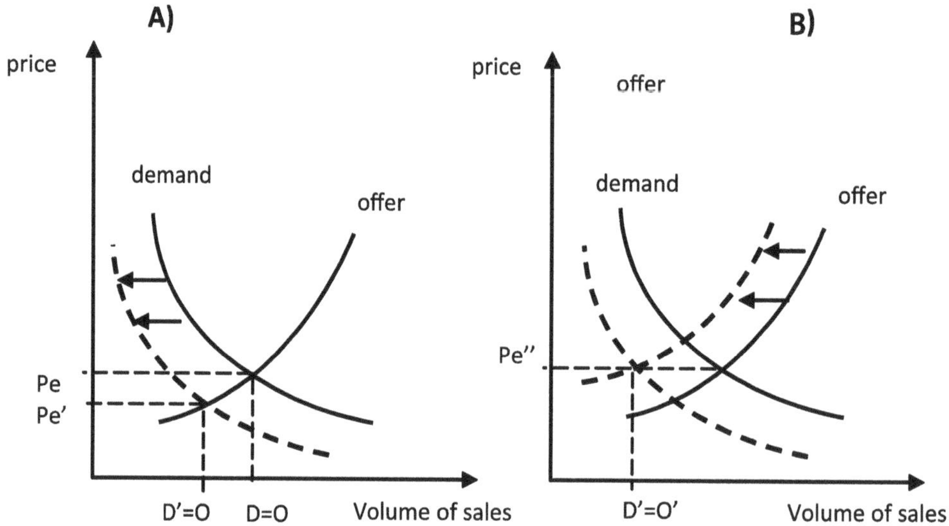

Figure 4.2: Illustration for equilibrium price theory

the volume of presented demand corresponded to the supply of goods on the market *(S = D)*. A new short-term equilibrium has been established *(S'= D)* , which corresponds to the new price *Pe*. According to the laws of the market, manufacturers will certainly respond to a decrease in the equilibrium price by reducing the supply of goods. The new price, without ensuring the previous rate of return, will lead to a partial curtailment of production and an outflow of capital from this market. The volume of supply will decrease (Fig. 4.2. b), as a result, a new equilibrium will arise *(S'= D')*, which will correspond to the new equilibrium price *Pe"*. The new equilibrium means that at the price *Pe*, the supply volume will be equal to the demand volume, i.e. Each seller will find a buyer, and each buyer will find a seller.

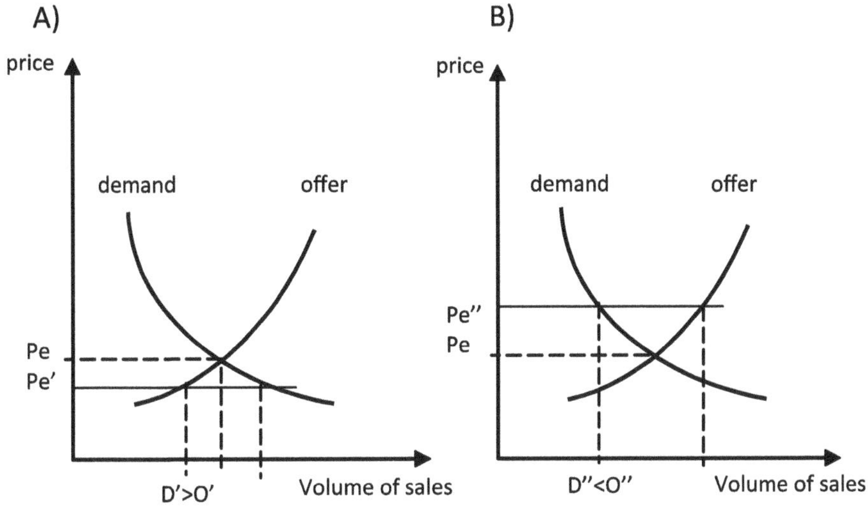

Figure 4.3: Illustration for equilibrium price theory: the occurrence of crises of deficit or overproduction

The ratio of the new and old equilibrium prices depends on the extent of the change in supply and demand. If this change is adequate (i.e. supply and demand change in equal measure), then the equilibrium price can be established at the same level ($Pe' = Pe$). However, as a rule, supply reacts to a drop in market demand more than to its recovery. The sellers of goods, trying to compensate for losses from the crisis, restrain supply volumes, keeping the price at a higher level. This is one of the most important factors of inflation in a market economy.

The illustration to the theory of equilibrium prices allows us to make another very important conclusion — when setting prices different from the equilibrium price level, we will inevitably upset the market equilibrium (Fig. 4.3).

If the price offered on the market is less than the equilibrium price, then the supply of goods will be less than the volume of demand (Fig. 4.3. a), and we will find ourselves in a situation of shortage of goods. If, on the contrary, the price of the goods is artificially high compared with the price of market equilibrium (Fig. 4.3.b), then inevitably falling demand will be less than the supply of goods on the market, and we will find ourselves in conditions of commodity overproduction, which is very fraught with economic shocks.

4.2 The concept of price. Pricing factors

The *price* category is closely related to such economic categories as *value, value, utility, rarity.*

This relationship can be represented in the following form (Fig. 4.4).

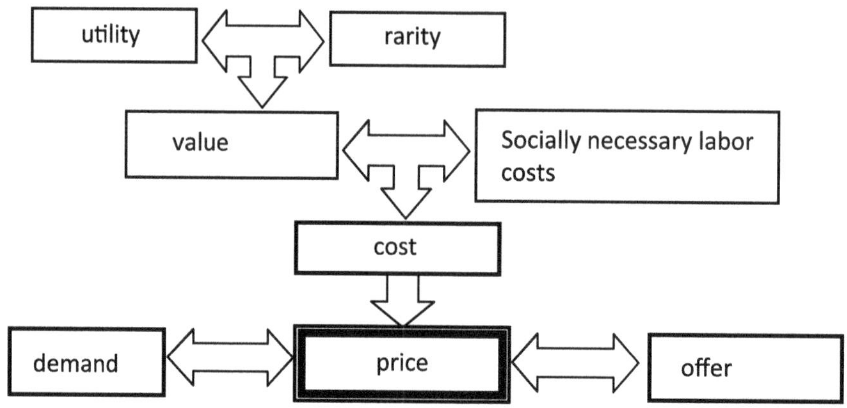

Figure 4.4: The relationship of economic categories: value, cost, price

However, in the future we will see that in economic practice these categories are often mixed, replacing one another. For example, in construction, an indicator that performs the function of price is called *estimated cost.* When evaluating real estate, the category of value is also used (market value, book value, investment value, etc.).

The simplest definition of a price category can be the following: the *price of a product is the sum of the monetary equivalent of the goods transferred by the buyer to the seller when the purchase and sale transaction is completed.*

The price of the goods is manifested in the exchange of goods, but its foundation is laid in the sphere of production and in the sphere of consumption (Fig. 4.5). The figure shows two approaches to determining the price: costly and value. The cost approach is based on the determination of production costs and determines the minimum price of the seller. The value approach is based on the recognition by the consumer of the significance of the given product for him and determines the maximum price of the buyer.

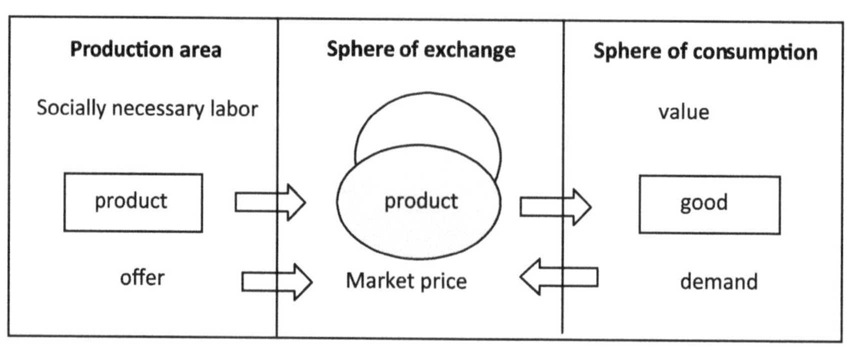

Figure 4.5: Transformation of pricing categories in the process of commodity exchange

In the process of market interaction, the seller's price and the consumer's price are transformed depending on the ratio of supply and demand, determining the market price. In the future, we will see that the cost-based approach prevails in the construction products market, taking into account the costs of construction companies for the construction of buildings and structures, and in the finished real estate market, a value-based approach characterizes the usefulness of this object for the buyer.

The bulk of the price of any product is production costs, i.e. producer costs for the production of goods (work, services). The price of the goods should provide the manufacturer with compensation for its production costs and some profit. Otherwise, the economic meaning of the production of goods is lost. Therefore, the general price formula has the form:

$$P = PC + PR, \tag{4.1}$$

where P is the price of the goods, rub.;

PC — production costs, rubles; PR — profit, rubles.

In the future, we will see that this general price formula underlies any manufacturers pricing strategy, however, the ratio of its components varies depending on the market situation and the goals of the company.

Demand and supply on the market are the main factors shaping the price of construction products. However, in addition to this, there are still a large number of pricing factors in the construction and real estate markets: exogenous, characterizing the impact of external factors on the construction and the real estate market, and *endogenous,* characterizing the internal factors and features of the functioning of the construction complex (Fig. 4.6).

All these factors can be divided into four groups: economic, organizational, architectural and technological and technological.

Exogenous factors are largely determined by the general economic situation in the country. The mechanism of action of these factors is complex and not always unidirectional. One and the same factor can cause both an increase in prices for construction products and its decrease. For example, high inflation increases the risks of investment projects, leads to a rise in the cost of resources used in construction, which naturally leads to a rise in the cost of construction products. Inflation expectations affect the consumer and investment priorities of potential buyers, sometimes leading to rush demand and a sharp jump in property prices as the most reliable asset. This happens, as a rule, in anticipation of another crisis, which we have already discussed a little higher. On the other hand, lower inflation leads to lower returns on financial instruments, which increases the investment attractiveness of real estate as a profitable investment. This leads to increased demand for real estate and higher prices. At the same time, deflationary expectations force investors to take a wait-and-see attitude, freeze investment projects, which leads to a decrease in supply on the market and can also cause a rise in prices for real estate. However, a decrease in credit rates and the cost of financial resources attracted by developers to implement projects will certainly reduce their costs and may lead to lower prices in the real estate market. Thus, consideration of these factors and state regulation of their impact should be based on a specific macroeconomic situation and the careful development of forecast scenarios.

Important factors affecting the price level in the construction and real estate markets are the presence of barriers to entry into the market and the level of competition between the main economic entities. Construction is a capital-intensive industry, so there are natural barriers to entry into the market that do not allow starting this business from scratch. These barriers are reinforced by the oligopolistic structure of the market, which is characterized by a high concentration of large producers in the market. Such manufacturers have great market power, dictate their policies on the market, and hinder the entry of new players into the market, which limits the development of competition and, consequently, leads to higher prices for products.

An effective regulatory effect on the market is provided by the presence of state and municipal targeted programs that not only allow attracting additional investments to the industry, but also inhibit price increases. So, for example, the program "Housing for the Russian Family", implemented in the country in 2014-2016, allowed not only to support the construction complex in the conditions of the crisis, but also helped to curb price increases, since the program set a limit for the cost of housing under construction in the amount of 35 rubles per sq.

A huge impact on the "cost-intensiveness" of the construction and operation of real estate is provided by the technical policy, the level of technological development of the industry, which is manifested in the formation of a new typology of construction, the introduction of scientific developments and innovative methods of production and life support of objects. Therefore, the support of industry science and innovation, the expansion of the raw material base and the development of new building materials and structural systems are important pricing factors.

Obviously, the main pricing factors lie inside the construction industry. These are endogenous factors that determine the level of producer costs and the reserves of cheaper construction. Managing these factors and using all reserves is the main task of effective management. Endogenous (intra-production) economic factors are associated with the cost and efficiency of the use of construction resources, primarily material, the costs of which are 60–80% in the structure of construction costs.

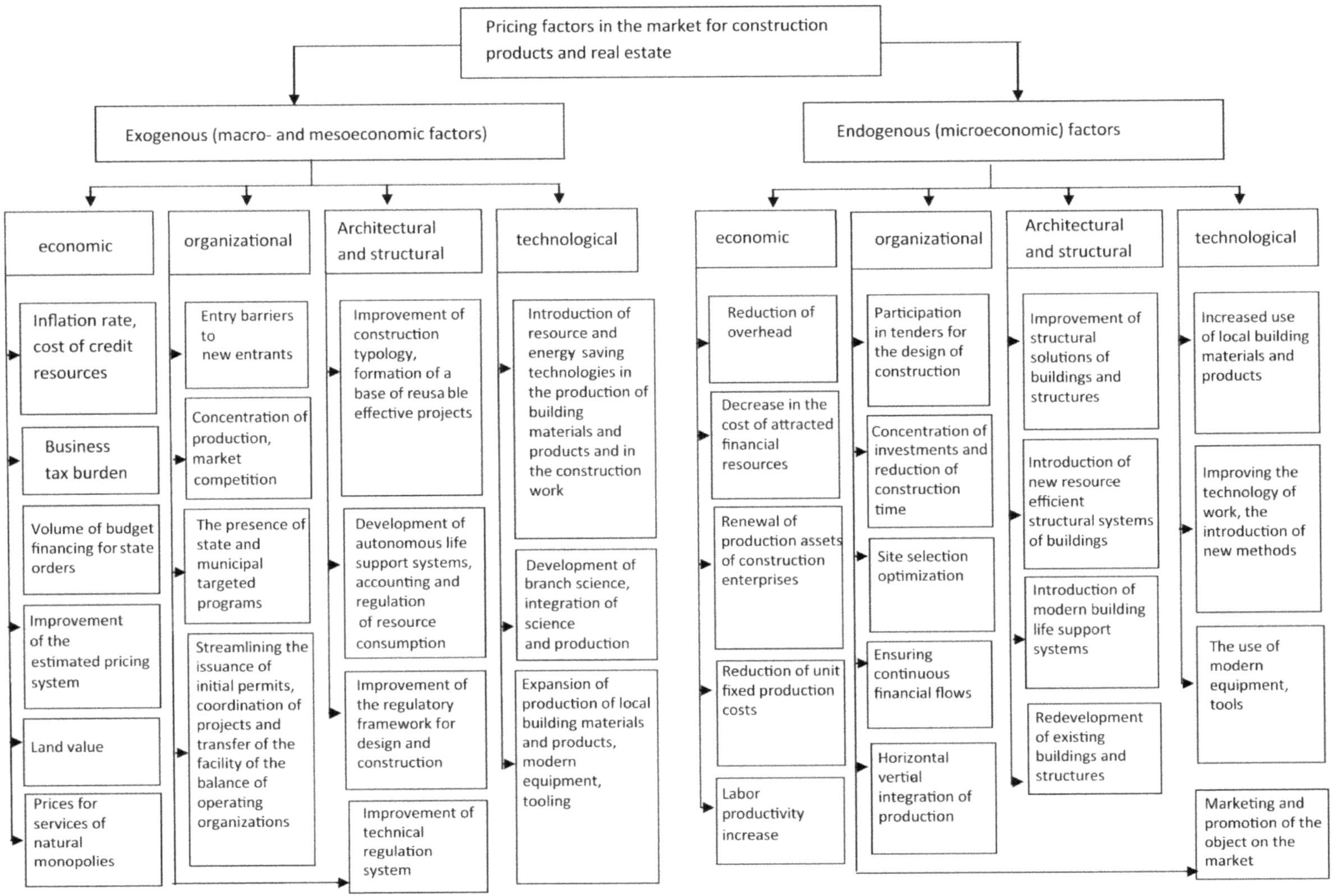

Figure 4.6: Pricing factors in the construction products and real estate market

To a large extent, the final cost of builders is influenced by the cost and terms of attracting financial resources. So, for example, in housing construction, the "cheapest" financial resources are attracted through equity participation agreements in housing construction, which until now are the main mechanism for financing housing construction. The use of borrowed financial resources at existing interest rates leads to some increase in the cost of construction. At the same time, the transition to project financing on the basis of escrow accounts can become a real alternative to financing through equity agreements, and restrain a significant increase in prices due to the inclusion of the banking construction control mechanism (for more details see Chapter 4, Section 4.6, Part II).

Intra-production organizational factors are associated primarily with the optimization of the production program of construction organizations. When forming the developer's investment and production portfolio, it is important to take into account the ratio of actual production volumes with the calculated break-even point for this enterprise. Calculations show that in small organizations building only one object, as a rule, the actual amount of work is less than the breakeven point, and the share of fixed (conditionally constant) costs is higher than the industry average. Such organizations have "long-term construction" and are forced to raise prices to cover losses. The increase in production volumes of construction organizations should not occur due to an increase in the number of simultaneously under construction objects, since this involves the spraying of production resources over a large number of simultaneously under construction objects, which leads to a complication of financial and resource flows, and an increase in production costs. Therefore, reserves for reducing the construction time, and, consequently, the prices of real estate under construction, can be found in the concentration of production resources on a small number of objects.

The value of real estate to a large extent depends on the adopted architectural and structural decisions in accordance with the structure of demand in the primary market, optimizing the number of storeys of buildings, introducing lightweight energy — efficient structural systems of buildings, modern engineering life support systems, and the use of flexible planning solutions.

Technological factors are associated with the introduction of modern resource-saving technologies for the construction of buildings at all stages of the investment cycle. The introduction of new technologies requires the use of modern tools, tooling and equipment, which can significantly increase labor productivity in construction.

The variety of pricing factors is due to the fact that real estate is the result of the activities of many entities of the construction complex and are complex engineering systems.

4.3 Types of prices in construction

Since the market for goods is diverse, and so are the forms of sales of goods, a whole system of prices operates in a market economy. This also applies to the construction industry. Consider the classification of prices, dividing them into groups according to several classification criteria (table. 4.1).

Table 4.1 Classification of prices in construction

Signs of classification	Price types
1. Action time	BaselineCurrent (current) Forecast
2. Method of determination	Market Regulatory Contractual (contractual)
3. Stage of the investment process	Investor Estimated Contractual (contractual) Actual
4. Organization pricing strategy	Cost cover cost. "Market gain" price Flexible price Monopoly price (oligopolistic) The price is psychological

We give brief comments on this classification.

In the practice of economic and investment analysis, basic prices are used — prices of a certain point in time (year), taken as a basis for economic comparisons. However, the most widespread *base prices* were received in construction, where the main method of pricing remains the method of calculating the cost of construction and installation works on the basis of basic level prices using indexes. For example, in the practice of pricing in construction, the prices of 1969, 1984, 1991, 2001, and 2001 were taken as base prices. *Current prices* are prices that are valid at a given (current) point in time. Accordingly, *forecast prices* are prices used in economic forecasts and calculated by multiplying current prices by the value of forecast price growth indices. Forecast prices are used to justify promising investment projects, plan budget expenditures, and make economic forecasts.

The determination of the *market price* was given by us above. Unlike market prices, which are formed under the influence of supply and demand, *regulatory prices are* determined by certain methods in accordance with established standards. Standard prices can be as unit prices, i.e. installed per unit volume of work, as well as enlarged, installed per unit of finished product. Normative prices are widely used in construction, where the cost of the final product is determined by special *estimates* based on *estimated standards.*

Contractual or *contractual prices are* the prices determined at the conclusion of contracts (contracts) for the production of goods, the performance of work or the provision of services and established in these contracts. The contract price in construction is the cost of construction and installation work for the facility, established in the contract. As noted in chapter 2, it can be solid (final) and open. The firm (final) contract price is fixed in the contract and remains unchanged for the entire period of its validity. The fixed contract price is used when concluding contracts for small facilities, the construction duration of which does not exceed 6-9 months. Short construction periods make it easy to predict the possible change in the cost of construction and installation works and take them into account immediately when determining the contract price. A fixed contract price is usually set in contracts for the execution of state or municipal orders. Open contract price — is set in the contract in the form of the initial contract price, i.e. in the amount fixed on a certain date (usually on the date of conclusion of the contract). The initial contract price is subject to subsequent clarification during the execution of the work, while the contract agreement must indicate the mechanism for adjusting thc contract price, which can be index or compensation

Depending on the stage of the investment process, the price may also be different. At the pre — investment stage, when determining the need for investments, the preliminary price of the object, which is called the *investor value, is calculated.* It is determined, as a rule, either on the basis of consolidated construction price standards, or on the basis of analogous facilities. Further, at the stage of development of the project, taking into account the project list and the volume of work, the *estimated cost of* construction is calculated. It is determined by the estimated regulatory methods using the estimated regulatory framework (we will consider this issue in more detail below). At the stage of contract bidding or conclusion of a contract, a *contract price (contract) is formed*, which may differ from the estimated cost, as a rule, in a smaller direction. And, finally, as construction and installation work is completed, the *actual cost of* construction is formed, which takes into account the actual costs of the participants in the investment process.

The pricing strategy of the enterprise is one of the main instruments of competition for the consumer. In search of their place in the organization's market, in addition to the strategy of covering production costs (this strategy is described by the general price formula — formula (4.1)), various methods of price competition are used. Those organizations whose level of production costs is lower than the costs of competitors have significant competitive advantages. Such organizations have the opportunity to use the "market conquest strategy" by approximating the price level to the level of production costs and setting prices significantly lower than competitors' prices. Under *monopoly price* refers to the price that consistently deviates from its potential level in a competitive market that has developed under the influence of supply and demand. The monopoly price is set by an economic entity that holds a dominant position in the commodity market in order to realize its economic interests due to the abuse of market power. The construction market is characterized by an oligopolistic market structure — when two or three large companies noticeably dominate the market, dictating, in fact, their prices to consumers. Therefore, in relation to the construction market, it would be correct to single out the *oligopolistic price.* Depending on the strategic and tactical goals of companies in the market, there may be other approaches to pricing.

4.4 Features of pricing in construction

Features of pricing in construction stem from the characteristics of construction products and construction production. This can be seen in table 4.2. So, for example, the individual nature of the products, the features of the construction site require an individual approach to determining the price of each object. The price is determined by *individual calculation,* which is called the *estimate* or *estimate.* Since real estate objects are being built in areas with different climatic and geographical conditions, their architectural, planning and design decisions should take into account the peculiarities of the construction site. For example, different temperature conditions impose different requirements on the heat-shielding properties of building envelopes, different freezing depths of soils are taken into account when designing the foundations and foundations of buildings, the seismicity of the area requires increased seismic resistance of

Table 4.2 The influence of the features of construction products and construction production on the formation of prices of construction products

Features of construction products and construction production	Features of pricing in construction
Individual character of objects	For each object, the price is determined by individual calculation
Dependence of architectural-planning and structural solutions of objects on climatic and natural-geographical conditions of construction	Prices for construction products are zoned (vary by territorial area)
Busy and multioperational production	The complexity of determining the price of the construction object, the determination of costs for each type of work
A large number of construction participants (subcontractors, subcontractors)	The need for budget estimates for each type or set of works
Long production cycle	The need for adjustment (indexation) of prices by time

buildings, etc. Therefore, *prices for construction products are differentiated by region, i.e. zoned.* Price differentiation takes into account not only the climatic features of the construction site, but also economic ones. For example, the level of demand for construction products in a certain territory and the prevailing price level. Construction is a complex technological process, including a large number of stages, types of work, individual operations. A large number of performers participate in this process. Accordingly, the *preparation of estimates is a rather time-consuming process,* since the costs are determined for each type of work and for each contractor. The larger the object, the more complex and larger the estimated calculations. This led to the need to automate the estimated calculations, because currently the estimate documentation is compiled using various software products for the preparation of estimates. And, finally, the length of the technological cycle determines the change in the cost of construction products at different stages of the investment process and the need to adjust (index) the cost as the project progresses.

But the main feature of pricing in construction is the combination of market pricing methods and the estimated normative method, which is based on the use of a *system of estimated standards.* Perhaps this is an exceptional feature of construction, due to its extreme resource and labor intensity. By approving the system of estimated standards that determine the normative need for resources necessary to carry out the corresponding type of work (labor costs of workers, expenditure of basic building materials and structures, labor time of machines and mechanisms), the state regulates pricing in construction. On the basis of estimated standards and design data on the physical volumes of construction work, the overall resource requirement for the construction and installation work on the object is determined. Further, using the standard prices of construction resources or their real market value, you can determine the cost of building the object. The estimate-normative method allows the use of two approaches: elemental and enlarged. In the *elemental approach, the* estimated construction costs are determined using *elemental estimated norms.* In an *enlarged approach, the* estimated cost of construction is determined using the *aggregated estimated norms or norms of the construction price.* Next, the estimated regulatory method of pricing in construction, we will consider in more detail.

4.5 Estimated cost and cost of construction products

The estimated cost of construction of enterprises, buildings and structures is the amount of money necessary for its implementation in accordance with the project. As part of the project, *estimated documentation* is being developed —

a set of documents containing calculations of the cost of design and construction of objects. These calculations are called *estimates, the* method used to determine the value is called the *estimated normative,* therefore, the indicator of value is called the *estimated cost.* The estimated cost is determined at the design stage of the investment process.

Based on the estimated cost, the total need for investments in fixed assets Ci(capital investments) is calculated:

$$C_i = C_e = C_{e,ds} + C_{e,ci} + C_{e,eq} + C_o \tag{4.2}$$

where C_e is the estimated cost of finished construction products (buildings, structures), rub.;

$C_{e,ds}$ — estimated cost of design and survey work, rubles;

$C_{e,ci}$- estimated cost of construction and installation works, rubles;

$C_{e,eq}$ — estimated cost of technological equipment and its installation, rubles;

C_o — the cost of other work (the cost of preparing the site for construction, obtaining technical specifications for design and construction, etc.).

Formula (4.2) shows the investor's costs for the creation of construction products and reflects the participation in the final product of all subjects of the investment process. Similarly, by the formula (4.2) the cost of reconstruction of buildings and structures is calculated.

The ratio of individual elements in the total cost of construction depends on the type of object, its purpose. The share of the cost of design and survey work in the total amount of capital investments, as a rule, is not large — on average 2–3%. In residential and public buildings, the main share belongs to the cost of construction and installation works. In industrial facilities, the share of the cost of construction and installation works and equipment can be almost the same. With the development of technology, the introduction of technological innovations, the share of the cost of equipment increases. For example, the introduction of the "smart home" concept has led to the emergence of "smart" life support systems, climate control equipment, and security systems in residential buildings. All this increased the cost of equipment and increased its share in the total investment need. During the construction of facilities as part of the redevelopment of built-up territories, other costs sharply increase, associated with the demolition of existing facilities, compensation for damage to their owners, taking into account urban planning restrictions and requirements, etc. Other costs associated with site preparation and construction situations in new undeveloped territories are high. Due to the complete lack of infrastructure, developers are sometimes forced to spend up to 20% of the amount of investment before starting the construction of the facility.

The estimated cost of construction may differ from the price of finished construction products on the market. This can be illustrated in fig. 4.7.

However, it should be noted that this situation is typical for the conditions of a growing or stably functioning market. In a crisis or market stagnation, situations are possible when a developer is forced to sell an object for less than the estimated cost. But such situations, as a rule, are short-lived, because either the industry gets out of the crisis and begins to rise in the real estate market, or the developer company, working at a loss, becomes bankrupt[3].

The participation of civil organizations in the creation of the final construction products is determined by the estimated cost of construction and installation works $C_{e,ci}$.

The basis of determining the estimated cost of construction and installation works is the general price formula, i.e. the estimated cost is the sum of the production costs of the construction company and profit (see formula 4.1):

$$C_{e,ci} = C_{e,pc} + PRe, \tag{4.3}$$

where $C_{e,pc}$ is the estimated cost of construction and installation works, rubles; PRe — estimated profit of construction works.

Using the same formula, the cost of repair and construction or restoration work is determined. The main part of the estimated cost construction and installation work is the cost of construction and installation works. *Cost* is the cost of the enterprise in manufacturing products, performing work or providing services. At each stage of the investment process, the cost of construction and installation works is determined: at the design stage, the *estimated cost* is determined, at the planning and preparation stage of the construction production, the *planned cost is* calculated, when the construction and installation works are performed, the *actual cost* is formed.

Estimated profit is included in the estimated cost of construction and installation works to ensure the profitability of construction production and create conditions for the normal financial activities of enterprises: taxes, settlements with creditors, expansion of own production, material incentives and social support for employees of the enterprise. Estimated profit may differ from the *planned profit*, which is determined at the stage of planning the activities of the construction organization, and from the *actual profit* received as a result of work and sale of construction products. *A feature of pricing in construction is the valuation of estimated profits, i.e. determination of*

[3]2016–2017 became record-breaking in the number of bankruptcies of senior developers, breaking the "records" of the previous crisis

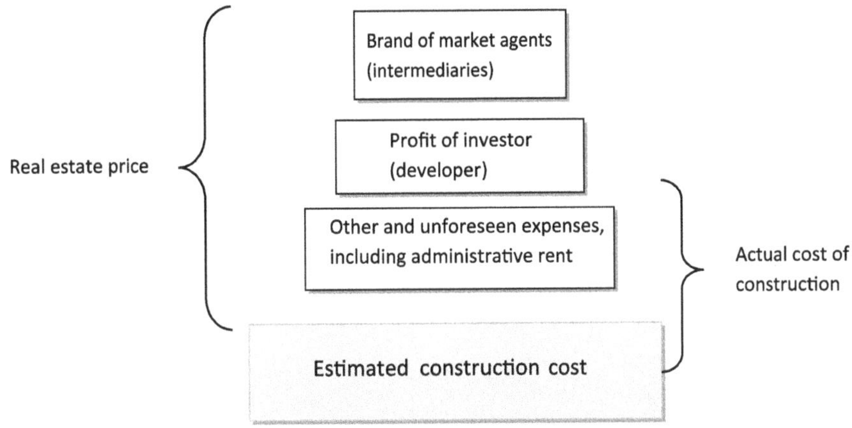

Figure 4.7: The ratio of estimated cost and market price of construction products

its size according to the standards. The estimated profit should cover the expenses of construction organizations for paying taxes (corporate income tax, property tax), development of production (modernization of equipment, updating of fixed assets, technical re-equipment) and material incentives and social development of workers. The procedure for determining the estimated profit will be considered by us further.

The cost of construction and installation works is an indicator that characterizes the organization's costs associated with the implementation of these works. For the purpose of planning, accounting and cost analysis, they are grouped by cost. In economic practice, different methods of cost grouping are used, the main of which are grouping by primary cost elements (used in accounting and tax accounting) and grouping by complex calculation items used in estimated pricing.

When using the *method of grouping by complex cost items* to determine the estimated cost, all costs of construction organizations are grouped into two complex costing items — *direct costs and overhead (indirect) costs* , which combine different *costs* along primary elements, but having a general purpose, costs:

$$C_{e,pc} = DC_e + OC_e, \tag{4.4}$$

where DC_e — estimated direct costs for the construction and installation, rubles;

OC_e — estimated overhead costs for the production of construction and installation works, rubles.

Direct costs are costs directly related to the construction and installation works, determined by a direct account and related to a specific object.

Overhead costs are the costs associated with the management, organization and maintenance of the construction industry. These costs are formed in the whole organization, and in relation to a particular object are indirect.

Direct costs and overheads are complex cost items, which, in turn, include costs (formulas 4.5 and 4.6):

$$DC_e = M + CL_m + CM, \tag{4.5}$$

where M is the cost of materials, structures and products used in the construction and installation works, rub.;

CL_m — the cost of labor of the main workers employed directly on the implementation of construction and installation works, rub.;

CM — the cost of operating machines and mechanisms when performing construction and installation works, rub.;

$$OC_e = AE + CS_w + CO_w + OC_o, \tag{4.6}$$

where AE — administrative expenses, rubles;

CS_w — the cost of servicing workers, rubles;

CO_w — the costs of organizing work at the construction site, rubles;

OC_o — other overhead costs, rub.

The estimated cost of materials, products and structures, which is part of direct costs, is determined at the price of "ex- warehouse"[4], i.e. includes the manufacturer's selling price, the cost of packaging, packaging and props, supply and marketing margins, transportation costs, loading and unloading costs, procurement and storage costs, i.e. all the costs of delivering materials to the construction site, to the place from where these materials are directly fed to the work area. *The labor* costs of *construction workers* include the salary costs of the main workers directly involved in the construction and installation works, and are determined on the basis of the normal working hours and normal working conditions. This cost item does not take into account the labor costs of workers performing auxiliary work, for example, the construction of temporary buildings and structures at a construction site, the improvement of a construction site, the preparation of an object for delivery, etc. *The estimated cost of operating construction machines and mechanisms* includes depreciation for the full restoration of equipment and vehicles directly involved in the production of labor, labor costs for machinists, repair and maintenance of machinery and mechanisms, fuels and lubricants, energy, installation costs dismantling and relocation of the machine from one construction site to another.

---

[4]The term "price- ex . . . " Means the price of the goods, including all expenses for the delivery of the material to the place indicated after the word ex

Administrative and administrative expenses include expenses for the remuneration of administrative staff and the amount of the single social tax (contribution) calculated from expenses for the remuneration of employees of administrative and administrative staff, postal telegraph and office expenses, communication services and information systems, expenses for maintenance and operation of computer and office equipment, maintenance and operation costs of buildings, premises occupied and used by administrative staff, expenses maintenance and operation of the service of passenger cars and other. *The cost of servicing the construction workers* include the costs associated with training and retraining of personnel, transfers to the unified social tax from the wage costs of workers employed in construction work and operation of construction machines and mechanisms, costs on ensuring sanitary-hygienic and living conditions, labor protection and safety *costs,* etc. The *costs of organizing work on construction sites* include wear and tear expenses for repairing tools and industrial equipment, depreciation and expenses associated with the repair, maintenance and dismantling of temporary (non-title) structures, maintenance of fire and watch guard, expenses for the implementation of advanced methods of labor organization, expenses for the development of work production projects, expenses associated with invention and innovation, the costs of maintaining production laboratories, the costs of improvement and maintenance of construction sites, the costs of preparing construction projects for construction And others. *Other overheads* include depreciation on intangible assets, payments on bank loans and budget loans, and expenses related to advertising.

Having summarized the above formulas into one, we can see that the estimated cost of construction and installation works is defined as

$$\begin{aligned} C_{e,ci} = C_{e,pc} + PR_e = DC_e + OC_e + PR_e = \\ M + CL_m + CM + AE + CS_w + CO_w + OC_o + PR_e, \end{aligned} \tag{4.7}$$

For clarity, we present a general scheme for the formation of the cost of construction products (Fig. 4.8).

When determining the estimated cost of construction at the design stage, direct costs are calculated by direct account for individual cost items for each type of work. And overhead costs, due to the fact that a significant part of them are formed as a whole for the organization, are allocated to individual types of work or objects by an indirect method — using standards. In the following sections, we will consider the methodology for determining the estimated cost of construction works and its individual elements.

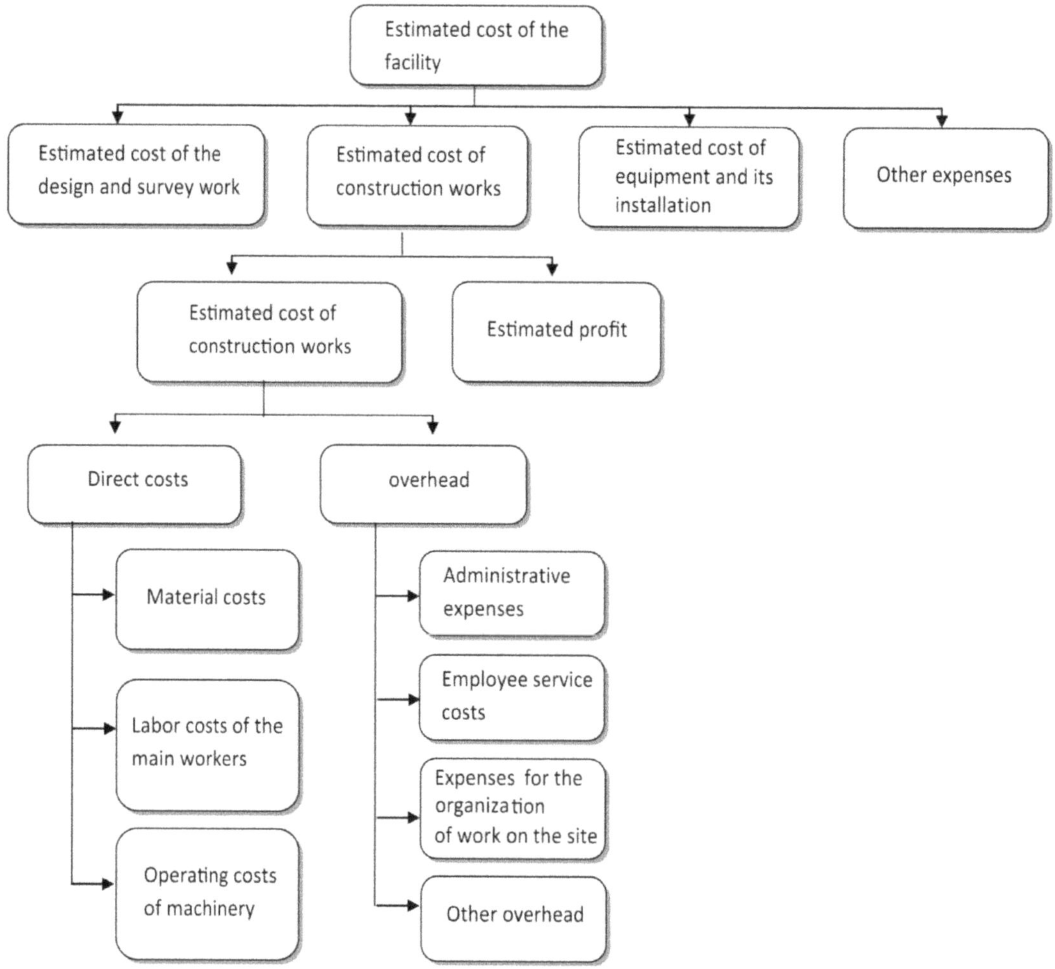

Figure 4.8: Formation of estimated cost of construction products

4.6 Approaches and methods for determining the estimated cost of construction and installation works

The estimated cost of construction products is calculated on the basis of design decisions that determine the list and scope of work on the facility using estimated standards. Depending on the stage of the investment project at which the estimated cost is determined, and the type of estimated standards used, it is possible to use various approaches and methods for determining the estimated cost. These approaches and methods are determined by the methodology of estimated normative pricing, fixed in the MDS 81-35.2004.

Methodology for determining the cost of construction products in the Russian Federation[5].

In fig. 4.9 presents a classification of approaches and methods of estimated normative pricing in construction.

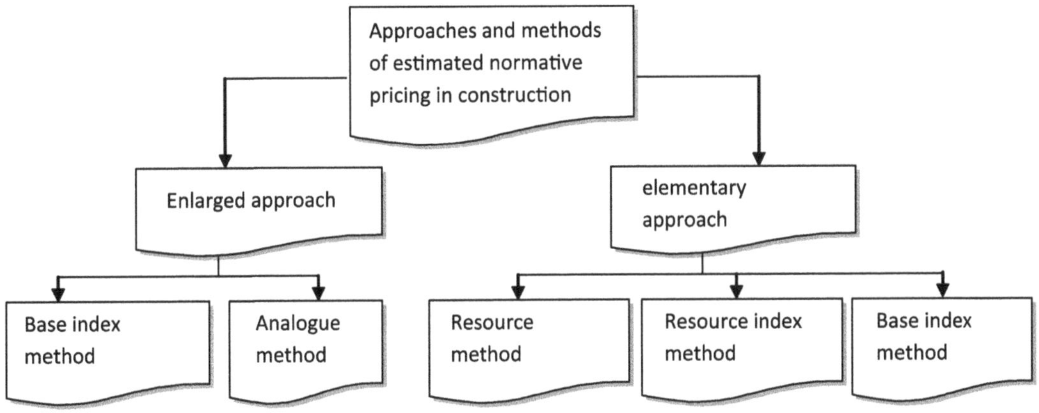

Figure 4.9: Approaches and methods for determining the estimated cost of construction products

The main difference in approaches is the use of various estimated norms and standards — aggregated or elemental[6]. *The enlarged approach is* used at the pre - investment stage when developing the rationale for investments and determining investor value, planning budget limits for capital investments, at the stage of conceptual design or developing the main architectural and planning solutions for a future object. The lack of complete information on the composition and scope of construction and installation work on the proposed construction does not allow a detailed calculation of the estimated cost. Therefore, at this stage, an enlarged approach is applied using *aggregated estimated standards or a databank on the value of previously constructed or designed analogous facilities.*

The aggregated estimated standards determine the estimated cost per unit of capacity of a facility under construction or units of its consumer characteristics (area, building volume, length, capacity, etc.), or per unit

[5]In the bowels of the Ministry of Construction of Russia, a draft of a new Methodology for determining the cost of construction products in the Russian Federation was developed and submitted for public discussion and professional examination in March 2018. The draft new document retains the basic methodological principles of estimated pricing in construction, but some adjustments are made to the application of various methods for determining the estimated cost. See in more detail on the Federal portal of draft regulatory legal acts : [Electronic resource] : URL http://regulation.gov.ru/projects#npa=79172

[6]Next, we will examine in more detail the composition of the estimated regulatory base used in determining the cost of construction

component or type of work. The difference between the indicators is the completeness of cost accounting — the integrated construction price standards take into account overhead costs, estimated profits and other costs per unit capacity of the facility, while the integrated standards for structural elements or types of work do not.

When using the *integrated standards of construction prices, the* estimated cost of construction and installation works will be determined by the formula:

$$C^e = NAC \cdot CP \cdot Zf + VAT, \tag{4.8}$$

where NAC is the aggregated norm of the construction price of an object per unit of its capacity or other quantitative indicator (area, construction volume, length, etc.), rubles / natural units ;

CP — the capacity of the facility or other quantitative indicator (area, construction volume, length, capacity, etc.), natural units.

Zf — zoning factors taking into account the regional and climatic conditions of the construction site;

VAT — value added tax, taken into account in the estimated cost of construction.

When using the *integrated standards for the price of structural solutions, the* estimated cost of construction and installation works will be determined by the formula:

$$C^e = \left(\sum_{i=1}^{n} NPCD_i \cdot V_i \cdot Zf \right) + OC^e + PR^e + LC^e + VAT, \tag{4.9}$$

where $NPCD_i$ — the integrated price standard of the *i-th* constructive solution

(i = 1... n), rub / natural units;

V_i — volumetric (quantitative) indicator of a structural element, natural units;

Zf- zoning factors taking into account the regional and climatic conditions of the construction site;

OC^e — estimated overhead costs, rub.;

PR^e — estimated profit, rub.;

LC^e — estimated limited costs (other costs and expenses included in the estimated cost at the established standards), rubles; *VAT* — value added tax, rubles.

The method of determining the estimated cost using a data bank on the cost of previously constructed or designed analogous facilities is used in forecast calculations of investment needs, in the budget process when planning limits for capital investments, etc. For example, knowing the cost of building a similar social purpose facility (school, kindergarten, hospital, etc.), you can determine the preliminary estimated cost (estimated investment need) of the designed facilities for inclusion in the draft budget. In this case, it is necessary to make an adjustment to the cost of the analogous object taking into account quantitative parameters, zoning, and inflationary processes:

$$C^e = (C^e_a / CP_a) \cdot CP \cdot Zf \cdot C_{inf} \tag{4.10}$$

where C^e_a is the estimated cost of the analogue object, rub. ;

CP_a — the capacity of the analogue object or another quantitative indicator of its consumer characteristics (area, construction volume, length, capacity, etc.), natural units.

CP — the capacity of the projected object or another quantitative indicator of its consumer characteristics (area, construction volume, length, capacity, etc.), natural units.

Zf — zoning factor;

C_{inf} — coefficient taking into account inflationary processes (index-deflator), with the help of which indexation of prices is carried out at the current level.

We emphasize once again that the enlarged approach to determining the estimated cost of construction is used at the preliminary stage of developing an investment project in the absence of complete information about the construction project or an incomplete set of design documentation, when it is impossible to determine the full composition and scope of construction and installation work being carried out at the facility.

The elementary approach to determining the estimated cost is used at the stage of project development and working drawings. In the elemental approach, the estimated construction costs are determined using *elemental estimated norms.* Depending on the used elemental estimates, the elemental approach involves the use of three methods for determining the estimated cost:

- resource method;
- resource index method;
- basic index method.

Resource and resource-index methods are based on the use of elemental estimated consumption rates for building resources. The basic index method is based on the use of elemental estimated norms of direct costs.

When using the *resource method, the* estimated cost is calculated as follows:

$$C^e = \left(\sum_{i=1}^{n} \sum_{j=1}^{m} CR_{ij}^e \cdot V_i \cdot P_j \right) + OCe + PRe + LCe + VAT, \qquad (4.11)$$

where CR_{ij}^e are the elementary estimated consumption rates of the j-th type of resource for the i- *th* type of work, natural units ;

V_i — the volume of the *i-th* type of work, natural units;

P_j — current unit prices of the *j-th* type of resource, rubles / natural units; OCe- estimated overhead costs, rubles; *PRe*- estimated profit, rubles.

LC^e — estimated limited costs (other costs and expenses included in the estimated cost at the established standards), rub.;

VAT — value added tax, rub.; type of construction and installation work, i = *1... n*;

type of resource used, j = *1... m.*

The resource-index method according to the application algorithm is similar to the resource method, but the basis for the calculation is not the current but the base prices of construction resources, which are subject to indexation in the calculation taking into account the inflation rate:

$$C^e = \left(\sum_{i=1}^{n} \sum_{j=1}^{m} CR_{i,j}^e \cdot V_i \cdot P_j^{basic} \cdot C_{inf} \right) + OC^e + PR^e + LC^e, \qquad (4.12)$$

where P_j^{basic} — unit prices of the j-th type of resource in the basic price level, rubles / natural units ;

C_{inf} — coefficient taking into account inflationary processes, with the help of which price indexation is carried out at the current level.

The base-index method is based on the use of estimated norms of direct costs per unit volume of construction and installation works (*unit rates*) calculated at the *base price level, with their indexing to the current price level:*

$$C^e = \left(\sum_{i-1}^{n} UP_i \cdot V_i \cdot C_{inf} \right) + OC^e + PR^e + LC^e + VAT, \qquad (4.13)$$

where UP_i is the unit rate that determines the amount of direct costs per unit of the *i-th* type of work at the base price level, rub.

Unit prices include unit costs for materials, basic wages and expenses for the operation of construction machinery and mechanisms. Therefore, formula 4.13 actually takes the form:

$$C^e = \left(\sum_{i-1}^{n} (M_i + CLm + CM_i) \cdot V_i \cdot C_{inf} \right) + +OCe + PRe + LCe + VAT, \tag{4.14}$$

It should be noted here that some unit rates include only part of the used building materials, products or structures. Such rates are called open. In these cases, unaccounted building materials should be considered additionally. Then the formula 4.14 will take the form:

$$\begin{aligned} C^e = \left[\left(\sum_{i-1}^{n} (M_i + CL_{m,i} + CM_i) + \sum_{j=1}^{m} M_j \right) \cdot V_i \cdot C_{inf} \right] + \\ +OC^e + PR^e + LC^e + VAT, \end{aligned} \tag{4.15}$$

The application of the above methods of estimated normative pricing in construction is described by the current Methodology for determining the cost of construction products in the Russian Federation (MDS 81-35.2004).

In the practice of estimated pricing, the prevailing method for determining the estimated cost of construction is the base-index method, since it is less time-consuming to use than the resource and resource-index method and more provided with a regulatory framework. The use of the resource method is limited by its high laboriousness — determining the amount of resources (material, labor, machines and mechanisms) required for each type of construction and installation or repair and construction work, and searching for data on the current cost of these resources significantly increase the labor costs of costing specialists. However, the concept of reform of the estimated normative pricing in construction, begun in 2016, provides for the transition, mainly, to the *resource method of determining the estimated cost as the most accurately reflecting the costs of participants in the construction process.* This concept is also embedded in the draft Methodology for determining the cost of construction products in the Russian Federation, proposed by the Ministry of Construction of Russia in 2018, which we mentioned above.

We have already noted above that direct costs arise directly during the construction and installation works and, when determining the estimated cost, are calculated by cost items by direct account. Overhead costs are indirect in nature, are formed as a whole for the organization, and their line-by-line calculation in determining the estimated cost of certain types of work or objects is impossible. Therefore, in the estimated calculations, the estimated overhead costs are determined by the indirect method according to the standards as a percentage of the amount of funds for the remuneration of the main workers and workers servicing machines and mechanisms.

At various stages of the investment process, various *standards for overhead costs are used*:

- consolidated standards for the main types of construction (industrial, housing, civil, transport, etc.);
- standards for the types of construction and installation works;
- individual standards for a particular construction organization.

These standards are defined in the Guidelines for determining the amount of overhead in the construction of MDS 81-33.2004[7].

When using the enlarged approach at the stage of determining the investor value of an object or a preliminary estimate of the estimated value when conducting contract bidding, the *integrated overhead standards for the main types of construction are used*

$$SOC^e = \frac{SOC^e_{mds} \cdot LC^e}{100} = \frac{SOC^e_{mds} \cdot (LC^e_m + LC_{e,e})}{100}, \tag{4.16}$$

where SOC^e_{mds} — the integrated standard of overhead costs determined by MDS 81-33.2004,%;

LC^e — estimated amount of funds for the remuneration of workers, rubles;

LC^e_m — estimated amount of funds for the remuneration of workers employed in primary production, rubles;

LC^e_e — the estimated amount of funds for the remuneration of workers employed in the maintenance of machinery and equipment, rub.

At the stage of development of working documentation, when a complete list of construction and installation or repair and construction works has already been determined, estimated overhead costs are determined using *the overhead standard for the types of construction and installation works* . When using the *resource method, the* calculation is carried out according to the formula:

$$SOC^e = \sum_{i=1}^{n} \frac{SOC^e_i \cdot iLC^e_m}{100} = \sum_{i=1}^{n} \frac{SOC^e_i \cdot (LC^e_m + LC^e_e)}{100}, \tag{4.17}$$

where SOC^e_i the standard of overhead expenses for the *i-th* type of construction and installation or repair and construction works,%;

LC^e — estimated amount of funds for the remuneration of workers for the *i-th* type of work, rub.;

LC^e_m — the estimated amount of funds for the remuneration of workers employed in the main production for the *i-th* type of work, rub.;

[7]During construction in the Far North regions, the norms defined in the Methodological Guidelines for determining the amount of overhead costs in construction carried out in the Far North regions and in areas equated to them are applied (MDS 81-34.2004).

LC_e^e — the estimated amount of funds for the remuneration of workers employed in the maintenance of machinery and mechanisms for the *i-th* type of work, rub.

When using the resource-index or basic-index method, additional indexation of the wages of workers, defined in the basic price level, to the current price level is necessary. Then formulas 4.16 and 4.17, respectively, will take the form:

$$SOC^e = \frac{SOC_i^e \cdot iLC_m^e \cdot C_{inf}}{100} = \frac{SOC_i^e \cdot (LC_m^e + LC_e^e) \cdot C_{inf}}{100}, \qquad (4.18)$$

$$SOCe = \sum_{i=1}^{n} \frac{SOC_i^e \cdot iLC_m^e \cdot C_{inf}}{100} = \sum_{i=1}^{n} \frac{SOC_i^e \cdot (LC_m^e + LC_e^e) \cdot C_{inf}}{100}, \qquad (4.19)$$

Standards for overhead costs by type of work are differentiated depending on the complexity of construction and installation works: from 80% for manual excavations to 155% for reinforced concrete works in civil engineering. For repair and construction work, the standards for overhead costs are slightly lower — from 75% to 108%.

Individual norms of overhead costs are calculated for a particular organization if the conditions of work are significantly different from the industry average. This rule is justified by special calculation and approved in the prescribed manner.

As we noted above, a feature of construction is that the profit when determining the cost of construction and repair or repair work is normalized, i.e. determined by the standards of estimated profit . The procedure for calculating the estimated profit when determining the estimated cost of construction and performing repair work is defined in the Methodological guidelines for determining the estimated profit in the construction of MDS 81-25.2001.

Depending on the design stage, the method for determining the estimated cost and the estimated regulatory base used, the following *estimated profit standards* can be applied:

- industry-wide standards;
- standards for the types of construction and installation works;
- individual norms of estimated profit.

As a base for calculating estimated profits, the amount of funds for the wages of workers of the main production and workers servicing machines and mechanisms defined in the estimated documentation on the estimated standards is taken.

Industry-wide standards for estimated profit are applied at the stage of developing a feasibility study for a project, when drawing up an investor estimate or in determining the initial (starting) cost of a project for contract bidding. When using the resource method, the calculation is performed according to the formula:

$$PR^e = \frac{SP^e \cdot LC^e}{100} = \frac{SP^e \cdot (LC_m^e + LC_e^e)}{100}, \tag{4.20}$$

where SP^e is the industry-wide standard for estimated profit,%.

When determining the estimated cost by the base-index or resource -index method, the calculation should be made taking into account the indexation of the base wage at the current price level:

$$PR^e = \frac{SP^e \cdot LC^e \cdot C_{inf}}{100} = \frac{SP^e \cdot (LC_m^e + LC_e^e) \cdot C_{inf}}{100}, \tag{4.21}$$

When determining the estimated cost of construction and installation works, the industry-wide standard for estimated profits is adopted, according to MDS 81-25.2001, in the amount of 65% of the amount of funds for the remuneration of workers (employed in the main production and servicing machines and mechanisms). When determining the estimated cost of repair and construction work, the industry-wide standard for estimated profit is taken at a rate of 50% of the amount of funds for workers' wages.

The estimated profit standards for the types of construction and installation works are applied at the stage of development of working documentation, when the full scope of construction and installation or repair and construction works is determined. At the same time, the formulas for calculating estimated profits take the form: with the resource method:

$$PR^e = \sum_{i=1}^{n} \frac{SP_i^e \cdot LC_i^e}{100} = \sum_{i=1}^{n} \frac{SP_{e,i} \cdot (LC_{m,i}^e + LC_{e,i}^e}{100}, \tag{4.22}$$

with basic-index or resource-index methods:

$$PR^e = \sum_{i=1}^{n} \frac{SP_i^e \cdot LC_i^e \cdot C_{inf}}{100} = \sum_{i=1}^{n} \frac{SP_i^e \cdot \left(LC_{m,i}^e + LC^e e, i\right) \cdot C_{inf}}{100}, \tag{4.23}$$

where SP_i^e — the estimated profit rate for the *i-th* type of construction and installation or repair and construction works,%.

The standards of estimated profit by type of work are differentiated depending on the complexity of construction and installation works: from 45% for earthworks performed manually, up to 100% for concrete and reinforced concrete works in civil engineering. For repair and construction work, the estimated profit margins are slightly lower — from 45% to 80%.

In those cases when the conditions for the production of works differ from those adopted in the averaged standards, an *individual standard of estimated profit* can be developed for a particular organization. However, MDS 81-25.2001 excludes the application of an individual standard for construction projects financed from the federal budget.

When calculating estimated overhead costs and estimated profits, different ratios can be applied to the norms, taking into account the characteristics of the organization (for example, when a construction company operates on a simplified taxation system, a reduction coefficient of 0.9 is applied to the standard for estimated profits) or features of the construction object (for example, when reconstruction of underground facilities, bridges, overpasses and other structures belonging to the category of complex, to the specifications of overhead applied boost to coefficient 1.2) etc. These coefficients are given in the current editions of MDS 81-33.2004, MDS 81-34.2004, MDS 81-25.2001 in the notes to the standards or in departmental normative acts.

4.7 Estimated regulatory base for determining the estimated cost of construction

Estimated standards are determined by special collections that form the estimated regulatory base, which is a key link in the estimated pricing system in construction. *Estimated and normative base is a system of estimated norms of resource consumption, cost standards, prices and rates for individual indicators of constructed (reconstructed, repaired) objects, work performed, resources used, as well as a system of rules and guidelines for their use* .

The estimated norms and standards included in the estimated regulatory base are diverse and can be classified according to the degree of detail (enlarged and elemental), to the meter (in-kind, value, percentage), and to the level of application (federal, industry, territorial, individual).

Since the formation of a system of estimated standards is an extremely complex and time-consuming process, such a base is formed on a specific date. So, in construction, when determining the estimated cost, the estimated normative bases were used in 1969, 1984, 1991, 2001, 2011. At present, a new estimated normative base is being formed, taking into account the change in construction technologies, the emergence of new constructive solutions and materials, new machines, mechanisms and equipment, as well as taking into account the transition from a predominantly basic-index pricing method to a resource method.

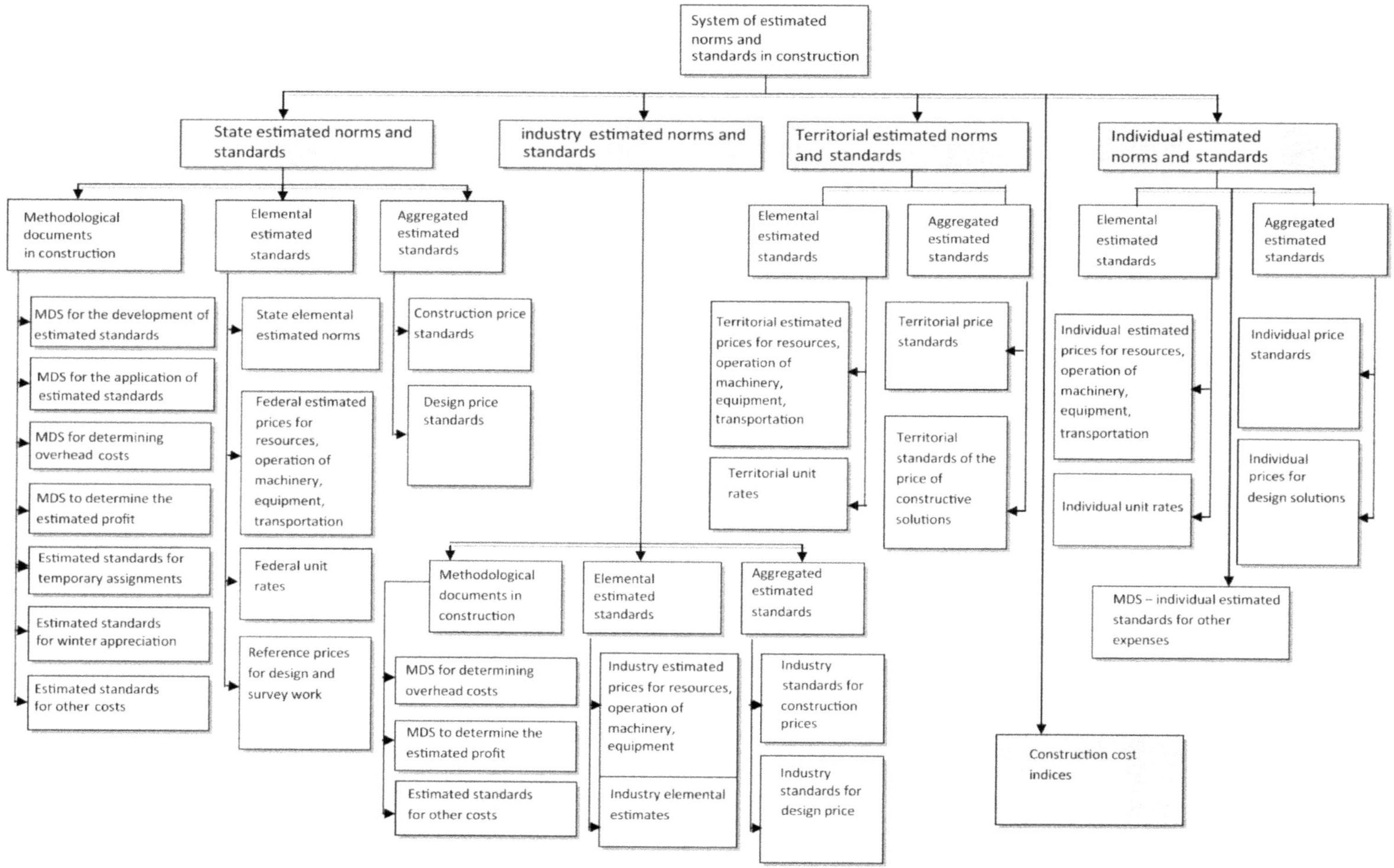

Figure 4.10: Estimated regulatory base in construction

In fig. 4.10 presents the structure of the current budget and regulatory framework in the Russian Federation[8]. Even from the analysis of the enlarged structure of the budget base shown in Fig. 4.10, it is clear how complicated the system of estimated standards used in construction is. This determines not only the highest complexity of estimated pricing in construction, but also the enormous cost of the state to maintain the estimated regulatory base in an up-to-date state.

When calculating the estimated cost of construction and repair and construction works by the base-index method, the cost standards presented in the collections of federal unit prices for construction and installation works (FER), repair and construction works (FERr), and repair and restoration (FERrr) are used, installation of equipment (FERM), commissioning (FERp), overhaul or modernization of equipment (FERMr) or territorial unit prices (TER, TERr, TERrr, TERM, TERp, TERMr) followed by indexing of pr direct costs at the current price level. When using the resource method, the basis for calculating direct costs is the state elementary estimated norms (GESN, GESNr, GESNm, GESNp, G ESN mr), which contain standards for the consumption of construction resources per unit volume or structural element of work performed:

- labor costs of workers (builders, installers) in person — hour;
- average level of work (workers link);
- labor cost drivers, in person — hour;
- the composition and duration of operation of construction machines, appliances, power tool in mach.- h;
- a list of materials, products, structures used in the manufacturing process, and their consumption in physical (natural) units.

Elementary estimated norms determine the normative amount of resources, the minimum necessary and sufficient to carry out the corresponding type of work.

Examples of tables from the collections of FER and GESN by type of work "Finishing work. Stucco of facades " are shown in figures 4.11, 4.12.

The cost of these resources is determined using federal or territorial resource price collections, which will include: estimated prices for construction materials, products and structures (FSSTS, TSSTS), estimated prices for the operation of construction vehicles and vehicles (FSEM), estimated prices for the operation of construction machines and vehicles (FSSC for equipment, TCCC

[8]This classification is approved by order of the Ministry of Construction and Housing and Communal Services of the Russian Federation of June 8, 2015 No. 413 / pr

Table FER **15-02-001** Improved cement-lime mortar stucco

meter **100 м²**

	Improved façade plastering with cement-lime mortar						
15-02-001-01	01 wall	1 713,34	681,87	51,77	24,77	979,70	70,88
15-02-001-02	02 Round columns (cylindrical and variable section)	3 833,01	2 837,77	10,36		984,88	263,00
15-02-001-03	03 rectangular columns	2 121,96	1 126,72	10,36		984,88	112,00
15-02-001-04	04 pilasters of variable section	2 785,92	1 790,68	10,36		984,88	178,00
15-02-001-05	05straight pilaster	2 433,82	1 438,58	10,36		984,88	143,00
15-02-001-06	06 eaves, drafts and platbands of rectilinear	8 979,96	3 892,59	60,22		5 027,15	351,00
15-02-001-07	07 curved rails, rods and platbands	13 470,87	8 383,50	60,22		5 027,15	810,00

Figure 4.11: Example of federal unit prices for facade plastering (FER 81-02-15-2001 fragment "Finishing work")

Table GESN **15-02-001** improved cement-lime mortar stucco

Scope of work:

01. surface preparation
02. applying the solution on the surface with leveling and grouting the topcoat
03. pulling rods with angle cutting
04. plaster care

meter **100 м²**

Improved façade plastering with cement-lime mortar:

15-02-001-01 01 wall
15-02-001-02 02 Round columns (cylindrical and variable section)
15-02-001-03 03 rectangular columns
15-02-001-04 04 pilasters of variable section
15-02-001-05 05straight pilaster
15-02-001-06 06 eaves, drafts and platbands of rectilinear
15-02-001-07 07 curved rails, rods and platbands

Resource code	Name of cost item		15-02-001-01	15-02-001-02	15-02-001-03	15-02-001-04	15-02-001-05
1 1.1	1 Labor costs of works 1.1 Average job	h	70,88 4,0	263 4,8	112 4,3	178 4,3	143 4,3
2	2 Labor costs of drivers		2,78				
3	Machines and mechanisms						
91.06.03-061	Electric winches with traction effort: to 12,26 кН (1,25т)	h	0,9	3,16	3,16	3,16	3,16
91.07.07-042	Mortar pumps: 3 м³/ч		2,78				
4	Materials						
01.7.03.01-0001	Water	м³	0,35	0,35	0,35	0,35	0,35
04.3.01.12-0111	Heavy finished mortar, cement-lime 1:1:6	м³	1,89	1,9	1,9	1,9	1,9

Figure 4.12: An example of state elementary estimated standards for plastering facades (fragment GESN-2001-15 "Finishing work")

for equipment), estimated prices for transportation of goods for construction (FSSC for freight, TSCC for freight).

The development of estimated standards is based on the principle of averaging, i.e. and resource standards and cost indicators take into account average indicators for the industry or territory.

Estimated norms and prices provide for the performance of work in normal (standard) conditions, not complicated by any factors. When performing work in special conditions: tightness, gas contamination, near existing equipment, in areas with specific factors (high altitude, etc.) — the coefficients given in general terms to the corresponding collections of standards and rates are applied to estimated standards and prices.

If there are no separate standards or prices in the current estimate and regulatory base, for example, according to the new work technologies provided for in the project, or when using innovative materials or equipment, it is possible to develop appropriate individual estimates and unit prices, which are approved by the customer (investor) as part project (working draft). Individual estimated rates and prices are developed taking into account the specific conditions of the work with all the complicating factors.

When using the base-index or resource-index method of determining the estimated cost for the conversion of base prices into current (forecast) prices, *cost-conversion indices* can be applied that take into account the level of inflation and price changes for individual cost elements. Indexes may apply:

- to certain types of resources as part of direct costs;
- to direct cost items (for a complex or for types of construction and installation works);
- to the results of direct costs or the full estimated cost (by types of construction and installation works, as well as by sectors of the national economy).

The current estimated regulatory base is presented on the official website of the Ministry of Construction and Housing and Communal Services of the Russian Federation[9].

4.8 The composition and procedure for the development of budget documentation

Estimated documentation is an essential part of the project for the facility. According to the Decree of the Government of the Russian Federation of February 16, 2008 No. 87 "On the composition of sections of project documentation and requirements for their maintenance" as part of the project, Section 11 "Estimates for the construction of capital construction projects" is mandatory, which should contain a text part as part of an explanatory note to the budget documentation and estimate documentation.

[9]Ministry of Construction of Russia. Official site : [Electronic resource] : URL www.minstroyrf.ru

The composition and procedure for the development of budget documentation is defined in MDS 81-35.2004. The general structure of the budget documentation section is presented in Figure 4.13.

In fact, this figure shows not only the composition of the budget documentation, but also shows the procedure for its development — the arrows going up show the sequence of development of documents included in the budget documentation.

The basis for determining the estimated cost of construction is the design documentation:

Initial customer data for the development of budget documentation, including information on the conditions of work, terrain features, characteristics of the building plot, etc.;

pre-project and project documentation, including explanatory notes to project materials, drawings, statements of volumes of construction and installation works, specifications and statements of equipment needs;

decisions on the organization and sequence of construction adopted in the construction organization project (POC);

information on concluded contracts for the supply of materials, transportation schemes for the delivery of materials, commercial offers (prices) for materials for which prices are not available in the estimated regulatory base.

On the basis of these initial data, a *statement of the physical volumes of work* is compiled, which is a list of the construction, installation or repair-construction work performed, corresponding to the technological sequence adopted in the project, and the physical volumes of these work in physical units. When determining the estimated cost by the resource method, resource sheets are compiled on the basis of a statement of the physical volumes of work, which determine the composition and need for basic construction resources. When using the base-index method, the resource list, as a rule, is not compiled.

The primary estimates are local estimates (local estimates), which are compiled for individual types or complexes of work. As a rule, general construction works are combined in one local cost estimate, while certain types of work in the estimate are distinguished by sections. Local estimated calculations are the most difficult and time-consuming part of estimated calculations, and the most responsible, since it is in these documents that the main costs of construction organizations are calculated and the estimated cost of construction and installation works is determined. This calculation, depending on the method used (resource or basic index), is carried out according to the algorithms defined by the above formulas.

Local estimated calculations are the basis for the preparation of *object estimates (estimates),* which include all the costs of the construction of the object. The cost determined in the object estimate calculation is the basis for

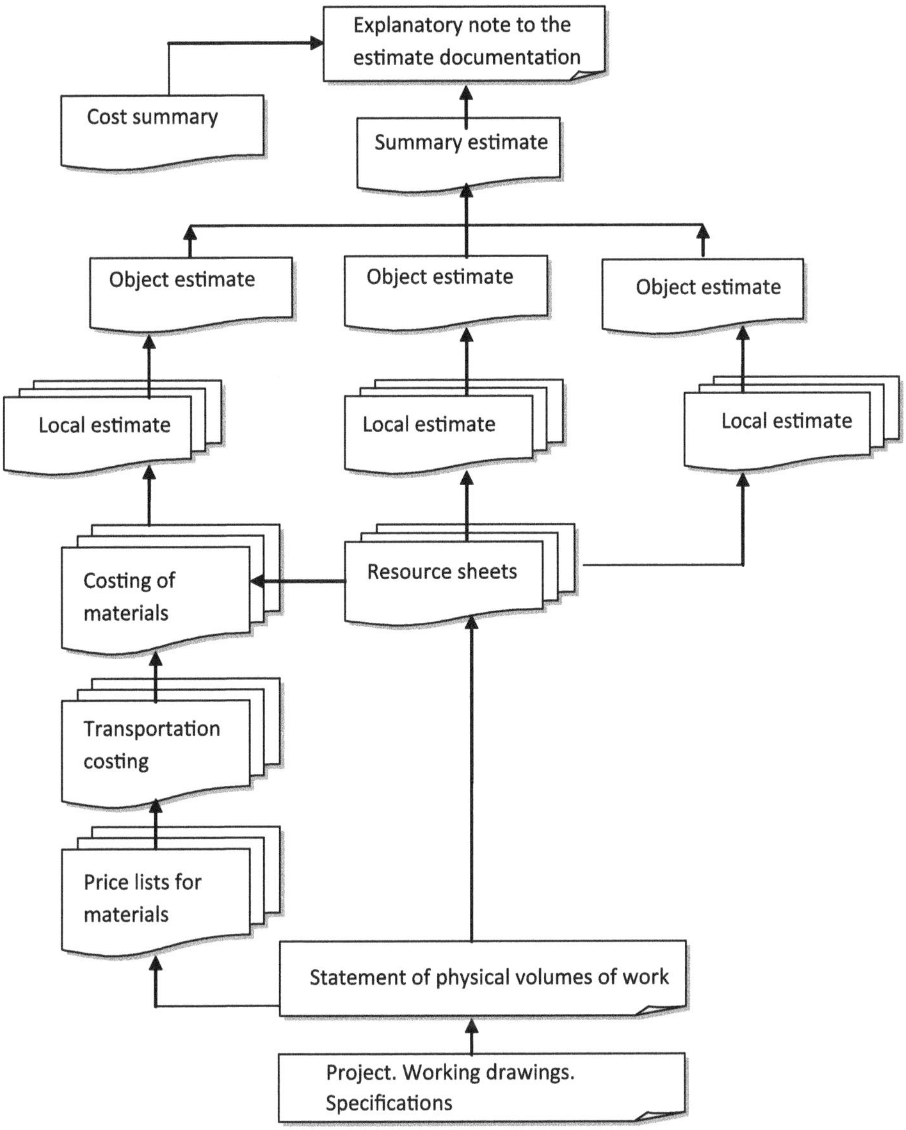

Figure 4.13: The composition of the estimated documentation for the construction of the facility

concluding a contract for the construction of the object (the implementation of a complex of works at the object). In addition to the estimated cost of construction and installation or repair and construction work directly carried out at the facility, other costs are taken into account in the estimated design: limited costs for the construction of temporary buildings and structures (GSN 81-05-01-2001 Collection of estimated cost standards for the construction of temporary buildings and constructions), additional costs associated with the production of work in winter conditions (GOS 81-05-02-2007 Collection of estimated norms of additional costs for construction and installation work in the winter) and unforeseen incurred costs.

All results of calculations on object estimates are summarized in the main estimate document — the *summary estimate calculation.* The summary cost estimate determines the total estimated cost of construction and the total investment need for the implementation of the investment project, including the costs of preparing the construction site (forming a land plot, obtaining rights, removing encumbrances, obtaining approvals, damages for demolition of facilities, etc.), directly works on the subject of network device work, objects of energy and transport sector, the costs of project development, etc. The methodology for determining the cost of construction products MDS 81-35.2004 defines the structure of the consolidated estimate calculation, which includes 12 chapters:

Chapter 1. Preparation of the construction site.

Chapter 2. The main objects of construction.

Chapter 3. Facilitics for utility and maintenance purposes.

Chapter 4. Objects of the energy economy.

Chapter 5. Objects of the transport sector.

Chapter 6. External networks and structures of water supply, drainage, heat supply and gas supply.

Chapter 7. Improvement and greening of the territory.

Chapter 8. Temporary buildings and structures

Chapter 9. Other work and costs

Chapter 10. Content of customer service. Construction control.

Chapter 11. Training of operational personnel.

Chapter 12. Design and survey work.

For *overhaul facilities, the* 9-main structure of the consolidated estimate is allowed[10]:

1. Preparation of sites (territories) for overhaul.
2. The main objects.
3. Facilities for utility and maintenance purposes.
4. External networks and structures (water supply, sewage, heat supply, gas supply, etc.).
5. Improvement and gardening of the territory.
6. Temporary buildings and structures.
7. Other work and costs.

[10]The draft new version of this Methodology of 2018 provides for a unified, 12-main structure of the consolidated estimate

8. Technical supervision.

9. Design and survey works, field supervision.

MDS 81-365.2004 determines the procedure for performing estimated calculations in the chapters of the consolidated estimated calculation and the standards of other expenses taken into account.

The relationship of the estimated documents and the calculation formulas in them of the estimated cost of construction are presented in Figure 4.14.

An *explanatory note is* being developed for the budget documentation, which should contain the following information:

- location of construction;
- a list of estimated standards adopted for the preparation of estimates for construction, methodological documents in construction, as well as departmental or territorial regulations used in the preparation of budget estimates;
- name of the general contractor (if known);
- norms of overhead costs (for a specific contractor or by type of construction);
- estimated profit margin;
- coefficients, corrective calculations, taking into account the specifics of determining the estimated cost of construction and repair or construction works for a given object;
- features of determining the estimated cost of equipment and its installation for a given construction site;
- features of determining for a given construction (facility) funds in chapters 8–12 of the consolidated estimate;
- calculation of the distribution of funds in the areas of capital investment (for housing construction);
- other information on the procedure for determining the cost specific to a given construction site, as well as links to relevant decisions of public authorities on issues related to pricing and benefits for a particular construction.

Forms of budget documentation and methods for their preparation are presented in MDS 81-35.2004. The complexity of the estimated calculations and their complexity led to the need to use for the preparation of budget documentation of various *software products.* Currently, various professional software products are presented on the market, which include the entire estimated regulatory base and algorithms for the preparation of budget documentation by various methods.

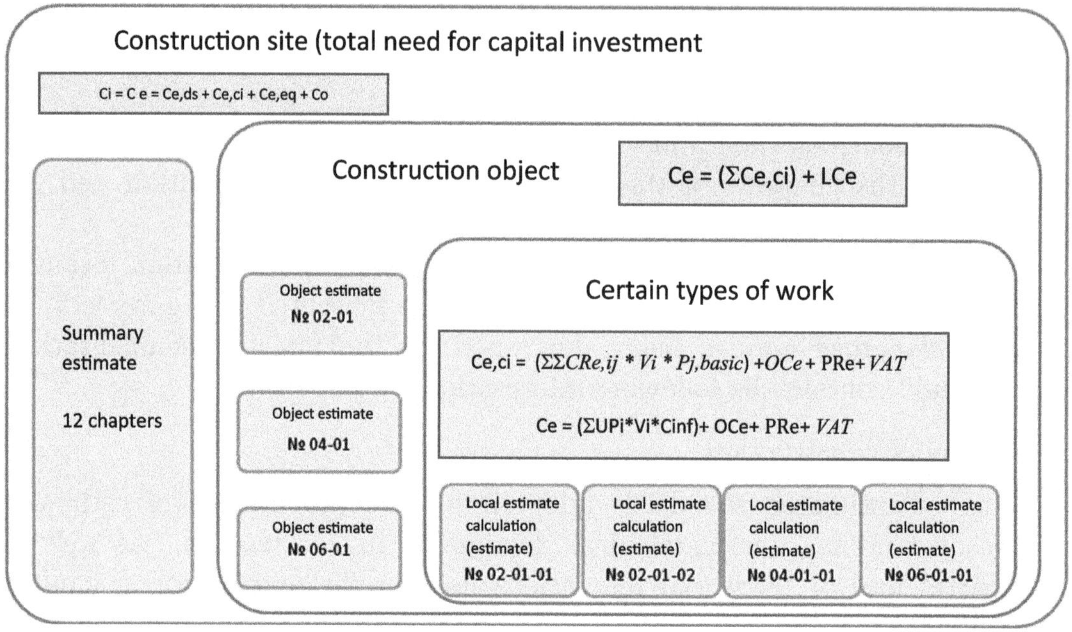

Figure 4.14: Relationship of documents in the estimate documentation (a description of the components included in the calculation formulas is presented above in section 4.6)

4.9 Contract strategy for the implementation of the investment construction project

Before forming a contractual strategy for ICP, it is necessary to determine the size of the direct production cost of the project. Under current conditions, there are a number of methods for determining the cost, each of which depends on the availability of analogues (the more reliable analogues of cost, the more reliable is the assessment of the cost of the work). The most important is the understanding of the typical (indicative) resources used in the selected technology of work. It should be understood that the existing construction norms and rules are based on the assessment of the technology of the 60s of the 20th century, therefore, for the purpose of their application in a particular construction organization, it is necessary to develop your own base of unit prices for the cost of standard work in ICP implemented by the organization. An enlarged scheme for estimating the cost of work is shown in Figure 4.15:

By analogy with standard approaches to assessing the value of a business, there are three approaches to valuation ("Cost", "Combined" (comparative) and "Profitable"), an agreed assessment of which can form a preliminary estimate of the direct cost of the project. You should be aware that the cost estimate changes dynamically during the implementation of the project,

Available information	❶ costly	❷ combined	❸ profitable
analogues	▪ Basic-index: base –past costs of an analog or a collection of basic prices (quasi-analogue); translates into current prices through indices	▪ Enlarged standards on the basis of analogues objects: if there is an analog, the method of enlarged standards, if not, the method of reduced market value	▪ Bringing the market value of an analog to a unit: bringing the cost of an analog to a unit (products, area, volume, personnel, etc.)
Analogues (partially)	▪ Resource-index: resources for which there is in the current price – the resource method, for which there is no price – basic-index	▪ Element-wise calculation: each object, title, type of work or installation complex is considered according to the most easily accessible information	▪ Resource-profitable: for known objects – by the inverse CAPEX method (distribution of the contract value), for unknown – by the method of bringing the market value to a conventional unit
resources	▪ Resource-expert: resources for which there are current prices – in fact, for which there is no – expert-analytical or technical method	▪ Aggregated resource value: for buildings, structures, installations, nodes, systems for which there is a price – in fact; for the rest – by the reverse CAPEX method (distribution of contract value)	▪ Reduction of the inverse CAPEX (distribution of the contract value) to the service life: operation expenses are considered the resource method at current prices; profit – estimated at full performance

Figure 4.15: An integrated scheme for assessing the cost of construction work

making changes and clarifications to the working documentation (RD), and will be final only at the end of the project. Accordingly, all approaches to evaluation up to this point are an assessment of the "plug" of the cost of the project.

With the **basic index** method of calculation, the cost of work is considered at the basic price level, and a system of indices is used to bring the prices to current prices. To date, the base-index method is the least popular for the following reasons:

- FER / TER includes industry average costs and resource costs, which must be adjusted depending on the conditions of work;
- many modern technologies differ from those laid down in the GESN. Normative guides lag behind updating equipment and the scope of work, and the rules for estimates do not contain clear descriptions of the use for such cases;
- the TEP databases themselves and the indices issued for them are not updated frequently enough;
- Estimated rules contain a number of assumptions about the availability of personnel that is most suitable for each job, which is true only for large

organizations, but not for medium and small ones, where simple work can be entrusted to an expensive worker without raising the cost of the project due to low overhead costs;

- the ability to perform work in different ways, balancing between cost and quality, is not always taken into account.

As a result, the application of the basic index method leads to inaccurate calculations, therefore, it is necessary to strive to apply this method to determine the cost of prospective construction. To assess the cost in the performance of work, it is necessary to strive to use the resource method (see section 4.7).

The resource method separately establishes the costs of materials and products, the time spent on the operation of machines and mechanisms, the labor costs of workers; resource prices are taken at the current level (at the time of calculation). The composition, consumption rate and cost of resources are set in accordance with the design data. The disadvantage of the resource method limiting its use is the high labor intensity (compared to the index index), which can also lead to an inaccurate calculation: while performing the detailed design and construction and installation work, there is no reliable estimate of the resources. There are several approaches to calculating valuations:

1. **The top-down assessment method is** used to estimate costs in the early stages of a project when information about the project is limited. The meaning of such an enlarged expert assessment is that it is carried out in a generalized manner and the project is evaluated as a whole by one indicator. Evaluation is convenient because it does not require much effort and time. The disadvantage is the low accuracy, incomparable with the result of a more detailed assessment.

2. **The bottom-up assessment method is** needed to develop an agreed base project price or a final project valuation. The name of the method reflects the method of calculating the valuation — the method provides for the assessment of costs at detailed levels of the project, and then the summation of costs at high levels. To carry out such a "convolution" of costs, the structure of the work decomposition (SDR or WBS) of the project is used. The advantage of this method is the high accuracy of the result, which depends on the level of detail when evaluating costs at the lower levels of detail of the work plan. The disadvantage of this method is the magnitude of the cost of funds and time to perform a detailed assessment.

3. **The "by analogy" assessment method** is one of the "top-down" assessment methods. To assess the cost of the project, actual data on the

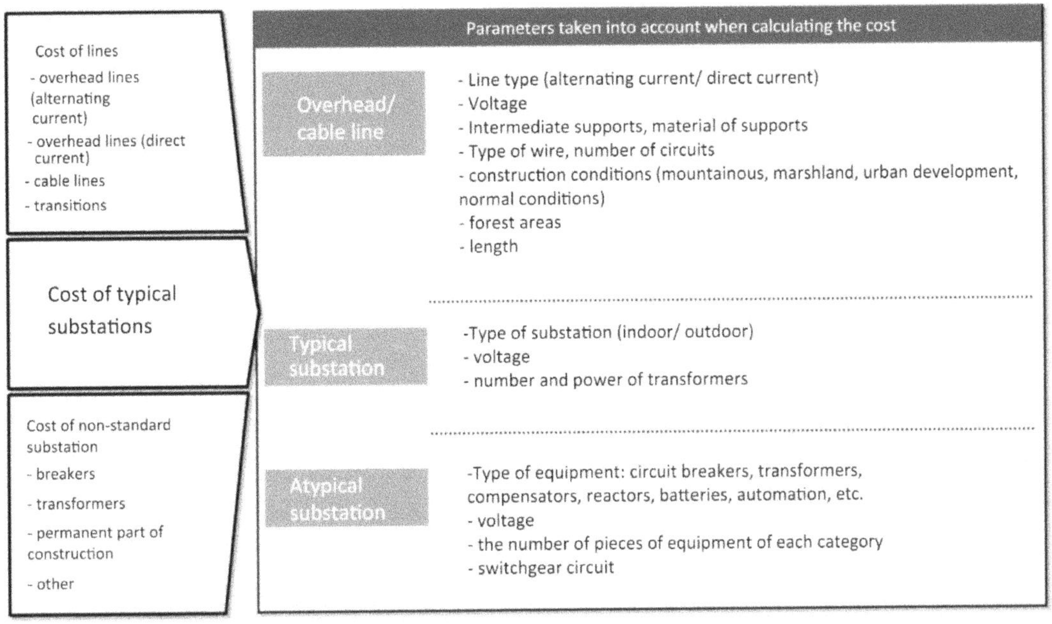

Figure 4.16: Consolidated Pricing Appraisal Model

cost of previously completed projects are used. The task is to determine the set of work in other projects, which can be attributed to the analogues of the estimated set of work in the project. The disadvantage of this method is the poor formalizability and the need to justify the choice of analogues and / or make adjustments to the actual data for similar works. It is also necessary to note the limitation on accuracy "within the order": the method gives the most reliable range of results if the analogue in physical volume is no more than 10 times different from the estimated object.

4. **The method of parametric estimates** is similar to the "by analogy" rating. The accuracy of the method is comparable to the accuracy of the "by analogy" method. The assessment task is to determine the characteristic physical volume for each significant type of work, the change of which entails a proportional change in the project cost. Then the determination of the unit rate of a given characteristic physical volume and the estimation of the physical volume can give a final estimate of the project cost. The disadvantage of this method is the need to justify the selection of a characteristic physical volume.

Price can be expressed both in estimated cost, and in aggregated prices for certain types of construction and installation works and constructs. The estimated cost of construction is determined on the basis of standards, on the basis of which, the price of each component that is included in the estimated cost is formed. Standards determine the estimated cost of the construction of the object.

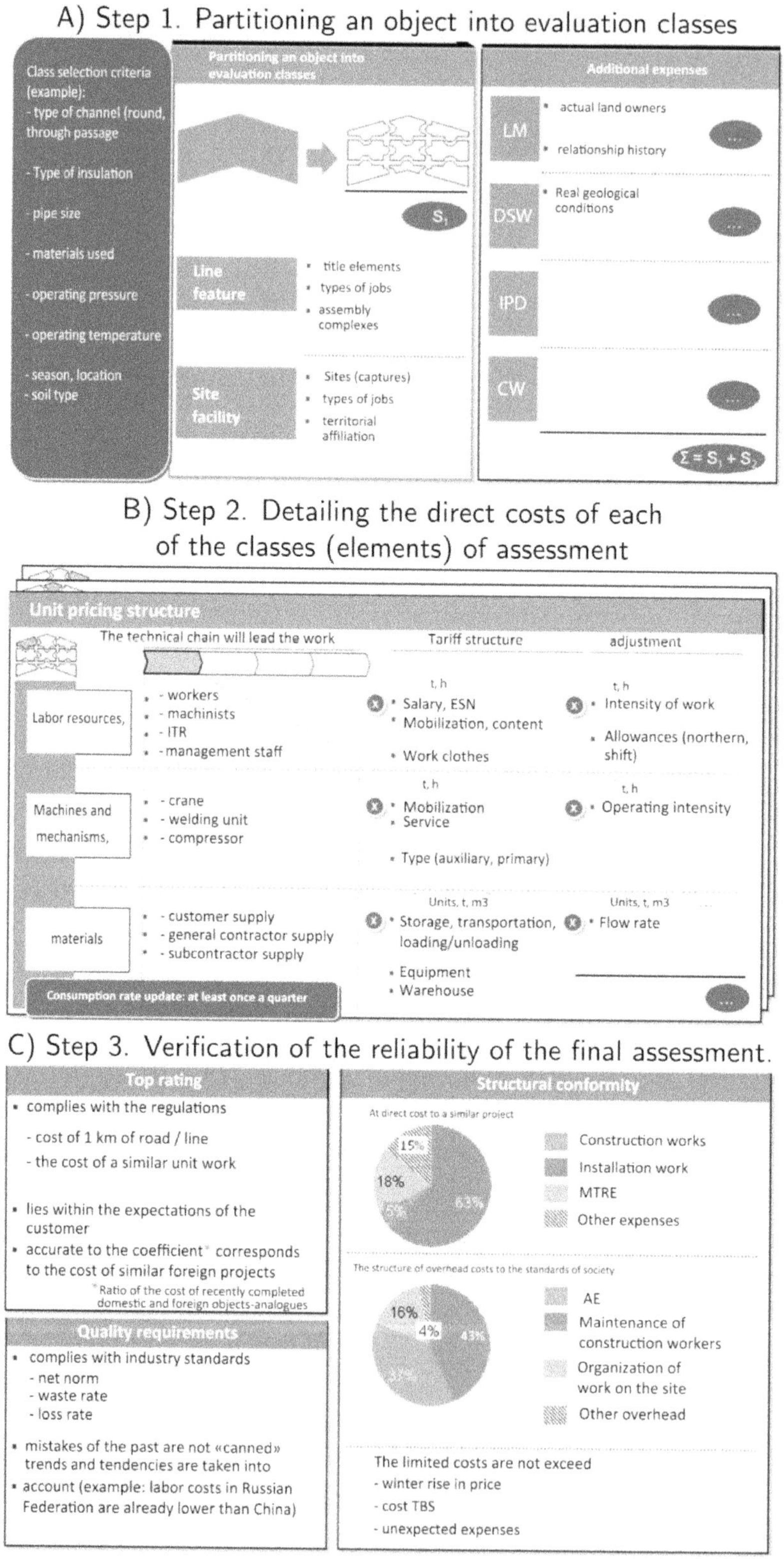

DSW — design and survey work, LM — land management, IPD — initial permit documentation, CW — commissioning works, TBS — temporary buildings and structures, AE — administrative expenses, MTRE — material and technical resources and equipment, MM — machines and mechanisms.

Figure 4.17: "Road map" of the formation of the cost of the object

An example of the application of consolidated prices (Fig. 4.16) is the application for assessing the cost of building an object under relatively stable project conditions (for example, infrastructure (road) construction or electric grid construction).

As you can see, the completely covered typification of the main works within the framework of electric grid construction allows us to quickly determine the cost of the work for further decision-making on the detailed elaboration of the project.

The "road map" of the formation of the cost of the object can be represented in the form of three "macro steps".

The characteristic *features of the class are* determined (the left part of Figure 4.17, a), then the object — depending on the type (linear or platform) is divided into *classes (elements) of evaluation* (Fig. 4.17, b) — the direct cost of the project is formed, the next step is to adjust the objective *features of a specific major project* , such as land management works, the geological structure of the place of production work, the necessary work on the preparation of initial permits, possible cost factors for commissioning, etc. (Fig. 4.17, c).

For each element of the assessment, a technological chain is allocated, which individually estimates the costs of labor resources, machines and mechanisms, materials and equipment. Each of the basic tariffs is adjusted for the actual conditions of work. It should be understood that the reliability of estimates is possible only with a fairly frequent updating (comparison with real market conditions) of the initial costs of labor, the use of machines and mechanisms, and MTRiO.

At first , it is necessary to understand whether, in our assessment, we "fell" into the expertly determined cost of a similar characteristic physical volume, whether the Customer is ready to talk about the identified cost of the work, how market-oriented (both from local — within the Russian Federation — and global — in the framework of BRICS and the world as a whole), the resulting estimate of the cost of the work looks like. Further, it is necessary to understand whether corrective optimism is formed that negates losses and waste, a realistic approach to cost estimates and whether global macroeconomic trends are taken into account. If it was possible to find the best option between these "clutches" of the valuation, it is necessary to determine how structurally reliable the resulting valuation is, both in terms of direct costs and in terms of not exceeding the limited costs, the structure of overhead costs.

After determining the project cost estimate and modeling the possible impact on the cost of the contract with the Customer, it is necessary to determine the feasibility of participating in the work on this project. The basic principles of decision making are:

- assessment of the effect of **direct** project **costs** (calculation of the "corporate tax" (overhead and management expenses) — after making a decision on participation in the project). Otherwise, fixed and semi-fixed costs can "eat" the entire calculation of the project effect;
- the effectiveness of the project is evaluated at the horizon of its **completion** , otherwise temporary redistribution of funds within the period of the project may give a distorted assessment of the effectiveness of the project and cause high expectations that are not economically justified;
- when managing the "gate" (gates), the actual costs incurred (sunk cost) cannot be the **only** factor in favor of the continuation of the project. Hopeless projects must be stopped, because, as practice shows, the situation — without clear elimination factors — is not corrected compared to the current one. If we take as a basis for understanding how much money has already been spent on the project, it is very difficult to recognize the inexpediency of continuing the work. Money can no longer be returned, and a loss-making project will continue to generate losses. And thus, the manager may be trapped in the failure to make a decision, resulting in ever-increasing losses from the project;
- temporary diversion / attraction of resources (not only financial, labor, material and technical) in other projects is based on **internal transfers.** It is unfair to attribute idle equipment temporarily not involved in the project (provided that the need for it is clearly defined by the project director) to the project. This action can significantly distort the real economic situation of the project;
- all project costs are allocated to the project budget (the project director should be able to **confirm the** planned costs). Otherwise, there is always the risk of "eating" the whole effect of the "business tourism" project, when regular VIP travels of senior management directly put a burden on the project budget without the ability to challenge or adjust this decision on the part of the project management team.

When making decisions on projects, it is necessary at the level of enterprise standards, including determining the answers to the following questions:

1. How is the distribution of costs? Options:
    - for all projects evenly,
    - in proportion to the duration, complexity, % of the prime cost of the standard type,
    - % of the cost of the object.

2. How is the distribution of the excess? If the total demand for materials (machines, personnel) for the projects is one year less than the total costs (10 cars are needed, 100 in the fleet), the balance between the projects:
    - distributed
    - not distributed.
3. How is the cost of resources determined (personnel, equipment). Options:
    - according to plan indicators;
    - taking into account downtime.

Contract strategy is a key document for project performance management. It is in it that decisions about options for generating profit, managing contracting organizations, a contracting schedule and linking it to the work schedule are recorded (Fig. 4.18).

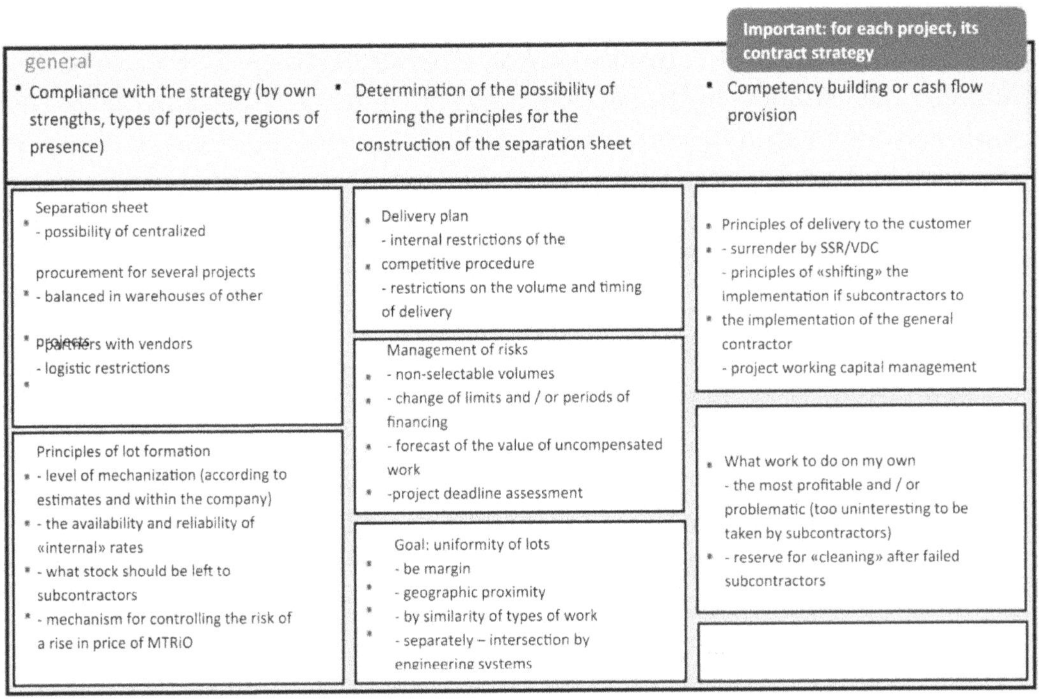

Figure 4.18: Schematic diagram (roadmap) of the contract strategy

Before forming a contract strategy, you need to decide on the answer to three key questions:

1. Does the project page comply with the development strategy of the Company (according to the principles of involving one's own forces, according to the type of project proposed for implementation, by region of work)? If the answer to any of these questions is negative, it is worthwhile to additionally

assess the appropriateness of participating in such a tender (it is possible that participation in the tender is justified to cover fixed costs, but in this case it is worth making sure that there are no truly relevant projects on the horizon).

2. Is it possible to distribute the risks of deliveries of the Customer, the general contractor and the supply transferred to subcontracting organizations? If distribution is possible, it is imperative to assess the possibility of centralized procurement in the interests of several projects (which obviously can affect the schedule of work), take into account the internal terms of the company for organizing and conducting competitive procedures, establish restrictions on the volume and timing of delivery, conduct an express audit of the balances in warehouses, possibly the required quantity and assortment of MTRiO, to update the status of possible partnerships with key suppliers, to clarify the logistical restrictions on delivery (including customs, availability of transport arteries, availability of a supply calendar, etc.)
3. A separate issue is the purpose of participation in the project. There are a number of customers in Russia (for example, Sibur LLC), which, due to their own maturity and understanding of construction technologies, do not allow general contracting organizations to earn extra profits. But, guaranteeing support in terms of organizational, technical and technological solutions, such a mature Customer allows the organization to grow and "build up" the necessary competencies. When entering the project, the task of determining current priorities is important.

Before forming lots, it is necessary to determine the principles for handing over the work to the Customer, including whether the work is being carried out according to the SE / VDC, how the subcontractors are "shifted" to the general contractor, how the project's working capital is managed (including in terms of calendar accounts receivable and payable, inventory management at the facility, a mechanism for identifying and managing unclaimed and / or non-liquid assets).

When dividing an object into lots, it is necessary to take into account the level of mechanization (determined by estimates and actual within the company), the availability and reliability of "internal" prices, the decision on the amount of excess profit left to subcontractors (for example, one of the key decisions will be to include or not include a high margin in the lot deliveries), a mechanism for controlling the risk of an increase in the cost of materials and equipment (it is especially important for large projects in which inert materials and equipment rental begin to rise in price one or two years before the official start of work in the region, etc.). The purpose of the partition is to ensure the comparative uniformity of lots by margin, geographical proximity, similarity of types of work. This will create economic uniformity of the contract field of the project, which will allow in the future to quickly redistribute resources between lots. Separate issues are the formation of so-called integration lots (for example, comprehensive testing of equipment, combination of engineering systems, "through" engineering network passing through the entire site, etc.).

When planning the use of own forces, it is necessary to determine the key areas of their involvement:

- the most profitable work (for example, installation supervision, integrated testing and commissioning);
- the most understandable work (work, possibly with a low margin, but known in the organization and giving a high probability of obtaining the planned effect). An example of such work can be excavation and excavation works, piling, foundation and foundation works;
- the most critical work (work, the performance of which by subcontracting organizations means the general dependence of the general contractor on these organizations). These include installation of auxiliary systems, electrical equipment, instrumentation, finishing, premises, landscaping and permanent roads;
- "problematic" (too uninteresting to be taken by subcontractors) work. In this case, it makes sense in the project budget to make a reserve for "cleaning" after subcontractors who have not managed. As a rule, such work is the installation of expansion joints, garbage removal, arrangement of slopes, construction of temporary roads, etc.

It is important to note that depending on the decisions made, the contract strategy may be adjusted both for filling lots and for the very structure of this management mechanism.

After completion of the formation of the contract strategy, it is advisable to "impose" a contract schedule on the work schedule. Key quality factors of the project summary schedule:

1. The optimal set was selected according to the performers used by M&M materials (in the logic of "price-quality" — delivery and involvement in production).
2. There is a plan "B" in case of failure to deliver the key equipment, etc.
3. Important areas of work are distributed in time (staggering) so as not to adjoin each other without a "gap".
4. When creating a cash flow schedule, we strive not to pay subcontractors and suppliers "better" than we receive financing from The customer.

5. We don't try to take advances that we can't work out by the end of the quarter (we don't work out — we get VAT), we try not to create NVI / NLL. If advances are made for the purchase of expensive equipment of long-term manufacture, VAT payments "withdraw" money from circulation earlier than a refund is received by offsetting VAT.
6. The cost structure of the project complies with corporate standards.

The objectives of a balanced project summary schedule are:

- optimize project costs both in size and in the cash flow schedule;
- assess the possibility of increasing revenue:
  - add. work
  - operation, training,
  - certification of alternative equipment,
  - logistics, centralized procurement;
- minimize the risks of VAT when receiving significant unspent advances in the reporting quarter.

The scheme of the consolidated project schedule is presented in Fig. 4.19:

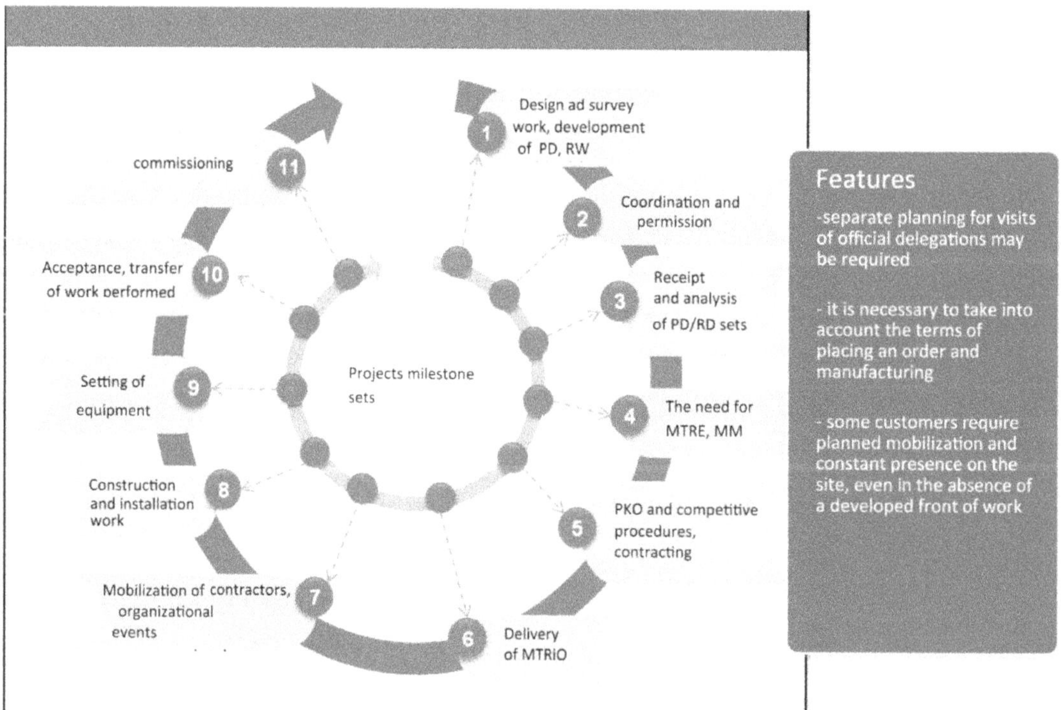

Figure 4.19: Project Summary Scheme

These sets of project milestones (including the physical volumes of work completed by construction) are a convenient tool for managing subcontracting organizations. As an annex to the contract, the milestone plan actually represents a task for a month in terms of work in relation to the specific geography of the object, physical volumes and average output for a specific planning period. This formation allows you to manage the risk from the fact that the subcontractor "bites" all the work (to make it harder to remove from the site), gain profitability and leave the general contractor alone with the cost of finishing the unprofitable work. Pay schemes depending on the performance of monthly tasks allow you to maintain a given pace and properly deploy the fronts of work. Contracting a unit of physical volume of work and development (rate of completion of work) instead of the total volume will allow for the comparison of subcontracting organizations on the site at comparable works and will facilitate the task of transferring part of the volume of work between subcontracting organizations depending on the fulfillment of the planned pace of work.

These activities serve as a management mechanism for subcontracting organizations selected for work.

For risk management purposes, the selection of sub-contracting organizations of poor quality is based on the prequalification system for subcontracting organizations, which is discussed in the next chapter.

Questions for self-control

1. What is the pricing mechanism in a market economy?
2. What is the demand for goods? What factors influence the volume of demand?
3. What is the offer of goods in the market? What factors influence the supply volume?
4. What is market equilibrium? How is the equilibrium price formed in the commodity market?
5. What is the price? How is this economic category related to such economic categories as value, value, utility, rarity?
6. What does the general price formula include?
7. What types of prices can be set for construction products?
8. What is the estimated cost of construction? What are the components of the estimated cost of a construction project?
9. What is the estimated cost and estimated cost of construction and installation (repair and construction) works? What do they include? Give the calculation formulas.

10. What are direct costs and overheads as part of the cost of construction and installation works? What is the difference? What are the features of the definition? give the calculation formulas.
11. What is estimated profit? How is it determined when determining the estimated cost of construction?
12. What are the approaches and methods for determining the estimated cost used in the estimated pricing in construction?
13. When and for what purpose is an integrated approach applied in determining the cost of construction?
14. When and for what purpose is the elemental approach used in determining the cost of construction?
15. What is the estimated regulatory base in construction? What does she include?
16. What are elemental estimated norms? What do they include? How are used in determining the estimated cost? Give the calculation formulas.
17. What are unit rates? What do they include? How are used in determining the estimated cost? Give the calculation formulas.
18. What documents consists of a section of the design documentation "Estimate for the construction of capital construction"? What is the order of their development? 19. What is a local estimate? What information does it contain? How is it compiled?
19. What is an object estimate calculation? What information does it contain? How is it compiled?
20. What is a consolidated estimate? What information does it contain? How is it compiled?
21. What should contain an explanatory note to the estimate documentation?

Questions for discussion

1. What is the importance of pricing ah functioning of a market economy?
2. What are the consequences of the imbalance of supply and demand in the market?
3. What are the features of pricing in construction and the real estate market?
4. What is the essence of the cost and value approach in pricing?
5. What features of construction products determine the features of pricing in construction?
6. Why is the estimated cost of construction usually different from the market price of construction products?

7. What is the essence of the resource, resource-index and base-index methods for determining the estimated cost in construction? What are the advantages and disadvantages of each of these methods?
8. Why is the estimate documentation compiled? Can construction be carried out without budget documentation? Why?
9. What explains the high complexity of the preparation of budget documentation? How can I reduce labor costs for the preparation of budget documentation?

Questions to solve the problem yourself

1. What pricing factors affect the cost of construction and real estate? Give examples. Explain the effects of specific factors in these examples. What determines the variety of pricing factors in construction? What pricing factors can and should a construction company manage? How? Build a chain: the pricing factor — its impact on the price of construction products — tools (mechanisms) for managing this factor.
2. Familiarize yourself with the methodological documents in construction that determine the methodology of estimated pricing in construction (MDS -81...). Make a list of them with the main provisions presented in each document.
3. Familiarize yourself with the structure of the estimated regulatory base in construction. Find the state elemental estimated norms for certain types of work (on the instructions of the teacher). Write down the composition of resources and their consumption rates for this type of work. Find the collections of prices for these resources in the estimated regulatory base. How to convert expenditure ratios to cost? Determine the estimated cost of these types of work.
4. Find in the estimate and regulatory base collections of federal unit rates for certain types of work (on the instructions of the teacher). Write down the composition of the costs included in the unit price for this type of work. How to determine the cost of construction works using unit prices?
5. Familiarize yourself with the forms of estimated documentation presented in MDS 81-35.2004. What is the difference between these forms? What information should contain. Try to draw up budget documentation for certain types of work on the capital construction project using standard Microsoft Excel capabilities (based on the source data provided by the teacher). Use the resource method and the base index method. Estimate your labor costs for completing this task.
6. Find information on professional software products used for automated budgeting. Describe their capabilities.

Chapter 5

CONSTRUCTION CONTROL, ACCEPTANCE, AND COMMISSIONING OF REAL ESTATE COMPLETED

5.1 Conformity assessment of buildings and structures. Conformity Assessment Forms

The definition of conformity assessment is given in the Federal Law of December 27, 2002, No. 184-FZ "On Technical Regulation"[1]: conformity assessment is a direct or indirect determination of compliance with the requirements for an object.

For the purpose of technical regulation of buildings and structures of any purpose (including the networks of engineering and technical support and engineering and technical support systems included in them), as well as the design processes (including surveys), construction, installation, commissioning related to buildings and structures, operation and disposal (demolition), the Federal Law of December 30, 2009 N 384-FZ "Technical regulation on the safety of buildings and structures" was adopted[2] (hereinafter — the Technical Regulations).

The technical regulation applies to all stages of the life cycle of a building or structure. However, it does not extend to the safety of technological processes corresponding to the functional purpose of buildings and structures. Only possible hazardous effects of these processes on the condition of a building,

[1]Federal law of 27.2002 N 184- FZ "On technical regulation"

[2]Federal Law of December 30, 2009 No. 384- FZ "Technical Regulations on the Safety of Buildings and Structures"

structure or parts thereof are subject to accounting. An assessment of the conformity of engineering survey results should determine the conformity of such results to the requirements of the Technical Regulations.

The conformity assessment of design documentation should determine the conformity of design documentation to the requirements of the Technical Regulations and the results of engineering surveys.

An assessment of the conformity of a building or structure during the construction process and at its completion should determine the conformity of the work performed during the construction process, the results of their implementation and the applied building materials and products to the requirements of the Technical Regulations and design documentation.

The conformity assessment of a building or structure during operation should determine the conformity of the building or structure with the requirements of the Technical Regulations and design documentation.

The technical regulation establishes the forms and rules for the mandatory assessment of the conformity of buildings and structures, as well as the processes of design (including survey), construction, installation, commissioning and disposal (demolition) associated with buildings and structures.

A mandatory assessment of the conformity of buildings and structures , as well as the processes of design (including surveys), construction, installation, commissioning and disposal (demolition) associated with buildings and structures, is carried out in the form of:

1) statements on the compliance of project documentation with the requirements of the Technical Regulations; it is carried out before the design documentation is approved by the designer by drawing up assurance that the design documentation is developed in accordance with the design assignment and the requirements of the Technical Regulations;

2) state or non-state examination of the results of engineering surveys and design documentation; carried out in accordance with the rules and within the time limits established by the legislation on urban development, and only in cases stipulated by the legislation on urban development;

3) construction control;

4) state construction supervision; carried out in accordance with the rules and within the time limits established by the legislation on urban development, and only in cases stipulated by the legislation on urban development;

5) statements of conformity of a constructed, reconstructed or renovated building or construction of design documentation; carried out by the contractor and builder (customer) after the completion of construction, reconstruction, overhaul of the building or structure before putting them into operation by signing a document confirming the conformity of the constructed, reconstructed

or renovated building or construction of design documentation (except for individual housing construction);

6) statements on the compliance of the constructed, reconstructed or renovated building or structure with the requirements of the Technical Regulations; carried out by the contractor after completion of construction, reconstruction, overhaul of the building or structure before putting them into operation by signing a document confirming compliance of the constructed, reconstructed or renovated building or structure with the requirements of the Technical Regulations;

7) Putting the facility into operation; carried out in accordance with the rules and within the time limits established by the legislation on urban development.

A mandatory assessment of the conformity of buildings and structures, as well as operating processes associated with buildings and structures with the requirements of the Technical Regulations and the requirements established in the design documentation, is carried out in the form of:

1) Operational control; carried out by the person responsible for the operation of the building or structure, in accordance with the legislation of the Russian Federation;

2) State control (supervision); is carried out by authorized federal executive bodies, executive bodies of the constituent entities of the Russian Federation in cases and in the manner established by federal laws.

In addition to the mandatory forms for assessing the conformity of buildings and structures, as well as the design processes (including surveys), construction, installation, commissioning and disposal (demolition) associated with buildings and structures, the Technical Regulations establish the Rules for voluntary conformity assessment of buildings and structures, as well as those associated with buildings and constructions of design processes (including surveys), construction, installation, commissioning, operation and disposal (demolition).

Voluntary assessment of the conformity of buildings and structures , as well as the processes of design (including surveying), construction, installation, commissioning, operation and disposal (demolition) associated with buildings and structures, is carried out in the form of a non-state examination of the results of engineering surveys and design documentation, architectural supervision[3], surveys of buildings and structures, the state of their foundations, building structures and systems of engineering and technical support and in other forms stipulated by the legislation of the Russian Federation.

[3]Code of rules SP 246.1325800.2016 "Regulation on the supervision of the construction of buildings and structures" (approved by order of the Ministry of Construction and Housing and Communal Services of the Russian Federation of February 19, 2016 N 98 / pr)

For the purposes of the Technical Regulations, building codes and rules approved before the date of entry into force of this Federal Law are recognized as codes of practice.

The technical regulation provides for the approval by the Government of the Russian Federation of a list of national standards and sets of rules, because of which, on a mandatory basis, compliance with its requirements is ensured[4]. The national standardization body of the Russian Federation approves, publishes and places the law a list of documents in the field of standardization, the application of which on a voluntary basis ensures compliance with the requirements of the Technical Regulations[5].

5.2 Examination of design documentation and engineering survey results

The design documentation of capital construction facilities and the results of engineering surveys performed to prepare such design documentation are subject to examination, with the exception of cases provided for by the Town Planning Code[6]. An examination of design documentation and (or) an examination of the results of engineering surveys is carried out in the form of a state examination or non-state examination. The developer or technical customer, at his choice, sends the design documentation and the results of engineering surveys to the state examination or non-governmental examination, unless, in relation to the design documentation of capital construction objects and the results of engineering surveys performed to prepare such design documentation, a state examination is provided.

Examination is not carried out in relation to the design documentation of individual capital construction projects. These include individual housing projects up to three floors; interlocked residential buildings (townhouses) with up to three floors and ten isolated blocks; apartment buildings up to three floors and four sections; non-residential and non-industrial buildings with an area of up to 1,500 square meters up to two floors; industrial buildings with an

[4]Decree of the Government of the Russian Federation of December 26, 2014 No. 1521 "On approval of the list of national standards and codes of rules (parts of such standards and codes of rules), as a result of which, on a mandatory basis, compliance with the requirements of the Federal Law" Technical Regulation on Building Safety and facilities

[5]Order of the Federal Agency for Technical Regulation and Metrology of March 30, 2015 No. 365 "On approval of the list of documents in the field of standardization, as a result the application of which on a voluntary basis ensures compliance with the requirements of the Federal Law of December 30, 2009 No. 384-FZ "Technical Regulations on the Safety of Buildings and Structures"

[6]Town Planning Code of the Russian Federation of December 29, 2004 No. 190-FZ, Article 49

area of up to 1,500 square meters up to two floors, not related to particularly dangerous, technically complex or unique.

Moreover, if the construction, reconstruction of such capital construction projects is planned to be carried out within the boundaries of the protected areas of pipeline transport facilities, examination of design documentation for the construction, reconstruction of these capital construction facilities is mandatory.

An expert examination of the design documentation of the capital construction object, which has received a positive expert opinion and is used repeatedly, or its modification, is not required. An examination of design documentation is not carried out if a construction permit is not required for the construction or reconstruction of the capital construction facility. Examination of design documentation is not carried out in relation to sections of design documentation prepared for overhaul of capital construction projects, with the exception of design documentation prepared for overhaul of public roads.

In the above cases, an examination of the results of engineering surveys is also not required.

The results of engineering surveys can be sent for examination simultaneously with the design documentation or before sending the design documentation for examination.

The project documentation of all facilities subject to state expertise is to be reconstructed in the territories of two or more constituent entities of the Russian Federation, embassies, consulates and representative offices of the Russian Federation abroad, in the exclusive economic zone of the Russian Federation, on the continental shelf of the Russian Federation, in inland sea waters, in the territorial sea of the Russian Federation, defense and security facilities, other facilities, information about which are state confidential secret of highways of federal significance, objects of cultural heritage (historical and cultural monuments) of federal significance (if constructive and other characteristics of the reliability and safety of such an object are touched upon while preserving the cultural heritage of federal significance), especially dangerous, technically complex and unique objects, objects used for the disposal and (or) disposal of waste of I–V hazard classes, other objects defined by the Government Of the Russian Federation, objects, construction, reconstruction of which are financed from the budgets of the budget system of the Russian Federation, public roads, major repairs of which are financed or are supposed to be financed from the budgets of the budget system of the Russian Federation, objects of cultural heritage of regional and local significance (in the case of if, when carrying out work to preserve the object of cultural heritage of regional or local significance, the constructive other and other characteristics of the reliability and safety of the specified object) and the results of engineering surveys performed to prepare such design documentation, as well as design documentation of facilities whose construction and reconstruction it is supposed to be carried out on the lands of specially protected natural territories, facilities used for placement and (or) neutralization of waste of I–V hazard classes.

In the event that there are changes in the design documentation affecting the structural and other safety characteristics of the capital construction project and (or) leading to an increase in estimates for its construction or reconstruction at comparable prices, the design documentation, as amended, is subject to examination.

The subject of the examination is the assessment of compliance of design documentation with the requirements of technical regulations, including sanitary and epidemiological, environmental requirements, the requirements of state protection of cultural heritage sites, the requirements of fire, industrial, nuclear, radiation and other safety, as well as the results of engineering surveys, and assessment of compliance with the results engineering surveys to the requirements of technical regulations.

It is not allowed to conduct other examinations of project documentation, except for the examination of project documentation provided for by the Town Planning Code, the state historical and cultural examination of project documentation for the conservation of cultural heritage objects, as well as the state environmental review of project documentation of objects whose construction, reconstruction is supposed to be carried out in exclusive economic zone of the Russian Federation, on the Ross continental shelf Federation, in inland sea waters, in the territorial sea of the Russian Federation, on the lands of specially protected natural territories, on the Baikal natural territory, as well as design documentation for facilities used for the disposal and (or) neutralization of waste of hazard classes I–V, artificial land on water bodies.

The result of the examination of project documentation is a *conclusion on compliance* (a positive conclusion) or *inconsistency* (negative conclusion) of the project documentation with the requirements of technical regulations and the results of engineering surveys, the requirements for the content of sections of design documentation, and also about the conformity of the results of engineering surveys with the requirements of technical regulations.

The negative conclusion of the examination may be challenged by the developer or the technical customer in court.

Decree of the Government of the Russian Federation of March 5, 2007 No. 145[7] determines the procedure for organizing and conducting in the Russian Federation a state examination of project documentation and the results of

---

[7]Decree of the Government of the Russian Federation of March 5, 2007 No. 145 "On the procedure for organizing and conducting the state examination of design documentation and engineering survey results"

engineering surveys (hereinafter referred to as the state examination), the procedure for determining the amount of fees for conducting a state examination, issuing an opinion on the modified project documentation of a capital construction object that has received a positive conclusion from the state examination of design documentation (hereinafter — the conclusion on the modification of design documentation), as well as The core of charging this fee.

The state examination begins after the applicant submits documents confirming the payment of the state examination in accordance with the contract, and ends with the submission (delivery) of the state expert opinion to the applicant.

The term of the state examination should not exceed 60 days. Within no more than 45 days, a state examination is carried out:

a) the results of engineering surveys that are aimed at state a new examination before sending design documentation to this examination;

b) design documentation or design documentation and engineering survey results for residential capital construction projects, including those with built-in non-residential premises not related to unique objects;

c) design documentation or design documentation and engineering survey results in relation to capital construction projects, the construction, reconstruction and (or) overhaul of which will be carried out in special economic zones.

The terms of the state examination can be extended at the initiative of the applicant for no more than 30 days in the manner prescribed by the contract.

When conducting a state examination of project documentation, operational changes may be made to the design documentation in the manner prescribed by the contract.

The conclusion of the state examination is prepared and signed by persons certified for the right to prepare conclusions of the examination of project documentation and (or) the results of engineering surveys (hereinafter referred to as the expert) and participating in the state examination, and approved by the head of the organization for conducting the state examination or his authorized person.

Project documentation cannot be approved by the developer or technical customer in the presence of a negative opinion of the state examination of project documentation.

The organization for the conduct of state examination shall maintain a register of issued conclusions of state examination. When conducting a state examination, a state examination case is opened. State examination cases relate to archival documents of permanent storage. Their destruction, as well as correction and (or) seizure of documents contained in them are not allowed.

The design documentation and (or) the results of engineering surveys are sent repeatedly (2 or more times) to the state examination after eliminating the deficiencies indicated in the negative conclusion of the state examination, or when making changes to the design documentation that received a positive conclusion from the state examination, in terms of changing technical solutions that affect the structural and other safety features of the capital construction facility.

The expert assessment during the repeated state examination is subject to the part of the design documentation and (or) the results of engineering surveys, which were amended, as well as the compatibility of the changes made with the design documentation and (or) the results of engineering surveys, in relation to which the state examination was previously conducted.

By the Decree of the Government of the Russian Federation of May 18, 2009 No. 427[8] (hereinafter — Resolution No. 427) approved the "Regulation on the verification of the reliability of the estimated cost of construction, reconstruction, overhaul of capital construction projects, the conservation of cultural heritage objects (historical and cultural monuments) of the peoples of the Russian Federation, which are financed from raising funds from the budgets of the budget system of the Russian Federation, funds from legal entities created by the Russian Federation, constituent entities of the Russian Federation, municipal and entities, legal entities, the share of the Russian Federation, constituent entities of the Russian Federation, municipal entities in the authorized (joint-stock) capital of which is more than 50 percent. "

The estimated cost is subject to verification of the estimated cost of the preservation of cultural heritage objects in the event that when carrying out such work, structural and other characteristics of the reliability and safety of cultural heritage objects are affected.

The subject of verification of estimated cost is the study and evaluation of the calculations contained in the estimated documentation, in order to establish their compliance with the approved estimated standards, information about which is included in the federal register of estimated standards, the physical

---

[8]Decree of the Government of the Russian Federation of May 18, 2009 No. 427 "On the procedure for verification of the determination of the estimated cost of construction, reconstruction, overhaul of capital construction objects, work on the preservation of cultural heritage objects (historical and cultural monuments) of the peoples of the Russian Federation, financing which are carried out with the involvement of budget funds of the budget system of the Russian Federation, funds of legal entities created by the Russian Federation, constituent entities of the Russian Federation, municipalities "burning entities, legal entities, the share of the Russian Federation, constituent entities of the Russian Federation, municipal entities in the authorized (joint-stock) capital of which is more than 50 percent."

volume of work, constructive, organizational, technological and other decisions provided for by the design documentation, as well as in order to not exceed the estimated cost of the aggregated norm of the construction price.

In the absence of aggregated standards for the construction price for facilities similar in purpose, design capacity, natural and other conditions of the territory on which it is planned to carry out construction, the calculations contained in the estimate documentation are also examined and evaluated for compliance with the estimated (marginal) construction cost calculated based on documented information about similar projects.

In cases where the development of project documentation is not required, an assessment is made of the conformity of the calculations to the physical volumes of work included in the statement of volumes of work or the certificate of technical inspection of the capital construction object and the defective statement when checking the estimated cost of capital repairs.

Verification of the estimated cost is carried out within the period stipulated by the contract, which cannot be more than 30 working days. When checking the estimated cost, changes to the estimated documentation can be carried out in time and in the manner prescribed by the contract. At the same time, the period for conducting an estimate of estimated cost can be extended on the basis of an agreement or an additional agreement to it, but not more than 30 working days.

The results of checking the estimated cost are made out in the form of a *conclusion on the reliability* (positive conclusion) or *inaccuracy* (negative conclusion) of determining the estimated cost of construction, reconstruction, overhaul of the capital construction object, work to preserve the cultural heritage object (hereinafter — the conclusion).

The conclusion should contain the justification of the conclusions on the reliability (inaccuracy) of determining the estimated cost of construction, reconstruction, overhaul of the capital construction object, work on preserving the cultural heritage object with links to specific provisions of the estimated standards and listing inconsistencies associated with the incorrectness and (or) unreasonability of the accepted in the calculations of the physical volumes of work, structural, organizational, technological and other solutions provided for by the design document orientation.

A negative opinion may be challenged by the applicant in court.

If, after receiving a positive opinion, changes were made to the design documentation, the estimated cost is checked again.

The state examination of project documentation and engineering survey results, as well as verification of estimated cost, are carried out at the expense of the applicant. Payment for state expert examination and estimated cost verification is made regardless of the result of the estimated cost verification.

By the Decree of the Government of the Russian Federation of March 31, 2012 No. 272[9] approved the "Regulation on the organization and conduct of non-state examination of project documentation and (or) the results of engineering surveys", which establishes the procedure for organizing and conducting non-state examination of the project documentation of capital construction objects (hereinafter referred to as project documentation) and (or) the results of engineering surveys, completed for the preparation of project documentation (hereinafter referred to as engineering surveys, non-state examination).

Non-state examination is carried out by legal entities accredited for the right to conduct non-state examination in the manner established by the Government of the Russian Federation (hereinafter referred to as the expert organization).

Non-state examination is carried out on the basis of an agreement between the applicant and the expert organization, concluded in accordance with the civil legislation of the Russian Federation.

Procedures for conducting a non-state examination, including the preparation of an expert opinion, its signing, approval, issuing to an applicant and appealing, as well as opening and conducting cases of a non-state examination, maintaining a register of issued expert opinions and providing information from the said register, are carried out in the manner established for state examination of project documentation and (or) the results of engineering surveys by the Regulation on the organization and conduct of state examination of the project documentation and the results of engineering surveys, taking into account the features established by this Regulation.

5.3 Construction control

In accordance with the Town Planning Code[10] construction control is carried out during the construction, reconstruction, overhaul of capital construction facilities in order to verify compliance of the work performed with project documentation, the requirements of technical regulations, engineering surveys, construction requirements, reconstruction of the capital construction facility established on the date of issue submitted for receipt permits for the construction of the urban development plan of the land plot, as well as the permitted use of land of land and restrictions established in accordance with the land and other Russian legislation.

[9]Decree of the Government of the Russian Federation of March 31, 2012 No. 272 "On approval of the Regulation on the organization and conduct of non-state examination of design documentation and (or) the results of engineering surveys"

[10]Town Planning Code of the Russian Federation of December 29, 2004 No. 190-FZ, Article 53

Construction control is carried out by the person carrying out the construction. In the case of construction, reconstruction, overhaul based on a construction contract, construction control is also carried out by the *builder, technical customer, the person responsible for the operation of the building, structure*, or the regional operator or an individual entrepreneur or legal entity employed by them based on the contract. The developer or technical customer, on his own initiative, may engage a person preparing the project documentation to check the compliance of the work performed with the project documentation.

During the construction, reconstruction, overhaul of the capital construction facility by the person carrying out the construction (the person carrying out the construction, and the developer, the technical customer, the person responsible for the operation of the building, structure, or the regional operator in case of the construction, reconstruction, overhaul on the basis of construction contract), control should be carried out for the performance of works that affect the safety of the capital construction facility Government and in accordance with the technology of construction, reconstruction, overhaul, control over the implementation of which cannot be carried out after other work is completed, as well as over the safety of building structures and sections of engineering and technical support networks, if the elimination of deficiencies identified during construction monitoring is impossible without disassembly or damage to other building structures and sections of engineering networks, for the conformity of the specified works, structures and network sections to the requirements of technical regulations and design documentation. In cases stipulated by the design documentation, the requirements of technical regulations, structural tests should be carried out. Based on the results of monitoring the implementation of these works, the safety of these structures, sections of engineering networks, inspection certificates are drawn up for these works, structures, sections of engineering networks.

The comments of the developer, the technical customer, the person responsible for the operation of the building, structure, or regional operator involved in the construction control of persons on the shortcomings of the work during the construction, reconstruction, overhaul of the capital construction object must be made in writing. An act is drawn up to eliminate these shortcomings, which is signed by the person who submitted comments on these shortcomings, and the person carrying out the construction.

By the Decree of the Government of the Russian Federation of June 21, 2010 No. 468[11] (hereinafter — Resolution No. 468) approved the "Regulation on the construction control during the construction, reconstruction and overhaul of

[11] Decree of the Government of the Russian Federation of June 21, 2010 No. 468 "On the procedure for conducting construction control during the construction, reconstruction and overhaul of capital construction facilities"

capital construction projects", which establishes the procedure for construction control during the construction, reconstruction and overhaul (hereinafter — construction) of objects capital construction, regardless of the sources of their financing, as well as the procedure for determining the amount of costs for conducting construction control and number of employers carrying building control, for the projects financed in whole or in part with funds from the federal budget.

The subject of construction control is to verify the execution of work during the construction of capital construction facilities for compliance with the design requirements and working documentation prepared on its basis, the results of engineering surveys, the requirements of the urban development plan of the land plot, and the requirements of technical regulations in order to ensure the safety of buildings and structures.

The functions of construction control are entitled to be carried out by the employees of the contractor and the customer, who are assigned the responsibility for the implementation of such control in the prescribed manner.

The construction control carried out by the contractor includes the following control measures:

a) quality control of building materials, products, structures and equipment supplied for the construction of the capital construction facility (input control);

b) verification of compliance with established norms and rules of storage and storage knowledge of the products used;

c) verification of compliance with the sequence and composition of technological operations walkie-talkies during the construction of the capital construction facility;

d) together with the customer, the examination of the works hidden by subsequent works (hidden works), and the interim acceptance of the erected building structures affecting the safety of the capital construction object, sections of engineering networks;

e) acceptance of completed types (stages) of work;

f) verification together with the customer of the conformity of the completed construction facility with the design requirements and the working documentation prepared on its basis, the results of engineering surveys, the requirements of the urban development plan of the land plot, technical regulations.

Construction control carried out by the customer includes the following control measures:

a) verification of the completeness and compliance with the established deadlines for the contractor to perform incoming control and the reliability of the documentation of its results; b) verification of the implementation by the contractor of control measures to comply with the rules of warehousing and storage of applied products and the reliability of documenting its results;
b) checking the completeness and compliance with the deadlines for the contractor to control the sequence and composition of technological operations for the construction of capital construction facilities and the reliability of documenting its results;
c) together with the contractor, the examination of the hidden works and the intermediate acceptance of the erected building structures affecting the safety of the capital construction facility, sections of engineering networks;
d) verification together with the contractor of the conformity of the completed construction facility with the design requirements and the working documentation prepared on its basis, the results of engineering surveys, the requirements of the urban development plan of the land plot, and the requirements of technical regulations; *Input control is* carried out until the products are used in the construction process and includes checking the availability and content of suppliers' documents containing information about the quality of the products they delivered, their compliance with the requirements of working documentation, technical regulations, standards and codes of practice. The contractor is entitled to carry out measurements and tests of the relevant products on its own in the established procedure during the incoming inspection or to entrust them with the accredited organization. In case of detection during the incoming inspection of products that do not meet the established requirements, their use for construction is not allowed.

If during the verification of compliance with the rules of warehousing and storage violations of the established norms and rules are revealed, the use of products stored in violation for construction is not allowed until the compliance of its quality indicators with the requirements of the working documentation, technical regulations, standards and codes of practice.

Until the completion of the examination procedure for hidden work, subsequent work is prohibited.

In the event that control measures are carried out jointly by the contractor and the customer, the contractor provides a notice to the customer about the date and time of these events no later than 3 working days.

If the customer was notified in the prescribed manner and did not appear to participate in the control measures, the contractor has the right to conduct them in the absence of the customer.

The control event and its results are recorded by drawing up an act. Information on the control activities carried out and their results are reflected in the general journal of work with the appendix of the relevant acts.

At capital construction projects being erected in whole or in part with the involvement of federal budget funds, the implementation of construction control by the contractor is financed by the overhead costs of the contractor provided for in the price of the construction contract.

The annex to Resolution No. 468 defines the standards for the cost of the customer for the implementation of construction control during the construction of capital construction projects, financed in whole or in part with the involvement of the federal budget, and the standards for the number of employees of the customer, which are assigned the responsibility for the implementation of construction control in the prescribed manner. These costs are indicated in chapter 10 of the consolidated estimated calculation of the cost of construction as a separate line "Construction control".

5.4 State Construction Supervision

State Construction Supervision[12] is carried out at:

1) the construction of capital construction projects, the design documentation of which is subject to examination or is a modified design documentation;

2) reconstruction of capital construction objects, including during the conservation of cultural heritage objects, affecting the structural and other characteristics of the reliability and safety of such objects, if the project documentation for the reconstruction of capital construction objects, including these works on the preservation of cultural heritage, subject to examination.

The subject of state construction supervision is the verification of:

1) the compliance of the work and the building materials used in the construction process, reconstruction of the capital construction facility, as well as the results of such work, to the requirements of technical regulations, design documentation, including the requirements for energy efficiency and the requirements for equipping the capital construction facility with metering devices for energy resources used;

2) the availability of a building permit;

3) the fulfillment of the requirements for membership in the SRO of construction participants and the right to carry out works that affect the safety of capital construction facilities.

---

[12]Urban Planning Code of the Russian Federation of December 29, 2004 No. 190-FZ, Article 54

Based on the results of the inspection, the state construction supervision body draws up an act, which is the basis for issuing to the person carrying out the construction, an order to eliminate the identified violations. The prescription shall indicate the type of violation, a reference to the regulatory legal act, technical regulation, design documentation, the requirements of which are violated, and also establish the deadline for eliminating the violations identified. The suspension of construction and reconstruction of a capital construction facility for a specified period shall be carried out in the manner established by the legislation of the Russian Federation.

It is not allowed to carry out other types of state supervision during the construction, reconstruction of capital construction projects, except for state construction supervision, as well as federal state environmental supervision in relation to objects whose construction is being carried out in the exclusive economic zone of the Russian Federation, on the continental shelf of the Russian Federation, in the internal sea waters, in the territorial sea of the Russian Federation, on the lands of specially protected natural territories, on artificial land plots on water bodies, and state supervision of the state, maintenance, preservation, use, popularization and state protection of cultural heritage sites during the conservation of cultural heritage sites, and during the construction, reconstruction of capital construction facilities related in accordance with legislation in the field of environmental protection to facilities of category I.

By the Decree of the Government of the Russian Federation of February 1, 2006 No. 54[13] approved the "Regulation on the implementation of state construction supervision in the Russian Federation".

The task of state construction supervision is the prevention, detection and suppression of violations of the laws on urban development, including technical regulations, and project documentation made by the developer, customer, and also the person carrying out construction on the basis of an agreement with the developer or customer (hereinafter — the contractor).

In the absence of technical regulations, the subject of state construction supervision is to verify the compliance of the work performed, the applied building materials and the results of such work with building codes, federal standards and rules in the field of atomic energy use, sanitary and epidemiological rules and standards, fire safety requirements, and environmental protection, energy efficiency requirements and equipment requirements and the capital construction facility with meters for used energy resources, the requirements of state protection of cultural heritage sites and the requirements for the preservation of cultural heritage sites, the norms and rules of civil

[13] Decree of the Government of the Russian Federation of February 1, 2006 No. 54 "On State Construction Supervision in the Russian Federation"

defense engineering measures, industrial safety requirements, reliability and safety requirements in the electric power industry, and hydrotechnical safety standards and rules facilities, other safety rules and state standards, as well as the requirements of other legal acts of the Russian Federation and normative legal acts of the federal executive authorities, subject to compulsory execution in the construction, reconstruction of capital construction projects (hereinafter — the rules and regulations).

If during construction, reconstruction of capital construction projects it is envisaged to carry out state construction supervision, then the state construction supervision body within the framework of state construction supervision shall carry out federal state fire supervision, federal state sanitary and epidemiological surveillance, state control (supervision) of compliance of the capital construction object with the requirements for its energy efficiency and requirements on its equipment metering devices used energy resources, as well as state environmental oversight.

Federal executive bodies authorized to carry out federal state construction supervision carry out such supervision during the construction and reconstruction of facilities specified in clause 5.1 of Article 6 of the Town Planning Code of the Russian Federation, with the exception of facilities of federal nuclear organizations. The State Atomic Energy Corporation "Rosatom" exercises federal state construction supervision during the construction and reconstruction of facilities of federal nuclear organizations.

The executive authorities of the constituent entities of the Russian Federation authorized to carry out regional state construction supervision (regional state construction supervision bodies) shall exercise such supervision over the construction, reconstruction of other capital construction facilities, if state construction supervision is provided for during their construction and reconstruction.

When organizing regional state construction supervision, a *risk-based approach is used.*

State construction supervision is carried out by the state construction supervision body from the date it receives a notice of commencement of work until the date of issuing a conclusion on the compliance of the constructed, reconstructed capital construction facility with the requirements of technical regulations (norms and rules), other regulatory legal acts and design documentation, including the requirements in regarding energy efficiency and requirements regarding the equipment of the capital construction project with metering devices used energy resources (hereinafter referred to as the conclusion on compliance).

In order to apply a risk-based approach to the organization of regional state construction supervision, construction, reconstruction of capital construction projects should be assigned to certain risk categories. The assignment of a risk category to a building under construction, reconstruction under reconstruction is carried out by the regional state construction supervision body after receiving notification of the start of work at such an object in accordance with the criteria for classifying construction and reconstruction of capital construction projects as risk categories when carrying out regional state construction supervision taking into account information from project documentation, received a positive conclusion of the examination of the project documentation. The assignment of a risk category is documented by order (order) of the head (deputy head) of the regional state construction supervision body and is reflected in the inspection program.

In accordance with the criterion of the severity of potential negative consequences of possible non-compliance by legal entities and individual entrepreneurs with the requirements established by federal laws and other regulatory legal acts of the Russian Federation adopted in accordance with them, in the course of construction and reconstruction of capital construction objects, such objects belong to the following risk categories:

- *high risk* — public buildings and structures, apartment buildings, overpasses, tunnels, bridges and overpasses, as well as capital construction projects with a span of 20 to 100 meters;
- *significant risk* — industrial buildings;
- *moderate risk* — capital construction projects not indicated in paragraphs three and four of this document.

State construction supervision is carried out in the form of inspections.

Verification of compliance of the work performed, applied building materials during the construction process, reconstruction of the capital construction facility and the results of such work with the requirements of technical regulations, norms and rules, as well as the requirements of other regulatory legal acts and design documentation, shall comply with:

a) during construction — the requirements for the preparation of the land and the implementation of earthwork, installation of foundations, structures of underground and aboveground parts, networks of engineering and technical support (including internal and external networks), engineering systems and equipment;

b) during reconstruction — the requirements for the preparation of the capital construction object for reconstruction in case of changes in the parameters of the capital construction object, its parts, as well as the replacement and (or) restoration of the supporting building structures of the capital construction object (with the exception of replacing individual elements of such structures with similar or other improving indicators of such structures, elements and (or) restoration of these elements), as well as requirements for the performance of work to change pairs meters of linear objects or their sections (parts), which entails a change in the class, category and (or) initially established indicators of the functioning of such objects (power, load capacity and others) or which requires a change in the boundaries of the right of way and (or) security zones of such objects;

Inspections are carried out by an official (officials) of the state construction supervision body authorized on the basis of the relevant order (order) of the state construction supervision body and on its behalf to carry out such supervision in accordance with the inspection program, as well as in the case of notifications, appeals from individuals and legal entities, state authorities and local governments.

The inspection program is developed by an official of the state construction supervision body taking into account the design and other features of the capital construction object and the implementation of work on its construction, reconstruction, conditions for subsequent operation, as well as other factors that must be taken into account in accordance with the requirements of technical regulations (norms and rules), other regulatory legal acts and design documentation.

When carrying out regional state construction supervision, the inspection program is compiled taking into account the following number of inspections for the construction period, reconstruction of the capital construction facility for the corresponding risk category of the capital construction under construction, reconstructed:

a) for the high risk category — no more than 12 inspections;

b) for the category of significant risk — no more than 10 checks;

c) for the moderate risk category — no more than 7 checks.

The indicated number of inspections for the period of construction and reconstruction of the capital construction object may be increased by no more than 2 inspections in the following cases:

a) construction, reconstruction of the capital construction facility in the conditions of cramped urban development (in accordance with the design documentation);

b) construction, reconstruction of the capital construction facility in difficult engineering and geological conditions (in accordance with the design documentation);

c) construction, reconstruction of the capital construction facility, total whose area exceeds 20,000 square meters.

The number of inspections for the period of construction and reconstruction of the capital construction object can be increased, respectively, with respect to the capital construction object to which the high risk category is assigned, up to 24 inspections, for the capital construction object to which the significant risk category is assigned, up to 20 inspections, in relation to capital construction facility to which the moderate risk category is assigned — up to 14 inspections in cases of:

a) bringing legal entities and individual entrepreneurs engaged in the construction, reconstruction of the capital construction facility within one calendar year 3 or more times to administrative responsibility for offenses provided for by the Code of the Russian Federation on administrative violations[14];
b) violation of the terms of construction, reconstruction of the capital construction facility, provided for by the construction organization project in the design documentation that has received a positive expert opinion for more than 6 months or its conservation, suspension of construction.

If violations are discovered by the official of the state construction supervision body as a result of the audit, an act is drawn up that is the basis for issuing orders to the customer, developer or contractor to eliminate such violations. The prescription shall indicate the type of violation, a reference to the technical regulation (norms and rules), other regulatory legal act, design documentation, the requirements of which are violated, and the deadline for eliminating the violations shall be established taking into account the structural and other features of the capital construction project.

Other inspection results are entered by the official of the state construction supervision body in the general and (or) special journals.

After completion of construction, reconstruction of the capital construction facility, the state construction supervision body conducts an audit, based on the results of which the work performed is evaluated and a decision is made to issue a conclusion on compliance or to refuse to issue such a conclusion.

The body of state construction supervision issues a conclusion on compliance, if during the construction, reconstruction of the capital construction object there were no violations of the compliance of the work performed with the requirements of technical regulations (norms and rules), other regulatory legal acts and design documentation, or such violations were eliminated before the date of issue of the conclusion about compliance.

[14]Code of the Russian Federation on Administrative Offenses of December 30, 2001, No. 195-FZ

In other cases, the state construction supervision body refuses to issue a statement of compliance. The decision on the refusal to issue a conclusion of conformity should contain a justification of the reasons for such a refusal with references to the technical regulation (norms and rules), another regulatory legal act, and design documentation.

The decision to refuse to issue a statement of compliance may be challenged by the developer or customer in court.

State construction supervision during the construction, reconstruction of nuclear facilities (including nuclear installations, storage facilities for nuclear materials and radioactive substances), hazardous production facilities, hydraulic structures is carried out in conjunction with inspections and inspections provided for by laws and other regulatory legal acts of the Russian Federation governing relations in the field of ensuring the safety of these facilities.

5.5 Issuance of permission to put an object into operation

Permission to put an object into operation[15] is a document that certifies the completion of construction, reconstruction of the capital construction facility in full in accordance with the building permit, design documentation, as well as the compliance of the constructed, reconstructed capital construction facility with the requirements for construction, reconstruction of the capital construction facility established on a date issuance of a land plot submitted for obtaining a permit for the construction of a town-planning plan Using the land or in the case of construction, reconstruction of a linear object project planning area and land survey design and limitations set forth in accordance with the land and other Russian Federation.

To put an object into operation, the developer applies to the federal executive body, the executive body of a constituent entity of the Russian Federation, a local government body or an authorized organization that carries out state management of atomic energy use and state administration in carrying out activities related to the development, manufacture, disposal of nuclear weapons and military nuclear power plants, or the State Space Corporation "Roskosmos", building permits issued, with an application for a permit for the facility to operate.

A refusal to issue a permit for putting an object into operation may be challenged in court.

[15] Urban Planning Code of the Russian Federation of December 29, 2004 No. 190-FZ, Article 55

The permission to put the facility into operation is the basis for state registration of the constructed capital construction facility, and for amending the state accounting documents of the reconstructed capital construction facility.

The permit for putting the facility into operation shall reflect information on the capital construction facility in the amount necessary for the implementation of its state cadastral registration.

The permission form for putting the facility into operation was established by order of the Ministry of Construction and Housing and Communal Services of the Russian Federation of February 19, 2015 N 117 / pr[16].

5.6 Construction and cost studies

In accordance with paragraphs. "G" p. 13 of the Decree of the Government of the Russian Federation dated 01.02.2006 No. 54 "On State Construction Supervision in the Russian Federation", the inspection may be associated with the conduct (designation) by the state construction supervision body of examination, surveys, laboratory, and other tests performed works and applied building materials.

The purpose of the research activities carried out as part of the audit is to establish the conformity of the results of work performed during the construction, overhaul or other form of repair, reconstruction, expansion, modernization, technical re-equipment to a specific norm, rule or regulation.

The objects of research are buildings, structures, structures, other construction objects, including those whose construction is not completed; their individual structures, elements and interfaces; land plots functionally associated with them; as well as initial permitting, design, executive, primary accounting, contractual, and other documentation related to the process of construction work.

A number of types of research that are significantly different from each other precedes the establishment of the conformity of the object of study to any norm, rule or regulation. Let us consider them in more detail.

1) *Establishing the presence of an object (existential research).* The basis, motive for solving this issue is a direct normatively fixed indication of the need for the existence of an object.

The life cycle of construction products — from the development of design estimates to the construction, modernization and reconstruction, demolition

[16] Order of the Ministry of Construction and Housing and Communal Services of the Russian Federation of February 19, 2015 No. 117 / pr "On approval of the form of a building permit and the form of permission to put an object into operation"

(dismantling) and disposal of buildings, structures and structures — is documented, in a strictly defined order, with mandatory regulation of the volume and cost of work performed, detailed and sequential recording of data on their implementation. Thus, the Civil Code of the Russian Federation (Civil Code of the Russian Federation) provides for the obligatory availability of technical documentation for the organization carrying out construction and related works that defines the scope, content of work and other requirements for them (Part 1 of Article 743 of the Civil Code of the Russian Federation).

Establishing the presence (absence) of documents provided for by special rules is usually the first stage of a study aimed at resolving subsequent issues.

2) *The establishment of quantitative characteristics of the object (volumetric studies)* includes the implementation of actions (measurements and calculations) in order to establish the actually performed amount of work, installed equipment, used structures and materials. Quantitative characteristics, for example, include the volume of erected monolithic reinforced concrete structures (m^3), the area of interior decoration (m^2), the length of installed utilities (m), etc.

The procedure for determining the volume of work performed is described in specialized literature[17]. The most complete and detailed technical norms, methods and rational techniques for calculating the volume of work and the consumption of building materials for various types of work are presented in thematic guides[18].

3) *Establishment of qualitative characteristics of the object (attributive research).* The properties of construction products are most often investigated. These objects, like any material formations, have an infinite number of properties, however, only those that are relevant in a particular situation become the subject of research. These are functional (destination properties), operational properties and safety properties. In the course of the study, it is necessary to identify, study, evaluate certain signs of the object and express their judgment on its properties. When determining the properties of an object under study,

[17]In general terms, see MDS-81.35.2004, "Methodology for Determining the Cost of Construction Products on the Territory of the Russian Federation," specified in the "Technical Part" sections of the relevant Price Collections used in calculating the cost of certain types of work.

[18]See, for example: *Golubev B.I.* Determination of the volume of construction work: Ref. M., 1991; *Zineva L.A.* Handbook of a civil engineer: in 2 volumes. Rostov n / a, 2006. These publications include a description of the studies under consideration in relation to the results of excavation, construction and installation (monolithic and prefabricated reinforced concrete, stone, wooden structures), roofing, finishing works, as well as thermal insulation, ventilation, waterproofing works, heat supply, water supply and sewage works (internal and external networks).

it should be assumed that it is characterized not only by the presence, but also by the absence of certain signs.

There is such a thing as a "negative circumstance", when what is supposed to be present is missing. For example, the absence of air draft in the ventilation opening of the natural exhaust ventilation system of a residential building indicates a clogged ventilation riser or unauthorized narrowing (reduction in cross-sectional area) of sections of the ventilation duct.

In order to obtain a more complete picture of the properties under consideration and the ways of their establishment, it seems appropriate to describe the most significant of them.

Functional properties determine the purpose of construction products. They are formed already at the stage of manufacturing building materials, therefore, research begins, as a rule, with their study, regardless of whether the issue of determining the causes and conditions of the emergence and development of destructive processes in building structures, or complete (partial) loss of functional or a separate element of thc building structure.

In addition to the technical aspect, the social aspect is clearly visible in the concept of "the property of designating construction products". The main purpose of individual rooms and the building as a whole is to satisfy housing, industrial and other human needs. The fullest compliance of the building and structure with the designation stipulated by the project is achieved, in particular, by observing the technology of construction production, carrying out design, engineering and survey and other works at a modern technical level.

Operational properties make it possible to use the object in accordance with its functional purpose. The law provides for the right of the construction customer to refuse to accept the result of work in the event that defects are found that exclude the possibility of its use for the purpose specified in the construction contract and cannot be eliminated by the contractor or customer (part 6 of article 753 of the Civil Code of the Russian Federation). Thus, the operating procedure for buildings provides for "consumption of constructed facilities", i.e. the use of their premises, systems, adjacent territories for specific purposes. If we are talking about a residential building, proper operation means the use of apartments for citizens to meet, the needs of which can only be met with the smooth functioning of all engineering systems, certain dimensions of the premises, noise level, insolation, lighting in them, etc.

When answering the question about the compliance of operational properties with special rules, it should be assumed that the requirements for them are divided into general and special. General requirements apply to all buildings, special — to certain groups of buildings that differ in the specifics of purpose or production technology. General and special operational requirements are formulated in the norms and technical conditions for the design of certain groups of buildings, and special requirements, determined by purpose or design solution, are contained in the design specification.

Security properties. In accordance with the law, the construction contractor is not entitled to use equipment during the implementation of works if this can lead to a violation of the mandatory safety requirements for construction works (part 2 of article 751 of the Civil Code of the Russian Federation). In the study of such objects, the establishment is subject to the safety of their operation. These properties should include, for example, the reliability of equipment — it is provided already at the design stage, and then manufacture, taking into account the mechanical, thermal and chemical effects to which it must be subjected during operation. In addition to the strength characteristics of machines and mechanisms that determine their ability to not collapse and, therefore, not to injure people, you need to keep in mind the hazards that are created in the process of working equipment.

The need for a study of the safety of an object arises when it becomes possible to use residential (industrial) premises in accordance with their functional purpose. Quite often, cases of using materials containing harmful substances for human health (formaldehyde, menthol, benzene, chlorinated hydrocarbons, etc.) are identified during construction and finishing works. Establishing their presence and concentration is impossible without conducting comprehensive studies — with the participation of specialists in toxic substances and materials.

The definition of the properties of the object of research carried out during the test is not exhausted. This is only one of their stages, among others, including classification and diagnostic, if the identified properties of the object serve as the basis for its attribution to any official set or for determining its technical condition.

4) *Establishment of an object belonging to a certain class, genus, species, group (classification studies).* A common feature of classification studies is the establishment of an object's belonging on the basis of determining its properties and characteristics to the official (provided by a state standard or other regulatory document) set of objects whose properties and characteristics are known in advance.

Quite often, the issue of the belonging of building products, parts, structures to products, parts, structures of one class or another, type, type, is solved. So, when examining masonry, you need to determine its type — simple, medium complexity, complex; in the study of the structure (structure) — the concrete grade and class of reinforcement, the brands of the structures and parts themselves, the type of soil on which the construction is carried out.

This type of research should also include the establishment of ownership:

- products of the building materials industry (parts, products, structures) to a specific type, brand, class;
- products of construction production (buildings, structures, structures) to a specific series, type of capitality, area of operation (industrial, civil, etc.);
- buildings and structures for a group involving the operation of facilities in special conditions (seismic and mudflow hazardous, with a high level of groundwater, in areas with unstable soils, etc.);
- carried out (planned) repair and construction work for the capital, current, preventive type of repair, etc.

5) *Establishing the value of the object (cost studies).* Studies of this type are aimed at determining the cost of construction and special works actually performed at a construction site. The cost of construction work is determined in accordance with the terms of the contract, based on the current estimated standards, as well as the provisions set forth in MDS 81-35.2004. These standards can be divided into two types.

The first type includes the following estimated standards: state (GOS[19]), sectoral (DOS) and territorial (TSN).

The second type includes company (FSN) and individual (ISN) estimated standards.

The first type of cost calculations is characterized by the fact that the basis for determining the cost of construction work here is the use of estimated federal territorial[20] or industry standards (the last two standards take into account the specifics of a particular region or industry). Estimated regulatory frameworks, as well as conversion factors for the cost from the base price level to the current (or for a certain period of the past), are periodically updated. To draw up estimates, licensed software systems are used (for example: Smeta.ru, Grandsmeta, etc.).

The second group of estimated standards is characterized by the fact that they (company and individual) are used in cases where:

- it is stipulated by the terms of the contract[21];

---

[19]The corresponding unit rates (FER, TER, etc.) are based on both the GOS and the DOS and TSN

[20]The use of territorial unit prices is mandatory subject to the financing of construction from the regional budget. In the case when financing is made from the federal budget or the terms of the contract stipulate the use of federal estimated standards, the cost is calculated according to FER.

[21]Under the current legislation, business entities are entitled on a contractual basis and on an equal footing to use any procedure for calculating the cost of construction that meets the actual conditions of work.

- state, industry and territorial standards do not regulate the procedure for calculating the cost of certain (specific[22]) types of work[23].

Consider the procedure for conducting cost calculations of these two types.

1. Determination of the cost of actually completed (unfulfilled) work using GOS (FER) and TSN (TER). Based on the data obtained in the course of previous studies, the structure of the future estimate calculation is determined: sections of the estimate are formed on various grounds (according to the types of completed or unfulfilled works, individual elements of a construction object, etc.). Each section is filled with prices for the types of work performed (outstanding)[24]; their volumes are affixed. When using the software package, the base cost of work is recalculated to the current price level automatically; the calculation of overhead costs and profit estimates for each rate also takes place. Here it is necessary to take into account the special conditions of the work (if any) by introducing the cost of each coefficient of the coefficient: increasing, for example, constraint as a condition that complicates the work, or lowering, for example, dismantling structures[25].

   Given the terms of the contract, the calculation of the winter rise in price is made for the total estimated cost or for each rate for cost items. If the contract does not provide a procedure for calculating the rise in price of winter, but it is assumed that the regional specifics of pricing must be taken into account, it is necessary to contact the State Customs Service 81-05-02-2007 (for new construction) and the GSNr81-05-02-2001 (for repair of civilian facilities). When calculating other limited costs, it is necessary to be guided by the terms of the contract and the provisions set forth in MDS 81.35-2004, using a licensed estimate complex.

   The result of the actions taken is the cost of actually completed (unfulfilled) work at the construction site.

---

[22]For example: "Venetian plaster", the installation of certain air conditioning fan coils, the installation of low-current video surveillance systems, etc. In other words, when the products of the construction industry are made using new technologies that are not provided for by the existing estimated standards of the state, departmental (industry) and territorial levels.

[23]The use of company and individual estimated standards for determining the cost of construction, the financing of which is carried out with the involvement of the federal (regional) budget, is recommended after their approval by the relevant authorized federal (regional) executive body in the field of construction

[24]To ensure the correctness of the cost calculation when choosing quotations, it is necessary to take into account the data provided in the Technical parts of the used collections of quotations.

[25]In relation to the dismantling of structures in the absence of a direct price, the price for the installation of the corresponding structures with the indicated reduction factor is applied

In practice, often when determining the cost of actually performed work using GOS (FER) and TSN (TER), it becomes necessary to establish the conformity of the applied rates of the estimated regulatory base in the estimates and acceptance certificates of the work performed (KS-2 form). When solving this issue, a comparative table is compiled, where one of the columns reflects the prices applied in the estimates and (or) acceptance certificates of the work performed, submitted for research, the other column reflects the prices necessary for use in accordance with the provisions of the current budget and regulatory base. The column "note" states the judgment on the correctness (incorrectness) of the application of one or another price.

In case of discrepancies identified, it is recommended to recalculate the estimate (acts of acceptance of work performed) in accordance with the verified rates and indicate the cost expression of the established discrepancy.

2. Determination of the cost of actually performed (unfulfilled) work using company and individual rates. The mechanism for conducting cost calculations here is similar to the calculation mechanism described above. The differences are as follows:

    - the basis of the calculation is not the prices of a certain estimated regulatory base (FER, TER, etc.), but the results of the analysis of publicly available information on the cost of performing those types of work (including the cost of structures, products and materials) that are subject to assessment;
    - the weighted average cost of these works and materials is determined.

When analyzing the information on unit prices of construction companies and trading enterprises, it is taken into account that some organizations include unit costs and others do not include certain types of costs (overhead costs, estimated profit, transportation, value added tax, etc.).

6) *Establishment of the state of the object (diagnostic studies).* During their conduct, deviations from the requirements of building codes and rules (SNiP) governing both design and construction itself can be established, and signs can be identified, the study of which will allow us to ascertain the occurrence and development of destructive processes in the structures of the structure under study — this may be indicated by cracks, deflections, chips, etc. in them Knowing the general laws of such processes will make it possible to formulate a predictive conclusion, for example: "Under these conditions, the building will inevitably be destroyed." When researching premises, during which only the presence (absence) of deviations from sanitary norms is established, there will be no prognostic component — the conclusions will contain only a statement of a fact, for example, the fact of a deviation from the standard value of the level of insolation, lighting, noise, as a result of which it was found that the condition of the investigated object does not meet the requirements for residential premises.

In accordance with Part 1 of Art. 754 of the Civil Code of the Russian Federation, the construction contractor is liable to the customer for deviations from the requirements provided for in the technical documentation and in building codes binding on the parties, and during the reconstruction (renovation, reconstruction, restoration, etc.) of a building or structure is assigned to the contractor responsibility for the reduction or loss of strength, stability, reliability of the building, structure or part thereof. In relation to the above circumstances, diagnostic studies of a stating nature will also be conducted.

During the diagnostic studies, the characteristics of the object of study are correlated with the requirements of special norms and rules, which can be divided into general and particular. The general ones should include the rules governing issues related to the construction industry, regardless of the specific activities of a particular construction organization. To private — rules, instructions, regulations developed for a specific construction organization (its subdivisions) and approved in the prescribed manner. Information about documents containing general rules is reflected in the relevant norms, rules, standards.

7) *Establishing the presence and types of causal relationship between events, phenomena, actions and processes (causal research).* Conducting research of this type is aimed, as a rule, at establishing the presence and types of causal relationship between deviations from the requirements of special rules and various negative events (phenomena).

Causal research is required when establishing:

- accidental or other nature of death or damage to the construction object (part 1 of article 741 of the Civil Code of the Russian Federation);
- the presence (absence) of a causal relationship between the death (damage) of the construction object and the poor quality of the used material, parts or structures or the execution by the contractor of erroneous instructions from the customer (part 2 of article 741 of the Civil Code of the Russian Federation);
- the possibility (absence thereof) of the use of certain building materials without compromising the quality of the work to be performed (part 2 of article 745 of the Civil Code of the Russian Federation);
- the possibility (absence thereof) of the negative impact of deviations from the terms of the construction contract on the quality of the work to be performed (part 2 of article 748 of the Civil Code of the Russian Federation);
- the possibility (absence thereof) of the negative impact of certain building materials, the results of the contractor's execution of the customer's in-

structions on the environment, as well as on the safety of construction work (part 2 of article 351 of the Civil Code of the Russian Federation);

- reasons for exceeding the construction budget and the presence (absence) of a causal relationship of such excess with the actions of the contractor (part 3 of article 744 of the Civil Code of the Russian Federation);
- causal relationship between defects in technical documentation and costs,
- incurred in connection with their establishment and elimination (part 4 of article 744 of the Civil Code of the Russian Federation);
- causal relationship between improper actions of the customer (contractor) and death (damage) of the results of work performed at a certain stage of their production (part 3 of article 753 of the Civil Code of the Russian Federation);
- a causal relationship between improper design and survey work and deficiencies discovered during construction, as well as the operation of an object created on the basis of technical documentation and survey data (part 1 of article 761 of the Civil Code of the Russian Federation);
- causal relationship between the suspension of work and the death (damage) of the construction object (part 4 of article 743 of the Civil Code of the Russian Federation);
- a causal relationship between construction work, the operation of the construction site and the harm or the threat of new harm (part 2 of article 1065 of the Civil Code and part 1 of article 1079 of the Civil Code).

The peculiarity of the attitude in practice to issues related to causality lies in the fact that the intermediate attention often does not fall into the intermediate phenomena that make up the causal chain — the study focuses only on those parts of it that represent the beginning and end of the corresponding chain, called the cause and consequence. At the same time, the completeness of the study will be ensured only if the entire set of phenomena and processes that led to the event is covered.

Studies related to the establishment of the causes, conditions, circumstances and the mechanism for reducing the quality indicators of a constructed or operated construction object are quite common: the construction contractor is responsible for defects (defects) found within the warranty period if it does not prove that they occurred due to normal deterioration of the facility or its parts, improper operation or incomplete instructions for its operation, improper repair of the facility, made about the customer himself or third parties attracted by him (part 2 of article 755 of the Civil Code of the Russian Federation), but is not responsible for minor deviations from technical documentation that he admits without customer's consent, if he proves that they did not affect the quality of the construction object (part 2 Article 754 of the Civil Code of the Russian Federation). The basis for solving this issue should be taken from the results of causal research.

8) *Establishment of compliance of an object with any norm, rule or regulation (regulatory and technical research).* Studies of this type are aimed at establishing compliance (absence thereof) with the requirements of special rules (any norm, regulation) of construction products. They are characterized by the process of comparing the existing and the proper; their distinguishing feature is the presence of a norm (the provision of a special rule) in the system of elements of comparison.

In the construction industry of Russia, regulatory and technical documents are systematized and are part of a single mechanism for regulating production and public relations. The regulatory framework governing the construction sector is represented by a wide range of documents. However, the following regulatory legal documents are most important for the implementation of the inspections under consideration:

1. The Town Planning Code of the Russian Federation of December 29, 2004 No. 190-FZ;
2. Civil Code of the Russian Federation of November 30, 1994 No. 51-FZ;
3. The Housing Code of the Russian Federation dated December 29, 2004 No. 188-FZ;
4. Federal Law of December 30, 2009 No. 384-FZ "Technical Regulations on the Safety of Buildings and Structures";
5. Federal Law of December 27, 2002 No. 184-FZ "On Technical Regulation";
6. Federal Law of April 5, 2013 No. 44-FZ "On the contract system in the field of procurement of goods, works, services to ensure state and municipal needs";
7. Decree of the Government of the Russian Federation of February 16, 2008 No. 87 "Regulation on the composition of sections of project documentation and requirements for their content."

To this list should be added codes of rules (building codes, building codes, updated building codes), national and international standards, guidance documents in construction (RD), methodological documents in construction (MDS) and estimated standards.

Regulatory documents that approve the forms of primary accounting documents in construction include:

- Decree of the Goskomstat of Russia of October 30, 1997 No. 71a "On approval of unified forms of primary accounting documentation for the accounting of labor and its pay, fixed assets and intangible assets, materials, low-value and wearing items, works in capital construction";

- Decree of the State Statistics Committee of Russia dated November 11, 1999 No. 100 "On approval of unified forms of primary accounting documentation for the accounting of works in capital construction and repair and construction works".

When conducting inspections, regulatory legal documents should be used as amended in the period in respect of which research is being conducted. In this case, it is necessary to comply with the requirements of the Decree of the Government of the Russian Federation dated December 26, 2014 No. 1521 "On approval of the list of national standards and codes of rules (parts of such standards and codes of rules), as a result of which, on a mandatory basis, compliance with the requirements of the Federal Law "Technical Safety Regulation buildings and structures."

5.7 Methodological basis of research conducted during the audit

The methodological foundations of the research conducted during the audit are a set of methods and techniques used in the study of construction sites and the territory functionally associated with them. Methods according to the sequence of their application can be divided into the following groups:

1. methods of systematization and subsequent study of documentary data to be investigated;
2. methods for detecting, establishing the location of individual building structures and products in buildings and structures, as well as their fixation;
3. methods of preliminary research of objects in order to establish their nature, method of manufacture and choice of direction for subsequent research;
4. methods of analytical and synthesizing research of objects;
5. methods for presenting the course and results of the study.

Research methods are also divided into two independent, but interrelated areas: general scientific and special.

General scientific methods include:

- analysis (mental breakdown of any complex phenomenon into components — simpler parts, elements);

- synthesis (combination, reproduction of individual parts, elements, sides, components of a complex phenomenon and the achievement of the whole in its unity);
- generalization (the logical method of transition from single to general, from less general to more general meaning);
- comparison (comparison of properties and attributes of two or more objects);
- professional observation (deliberate and organized in a certain way with the designation of tasks and the formulation of the ultimate goal, the perception of the subject, the phenomenon as a whole or its individual parts, parts, properties, as well as relationships with other objects);
- modeling is the study of objects on models, that is, on conditional images, diagrams, or physical structures similar to the object under study, using the methods of analogy and similarity theory;
- reconstruction — a special case of modeling, that is, restoration of the original appearance, condition, appearance of an object from its remains or descriptions; process or phenomenon — according to available information about them;
- idealization — the creation and study of ideal, mentally constructed objects;
- measurement — a set of actions performed using measuring instruments to find the numerical value of a quantity. It should be noted that the use of this method involves the mandatory observance of metrological requirements (verification, calibration, certification) to the measuring instruments used in the research;
- description (recording the results of observations by means of plain text, figures, numbers, graphs, charts, symbols) [26]

Special methods include:

- acoustic, electrophysical, electromagnetic and thermal methods;
- regulatory control (provides for the study of the contents of a single document from the point of view of its compliance with the current regulatory documents);
- formal verification (a verification method in which the completeness of filling all the details in a document is established);

[26]Distinguish between *direct* and *indirect* description. The first is carried out to consolidate the results of direct observation, it consists in fixing the signs in the process of observation or at the end of it (from memory). The second — includes signs of objects that are perceived by others or identified through technology.

- comparison of documents (a method that allows mutual control of two or more types of documents);
- calculation methods, including those based on the use of specialized licensed software systems.

The main research methods are also divided into *solid* and *selective.*

The choice to conduct a continuous or selective study in relation to the objects of construction, reconstruction, modernization, technical re-equipment, overhaul depends on the specifics of the object of study, as well as on the conditions of a particular situation.

The project, estimates and control measurements are selectively checked in relation to specific types and specific volumes of work, which are among the largest and most expensive in their total volume.

To conduct research on construction sites are used:

1. measuring instruments (tape measures, rangefinders, calipers, instruments for measuring the thickness of the protective layer of concrete, ultrasonic thickness gauges, probes, curvimeter, electronic levels, total stations, etc.);
2. means of fixation and observation (cameras, video cameras, video scopes, binoculars, magnifiers, quadcopters);
3. construction tools and equipment (lamps, step-ladders);
4. organizational and computing devices;
5. specialized software systems and reference systems (GRAND-Estimate, AutoCAD, Tehekspert, ADEPT-Project).

The measuring instruments used in the research should be of the approved type, verified in accordance with the requirements of the Federal Law of 06.26.2008 No. 102-FZ "On ensuring the uniformity of measuring instruments".

When checking the quality of work performed and used building materials, the following methods can be used:

- organoleptic method, in which a visual inspection of the work performed and applied building materials is carried out;
- instrumental method, when the quality and the exact amount of the materials used are actually used up for construction and installation works;
- laboratory method, which establishes the quality of building materials, the conformity of their design estimates. It is used in stationary or field laboratory conditions on samples, samples extracted from the structures of buildings and structures. It uses physical, chemical, physico-mechanical and physico-chemical research methods designed to analyze morphology (external structure), composition (elemental, molecular, phase — qualitative

and quantitative), structure, physical and chemical properties of substances and materials used in construction industry.

All these three methods can be used both individually and comprehensively, when there is a need to use not one, but two or all three methods (if the building object is fully tested, then all three verification methods are used).

The list of research tools and methods presented here, of course, is not exhaustive — in fact, it is much wider, more diverse and constantly increasing with the development of science and technology, as well as construction technology and the construction industry as a whole[27].

5.8 Acceptance and commissioning of completed real estate

5.8.1 General provisions for the acceptance of a completed construction project commissioning

In the codes of practice for the organization of construction and acceptance into operation of objects completed by construction (SP 48.13330.2011 and SP 68.13330.2017, respectively), two concepts are distinguished:

- *acceptance of an object completed by construction* — a set of technical, technological and legal actions for the commissioning of an object completed by construction from the construction and installation work contractor (general contractor) to the developer (technical customer) or another person authorized by the developer. As a result, the developer (investor) receives ownership of the accepted object. Next, the developer (technical customer) proceeds with the preparation of this facility for commissioning;
- *commissioning of the facility* — a set of technical, technological and legal actions of the builder (acceptance committee) confirming the readiness of the completed construction of the property for operation for its intended purpose.

Acceptance of the object is the final stage of the investment stage of the project management for the construction of the building (a complex of buildings and structures), and the commissioning of the object is the first stage of the operational stage of the project management. Therefore, in the theory of project management and in the regulations for the organization of construction, two concepts are used for the finished construction object:

[27] For more on this see: K.P. Hornbeam. Guidelines for the implementation of construction and technical research in relation to the construction, reconstruction, modernization, technical re-equipment and overhaul facilities. — M., Treasury Publishing House, 2018.

ready for acceptance by the customer (developer) from the contractor (general contractor); ready for commissioning. The construction object is understood as a complex of buildings and (or) structures, a separate building or structure, or its autonomous part, erected for a particular developer under one building permit. Building — a ground construction with premises for living and (or) activities of people, production facilities, storage of products or keeping animals. Construction — a single result of construction activities, designed to carry out certain consumer functions. Finished construction project — a construction project in a structure that allows its independent use for its intended purpose, on which the supporting, enclosing structures and engineering systems are provided, in accordance with the requirements of the design, regulatory and technical documentation, which together provide the strength and stability of the building (structure), weather protection, temperature, safety of users, the public and the environment.

At the *investment stage of the project*: an object completed by construction — a complex of buildings and structures (a separate building or structure), or its autonomous part, allowing the possibility of its independent operation, on which all the construction and construction contracts provided for in accordance with the requirements of the project and regulatory documents are executed and accepted installation work.

At the *operational stage of the project*: an object completed by construction and prepared for operation — an object on which all construction work has been completed in accordance with the project, the installation of engineering systems and technological equipment has been completed, a set of testing and commissioning works has been carried out, production has been conducted in trial mode (provision of services) in the amount established by the project for the end of the launch period. Transfer of external communications for maintenance to operating organizations has been ensured, special permits for the operation of the facility and equipment have been obtained in the relevant state supervision bodies.

Acceptance and commissioning of the completed construction object are important functions of the developer, who can entrust the fulfillment of his functions on a contractual basis to the technical customer. The technical customer carries out its activities on behalf of, at the expense of financial resources and in the interests of the developer.

Under a construction contract, the contractor undertakes to build a specific object on the instructions of the builder within the time period specified by the contract, and the builder undertakes to create the necessary conditions for the contractor to perform the work, accept their result and pay the stipulated price (Article 740 of the Civil Code of the Russian Federation). Upon completion of the work stipulated by the contract, the developer must accept the completed building from the contractor, and then, at the production facilities, arrange for the adjustment and testing of equipment, trial production and other activities for preparing the production facility for operation.

5.8.2 Procedure for acceptance and commissioning of capital construction facilities

The customer (developer) independently determines the procedure (scheme) for the commissioning of the completed real estate object, being guided by the provisions of SP 68.13330.2017. This set of rules is an updated version of SNiP 3.01.04 - 87 “Acceptance of the completed construction projects” and was put into effect on January 28, 2018. According to the generally accepted scheme, an object is put into operation in two stages. At the *first stage, the* object is accepted from the contractor by the developer in accordance with the terms of the construction contract and is executed by the Acceptance Certificate of the completed building for a certain purpose and the Acceptance Certificate of the object in the form of KS-11; at the *second stage, the* customer, after organizing and performing the necessary additional work (commissioning with trial operation and production, connecting the facility to external engineering systems, transferring the facility to the operating organization and a number of other works) puts the facility into operation through acceptance commission (or without it) under the control of state construction supervision, state technical supervision, state supervision, state sanitary and epidemiological surveillance, operating organization and other representatives of the organization basics. If the construction of the object was carried out with the attraction of budgetary funds or by order of the executive authorities (social and cultural facilities, engineering infrastructure of the city, municipality, apartment buildings and their complexes), then their representative is appointed as the chairman of the acceptance committee. The commissioning of the facility is made out by the Permission of the executive authority to commission the facility, which is issued on the basis of the State Construction Supervision Act and the Acceptance Certificate of the completed construction of the facility by the acceptance commission, drawn up in the form of KS-14.

Completed construction projects constructed at the expense of private investments and other extra budgetary funds are accepted and put into operation by the customer in accordance with the provisions of the building permit, design documentation. Acceptance of an object that is not fully ready for operation is possible (for example, retail premises on the ground floor of an unfinished construction of a retail and office center). Further, the customer may not complete the remaining set of works for some time, that is, temporarily “freeze” the construction and commissioning of the facility in full, waiting for more favorable conditions for doing business. A private customer has the right to involve a future operating organization, project authors, specialized organizations, insurance companies in the acceptance of the object, but only with the right of an advisory vote. The costs of organizing the acceptance of objects into operation are borne by the developer. Upon acceptance into operation of a private facility without an acceptance commission, the date of commissioning of the facility is the date the executive authority adopted the legal act on operation.

The process of acceptance into operation of the completed construction facility (after state registration) is being completed by registering it with the developer in the form of KS-14 as an asset.

Upon completion of the construction of the building or structure, its compliance with the requirements of applicable law, technical regulations, design and working documentation is evaluated, the results of which are the acceptance and commissioning of the completed building or structure.

When accepting buildings or structures, it is necessary to comply with the requirements specified in the exhaustive list of procedures in the field of housing construction, the exhaustive list of procedures in the field of construction of capital construction projects of non-residential buildings and the exhaustive list of procedures in the field of construction of heat supply networks.

The builder shall inform the federal executive authorities, executive authorities of the constituent entities of the Russian Federation or local authorities and state construction supervision in advance of the readiness of the facility for commissioning.

To fulfill its functions, in accordance with applicable law the developer may involve a technical customer — a professional or legal entity acting on a professional basis. In this case, the technical customer is authorized by the developer to organize the acceptance procedure of the object and sign the necessary documents on its behalf.

Organization of object acceptance is assigned to the developer (technical customer), the basic functions of which in this case are:

- Acceptance of the construction project completed by the construction company from the person carrying out the construction, in case of performance of work under an agreement (contract);

- organization of adjustment and testing of equipment, trial production of products and other measures to prepare the facility for operation;

- Presentation of the completed construction to the state construction supervision authorities;

- presentation of the completed construction facility to the federal executive body, the executive body of the constituent entity of the Russian Federation, local government or an authorized organization that issued the building permit;

- acquisition, storage and transfer to the relevant organizations of executive and operational documentation.

The developer (technical customer) accepts the object or part of it from the person carrying out the construction, if there is a building permit obtained in accordance with the provisions of SP 48.13330.2011 "Organization of construction" and the requirements of Article 51 of the Town Planning Code of the Russian Federation.

Upon acceptance of the facility, its compliance with the requirements of the permit for the construction of the facility, SNiP and design documentation, technical regulations, established by the provisions of federal laws of December 27, 2002 No. 184-FZ "On Technical Regulation", dated December 30, 2009 No. 384-FZ "Technical Regulation on the safety of buildings and structures ", dated 23.112009 No. 261-FZ " On energy supply and improving energy efficiency "and other regulatory documents.

In the case of the construction of the facility by a legal entity performing two or more functions (developer, technical customer, designer, contractor), the head of this legal entity may involve responsible executives of the relevant structural divisions of the organization for acceptance of the constructed (reconstructed) capital construction facility.

Until the presentation of the completed construction project for acceptance, all changes in the design documentation must be made in the prescribed manner.

The person who carried out the development of project documentation may make additions to the project documentation related to changes in the urban development plan of the land plot, as well as the need to take into account the technical capabilities of the person carrying out the construction, and (or) coordination of the deviations from the design documentation between the construction participants.

After the full implementation of all the work stipulated by the project documentation or the construction contract (contract), the person carrying out the construction is sent a statement to the builder (technical customer) along with certificates of compliance of the completed construction with the requirements of technical regulations and project documentation with the following attachment:

- a list of organizations involved in the construction, installation and commissioning works, indicating the types of work they perform and the engineering and technical workers directly responsible for their implementation, copies of certificates of admission to work that affect the safety of capital construction projects;

- executive documentation, general and special journals of accounting for the performance of work, corresponding in terms of composition and procedure for maintaining the requirements of regulatory documents;
- the supervision magazine for the construction project as a whole or for individual buildings and structures, as well as for launch complexes, if such are provided for in the design documentation, during the supervision;
- certificates, technical passports, test reports and other documents certifying the quality, safety and properties of materials, structures and products used in the performance of work;
- test reports of indoor and outdoor electrical installations and electrical networks, telephone, radio, television, alarm and automation devices, devices providing explosive, fire safety, lightning protection, and fire protection systems, adhesion strength in masonry of load-bearing walls of stone buildings located in seismic areas;
- materials of inspections carried out during the construction process by state and departmental supervision bodies;
- confirmation of compliance of the facility with the requirements of energy efficiency and equipping them with meters of used energy resources;
- conclusions of the authorized bodies of the State Labor Inspectorate on the possibility of putting into operation new or reconstructed industrial facilities.

After receiving from the person carrying out the construction, a written statement about the readiness of the object for acceptance, the technical customer accepts the object.

A person carrying out construction, declaring compliance on the basis of both his own evidence and evidence obtained with the participation of third parties, has the right to independently generate evidence to confirm the conformity of construction products with the requirements of project documentation and technical regulations.

In order to receive a conclusion from the state construction supervision authorities on the compliance of the constructed (being reconstructed) capital construction facility with the requirements of technical regulations (norms and rules), other regulatory legal acts and design documentation, the builder (technical customer) shall notify the state construction supervision authority of the completion of construction (reconstruction) of the facility or parts thereof, if the commissioning of a part of the facility is provided for by the design assignment, by the contract (act) and project documentation.

The notice shall be sent by the developer (technical customer) after the actual completion of the construction (reconstruction) of the capital construction facility, elimination of all violations during the construction (reconstruction), execution of executive documentation related to all construction (reconstruction) of the capital construction facility, as well as with building materials, products and structures.

The decision on the possibility of issuing a conclusion on the compliance of the constructed, reconstructed capital construction facility with the requirements of technical regulations (norms and rules), other regulatory legal acts and design documentation or on refusal to issue such a conclusion is made after the state construction supervision body conducts an audit performed at the end of construction, reconstruction of the facility. Based on the results of the audit, an act is drawn up.

When conducting an inspection carried out upon completion of construction, reconstruction of an object, the developer (technical customer) must provide the state construction supervision authorities with the opportunity:

- visual inspection of the constructed (reconstructed) capital construction facility in full (including individual work performed, building structures, sections of engineering networks and applied building materials (products);
- verification of all acts (regulations, notices) on elimination of violations (deficiencies) identified during the implementation of state construction supervision and construction control.

To verify the completion of construction, reconstruction of the facility, the following documents must be submitted to the state construction supervision authorities:

- general and (or) special magazines;
- executive documentation, including certificates of inspection of works, structures, sections of engineering networks affecting safety, the monitoring of which cannot be carried out after other works are performed, as well as without disassembling or damage to building structures and sections of engineering networks — technical support;
- acts on elimination of violations (deficiencies) in relation to the work performed, identified in the process of construction control and the implementation of state construction supervision;
- the results of examinations, examinations, laboratory and other tests of work performed during construction control;
- documents confirming the quality control of the applied building materials;

- documents confirming the execution of decisions on cases of administrative offenses.

Prior to signing the acceptance certificate, performed upon completion of construction, reconstruction of the facility, the technical customer arranges the connection of the capital construction facility to the networks of engineering and technical support in accordance with the technical conditions and the provision of the documentation specified in the exhaustive list of procedures in the field of housing construction, section 4 “Procedures, related to the granting of permission to put the facility into operation, state registration of rights to the constructed facility, the conclusion of contracts for energy, heat, water, gas supply) and wastewater disposal ”, an exhaustive list of procedures in the construction of non-residential capital construction projects, section 5“ Procedures related to the granting of permission to commission a capital construction of non-residential premises into operation, state registration of rights to constructed object, by the conclusion of energy, heat, water, gas, and wastewater agreements ”and an exhaustive list of procedures in the field of construction of heat supply networks, section 5“ Procedures linked with submission of permits for the facility to operate, the state registration of rights to the built object.”

The connection of facilities under construction (reconstructed) to the networks of engineering support is carried out in the following order:

- submission by the technical customer of an application for connection indicating the required amount of connected load to the organization operating the engineering networks, or to local authorities;

- conclusion of a contract with an organization operating engineering networks for the subject of connection, taking into account the technical conditions previously received by the technical customer from the contractor or local government, or from the previous owner of the land, provided that they have not expired;

- fulfillment by the parties of the terms of the connection agreement (taking measures for the actual connection of the facility to the networks of engineering and technical support), verification by the parties of the implementation of these measures;

- connecting the completed construction facility to the engineering and technical support networks and signing by the parties of the acts specified in the exhaustive list of procedures in the field of housing construction, non-residential capital construction projects and construction of heat supply networks.

During the verification carried out upon completion of construction, reconstruction of the facility, state construction supervision bodies must be provided with documents establishing the compliance of the constructed (reconstructed) capital construction facility with energy efficiency requirements and the equipping of energy meters used with them.

The built-in and built-in attached civil defense premises are accepted by the developer (technical customer) together with the relevant territorial operating services and state oversight bodies.

The result of the audit, carried out at the end of construction, reconstruction of the facility, is issued by the relevant act. This act is the basis for the application of the builder (technical customer) to the state construction supervision authorities to issue a conclusion on the compliance of the constructed (reconstructed) capital construction facility with the requirements of technical regulations (norms and rules), other regulatory legal acts and design documentation.

The Conclusion of Conformity is issued by the state construction supervision body if during the construction (reconstruction) of the capital construction facility there were no violations of the compliance of the work performed with the requirements of technical regulations (norms and rules), other regulatory legal acts and design documentation, including requirements, equipment requirements capital construction facility with meters for used energy resources, or such violations were eliminated before the date of issue of the opinion on conformity.

The compliance statement should contain information on the class of energy efficiency.

The state construction supervision body may refuse to issue a statement of conformity if previously identified violations have not been eliminated.

A conclusion on the compliance of the constructed (reconstructed) capital construction facility with the requirements of technical regulations (norms and rules), other regulatory legal acts and design documentation, or a decision to refuse to issue such a conclusion shall be provided to the developer (technical customer) or the representative of the state building authority who has applied for the conclusion supervision in a single copy within 10 working days after receipt of the notice.

The adoption by the state construction supervision body of a decision to refuse to issue a conclusion of compliance does not preclude the repeated application of the builder (technical customer) to issue a conclusion of compliance after eliminating the reasons that served as the basis for the refusal to issue a conclusion of compliance.

To commission the facility, the developer applies to the federal executive body, the executive body of the constituent entity of the Russian Federation, the local government or an authorized organization that issued the building permit, with an application for the issuance of permission to put the facility into operation.

An application for a permit to put an object into operation and the attached documents shall be submitted by the developer or his authorized representative in person or by post, or may be sent to the email address in the form of an electronic document drawn up in accordance with regulatory requirements for the provision of state and municipal services and electronic signature.

The documents attached to the application for the issuance of permission to put the facility into operation must be authentic or duly certified copies.

1. Title documents for the land.
2. The urban development plan of the land plot or, in the case of construction, reconstruction of a linear facility, a project for the planning of the territory and a project for land surveying.
3. Building permit.
4. The acceptance certificate of the capital construction object, in case of construction, reconstruction on the basis of the contract.
5. A document confirming the compliance of the constructed, reconstructed capital construction facility with the requirements of technical regulations and signed by the person who carried out the construction.
6. A document confirming the compliance of the parameters of the constructed, reconstructed capital construction project with project documentation, including the requirements of energy efficiency and equipment of the capital construction project with meters for energy resources used and signed by the person who completed the construction (the person who completed the construction and the developer or technical customer in case of implementation of construction, reconstruction on the basis of the contract, as well as by the person who carried out construction control, in the case of construction control under the contract), with the exception of cases of construction, reconstruction of individual housing construction.
7. Documents confirming the compliance of the constructed, reconstructed capital construction facility with the technical specifications and signed by representatives of organizations operating engineering networks (if any).
8. A diagram showing the location of the constructed, reconstructed capital construction object, the location of the engineering and technical support networks within the boundaries of the land plot and the planning organization of the land plot and signed by the person conducting the construction (the person carrying out the construction, and the developer or technical

customer in case of construction, reconstruction based on the contract), with the exception of cases of construction, reconstruction of a linear facility.

9. Conclusion of the state construction supervision body (in the event that state construction supervision is envisaged) on the compliance of the constructed, reconstructed capital construction facility with the requirements of technical regulations and design documentation, including the requirements of energy efficiency and the requirements for equipping a capital construction facility with meters for the use of energy resources, conclusion of federal state environmental supervision in the case of s provided [Art. 54, part 7 of the Civil Code].
10. A document confirming the conclusion of a contract of compulsory civil liability insurance of the owner of a hazardous facility for harm resulting from an accident at a hazardous facility in accordance with the legislation of the Russian Federation on compulsory civil liability insurance of the owner of a hazardous facility for harm resulting from an accident at a hazardous facility.

In the case of a decision on the commissioning of several buildings, structures, information is provided on all technical plans for the created buildings and structures. The term for the procedure for issuing or refusing to issue a permit for putting an object into operation indicating the reasons for refusal is no more than 7 working days.

Permission to put an object into operation is issued to the developer for each specific capital construction object, for several objects included in the technological complex, for a separate stage of construction in accordance with the building permit and approved project documentation.

The permission for putting the facility into operation reflects information on the capital construction facility in the amount necessary for the implementation of its state cadastral registration. The composition of such information must comply with the requirements for the composition of information in the graphic and text parts of the technical plan.

Permission to commission unique, especially dangerous and technically complex facilities is issued upon the proposal of the developer (technical customer) by the body or authorized organization responsible in the relevant industry.

Permission to commission the facility to the developer (its authorized representative) is issued in duplicate. Simultaneously with the issuance of a permit to commission the facility, the developer must return the originals (duly certified copies) of the documents submitted by him for obtaining permission to put the facility into operation.

Permission to enter a residential building into operation is the basis for the supply of resources through networks of engineering and technical support.

Settlement of residential buildings, sections and premises, the operation of other non-residential non-production facilities, as well as the industrial operation of production facilities before their acceptance and commissioning are not allowed.

Commissioning of built-in, attached and built-in-attached premises must be issued separately from the main building.

Permission to put an object into operation is the basis for state registration of a completed capital construction object or amending the state accounting documents of the reconstructed capital construction object, as confirmation of the existence of powers in relation to the real estate object.

After putting the object into operation, the builder (technical customer) is obliged to transfer to the organization that will operate the capital construction object, the results of engineering surveys, design documentation, inspection certificates of works, structures, sections of engineering and technical support networks of the object, other documentation for the object, which is necessary for its operation.

A warranty period of 2 years shall be established for capital construction projects accepted for operation, unless otherwise provided by federal law or a contract (contract) agreement. The calculation of the warranty period is carried out from the moment of signing by the customer and the person carrying out the construction of the acceptance certificate of the completed construction facility.

5.8.3 Features of acceptance into operation of residential buildings and industrial facilities

Sectional residential buildings, consisting of several sections, with the exception of specialized residential homes for the elderly and families with disabilities, can, in the cases provided for by the project, be accepted and put into operation in separate stages (block sections), provided that the installation of the supporting and enclosing structures is completed, roofing devices, heating connections in the adjoining section and completion of landscaping adjacent to the rented section.

Residential buildings with built-in and built-in premises for placing public facilities should be presented for acceptance after all general construction and special construction works have been completed, including work on the indicated premises, taking into account their purpose.

Acceptance and commissioning of residential buildings can be carried out with incomplete decoration, internal engineering or technological equipment in the built-in and built-in-attached premises, if this is provided for by the design documentation for the construction.

The necessary conditions are:

- erection of load-bearing and enclosing structures in full accordance with the design documentation;
- provision of standardized resistance to heat transfer of the building envelope of a residential building at the junction of built-in and attached premises;
- creating a safe environment for the operation of the facility.

If the built-in or built-in-attached premises belong to several residential sections, sectional acceptance should be carried out if all construction and installation works are completed and the presented part of the building is provided with all engineering networks for the normal operation of the premises of a particular section. The acceptance of the built-in and built-in attached premises in this case is carried out simultaneously with the acceptance of the last section.

When commissioning normal and high-energy efficiency multi-apartment residential buildings in *warranty* terms, *the* developer must confirm the standardized energy indicators both at their commissioning and subsequent confirmation after *5 years*, and for multi-apartment residential buildings of the highest energy efficiency classes — at least than in *10 years.*

When accepting the completed construction projects in winter, it is allowed to postpone the execution of works on the arrangement of the top cover of intra-quarter roads and sidewalks, utility, playgrounds and sports grounds, on the installation of small architectural forms, landscaping for the near favorable period.

Greening of the built-up territories can be carried out in the nearest favorable agro-technical period following the moment of putting the object into operation.

The list of transferred types of work, their volumes and deadlines are approved by the developer (technical customer) in agreement with the state construction supervision body and are reflected in the acceptance certificate and the act of verification of the completed construction facility.

The transfer of the transferred types of work to the developer (technical customer) is carried out in the presence of a representative of the state construction supervision body with full improvement and landscaping of the territories adjacent to the object.

The possibility of delaying the completion of improvement work in the case of shared construction of multi-apartment residential buildings being built with the funds of citizens and legal entities and to be transferred to the participant in shared construction after receiving permission to put into operation should be reflected in the contract for participation in shared construction indicating the types of work, volumes and terms of their implementation.

Residential buildings with free planning apartments, providing for the possibility of their transformation, at the end of construction can be commissioned without building partitions and carrying out in these apartments a full range of finishing, part of special construction work and the installation of internal equipment. In this case, the developer (technical customer) must have a positive expert opinion and a building permit according to the developed project documentation.

The design documentation for residential buildings with freestanding apartments, as well as in contracts or other documents regulating relations between participants in the investment process, indicate the composition of construction and installation works and installation of engineering equipment. At the same time, it is necessary to take into account the need to fully perform all the work that should be provided for by the project documentation in public places (decoration and arrangement of stairwells, vestibules, installation of elevators, building engineering equipment, and fire safety systems). Contracts for shared construction often list works that are not performed by the developer, but are carried out by the owners of the premises (after they have been transferred by the developer) to bring the premises to full readiness:

1. the device of interior partitions and internal doors;
2. final (fair) decoration of apartments (rooms);
3. installation of window sills, electric and gas stoves;
4. in -house wiring of utility networks with the installation of plumbing fixtures and products;
5. the device of built-in furniture and mezzanines.

The legal act on the operation of an apartment building is issued by the head of the municipality (prefect) upon confirmation by the operating organization of the availability of certified operating personnel and contracts with utilities.

5.8.4 Features of acceptance for operation of industrial facilities

The result of a comprehensive testing of equipment at operating conditions for industrial facilities should be the beginning of production (services) provided for by the project documentation in an amount that meets the standards for the development of design capacities in the initial period.

Pilot (experimental), pilot industrial enterprises, workshops and installations are subject to acceptance into operation when they are prepared to conduct experiments or release products provided for in the design documentation.

Acceptance into operation of industrial facilities is not allowed, for which, in violation of the established procedure, changes have been made to the composition of the launch complexes provided for by the design documentation.

In exceptional cases, changes may be made to the launch complexes before issuing permission to put the facility into operation. At the same time, the following should not be excluded from the start-up complexes: buildings and sanitary facilities providing working conditions in accordance with the requirements of industrial sanitation, effective cleaning, neutralization, capture of harmful emissions into the atmosphere, water and soil; buildings and facilities for the processing of industrial waste; driveways; communication lines.

The commissioning of the final launch complex should be carried out simultaneously with the acceptance of the facility as a whole or its last stage.

First, individual testing of the equipment is carried out, and then its comprehensive testing, which is executed by relevant acts in the forms established by SP 68.13330.

Before drawing up the acceptance certificate of the finished industrial construction object, its readiness to start production or provide the services provided by the project is checked to the extent that it meets the standards for the development of projected capacities in the initial period, uninterrupted operation and the development of projected capacities in standard terms, provided with technological documentation for the production of products, energy, raw materials, semi-finished products and components necessary for the maintenance of sanitary but household-rooms and canteens.

Questions for self-control

1. What federal law defines the forms of conformity assessment of buildings and structures, as well as the processes of design (including surveying), construction, installation, commissioning, operation and disposal (demolition) associated with buildings and structures?
2. What regulatory act contains a list of national standards and codes of practice?
3. What are the forms of voluntary conformity assessment of buildings and structures, as well as the processes of design (including survey), construction, installation, commissioning and disposal (demolition) associated with buildings and structures.

4. What are the forms of mandatory conformity assessment of buildings and structures, as well as operating processes associated with buildings and structures.
5. What is the result of the examination of project documentation and engineering surveys?
6. What is the result of state construction supervision?
7. List the types of objects subject to research carried out as part of the audit.
8. What types of studies are conducted as part of the audit?
9. What characteristics of construction objects are established during volumetric studies?
10. What are the properties of construction objects are established during attributive research?
11. What are the estimated standards used in determining the cost of construction work?
12. What is the purpose of regulatory and technical research?
13. What are the main technical means, providing a modern level of research of construction objects.
14. What is the difference between the acceptance and commissioning of a completed construction facility?
15. In what form take into account the transfer of the completed construction project from the contractor to the developer?
16. What are the differences between the forms KS-11 and KS-14?
17. In what cases is the developer obliged to create an acceptance committee for putting the facility into operation?
18. List the work that cannot be performed in the winter season?
19. What is the procedure for obtaining permission to put the facility into operation.
20. Which organization issues this permission?

Questions for discussion

1. In your opinion, when implementing regional state construction supervision with a risk-based method, does the number of inspections conducted by the state construction supervision body increase or decrease in comparison with the "traditional" approach?
2. Can an inspector of state construction supervision independently measure the work performed, structures, etc. to determine their compliance with the design documentation?

3. What role does the project documentation play in establishing compliance with the main characteristics of construction projects with regulatory requirements? What information does the executive documentation supplement in this situation?
4. In what order is it preferable to conduct research aimed ultimately at determining the conformity of the technical characteristics of a building object with normatively defined requirements? Justify the proposed procedure.
5. What are the official grounds for classification to most efficiently streamline one or another set of construction objects or products for the production of building materials, products and structures?
6. What are the reasons for exceeding the construction budget should be considered reasonable, and which — unreasonable? In what situations is the justification for exceeding estimates becoming less convincing?
7. What types of causal relationships can arise between the suspension of work and the destruction of a construction project?

Questions to solve the problem yourself

1. Establish a chronology (sequence) for the preparation of the following documentation: executive, contractual, design, initial authorization, primary accounting.
2. Determine belonging to a particular class, genus, species, group of the building in which you are currently located. Follow the same steps for the individual structural elements of this building.
3. Determine the technical condition of the decoration of the room in which you are currently located.
4. Establish compliance (absence thereof) with the condition of the external decoration of the room in which you are located, with the normatively defined requirements for the quality of the internal decoration of the premises.
5. What modern instrumental methods should be used to determine the structure and texture of the material of the external walls of the building in which you are currently located?
6. What means of fixation should be used to study the entire complex of buildings of the university where you are studying, and which ones to determine the technical condition of floor slabs between floors of a separate building of the specified complex?

Chapter 6

FIXED ASSETS OF CONSTRUCTION AND ITS RESOURCE SUPPORT

6.1 Place of fixed assets in the structure of production

For the production of any type of goods, work, services, including in the construction industry, the presence of three elements is necessary: means of labor, objects of labor and workers. In fig. 6.1. A systematization of the means of production (production costs) is presented taking into account the "labor" theory, when the means of labor and objects of labor form the so-called "materialized labor", and the activities of workers' form "living labor". In the economic theory of living labor, it is used as part of the "value added" (and related tax) and gross domestic product (GDP). All three parts (elements) can be measured in physical meters (machine shift, man-hour, Kg, m^2, m ^{3}, etc.,), in monetary terms (price of a machine change, price kg, m^2, m ^{3}) and wages (person-hour). This duality of valuation is reflected in the systematization of fixed and current assets, when the means of labor valued at historical cost for accounting and tax accounting of more than 100,000 rubles are fixed assets and depreciation is accrued on them, and those valued at less than 100,000 rubles relate to current assets (labor) for which depreciation is not charged (i.e., the accounting technique is facilitated).

6.2 The composition of the means of labor

Means of labor are tools, implements, devices with which a person (worker) produces material goods, work, services. Moreover, the means of labor are of primary importance in the progress of human society (see. "Capital" by K.

Marx), because they allow to increase social labor productivity by tens or even hundreds of times, and at the enterprise level they increase profits and increase its competitiveness. Means of labor can be divided into:

- fixed assets;
- intangible assets;
- current assets.

Fixed assets (OS) in their physical form can be divided into production fixed assets (PIC) and non-production fixed assets (NPOS).

Production OSs are directly involved in the manufacture of goods, works, services in the construction industry.

Non-production fixed assets take place in those enterprises, organizations and institutions that have developed a social sphere for servicing their own personnel — residential buildings have been built at the expense of their own profit; created utilities (roads, engineering networks, repair units for housing and communal services), cultural and sports facilities (cultural houses, stadiums, sports grounds, etc.); healthcare facilities (clinics, dispensaries), education, religion; educational facilities (own advanced training courses, technical schools, etc.).

Further, PIC can be divided into active (APOS) and passive (FPOS) production fixed assets.

APOS are directly involved in technological or managerial processes at the enterprises of the construction sector (construction complex). These include:

- working machines and equipment;
- power and energy machinery and equipment;
- vehicles;
- valuable tools and production equipment; measuring and adjustable instruments and devices;
- computer engineering, communications.

The property of construction enterprises that creates convenience for the main work can be attributed to the EPPO:

- industrial buildings and structures (reinforcing, carpentry, and other workshops) for passive and auxiliary industries;
- administrative buildings;
- storage facilities;
- construction laboratories;
- flyovers, industrial roads.

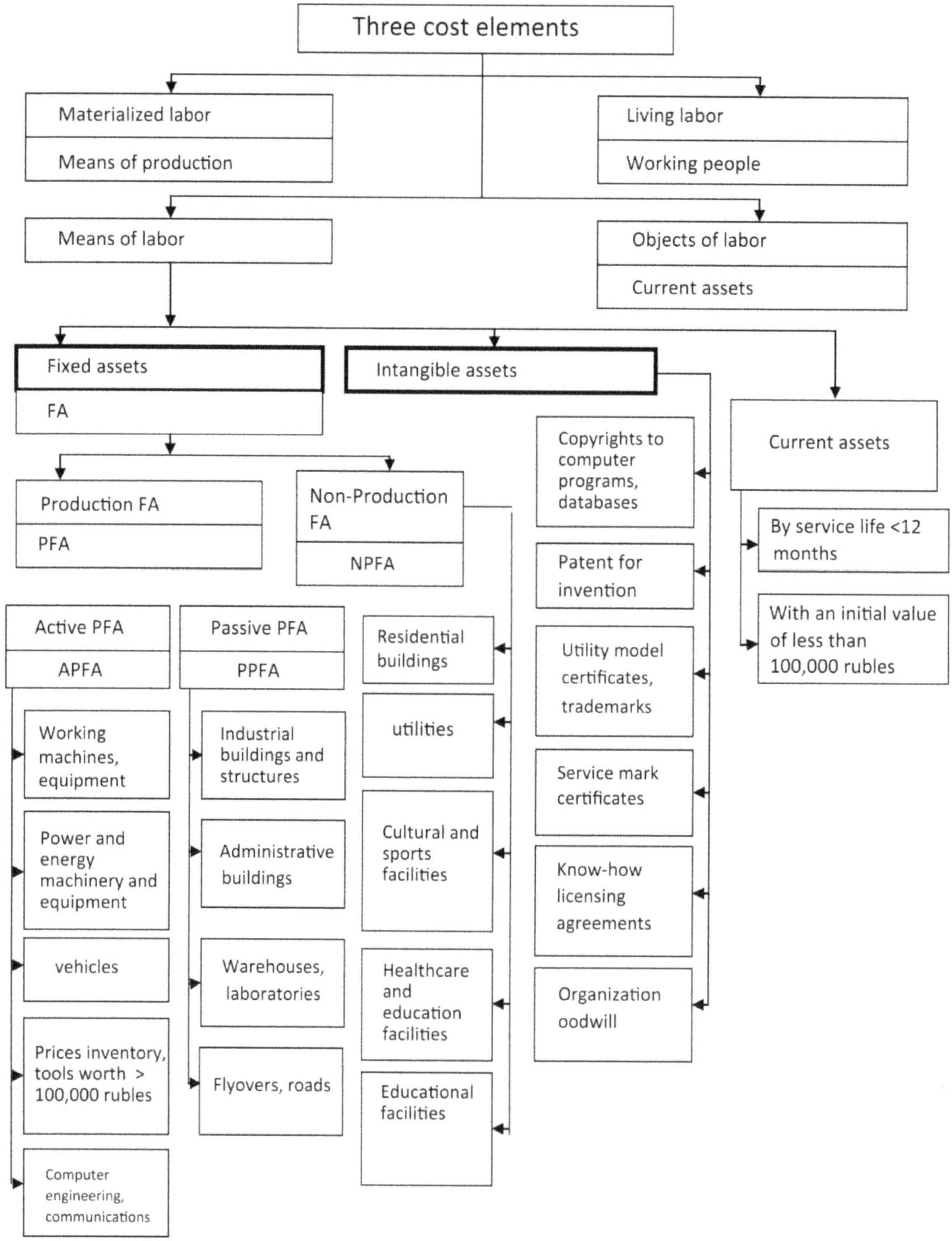

Figure 6.1: Systematization of the means of production

Industrial buildings include: buildings occupied by offices, warehouses, laboratories, checkpoints, weight points, fire stations, garages. Structures include: bridges, overpasses, ramps, power lines, water towers, highways, railways, bunkers for storing bulk materials, etc.

Production OSs in their material essence will differ in different enterprises performing specific activities in the construction sector. For example, you can imagine the construction complex in the form of a concentric model (Fig. 6.2), where in the center (1st concentrate) are construction organizations that perform work directly on the construction site.

The group of "*working machinery and equipment*" includes: earthmoving machinery (excavators, bulldozers, scrapers, etc.); pile driving machines (copra with diesel hammers, electric vibration loaders, drilling machines; hoisting machines (electric tower, tower jib, jib cranes; diesel-electric construction and assembly cranes, truck cranes, freight and passenger-and-freight lifts, etc.); other machines and mechanisms, used directly in the production of construction and installation works in the budget and production of regulatory literature installation works work:

- installation — installation on the place of work equipment Nia (elevators, machine tools, pumps, electrical panels, etc.);
- electrical work (both inside buildings and outside);
- installation of metal structures of the building itself, structures.

For installation works, mounting cranes (MKG) are used, unlike construction cranes (SKG), the lowering speed of which can be significantly reduced (with the aim of filigree installation of the cargo in place).

For concrete monolithic works, wound bases are used if there is a crane or concrete pumps at the construction site (stationary self-lifting, or concrete pumps with a small number of storeys).

At the construction site, they sometimes install their own concrete-mortar unit with adjoining warehouses of sand, coarse aggregate, cement, water, which is equipped with its own set of machines (concrete mixers) and equipment (weighing machines, bulk material conveyors, control electronics, etc.).

For internal work, equipment and small-scale mechanization are used for putty, whitewash, paint, and parquet works. The list of this equipment can be found in special catalogs, which are periodically updated, as Many domestic and foreign copies appear on the market.

The group of "power *and energy machines and equipment*" includes: generators producing thermal and electric energy in the case where it is not possible to use a permanent network, gas generators, steam boilers, mobile power plants (PES), compressors, equipment for cooling water and air, equipment transformer substations, etc.

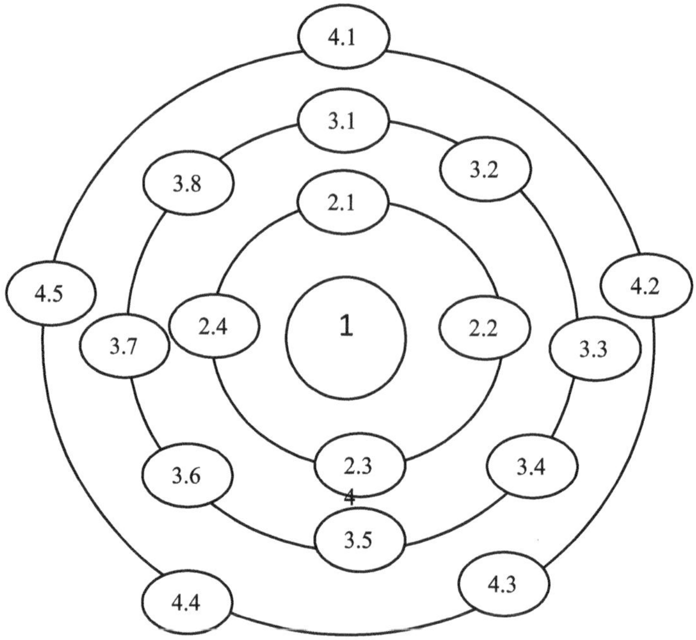

Figure 6.2: Concentric model of a building complex

Legend: 2.1 – mechanization enterprises; 2.2 – trucking enterprises, 2.3 – construction industry enterprises, 2.4 – logistics companies, 3.1–3.3 – industrial enterprises, 3.4 – transport, 3.5 – banks, 3.6 – government agencies, 3.7 – authorities, 3.8 – service organizations, 4.1 – research institutes, 4.2 – universities, 4.3 – colleges, 4.4 – vocational school, 4.5 – Ministry of Construction and Housing

The group of "vehicles" includes: vehicles (both indoor and outdoor, railway (if a large industrial complex is being built, a large bridge (for example, Crimean)) consisting of cars, locomotives, platforms; conveyors; vibration conveyors of various designs; cable- cranes; aerial cable transport; helicopters (the most expensive form of transport, but sometimes the only one possible according to the terrain); horse-drawn vehicles are sometimes used in mountainous areas. not only transport, but also technological functions (for example, a concrete truck delivers concrete mixture to a construction site and feeds it through a gutter to the place of concreting the concrete foundation foundation.) Materials transport can be divided into the following stages:

- external transportation to the warehouse at the construction site;
- from the warehouse to the crane hook;
- vertical transport of cargo to the desired elevation of the building;
- horizontal transport at the desired elevation to the place of use of the material (semi-finished product, structure).

Therefore, a group of machines is called "hoisting-and-transport machines".

APOS includes such means of labor as: mechanized tools, geodetic instruments (optical, laser, space), computer equipment, communication devices whose service life is more than 12 months and the initial cost (purchase, transportation, installation, commissioning) of which is more than 100,000 rub. (see. Tax Code of the Russian Federation).

The closest production relationships with construction are *enterprises of the 2nd concentration:*

2.1 — enterprises of mechanization. They are created in well-developed territories, big cities where it is economically feasible to specialize mechanization enterprises (it is better to organize maintenance, repairs, fleet renewal, train drivers, etc.), while the management of construction organizations are exempt from activities not characteristic of them.

PMs themselves can be highly specialized (for example, only for tower cranes, only for truck cranes, etc.). The composition of APOS is sharply limited in the "working machines" group. In the group "tools and production equipment" the assortment is wider if there are workshops for maintenance and repair of machines.

2.2 — motor transport enterprises (ATP), which may be specialized, but legally (promptly) not part of the mechanization departments. ATP services are provided on the basis of contracts with construction organizations. In the APOS group "vehicles" in the structure of the ATP there is a small assortment of types of vehicles, especially if the ATP is narrowly specialized (for example, only panel trucks or concrete trucks, etc.).

2.3 — enterprises of the construction industry (concrete and mortar units, woodworking enterprises for the production of windows, doors, etc.). At these enterprises, the main group of APOS is "working equipment", "tools and production equipment" in accordance with the production technology. A large proportion of them is in the form of "production buildings and structures", "administrative buildings".

2.4 — management of production and technological equipment (OITE). This is another type of activity of construction organizations, which stood out in an independent production and management direction. Its functions have two directions:

- *production* (on the territory of a large indoor premises, preparation for deliveries to the construction site of all oversized materials strictly according to the schedule of work (cutting wallpaper, preparing paint, cutting wires and cables for electrical work, bending pipes for independent work, selecting rolls, etc.;
- *management:* a responsible engineer is appointed from OITE for each construction site. He contacts the PTO (production and technical de-

partment of builders), receives all the data on the schedule of work (the beginning and terms of work, the schedule for the need for construction machinery and equipment, the schedule for the demand and supply of all materials, structures). After that, he arranges contracts with the UM, ATP, construction industry enterprises for deliveries to the construction site according to the calendar work schedules.

In this regard, in the OITE, the structure of fixed assets includes the group "production buildings" (for example, a large indoor hangar) as part of the PEP, as well as "tools and production equipment" in the active part of the OS.

The 3rd concentrator is represented by the following organizations:

3.1 — enterprises carrying out engineering surveys under a contract with a customer (geological, hydrogeological, soil-geo-botanical, sanitary-epidemiological, seismic, etc.), as well as economic surveys (availability of roads, labor, electricity supply, etc.). Here, the APOS of each specialized organization will mainly consist of "vehicles", "tools and production equipment", and the composition of the EPOS will include "administrative buildings for office processing of data received "in the field";

3.2 — design organizations, they have the "computer engineering" group as part of the APOS, and "administrative buildings" as part of the EPOS;

3.3 — external industrial enterprises (ferrous metallurgy, chemical industry, whose industries supply their products to the construction site). At these large enterprises, as a rule, there is a complete set of all groups in APSS and PEPO;

3.4 — external transport — these are specialized large companies (railway, water, automobile, aviation) with specifics in the composition APOS;

3.5 — commercial banks: as part of APOS — "computer technology", as part of EPOS — "administrative buildings";

3.6 — government agencies (Moskompriroda, Ministry of Emergency Situations, etc.); as part of APOS — "computer technology", "vehicles", as part of EPOS — "administrative buildings";

3.7 — state and municipal authorities; APOS — "computing equipment", "vehicles", as part of EPOS — "administrative buildings";

3.8 — serving organizations, management companies; APOS — "working machines and equipment", "vehicles", "computer technology", as part of EPOS — "administrative buildings". In the *4th concentrate is* presented:

4.1 — research institutes;

4.2 — Universities;

4.3 — colleges;

4.4 — vocational schools;

4.5 — Ministry of Construction and Housing and Public Utilities.

On the balance sheet of these organizations and institutions are in the composition of APOS — "tools and production equipment", "computer technology", as part of the EPOS — "administrative buildings and structures".

As can be seen from the above review, in construction organizations, the composition of production work is dominated by APOS in relation to FPOS. This is explained by the fact that in the construction sector, products remain in place, and only means of production move, i.e. their active part.

6.3 The Reproduction of production fixed assets and their update

Reproduction of production fixed assets (PIC) is understood as a simple replacement of a worn-out fixed asset with the same in its main function (automobile — for automobile, tractor — for tractor, etc.).

PIC wear is not an easy process. The *physical wear is* separated (the parts wear out from work, corrosion from atmospheric influences occurs, accidents, catastrophes, etc. occur) and *moral* — this is the result of technological progress. Mankind is constantly improving the means of labor, increasing productivity, inventing new machines, computers, means of communication with the same functions, cheapening the OS itself, not forgetting to improve aesthetics, comfortable conditions, etc.

The term "moral" does not quite adequately reflect the factors listed above, it could be replaced by depreciation of the "consumer value" of the OS, since consumer value depends on functional, aesthetic features, on comfortable conditions during operation (for example, from the newsreel, that in the 30s the tractors didn't even have cabs), from the financial costs of the purchase and the operation process.

Over the past decades, specialists have done a lot of scientific research and collected rich statistics on the processes of physical deterioration. Based on this, the terms of use of various groups of fixed assets were determined and the RF Government Resolution No. 1 of 2000 was issued, where 10 groups of fixed assets with their physical characteristics and useful lives were recommended:

Group 1 — from 1 year to 2 years inclusive;

2 group — over 2 years to 3 years;

3 group — over 3 years to 5 years;

4 group — over 5 years to 7 years;

5th group — over 7 years to 10 years;

6th group — over 10 years to 15 years;

7th group — over 15 years to 20 years;

8 group — over 20 years to 25 years;

9th group — over 25 years to 30 years; Group 10 — over 30 years.

In order for the fixed asset to physically last a specified number of years, appropriate technical measures are provided, namely:

- maintenance;
- current repair;
- overhaul.

From the point of view of financial support for the process of replacing a fixed asset (buying a new fixed asset after the old one is written off), regular (once a month) replenishment methods are used, the so-called *depreciation deductions* as to the individual accounting card of each fixed asset unit (to the account "02", when this account 01 "Fixed assets" is reduced by this amount). Therefore, the fixed asset in the balance sheet is presented in the form of residual value and by the end of its full useful life the residual value of this fixed asset will be "0", and the accumulated money equal to the initial cost of fixed assets will be reflected in the off-balance account "010". If inflation were zero, then this money would be enough to buy a new car (at a constant price for it), but taking into account inflation, it became necessary to introduce the concept of *replacement cost,* which, naturally, would be more than the initial cost of a worn-out car, which is not supposed change, but it is allowed once a year to reassess fixed assets, thereby increasing depreciation.

The amount of annual depreciation deductions is equal to the initial cost divided by the number of years of normative service, and monthly deductions will be 12 times less, respectively (this is a linear method of depreciation).

If there is not enough amortization money to buy a new car, then enterprises should add account "82" from reserve capital or from retained earnings, account "84". The costs of all types of repairs are not limited to modern accounting and tax accounting and are included in the cost of production costs. Until 1991, there were two columns in depreciation rates: one for renovation (reproduction, that is, the purchase of a new car to replace a worn old one), and the other for major repairs. This limited the extension of the service of a worn-out machine, made it necessary to write off old cars faster, thereby "spurring" technological progress.

There is also the concept of "updating *fixed assets"*. This is understood as the acquisition of updated OS, taking into account the eliminated obsolescence of the old machine, other OS.

There are two ways to do this:

- buying a new car, building a new house;

- carrying out updating activities on an old machine, which still has a certain period of work before being written off, this is depreciation and reconstruction.

By *modernization* is meant the improvement of some parts of the machine or the house (for example, more modern parts in the control, light-on-light sensors are installed in the house when a person appears, etc.).

Under *reconstruction* understood more substantial changes and improvements (e.g., in a house superstructure do upper floors or parked outside the elevator shaft in a 5-storey building, etc.).

The costs of this work are recorded from net profit and are capital investments. After these works, the operating life of the OS can be increased, which should be reflected in the OS card.

6.4 Fixed Asset Efficiency

There are many complex formulas for calculating the effectiveness in the construction sector, including the use of labor, especially the active part of production fixed assets. This complexity is also associated with the very definition of the term "efficiency". We assume that efficiency is the result of dividing the effect by the costs that caused it. Then you need to determine what the effect is in construction. The effect can be at the enterprise level and at the state level. The effect can be economic, financial — when it is expressed in money; the effect can be expressed in physical meters (duration of construction — in years; output of finished products — in m^{2of}housing, m ^{3of}buildings, etc.). This effect is called organizational and technical.

After determining the effect (Profit) and costs (Cost of work) determines the financial efficiency (Profitability) of work using the OS:

$$Profitability^{mech}(E^{mech}) = \frac{Profit_{mech}}{Cost_{mech}}, \tag{6.1}$$

and Profitability (efficiency) of work performed without using the OS

$$Profitability^{man}(E^{man}) = \frac{Profit_{man}}{Cost_{man}}, \tag{6.2}$$

Now we calculate the comparative effectiveness (profitability) to identify the benefits of using the OS:

$$Profitability^{comp}(E^{comp}) = E^{mech} - E^{man} \to \max \tag{6.3}$$

As mentioned above, organizational and technical efficiency is determined by the technical effect (for example, m^2 ofbuilt housing) and costs (for example, cost), then the comparative efficiency will be written as follows:

$$E^{comp} = \frac{\sum^{mech} m^2}{\sum^{mech} Cost} - \frac{\sum^{man} m^2}{\sum^{man} Cost} \to \max . \tag{6.4}$$

If we take the duration of construction (T) as the effect, then the comparative efficiency will be written as follows:

$$E^{comp} = \frac{T_{mech}}{\sum^{mech} Cost} - \frac{T_{man}}{\sum^{man} Cost} \to \min . \tag{6.5}$$

The use of mechanization, complex mechanization, automation, computers, modern means of communication increase the efficiency of construction production, and then of all social progress.

6.5 Resource support for construction

Material and technical resources used in the construction industry are divided into natural, industrial, and non-production. Some of them, being objects of labor, are part of the final product — buildings and structures. Others — actively participate directly in the construction process (construction machines, equipment, small-scale mechanization, tools, vehicles, etc.) or are passively used to create normal production and sanitary conditions (industrial, warehouse, sanitary and administrative buildings, roads, etc. — see section 6.1).

Natural resources are mineral resources, mining products, water and energy resources.

The most rational form of providing construction with energy resources is to bring the capacities of engineering systems in line, which provide both the construction phase and the subsequent operation of buildings. The sequence of stages of the construction of buildings and the operation of real estate during their life cycle determines a *balanced choice of resource support for engineering systems,* both the construction site and the operated real estate, mainly on an ongoing basis.

6.5.1 Construction site energy supply

Providing a construction site with various types of energy resources depends on the volume of construction, the nature of the work and the accepted methods for their implementation, the purpose and size of the auxiliary production, the number of workers and machines employed, and regional climatic conditions.

The organization of resource support for the construction site can be carried out both on a temporary and permanent basis and is based on the results of engineering surveys in the construction area, which allow you to choose the most economical sources of power for the construction of electricity, steam, compressed air, gas, hot and cold water.

Engineering preparation of the territory, carried out before the start of construction, including the laying of permanent communications, should ensure the timely connection of temporary networks needed to service the construction.

Temporary networks, as well as permanent ones, are arranged in the preparatory period, and work on their arrangement is taken into account in calendar planning in the schedule of the preparatory period.

The main requirements for their device are reducing the time and complexity of installation. When designing temporary engineering communications, it is necessary that their length and cost are minimal.

6.5.2 Determination of electricity demand

In the construction industry, most of the electricity is spent on powering the electric motors of building machines and mechanisms (up to 70%), significantly less (about 20%) — on technological needs (electric heating, electric welding, electric drying, etc.) and about 10% is spent on external and internal lighting of the territory of the construction site, workplaces in the dark, objects under construction and administrative, cultural, utility, utility and warehouse premises.

For the energy supply of all types of consumers, permanent and temporary power supply networks are used, which are designed for power and technological consumers, devices for external and internal lighting of construction sites, auxiliary buildings, construction and installation sites and construction sites.

To organize the power supply of the construction site, first of all, transformer power is installed, i.e. determine the total demand for electricity, then select the source of energy, and then design the power grid.

The parameters of electric networks (or their individual elements) are set in the following sequence:

- calculation of electrical loads;
- selection of sources of electricity;
- identification of service facilities of the first category (facilities requiring backup power;

- water reduction, electric heating, boiler rooms, fire pumps, etc.) located on the territory;
- drawing up a working power supply scheme.

On the basis of the schedule or network schedule of the work, the schedule of machines and mechanisms, as well as the object construction plan, the consumers and their power (kW) are determined during the period of maximum electricity consumption.

The calculated indicator of the required power P_{tr} is determined when all consumers are known, for a construction site (kW) from the expression:

$$\begin{aligned} P_{tr} = \alpha(K_1 \sum P_m/cos\varphi_1 + K_2 \sum P_t/cos\varphi_2 + \\ +K_3 \sum P_l + K_4 \sum P_{el} + K_5 \sum P_w), \end{aligned} \tag{6.6}$$

where α is the power loss coefficient in networks depending on the length, cross-section, etc., is 1.05 ... 1.1;
$\sum P_m$ the sum of the rated power of all installed in the network of electric motors, kW;
$\sum P_t$ — the sum of power consumption for technological needs (concrete electrical heating, concrete heating, soil thawing, etc.), kW;
$\sum P_l$ — total power of lighting devices and devices for indoor lighting of objects, kW;
$\sum P_{el}$ is the same for outdoor lighting of objects and territory,
P_w — the same, of all installed welding transformers, kW;
$\cos(\varphi_1)$ — power factor for power consumer groups electro motors (average 0.8);
$\cos(\varphi_2)$ — the same for technological consumers (average 0.8);
K_1 — coefficient of simultaneous operation of electric motors (up to 5 pcs. — 0.6; 5...8 pcs — 0.5 and more than 8 pcs. — 0.4);
K_2- the same for technological consumers (on average 0.4);
K_3- the same for indoor lighting (average 0.8);
K_4- the same for outdoor lighting (average 0.9);
K_5- the same for welding transformers (up to 3 pcs. — 0.8; 3...5 pcs. — 0.6; 6...8 — 0.5 and more than 8 pcs. — 0.4).

The indicator P_m can be determined by the list and passports (catalogs, directories) of machines, mechanisms and installations of the construction site according to the total area of electric motors.

The power of power plants for industrial needs is set by the schedule in the form of table 6.1.

The required power for outdoor lighting is calculated based on lighting standards. The power capacity for indoor and outdoor lighting of workplaces and the territory of work is calculated according to the form of table 6.2.

Table 6.1 Schedule of the required installed power of electric motors for production needs

The mechanisms	units	Number	installed motor power	general power	Months: january	february	march	Etc.
Tower crane (brand...)	PCS.	...	...	...	...	...	...	
Concrete mixer (brand..., Volume..., L)	PCS.	...	...	...	...	...	...	
Concrete pump (brand ... , Productivity .... , M ^{3}/ h)	PCS.	...	...	...	...	...	...	
Mast Lift (brand...)	PCS.	...	...	...	...	...	...	
Vibrator (brand...)	PCS.	...	...	...	...	...	...	
Painting unit	PCS.	...	...	...	...	...	...	
Mosaic grinding machine (brand...)	PCS.	...	...	...	...	...	...	
...	PCS.	...	...	...	...	...	...	
Total: $\sum$Pm					...	...	...	

Based on the calculated capacity, a selection of power sources and transformers is made. The most rational way to meet the demand for electricity is to connect to the existing regional high-voltage networks in the preparatory period of construction with the installation of a transformer substation. In the absence of district high-voltage networks, as well as the possibility of obtaining electricity from nearby industrial enterprises, temporary stationary or mobile power plants are installed.

Power supply to the construction site from the district high-voltage line (voltage of 6 and 10 thousand V) is carried out with current transformation to a voltage of 220 or 380 V at temporary complete transformer substations (KTP) of collapsible type or from a constant transformer substation (TP). With a large construction site and high electrical loads, several KTPs with a service radius of about 400 m are installed.

For transmission and distribution of electric energy to consumers, air and cable electric networks are used. From a transformer substation on the territory of the construction site, a distribution network is laid to the places of installation of power points, through which power is distributed between various consumers. In the conditions of the construction site, the most widely used are air posting along poles, ensuring the safety of networks and reuse. When laying inside the building, insulated wires are used. Cables, in comparison with wires, have a higher cost, so their use is determined by the specific conditions for the safe execution of work, for example, such as the operation of a tower crane, etc.

Table 6.2 Power supply for indoor and outdoor lighting of workers places and territories of work

Electricity consumers	unit of measurement	number	Norm of illumination, kW	power, kWt
Interior lighting:				
Office and public premises	m 2	...	...	...
Sanitary facilities	m 2	...	...	...
Workshops	m 2	...	...	...
Closed warehouses	m 2	...	...	...
Total: $\sum Pl$				...
Outdoor Lighting:				
Open warehouses	m 2	...	...	...
Main walkways and driveways	Km	...	...	...
Minor passages and driveways	Km	...	...	...
Security lighting	Km	...	...	...
Installation of prefabricated structures	m 2	...	...	...
Total: $\sum$Pel				...

Cross-sections of wires of external networks are selected depending on the rated current strength (the condition for heating the wire is not more than 70° C). The current strength I *is* determined by the formulas: with three- and four-wire lines (with zero wire)

$$I = 1000P/1.73U \cos\varphi; \tag{6.7}$$

for two-wire lines

$$I = 1000P/U \cos\varphi, \tag{6.8}$$

where P is the power of current consumers in the design area, kW; U is the line voltage, V; cos 3 is the power factor; for temporary networks cos (phi) = 0.7 – 0.8.

The cross-section of the wires is determined by the current strength according to the formulas: for three- and four-wire lines (with a zero wire)

$$s = 173 \sum L \cos\varphi/K\ U^2 \Delta U; \tag{6.9}$$

for two-wire lines

$$s = 100 \sum L \cos\varphi/K\ U^2 \quad \Delta U, \tag{6.10}$$

where L is the length of the line at one end, m;

K is the specific conductivity of the wire material, which is taken for copper equal to 57, for aluminum — 34.5, for steel — 83;

ΔU — permissible voltage losses in the calculated line, for power three- and four-wire networks $\Delta U \leq 8\%$, for two-wire $\Delta U \leq 6\%$.

At the time of high tension networks need to check the voltage in the network ΔU. For power three- and four-wire networks, the calculation is performed according to the formula

$$100 \sum PL/K\, U^2 s = \Delta U \leq 8\,\%; \tag{6.11}$$

for two-wire lines is determined by the formula

$$200 \sum PL/K\, U^2 s = \Delta U \leq 6\,\%; \tag{6.12}$$

where $\sum PL$ is the total load moment, $W \cdot m$, equal to the sum of the products of the applied loads flowing along the section by the length of this section or equal to the sum of the products of the applied loads, W, by the length from the beginning of the line L , m, ($\sum PL$).

To illuminate walkways, driveways and workstations, a separate line can be provided for which the cross-section of the wires is calculated based on the loads in the network (see table 6.2). In this case, the power consumption for lighting is not accepted as the total at the end point, but dispersed through 100–200 m (the distance between the spotlights).

Separately, the calculation of the wire cross section for supplying electricity to industrial and technological needs with a voltage of 220/380 V is performed according to the formulas for three- and four-wire lines (with a zero wire).

To account for energy consumption at construction sites, meters are installed. In addition, power supply organizations apply a system of discounts and allowances to the tariff value of electricity, depending on the deviation of $\cos\varphi$ from the established norm (0.85). If the weighted average $\cos\varphi$ exceeds the value of 0.85, the construction company receives a discount from the energy supplying organization, otherwise, a fine. The reasons for the decrease in $\cos\varphi$ are most often low load of motors and transformers, as well as their idling.

6.5.3 Construction site heat supply

Heat supply at construction sites is carried out for industrial and household needs in order to provide heat to technological processes, heating and drying of facilities under construction; heating, ventilation and hot water supply of temporary sanitary and administrative buildings (locker rooms, dining rooms, showers, offices, etc.). The structure of temporary heat supply systems includes heat sources, temporary heat supply networks and end devices (heaters, units, boilers, heaters, etc.). Design, placement and construction of heat supply networks is carried out in accordance with current regulatory and technical documents.

The design of temporary heat supply is carried out in the following order:

- the heat demand for individual consumers and the total consumption for the facility as a whole are calculated;
- sources of heat supply are determined and the need for fuel is calculated;
- heat conduit routes are calculated and designed;
- local units and devices are selected for heating, drying, heating, steam supply, etc.

The total heat demand Q_{total}(kJ) is determined by summing the estimated consumption for individual consumers with the introduction of increasing factors: R_1 for unaccounted heat consumption, equal to 1.1...1.2 and R_2 — losses in the network (tentatively take R_2 — 1.1...1.5):

$$Q_{total} = (Q_h + Q_{tech} + Q_{dry}) \cdot R_1 \cdot R_2, \tag{6.13}$$

where Q_h — the amount of heat for heating buildings and greenhouses; Q_{tech} — the same for technological needs; Q_{dry} — the same for drying buildings.

The heat demand for heating buildings and structures is determined taking into account their nomenclature, which depends on the maximum number of working and building materials that require storage in heated warehouses.

The heat consumption for heating buildings Q_h (kJ / h) is calculated by the formula

$$Q_h = [\alpha \cdot q_o \cdot (t_{int} - t_{ext})] \cdot V_b, \tag{6.14}$$

where α is a coefficient depending on the calculated outdoor temperatures (at $t_{ext} \geq -10°C$ $\alpha = 1.2$; at $t_{ext} \geq -20°C$ $\alpha = 1.1$; at $t_{ext} \geq -30°C$ $\alpha = 1.0$; at $t_{ext} \geq -40°C$ $\alpha = 0.9$;

q_o — specific heating characteristic of the building, kJ / (m $^3 - -\cdot$ h $\cdot$°C);

t_n- calculated outside temperature, °C (average temperature is the most five-day boat week of the construction area, t_{int} — estimated temperature inside the heated premises, °C;

V_b- the volume of buildings by external measurement, m^3.

Calculation of heat demand for technological needs for work in winter conditions is carried out after identifying the timing of their implementation according to the schedule of the construction of the facility, the simultaneous implementation of various works and the adopted technology for the production of these works. To establish the maximum heat demand, a schedule is drawn up (table 6.3).

Table 6.3 Schedule of heat demand for technological needs

Types of jobs	unit	quantity	Specific heat consumption per unit volume of work, MJ	Estimated time of heat consumption, t, h	Heat flow unevenness	Months			
						january	*february*	*march*	Etc.
. . .									
. . .									
. . .									
. . .									
Total: $\sum$Pm									

The data in table 6.3 are entered after determining the hourly heat consumption for technological needs Q_{techn}, kJ / h for each work according to the formula

$$Q_{tech} = V \cdot M/t \cdot k_n, \tag{6.15}$$

where V is the amount of work per day, m^3;

M — specific heat consumption per unit volume of certain types of work; t is the estimated time of heat consumption, h;

k_n — the coefficient of non-uniformity of heat consumption, taken equal to 1.1…1.2.

The maximum heat demand for technological needs is included in the formula (6.15).

Determining the amount of heat and air for drying buildings requires special calculations that take into account the necessary amount of heat to evaporate moisture from materials and heat the air supplied to the room.

Sources of temporary heat supply are accepted, as a rule, existing or planned heating systems of boiler houses of the district, enterprise or thermal power plant under construction. If necessary, heating devices can be selected according to the reference data. As a result of the calculations, the diameter of temporary pipelines is tentatively determined taking into account the selected type of coolant.

The type of coolant (water, steam, air) is selected depending on the production, technological and economic needs of the construction. It is preferable to use one type of coolant, if this does not contradict hygienic and technical requirements. Typically, construction sites and temporary settlements use a water heating system. The temperature of the coolant is accepted: for heating and work systems, sanitary facilities, baths, laundries, canteens and shops with a steam or water system — 130…150°C; for residential buildings, dormitories, schools, clinics, health centers, offices — 95 °C; for nurseries, kindergartens and hospitals — 85°C; for gyms and clubs — low pressure steam (115°C).

In the absence of special requirements and reliable thermal insulation, the minimum vapor pressure can be taken taking into account the most distant point of consumption to the boiler room, m:

- up to 300 — 0.05…0.07 MPa;
- up to 600 — 0.20 MPa;
- up to 1000 — 0.30 MPa.

When choosing circulation pumps, the pressure loss in the network can be considered equal to 100-120 Pa for each meter of the length of the pipe farthest from the boiler room.

Based on the total heat demand calculated according to formula 6.15, the accepted type of heat carrier and its parameters, the diameter of temporary pipelines is determined.

Inventory mobile and container domestic premises often have local heating units, in which water or steam serves as a heat carrier.

Combination of heating with drying of the building has become widespread, for which installations with air coolant — heating and ventilation units are effectively used.

Heat generators are used as the main source of heat when working in the open air (thawing soil, heating bitumen, etc.). Gas cylinder installations with infrared burners are designed for drying individual places in buildings under construction. In cases where heating systems are used for some needs, and installations and units for others, the diameter of temporary pipelines is determined only taking into account the heat demand that is provided from the heating systems, and the type of unit is selected so that its heat output is sufficient for other purposes. Then the total heat demand by the formula (6.15) is not determined.

The estimated amount of heat also determines the need for fuel for the entire heating period, the value of which is set depending on regional climatic conditions.

To supply steam or hot water to the place of consumption, it is preferable to use permanent pipelines of the facilities under construction, laid in the preparatory period. When installing temporary heating networks, the most rational routes for their laying to consumption objects are determined.

For heating buildings under construction in the winter, as a rule, use a permanent heating system. In multi-storey residential buildings, where a heating system with a lower wiring is provided, you can turn on the heat supply as the floors are erected. For heating temporary buildings and structures, mainly individual use devices are used.

6.5.4 Determining the need for compressed air and determining the cross-section distribution pipelines

Compressed air is used to ensure the operation of pneumatic machines. The parameters of temporary networks or their individual elements are set in the following sequence:

- calculation of the required amount of resources;
- determining the capacity of resource providers;
- determination of the nature of the distribution network.

Calculation of resource requirements is carried out according to construction periods (or stages and types of work) by a phased calculation of actual costs.

The total demand Q $_{St}$, m ^{3}/ min in compressed air is determined by the formula

$$Q_w = n_1 Q_1 K_1 + n_2 Q_2 K_2 + \ldots + n_m Q_m K_m, \tag{6.16}$$

wherein n_1, n_2, ..., n_m is the number of homogeneous consumers;

Q_1, Q_2, ..., Q_m is the flow rate of compressed air per consumer, m^3/min;

K_1, K_2, ..., K_m — coefficients that take into account the simultaneous operation of homogeneous consumers (for two consumers 1.4...0.85; for six — 0.8; for ten — 0.7; from fifteen to twenty — 0.6 and more than twenty — 0.5).

The estimated capacity or performance of the compressor unit Q_{comp}, m^3/h, is determined by the formula

$$Q_{comp} = Q_w(100 + P_c + P_o + P_n + P_p)/100, \tag{6.17}$$

where P_c —air loss in the compressor (up to 10%);

P_o — the same from cooling in the pipeline (up to 30%);

P_n — the same from leaky connections in pipelines (5...30%);

P_p — the flow rate of compressed air for purging (4...10%).

To establish the maximum flow rate of compressed air to ensure the operation of pneumatic machines on the basis of the schedule, the range of machines used, their technical characteristics and the number of homogeneous consumers working simultaneously, a schedule is drawn up (table 6.4).

Table 6.4 Schedule of compressed air demand

Types of jobs	Name of the used tool and devices	The highest air consumption m ^{3}/ min	Quantity of one new tool	Months			
				1	2	3	etc.
...							
...							
...							
Total:							

The source of compressed air at the construction site is mobile and stationary compressor units and production stations with a duration of 5...10 m ^{3}/ min or 5...40 m^3/min, placed in inventory and collapsible buildings.

The wiring of compressed air from mobile compressors is carried out with rubber hoses with a diameter of 20 ... 40 mm, and from stationary compressor stations with steel pipelines laid for condensate drain with a slope of 0.005 ... 0.01 in the direction of air movement. The diameter of the air duct (d) is determined according to the norms depending on its length and the amount of compressed air passing through it, approximately according to the formula

$$d = 3.18\sqrt{Q_w}, \tag{6.18}$$

where Q_w — air flow, m^3/min flowing through the calculated area.

The inner diameters of the pipes are rounded to the nearest larger diameter: 25, 38, 80, 100, 125, 150, 200, 300 mm.

6.5.5 Organization of providing construction materials and products

Materials and products occupy the largest share in the estimated cost of a construction project. The share of the cost of building materials in the total cost of construction and installation works is more than half of all costs.

According to technical properties, the classification of materials is divided into sections, groups, subgroups, brands and grades. Each group is divided into subgroups; they, in turn, are divided into brands, grades and profiles. This classification is established by the State Statute of the Russian Federation.

The classification of materials according to their technical properties forms the basis for the development of nomenclatures, i.e. systematic lists of materials consumed in production. It indicates the name of each material, type, grade, size, unit of measurement, as well as the code assigned to it, called the item number, which is indicated in all primary documents associated with a particular type of material.

All material resources spent in the construction industry are divided into the following groups: basic materials; constructions and details; equipment and inventory; other (auxiliary) materials; low value and wearing items.

The **main materials** include all materials that are materially included in the construction of buildings and structures — cement, sand, gravel, gravel, brick, reinforcement, metal, lumber, paints and other materials.

For **structures and components** are reinforced concrete, wood, metal, asbestos cement and other structures, prefabricated buildings and structures, pipes of different materials, rails, sleepers, prefabricated elements for plumbing works, etc.

In construction, industrial, technological, energy and other types of **equipment are used** — transformers, elevators, machine tools, escalators and other mechanisms.

To **support** include materials that do not create the material basis for the production of construction, — fuel, lubricants, spare parts for construction machinery and equipment, and others.

Items with a service life of less than one year (household equipment for temporary buildings, etc.) are considered to be of **little value and wearing out** (see section 6.2.).

As part of the design and estimate documentation for construction, data on the need for materials, products, structures and equipment should be provided. These data are the basis for determining the need for materials at construction sites and drawing up applications for materials in the material and technical supply units of construction organizations.

The need for materials, structures and products is determined on the basis of working drawings. In the working drawings for this purpose, specifications of materials, products, equipment should be given.

Specification of materials, products and equipment — a text design document that defines the composition of materials, products and equipment intended for acquisition, preparation and implementation of construction.

The specification, as a rule, is made up of sections (under sections), the composition of which, and the sequence of recording, in them equipment, products and materials are established by the relevant standards.

Material specifications are developed for each basic set of working drawings of buildings and structures, for example: architectural solutions (AR); reinforced concrete structures (KZh); metal structures (KM); wooden structures (KD); architectural and construction solutions (AS); heating, ventilation and air conditioning (OV); domestic water supply and sewerage (VK); master plan and transport (GT); heating networks (TS); gas supply (HS); external networks of water supply and sewerage (NEC); anticorrosive protection of structures (AZ); architectural interiors (AI), etc.

Formation of specifications of equipment, products and materials is carried out by special units of design organizations involved in the development of working documentation (working drawings) and estimates.

As part of the PIC, a statement of the need for building structures for products and materials and equipment is developed with a distribution by calendar periods of construction, compiled on the construction site as a whole and on the main buildings and structures based on their scope of work and current norms for the consumption of building materials.

At the stage of development of PPR, schedules for the receipt of building structures, products, materials and equipment with data on the supply of these resources for each contract team and with the application of picking lists are compiled.

Schedules of receipt of material resources at the facility are compiled on the basis of working drawings and a work schedule, in which the sequence and timing of work is established.

The assembly of construction sites is based on the picking lists and delivery schedules. The picking lists are developed by the production and technical departments of construction organizations for each object.

When determining the need for materials, **production and estimated norms of material consumption** are applied.

The rate of consumption of materials determines the maximum permissible level of costs of materials and products in physical terms for the production of a unit of finished products or for a certain amount of work, taking into account compliance with the established requirements for the quality of materials and products made from them.

Production standards determine the amount of materials needed to produce a unit of work, unit or group of products. They are compiled taking into account difficult to eliminate losses and waste during the manufacturing process (for example, the amount of paint remaining on the brushes after painting), in preparing materials for production consumption (cutting, trimming, sawing, etc.), as well as during their transportation from the warehouse to the construction site site to the place of laying (for example concrete mix). Production standards take into account the consumption of materials in physical terms (t, m3, pcs., Etc.) Based on the production norms of consumption, materials are dispensed to construction sites, teams, and workers. These standards serve as the main measure for monitoring the actual expenditure of building materials in the performance of work.

Estimated consumption rates for materials are mainly intended to determine the estimated cost of construction work. Estimated standards are compiled in physical terms by a more integrated nomenclature in comparison with production.

Norms of natural loss are called characteristic for certain materials under normal conditions of storage, transportation, loading and unloading and the sizes of natural loss (loss) approved in the established manner.

The types of natural loss, which depends mainly on the physicochemical properties of materials, include:

- drying, weathering, freezing, evaporation of the moisture contained in the materials or the volatilization of individual particles due to temperature changes, such as volatilization of paints, varnishes, etc.
- leakage and spillage — when pumping liquid materials from one container to another

- spraying cement, dry paints, chalk and other materials during loading and unloading
- battle of materials (brick, glass, etc.)

The supply of construction materials, products, structures is one of the functions of material and technical support (MTO) of construction production.

The functions of the MTO include the functions of warehousing, storage, processing of the supply of raw materials at the request of construction organizations; provision with tools, fixtures and repairs of technological, energy, transport and other equipment, their care and supervision, constant maintenance of equipment in working condition; providing the enterprise with electric and thermal energy, compressed air and water; movement of goods inside and outside the site; all loading and unloading operations.

The supply process is a set of operations that provide the enterprise with the necessary materials, raw materials, products, structures, tools and equipment. The main objective of the supply organization is the timely, uninterrupted and complete supply of construction materials with necessary material resources at minimum cost.

Providing construction projects with raw materials, materials and finished products is associated with the performance of such functions as procurement, transportation, warehouse processing and others. All these operations are planned, carried out, controlled and regulated by specialized units — supply services based on the supply plan.

The supply plan reflects and substantiates the need of the construction organization for all types of material, technical and energy resources, equipment necessary for the production of construction products and other needs, as well as determines the size of inventories and establishes an inventory management system.

The development of a supply plan can be divided into the following stages:

1. The preparatory phase — the preparation of the necessary data for the preparation of the plan, the study of:
   - the production program of the construction organization in the planning period;
   - norms of material consumption, terms of wear of tools, spare parts, and other means and items of production;
   - applications and calculations of building sites for materials, raw materials, tools, etc.;
   - data on the balances of materials at the facilities, work in progress at the beginning of the planning period, the balances of materials in warehouses,

their consumption in the past period, the state of the supply process in the past period;

- price lists of firms — potential suppliers, transportation tariffs, delivery terms for each type of product.

2. Calculation of the need for material resources for the implementation of the production program of the organization.

3. The calculation of the expected inventory balances at the end of the planning period and carry-over stocks of materials.

4. Determining the need for material resources for delivery is the main indicator of the plan of material and technical supply, which should be sought to minimize.

5. Identification of suppliers.

6. Drawing up a supply plan in accordance with the selected inventory management system, signing contracts with suppliers.

As a rule, in construction organizations these problems are solved in the supply department, which collects information about the need for building materials from the production and technical department, applications from construction sites and data from the warehouse on the availability of materials. Material supply of the construction industry is carried out in accordance with the production program of the construction organization.

The versatility of the supply department is aimed at solving problems of ensuring construction in a timely manner with materials, their delivery to construction sites, the organization of their acceptance, storage, proper rational use, identification of surplus stocks and their further distribution. The supply department submits materials specifications to suppliers, enters into relevant agreements, monitors the accuracy and timeliness of suppliers' fulfillment of contractual obligations.

In the supplying activities of the construction organization, two main types of functions can be distinguished: external and internal.

External supply functions determine the relationship of the construction organization with suppliers, wholesale and retail firms, transport organizations and include:

- search for potential suppliers of material resources, analysis and selection of the most suitable of them; conclusion of contracts with suppliers;

- establishing economic relations with enterprises for the supply of products to construction sites;

- selection of means and methods for the delivery of material resources from suppliers to construction sites, conclusion of contracts with transport companies.

Internal supply functions characterize the interaction of the supply service with the management and production units of a construction organization:

- planning of material and technical supply on the basis of a plan of the need for construction projects in material resources;
- planning and organization of the supply of means and objects of labor of production units;
- limiting the release of materials from the warehouse;
- preparation of material resources for production consumption, vacation and delivery of material resources from the warehouse to the place of their consumption;
- operational regulation of the movement of material resources, control over their use in the organization.

There are two forms of supply:

- a **transit** form of supply, in which the construction organization receives materials, raw materials directly from enterprises extracting, processing or producing them, the organization of procurement of materials for supplying construction sites is carried out by concluding direct agreements with industrial enterprises — manufacturers of building materials;
- a **warehouse** form of supply in which the construction organization receives material resources through intermediaries — wholesalers, retailers, commodity exchanges, territorial and supply bases and production and technological equipment departments.

Currently, construction organizations are provided with material resources through auctions, tenders, bulk purchases, regular purchases in small batches, purchases as necessary, supply of production on demand, as well as supply through materials of own production.

Forms of organization of material and technical supply of construction at present can be reduced to three main groups.

- The organization of the supply process mainly on direct ties with suppliers of material resources and is completely confined to the framework of the construction organization. A similar organization of supply of construction is characteristic of fairly large construction organizations that have stable volumes of work and retain a certain specialization. As a rule, they have their own network of economically dependent supply units, including production and technological equipment units.

- Organization of the supply process, in which both direct economic relations and the services of commercial intermediaries are used. Usually these are medium and small construction companies, prone to universalization and diversification of production. Most often they use only some elements of the production and technological equipment at individual facilities.

- The organization of the supply process is based on specialized enterprises of material and technical supply of construction, including OITE.

The composition of the production units of the supply service of the construction organization is also quite diverse and depends primarily on such factors as the scale and geography of the construction organization, the size of the organization, the availability of a portfolio of orders, industry affiliation and specialization, level of cooperation, etc.

The selection of a potential supplier of building materials is carried out on the basis of research on the supplier market, which is carried out by the employees of the supply department or marketing group in the construction organization under the supervision of the deputy supply manager. The selection criteria for the supplier are the price level for construction materials, the location of the supplier's warehouses and production bases, the market's existence and reputation of the supplier, the conditions for the supply of materials, the payment terms for the purchased materials under the supply and sale contracts for materials, etc.

For a construction organization, it is very important to conclude a contractual relationship for the purchase of materials and then maintain a stable relationship with a reliable seller of building materials, since the quality of the materials used and the timely delivery of them to the site determines the fulfillment of contractual obligations of contractors to customers and the release of high-quality finished construction products.

In wholesale trade in material resources, prices for materials, products and structures are lower than in retail trade, since the goods are sold not in units but in large quantities. Wholesale trade is carried out through wholesale bases, commodity exchanges, brokerage firms, and territorial supply bases.

Commodity exchanges — commercial organizations created for conducting trade operations, as a rule, specialize in certain types of goods (for example, metal, timber, etc.). At commodity exchanges, intermediary services are provided for concluding trade transactions, the supply and demand for a certain type of goods are recorded, information is collected on prices of products, enterprises, state of production, etc.

The bulk of transactions on commodity exchanges are the so-called **derivatives transactions,** in which trade transactions are performed within a certain period, to **cash transactions,** the transfer of goods and payment of which occurs immediately or within 2-3 days, they occupy a small share.

Brokerage firms (trading houses) — intermediary organizations that receive a certain fee — mediation fees for contracts between sellers and buyers of goods.

Territorial supply bases provide construction organizations with materials, products and structures through bulk purchases and sales. They can be independent enterprises, and can be part of large construction organizations, such as the **Office of Industrial and Technological Equipment (OITE).**

The functions of the material and technical supply bodies in large construction organizations are performed by the units of production and technological equipment (OITE) as production units.

The main objective of OITE is the complete provision of construction objects with materials, structures and parts according to annual, quarterly, monthly plans and weekly daily schedules.

In accordance with this task, the main functions of the OITE are defined: planning of material and technical supply; the implementation of material assets and the organization of decentralized procurement; centralized complete delivery of constructions, products and materials to construction sites; the maximum possible support for the installation of structures and assemblies directly from vehicles "from the wheels" and the implementation of a series of preparatory work, as well as acceptance of incoming material resources, their storage and storage, manufacturing of non-standard parts and structures, bringing incoming materials to a high degree of technological readiness, organization of timely delivery of kits to construction sites.

OITE has organized production and assembly bases for processing materials into semi-finished products and products, enlargement and assembly of units, acquisition, containerization and packaging, and, if necessary, for the manufacture of non-standard structures and products.

OITE, according to the concluded agreements and schedules, accepts products from suppliers and intermediary organizations only according to the established sets.

The forms of organization of the OITE are diverse and depend on the specifics of the construction of facilities, their territorial location, level of assembly, the types and volumes of work, and other specific conditions. OITE, on behalf of the builder, as a customer, carries out the material resources necessary to carry out the planned volumes of construction and installation works, and enters into contractual relations with transport organizations.

By the power of attorney of the builder (development company), OITE can represent its interests in all matters of material and technical supply and assembly, in supply and sales, components, industrial and transport organizations. It is a single supplier of material and technical resources to all production units of the developer and a single buyer of these resources from manufacturers, as well as from all suppliers of supply and marketing and component organizations.

OITE disposes of fixed and circulating assets assigned to it, labor and material resources; carries out its activities, as a rule, on the basis of internal economic accounting within the framework of the rights established by law, as well as the rights transferred to it by the trust; It is on a separate balance sheet, has a current account in a separate bank, as well as a seal with its name.

The rights and obligations of OITE are determined by the construction organization (holding) in accordance with applicable law, on the basis of the model regulation on OITE.

In addition to ensuring the integration into a single whole of the processes for preparing materials and parts, the manufacture of semi-finished products, structures and their complete delivery to construction sites in accordance with the schedule of construction and installation works, the tasks of OITE are:

- timely implementation of the resources allocated to the trust — building structures, parts and materials, equipment and means of mechanization;
- organization in accordance with the established procedure for orders and through wholesale trade through territorial bodies for the supply of materials and products, based on their needs, determined by projects and estimates, taking into account the schedules for construction and installation works, as well as industrial enterprises;
- processing and improving the technological readiness of materials, semi-finished products and products for industrial consumption;
- selection of sets, containerization, packaging, organization and centralized delivery of building structures, products, materials, semi-finished products to objects;
- providing construction organizations with auxiliary materials, inventory, fixtures, tools, work clothing and other personal protective equipment;
- quality control of incoming building structures, parts, materials and other resources, storage and rational use of material resources in all divisions of a construction holding;
- improving the efficiency of the production and technological system based on the achievement of scientific and technological progress and best practices.

When creating and developing the OITE, it is recommended that all the functions of material and technical supply and equipment previously dispersed between individual divisions, departments and services in a single organization (OITE) be concentrated.

OITE is transferred to industrial units (plant, workshops, workshops) that manufacture non-standard or non-serial products.

All manufacturing enterprises included in the OITE receive technical and economic indicators of their activities from him and hand over balances and reports on the results of their activities to the OITE. OITE reports on the results of its activities to the construction and assembly holding.

The fundamental difference between OITE and the departments of material and technical supply in construction and installation organizations is that OITE, by the nature of its activity, is a combined body that combines the functions of industrial production, supply and assembly.

Currently, construction organizations, incorporating independent structural units that perform the functions of material and technical supply of construction, are carrying out a reorganization, the essence of which is to liquidate the supply units as legal entities and subordinate them to the rights of departments or administrations.

The form of organizing the supply of construction, which is based on predominantly direct relations with suppliers and is completely organizationally closed by the framework of the construction organization, is the most effective in the current conditions and allows achieving minimal costs in the implementation of the supply process.

Construction organizations can receive material assets from different suppliers on the basis of contracts, which are legal documents that determine the rights and obligations of the supplier and buyer.

For materials coming under sales and supply agreements, the construction organization receives from the supplier settlement documents (invoices, waybills, invoices, etc.) and supporting documents (specifications, certificates, etc.).

The organization establishes the procedure for acceptance, registration, verification, payment and passage of settlement documents for incoming materials.

Suppliers' **supporting** and settlement documents must be carefully checked and recorded in the **Logging register of incoming goods.** In this case, it is necessary to pay attention to how the terms of the supply agreement are met by the timing, quantity, assortment, quality of goods, as well as the correctness of prices, possible discounts on transportation costs, arithmetic calculations. Acceptance of building materials should be carried out according to the supplier's transport and accompanying documents (invoice, specifications, waybills, etc.) and should consist in determining whether the quantity and quality of received products matches the quantity and quality specified in the transport and accompanying documents, as well as in contracts, GOSTs and specifications.

Acceptance of incoming materials is carried out on the basis of a **bill of lading** received from the consignor.

Bill of lading — a document that combines an order for the release of inventory, an acceptance bill, a bill of lading and a pass for the export of inventory from the territory of the enterprise.

When establishing the discrepancy between the materials received and the assortment, quantity and quality specified in the supplier's documents, as well as in cases where the quality of the materials does not meet the requirements (dents, scratches, breakage, damage, leakage of liquid materials, etc.), acceptance is carried out by the Commission, which draws it up with the **Act on the acceptance of materials.**

The following operations must be performed during the acceptance of building materials:

a) determination of the quantity and quality of the materials received;
b) acceptance of materials for registration;
c) preparation for laying materials for storage.
d) laying materials at storage sites.

Acceptance of products is carried out by the head of the warehouse (storekeeper) or a person replacing him. To receive materials from the supplier's warehouse or from a transport organization, the storekeeper is issued a **Power of Attorney for receiving materials.**

The warehouse manager or storekeeper must, in advance, before building materials arrive at the warehouse, prepare for their acceptance:

a) determine the place for their installation;
b) instruct the workers on how to carry out the upcoming unloading part-time work in compliance with safety regulations.

When accepting building materials from transport organizations, you must check:

a) the presence of seals on vehicles (wagon, container, etc.);
b) the serviceability of the container;
c) the conformity of the name of the cargo and the transport marking with the indicated in the transport document.

The acceptance of materials by quantity should be determined in the same units of measurement that are indicated in the accompanying documents (invoice, specification, waybill, etc.).

Acceptance of construction products for quality to completeness is made at the consignee's warehouse.

If the acceptance process reveals the absence of certain documents, the acceptance of building materials and products in such cases is not suspended, in this case an act is drawn up on the actual availability of products indicating the missing documents.

Persons competent in matters of accounting, storage, acceptance and dispensing of material assets are distinguished as representatives for participating in the acceptance of construction products.

The act on hidden product defects should be drawn up within 5 days upon detection of defects, but no later than four months from the date of receipt of the products at the recipient's warehouse.

If a representative of the manufacturer (sender) is called in to draw up the act, then the time required for his arrival is added to the established 5-day period.

Hidden defects are recognized as defects that could not be detected during the usual inspection for a given type of product and revealed during processing, preparation for installation, during installation, testing, use and storage of products.

Acceptance is considered to be done on time if the quality control and completeness of the products, carried out simultaneously with the acceptance, is completed in a timely manner. At the same time, packaging, packaging and labeling must comply with the requirements of GOSTs, technical specifications, special conditions, other rules binding on the parties, as well as the relevant drawings and samples.

Acceptance of products for quality and completeness is carried out in strict accordance with standards, specifications, basic and special conditions of delivery, as well as accompanying documents certifying the quality and completeness of the delivered products (technical passport, certificate, certificate of quality, invoice, specification and etc.).

The release from the warehouse of materials is carried out on the basis of consignment notes to the driver of the transport organization engaged in transportation, and in cases where the forwarding of the drivers is not possible, the release of the cargo is made to the forwarder of the supplier.

The driver (forwarder) checks the amount of cargo accepted for transportation by measuring, counting places. Without verification, only goods that are transported in special bodies or containers sealed by the supplier are accepted for transportation. The driver monitors the correct placement of construction products in the car, its reliable fastening, as well as the safety of tags.

Upon delivery of the cargo to the object, the driver hands it in the same manner in which the cargo was received from the supplier to the recipient's materially responsible person, who signs the invoice and confirms receipt of the cargo and puts the organization's seal.

Loading is carried out by the supplier, unloading by the recipient.

In the event the recipient refuses to accept the cargo, an act is drawn up for the signatures of the driver of the car (forwarder) and the representative of the recipient, and if the latter refuses to sign, the driver of the car (forwarder) draws up a unilateral act indicating the name and position of the person who refused the signature. In this case, the goods will be returned to the supplier, who must immediately accept it.

Proper organization of storage of materials should ensure its qualitative and quantitative safety:

When storing materials, it is necessary to ensure: a) rational distribution of products;

b) the safety of consumer qualities;

c) ease of accounting and inventory;

d) continuous updating of stocks;

e) safe working methods.

According to the storage method, all construction products are divided into the following four groups:

I — products that do not require protection from atmospheric precipitation, to be stored in open areas (mineral aggregates, coarse metal, timber, brick, precast concrete and reinforced concrete products, asbestos-cement pipes, etc.);

II — products requiring protection against direct atmospheric precipitation, but not sensitive to temperature fluctuations, to be stored under a canopy (carpentry, dry plaster, asbestos-cement sheets, bitumen in containers, cable in drums, radiators, sheet metal, etc.);

III — products requiring protection from atmospheric precipitation and dampness, not very sensitive to temperature fluctuations, to be stored in closed unheated warehouses (lime, cement, gypsum, chalk, glass, felt, wallpaper, paints, drying oil, fasteners, refractory products, ceramic tiles, wire, window devices, etc.);

IV — products sensitive to temperature fluctuations, to be stored in closed insulated warehouses (parquet, electrical materials, linoleum, measuring instruments and tools, laboratory equipment, etc.).

Losses resulting from damage to building materials and products due to the careless performance of transport and storage operations, do not apply to losses of natural loss.

Documentation and accounting of materials at the enterprise is carried out in accordance with the Basic Provisions for Material Accounting and the unified standard forms of primary accounting documentation developed by the State Statistics Committee.

The organization should establish control over the receipt of materials (over shipment by suppliers), as well as over settlements with suppliers and customers.

To register the receipts and expenditures submitted to the accounting department, the warehouse manager fills out the register, which is drawn up in two copies, and the receipts and expenditures are registered separately. At the same time, registration should be done on a daily basis, and within a day — on operations.

One copy of the registry with the primary documents attached to it (receipt orders, acceptance certificates, invoices, transport documents, etc.) is transferred to the accounting department against receipt on the second copy of the registry, which remains with the materially responsible person.

The accounting policy of the construction organization should provide for the procedure for the release of materials from warehouses to production.

The **release of** materials for production is understood as their delivery from the warehouse directly for construction and installation works.

Materials, fuel, semi-finished products, raw materials and other material values should be released from warehouses into production by weight, volume or account, in strict accordance with established production standards and the volume of the production program.

The lists of persons agreed to with the chief accountant who are granted the right to demand materials from the warehouses, as well as samples of their signatures, must be communicated to the appropriate warehouse. The release of materials for production by warehouses is carried out only by construction and assembly workers allocated for their receipt.

The release of materials from the construction organization's warehouses to sections, teams, and workplaces, as a rule, should be based on pre-established limits.

At construction sites, the consumption of materials is limited by the planning or production department when drawing up production plans. The limits are based on the approved production norms for the consumption of materials per unit of a structural element or type of work, taking into account organizational and technical measures that form the basis of the approved plan for reducing the cost of construction.

The limits for the release of materials for production are established by the procurement department or other units by decision of the head of the organization.

The primary accounting documents for the release of materials from the organization's warehouses to the sites are the **limit-intake card,** the **requirement-invoice,** the **invoice.**

Limit-fence cards are intended for dispensing materials systematically consumed for work, as well as for monitoring compliance with limits.

Limit-intake cards are issued by organizational units that perform procurement or planning functions, in two or three copies for a period of a month.

With small volumes of goods dispensing, they can be written out per quarter. A separate limit fence card is issued for each warehouse.

One copy of the limit-withdrawal card is transferred to the recipient of the materials before the start of the month (quarter) of its validity, the second copy to the corresponding warehouse. The third copy remains in units performing procurement or planning functions for control.

The person who issues the goods shall note in both copies of the limit-sampling card the date and quantity of materials supplied, which are confirmed by the signatures of thc rccipicnt and the warehouse manager. Only those materials that are indicated on the limit-intake card, and within the established limits, are released.

The limit-fence card can be issued in one copy. In this case, the recipient signs the receipt of materials directly on the warehouse accounting cards, and the person responsible for the release of the material from the warehouse signs on the limit intake card. The limit-intake card can also be used to return unused materials to the warehouse.

At enterprises and construction sites, control should be organized for the timely delivery of limit-intake cards at the end of the month to the accounting department.

In the case of materials being released over the limit, the stamp "Over the limit" is put in the primary accounting documents (limit-intake cards, bill of lading requirements). The release of materials in excess of the limit is subject to the permission of the manager or persons authorized by him. The documents indicate the reasons for the excess release of materials.

Extra-maximum supply of materials includes additional holidays related to the correction or compensation of defective products and covering over-expenditures of materials, i.e., expenses in excess of norms.

When replacing the material provided for by the technology established for this type of work, another material draws up **a replacement request.**

Waste generated in organizational units is collected in accordance with the established procedure and handed over to warehouses according to delivery invoices with an indication of their name and quantity.

The cost of recorded waste is included in the decrease in the cost of materials released into production.

In case of subsequent use of the waste during the performance of work, its release into production is made out by the statement of **Requirements (requirements-invoices).**

Requirements ***I*** write out sections for each item number material or material group. The warehouse must release materials in strict accordance with the requirements of the facilities. Requirements are the grounds for the operational accounting of the release of material at the warehouse, as well as accounting. They are also used when receiving materials in excess of the established limit with the permission of management.

Return of unused materials to the organization's warehouse is executed by waybills or limit-fence cards. Materials handed over to the warehouse are received in the warehouse with simultaneous debiting from the report of the organization's subdivision. If these materials were written off in production, their cost is charged to reduce the associated costs.

The release of materials, structures, parts, fuel from the on-site warehouse to production at construction sites is reflected in the material report of the superintendent without registration with primary documents if the superintendent is a financially responsible person.

Moving materials from one warehouse or pantry to another warehouse or another pantry of this organization is issued a **waybill for the internal movement of materials.**

When an organization sells materials to individuals and legal entities, the sale price is determined by agreement of the parties (seller and buyer). Materials should generally be sold at market prices, taking into account their physical condition. Calculation and payment of taxes to the price of materials sold (transferred) is carried out by the organization in the manner prescribed by applicable law.

The sale of materials is made out by the appropriate division of the organization, performing supply and marketing functions, or by an official performing similar functions, by issuing **an invoice for the release of materials to the side,** on the basis of contracts or other documents and the permission of the head of the organization or persons authorized by it.

In order to reduce the complexity of accounting work, enterprises (construction sites) should issue primary documents for the release of materials, as a rule, in a centralized manner. In this case, using the technological documentation for the manufacture of products, a preliminary calculation is made of the amount of materials required for each construction site, based on the monthly program. Based on such calculations, the required number of primary documents is written out, which are transmitted in advance to the plots.

In all construction organizations, **accounting and control** over the use of materials, raw materials, fuel and other material values in production should be organized. In this case, the basis of accounting is the quantitative accounting of the use of materials in the plots.

The basis for controlling the expenditure of building materials is to compare their actual consumption with those established by production standards.

On a monthly basis, site managers (work manufacturers) compile a report on the consumption of building materials in comparison with production standards. The report in the prescribed form serves as the basis for writing off building materials to the cost of construction and installation works, therefore it should be submitted to the accounting department no later than the 5th day of the month following the reporting one. Such a report is compiled for individual objects or sites on the basis of data on the implementation of construction and installation works for the month. The number of construction and installation works performed per month is determined on the basis of the volumes of work indicated in the logbook of work performed in a specially established form.

Material reports approved by the head of the construction organization with all the primary documents for the receipt and consumption of materials are handed over to the accounting department.

Undocumented deviations, comparing the quantity and cost of materials released during the reporting period to the site or to the contractor, are revealed during the inventory of the residues.

During the inventory, the safety of material values, the correctness of their storage and consumption, and the procedure for recording their movement are checked.

In construction, many types of materials are used that are stored in open areas and which are accounted for by the method of periodic inventory. These materials include sand, gravel, gravel, blocks, boards, etc.

Open storage materials are usually stored at construction sites where they are used. When used for the construction of facilities, expenditure documents are not prepared. The actual availability and consumption of materials in quantitative terms is determined by monthly inventory of them as of the last day of each month.

The results of the inventory, as well as the amount of materials used in the production, are determined according to the inventory act for the write-off of open storage materials. In accordance with the inventory data, the actual consumption of materials is determined as the difference between the amount of the balance at the beginning of the month and the receipts of materials for the month minus their actual balance at the end of the month and the amount of materials sold and released to the side. In the inventory method, records of the use of materials are kept, where, on the basis of primary documents, the quantity of materials transferred to production, production waste and unused materials is recorded.

According to the inventory data, the remains of unused materials are entered in the cards. Comparing the actual consumption of materials with the norm, the magnitude of the deviations is revealed.

The warehouse manager compares the balance of the material displayed on the card with the minimum and maximum inventory rates indicated in its heading. If the rest of the material displayed on the card deviates from the norms, he informs the supply department about this by means of a signal certificate. It indicates the item numbers, the names of the materials and the marginal stock standards reached on them.

6.5.6 Organization of operation of a fleet of construction vehicles

The modern construction industry is a complex mechanized process for carrying out construction work in which a large fleet of construction equipment is used: earthmoving, installation, general construction, road, transport, loading and unloading, etc.

The general need for construction vehicles necessary for completing the fleet of vehicles of a construction enterprise is determined by summing up the needs for individual types of machines designed to carry out each type of work. Determination of the type and brand of machines, the availability of replaceable equipment, the value of the main parameter, productivity, etc. should be based on an analysis of the volume and structure of construction work included in the program of the construction organization (structural characteristics of buildings and structures, types and volumes of work, the number and distance of movement of building materials and structures, climatic, regional and other conditions), methods of organizing construction (in-line complex), the form of operation and the range of delivery of machines, their mode of operation, etc.

The composition of the fleet and the number of vehicles required to carry out the adopted construction program are determined in one of three ways.

1. The need for construction vehicles is determined on the basis of the volume of work, the adopted methods of mechanization in the project for the production of work and the operational productivity of the machines or the norms for the production of machines that are established taking into account local construction conditions.

The average number of machines required to perform the accepted amount of work for the corresponding period of time is determined by the formula:

$$M = \frac{Q}{{}_cP_{op} \cdot K_{us} \cdot T}, \tag{6.19}$$

where Q is the volume of work of this type in physical measurements, units, t, m^2, m^3, pm;

P_{op} — operational performance of one machine in physical measurements of the volume of work per hour or work shift, units, t, m^2, m^3, m/hour, shift;

K_{us} — factor inter shift use of machines; T — working time of one machine for the corresponding period, hour, shift.

2. The calculation is made according to the norms of the cost of machine time per unit of work performed in the physical dimension, set forth in the EniR or VNiR and accepted methods of mechanization in the project of work:

$$M = \frac{N_{vr} \cdot Q}{K_{us} \cdot T} \tag{6.20}$$

where: N_{vr} — the number of machine-hours per unit of volume of work in physical

metric measurement, machine-hour/unit, t, m^2, m^3, m;

T is the operating time of one machine for the corresponding period of time, h.

The following indicators are used to assess the use of the construction machinery fleet:

- **the utilization factor of the calendar time of machines** (K_k) is determined by the ratio of the number of hours of working time (T_k) in hours of one average payroll machine to the duration of the corresponding calendar period of time in hours (T)

$$K_k = \frac{T_k}{T} \tag{6.21}$$

- **utilization of machine time** (K_{us}) is determined by the ratio of the actual working time (T_f) in the average car audio clock to set the duration of the working time (T_p) Percentage

$$K_{us} = \frac{T_f}{T_p} \cdot 100 \tag{6.22}$$

- the **coefficient of use of intra-shift time** (K_t) is determined by the ratio of the number of hours of useful work of the machines during the shift (T_{sh}) to the total set duration of the shift (T_{cm}) in hours

$$K_t = \frac{T_{sh}}{T_{cm}} \tag{6.23}$$

- **the shift index of the machine** (K_{sh}) is determined by the ratio of the average hours of one day of the machine ($T_{wd.}$) The total duration of the set shift (T_{sh}), hours

$$K_{sh} = \frac{T_{wd.}}{T_{sh}} \tag{6.24}$$

- the **rate of fulfillment of machine production norms** (K_e) is determined by the actual operational production of machines (P_{ef}) for the corresponding period of time to the norm (P_{en}) established for the same period, expressed as a percentage

$$K_e = \frac{P_{ef}}{P_{en}} \cdot 100 \tag{6.25}$$

The existing fleet of construction vehicles is mainly focused on the enterprises of the construction complex.

Depending on the specific construction conditions, the type and dimension of the enterprise, the volume and structure of construction work, the operation of construction machines can be carried out in various organizational forms.

1. Construction machines and mechanisms are on the balance of small construction organizations or their structural divisions in their direct submission, which allows them to be managed quite quickly. However, with this form of operation of the machines, it becomes impossible to create conditions for their maintenance and repair. In these conditions, there is no economic opportunity to create the necessary base with the availability of modern diagnostic and repair equipment. After-sales service of machines in specialized enterprises will entail a large amount of time for diagnosis, waiting, transportation and the service itself, which reduces the rate of its use.

2. Construction machines and mechanisms are on the balance of specialized mechanization units that are part of large construction organizations. This form of operation of construction machines provides an economic opportunity to create their own repair base, which ensures the proper maintenance of construction equipment and its effective use. Mechanization units and general construction units are administratively subordinate to the mechanization enterprise, which ensures the efficient use of construction equipment.

3. Construction machines and mechanisms are on the balance sheet and as part of mechanization enterprises. The concentration of construction machinery, equipment and mechanisms in large enterprises of mechanization ensures the efficient use of the fleet of construction machinery, the introduction of new means of mechanization and the most progressive methods of work, the growth of labor productivity and the reduction of manual labor in construction by further developing and raising the technical level of mechanization of construction work, improvement methods of maintenance and repair of construction equipment.

The mechanization enterprises, by the nature of the construction work performed, can be specialized in the operation of similar machines and operating a diverse fleet of construction equipment.

4. Construction vehicles and mechanisms on the balance of leasing companies specializing in leasing (renting) construction vehicles (earthmoving machines, truck cranes, tower cranes, small-scale mechanization equipment, etc.).

Leasing companies enable construction companies to use long-term and short-term use of construction machinery and equipment types of work, accompanying them with maintenance and repair services, which eliminates the need for construction organizations to create or develop an operational base and include all types of vehicles in their fleet their construction work.

Currently, leasing companies are a developing form of operating a fleet of construction vehicles, the concentration of which is currently located mainly in the mechanization divisions of construction enterprises and mechanization enterprises.

The development of leasing in construction involves the formation and development of the infrastructure of the leasing market for construction equipment by creating a network of regional leasing companies, as well as expanding the scope of services provided by mechanization enterprises.

Based on leasing, construction companies are successfully re-equipping their fleet of construction vehicles and mechanisms with new generation equipment, which increases their competitiveness in the construction market.

The use of small-scale mechanization is one of the main factors in reducing manual labor, increasing efficiency and quality when performing construction work.

Small-scale mechanization means include construction machinery and equipment of low power: wheeled tractors and bulldozers and caterpillars up to 75 hp; excavators with bucket capacity up to 0.4 m^3; truck cranes with a lifting capacity of up to 7.5 tons; fork electric and auto-loaders; single-bucket loaders with a loading capacity up to 2 t; concrete and mortar mixers with a capacity of up to 250 l. ; plastering and painting stations; winches, hoists, portable jib cranes with a lifting capacity of up to 1 t, hoists; compressor and electric welding units, as well as tools with manual and mechanized drives: various trowels, grinders, parquet grinders, polisher, mosaic grinders; machines for applying mortar and putty, cutting and welding linoleum, for transportation of building materials with a body up to 0.15 m^3 on the basis of a scooter and other means designed for the mechanized execution of basic and auxiliary processes and construction operations of various kinds.

The main most effective form of organizing the operation of small-scale mechanization means is to concentrate them in specialized units, the activities of which are aimed at performing certain types and complexes of work on their own, transferring available funds to construction enterprises on lease (rental) with or without maintenance personnel, organizing and completing stationary or mobile tool-dispensing points with the necessary technical means of mechanized execution of construction work, maintenance and repair of machines, equipment and tools, they are in charge.

Subdivisions of small-scale mechanization are formed as part of mechanization enterprises or large contracting construction organizations, where it becomes necessary to organize their own repair and maintenance base.

The complete set of instrumental and distribution points includes:

- volumes of work carried out in-house or jointly with construction organizations;
- volumes of work performed by small-scale mechanization transferred to construction organizations on lease (lease) with or without staff;
- the scope of work on the manufacture of devices, equipment, accessories, etc., sold as industrial products, as well as the repair of machinery and mechanisms of other enterprises.
- The interrelations of small-scale mechanization units with construction organizations are determined by the terms of the agreements, which stipulate: volumes and terms of performing certain types of work on their own with small-scale mechanization units;
- the composition of technological sets of small-scale mechanization facilities, the duration and conditions for providing them to a construction organization;
- the obligation of the construction organization to prepare the front of construction work and ensure their safe conduct, the protection of small-scale mechanization equipment at construction sites;
- settlement procedure for the volume of work performed; operation of small-scale mechanization facilities and other services;
- property and legal liability of the parties for violation of the terms of the contract.

On the basis of the adopted own production program and the concluded agreements with construction organizations, monthly schedules for the work of the brigades and the distribution of small-scale mechanization equipment are developed.

Integrated mechanization is a way of carrying out construction work, in which all the main and auxiliary processes that make up the construction work are carried out in a mechanized way using construction machines, small-scale mechanization and various types of mechanisms, equipment and devices, interconnected by basic parameters. At the same time, the use of manual labor can be allowed only to perform auxiliary work that is insignificant in labor intensity.

When interconnecting the performance of each element of this set of machines and mechanisms should be created by the flow organization of construction.

The formation of a set of machines and mechanisms begins with determining the type and number of leading machines (M_3) required to perform a given amount of construction work for the corresponding period:

$$M_3 = \frac{Q \cdot U}{100\, n_{hour} \cdot T \cdot K_{us}}, \tag{6.26}$$

where Q is the volume of work of this type in unit quantities, pcs, t, m^2, m^3, lm.;

U — the share of work performed by the leading machine, in the total volume, percent;

n_{hour} is the hourly productivity of the driving machine in physical quantities;

T — working time of the host machine for the corresponding period of time, hour;

K_{us} — an indicator of the use of machines in time.

The types and number of auxiliary machines and kit mechanisms are selected in such a way that their productivity is equal to or slightly greater than the productivity of the host machine.

The use of integrated mechanization in construction organizations is characterized by indicators of the level of mechanization of construction and installation works and the level of mechanization of labor.

The level of mechanization of construction work (U_m) characterizes the degree of replacement of manual labor by machines and mechanisms and is determined as a percentage for each type of work and is determined by the formula

$$U_m = \frac{Q_m}{Q_{total}} \cdot 100, \tag{6.27}$$

where: Q_m — the volume of mechanized or complex mechanized work;

Q_{total} — the total amount of work.

The level of mechanization of labor (U_{mt}) characterizes the complexity of mechanization and the degree of application of manual labor

$$U_{mt} = \frac{N_m}{N_{ss}} \cdot 100, \tag{6.28}$$

where: N_m — the number of workers on mechanized or integrated low-grade works;

N_{ss} — the average number of workers.

The production program of mechanization enterprises in the conditions of competition among themselves in the market of contracting works and services of the construction complex is formed due to: the volume of construction work carried out on its own on a subcontract basis; loading and unloading and auxiliary works carried out jointly with construction organizations, allocating them construction machines with maintenance personnel; the rent of leased (rented) construction machines and mechanisms with and without staff; maintenance and repair of construction equipment of other enterprises; implementation of commercial and intermediary activities for the acquisition and sale of new construction equipment, repair and sale of previously used mechanization equipment, etc.

Settlements of construction organizations with mechanization units are carried out: at the estimated cost of construction work carried out on their own; at planned prices for the amount of work actually performed or the operational cost of the machines for the actually worked time allocated to them by equipment with maintenance personnel; under leasing agreements for leased (rented) construction equipment with or without staff; at contractual prices or estimated prices for the transportation of construction equipment, installation and dismantling of large construction machines, installation of crane ways for tower cranes, etc.

Estimated operational costs ($C_{c.e.}$) The construction of the machine is determined by the formula:

$$C_{c.e.} = C_{m.h} \cdot K_{n.p} \cdot T \ , \tag{6.29}$$

where: $C_{m.h}$ — the cost of 1 machine-hour of the construction machine;

$K_{n.p}$ is the overhead ratio;

T — the number of machine hours of construction machinery at the facility.

The cost of 1 machine-hour of work of any construction machine is determined by the formula:

$$C_{.} = \frac{C_e}{T_0} + \frac{C_g}{T_g} + C_{th} \tag{6.30}$$

where C_e — one-time costs, which include the cost of transporting cars to the construction site, the cost of installation and dismantling of cars, the relocation of non-self-propelled cars within the territory of the facility under construction, the cost of erecting auxiliary structures and devices necessary for normal operation of the machines;

C_g — annual costs, which include annual depreciation, capital repairs of construction equipment, modernization of machines during their operation;

C_{th} — current operating costs for 1 machine-hour of the construction machine: the salary of staff, the cost of electricity and fuels and lubricants, the cost of operating materials (wipers, ropes, tires, etc.), maintenance and repair;

T_0 — the total number of working hours of the machine at the facility, h;
T_g — the amount of working time using a construction machine during the year, hours

The planning of the work of mechanization enterprises is carried out on the basis of direct agreements with construction organizations, in which, in addition to the volumes, terms and methods of construction work, organizational and technical issues are specified, the implementation of which requires:

- mechanization enterprises to allocate machines in technically sound condition, and in the case of staffing them, send drivers of appropriate qualifications with documents on the right to drive the machine;
- carry out diagnostics of machines, their maintenance and repair according to previously provided schedules;
- provide fuels and lubricants and other services that ensure the efficient use of the equipment they provide;
- construction organizations to provide the cars provided to them with a front of work, as well as entrances to the place of their work;
- organize the perfect operation of machines in compliance with the rules for the safe execution of construction work;
- to equip the crews serving the work of the machines with a permanent staff of workers of relevant qualifications;
- provide illumination of the object of work and protection of machines and mechanisms outside working hours;
- take into account the work performed using the machines, their actual location at the facility with the preparation of relevant documents.

Upon receipt of machinery and mechanisms for leasing (rental), construction organizations must: accept the equipment provided to them under the act in accordance with the leasing (rental) agreement, which also stipulates the conditions for the delivery, maintenance and repair of the leased equipment; organize the proper operation, maintenance and protection of machines; at the end of the lease, return the lessor the machinery and mechanisms under the act or, under the terms of the contract, redeem it at the residual value.

The operational management of a mechanization enterprise consists in coordinating the work of all its divisions and the machines and mechanisms that are in their composition, organizing operational control over the implementation of adopted plans in cooperation with construction organizations.

The main tasks of operational management are: monitoring the implementation of construction schedules of construction machines and mechanisms, their movement and regulation of the implementation of work plans in case of failure; ensuring constant interaction with construction and installation organizations on issues arising in the course of construction work: monitoring the implementation of the schedule of maintenance and repair of construction vehicles and mechanisms; collection, analysis and transmission of information on the progress of construction schedules of construction machines for the period (day, week, decade, month); collection from serviced enterprises of applications for the supply of necessary machines and mechanisms; development of monthly operational plans and the work of construction machines and mechanisms.

The effective use of construction machines and mechanisms largely depends on their technical condition.

A guarantee of reliable and safe operation of construction machines, increase of their productivity and increase of term of work is **maintenance and repair**.

Maintenance and repair of construction machines is carried out on the basis of diagnosing their technical condition, which aims at identifying, analyzing and recording information in the diagnostic cards of machines, allowing to evaluate their technical condition without disassembly.

A. Technical diagnostics determines the possibility of operating a construction machine in the appropriate technical condition, the need for maintenance, repair or overhaul and their volume. After each type of maintenance or repair is carried out, construction machinery is diagnosed in order to obtain initial data on the assessment of measures taken and the establishment of a residual resource.

Measures for maintenance and repair of construction vehicles are planned and implemented on the basis of operational and repair documentation of manufacturers, requirements and rules for the technical condition of the machines and their safe operation established by the Gosgortekhnadzor, the State traffic inspectorate, Gosenergonadzor, as well as state regulatory and technical documents.

In the process of operating construction machines, the following types of maintenance are carried out: **shift, periodic and seasonal.**

To maintain the operability of construction vehicles during transportation and during storage, special maintenance is carried out in accordance with the requirements of the operational and repair documentation.

B. Shift maintenance is performed before, during, or after the end of the shift by the driver (crew members), who are assigned the machine and includes a visual inspection of the technical condition of the machine and its completeness, checking the fuel level in the tank, fluid in the radiator, oil in the crankcase of the mechanisms, fastening of aggregates, etc. If the driver or crew members of the construction machine are assigned the function of only managing it, then monthly maintenance is carried out centrally in non-work time staff dedicated sites of maintenance and repair of machines.

Maintenance carried out through the planned periods of development of construction machines, regulated by manufacturers, involves mainly their cleaning, inspection, technical diagnosis, regulation, lubrication and testing. **Each type of maintenance, depending on the frequency of the work and the scope of work, is assigned a serial number: TO-1, TO-2, TO-3** . The structure of the maintenance work, having a higher number, includes the work of each previous type of maintenance, including the daily maintenance of construction vehicles.

Depending on the complex of works that provide for the elimination of damage and failures to restore the operability and serviceability of construction vehicles, two types of repairs are installed: current and overhaul.

C. Current repair ensures the restoration of the machine's life to the next scheduled repair, in which partial dismantling of construction machines is allowed, malfunctions in individual assembly units and parts in the amount determined by the technical condition are eliminated.

D. Overhaul ensures the restoration of a complete or close to the full resource of the machine by repairing and replacing individual units, components and parts, including basic ones, assuming their complete disassembly.

Maintenance and repair of construction machines is carried out on the basis of annual and monthly schedules developed by construction organizations, on the balance of which they are available. The data for the development of annual plans is the actual operating time at the beginning of the planned year from the time of the corresponding maintenance, repair or from the beginning of operation and the planned operating time of the machine for a year.

The annual plan determines the need for material and labor resources, as well as the number of planned maintenance and repairs for each machine.

The number of technical services and repairs in the planned year (K_{tor}) is determined using special tables and nomograms or by the formula:

$$K_{tor} = \frac{N_f + N_{pl}}{T_n} - K_n \ , \qquad (6.31)$$

where: N_f — the actual operating time of the machine at the beginning of the planned year since the last similar type of maintenance, repair or from the beginning of its operation, year;

N_{pl} — the planned operating time of the machine for the accounting year, year;

T_n — the frequency of maintenance or repair, which is the calculation, year;

K_n — the number of all types of previous maintenance and repairs that are being calculated (when calculating a major overhaul, K_n is zero).

The calculation according to the formula (6.31) is performed in the following sequence: overhaul, current repair, maintenance (TO-1, TO-2, TO-3); calculation results are rounded down to integers.

The month of the year in which the machine is to be overhauled is determined by the formula:

$$K_m = \frac{12(T_n - N_f)}{N_{pl}} + 1 \,, \tag{6.32}$$

where K_m — serial number of the month in which the repair was conducted.

If during the calculation it turns out that $K_m > 2$, overhaul of the machine in the planned year is not carried out and is transferred to the next year.

The monthly schedule of maintenance and repair of machines establishes the date of its stop for maintenance or repair and the duration of machine downtime.

The ordinal working day of the month (D_{tmr}), on which the start of maintenance or repair of machines, is determined by the formula:

$$D_{tmr} = \frac{N(T_n - N_f)}{N_{pl.m}} + 1 \,, \tag{6.33}$$

where: N — the number of working days in the planning month, taking into account the established at this enterprise operating mode;

$N_{pl.m}$ — the planned operating time of the machine for the billing month,

If during the calculation the value of D_{tmr} turns out to be greater than N, the corresponding type of maintenance or repair is not performed in the planned month.

Maintenance and repair of construction machines is carried out at repair enterprises, which are classified by purpose, specialization, production volume and degree of mobility.

Overhaul of complex construction machines (excavators, bulldozers, scrapers, pipe layers, crawler cranes and pneumatic wheels, etc.) is carried out at mechanical repair plants.

Maintenance, current repair of all machines and major repairs of simple machines are carried out by mechanical and repair units of mechanization bases.

The mechanization bases can be universal, for servicing a mixed fleet of construction vehicles or specialized, for servicing certain types of machines or groups designed to perform certain typcs of construction work, for example, excavation, installation, lifting and transport, etc.

Repair and mechanical units of mechanization bases incorporate production sites, the structure of which depends on the type of base and its annual production program for the repair and maintenance of construction vehicles.

In cases where construction machines cannot be returned to the base for maintenance or repair during the construction of geographically dispersed and linearly extended objects, mobile workshops are used that are usually mounted on the chassis of automobiles.

On construction sites with a large number of construction machines and the duration of their work in one place, stationary or collapsible repair shops and dispensaries are used.

Repair of construction vehicles is carried out by the following methods: **individual, modular and complete.**

In the individual (detailed) method, the installation of repaired parts and assemblies is carried out on the same machine from which they were removed for restoration and, therefore, the machine has been under repair all this time.

The essence of the aggregate (depersonalized) method lies in the fact that the components and assemblies removed from the machine are sent for repair, and other, pre-repaired or new oncs from the revolving repair fund are immediately installed in their place.

With the complete repair method, the construction machine is divided into sets consisting of several units and, when the established resource is used up, they are periodically replaced. For these purposes, repair enterprises should create a revolving repair fund of sets.

The application of the last two methods allows to reduce the stay of the machine in the repair, and with the complete method the number of repairs.

6.5.7 Organization of transport in construction

One of the most important conditions for increasing the efficiency of construction production is the timely and high-quality delivery of construction materials. By type of construction cargo are:

- powder materials — gypsum, alabaster, cement, fluff lime, etc.;
- bulk materials — crushed stone, gravel, expanded clay, slag, sand, various types of soils, etc.;
- piece goods — brick, facing and finishing materials, window and door blocks, reinforced concrete and additional elements, glass, roofing and insulation materials, plumbing equipment, etc.;
- large-sized products — roof trusses, flights of stairs, wall panels of prefabricated house-building, starting elements of arches or beams of the superstructure of bridges, etc.;
- long materials and products — piles, pipes, fittings, rolled products, timber, etc.;

- flat elements — floor slabs and coatings, partition panels, slabs you are paving, etc.;
- thin-walled elements — arches and shells, reinforced cement slabs, etc.;
- volumetric elements — plumbing cabins, blocks of underground collectors, sections of drains, sewers and manholes, etc.;
- heat-insulating materials — mineral and glass wool, aerated concrete, foam silicate, etc.;
- viscous (mobile) materials — concrete mix, mortar, asphalt mix, etc.;
- liquid materials — heated bitumen, lime paste, primers, etc.

The above types of cargo allow for practical purposes to predict the type of vehicle and the method of transportation.

Transportation of construction materials can be carried out in an open way, and goods requiring protection from atmospheric influences, special safety conditions, compliance with more complex conditions for the preservation of quality and quantity — closed.

According to the method of position in vehicles, cargo can be in a vertically-inclined and horizontal position. The method of position of the cargo is determined by the maximum use of the vehicle in terms of carrying capacity and volume of rolling stock or the physical condition of the cargo during transportation.

According to the method of transportation, construction cargo can be in vehicles in bulk, in pieces, packages, containers, special containers, etc.

For the transport of construction materials, transport is used: **railway, automobile, tractor, water, air, pipeline, suspended cable and continuous operation.**

All types of transport used in construction are divided:

- **in relation to the construction object, on the internal and external;**
- **in the direction of movement of the load — vertical and horizontal.**

Intra- construction **transport is** carried out transportation of building structures, materials and products at the construction site from the on-site warehouse to workplaces, and on-site transport — from warehouses of production and technological equipment bases to on-site warehouses or workplaces within the construction organization.

External transport carries out transportation of building materials from suppliers (manufacturers, trade and intermediary enterprises, etc.) to their consumers (warehouses of construction companies or their bases of production and technological equipment, on-site warehouses of construction sites).

Vertical transport is designed to lift building structures, materials, products and equipment and is carried out by various types of cranes, hoists, pneumatic superchargers and concrete, mortar pumps, screw conveyors, etc.

Horizontal transport moves goods from the place of their production or storage to the place of their consumption. It includes all modes of transport listed at the beginning of this section.

In terms of fitness for the transportation of building materials, transport can be:

- universal — for the transportation of goods of a wide range;
- specialized — for the transportation of goods of certain types;
- special — for a specific type of cargo or single transportation.

Depending on the transport belonging to different structures, there **are general-purpose transport and departmental transport** belonging to a particular organization.

Consider the main modes of transport and their structure.

A. Railway transport

Rail transport is the main freight trunk transport and transport, providing bulk transportation of building materials over long distances.

Rail transport is of normal gauge (1524 mm) and narrow gauge (750 and 600 mm).

Normal gauge railway transport is used for external transportation of construction materials, delivery of non-metallic materials and metal rental to construction industry enterprises and others. How intra-building transport is used in cases when the project of the industrial plant under construction provides for permanent railway tracks, and their construction was carried out in the preparatory period, and also — during the reconstruction of existing enterprises or after commissioning of the starting complex (line) of the building Xia industrial plant with the existing railway tracks.

Narrow gauge railway transport is mainly used in quarries for the extraction of stone, gravel, sand, sand and gravel, etc., timber industry enterprises, peat mining and other enterprises when there are stable freight flows.

Rolling stock of railway transport includes:

- locomotives with electric and diesel traction for freight transportation and shunting, export, transmission and traction units (motor cars, motor vehicles, etc.);
- universal and special wagons.

Universal wagons are covered, open wagons and platforms, and **special ones** adapted for the transportation of certain goods — **dump cars** for transporting gravel, crushed stone, sand, other bulk goods, **hopper cars** — cement, lime, and other goods requiring protection from atmospheric influences, **tank cars** — for loose and bulk cargoes.

Covered wagons have lateral sliding openings, and some types have a roof, which allows the transportation of various types of cargo.

Gondola cars have hatches in the side walls and the floor, opening end walls and are intended for the transportation of bulk, long and other goods.

Platforms are carried out with and without sides and are intended for the transportation of various construction materials: reinforced concrete structures and products, rolled products, equipment, containers, timber, etc.

There are 54...135 tons of wagons in carrying capacity, and up to 130 m^3 in body volume.

According to the method of unloading, cars are divided into **self-unloading, unloaded using mechanisms and manually**.

Rail transportation of construction cargo is carried out by wagons belonging to the joint railway facilities, Ministry of Railways, own or leased wagons of construction enterprises and cargo suppliers.

The organization of work of railway transport is carried out by industrial enterprises of railway transport, as well as by transport divisions of large construction associations, construction industry enterprises, quarries and other farms.

B. Road transport

Road transport is the most mobile and maneuverable of all types of transport for the transport of construction materials and is classified by engine, body type, load capacity, type of cargo carried, and traffic.

By the type of body, vehicles can be universal, specialized and special.

According to the carrying capacity determined by the manufacturer in accordance with a specific type of body, motor vehicles are divided into the following classes: small — up to 2 tons; medium — up to 5 tons; large — over 5 tons and up to the limit set by road restrictions; especially large — over the limit established by road restrictions (career, off-road cars). The most common in construction vehicles with a carrying capacity of 3, 5, 8, 10, 12, 16, 27, 40, 60, 75, 120 tons.

By the type of cargo transported, motor vehicles are divided into general purpose vehicles, dump trucks (general construction, mining, land trucks), truck tractors with semi-trailers (farm trucks, panel trucks, plate trucks, block trucks, plumbing trucks, bitumen trucks, cement trucks, etc.).

By cross-country vehicles are divided into road, off-road and high cross, and off-road.

The main vehicle in construction is road transport, which accounts for more than 80% of all transported construction cargo.

Motor transport is located in motor transport enterprises, which differ in the nature of ownership and legal status, as well as in the composition of construction organizations, enterprises of the construction industry and mechanization.

Concentration of transport in large motor transport and construction enterprises, concerns, holding companies, etc. allows to significantly increase the use of vehicles and reduce the cost of transportation of goods due to the balanced structure of vehicles and freight flows, as well as improving maintenance and repair of vehicles.

Vehicle structure of a motor vehicle enterprise, i.e. the quantitative composition of the fleet according to classification principles should correspond to the maximum extent to the volumes of goods transported and their types, the standard of deliveries and the intensity of consumption, the conditions of transportation and loading and unloading, the degree of dispersion of construction objects and the condition of roads, the remoteness of suppliers and consumers of goods between them and to the car company and other requirements.

By the structure of the rolling stock, motor transport enterprises can be general-purpose for the transportation of goods of a wide range and specialized.

The relationship between transport enterprises and consignees is determined by agreements that govern their obligations and responsibilities of the parties.

The organization of the work of vehicles must be consistent with the work of suppliers and consignees, repair of vehicles, the work schedule of drivers and maintenance personnel and can be one — two-shift and around-the-clock, and release to the line — one-time, sequential and periodic (group) depending on the conditions of loading unloading operations, frequency of deliveries, etc.

Maintenance and repair of road transport is provided by the enterprises on whose balance they are located, according to the planning and warning system after a certain mileage of rolling stock. The following types of maintenance are carried out:

- **daily maintenance** (SW) of the rolling stock is carried out at the end or before the start of the shift for the overall control of its technical condition and availability, ensuring traffic safety;
- **maintenance of the first** (TO-1) and second (TO-2) is carried out with the aim of identifying, preventing and eliminating failures and malfunctions for reliable and safe operation of all systems, units and assembly units

of rolling stock through certain runs set depending on the type and its operating conditions. For example, for freight vehicles, trailers and semi-trailers in the first category of operation, the frequency of TO-1 is 2,200 km, and that of TO-2 is 11,000 km;

- **seasonal maintenance** (C) is designed to prepare rolling stock for work in the spring-summer and autumn-winter season and is performed twice a year, combining it with the shortest time for the TO-2 and TO-1.

For enterprises with a small number of vehicles or multi-brand rolling stock, maintenance can be performed at universal posts. For large specialized motor transport enterprises (ATP), car maintenance should be carried out on production lines, which can increase the productivity of repair workers and thereby reduce vehicle downtime.

The current repair of vehicles is intended to eliminate the arising failures and malfunctions and is aimed at fulfilling the established mileage standards before their overhaul.

Repair (TR) should be carried out mainly by aggregate and aggregate-node methods.

Carrying out maintenance and repair of vehicles should be preceded by a diagnosis of their technical condition, which determines the scope and composition of repair work.

Diagnosis can be general (D-1), which determines the condition of assembly units and assemblies that ensure traffic safety and is carried out at intervals of TO-1, in-depth (D-2) to detect hidden malfunctions, which is carried out before the next TO-2 and performed in the form of separate operations (dr).

Diagnosis allows you to timely assess the technical condition of vehicles, reduce the complexity and cost of maintenance and TR, as well as increase the reliability and efficiency of cars.

C. Water transport

Depending on the navigation conditions, construction cargoes are transported by sea and river vessels, which are designed for inland river routes and mixed navigation (river — sea).

Water transport can be transport, cargo, service and auxiliary (towing, tugboats, pushers, traveling, etc.) and technical.

Inland navigation freight transport is divided into self-propelled, non-self-propelled, barges and sections (half sections).

Self-propelled and non-self-propelled crafts, in turn, are for **dry cargo vessels** (closed, open and with hatch closure, platforms), **bulk** (tankers) and **combined** (dry cargo and bulk), and **barges and sections are open and platforms**.

D. Air transport

Air transport is used to deliver building materials to places inaccessible to other modes of transport (water barriers, lack of roads and railways), as well as specific technological conditions (construction of the upper elements of blast furnaces, pipes, TV towers, power transmission towers, etc.).

Air transport means are classified:

- by way of transportation — aircraft (airplanes and helicopters) and airships;
- by engine type — piston and gas turbine;
- in carrying capacity — I class (more than 10 t), II class (5 ... 10 t), III class (2 ... 5 t) and class IV (up to 2 t).

In construction, when transporting goods, aircraft with increased carrying capacity are mainly used, for example, Antei, IL-76, MI-1,2,4,6,8 and 10K helicopters, Ka-26, airships and other types.

All aviation work is carried out in compliance with the requirements of the Air Code of the Russian Federation and other documents governing flight operations and operation of air transport.

For the transport of construction cargo can be used all types of vehicles used in construction.

When choosing a type of transport, production and technical factors are taken into account (volumes, types, dimensions and partionality of the transported goods, range and delivery time, conditions of loading and unloading operations and the possibility of non-reloading delivery, the presence and condition of transport routes, technical characteristics of vehicles, etc.), natural and climatic conditions (seasonality of delivery, condition of transport routes at different periods of the year, etc.) and other construction features in each specific case.

The choice of vehicles is made sequentially.

At the first stage, specific conditions of transportation of construction cargo are analyzed and the possibility and rationality of the use of a particular type of transport are determined.

For example, it is advisable to use road transport for transportation of goods up to 200 km, and for dispersed construction, delivery of oversized cargo under the conditions of railway transportation, during construction in remote areas and over long distances.

It is rational to use railway transport with high productivity and relatively low cost of transportation for the delivery of large volumes of goods at a distance of at least 200 km due to the long duration of loading and unloading operations and the short average daily mileage of rolling stock.

Water transport is advisable to use for the delivery of bulk cargo in concentrated construction of facilities directly adjacent to water areas and having the appropriate port equipment.

Due to the high cost of transportation, it is advisable to use air transport if it is impossible to use any other type of transport or to overcome natural barriers in the transport scheme for the delivery of goods.

The value of cargo turnover, as well as the power and stability of cargo flows, are essential for the choice of transport.

The value of cargo turnover (Q_{gr}) is the volume of construction cargo to be transported for a certain period of time (year, quarter, month). Calculation of cargo turnover allows you to determine the size of the daily cargo turnover ($Q_{gr.days}$):

$$Q_{gr.days} = \frac{Q_{gr}}{n_{sh}} \cdot K_{n.p.} , \tag{6.34}$$

where: n_{sh} — the number of work shifts for the adopted period of time;

$K_{n.p.}$ — the coefficient of uneven transport, is equal depending on the type of construction $1.1 \div 1.3$.

The capacity of the cargo flow $Q_{gr.n}$ is determined by the value of the transported cargo in one direction for a certain period of time, **and the** stability is the intensity of the cargo flow ($J_{gr.P}$) per accepted unit of time

$$J_{gr.n} = \frac{Q_{gr.n}}{n} \cdot K_{n.p.} , \tag{6.35}$$

where n is the number of units of time for the adopted period in comparable quantities.

At the second stage, possible options for vehicles for the transportation of goods using one or more modes of transport are formed. Combined delivery methods are used in cases where for technical reasons it is impossible to use one of the modes of transport or it is more expedient to use several modes of transport taking into account overloads than one of them.

The number of vehicles (N) of each type in the accepted options is determined by the formula

$$N = \frac{Q \cdot g}{P_e \cdot K_u} \cdot 100 , \tag{6.36}$$

where: Q — the total volume of the transported cargo for a certain period of time, t, t.km. ;

g — the share of goods transported by a vehicle of this type in total volume,%;

P_e — operational performance of the vehicle for a certain period of time, t., t.km.;

K_u — the utilization rate of the fleet of vehicles.

At the third stage of the choice of vehicles, a feasibility study is made of the accepted options for transporting construction materials.

The basis for choosing a cost-effective option for vehicles is the method of comparative assessment of the value of operating costs (E).

Operating costs for the maintenance of vehicles are the sum of the cost of maintenance and repair work, depreciation for full restoration and overhead costs, the cost of energy and maintenance materials, wages of operating and maintenance personnel and are determined by the formula:

$$E = \sum_{1}^{N} E_i \cdot N_i \ , \tag{6.37}$$

where E_i — operating costs for each type of vehicle;

N_i — the number of vehicles of each type.

For the transport of construction cargo, the option is accepted, the total cost of which is the smallest.

Questions for self-control

1. What do the means of production include?
2. What elements are included in the concentric model of the building complex?
3. Types of depreciation of fixed assets
4. Types of material and technical resources in the construction industry.
5. What are the requirements for utilities to provide energy resources for a construction site?
6. The composition and structure of electricity consumers at the construction site.
7. How to determine the volume of heat supply to the construction site?
8. For what purposes is it necessary to provide the construction site with compressed air?
9. How is the required capacity of electric consumers at a construction site determined?
10. How is the period of maximum consumption of certain types of resources determined during the construction period?
11. Classification of building materials by type and method of transportation.

12. The structure and composition of the fleet, depending on the volume and type of construction work.
13. The value of cargo turnover, power and stability of cargo flows when choosing a mode of transport and determining their quantity.
14. Forms of organization of vehicles in construction and their structure.
15. Methods of organizing the transport of construction materials.
16. Technical and economic performance indicators of vehicles.
17. Organization of maintenance and repair of automobiles.
18. Ways to develop the structure of the park of construction vehicles.
19. Ways to determine the quantitative composition of machines to implement the adopted program of construction work.
20. Technical and economic indicators of the use of the fleet of construction vehicles.
21. Means of small-scale mechanization: structure, organization of operation and their relationship with construction organizations.
22. Planning activities of enterprises of mechanization and their production program.
23. The main tasks of the operational management of enterprises of mechanization.
24. How is the determination of the need for construction materials and the timing of their delivery?
25. What is meant by the consumption rate of building materials?
26. What are the functions of the management of production and technological equipment in a construction organization?
27. How is the acceptance procedure for building materials?
28. On the basis of what accounting documents is the vacation of building materials made?
29. How is the process of controlling the expenditure of building materials?

Questions for discussion

1. To evaluate the role of various elements in a concentric model of a building complex
2. To conduct a comparative analysis of various forms of reproduction of fixed assets

3. Systematize all types of resource support for construction production.
4. Decompose the energy resources of the construction site and identify the advantages and disadvantages of permanent and temporary sources of supply of resources and utilities.
5. Define rational methods and forms of providing construction materials for construction sites.
6. The principles of the organization of the work of various modes of transport while ensuring a continuous sequence of the technological chain at the construction site.
7. Progressive forms of interaction between specialized construction organizations to ensure an integrated supply of all types of resources.

Questions to solve the problem yourself

1. What is the manifestation of obsolescence for various types of fixed assets?
2. To analyze the possible composition of the means of labor on the example of a specific construction organization.
3. Ways to save energy while maintaining the functioning of the construction site
4. Measures to reduce energy consumption in the construction industry.
5. Use of competitive innovative building materials for resource support of construction.
6. Systematization of evaluation criteria for the selection of building materials, products and structures on an alternative basis in the construction work.
7. A comparative analysis of modern means of mechanization in construction and variant design of the operation of machines and mechanisms.
8. Provision of construction production with material and technical resources with specified technical and economic parameters.

Chapter 7

CONSTRUCTION OF OBJECTS OF ENGINEERING INFRASTRUCTURE

7.1 General information about engineering networks as objects of infrastructure for the development of the territory and their development prospects

Modern construction is characterized by the presence of a significant number of infrastructure facilities, which includes a whole range of interconnected *engineering structures and networks* providing the basis for a comfortable and safe life of people by supplying industrial and civil facilities with various types of energy (thermal energy, gas, electricity) and water, as well as by removing industrial, domestic, storm water. These infrastructural structures are a network of linearly extended facilities, laid mainly underground for a number of reasons, the leading of which is the economics of the built-up space and the convenience of further operation of construction facilities served by infrastructure networks. Underground laying of utility networks together with this makes their operation difficult due to the presence of the environmental impact factor and the difficulty of access to them during their operation. Therefore, if possible, when designing engineering networks, preference is given to ground laying, which does not always look aesthetically pleasing and requires certain actions by designers for its organic integration into the surrounding building.

At present, *integrated solutions* for new construction and development of existing buildings have become common practice, implying a balanced approach to the placement of objects of various functional purposes, utilities, transportation facilities, landscaping and landscaping. Therefore, engineering networks, being an important part of the infrastructure of the modern human environment, largely determines the level of its development. This, in turn, necessitates studying the issues of ***organizing their construction,*** starting with design decisions on placement and structures, laying engineering networks, and ending with the stage of their operation.

Currently, the organization of the construction of each type of engineering network is formed on the basis of a significant amount of regulatory and technical documentation of various levels, which is a set of mandatory or recommended documents adopted in the manner prescribed by the authority authorized for these actions, and carried out in practice by specialized organizations engaged in the construction of engineering networks. Regulatory and technical documentation includes rules, norms, instructions, standards and other types of regulatory documents. Their composition and content varies depending on the functional purpose of the engineering network, however, the basis for the development of documents for the organization of its construction — work organization projects (POR), work production projects (PPR) is the project of its design solutions, which are quite diverse. Consider the general characteristics of the design decisions of engineering networks and the conditions for their placement

Structurally, the *engineering infrastructure networks* laid underground are **pipelines cables and collectors.**

A) Pipelines *in the engineering network of the* appropriate purpose, depending on the function they perform, are divided into:

- *trunk,* usually starting from a source of a resource (water, energy of a certain type) and transferring transported resources from it further down the supply chain. The functional purpose of the backbone networks determines the necessity of choosing, when designing the maximum diameters from the intervals used, the values for the corresponding type of networks due to the volumes of the resource transported by them. As a rule, main engineering networks, depending on the size of the settlement, can serve the city (with its small size) or its individual areas (in the case of larger cities);
- *distributing (distribution),* which is an intermediate link in the engineering network of the corresponding purpose, which are connected through certain technological devices and structures to the main networks and transporting the resource to the consumer or other networks that directly end with the consumer's receiving device. The diameters of this type of network are, in most cases, less than the main ones. They differ from the main modes of operation — temperature, pressure, etc., characteristic of a certain type of

transported resources. As a rule, distributing engineering networks form part of the infrastructure of a micro district or quarter of a city;

- *intra-quarter ones* that are connected to distribution (distribution) networks and terminating directly at the receiving device of the consumer of the supplied resources — an industrial or civil facility. Modern design solutions of engineering networks no longer provide for this link in the supply of a resource in the engineering network, assigning the function of supplying a resource to a consumer directly to *distributing networks (distribution networks).*

B) Cables (cable networks) of *engineering infrastructure networks* are electric networks of high (up to several tens of kilovolts) and low voltage, as well as low current networks — telephone, telegraph, broadcasting, television broadcasting. High voltage cables serve to transfer electricity from sources to transformer substations or between transformer substations. Material, number and cross-section of cores, type of protective shells, distinguish cables. In urban environments, cables are often laid in the form of cable ducts made of ceramic or asbestos-cement pipes. To pull the cable at all corners of the cable duct, wells are arranged.

C) Collectors of *engineering infrastructure facilities,* which can be walk-through and pass-through, vary in their functional purpose. Collectors have a predominantly rectangular or square section. For the operation of collectors, cameras are arranged, mainly, at the points of connection of pipes or cables. Depending on the nature of use, there are:

special collectors (channels for a certain type of piping or cables) that perform enclosing functions for underground networks. The most applicable in modern buildings for the placement of heat supply and electricity networks;

collectors — pipelines and tunnels, which are pipes of large diameter (more than 1.5 m), made primarily of reinforced concrete, designed to perform the functions of drainage of liquids of domestic and industrial origin, storm water;

common collectors used for joint laying of utility networks for various purposes, which are the most economical solution in terms of material consumption and the use of the underground space of the built-up territory, the deficit of which has already become evident in many Russian cities.

Along with their design features, the decisions on the organization of the construction of engineering networks are also affected by the placement of these objects on the construction site. As a rule, engineering networks are located under the streets, which are part of the urban area (limited by red lines), designed for traffic and pedestrians, equipped with traffic control, lighting, a green zone, etc. The underground engineering networks can also be located directly under the roads on which the movement of transport occurs, which necessitates taking into account the factor of its intensity in the design of networks and organization of it construction. The size of the city and the features of its layout determine the nature of the roads, which is essential for the location of underground utilities: trunk roads, expressways, roads inside residential areas or inside an industrial territory, with regulated or unregulated traffic, etc.

The location of engineering networks in relation to ground objects for various purposes, green spaces and their relative position should exclude the possibility of undermining the foundations of the foundations of buildings and structures, damage to other nearby networks and green spaces, and ensure the possibility of repairing networks without obstruction for urban transport. Regardless of the possibilities of placing engineering networks for various purposes on the *built-up* territory, the normative and technical documentation governing their construction defines the basic provisions, the observance of which is mandatory throughout our country. These include the following provisions for underground networks:

- engineering networks are placed ***in a straight line*** parallel to the axis of the street and the line of location of objects located on the street. If there are branches and intersections of the networks, they are designed and laid at right angles to the line of location of objects located on the street. If there is a street width of more than 60 m and the technical need is present, engineering networks can be laid on both sides of the streets in the case of economic feasibility of such a solution;
- ensuring ***safe*** distances from the point of view of operation of engineering networks — in the light horizontally to the nearest buildings and structures should be taken from 0.4 to 10.8 m, to green spaces (taking into account the prevention of the possibility of damage) is accepted in the range from 1.5 up to 2 m., to the objects of ground construction in order to prevent their subsidence, a distance of 2 to 5 m should be provided, depending on the depth of laying; when crossing underground engineering networks between themselves, the minimum distance between them in the light is from 0.15 to 0.40 m, depending on the pipe material and the purpose of the network;
- the ***smallest depth of engineering networks is*** regulated, which depending on the type of engineering network is in the range from 0.5 m to 0.9 m from the ground level to the top of its structure, including the design of engineering networks provides for laying to the depth — there are no heating networks less than 0.5 m, gas pipelines not less than 0.8–0.9 m, water pipelines not less than 0.5 m, sewer networks not less than 0.7 m, cables not less than 0.7–1.0 m and common collectors for joint laying of networks of at least 0.5 m.

In a systematic form, the location of engineering networks relative to the main objects of the construction area is presented in Table 7.1

In modern conditions, it is common practice to lay engineering networks in **common collectors** *for new construction and reconstruction,* which ensures cost-effective solutions and improved conditions for their operation. Placing underground utilities in collectors lengthens their service life due to less corrosion and the possibility of unhindered maintenance, and generally creates significantly better conditions for the operation of networks. The complexity of laying utility networks in collectors is the need to accumulate significant financial resources. In common collectors usually place water supply networks, heating networks, pressure drainage, electric cables of high and low current.

Table 7.1 Distances in horizontal section between utilities

Type of engineering networks	The horizontal distance from the engineering networks of the underground installation to objects, m				
	Foundations of buildings and structures	Side stone streets, edges roadway	Foundations of the supports of overhead power lines		
			Before 1 kV *	From 1 kV to 35 kV	35 to 110 kV and higher
Water supply and pressure sewer	5	2	1	2	3
Gravity drainage (domestic and rain)	3	1.5	1	2	3
Channel heat networks (from the channel surface)	2	1.5	1	2	32
Non-channel heating networks (from the pipeline shell)	5	1.5	1	2	3
Power cables	0.6	1.5	0.5	5	10
Channels and communication tunnels	2	1.5	1	2	3

* Outdoor street lighting, contact network of trams and trolleybuses

Gas networks laying in collectors together with pipelines and electric networks is permissible if the collectors are equipped with permanent supply and exhaust ventilation and automatic alarms. Under certain conditions, it is with an appropriate longitudinal slope of the collector that gravity networks can also be included in it. Common collectors are equipped with lighting, ventilation, alarm and other devices that provide normal conditions for the operation of networks. With a significant number of networks or with large diameters of pipelines, two-section collectors are used. The construction of circular collectors is possible. A typical solution within the framework of this approach is presented in Fig. 7.1 a, b.

Engineering networks in modern buildings are located mainly along streets and roads, which is why, at the stage of their design, it is necessary to provide places for laying networks in their transverse profiles: on the strip between the red line and the building line — cable networks and low-pressure gas networks under the sidewalks — heat networks or walk-through collectors; on dividing strips — water supply, gas pipeline and sewage for household purposes. It is especially necessary to distinguish two situations of location of engineering networks relative to the carriageway of streets and roads, which are presented in a systematic way as follows:

under the central carriageways of the highway, city highway and district highway, the laying of utility networks underground is strictly prohibited;

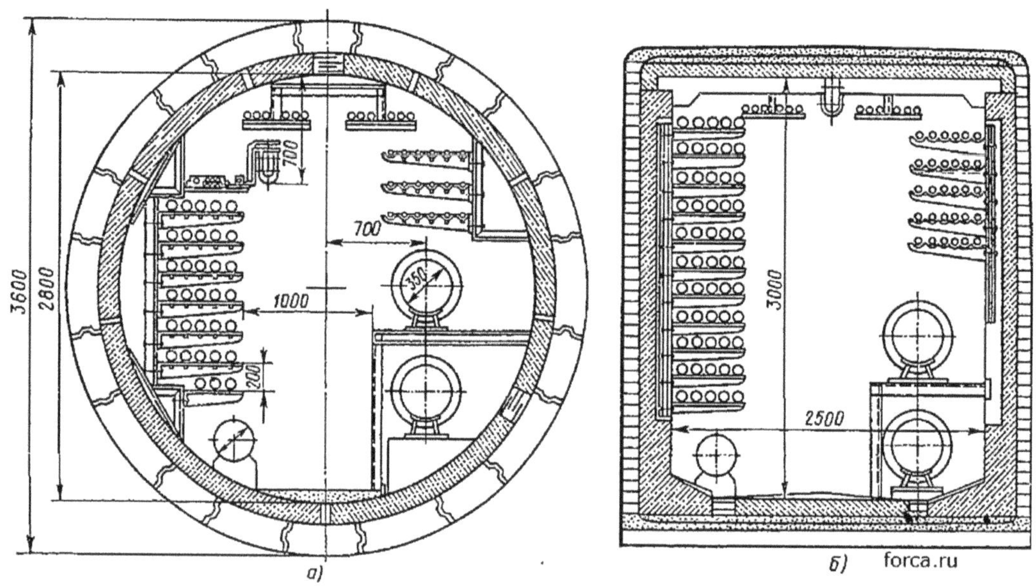

Figure 7.1: Placement options for engineering underground networks in a common collector of circular and rectangular cross-section

if there is justification, it may be permissible to lay utility networks under local passages and under carriageways of streets and local roads.

When installing engineering networks in the first situation, as a rule, duplicate layings are provided in order to avoid transverse intersections of these highways. It is allowed to lay networks in the right of way of highways that only serve these roads directly. In the second situation, you can arrange gravity underground networks — drains, drains. The removal of underground networks from the edge of the roadway should take into account the parameters characterizing the collapse of the soil in the trenches of the underground installation. When reconstructing the carriageways of streets and roads with the installation of road capital coatings, under which underground engineering networks are located, the provision of these networks to dividing strips and under sidewalks is provided. With appropriate justification, the preservation of previously existing engineering networks under the carriageways of the streets, as well as the laying of new networks in canals and tunnels, are allowed. On existing streets during reconstruction, without dividing strips, it is allowed to place new engineering networks under the carriageway provided that they are placed in tunnels or canals

Modern urban development includes the most comfortable form of transport for the population — the subway. The location of engineering networks relative to the subway is also regulated by regulatory and technical documentation and determines certain requirements for the organization of their construction. Intersection of subway structures by engineering networks is provided at an angle of 90 °, in the conditions of reconstruction it is allowed to reduce the intersection angle to 60 °. In this case, the intersection of engineering networks of underground station construction is not permitted under any circumstances. At the intersection sections, the pipelines of engineering networks should have a one-side slope and be enclosed in protective structures (steel cases, monolithic concrete or reinforced concrete channels, collectors, tunnels). The distance from the outer surface of the lining of subway structures to the end of the protective structures of underground engineering networks should be at least 10 m in each direction, and the vertical distance (in the light) between the lining or the sole of the rail (with land lines) and the protective structure of the networks should be at least 1 m. Transitions of engineering networks under the underground lines of the subway should be provided taking into account the requirements of GOST 23961-80. At the same time, the networks should be located at a distance of at least 3 m outside the fences of the underground sections of the underground.

Based on the foregoing, it is possible to determine the specificity of engineering networks affecting decisions on the organization of the construction of these infrastructure facilities of modern development an important requirement for the organization of construction in modern conditions is the need to complete the laying of underground engineering networks before the construction of the territory by ground facilities, including before the construction of roads. It should be noted that along with the permanent engineering networks included in the infrastructure of modern buildings, the construction process also provides for temporary engineering networks designed and built only for the construction period, after which they are subject to dismantling. Their arrangement is a mandatory component in the complex of organization of construction at the preparatory stage; therefore, regarding this type of engineering network, *separate* design and use *principles are* used during the construction process, which differ from the creation of constantly used engineering structures despite the same functional purpose — the supply of energy resources and water to consumers.

The above conditions for the placement of utilities as part of the infrastructure of modern development, taken into account when organizing the construction, are a technical part of the implementation of both the general urban development policy of the territory and the policy to improve resource supply, presented in a number of fundamental documents of the Russian Federation [2,10,23] Their provisions make it possible to determine priorities and specify the directions of development of construction infrastructure facilities.

In terms of placing engineering networks on the construction site, an important role is played by the compilation of promising schemes for the development of the engineering system of a certain functional purpose in the territory of a city or another settlement. In the past — 2017, the main laws were updated that regulate the supply of industrial and civil facilities with thermal energy, gas, water, which imply further improvement of tariffs for these resources [12,15,16] At the same time, compilation of promising schemes for developing resource supply systems is a prerequisite a certain territory, taking into account the existing engineering networks and based on the identification of promising needs to minimize the cost of transportation and distribution courses on engineering networks. This work is currently in its infancy in our country, but its prospects cannot be underestimated. Consider its main aspects on the example of heat supply networks.

The development of engineering networks for the heat supply of the territory of the city district or settlement is based on *the heat supply scheme,* which must comply with the territorial planning documents, including the scheme of the planned placement of heat supply facilities within the boundaries of the city district or settlement. ***The heat supply scheme*** is a document containing the necessary pre-design developments, including the justification of the conditions for ensuring the safety and reliability of operation of the functioning of engineering heat supply networks, their development, taking into account compliance with the requirements of legislation on energy conservation and improving the energy efficiency of resource supply networks of construction territories. The content of *heat supply schemes* and the principles of their development are determined by the rules approved by the Government of the Russian Federation. It is envisaged that in the process of developing heat supply schemes for a certain territory, the openness of all development procedures, discussions, and approval should be ensured, in which all interested parties can participate — representatives of heat supply organizations, heat supply organizations, and heat energy consumers.

The *heat supply scheme* establishes the conditions under which it is possible to organize the supply of thermal energy to consumers from centralized or decentralized sources of thermal energy while maintaining the required heat supply parameters. In the presence of such conditions, the distribution of the heat load between different types of sources of thermal energy based on competitions, the selection criterion being specific variable costs for the production of thermal energy by its various producers. They are determined by application — from heat producers, which, in turn, use the pricing provisions in the field of heat supply, approved by the Government of the Russian Federation and the standards used to regulate tariffs in the field of heat supply for a certain regulation period.

The organization of events included in *the heat supply scheme* in the direction of developing the existing engineering heat supply networks of the territory is carried out in accordance with the investment programs of organizations that own heat sources and heat networks, which, in turn, are subject to approval by the authorities authorized in accordance with the legislation of the Russian Federation in the manner applicable for coordination and approval of investment programs in the field of heat supply. This ensures a single nationwide approach to the development of this type of engineering systems, which allows to provide a new level of quality of design and organization of construction of heating networks in the direction from local solutions to their system development, harmonized with the development of other objects in the construction territories.

When developing *a heat supply scheme,* important safety indicators of the engineering network are taken into account, which should be ensured during their design and organization of construction in modern conditions:

1) reservation of the heat supply system;
2) uninterrupted operation of heat sources, heating networks and the heat supply system as a whole;
3) then "vitality" of sources of thermal energy, heating networks and the heat supply system as a whole.

Taking into account redundancy in the engineering networks of the territory, a balance of thermal energy and heat load must be ensured both under design conditions and in probable off-design weather conditions (taking into account backup sources of consumers, and redundancy in the territory's heat supply system).

Among the documents that determine the **prospects for the development of engineering networks** in modern buildings, **in terms of design decisions, the** most relevant *in terms of time* is the Forecast of scientific and technological development of the Russian fuel and energy sector for the period up to 2035, approved in 2016 and representing (hereinafter — the

Forecast NTR) is the first long-term document in our country since the days of the USSR on technological forecasting of the possibilities of introducing *innovations in the energy sectors* [17,23,24]. The document provides an important systematization **of the global energy development scenarios**, which are important for understanding the context of these processes on a global scale, which are reduced to three alternative options:

- the first, **"the formation of a new era of hydrocarbons",** the most favorable. It is based on an increase in hydrocarbon prices and demand for them, the result of which is the expansion of financial opportunities for introducing innovations in the field of constructive engineering networks of energy supply solutions and the corresponding changes in the field of construction organization;
- the second, **"the era of low hydrocarbon prices,"** which is based on maintaining unfavorable price trends for them. Economic realities will not allow radically increasing the prices of energy resources, while the necessary investments to improve generation and transportation technologies through utility networks cannot be formed;
- third, the "energy **revolution",** which consists in moving away from hydrocarbon sources, developing and introducing new technologies for the use of renewable energy sources. A favorable change may be a reduction in the cost of energy due to a reduction in the cost of the resources required for generation and the formation of funds for innovation at the expense of this. Suggestions are not ruled out for a radical change in the construction objects themselves, in the direction of reducing engineering networks to the level of power supply networks, the supplied energy of which will ensure the functioning of buildings and structures with a new quality of design solutions.

The authors of the NTR Forecast expressed their preference for the **scenario of the new era of hydrocarbons** (with various variations) as the most realistic, noting the conditions of uncertainty regarding a number of key factors of world development, as well as the **infrastructural nature and high inertia of the energy sector.** Likely enough to consider it is the low price scenario. The next most probable scenario in the forecast period until 2035, but the most critical one, is the scenario of the energy revolution, albeit not in full. Thus, in the estimated future, innovative changes are possible both in the structure and in the structures, location, conditions for organizing the construction and operation of engineering networks for the construction of various territories, which can positively affect the use of the space of cities and other settlements of the Russian Federation.

7.2 Certain types of infrastructure and their characteristics that determine the organization of construction

Along with the general characteristics of the design decisions of engineering networks and the conditions for their placement discussed above, there are also certain specific features of infrastructure facilities. Depending on the type of engineering network, the technological processes of transportation and distribution of resources are different, which determines the differences in design solutions that are essential for the organization of their construction and operation. Consider each type of engineering network in these aspects.

7.2.1 Engineering heat supply networks

The Russian Federation is the leading country in the world in the volume and length of district heating networks. Our country accounts for 40% of the global centralized production and supply of thermal energy. The total length of heating networks in the Russian Federation is 17 thousand km in two-pipe terms in district heating systems

Heat supply in accordance with the law of the Russian Federation "On heat supply" is a process of "providing consumers of thermal energy with thermal energy, heat carrier, including maintaining power". Three main elements are distinguished in the heat supply system: a set of sources of thermal energy, heat-consuming installations of consumers — industrial and civil facilities, technologically connected by heating networks. Two elements in accordance with the edition of the law "On Heat Supply" — heat sources, heat networks or their combination were called "heat supply objects", which in practice were previously associated with consumers largely. In this connection, the concept of "thermal energy consumer" was clearly defined as a person acquiring thermal energy (power), a heat carrier for use in hot water supply and heating.

In large cities, the heat supply source is the heat and power plants (CHP), where cogeneration processes are carried out — electricity is generated, and the resulting steam is used for heat supply. Along with thermal power plants, boiler houses producing only thermal energy are used as a source of thermal energy, which is less economical and should be used only with the appropriate feasibility study. By type of coolant, district heating systems are divided into water and steam. For consumers who use the supplied resources for domestic needs, in most cases water heating is used, since there is a simultaneous supply of heat and hot water.

Engineering networks of heat supply systems can be one, two or three four-pipe. In a one-pipe system, the coolant delivered to the consumer does not return to the source: it is either completely consumed at the facility or the spent resources are dumped into the sewer network.

The two-pipe heating system has a main pipeline — supply and auxiliary — return. The combination of these systems gives a three- and four-pipe system. The most common of these is a two-pipe system.

The main structural elements of heat supply networks that determine the organization of construction are linear sections of pipelines, fittings, expansion joints and chambers. For pipeline heat supply systems, mainly seamless steel hot-rolled pipes are used. When laying heating networks in places inaccessible for repair and inspection, the use of reinforced gas pipes with a weld is allowed. Steel pipes are connected by welding, and the fittings are attached to them on flange joints. Along with steel pipelines, there is experience in using asbestos-cement pipes. Their use is associated with certain difficulties due to the increased fragility of asbestos-cement pipes and the need to provide increased tightness of heating networks for operation at high temperatures of the coolant. The main advantage of asbestos-cement pipes is thcir high corrosion resistance.

When the heat carrier moves with high temperature through the pipes, stresses arise in their walls that cause the pipes to elongate or shorten. To compensate for deformations, turns and bends of pipelines are usually used, and in their absence, compensators are arranged. The most common are stuffing box and bent compensators. Cameras made of reinforced concrete or brick in the heat supply system are designed to accommodate shut-off and control valves and compensators.

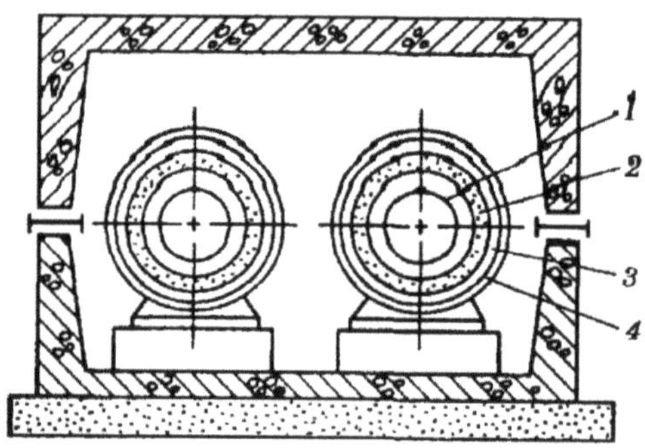

Figure 7.2: The design of the heat network laid in an impassable channel: 1 — pipeline heat network, 2 — anti-corrosion coating, 3 heat-insulating layer, 4 — mechanical protective coating.

There are several ways to lay heating networks: ground and underground in non-passage, semi-passage and passage channels, as well as channel-free (Fig. 7.2). Their main differences are as follows:

Channel less laying has recently become widespread, as 25–35% cheaper than in impassable canals. With this type of laying, the thermal insulation is in direct contact with the ground, so it must be durable and waterproof. The insulation designs of heating networks in this case can be printed, cast, precast cast and precast.

Impassable channels are used quite often; they are rectangular, cylindrical, vaulted, etc. non-passable channels of brick are now used only for small volumes of construction.

Semi-aisle channels are used for laying heating networks within urban driveways with improved coatings. In semi-aisle canals without opening the pavement, it is possible to not only carry out operational work, but also partially replace damaged pipes.

The choice of thermal insulation materials for their thermal outdoor installation is quite large. They come in a roll type or in the form of mats, they can be given a cylindrical or other figured shape that is convenient for installation, there are heaters that are applied in liquid form and acquire their properties only after solidification.

7.2.2 Gas supply engineering networks

The Russian Federation owns about 20% of the world's natural gas reserves, which made it possible to create a powerful network of main gas pipelines in the country, the length of which is the largest in the world, amounting to more than 165 thousand km. For the first time, work on the formation and approval of annual gasification programs for the constituent entities of the Russian Federation on the basis of an integrated approach to identifying promising construction projects was launched in our country in 2001, as a result of which gasification by network natural gas in Russia reached 67.2% by the beginning of 2017 (in urban areas — 70.9%, in rural areas — 57.1%).

Gas supply in accordance with the law of the Russian Federation "On gas supply" is "one of the forms of energy supply, which is the activity of providing gas to consumers, including the formation of a fund of explored gas fields, production, transportation, storage and gas supply" [15]. The law identifies two concepts: "gas supply system" as a more general concept, covering the production, transportation, storage, supply of gas and "gas distribution system" defined as a property production complex, through which gas is transported and supplied directly to its consumers — facilities located at building area (Fig. 7.3).

Gases delivered to consumers should have a sharp characteristic odor, for which the gases are technologically processed — odorized. It is necessary that when the content in the air of 1% gas was noticeable immediately. There are

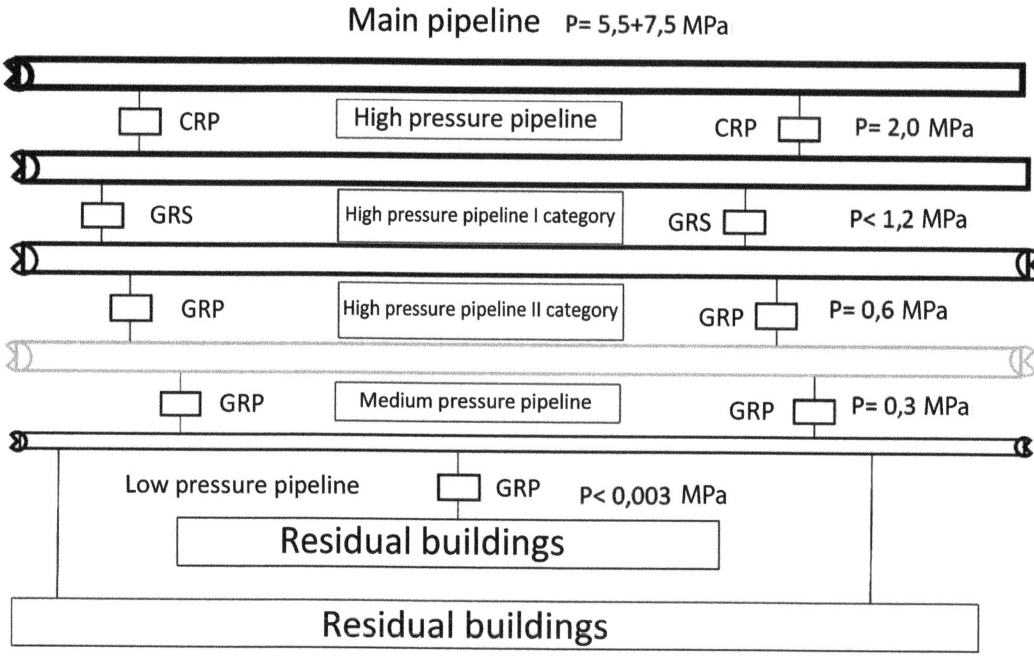

Figure 7.3: The scheme of multistage gas supply of a large city from the main gas pipeline (MG) to end consumers

three types of gas pipelines that differ structurally depending on the maximum working pressure:

- low pressure — with a pressure of not more than 0.005 MPa;
- medium pressure — up to 0.3 MPa;
- high pressure up to 0.6 MPa and up to 1.2 MPa.

The first type of gas pipelines is used to supply residential and public facilities, while various types of industrial production are supplied through medium and high-pressure gas pipelines. Depending on the construction, gas distribution pipelines can be **ring, dead-ends and mixed (ring and dead ends)**

Two types of gas networks are used:

- underground, for various purposes and various pressures, along the streets and roads in the built-up area at a depth of 0.6 to 0.9 m, depending on their coverage and traffic;
- ground, possible on the territory of industrial facilities, utility companies, inside residential areas.

The main structural elements of gas pipelines that determine the specifics of their construction are: pipelines, fittings, expansion joints, hydraulic locks, condensate collectors, wells.

For the construction of gas pipelines mainly **steel pipes are used** (seamless, welded straight-seam and spiral-seam), as well as relatively rarely non-metallic: asbestos-cement, plastic (polyethylene) pipes. Steel gas pipelines are connected by welding. Gate valves, valves and other valves are connected to the gas pipelines on the flanges. In places of installation of cranes, plugs and couplings on condenser collectors and water seals with underground installation and with the connection of instrumentation, threaded connections are allowed.

Valves in gas pipelines (valves, gate valves) are stopping devices for stopping or adjusting gas flow in the pipeline. Gate valves in the gas pipeline networks are mounted both in wells and located directly in the ground with a protective casing. Gate valves are used cast iron and steel. Parallel gate valves are installed on gas pipelines with a pressure of 3 kg / cm2, and wedge valves are installed on gas pipelines of other pressures. When installing the valve in the ground under the hood, the valve actuator assembly is brought to the surface. Cranes (bronze, cast-iron, steel cranes with a nominal diameter of 15 to 700 mm) are used with a lubricant, which ensures their tightness, corrosion resistance, and reduces wear on sealing surfaces.

Compensators are installed on gas networks in order to reduce stresses caused by temperature fluctuations in pipes and fittings. On gas networks, special compensators or stuffing boxes are used, as on heat supply networks. Disconnecting devices on low-pressure gas pipelines are **hydraulic locks.** During manufacture in the factory, tests are carried out for density and strength, after which these results are recorded in the passport. The surface of the water seal, including the tube for water inlet, is waterproofed. At the construction site, a water seal is installed on dense soil or sand preparation, observing the requirements for vertical placement of the element on the pipeline. The water trap tube, as well as the ground electrode, is led out under the carpet. **Condensate collectors are delivered to the facility coated with anti-corrosion insulation.** Each condensate collector must have a number welded onto the body and have a registered passport that contains data on compliance with the technical requirements for its manufacture and testing. An electrode is welded to the tube of the condensate collector installed in the places of propagation of stray currents to measure the potential difference between the ground and the pipeline. A ground electrode is installed in the ground near the condensation tube.

Wells are built on underground gas pipelines in the places of installation of valves and compensators. Structurally, wells can be made of concrete or reinforced concrete, as well as brick. Their various configurations are admissible: round or rectangular in the plan. Construction of wells should be waterproof construction is not dependent on the technology: prefabricated monolith or to ensure water tightness wells located in the ground, waterproofing is performed. To ensure the water resistance of wells in soils, waterproofing is used. To do this, the external walls are glued with borulin or plastered with waterproof cement to a height of 0.5 m above the maximum groundwater level.

Prefabricated elements of the wells are connected on a cement mortar with grouting. During the construction of brick wells, masonry seams from the inside are embroidered and rubbed with cement mortar.

7.2.3 Engineering networks of water supply and sanitation

A. Water supply In the Russian Federation, there are currently over 12 thousand municipal and 50 thousand departmental water pipelines providing 68% of the population with tap water from surface water bodies and 32% from underground sources.

Water supply in accordance with the law of the Russian Federation "On water supply and sanitation" consists of "water treatment, transportation and supply of drinking or technical water to subscribers using centralized or decentralized cold water supply systems (cold water supply) or preparation, transportation and supply of hot water to subscribers using centralized or non-centralized systems of hot water supply (hot water supply) "Depending on the type of consumption, household-drinking, etc. industrial and fire engineering systems separate water supply. Along with this, there are integrated water supply systems. Distinguish between local (for one object), group (for several objects) and the most common — district water supply schemes. In most populated areas, centralized water pipelines are currently under construction. In this case, supply all consumers arranged from one or more supply sources at one common or several networks. Water supply systems are a complex of structures designed to supply consumers with water in the required quantities, of required quality and at the required pressure. The complex of centralized external water supply structures includes: water intake facilities, pumping stations and pressure-regulating reservoirs, treatment facilities, transit and distribution networks.

According to the *configuration,* the water supply networks are divided into dead-end (branched) and ring (Fig. 7.4). The first type is more risky in operation, since it does not guarantee uninterrupted supply, while the second — due to the presence of parallel lines, the water supply during an accident does not stop (except for the damaged area)

Consider the main structural elements of water supply networks that determine the specifics of their construction, are pipelines, fittings, wells.

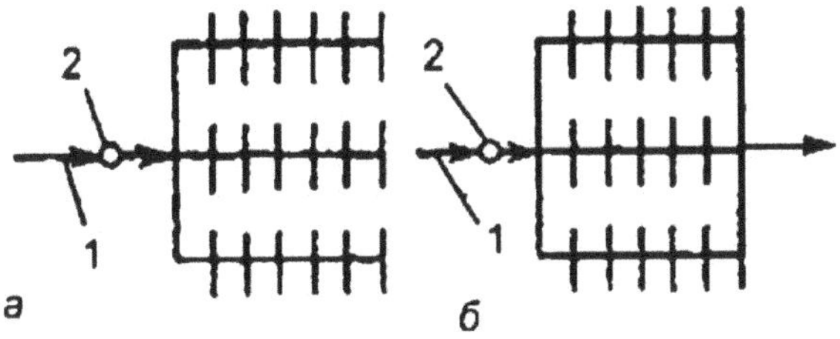

Figure 7.4: The configuration of the water supply engineering networks: *a* — dead end and *b* — ring, providing for the flow of water from the intake (1) through the water tower (2)

For the installation of external water supply networks, ***cast-iron, steel and asbestos-cement pipes*** are usually used. In recent years, pipes have also been found to be used to a limited extent from other materials — polyethylene, concrete, reinforced concrete, plywood, glass, etc.

For underground water pipelines in the construction areas, *cast-iron pipes* are predominantly used, which are produced with a diameter of 50 to 1000 mm and a length of 2 to 5 m, while a larger length is used for a larger diameter. To protect against rust, pipes and fittings (tees and crosses for branches, elbows and elbows — to change directions, transitions — when changing diameter, pipes) are paved with hot asphalt during manufacture. The joints of the bell pipes are sealed with a tar or tarred strand, followed by asbestos cement, cement and sulfur alloy. The first type of termination is more elastic, therefore, it is preferable from the point of view of operation.

Steel pipes that withstand greater internal pressure are also used for pipelines of engineering water supply networks, the wall thickness is less than that of cast iron: from 3 to 14 mm with a diameter of from 20 to 1400 mm. However, the susceptibility to corrosion determines the need for a mandatory waterproofing device — when laying steel pipes in the ground, they are covered with insulation based on petroleum bitumen and crumb rubber. They connect steel water pipes with welded joints, the advantage of which is strength and tightness. Valves (valves, valves, etc.) are connected by flange connections.

The use of *asbestos-cement pipes* (diameters from 100 to 500 mm, 3–4 m long) in the construction of water supply networks is due to their low weight, resistance to corrosion, and dielectricity. However, at the same time, the disadvantages are obvious: low resistance to shock, which causes additional difficulties during installation. These types of pipes are connected using asbestos-cement couplings with a rubber seal or cast-iron couplings with bolt ties with a rubber seal. Reinforced concrete pipes with an inner diameter from 500 to 1600 mm, length 5 m are also used, which are connected at the installation using bells or sliding couplings with rubber laying.

The fittings of water supply networks, installed, as a rule, in wells are divided into shut-off and regulating, water-folding, and safety. For reinforced concrete structures of ***manholes*** and chambers, concrete is used, normalized by strength, frost resistance and water resistance, depending on the climatic region of construction and the category of structures according to their working conditions under load.

B. Wastewater in recent years, an average of 340 km of sewerage was commissioned in Russia annually (calculated for 2000–2016), including 236 km of sewage networks with a capacity of 267 thousand cubic meters of wastewater per days in 2017. In accordance with the law of the Russian Federation "On Water Supply and Sanitation", sanitation is "reception, transportation and treatment of wastewater using a centralized sewage system" [12]. Depending on the origin, wastewater, which always has a certain degree of pollution, is divided into:

- domestic (household-fecal), which are formed in different facilities for the purpose of human life;
- production, which are formed when water is used in production processes;
- rainfall, which are caused by the melting of the snow cover of the territories and precipitation;

Depending on the functions performed for collecting and transporting a certain category of wastewater, there are several drainage systems laid underground, the construction volumes of which are different:

- an *alloy system* in which all categories of wastewater are discharged through a single network of canals and pipes;
- *separate system, (complete and incomplete).* In the first case, two independent systems of canals and pipes are laid: domestic, diverting domestic and contaminated industrial wastewater, and separately, diverting rainwater and conditionally clean industrial water. If with a separate drainage system only a domestic network is built, then the system is defined as an *incomplete separate*
- a *semi-divided system,* provides for the construction of two networks, one of which discharges domestic wastewater, contaminated industrial effluents and the first dirty rainwater flows, and the second (storm) relatively clean rain and relatively clean industrial wastewater are removed.

Network design gravity drainage (pressure less) and with calculation incomplete filling (diameter from 0.6 to 0.8) with the required speed of (minimum — from 0.7 to 1.5 m/s) provided by the bias device, the technical need network heating is provided. When placing drainage networks, the city territory is divided into drainage pools (territories limited by watersheds), where, according to the terrain, gravity pipelines of the street network and collectors are laid, i.e. collectors of wastewater from one or several pools with small slopes of the built-up land surface and a long engineering network, the collectors are buried, which significantly increases the cost of construction. The minimum allowable depth of the pipeline tray is up to 0.3 m for pipe diameters of 0.3 m, and for a larger diameter, 0.5 m less than the greatest depth of penetration into the ground of zero temperature, but not less than 0.7 m to the top of the pipe. For pumping wastewater, pumping (pumping) stations are arranged, those of them that pump wastewater from buried sewers to treatment facilities are called the *main ones.* The most common cost is pumping stations of a mine type with a ground pavilion, consisting of an engine room with pumps and a receiving tank. The underground part of the pumping stations is made of concrete or reinforced concrete, and the ground part is made of brick.

When organizing the construction, it is important to trace street networks, which include: *comprehensive,* when the networks encircle each quarter from all four sides, the *trace along the lowered side of the quarter is quarterly,* when the networks are laid inside the quarters. The principles of tracing a drainage network are similar to the principle of tracing a household drainage network, shown in Fig. 7.5.

The main structural elements of drainage networks that determine the specifics of their construction are: pipelines, fittings, chambers and wells. ***Pipes*** for laying drainage networks are used cast-iron, ceramic, reinforced concrete, concrete, asbestos-cement and plastic, differing in geometric parameters and interface designs.

Pipe diameters are calculated, while the minimum diameter is in the range from 150 to 250 mm. Pipe connections during construction are carried out in accordance with the material selected in the project, which also determines the installation requirements. For example, with reinforced concrete pipes with a socket end type A, the joints are sealed with caulking with the appropriate sealant; at the end of the pipe type B, the joints are sealed with rubber rings. The folded pipe joints are sealed with mastic or cement mortar with a continuous belt along the diameter of the pipe. Asbestos-cement pipes are connected in a slightly different way — with the help of asbestos-cement couplings supplied with the pipes.

Wells and chambers are also being constructed on drainage networks. Precast concrete chambers are built on all networks at the junctions of several lines of large diameters into one collector. Depending on the purpose, wells are arranged on the sewer networks: inspection, linear, rotary, nodal, control, flushing, and overflow (with a riser, with a spillway and a water well). Pipes

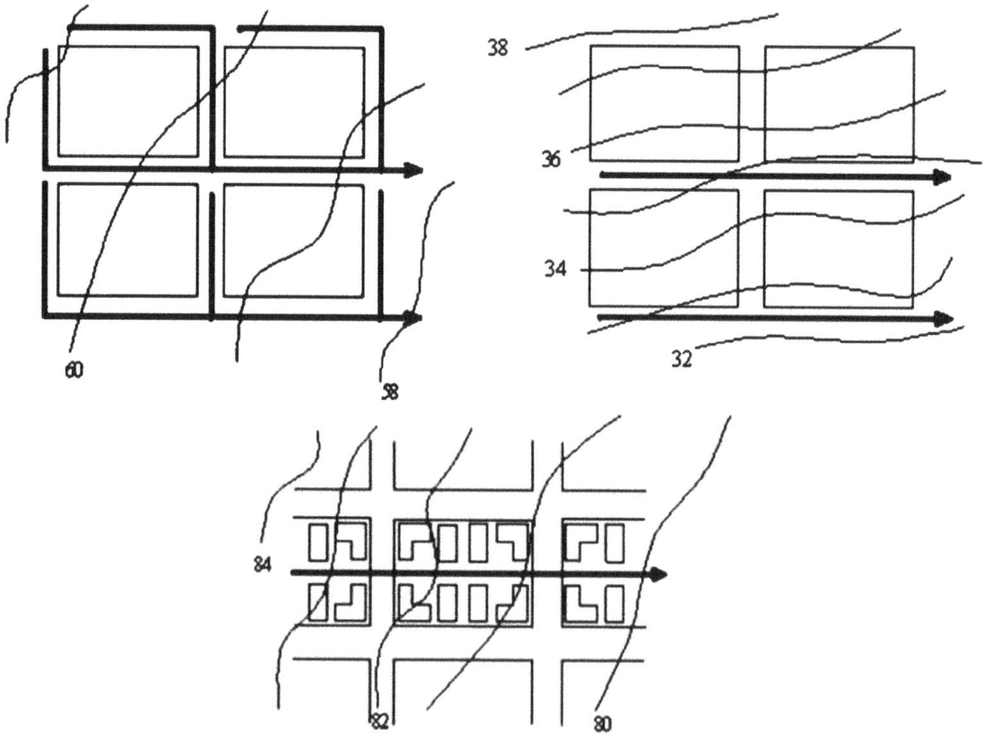

Figure 7.5: Three types of tracing of engineering water disposal networks: bulk, on the lowered side of the quarter, per-quarter

inside wells and chambers are replaced with open trays and a slight slope from the walls of the well to the tray.

The structural characteristics of engineering networks discussed above, which determine the organization of the construction of these modern infrastructure facilities, make it possible to single out work packages common to all linearly extended objects, which include preparatory types of work: preparatory, excavation, installation insulation, commissioning. There are certain differences in the technology of their implementation and the organization of the construction of engineering networks interconnected with it, which depend on their design decisions — material, thickness and diameter of pipelines, design features of fittings, types of various types of fittings for piping equipment, type of insulation coatings, presence or absence of channels. They affect the size of the territory for construction, the choice of machines and mechanisms, equipment for the production of works, the organization of the storage of building materials and structures. However, the concept of the organization of construction of infrastructure facilities, discussed below, is similar for all engineering networks for various functional purposes.

7.3 Organization of the construction of infrastructure infrastructure engineering networks

All engineering networks of modern buildings, regardless of their functional purpose, have similar structural elements, which include linearly-extended parts — pipelines, cables, channels, located on the built-up area. In this regard, it is obvious that they have a certain similarity in matters of the organization of construction, which is carried out on the basis of previously developed documents — POR or PPR, which contain all the necessary conditions for the construction of the engineering network. The same features of engineering networks determine the possibility of using the in-line method of organizing construction based on a certain technological sequence of the implementation of work packages. The flow in the construction of engineering networks is organized in such a way as to use the resources and means most economically, to carry out a large amount of work in a short time, at low cost and with high quality construction.

Consider the general characteristics of the organization of the construction of engineering networks as an infrastructure object during the development of the territory, starting from the issues of providing construction with material resources, ending with environmental protection.

7.3.1 Ensuring the construction of the engineering network with material resources

When organizing the construction of engineering networks, the delivery of the required quantity and nomenclature of building materials, products and structures, in accordance with the planned scope of work, to the place of their production is provided by centralized road transport. Due to the specifics of the construction object — engineering networks, which are characterized by relatively small needs for temporary supply of energy and water, the construction is provided with electricity from a mobile power station, and water, acetylene and oxygen are delivered by road. Providing construction with compressed air is carried out from mobile compressors.

The applied materials, products, equipment, inventory must have certificates confirming their quality. It is forbidden to use building materials and products that do not have an enclosed document, as well as a trademark on the product. Storage of the supplied resources is carried out differentially according to their types in the places provided by the construction plan: pipes are stacked in piles on linings with end stops, shutoff valves in one row on the liners, insulation materials — depending on the type of application (stacks or in one row), floor slabs canals, reinforced concrete rings — stacked on linings and layings, crushed stone and building sand — are stored freely within the allotted territory for construction.

7.3.2 Organization of a site for the construction of an engineering network

The organization of the construction of the engineering network is carried out on the basis of the construction plan (CGP), developed in accordance with regulatory and technical documents. The procedure for the development of EGR to engineering networks, taking into account their design characteristics and placement requirements, is adopted as follows:

- on the topographic plan, the boundaries of the construction site construction area are indicated;
- apply existing and planned engineering networks and other development objects located in the construction zone;
- determine the location of the main mounting cranes, construction machines and devices;
- determine the sites for the enlarged assembly and storage of structures of engineering networks and their technological equipment;
- a scheme is being developed for moving construction materials and technological equipment with justification of parameters and road structures;
- determine the location of temporary auxiliary buildings;
- types of temporary communications and networks are selected with indication of points of connecting them to existing systems;
- determine the technical and economic indicators of SHP.

Symbols on the construction plan are accepted in accordance with the current regulatory and technical documentation. Depending on the location of the engineering network, it may be necessary to develop, as a separate element of the organization of the construction of the project for the organization of road traffic — POD. It is necessary to streamline the movement of vehicles and pedestrians outside the construction territory when laying engineering networks, fulfilling the requirements to change the existing arrangement of technical means of organizing traffic. In terms of content, the SOD is a layout of road signs, technical means of organizing traffic, the layout of markings and other elements that determine traffic.

It is formed in accordance with the technical conditions issued by the traffic police, road owners and other authorized bodies.

There are mandatory requirements for the organization of a construction site for the construction of engineering networks. Construction sites are fenced

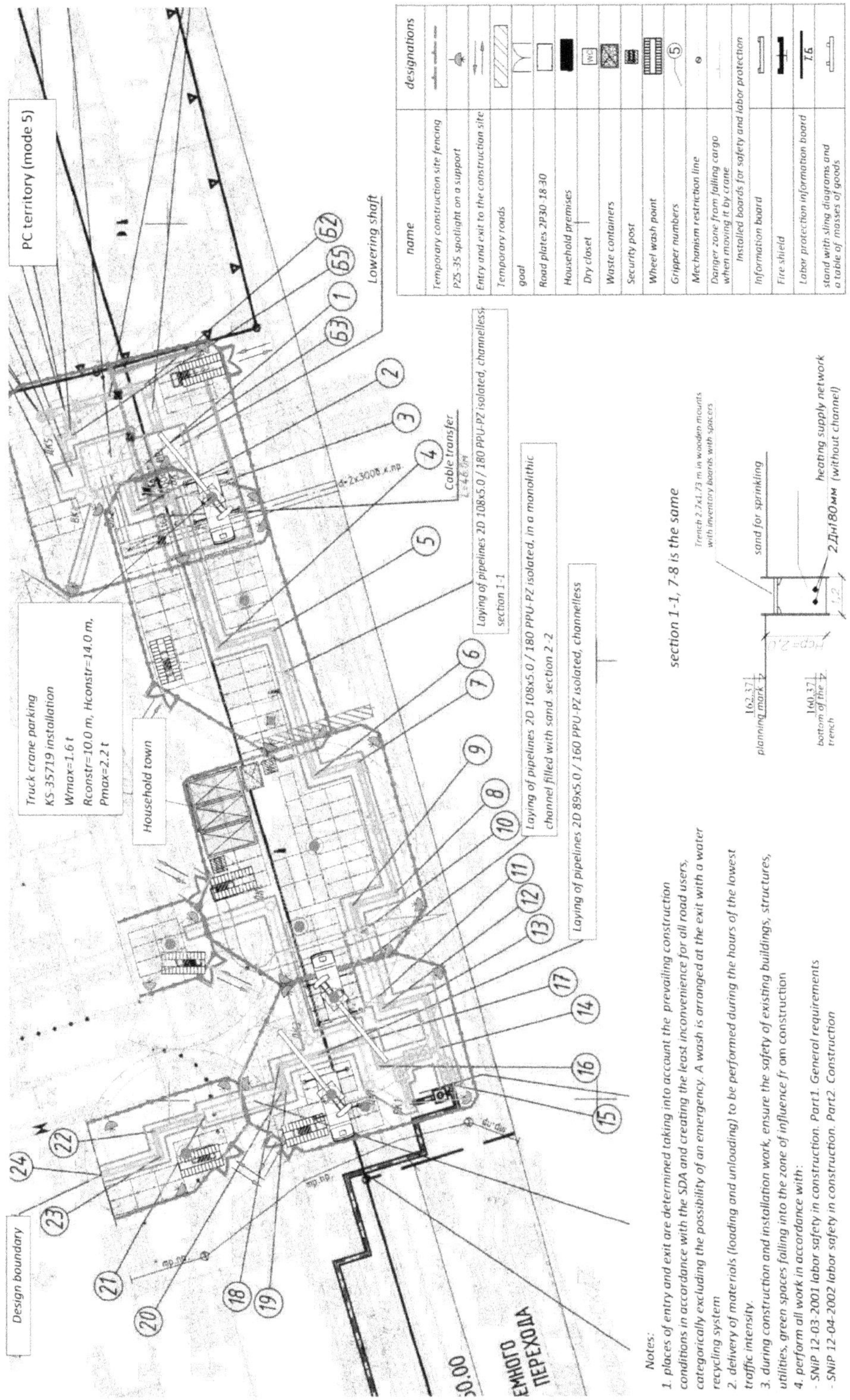

Figure 7.6: Construction master plan for the construction of a heating network to connect the capital construction project of an existing public building (at the stage of construction installation)

with an inventory panel fence and, as the front of work on a dedicated grab is completed, they are moved to the production area of the next stage of work. In accordance with the rules for the production and acceptance of work on construction sites, safe and harmless working conditions for people and mechanisms should be created alternately. On the territory of the construction site, entrance signs, light road warning signs for vehicles and pedestrians, signs on hazardous areas and rules of conduct in them should be installed. In places of transitions through trenches, bridges are installed with a width of at least 1.0 m with a railing and a height of 1.0 m. An example of a site construction plan during the construction of a heating network at the PPW stage is shown in Fig. 7.6.

7.3.3 The implementation of individual work complexes in the construction of engineering networks

The beginning and conditions for the implementation of construction work are determined by the "Warrant for Work" (OPS). There are several production complexes for laying the engineering network, which include:

- preparatory work;
- earthwork before and after installation of pipeline structures;
- installation work, including protection devices (electro-, chemical);
- insulation work, the composition of which depends on the presence (or absence) of factory insulation;
- testing, commissioning and commissioning.

If there is a canal network in the design solution, this list is supplemented by construction work on the canal after the excavation works and at the end of the pipeline. The specified sequence of work is carried out in accordance with the allocated captures of the construction zones within the framework of the accepted in-line method of organizing construction.

The composition of the *preparatory work* during the construction of the engineering network, as a rule, includes:

- breakdown of the route of the engineering network on the ground;
- arrangement of access and assembly roads to the construction site;
- fencing of the construction zone;
- wiring along the electricity route for construction needs;
- suspension of existing intersected underground utilities;
- delivery of building structures, pipes and other materials for construction.

Prior to the commencement of work, a commission is convened from representatives of the operating organizations, which are in charge of the facilities that fall into the construction zone for the coordination of all necessary issues. A large number of underground communications of modern buildings determines the need to strictly comply with the requirements for approvals. Three days before the start of excavation, the producer of the work calls in place the representatives of the organizations coordinating the excavation, as well as the representatives of the organizations indicated in the approval of the TSA. During a call, the owners of underground utilities must arrive at the excavation site, and for facilities where there are no underground networks and utilities belonging to them, they must inform the organization that made the call about this. *Prior to the arrival of representatives of operating organizations, work is not permitted.* Prior to commencement of work, all underground utilities located in the work area must be opened by pits in order to clarify the depth of their laying and location in the plan in the presence of the workers responsible for the operation of these utilities, and are marked with warning signs. Together with the operational services, the actual drawings of the cables and pipelines, the places where the pits are opened and the trench (pit) are manually excavated, as well as signs indicating the location of the underground utilities in the work area. Representatives of the operational services shall be given instructions to the work producer on measures to ensure the safety of their underground facilities and communications. Opened underground utilities should be enclosed in protective boxes and suspended according to standard drawings.

When performing *earthwork,* soil development is carried out by a single-bucket excavator E-3322A with "backhoe" equipment (or an analogue). The choice of excavator should be determined by the size of the trench and the pit, as well as the required radius of unloading of soil into the dump and into motor vehicles. The development of trenches and pits in the immediate vicinity of buildings and structures, as well as existing underground utilities, must be carried out in accordance with the design documentation in strict accordance with the building codes for labor safety in construction. Near existing communications, soil development is done manually. To ensure the protection of surrounding buildings and structures, during the construction of the engineering network for fixing trenches and pits, the method of pipe drilling is used. Pipe drilling should be done with the PBU-2 drilling rig (or equivalent) followed by soil extraction. If the construction of the engineering network takes place in cramped conditions, the development of trenches and pits is carried out in metal and wooden fixtures. The procedure for the development of trenches and pits, their fastenings are carried out in accordance with the PPW. The condition of the fixtures must be systematically monitored. If the work is carried out in cramped conditions, then during construction and installation work, the storage of structures and materials on the site of each stage of construction is carried out in a limited space, so the supply of building elements to the installation area should be made from the "wheels". Soil from the trench can be developed into a dump, and under cramped construction conditions — transported by vehicles to pre-selected places. When developing into the dump, the soil is fed by the excavator to the most remote places of the dump with the expectation that after the excavator passes there will be a brow with a width of at least 0.5 m between the slope of the trench and the dump. The height of the blade should be 0.4-0.5 m less than the height of the excavator unloading. Backfilling of trenches and pits after construction and installation work is carried out using a DZ-37 bulldozer (or equivalent).

The scope of work the *installation of pipelines* during the construction of engineering networks can be divided into several successive actions: laying pipes in a trench welding, flushing the pipeline, installation of systems of operational dispatch control (UEC) installation of couplings, foam joints, sealing couplings (Fig. 7.7) Bcforc installing the pipe they are cleaned inside and out of dirt, ice, snow, etc. They lay pipes on a prepared foundation always towards the slope; with bell-shaped and folded pipes — bell-shaped pipes forward along the course of laying, while the smooth end of the pipe being laid is inserted into the laid-in bell. Correct installation is checked with geodetic tools. It is important to maintain the given sequence of work. Pipeline welding outside the trench is not allowed. If this requirement is not met, then when trying to lower the finished structure to the bottom of the trench, the welded joints, as well as all other parts, are exposed to dangerous voltage and there is a high probability of hidden subsurface defects.

Manufacture of *insulation works,* which mainly refers to the heating networks (heat and hydro) in modern construction is rarely done enough on the building site. To protect the surface of metal elements from corrosion located in the channels, a layer of wrapping (roll on various mastics) or coating (mastics with paints or varnishes) is applied to their surface. The choice of thermal insulation materials may vary depending on the design decisions of the engineering network channel-laid (through passage, through passage) and channel less. When the latter is technically feasible, an advantage is given when choosing the type of laying, however, the design of the insulation of pipelines of the channel less laying, in addition to the main heat-insulating properties, must meet the following requirements: withstand the loads from the mass of soil passing through the transport, prevent the pipeline from moistening, etc. Therefore, to obtain high-quality insulation of pipelines, it is performed in the factory. At the construction site, only the joints of insulation are sealed at the places of welding of the pipelines, as well as at the places where the pipelines exit to the chambers and wells. To seal the joints of pipelines, finished products

Figure 7.7: Installation of a pre-insulated heating network in a trench

(shells or segments) are used, made of the same material as the main insulation, and delivered completely for installation together with the insulated pipeline.

After the network is installed, a *series of tests* should be *performed.* First of all, hydraulic tests are carried out. The purpose of this test is to assess the strength of welded joints and the effect of pressure on the pipeline of the engineering network as a whole. You should also check the UEC system. Remote control test results should be documented and stored for future use. Also, for a subsequent assessment of wet insulation, you need to know what its dryness was originally.

Backfilling of pipelines of channel less laying is carried out in layers. The first layer is sand. A small layer of soil is poured next. A signal tape is laid on it — a thin polyethylene strip of bright coloring with the inscription (for example, for a heating network): "carefully the heating network." Everything is filled up with soil, a fertile layer returns on top and grass cover is sown. Backfilling in crowded places and at the intersection with existing communications is done manually. The track is filled up under existing and planned passageways with sand with a layer-by-layer compaction; in other areas, the developed soil with layer-by-layer compaction. Sand and soil are carefully rammed by electric rammers IE-4502 (or equivalents). At the intersection of the trench with underground utilities laid within the trench, the latter is filled up manually with sand in layers of a thickness of not more than 0.1 m with thorough layer-by-layer compaction. To restore the pavement disturbed during the construction of the engineering network, a small-class skating rink should be used. In small areas inaccessible for compaction by the roller, it is allowed to use vibration seals (vibration plates).

7.3.4 Quality control of work

In the process of performing work, it is necessary to constantly monitor their quality (according to operational control schemes) with the preparation of the necessary acts for covert work with the participation of customer technical supervision services. This is mandatory for the organization of the construction of any objects, however, the specificity of engineering networks is their predominant underground installation, which greatly complicates their maintenance during operation and almost completely determines the technical condition of the network during the performance of its functions. The most responsible are laying and isolating the pipelines and organizing their backfilling with soil from the standpoint of eliminating the conditions of adverse effects of the surrounding soil on the protected network structure — mechanical, chemical, thermal.

We give controlled positions on the main complexes of work performed during the organization of the construction of underground engineering networks. During excavation, the following are monitored prior to commencement of work: the accuracy of the breakdown of the route; during the execution of work, deviation of the bottom marks of the excavations from the design during rough and final excavation of the trenches and pits, ensuring a longitudinal slope, the steepness of the slopes, the width of the trench and the dimensions of the pits along the bottom. When backfilling, the soil content, the thickness of the layer to be poured, and the density of the compacted soil are controlled. The implementation of the second major complex of works — installation of pipelines, also requires the full quality of work: control of the tightness of the pipes to the base, the presence of mounting marks, the cleanliness of the surfaces of the pipes being welded, the gaps between the ends of the pipes to be mated, and the operating condition of the equipment used for welding. When installing pipe insulation at the plant, it is also necessary to carry out incoming inspection of previously insulated pipelines for the correspondence of the wall thickness of the steel pipe and the wall thickness of the insulating layer to the design, dry insulation. The same control points apply to fittings. All fittings are additionally checked for closing / opening. Couplings are rated for ovality and inner diameter. In the case of the construction of engineering networks laid in the channels, it is necessary to check before installation that there is no dirt, ice, snow on reinforced concrete products, the quality of the sand or gravel preparation device, the degree of compaction of the concrete mixture during the concrete preparation device, during installation — the size of the installation clearance during assembly, the accuracy of the installation of reinforced concrete structures of the engineering network in the design position.

Studies conducted on a representative sample of one of the types of utilities — heating mains, obtained quantitative estimates of damage and failures during operation, arising from inadequate quality control of works at the construction stage (Table 7.3).

Table 7.3 Distribution of damage and failures of heating networks by type

Type of laying of heating networks	External corrosion,%			Internal corrosion,%		
	fistulas	breaks	weld cracks seam	fistulas	breaks	weld cracks seam
1	2	3	4	5	6	7
Impassable channel	86	13.9	0.1	92	7.4	0.2
Half bore	85	148	0.2	88	10.6	1.4
Channelless, in polyurethane foam	80	20		76	17	7
Channelless, in reinforced concrete	69	31		67	32	1

In the vast majority of cases, the cause of various types of failures in the operation of heating networks is the corrosion of metal structural elements, mainly on their outer surface, which arose in connection with poor-quality work at the construction stage, which leads over time to the appearance of metal contact with water penetrating to the pipeline. The other part of the damage — non-corrosive, as a rule, accounts for no more than 10% of the total number of damage and failures. All this indicates the need to pay due attention to the quality control of the construction of engineering networks, the malfunctions of which during operation can lead to significant malfunctions in the operation of all facilities throughout the territory of the network.

7.3.5 Occupational health and safety measures

A. The labor protection of workers during the construction of the engineering network should be ensured:

- issuing the necessary personal protective equipment (helmets, special clothing, shoes, etc.);
- implementation of measures for collective protection of workers (fences, lighting and safety devices);

- the presence of sanitary facilities and devices in accordance with applicable standards.

Before starting work, it is necessary to install fencing signs indicating the location of underground utilities. In the security zone of communications, earthwork should be carried out under the supervision of a superintendent or supervisor and under the supervision of the owners of these lines.

B. Environmental protection when laying utility networks is a mandatory element of the organization of work. To do this, when developing methods for the production of basic construction and installation works, hydrogeological conditions of construction are considered, the features and purposes of the network being laid, the features of the construction site, essential for ensuring environmental protection conditions, are taken into account.

To protect the land during the construction period, it is necessary to maximize the use of the existing infrastructure for the engineering support of the construction in one technical corridor, namely: roads, level crossings and temporary construction sites, which will reduce the area of temporary land allocation. Demolition of green spaces in connection with the need to carry out work on the construction of engineering networks is carried out only with the appropriate permits. After the construction is completed, restoration of the disturbed landscaping is carried out. Typical sources of negative impact during the period of work during the construction of engineering networks are construction and transport vehicles and mechanisms. The main factor in their impact is noise, which should be minimized during the organization of construction due to various measures, which include:

- carrying out construction work only in the daytime, with a complete prohibition of work at night;
- arrangement of working machines at a construction site taking into account mutual sound barriers and environmental barriers;
- implementation of preventive repair of mechanisms.

There are other factors of negative impact in connection with the operation of construction machines and mechanisms in the form of emissions into the air. In connection with these, it is necessary to provide for the organization of construction: control over the operation of equipment during a period of forced downtime or a technical interruption in work (parking of equipment only with the engine off);

- dispersion over time of the operation of construction machines and mechanisms that are not involved in a single continuous technological process;
- ensuring timely preventive maintenance of diesel mechanisms.

The measures listed above should be supplemented by regular work to control the toxicity of exhaust gases in accordance with GOST R 52160-2003.

The negative impact on the environment during the construction of engineering networks can also be as follows:

- the destruction of natural soil covers as a result of earthwork;
- pollution and cluttering of the soil surface with waste from building materials, household garbage, etc.

Typical wastes during construction work are asphalt concrete scrap and metal scrap, cinders of welding electrodes, household waste from the life of people working in production. Therefore, in order to prevent pollution of the territory, special measures for the disposal of waste during the construction period are necessary. Along with this, measures should be envisaged to reduce the amount of waste to the maximum extent possible and the obligation to conduct regular cleaning of the territory from construction waste. It is envisaged that there will be a metal container on the territory of the construction site for the collection of household waste, followed by their mandatory removal and the conclusion of an agreement between the construction organization and specialized organizations of the waste processing units. When designing the construction organization, measures to reduce the environmental impact of waste should also include:

- regular transportation of building materials as construction progresses;
- temporary storage of building materials and waste on the construction site in specially equipped places. At the same time, temporary storage of building materials in places not equipped with a hard surface is prohibited.

The features of laying engineering networks in built-up areas in predominantly underground construction impose special requirements not only on the organization of construction of these infrastructure facilities, but also on the organization of their operation, taking into account environmental adverse factors. The main guideline of modern organizations operating engineering networks, regardless of their functional purpose, are the same — it is ensuring the fulfillment of all production processes of transportation and distribution of resources with the required level of safety and reliability, with a minimum of energy losses. Therefore, a reasonable approach to its provision is the management of these characteristics of the operation of engineering systems from the stage of development of technical specifications for design, and sequentially continuing at the next stages of the life cycle of the infrastructure object. As a result, throughout the entire life of the engineering network, the proper *technical condition of the engineering networks* must be ensured. It is understood as the state of the operating engineering system, which is characterized at a certain point in time, under certain environmental conditions, with parameter values established by the requirements of normative and technical documentation for their design, installation and operation.

A modern solution for organizing the effective use of engineering systems in the process of fulfilling their functions is to organize *monitoring of their technical condition,* the first step in organizing which is to generate information on the characteristics of the engineering network based on executive documentation on the results of construction and installation work. In accordance with the above definition, three conditions can be identified for monitoring the state of the engineering network, which allow obtaining objective data as a result to assess the level of safety and reliability of its operation:

- regulation of the timing of activities to diagnose the state of engineering networks, which are indicated in the design documentation for infrastructure facilities;
- the need to take into account the conditions of the "external" environment in which the engineering network is operated, since it is the change in the external environment in dynamics that causes a decrease in the ***operational characteristics of networks,*** their inconsistency with the established parameters;
- selection of methods for obtaining information on the state of engineering networks in the range from the use of technical diagnostics to statistical monitoring of failures of operating facilities; creation of an automated monitoring information base based on the transfer of information from all interested structural units of the organization operating the engineering networks about any changes that are essential to ensure the functioning of the network.

Studies of the relationship between the quality of design, organization of construction and operation relative to engineering systems based on monitoring have shown that it is the quality of the organization of construction of engineering networks that determines to a large extent the presence (or absence) of damage to network structures and failures in operation during its operation. That is why the issues of the organization of construction are relevant now and in the estimated future, which is associated with the introduction of various types of innovative solutions to improve engineering networks.

Questions for self-control

1. List the engineering networks that are part of the infrastructure facilities of a modern city and give a brief description of them.

2. What are the current trends in the field of scientific and technological development of resource supply engineering networks that affect the infrastructure of modern buildings, are presented in the document "Forecast of scientific and technological development of the Russian energy sectors for the period up to 2035"?
3. What requirements for the placement of engineering networks of urban buildings should be observed and why?
4. What types of pipelines of engineering networks are usually distinguished and their design features?
5. What are the advantages of laying utility networks in collectors and what features of their design are available?
6. Describe the design features and placement conditions of engineering heat supply networks, essential for decisions on the organization of their construction.
7. Describe the design features and placement conditions of engineering water supply networks, essential for decisions on the organization of their construction.
8. Describe the design features and placement conditions of engineering water disposal networks that are essential for decisions on the organization of their construction.
9. List the main sets of work that must be performed on the construction site when laying utility networks, and briefly describe the features of their organization.
10. List the key issues of the organization of construction of engineering networks that are addressed in the design of the construction plan.

Questions for discussion

1. What conditions must be observed when designing the location of underground engineering networks in modern buildings?
2. Why and how are development schemes for engineering networks of a certain functional purpose drawn up?
3. In what sequence is the construction plan planned for the construction of engineering networks taking into account the design features of these facilities?
4. How is the design, organization of construction and operation of engineering networks interconnected?

5. What are the three scenarios for the development of energy in the Russian Federation and in the world that have been formed and how do they affect the change in the characteristics of utility networks in the estimated future?

Questions to solve the problem yourself

1. Compare the advantages and disadvantages of separate and joint (in collectors) laying of underground engineering networks from the perspective of the organization of construction.
2. How is the construction site organized for the installation of utilities: individual elements and features of their design.
3. In what sequence and how is the implementation of work packages during the construction of utility networks carried out?
4. What is the role of environmental protection in the construction of engineering networks in the modern development of territories?
5. How is it necessary to organize the obtaining of objective data to assess the level of safety and reliability of the engineering network during its operation?

Chapter 8

PLANNING OF CONSTRUCTION PRODUCTION AND MANAGEMENT OF THE CONSTRUCTION ORGANIZATION

8.1 Operational planning of construction production

8.1.1 Goals and objectives of operational planning

Planning for construction production is carried out by developing long-term (strategic), medium-term (tactical) annual, operational (quarterly and monthly plans). It is obvious that planning without control loses all sense, and control without a plan is impossible, because the plan, in fact, is a model for the implementation of the project — a scenario for the development of events. Operational planning is the final stage of the overall process of planning the production activities of construction organizations and enterprises — a management function that involves the distribution of estimated indicators of the production process over time and is certainly accompanied by planning to ensure production of all types of resources. It must be remembered that construction is one of the phases of the general life cycle of COI and the tasks of managing construction production are inseparable from the general tasks of managing COI. With the current coordination of work, deviations of the actual project progress from the given should be taken into account. This is the main task of operational project management. When managing

COI, which covers not only a comparison of the given and actual conditions of the project and analysis of deviations, but also regulation, the complex relationships between the timing, costs and goals of the project should be taken into account. The instrument of such regulation at the project implementation phase is *operational planning of* construction production.

Operational planning is the leading way to organize, manage and regulate the production activities of specialized construction, construction and installation organizations and their units and is based on rational production technology, and also serves as a means for further development and detailing of the main tasks of the annual plan for shorter periods of time and bringing these tasks to direct executors of works and deliveries. It is organically associated with the design of production work. Projects for the production of works and their schedules, routings with estimated indicators and labor costing serve as the technical basis for operational planning.

Operational plans are drawn up, in contrast to long-term (strategic) and medium-term (tactical) plans, covcring planning periods from one to three to five years, only for the current year, quarter, month, sometimes with a breakdown into weeks (decades) — *short-term plans.* They are the most important component of a unified system of preparation and planning of building production and serve the purpose of increasing the level of coordination of the work of all departments and organizations involved in construction and its material and technical support, as well as creating conditions for the proper organization of labor and the most efficient use of labor and material resources, determining the most important areas of work for the greatest concentration of forces in "narrow" places or work lying on the "critical" path.

Their development is based on several generally accepted principles. This is the so-called **balance** planning **method**, which involves linking the planned volume of construction and installation work with the production capabilities of construction (installation) organizations. Balanced plans are carried out for all types of resources used — labor, material, technical, and financial ones.

The second mandatory principle is **continuity of planning,** which provides for linking medium-term, operational and short-term plans. As the production process develops, the indicators of plans drawn up for a longer period are specified in plans (schedules) developed for shorter periods. All calendar plans that are developed for a single object or complex of objects must be mutually linked.

The principle of **comprehensive planning** — taking into account all areas of activity of construction and installation organizations: industrial, entrepreneurial, economic, social, scientific, technical, and environmental. **Stability of planning** involves the timely delivery of tasks to direct executors and their invariability throughout the entire planned period, which eliminates the violation of the rhythm of work, downtime of workers and mechanisms. In addition, finally, the **scientific nature of planning,** which consists in using the modern achievements of scientific and technological progress and the science of management in the preparation of implementation plans and work schedules.

The initial data for the development of operational plans are:

- Contract agreement (contract) for the construction of an object (complex of objects);
- Contract for the implementation of certain (special) types of work — for subcontracting organizations;
- Integrated enlarged network diagram;
- Scheduled production plans for the planned year and current quarter;
- Nodal network diagrams — for complex objects where the nodal method of construction management is used;
- work production projects;
- Technological maps for the implementation of certain types of work;
- Information on the status of the implementation of volumes and types of work at the beginning of the planning period, an assessment of deviations;
- List of works of the "critical" path;
- Availability of a work front for performers of certain types of work;
- Information on the availability of human, material, and technical resources;
- established tasks to fill in the previously admitted lag in the implementation of the work schedule.

The main objective of the operational planning of construction and installation works is to organize the most cost-effective implementation of tasks for the construction of the facility in a given time period, ensuring the fulfillment of the general conditions of the contract and / or the established deadlines for putting it into operation. Ensuring reliable performance of work on schedule is also one of the main indicators of the organizational and technological reliability of construction. The presence of an object construction model is, in turn, an indispensable condition for the automation of construction management. As the most common form of modeling the building process, modeling of relationships between works is used within the framework of calendar tasks, primarily operational planning.

Thus, obtained organizational and technical models of the construction process contain the following information:

- List of work performed;

- Sequence of their implementation;
- The nature of organizational, technological and temporal relationships between them;
- Data on the demand and consumption of various types of resources.

At the stage of operational planning, the tasks of organizing clear, rhythmic and coordinated work of all departments involved in the construction of the facility (complex of facilities) are solved, taking into account the possibility of ensuring the fulfillment of the planned volumes of work with the necessary labor and material and technical resources. That is why, among the tasks of construction management, organization of construction production, operational planning occupies a particularly important place. At this stage, the main management task is determined and solved — to "keep" the construction in the rhythm that will allow achieving the result with the lowest cost — putting the facility into operation on time. At the same time, the current management tasks are being solved — the completion of certain stages (types) of work, filling the previously allowed backlog for certain types of work, opening the fronts of work to related organizations, preparing for seasonal features of the work, for example, in the autumn-winter period, achieving readiness for work on the supply of heat, the inclusion of a constant power supply, integrated testing and commissioning of electrical and technological equipment, etc.

8.1.2 The content and procedure for the development of operational plans

As mentioned above, operational plans serve as one of the main construction management tools, i.e. a set of production processes for the construction of buildings and structures included in the production program of the enterprise. To carry out the management functions, an appropriate hierarchical management structure is always created in which the top managers are vested with all the powers necessary to ensure the effective operation of the building organization divisions — participants in production processes — and to achieve the required results. They exercise their powers and rights not only because of the direct subordination of the heads of the lower divisions to them, which is the case, but also (as a rule, under the conditions stipulated in the contracts) in relation to all organizations participating in the construction of the facility, regardless of their departmental affiliation or organizational -legal form. The composition and organizational form of the management structure depend, first of all, on the chosen scheme for implementing this project, its scale, type, number of participants, features of contractual relations between them and other factors. Construction, as one of the most important phases of the project life cycle, characterizes at the same time the optimality of the selected project management scheme and the level of its effectiveness. The main management schemes that are most common in domestic practice:

- the customer-developer organizes the work independently, performing all management functions, including under construction;
- All construction work is managed by a general contractor appointed by the customer and acting in accordance with the concluded agreements;
- construction is managed by a specialized developer company, which, in accordance with the contract, performs the functions of the customer and general contractor at the same time.

To perform management functions, the organizational structure at each hierarchical level is decomposed into areas of activity. The management functions are production-planning, organization of work, control, regulation, accounting and analysis. In relation to the established decomposition, a matrix for managing production processes and the entire production program is built. In this matrix, the incoming and outgoing information is linked: the first — in the form of initial data on the progress of the production process, i.e. previously established tasks and deadlines for completion (completion) of work, as well as deviations that arose, the second — in the form of management decisions. These decisions constitute, in essence, the basis of operational plans. At the same time, the main indicator of the effectiveness of the actions of an organization involved in the construction of an object (complex of objects), from the point of view of the managing structure, is not the general technical and economic indicators of its activity, but the level of fulfillment of obligations arising from the concluded contract for the construction of this object. Operational management and planning do not involve the intervention of construction management in the economic activities of organizations participating in the construction.

Construction organizations operate in conditions of the probabilistic nature of construction production. Under the influence of various random factors, the construction process objectively deviates from the previously planned — there are disruptions to the established terms of work, supply of materials and structures, there is a need to carry out additional volumes, forcing certain types of work, etc. Based on the real situation at the construction site, the status of the work, the supply process and the availability of material resources, announced decisions on construction management, each organization participating in the construction at least 5 days before the end of the current month prepares and submits an object-by-set set of volumes to the appropriate division of the management structure works in physical and cost terms, which she plans to carry out next month. At the same time, the deadlines for the completion of individual stages and types of work, the presentation of the work front to related organizations are highlighted; the required time for opening the front for the performance of their own work by other organizations is indicated. Operational (monthly) production plans are prepared in accordance with a single form established by the management of construction management, and may have a tabular form, a linear or network schedule.

Each work is assigned a list of material and technical resources necessary for its implementation. Varying the schedule, changing the execution time automatically cause the correction of the schedules of the cost of work and the need for material and technical resources. In accordance with the picking list, simultaneously with the work execution plan for the planned month, applications for the required materials, structures, products and equipment are issued, the supply of which under the terms of the contract is ensured for the contractor by the general contractor or customer. Requests are linked to information on actually delivered deliveries, the availability of required resources in warehouses, possible adjustments to requirements due to changes in volumes, terms or types of work. Materials and products, the provision of which is the responsibility of the contractor, are not usually indicated in the application for construction management, however, the list of them and the required delivery time are at the same time transferred to the own supply service of the construction or installation organization.

Having received operational plans for the execution of work and their material and technical support from all the organizations participating in the construction, the construction management apparatus within three days checks their compliance with contractual obligations, decisions previously adopted for the work of this organization, the deadlines established in the general schedule work taking into account the real state of affairs, compliance with the planned volumes of construction and installation work declared for the supply of resources. When checking the monthly work plans, special attention is paid to the careful coordination of the work of the general construction (general contracting) organization and subcontracting (specialized) organizations, which often carry out more than 50% of the volume of work at the facility or facility complex. Identified inconsistencies and deviations are discussed with the implementing organization, if necessary, the necessary amendments are made to the submitted operational plans, after which they are submitted for approval (approval) to the construction management. Applications for the supply of material and technical resources are transmitted by affiliation to the supply services (equipment) of the general contractor or customer.

Designed in this way, the operational plans of construction organizations — construction participants, agreed (approved) by the construction management, are transferred for execution both directly to the organization — the contractor and the construction management apparatus and serve as a working document for organizing monitoring of the progress of work and their material and technical collateral in the current month. On the basis of this plan, the management of the construction organization develops specific plans and tasks for the planned month for the direct performers of the work — site managers, work manufacturers, craftsmen — depending on the structure and composition of the organization, the number of personnel at this facility, and also sets the tasks for the supply service by volume and delivery dates of the necessary material and technical resources. Linear engineering workers (supervisors), in turn, prepare and issue specific tasks to brigades.

In a similar sequence, internal operational plans for the coming month are developed in any construction organization that can be involved in several construction projects. Such plans are necessary for the optimal arrangement of the work teams and mechanisms available in the organization, the rational use of the existing and proposed material and technical resources. The organization's operational plans establish financial and economic objectives and performance indicators for each operating unit.

Operational (monthly) plans for the production of construction and installation works and their material and technical support serve as the basis for short-term (weekly, daily, less often decade-daily) planning. The purpose of *weekly planning* of construction and installation works is the most cost-effective implementation of construction plans for the facility directly in a given period, taking into account the specific possibilities of providing it with material, technical and human resources. 24-hour planning is the basis for the development of weekly-daily schedules.

8.1.3 Weekly daily schedules of work and their material and technical support

Weekly daily schedules (WDS) of construction and installation works and their material and technical support are documents that link together the work of engineering services of construction and installation organizations, supply and assembly services, utility industrial enterprises and transport facilities, line personnel and relevant customer services and direct it to the implementation of the approved operational plans and construction schedules for a short, really visible period of time — weeks with distributed it jobs every day. The idea of weekly-daily planning is based on the principle, usual for the vast majority of people, of the distribution of ordinary everyday and production issues and problems by day of the week, i.e. in the assumption and calculation of what should and can be done at the beginning of the week (Monday, Tuesday), in the middle (Wednesday, Thursday) and at the very end (Friday, Saturday).

They are designed to ensure on their basis the operational planning of construction production and are based on a balanced monthly work plan, which is part of the quarterly and annual plans, providing for continuous loading of work crews and the concentration of necessary resources for the construction of the facility.

The weekly-daily schedule allows you to organize a clear operational work on the implementation of the tasks assigned to the construction of the facility and establish a reliable monitoring system. It stipulates the responsibility of all construction workers, from the construction manager to the team leader, for fulfilling each position in the schedule, both in the field of organizing construction production and providing them with structures, materials, semi-finished products, transport and mechanisms on time. The source data for the development of weekly-daily schedules are the calendar plans for the construction of facilities and operational monthly plans. An indispensable condition for their compilation is a detailed analysis of operational information on the progress of work and the specific results of the implementation of the schedules of the previous and current week. WDS are compiled for all construction and installation works outlined by the monthly plan for implementation at this facility.

The approved weekly-daily schedule is transmitted to the construction dispatching service for monitoring, as well as to the direct performers of the work, who on its basis daily resolve current issues of work organization at their sites.

8.2 Monitoring the implementation of operational plans, dispatch control in construction

8.2.1 General principles for the organization of operational control of the implementation of plans and work schedules

The system of operational production management in the most elementary forms appeared long ago and even at the beginning of its appearance, it sharply accelerated production processes. In a general sense, *the operational management system* is a complex of organizational and technical measures developed taking into account the specifics of the corresponding industry, which is an integral part of the management of any construction organization, association, energy system, transport system, investment project, etc. Competent formulation of operational production management and control is the most important factor ensuring the successful operation of construction and installation organizations and the effective management of a specific project. The construction manager must systematically analyze the construction conditions, choosing from a variety of questions the main ones, the normal course of the production process depends on the solution of which. If a gap occurs in the complex chain of construction production that has been left unattended by management, the entire production cycle will be disrupted, and it will be practically impossible to restore it without additional time and resources. The operational control system should be built in such a way that any serious deviation from the established deadlines and volumes of work and supplies of material and technical resources could not go unnoticed, because it is easier to strengthen one weak link in a particular place than to restore the entire chain after its destruction.

The choice of a method and system for monitoring the implementation of construction schedules, tasks established by contractors upon completion of certain stages or types of work depends on several circumstances characterizing the COI, the object itself or a group (complex) of construction objects:

1. The purpose of the object, type of construction (industrial, housing, civil, concentrated, linear in nature and other parameters).
2. The scale of construction (a separate object, a group of objects, a complex of objects).
3. The presence of its own production base, sources of construction support with material and technical resources.
4. The entire project management system (customer, general contractor, developer).
5. The nature of the construction (back-up, start-up), stages of work (preparatory, main, final).

If the project is carried out as part of the reconstruction of an industrial enterprise, the task of its management is to unequivocally convey to all project participants the purpose of the ISP and to regulate the distribution of responsibility. The tasks of the project manager and construction manager include, in addition to project-oriented planning, task control and management, also creating a working climate in the project and for the project, which ensures targeted and cost-effective implementation of the project and gives each of its participants the possibility of self-realization. In the process of performing work, careful monitoring of the status of the progress of work and other elements of the project, as well as a forecast of the achievement of the planned results, are also required. For such control, it is necessary to have well-established information links aimed primarily at *managing change.*

It should be borne in mind that if the construction manager can make the necessary decision on the progress of work on the construction of small facilities and even complexes, then on large-scale construction projects this is not only impossible, but also unacceptable. At such construction sites, there is a need to ensure clear planning, control and management of the activities of numerous construction participants — designers, general contracting and specialized construction and installation organizations, enterprises of the construction industry, vehicles and suppliers. These requirements are best met by the **nodal method of** organizing and managing construction, which consists in dividing a complex industrial, transport or social complex of objects into structurally or technologically separate parts (nodes) connected by technological and time dependencies, and creating on this basis a unified training system planning, management and control.

Work nodal network schedules, operational plans and weekly daily schedules of work are compiled separately for each node that is part of the complex, and each of them shows the initial and emerging work and events. These schedules are clearly limited, small, organizationally and technologically interconnected, their degree of detail is practically unlimited, convenient in organizing management and control, visual and accessible for use. Changes and deviations that occur during construction are reviewed and resolved autonomously within the framework of the site schedule, without affecting the overall schedule of work for the complex as a whole.

With this management and control method, engineering groups are created as part of the overall construction management structure that focus on the organization of work for a specific unit, which independently conduct work planning based on the requirements of the overall work schedule for the complex, management and control. The activities of such groups are identical to the activities of the management structure, which is created on the construction of small or uncomplicated objects. The degree of organizing influence of the schedule during the construction period largely depends on the possibility of carrying out at any time a subject analysis of the status of work for each of its positions. The implementation of the physical volumes of work in a given schedule does not always objectively reflect the state of affairs. For example, the construction and installation organization carries out tasks for the installation of metal structures of the building frame according to the tonnage in the terms established by the schedule, however, for the subsequent types of work — roofing, installation of bridge cranes or suspension hoists necessary for equipment installation, the frame structure is not transferred. The reason is that work is not being done to refine the structures to the design state (final welding and fixing of parts, installation of stairs, platforms, walkways, links, etc.). Failing to complete these works during the installation process, the organization will now have to attract a large number of workers for fine-tuning for a long period. To pay attention to this circumstance during the work is the task of the engineering management group.

Effective construction management and monitoring of the implementation of network schedules, operational and weekly-daily plans is possible only when these documents allow systematic monitoring of three main parameters — volumes, terms, quality. For a correct assessment of the state of work, in general for the construction of the complex or its individual units, it is necessary to know the degree of their technical readiness. The presence in each position of the network graph of data that determine the physical volumes, estimated cost and laboriousness of the work, the deadline for their completion, as well as the specified level of technical readiness, allows you to link the overall schedule with operational and weekly planning.

There are generally accepted principles for the organization of operational control, which can be combined into two main groups — periodic and continuous control. The fulfillment by the engineering team of the construction management of an object or unit of the functions assigned to it for the management of construction and control of work schedules (often these functions are combined with technical supervision) directly on the site requires each employee to know the working environment to quickly resolve issues arising during the work, assess the situation with point of view of deviations. To this end, the employees of the group (their number and specialization depend on the above factors) in the first 1.5–2 hours of the shift bypass work areas and quickly solve specific issues of work on the ground, and in the following hours solve those problems that require involvement other specialists, designers, suppliers, transporters, heads of related organizations. At the same time, the fulfillment of tasks and the schedule for the last day for each performer is checked, the reports of the performers on the implementation of the weekly-daily schedule for the past day are examined, the reasons for non-fulfillment, if any, are analyzed, and measures are taken to eliminate them.

At the time set by the construction management, as a rule, in the afternoon, an *operational technical meeting is held,* at which responsible representatives of the contractors, customer services, designers and other specialists necessary for a comprehensive solution of current problems should be present. The purpose of the meeting is to consider the implementation of the schedule, clarify or change the adopted technical solutions, supply equipment, materials and structures, i.e. those tasks that for various reasons could not be solved before. At the beginning of construction and at the stage of expanded construction, operational technical meetings are held two to three times a week and daily during the start-up period. The leaders of construction and installation organizations, customer services, designers, specialists of the engineering group briefly report on the implementation of the daily schedule and decisions taken at the previous meeting, on the problems associated with the work of allied and suppliers, design and others that arose during the work that could not be resolved in a working order and require the intervention of a construction manager. Simultaneously with the clarification of the reasons for the failure to fulfill the tasks, the construction manager takes appropriate decisions.

Operational meetings are carefully prepared and last no more than an hour. In the days when an operational meeting is not held, specialists of the construction management structure, engineering groups verify the implementation of the weekly-daily schedule by each organization separately. In large complexes, a weekly meeting plan is usually drawn up. In this plan, objects, units or types of work are outlined, on which, on certain days and hours with the involvement of a minimum number of participants, issues are considered and technical and organizational decisions are made. Having such a plan, each participant in the work on this object or unit can prepare in advance and think over questions that can be posed by allies, as well as prepare their claims. The content of operational meetings, the methods of their conduct and preparation vary depending on the stage of construction. In the initial period, the main focus is on monitoring the implementation of the preparatory work schedule. In the future, at the stage of expanded construction, when the main organizations are included in the work, the implementation of the schedule and operational plans for the main types of work is monitored at operational technical meetings.

At different stages of the construction of individual objects or a group of objects, a certain type of work may become decisive, therefore, at meetings, the main subject of consideration is monitoring the schedule of the organization that performs these works. In the final period of construction, the main attention is paid to monitoring the implementation of testing schedules, testing networks, equipment and mechanisms, preparing them for commissioning. Many years of experience indicate that such a management and control organization system allows you to quickly resolve issues arising during construction and to ensure timely commissioning of facilities under construction at the lowest cost. However, the successful operation of such a system is unthinkable without supervisory control.

8.2.2 Construction Supervision

The main task of dispatching construction is to monitor the implementation of weekly-daily work schedules and the operational management of material and technical support for construction. It can be summarized that **dispatching** is a management process in which a special dispatching service, using dispatch communication, collects information on the implementation of weekly-daily work schedules and their material and technical support, communicates to the executors the decisions made on the deviations and carries out constant monitoring of implementation of the WDS and management decisions. Joint implementation of weekly schedules and a dispatching control system, regardless of other factors, dramatically improves the efficiency of construction organizations, creates the required rhythm in the activities of all construction participants and ultimately ensures work acceleration. The tasks of the dispatching service in construction are:

- implementation of measures aimed at the unconditional fulfillment of weekly construction and installation work schedules;
- clear regulation of the delivery of materials (concrete, mortar, crushed stone, sand) during the day and ensuring the schedule of cargo transportation;
- taking measures to quickly eliminate malfunctions and accidents, downtime of workers, as well as vehicles, construction vehicles and mechanisms;
- control over the targeted use of labor and material and technical resources.

By *dispatching in the building* means a system of operational management of construction and installation works based on week daily schedules at constant dispatching regulation and control over the execution. There are various forms of dispatching, which depend on the nature and scale of construction, type of facilities, main types of work, and many other factors. There are three stages — initial dispatch, dispatch control and dispatch management. The introduction of dispatching at the construction site to perform auxiliary functions facilitating production management (monitoring the implementation of individual instructions of the management, collecting reporting data, applications, etc.) is the *initial stage of* dispatching, at which the dispatcher is not the operational manager of production. It mainly performs the functions of controller and signaling device, i.e. an observer who does not have the opportunity to delve into the essence of the situation and influence the course of the production process. This form of scheduling is usually applied at small construction sites or in the preparatory period at large facilities.

Dispatching *management of* construction production — the dispatching stage, in which the dispatching service performs centralized operational management of the production activities of all participants in the construction of an object (complex of objects), starting from construction sites and ending with all auxiliary and service enterprises, as well as operational services of the construction management apparatus (supply, transport, mechanization, etc.) within the approved schedule and regulations on their tasks, right and responsibilities. Dispatch control is carried out using modern means of communication and communications, a system of accounting and control at this construction site, ensuring the rapid transfer of information, management orders, applications and summaries.

Dispatch *management* is the stage of dispatching, in which the dispatcher, using the capabilities of the dispatching service apparatus, communications and information about the current production situation, personally manages the production processes. In construction, such a system is most often used in concrete-mortar plants, some automated workshops and small enterprises.

The structure of dispatching construction management is determined depending on the volume, scale, nature and methods of construction. At the same time, the main thing in the organization of the dispatch service is:

- Correct determination of the place of this service in the structure of the construction management apparatus;
- Compliance of the dispatching construction scheme with the requirements of a specific construction site;
- The accuracy of the construction of the dispatching service for the control of construction production based on weekly-daily schedules;
- Clarity and specificity of dispatching forms of accounting and control.

When organizing dispatch control at a construction site, it is necessary, first, to proceed from real production plans reflected in operational plans and schedules and to ensure constant monitoring of their implementation. However, dispatch service employees should not interfere in the process of preparing, adjusting, and optimizing these plans and schedules. The construction manager regulates and monitors the implementation of weekly daily work schedules and their material and technical support, not replacing technical and production personnel, but by their operational intervention increases its impact on production and thereby enhances the effectiveness of the entire construction management system. He does not replace the planning and production services of the rack, but takes on the operational management of the organization of the implementation of weekly daily schedules. The head of the dispatching service (chief dispatcher) and its employees perform the following functions:

- participate in the preparation of monthly work plans based on common schedules for their implementation, as well as in the development of weekly daily schedules;
- take into account, analyze, according to the received operational reporting data from construction units and suppliers, the implementation of the work, and supply schedule;

- daily report to the construction management (there is, as a rule, a special form of the daily dispatch report) on the progress of work, the implementation of the weekly-daily schedule, and measures taken and required to additionally be taken to eliminate malfunctions;
- resolve controversial issues of an operational nature arising in the production process between construction participants;
- prevent and organize the elimination of accidents, downtimes and other malfunctions that arise during the operation;
- confirm on the next day the assignment for the supply of concrete, mortar, crushed stone and other bulk cargoes, as well as for the operation of on-site transport.

In the dispatch service in each shift, there are duty (shift) dispatchers who supervise all operational work. Using the means of communication and information at their disposal, they, in addition to the functions listed above, keep a log of orders of instructions from the construction management and the chief dispatcher, monitor their implementation, a journal of operational data on the implementation of weekly-daily schedules for the execution of work and the supply of necessary local resources, as well freight schedules. The dispatcher is obliged to study the weekly-daily schedule in detail, to know perfectly the structure of the construction site, auxiliary production, service and transport organizations, the names and phone numbers of the managers, whom he should contact if necessary.

The most effective form of coordination of efforts of all participants and construction links aimed at organizing and monitoring the implementation of weekly work schedules and their material and technical support is the dispatch report (conference call). Such meetings at large construction sites with an established management and control system are held daily at a strictly set time and are held personally by the construction manager or a person directly replacing him during his absence. The workplaces of the heads of construction and installation organizations involved in the construction should be equipped with communication facilities that allow all participants in the meeting to hear each other and respond quickly to calls to them. Typically, a dispatch report begins with a brief report by the chief dispatcher on the progress and implementation of schedules over the past day, as well as on the implementation of decisions of the previous meeting. After the report of the chief dispatcher, brief reports of the heads of auxiliary and transport and auxiliary units serving the construction site follow. Having listened to the general report of the chief dispatcher and reports on the work of the rear of the construction site, the leading report has the opportunity to make more clear and balanced decisions when listening to the reports of the heads of organizations that are direct executors of the work following them.

The reports of all managers in the dispatch report should be extremely clear and concise. The construction manager considers only those issues that could not be resolved during the day when contacting the relevant services and construction divisions. The decisions made during the report, the dispatcher records the instructions of the manager, and control over their implementation is established. The data recorded in the daily report forms on the implementation of the weekly-daily schedule of work allows the construction management to daily analyze the production situation, the status of the progress of the schedule and take effective measures to eliminate deficiencies and deviations.

Thus, operational management and control consist of a systematic verification of the implementation of operational plans and a weekly-daily schedule, production instructions and instructions, rational methods of organizing work, and wide disclosure of work fronts for subcontractors. Control can be effective only if it is systematic and constant, covering all aspects of the organization of work, as well as all stages and / or construction projects. Only in this case operational planning reaches its goal.

8.3 Construction business planning

Planning is one of the central links in the management of a construction organization, carried out with the aim of ensuring the consistent implementation of measures aimed at obtaining the maximum possible profit from its activities, without harming the interests of citizens, legal entities, and the state protected by the legislation of the Russian Federation.

The basic principles of planning: economic feasibility; maintaining a balance of interests of the construction organization and society; accounting for market conditions; continuity — a combination and continuity of long-term, current and operational plans.

The main indicators of the plan, as a rule, are the profit and completion of work in accordance with the work contracts, the remaining indicators are the volumes of construction and installation works, the wage fund, labor productivity, taxes and payments, the development of new equipment, the volumes of supplies of construction materials; machines, equipment are calculated.

The construction organization independently determines acceptable forms and methods for planning its activities.

The key to the success of a construction organization in an ever changing and little predictable market environment and fierce competition is the existence of a well-founded action plan for managers to achieve specific business positions. Such a plan is the strategy of the construction organization, which is a combination of goals and competitive actions of managers to achieve them.

Creating a strategy falls into three tasks, the *first* of which is the formulation of the *mission* (mission) of the construction organization, which should contain an answer to the question of what its activities are and what it intends to do. The strategic vision is connected with the mission and represents a perspective view on the direction of development of the organization, the basic concept of what the organization is trying to do and what to achieve.

A well-founded and carefully formulated mission has real management value:

- It formulates the views of senior management on the long-term plans of the company for further development;
- Reduces the risk of shortsighted management and unreasonable decisions;
- Expresses the goals of the organization and serves as an incentive for employees to work in good faith;
- Helps middle managers formulate the tasks, goals and aspirations of their subordinate services and combine the main work with the policy and direction of development of the entire company;
- Greatly facilitates the preparation of the organization for potential difficulties on the way to the future.

The second task — setting goals is an obligation for the management personnel of a construction organization to achieve certain results on time. At the same time, strategic and financial goals are distinguished: the former should be focused on creating competitive advantages; the latter should be aimed at achieving the designated financial indicators.

The third task — the development of strategies involves obtaining an answer to the question of how to bring a construction organization from a real state to a target one. It is obvious that this task is invariant — the achievement of the goal can be achieved in different ways and means, as well as their combination.

One of the main requirements for the developed strategy is its compliance with the current market conditions and internal capabilities of the company. Given the constant and dynamic variability of the external environment of the organization, as well as the emergence of new opportunities as the company develops, it is necessary:

- consider the implementation of the strategy as a dynamic process, consisting of the proposed actions and immediate decisions on their adaptation to environmental conditions;

- include a mechanism for its monitoring in the design (reorganization) of the company management system.

The place of monitoring in the process of restructuring the construction organization is presented in table. 8.1.

The main elements and stages of developing a strategy and pricing policy, measures and the relationship between them are presented in Fig. 8.1.

Table 8.1 Monitoring scheme during the reorganization of the construction organization

Reorganization Stages	**Directions**
Enterprise Diagnostics	Evaluation strategy. Situational analysis.
Organizational project	Analysis of diagnostic results.
Improving management structure and functions	Change of strategy. Logistics. Business reengineering.
Development of financial management practices	Supply and sales. Pricing.

In order to fully account for the main factors ensuring the efficient use of production resources, their planned development over time, timely analysis of their implementation and the adoption of targeted operational management decisions of a construction organization, it is recommended to develop interrelated:

- Long-term (strategic and tactical) plans for economic and technical development;
- The current annual production and economic plan (business plan);
- Operational (monthly) production plans and weekly daily schedules.

The long-term plan for economic and technical development provides for long-term measures aimed at developing production volumes, mastering new equipment and technology, increasing the competitiveness, profitability and financial capabilities of the construction organization.

The long-term *plan* in its form is a detailed plan of organizational and technical measures to solve the tasks set in it, indicating the economic effect, the timing and cost of their implementation, the duration of the cost recovery. The initial data for the formation of this plan are: a forecast of changes in market conditions; the existing organizational and technical level and economic indicators of the construction organization, information on the achievements of scientific and technological progress in domestic and foreign construction.

The content of the long-term plan of technical and economic development, the duration of the period for which it is designed, are determined by the construction organization based on the specific strategic goals that it sets for itself.

The current annual business plan of the construction organization is a comprehensive production and economic program, providing for:

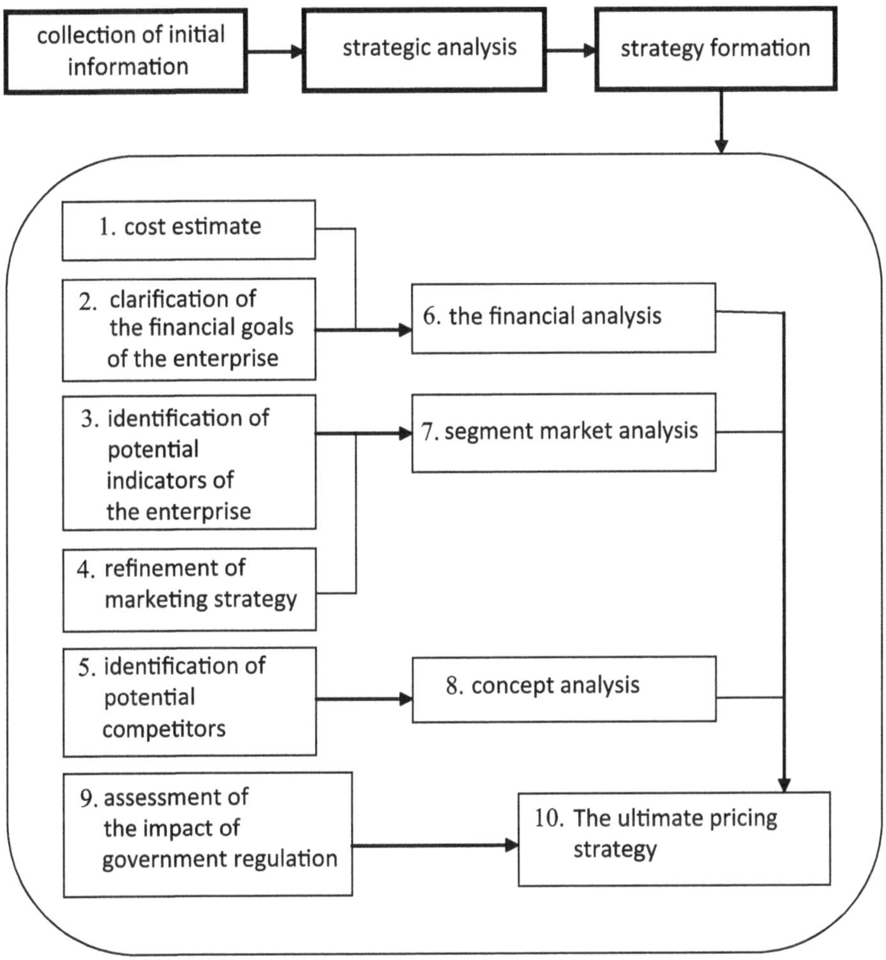

Figure 8.1: The main elements and stages of developing a strategy and pricing policy of a construction organization (enterprise)

Fulfillment of concluded construction contracts and other types of activities, compliance with the requirements of the legislation of the Russian Federation imposed on an economic entity, mobilization of production resources, obtaining the maximum possible profit from the activities of the organization.

In the general organization's business plan, it is recommended that the following sections be included:

1. Plan for construction production;
2. Industrial production plan (work of auxiliary production;

3. Design and survey work plan;
4. Plan for the technical development of production and own capital investments;
5. Work plan;
6. Plan of mechanization of work;
7. Logistics plan;
8. Profit plan;
9. Action plan for labor protection;
10. Action plan for environmental protection and rational use of natural resources;
11. Estimate of overhead costs;
12. Balance of income and expenses, etc.

The initial data for the development of a business plan for a construction organization are: a long-term plan for economic and technical development; construction contracts for facilities; agreements (contracts) with subcontract organizations, suppliers, design enterprises; design and estimate documentation; the need for materials, prefabricated structures, products, equipment, labor, work schedules, picking lists defined by the projects for the organization of construction and work. The sections of this plan have the following main content: the construction production plan is the central section of the annual plan and serves as the basis for the development of all its other sections.

The construction production plan contains tasks for the execution of construction contracts and the provision of services; it is developed by customers and contractors, based on the concluded contracts, for two years, taking into account the rolling stock. If the production plan for the second year is not secured by contracts, then it remains open for replenishment within the limits of the enterprise's capacity. For the next year, the former plan for the second year becomes the plan for the current year. Next, the planning cycle is repeated, ensuring its continuity.

Other sections of the business plan are subject to detailed development only for the first planned year of the construction production plan and are adjusted using electronic computers as new contracts are concluded and production preparations are made for them.

The construction production plan contains the start and end dates for the works in accordance with the work contracts, their total estimated cost, and the volume of work in monetary terms, completed at the beginning of the planned year, to be completed in the planned year and transferred to the next year.

The industrial production plan (work plan of auxiliary production) is primarily aimed at ensuring the implementation of the construction production plan. Surplus capacities of auxiliary industries are used to produce products sold under contracts with third parties.

The design and survey work plan includes the fulfillment of the obligations of the construction organization to ensure the construction of design and estimate documentation provided for in the construction contracts. The plan consists of two sections: on the development of technical documentation by the forces of our own design department and on contracts with design enterprises.

The plan of technical development and own capital investments are combined into a single section. It includes measures for the development of new equipment and technology, provided for by the long-term plan, and required to implement the current plan for construction production. The plan provides for the implementation of own capital investments related to this, as well as with the development of production, sources of financial resources for these purposes.

The labor plan contains the results of justification of labor productivity, the number of certain categories of workers, wage bill.

The plan of mechanization of work determines the sources of coverage of the need for means of mechanization, measures for effective use in the implementation of construction, loading and unloading, for production processes in auxiliary industries, the costs of mechanization of production.

The material and technical support plan determines by construction objects and auxiliary production: volumes, delivery times of materials, semi-finished products, equipment parts to ensure production plans; names of suppliers; delivery costs.

A plan for profit and cost of construction and installation works is developed for all construction projects, taking into account all cost items and the possibilities of saving them.

The plan of measures for labor protection provides for measures to ensure optimal working conditions, medical care, safety measures, industrial sanitation and material costs for these purposes.

The action plan for the protection of the environment and the rational use of natural resources provides for measures and material costs associated with the prevention of damage to the natural and social environment from the production activities of the construction organization, and compliance with applicable laws on the rational use of natural resources.

The estimate of overhead costs includes the overhead costs of construction and installation works for subsidiary enterprises and service farms that are on the balance sheet of a construction organization.

Moreover, for administrative expenses, including advertising costs, it is recommended to draw up an independent estimate in the form of an appendix to the general estimate of overhead costs.

The balance of income and expenses (financial plan) is the final section of the business plan. Its main task is to calculate the needs of a construction organization in cash for its production and economic activities and the implementation of planned measures. In the balance of income and expenses is reflected in value terms the final annual result of the production and economic activities of the organization.

8.4 Business management of a construction organization

8.4.1 Management of a construction organization based on a value concept

8.4.1.1 The essence of the value concept of business management

The problem of assessing the performance of construction organizations is relevant, and a search is constantly being made for a system of indicators that can characterize the results of activities in all areas that are most significant for maintaining or strengthening competitive positions, and be an indicator of internal and external changes. Research has led to the creation of such tools as a balanced scorecard, a comprehensive analysis of the economic activity of the enterprise, a comprehensive analysis of the indicators of sustainable development of the enterprise. They are based on systemic management concepts that provide a comprehensive review of business performance issues. Each system has made a definite contribution to the development of management information support.

Given the dynamics of problems, increased competition, increased requirements for social and environmental responsibility of construction organizations, indicator systems are constantly being reviewed, expanded, enriched with new indicators, and requirements for the level of indicators are changing. At the same time, the search for one integral indicator that is able to unequivocally answer the question of the stability of the development of the organization does not stop. The cost concept of business management, which has spread in recent decades, is based on the use of an organization's market value indicator. The market value based on standard approaches and methods in domestic practice is currently used for the purposes of sale, collateral, and other purposes related to the formation and circulation of property, and this extensive toolkit can be applied for strategic business management.

The potential of a construction organization can be considered as the sum of market, innovative, managerial, production, economic, environmental, technical, technological, informational, human and organizational potentials. The market value of the company as an integral indicator is able to take into account the synergistic effect of their interaction.

An indicator of the market value of a business has several advantages that are important for ensuring the selection of the right business strategy, in particular:

- Reflects changes in the current and potential capabilities of the organization;
- Provides an interpretation of the real state of the organization for potential investors;
- Individual elements of the assets and liabilities of an enterprise are measured at market value;
- Retrospective, current and forecast information is used for cost calculations;
- Forecasting profitability indicators takes into account the potential capabilities of not only means and objects of labor, but also of personnel potential;
- Taking into account the possibilities to influence the profitability of intangible assets, including the business reputation of the enterprise;
- The market position of the enterprise relative to competitors is taken into account.

The most effective cost concept is recognized in business areas characterized by the following features: high probability of significant changes in the industry related to government regulation; long investment cycle; complex business portfolio structure. The construction industry fully possesses all of these characteristics.

The cost of a construction enterprise as a general indicator of its activity does not replace the system of indicators traditionally used for a comprehensive analysis of economic activity, but only supplements it and expands the analytical capabilities of the system.

8.4.1.2 Market value assessment based on the cost (property) approach

One of the standard approaches to assessing the value of an enterprise is a costly (property) approach, which is based on a comparison of the assets and liabilities of the organization. The most common method is the net asset method, which is based on the method of determining the value of net assets (the procedure for determining the value of net assets of a joint stock company, approved by Order of the Ministry of Finance of the Russian Federation No. 84n dated August 28, 2014). The source of information is the balance sheet of the enterprise at the end of the reporting year.

The calculation formula that reflects the essence of the specified method is as follows:

$$K^P = A^S - L^E \ , \tag{8.1}$$

where K^P — pure assets of the enterprise;
A^S — settlement assets;
L^E — estimated liabilities.

The information value of the indicators reflected in the financial statements is reduced if the carrying value of assets differs significantly from their market value. Adjustment of balance sheet indicators can be carried out by applying standard valuation methods taking into account the specifics of the objects being evaluated. In relation to certain types of property of an enterprise, the following valuation methods can be applied (table 8.2).

One of the intangible assets that should be evaluated, taking into account the specifics of the construction activity, are the concluded contracts for construction, the acquisition of material resources for construction. As noted in Chapter 2, Section 2.5, the value of contracts (VC) can be determined by capitalizing additional profit by ensuring the stability of prices for resources for construction and construction products: ΔP

$$C_k = \frac{\Delta P}{K} \ , \tag{8.2}$$

where ΔP — additional profit,
K is the capitalization ratio.

In construction, it is important to obtain land for construction, and these assets should be assessed using standard methods, taking into account the potential increase in the value of land.

8.4.1.3 Assessment of construction in progress

In the framework of the cost approach, assets under construction are subject to assessment. Regardless of the degree of technical readiness, the construction in progress object has marketability and may have market value. An important stage in the assessment process is a technical examination, which allows a detailed examination of all erected structures, engineering systems. In the process of examining the object, it is necessary to identify the actual state of structural elements and the degree of readiness of the object, if the construction period is significantly violated, the degree of aggregate depreciation of the object, the amount of necessary investments to complete construction.

Table 8.2 Asset valuation methods in determining the market value of an enterprise using the cost approach

Asset type	Assessment Methods
Land plot	Sales Comparison Method Extraction method Distribution method Land rental capitalization method Residue method Intended Use Method
Intangible assets	Excess profit method Option method Cost Benefit Method Profit advantage method Royalty exemption method Replacement or reproduction cost method
Real estate	Net operating income capitalization method Discounted Cash Flow Method Replacement or reproduction cost method Pair Sales Method
Building machines and mechanisms	Index method Direct Sales Comparison Method Replacement cost method The method of direct capitalization of net operating income Equivalent Method
Vehicles	Equivalent Method Multidimensional Indirect Method Statistical method
Construction in progress	Cost approach based on price change index Discounted cash flow method
Productive reserves	At current prices, including transportation costs
Future expenses	At face value
Accounts receivable	The probabilistic method of accounting for the risk of default on obligations Option method The method of discounting receivables taking into account the period of overdue
Financial investments	Average values for actual transactions or adjustments prices (for liquid securities) Capital market method Dividend Capitalization Method Discounted cash flow method (for blocks of shares) adjusted for minority or majority nature
Cash in foreign currency account	At the exchange rate on the valuation date

Based on the above information and the results of the technical expertise of the facility, the readiness coefficient and the necessary time and money spent on completion of construction are determined. In the evaluation of construction in progress, the principles, approaches and methods for assessing real estate are applied.

The cost approach is the most common in the assessment of construction in progress, because at the date of the assessment the facility is not in operation. It is necessary to determine the cost of reproduction at current prices for materials, parts, structures; construction and installation work on the facility.

The error in the calculation of replacement cost may decrease when applying the method of dividing an object into components. Then the replacement cost formula will take the form:

$$C = \sum_{j=1}^{n} V_j \cdot C_j \cdot K_{pj} \cdot K_{rj} \cdot K_{uj} \ , \tag{8.3}$$

where V_j is the unit of measurement of the j-th component of the building; C_j — unit cost of the j-th component, rub. ;

n is the number of building components provided by aggregated indicators of the base cost for the types of work;

K_{pj}, K_{rj}, K_{uj}, respectively, are the conversion factors for prices, the readiness of the j-th component of the building.

The total accumulated deterioration takes into account physical, functional and external deterioration and is determined by the formula:

$$D = 1 - (1 - D_{phys})(1 - D_f)(1 - D_{ext}), \tag{8.4}$$

where D_{phys}, D_f, D_{ext} — respectively, physical, functional and external deterioration.

As part of the income approach, the discounted cash flow method can be applied. The formula for the value of the object is:

$$C = \sum_{n=1}^{l} \frac{E_n}{(1 + r_f)^n} + M \cdot \frac{1}{(1 + r_{op})^{l+1}} - \sum_{t=1}^{m} \frac{S_t}{(1 + r_0)^t}, \tag{8.5}$$

where S_t is the future cost of completion of construction, taking into account the actual condition and the necessary changes to existing elements, taking into account functional and physical depreciation, rub.;

E_n — cash flow during the operation of the completed facility, rub.;

M — the cost of reversal from the sale of the object after completion of operation;

m — construction completion period, years; l is the forecast period of operation of the facility, years;

r_f, r_{op}, r_0 — discount rates, respectively, for periods of completion of construction, operation of the facility and post-forecast year.

Discount rates are calculated by the method of cumulative construction based on the risk-free rate, taking into account the risk of illiquidity of the object and the risk of unforeseen costs associated with its completion and further operation for its intended purpose.

8.4.1.4 Income approach to business valuation

The income approach to business valuation takes into account the impact on business value of such an important factor as profitability, which compensates for the shortcomings of the property approach. Since acquiring a business is an investment option, profitability is the main criterion for the investment attractiveness of an enterprise.

Evaluation theory offers a number of income approach methods, each of which has a rational scope. The excess income method allows you to take into account the value of the business reputation of the enterprise. The net profit capitalization method is used if the profitability is stable and stability is predicted. The method of discounted cash flow is used if the profitability of an enterprise is unstable and for the correct assessment, it is necessary to form a cash flow and justify the forecast horizon.

Business value (C) using the net profit capitalization method:

$$\mathrm{C} = \frac{P^p}{K}, \tag{8.6}$$

where P^p — annual pure profit (forecast);

K is the capitalization ratio at the valuation date.

Capitalization ratio is an indicator used to convert a company's income into its value. The capitalization ratio (K) can be calculated based on the discount rate:

$$K = (d - g) \tag{8.7}$$

where d is the discount rate calculated for the future income stream, predicted for an unlimited period of time, %;

g — constant annual growth rate of future capitalized income for an unlimited period of time, %.

The capitalization ratio can also be determined based on information about similar enterprises put up for sale.

The application of the discounted cash flow method with long-term forecasting is based on the formula:

$$C = \sum_{i=1}^{T} \frac{E_i^q}{(1+r)^{i-0.5}} + C_{od} \,, \tag{8.8}$$

where C is the value of the business;
r is the discount rate;
E_i^q — cash flow taking into account attracted external sources of financing;
T — forecast period (3–5 years);
C_{od} — residual present value of the enterprise.

The method of cumulative construction of the discount rate involves the summation of the risk-free investment rate and risk premiums. The most typical risk premiums in assessing the value of a business are:

- Risk premium on the financial structure of the business;
- Risk premium on business scale;
- Risk premium for product diversification;
- Risk premium for diversification of consumers.

The above list of risks can be expanded taking into account the specifics of the functioning of a particular enterprise, including country risk.

8.4.1.5 Comparative approach to business valuation

A common method of comparative approach is the method of industry multipliers, which reflect the ratio of the market price of the enterprise — an analogue and one of the key indicators of its activity. The most common multipliers are:

- Enterprise price / profit;
- Business price / cash flow;
- Enterprise price / revenue from the sale of products;
- Enterprise price / book value of the property of the enterprise;
- Business price / net assets.

The comparative approach is focused on the study of information about real transactions for the sale of construction enterprises, or their stock prices on the stock market. At the same time, enterprises sold on the market should be analogues in the following ways: industry similarity; the same scale of business, determined by the annual volume of construction and installation works; the same chronological age of the enterprise; the same phase of the life cycle.

In assessing construction organizations, it is important to take into account not only the profitability of the business, but also the property status of the business entity. The cost of the enterprise (C) should be determined by the formula:

$$C = P^{v} \cdot \bar{M}_p \cdot d_1 + K_p \cdot \bar{M}_{ra} \cdot d_2 \ , \tag{8.9}$$

where P_v — the actual gross profit of the enterprise from sales of construction products;

K_p — pure assets;

$\bar{M}_p$ — the average value of the multiplier "price / profit before taxes" for similar enterprises;

$\bar{M}_{ra}$- the average value of the multiplier "price / net assets" for similar enterprises; d_1, d_2 — weighting coefficients for summarizing the results of determining the value obtained, respectively, on the basis of the multipliers "price / profit before tax" and "price / net assets" ($d_1+d_2=1$) are established taking into account the priority of profitability or property condition.

If there is an active stock market for construction companies whose quotes indicate the market position of the enterprise, the following value formula (C) can be applied:

$$C = P^{p} k_{rp} \ , \tag{8.10}$$

where P_p — net profit of the enterprise in the analyzed period;

k_{rp} — the average coefficient of market attractiveness for enterprise taxes.

$$k_{RP} = \frac{C_{PAi}}{P_i^p}, \tag{8.11}$$

where C_{PAi} is the market value of the block of shares of the i-th enterprise;

P_i^p — *i*-th net profit enterprise counterpart.

The procedure for applying valuation techniques provides that, based on a synthesis of the results of various approaches, the final cost of the enterprise is determined. It is advisable to take into account the cost indicators obtained by various approaches, since each approach characterizes different aspects of the enterprise:

Cost measurement based on the cost approach characterizes the development of the property complex;

Measurement of value based on the income approach characterizes the growth of business profitability;

Cost measurement based on a comparative approach characterizes the investment attractiveness of the enterprise relative to competitors.

Summarizing the results of enterprise valuation:

$$C = C_1 d_1 + C_2 d_2 + C_3 d_3 \ , \tag{8.12}$$

where C_1, C_2, C_3 — the value of the business, calculated by the costly methods, income and comparative approaches, respectively; d_1, d_2, d_3 — weighting coefficients of costs, determined respectively using costly, profitable and comparative approaches.

The market value indicator is determined after the end of the reporting year and its dynamics (positive or negative) is a guideline for choosing a business strategy.

8.5 Rating Methods for Construction Organizations

8.5.1 Types of ratings and rating methods

Statistical and economic-mathematical methods that provide a comprehensive assessment of the economic activities of organizations and are most common in practice are as follows: the method of amounts, which involves summing up the growth rate of the main indicators used for a comprehensive assessment; a method for determining the growth of the total resource by 1% of the growth in sales of products; a method for determining the share of the effect of intensification on a 100% increment in production volumes; the method of the amount of relative savings in production and financial resources; rating methods.

Rating methods occupy a significant place in this list, as they provide an opportunity for inter-farm analysis, presenting the results in an accessible form for any user. The rating is considered as a complex quantitatively measurable characteristic of the company's competitive positions. It is based on a system of indicators, in a complex capable of characterizing the activities of an economic entity from the standpoint of specific users of information, which implies a certain differentiation of approaches, methods and indicators used for rating assessment.

The advantages of rating ratings can be fully realized if the following conditions are met:

- The rating system is based on a system of indicators that adequately reflects the qualitative and quantitative characteristics of the activities of a construction organization;
- The method of transforming individual ratings into a generalized rating score has been reasonably chosen;
- The basis of the assessment is quality information support.

Theoretically, there are two types of ratings: ordered and classification.

Ordered ratings mean ranking enterprises in ascending or descending order using one or more indicators. Heterogeneous indicators are reduced to a comparable form and are transformed into an integral indicator, according to which ranking is performed.

A classification (unordered) rating represents a participant's position on a particular rating scale. A scale with rating classes is developed in advance, and then the enterprise indicators are determined, the achieved level of which allows it to be attributed to a certain rating range. The ordering of objects within a specific range is not performed.

As the main approaches to rating assessment, accounting and expert approaches are used, each of which has a system of rating methods. The accounting approach is based on the use of available financial reporting data, which is processed by statistical methods, and the necessary relative values are determined that are used to build a comprehensive rating score. The expert approach is based on the study and synthesis of quantitative and qualitative information and expert assessments of various areas or subsystems of the enterprise. In a generalized form, the system of methods is given in table 8.3.

Table 8.3 The main methods of rating enterprises

Rating Type	Rating Approaches	
	Balance	Expert
Ordered	•The method of the "reference" enterprise •Evaluation Express Rating Method •Method of regression residues	•Method of advantages sum •Method of direct alternative ranking
Classification	•Cluster analysis (classification without training) •discriminant analysis (classification with training)	•Hierarchical classification procedures

The choice of rating method depends on the specific group of users of the information, and the purpose of the rating, in particular: rating for choosing a business strategy; rating for competitive selection of a contractor; rating score for forming rating lists. The purpose of the rating assessment predetermines the list of indicators used and the method of their transformation into the final rating.

The reference enterprise method establishes the degree of proximity of each object of the studied population to the reference enterprise, which will determine its rating position. Approaches to the formation of a reference enterprise can be different: standard values of rating-forming indicators, maximum values of indicators for the studied set of organizations.

The express rating method is mainly used to assess the financial condition by comparing actual indicators with their normative values. The rating number

(ρ_j) of the j-th organization is determined as follows:

$$\rho_j = \frac{1}{m}\sum_{i=1}^{n}\frac{a_i}{N_i}, \tag{8.13}$$

where N_i is the normative value of the i-th indicator (i = 1, 2, ..., m);
a_i is the actual value of the i-th rating-forming indicator.

The method of regression residuals is based on the construction of a multifactor model of the dependence of the results of the enterprise on several parameters that can affect the results. For each object of analysis, a model is built of the dependence of the results of activities on various factors:

$$R_j = f(x_{1j}, x_{2j}\ldots x_{nj}) + \mathit{Eff}\ , \tag{8.14}$$

where $x_{ij}...x_{nj}$ — factors affecting the results of the j-th enterprise; j is the number of the analyzed enterprise ($j = 1...m$);
R_j is an indicator characterizing the performance of the j-th enterprise;
Eff is the regression residue.

The regression residue *Eff* is determined as follows:

$$\mathit{Eff} = R_j - \bar{R}_j, \tag{8.15}$$

where $\bar{R}_j$ is the average result of enterprises in the study population.

If there are several characteristics that are significant for the analysis, both initial and generalizing, the classification problem can be solved *by the cluster analysis method,* which differs from other methods by the absence of training samples, i.e. a priori information on the distribution of the general population of objects — construction enterprises. Clusterization methods differ in their approaches to the concepts of “similarity” and “degree of similarity” of objects. In the analysis process, it is necessary to justify the number of groupings of objects. *The discriminant analysis* assumes that the training samples are known, classes are formed on their basis, and it is required to determine to which class the studied object belongs.

The advantage of expert evaluations in rating building is that they allow you to cover a more complete range of characteristics of a construction company, both quantitative and qualitative. The method of summing up the benefits consists in sequentially comparing pairs of alternatives and choosing one of them. Based on comparisons, a preference matrix is built:

$$A = \left\{a_{ij}^{k}\right\}, \tag{8.16}$$

where k is the expert number;

$a_{ij}^k$is the result of comparison by the kth expert of the i-th and j-th objects;

$a_{ij}^k = 1$ if object i *is* preferable to object j ;

$a_{ij}^k = 0.5$ if the objects are equivalent;

$a_{ij}^k = 0$ if object i_{is} less preferable than object j .

Based on the private matrices, the final one is built, the sum of the ranks is calculated, and the final ordering of the population occurs in descending order of the ranks.

The method of direct ranking of alternatives provides that each expert "k" conducts ranking of the population, the ranks of experts are compared and a matrix is built:

$$R = \{r_{ik}\}, \tag{8.17}$$

where r_{ik} is the rank of the i-th object in the k-th ordering.

The total rating is equal to the total amounts of all elements and the totality is ordered in descending order of the rating number.

The method of constructing a classification rating using hierarchical procedures is similar, in fact, to cluster analysis, but unlike cluster analysis, it does not use strict mathematical procedures to establish the similarities and differences of objects, but rely on expert judgments.

For various users of rating information, the significance of individual groups of indicators cannot be equally weighty and the assignment of weighting factors is possible.

8.5.2 Rating for positioning construction organizations contractor market

Registers of construction organizations with the basic parameters of their activities, their level of reliability, are necessary for establishing business contacts, making decisions on the provision of state support, inclusion in investment programs. This stimulates the development of construction organizations, and, therefore, contribute to increasing the competitiveness of the industry as a whole.

The rating system of construction organizations for the formation of rating lists should reflect the interests of potential users of information. The system should reflect indicators of the quality of construction, the condition of the material and technical base of contractors, financial condition, staffing, the progressiveness of the technologies used, resource conservation, reliability in fulfilling contractual obligations, and social and environmental responsibility of organizations. The market situation is changing; additional regulations are emerging, which determines the need to periodically review the rating system and the list of rating-forming indicators. Table 8.4 shows an approximate list of rating-forming indicators.

Table 8.4 Recommended indicators for determining the rating of a construction company

No.	Indicators	Number of points (max. Value)
1	*Quality of work*	20
1.1	Lack of customer complaints on commissioned construction sites	20
2	*Volume indicators of the organization*	10
2.1	The growth of construction and installation work performed over the past 3 years	4
2.2	Average labor productivity at facilities under construction	4
2.3	Growth in average workload at construction sites	2
3	Fulfillment of contractual obligations	20
3.1	Fulfillment of obligations on the timing of the commissioning of construction projects	15
3.2	The number of objects for which the estimated construction cost exceeded	5
4	Material and technical base of construction	18
4.1	The proportion of their own machines and mechanisms in their total cost	4
4.2	The degree of deterioration of construction machines and mechanisms	8
4.3	Availability of own repair base	6
5	HR potential	10
5.1	The proportion of the constant staff in their total number, ensuring the implementation of the volume of construction and installation works	2
5.2	Qualification of staff	2
5.3	Average salary of employees	2
5.4	Staff turnover	2
5.5	Equipping jobs with modern means of production	2
6	Financial condition	10
6.1	Net asset growth	2
6.2	Profitability of construction products	2
6.3	Stock price growth	2
6.4	Current ratio	2
6.5	Factor security own means	2
7	Organization competitiveness	2
7.1	The number of trades won in the last 3 years	2
8	Resource efficiency	10
8.1	Resource intensity of construction products	4
8.2	Number of innovations aimed at increasing energy efficiency in the operation of facilities	3
8.3	Number of innovations aimed at increasing energy efficiency in the construction of facilities	3
	TOTAL	100

The recommended scorecard is transformed into a score and then into a rating as follows.

1. Quality of work

1.1 The absence of customer complaints on the commissioned facilities

Base	Points
1. The presence of objects for which there are comments from customers (regardless of whether they are eliminated or not).	0
2. No comments	20

2. Volumetric indicators of the organization

2.1 Growth in construction and installation work performed over the past 3 years

Base	Points
1. The growth rate of the volume of work on average over 3 years amounted to more than 10%	4
2. The same is less than 10%	2

2.2 Average labor productivity at the facilities under construction

Base	Points
1. Labor productivity in the organization above the industry average	4
2. The same at the industry average	2
3. The same below the industry average	0

2.3 Growth in the average volume of work at construction sites

Base	Points
1. The growth of the average volume of work per building project	2
2. The decrease in the average volume of work per building project	0

3. Fulfillment of contractual obligations

3.1 Fulfillment of obligations on the timing of the commissioning of construction

Base	Points
1. All objects were delivered within the period stipulated by the contract	fifteen
2. Objects (regardless of their number and reasons) surrendered in violation of the terms	0

3.2 The number of objects for which the estimated cost of construction exceeded.

Base	Points
1. The excess of estimated cost averaged no more than 2%	5
2. The same no more than 5%	4
3. The same no more than 10%	3
4. The same is more than 10%	0

4. Material and technical base of the organization

4.1 the proportion of their own machines and mechanisms in their total cost

Base	Points
1. The proportion of their own machines and mechanisms is more than 40%	4
2. The proportion of their own machines and mechanisms is less than 40%	2

4.2 The degree of deterioration of the used construction machines and mechanisms

Base	Points
1. The park of construction vehicles and mechanisms has a 30% production year of no more than 3 years	8
2. The same no more than 5 years	4
3. The same for more than 5 years	0

4.3 Availability of own repair base

Base	Points
1. The organization has its own repair base	6
2. Does not have a repair base	0

5. Human resources

5.1 the proportion of the permanent composition of workers in their total number, ensuring the implementation of construction and installation works

Base	Points
1. Permanent staff of at least 80%	3
2. The same at least 70%	2
3. The same less than 70%	0

5.2 Qualification composition of linear management personnel

Base	Points
1. At least 70% of the staff has higher and secondary specialized education in the field of activity	2
2. At least 60% of the staff have higher and secondary specialized education in the field of activity	1

5.3 Average salary of employees

Base	Points
1. The average salary of employees is higher than the industry average	2
2. The same below the industry average	1

5.4 Staff turnover

Base	Points
1. The turnover rate of not more than 10%	3
2. The same no more than 15%	2
3. The same is more than 15%	0

6. Financial condition.

6.1 Growth in net assets over the past 3 years.

Base	Points
1. Net asset growth averaged over 10%	2
2. The same at least 10%	1

6.2 Profitability of construction products

Base	Points
1. Product profitability is above the industry average	2
2. The same at the industry average	1
3. The same below the industry average	0

6.3 Stock price appreciation

Base	Points
1. The stock price has grown over the past 3 years on average by more than 10%	2
2. The same no less than 10%	1

6.4 current ratio

Base	Points
1. Current ratio ≥ 2.0	2
2. The same less than 2	0

6.5 Equity ratio

Base	Points
1. Equity ratio ≥ 0.1	2
2. The same below 0.1	0

7. Competitiveness of the organization

7.1 Number of trades won in the last 3 years

Base	Points
1. The number of trades won (in% of the total number) for the last three years amounted to more than 20%	2
2. The same is less than 20%	1
3. No tenders won (regardless of the reason)	0

8. Resource Efficiency

8.1 Resource consumption of construction products

Base	Points
1. Below industry average	4
1. At the industry average	2
3. Above industry average	0

8.2 Number of innovations aimed at increasing energy efficiency in the field of operation of facilities introduced over the past 3 years

Base	Points
1. More than 2	3
1. Less than 2	2
3. Not implemented	0

8.3 Number of innovations aimed at increasing energy efficiency in the construction of facilities introduced over the past 3 years

Base	Points
1. More than 2	3
1. Less than 2	2
3. Not implemented	0

The rating of a construction company will be more objective if the rating model takes into account the priority of each group of indicators using the weighted values method.

Questions for self-control

1. What are the main goals and objectives of the operational planning of construction production?
2. Weekly daily schedules for construction and installation works and their material and technical support: composition, purpose.
3. What is scheduling and dispatch control in construction?
4. What is a long-term plan for economic and technical development?
5. The main elements and stages of developing a strategy and pricing policy of a construction organization (enterprise).
6. The content of the business plan of the construction organization.
7. What is the essence of the value concept of business management?
8. The main approaches to assessing the value of a business: content, specific features.

9. Asset valuation methods in determining the market value of an enterprise using a costly approach.
10. What is the specificity of the assessment of construction in progress?
11. List and describe the main methods of rating an enterprise.
12. What is included in the list of recommended indicators for determining the rating of a construction organization?

Questions for discussion

1. Describe the basic baseline data for the development of operational plans.
2. Describe the main elements and stages of developing a strategy and pricing policy.
3. What are the main sources of input data for the formation of a business plan? 4. The specifics of determining the value of a business using a costly approach.
4. The specifics of determining the value of a business using a comparative approach.
5. The specifics of determining the value of a business using the income approach.

Questions to solve the problem yourself

1. Consider the content and procedure for the development of operational plans on the example of specific construction organizations.
2. Analyze the features of business planning in the construction of facilities for various purposes.
3. Conduct a comparative analysis of project management schemes in construction.
4. Give examples of informative content of operational technical meetings in construction.
5. What are the advantages of the value concept of business management? What are the specifics of the implementation of this concept in construction?
6. Conduct a comparative analysis of rating methods

Chapter 9

INFORMATION TECHNOLOGIES IN CONSTRUCTION

9.1 The main prerequisites for the implementation of information modeling technologies in construction

Investment and construction activities can be considered as a set of targeted measures, in one way or another, related to the creation and processing of information relating to various aspects of the existence of a building project at all stages of its life cycle — from a feasibility study of the need for its construction to demolition and waste disposal. This is not only a formalized design and estimate documentation related to a building or structure, but also a significant amount of data related to participants in investment and construction activities and their interaction with each other, management decisions at various stages of planning, organization and control of design, construction and operation object.

Effective work with significant amounts of information is possible only in an automated mode. That is why a significant breakthrough to the introduction of information technology in the practice of ICP implementation has given the development of computer technology, the emergence of appropriate computing power and data warehouses.

However, technical capabilities alone are not enough. Prerequisites are also needed related to the social, sectoral need for the development of one direction or another. In the construction industry, a significant demand for intensive work with extensive data sets characterizing ICP as a whole, for the use of information modeling technologies has arisen relatively recently. First of all, this is due to the sharp complication of ongoing projects, and as a result, to an increase in the number of participants in the process, an increase in the criteria for assessing success and quality of implementation, a significant increase in the number of risks and uncertainties at all stages of the life cycle.

In practice, a significant complication of construction turned out to be due to a significant increase in the number of accidents at large-scale construction and real estate objects, regular failures in the process of erecting such objects, serious deviations of the actual cost characteristics from the planned ones, etc.

The organizational structure of ISP is such that the general project management methodology can very organically be tied to the needs of the construction industry, taking into account the existing features in the design, construction of real estate construction and operation facilities. In practice, for example, mechanical engineering, proven techniques and methods of project management are much more difficult to implement. Unfortunately, the situation is the opposite with information modeling. Existing approaches are much more focused on the specifics of non-construction sectors. That is why the information modeling technologies in construction are still used separately, the established methodology and even the terminology as a whole have not yet been formed.

In the 1980s, the American Boeing Corporation proposed organizing automated data accounting for all components and parts of aircraft assembled at the corporation's factories. The attractiveness of this idea was based on the fact that any Boeing aircraft is constantly monitored by corporation specialists throughout its life. It is they who carry out not only the design and assembly of the aircraft, but also provide all routine and repair work throughout the flight history of the aircraft. The creation of an information base made it possible in a matter of seconds to get an answer to any questions related to the date and composition of all completed production manipulations (including information on responsible persons). It became possible to quickly plan all routine maintenance operations on the aircraft, replacing used components, parts, and so on.

In 1985, the US Department of Defense organized the introduction of an automated electronic description system for all stages of the design, manufacture and operation of military products. During this period, the so-called **CALS-technologies** (Continuous *Acquisitionand Lifecycle Support)* were developed — continuous information support of deliveries and product life cycle. In fact, a certain approach to the design and production of high-tech and high-tech products was formed, consisting in the use of computer equipment and information technology at all stages of the product's life cycle.

An important characteristic of the developed technologies was that the information model of the object in question was created and developed throughout the entire life cycle by the forces of one "owner" of information interested in using the accumulated data. As an interested party, the holder of the information model was ready to incur certain costs associated with the collection, storage and processing of the information collected. The resulting benefits from the use of information technology fully recouped the necessary costs in the early stages of the life cycle, when the information model is just being formed, when in fact you have to do the "extra" work of entering data that may be needed "not for me and not now", i.e. future generation.

Unfortunately, in the construction industry, the presence of a single owner of an object at all stages of the life cycle from a feasibility study on the need for construction to demolition and waste disposal is a rarity. The stages of the life cycle of a construction project are very fragmented both from the point of view of the main participants and from the point of view of their interests. In addition, the life cycle of the construction object is such that during the work with the information model generations of information owners can change, computer technologies, principles of information storage and transmission, data cxchange formats, etc. can change.

Unlike other industries, it often turns out that the costs of creating an information model, collecting and storing data are one, and the benefits should be given to completely different people who have nothing to do with the first legal or economic relationship. Accordingly, the former do not have not only economic interest, but also a legal basis for economic interest to appear (in fact, there is no understanding of who and under what conditions it is possible to sell the right to own this or that information on a construction project).

In practice, investor interests have a significant impact on how information technologies are introduced. If an object is being prepared for sale, then there is usually no interest in investing in further efficient operation. This applies equally to the costs of energy efficiency, resource conservation, environmental friendliness, etc. Even if an investor appears willing to finance the creation and use of an information model, which will certainly pay off during operation, and even during demolition and disposal, there are still problems associated with the specialists' unwillingness to provide a complete description of the composition of such a model. To date, there is no unambiguous understanding of which data may be needed after several decades, and which, on the contrary, will turn out to be superfluous. In addition, there is no complete spectrum of mathematical and physical models that allow accurate interpretation of the collected data characterizing the object, i.e. make an unambiguous conclusion about the need for certain operations to maintain the life cycle.

Nevertheless, the direction of information modeling in construction is developing very intensively, various software and hardware are being developed, new approaches to integrated information modeling of investment and construction processes are being proposed.

9.2 The evolution of the use of information technology modeling in construction

Historically, automation in construction began to the greatest extent from the design stage. It was the project activity that turned out to be the most formalized and algorithmic, which allowed the active use of computers in the development of design estimates. However, to a greater extent, automation touched on routine drawing procedures. You can trace the evolution of information processes in building design — Fig. 9.1.

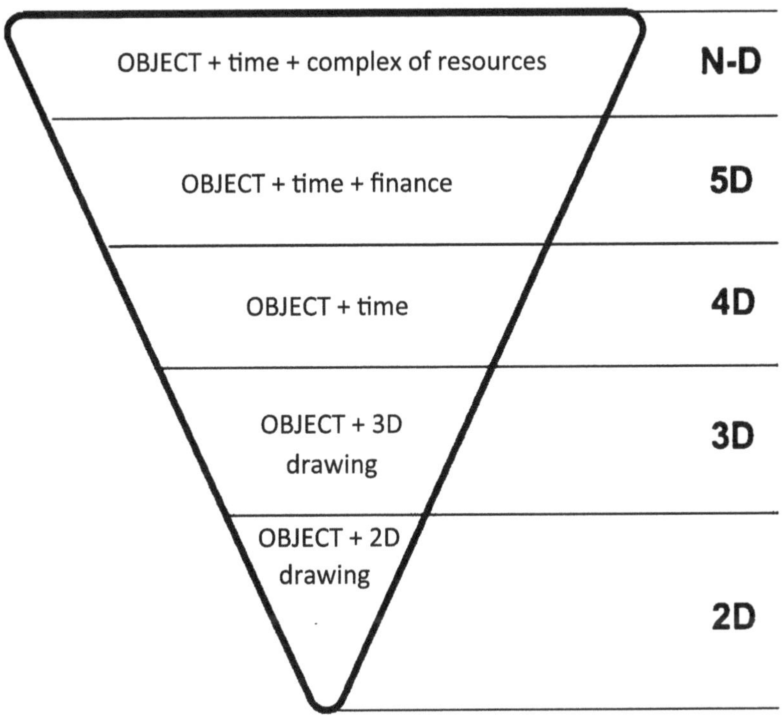

Figure 9.1: Levels of information models in building design.

The first **Design Automation Systems** (CAD) worked as an electronic shuttle, allowing you to reproduce the work of creating a classic flat two-dimensional (2D) drawing.

The rapid development of the ability of computers to display high-quality graphics allowed developers of software for building CAD systems to take the next step — to automate the formation of a three-dimensional model of an object (3D). This stage clearly reflects the complex interaction of programmers and users (in this case, designers). Often, not users set the prospects for the development of their own industry, but programmers actively dictate the implementation of those technologies that are determined by the capabilities of equipment and software. In fact, a qualified civil engineer must be able to read a flat drawing and no additional information is required to understand the structural characteristics of the object.

Of course, the volumetric model is more visual than the classic drawing. It can be effectively used to present the object to investors, customers, potential consumers of construction products. The ability to use color in the drawing in particularly difficult cases allows us to detect various conflicts at the design stage, which are associated with errors in the coordination of various, primarily, engineering systems of the building. Nevertheless, the active use of 3D-models is determined, first of all, not by serious engineering needs, not by the ability to solve new classes of problems, but by the ability of modern software without significant additional computing power and time consumption to depict the corresponding figure.

Any drawing in itself carries a significant amount of information about the object. A drawing made on a computer can be easily transferred, copied, corrected. In fact, it is an information model of a building (structure) or, what is commonly called **BIM** (from the English *Building Information Model*). However, is such an information model comprehensive? — Of course not. It is clear that the design documentation is not limited solely to the description of the geometric shapes and dimensions of the building or structure. Unlike the first years of the introduction of BIM-technologies, now no one identifies the BIM-model with the usual 3D-drawing.

A fairly natural development of modeling of a building object is an attempt to describe the process of its construction. One of the most important sections of organizational and technological design is scheduling. That is why the next indicator taken into account in the information model was time. By analogy with multidimensional models in classical physics, they began to call them four-dimensional or 4D-projects.

In modern conditions, construction, like other industries, cannot be considered in isolation from the comprehensive consideration of economic factors. Accordingly, projects appeared that considered not only the duration of the work, but also the corresponding cash flows, which allowed us to talk about 5D design (3D + time + finance).

Modern software products focused on architectural design allow you to work not at the level of graphic primitives, but at the level of building products, structures, modules. The object is formed not from ordinary lines, but from images that already contain information about the type of object being built, the necessary resources (materials, machines, mechanisms, work frames, equipment used), etc. In fact, many (N) indicators are included in the object's information model, characterizing both the object itself and, to a certain extent, the processes occurring at the construction site and outside it. In general, we can talk about N-dimensional or ND design.

At the same time, an unambiguous, universally recognized understanding of what exactly a full-fledged BIM model should include has not yet been formed. This is determined by many problems associated with the practical implementation of BIM-technologies. Many of these problems are not technological, but organizational and ideological.

9.3 Basic concepts and terminology of information modeling in construction

Since in the Russian Federation there is currently no comprehensive legislatively approved regulatory framework for information modeling in construction, there is no uniform universally recognized terminology in this area. Nevertheless, social consensus is gradually being formed on the basic, most frequently used concepts. In some cases, several definitions are used that characterize a particular phenomenon from several different sides that complement each other.

In addition to the already mentioned term **BIM** (*Building Information Model),* disclosed as an information model of a building (structure), they talk about **BIM**

(Building *Information Modeling),* referring to the modeling of all information about the object — not only geometric shapes, but also data on the processes associated with the functioning of the building object at all stages of the life cycle. Under **information modeling** in this case refers to:

- The creation and use of building information models (facilities);
- Digital representation of the physical and functional characteristics of the building (structure).

In some cases, they also talk about **BIM** (*Building Information Management*) as about managing information about a building object.

The following definition seems most complete: **Information modeling of a construction object** is a process of collective creation and use of information about a building, construction, forming a reliable basis for decision making throughout the entire life cycle of the object.

The most important thing that involves work in the format of information technology is the interaction between participants in an investment construction project in digital format in a common data environment **CDE** - *Common Data Environment.*

Actually, the creation of a unified information environment in which the construction object exists throughout its life, and makes it possible to significantly change the technology of managing the object and the technology of organizing joint work of many people, ensuring the creation and operation of the building (structure).

An information model is a collection of electronically presented documents, graphic and textual data on a construction project, placed in the **CDE** and representing a single reliable source of information on the construction at all or individual stages of its life cycle.

The content of the information model (the composition of the BIM-model) is determined by those tasks that are planned to be solved during the life cycle of the object. To date, there is no formalized, agreed upon list of all such tasks. Accordingly, there is no common understanding of what data needs to be collected, stored and processed in order to successfully achieve its goals. Nevertheless, already at this stage in the development of information technology, it is clear that information modeling opens up the possibility of achieving a fundamentally new level of posing and solving a wide range of issues relating to the entire human environment, in which a building object acts only as a separate element of a higher level system.

Consolidated Model (*Federated Model)* — a set of BIM-models, consisting of interconnected separate models for various disciplines or parts of the construction site, so that making changes to one of the models does not lead to changes in others.

In turn, each BIM model is a collection of elements.

A model element is a part of a BIM model that represents a component, system, or assembly within a construction site or construction site.

Component — a digital representation of the physical and functional characteristics of an individual element of a construction object, intended for repeated use. The component applied in the model becomes an element of the model.

The formalized presentation of the construction object in digital format is the most important step towards the transition from today's (practically artisanal, practically unchanged for centuries) construction technologies to the technologies of modern high-tech production.

When preparing an article in a text editor on a computer, the author does not need to look for any differences between the text he typed on the screen and the text printed on the printer. In the manufacture of a machine-building part on a machine with numerical control, discrepancies between the drawing (digital model) of the part and what is left under the computer-controlled cutter cannot occur. Today's construction site, built virtually "manually", according to paper drawings, has not single, but massive deviations from the approved project. Moreover, the more complex the object, the more significant the deviations can be, the more dangerous the consequences can be. This leads not only to problems directly at the construction site, but also to a decrease in the reliability of buildings and structures during their operation. The low quality of existing technologies for the construction of the facility leads to the need for designing to lay additional tolerances for the allocation of office spaces. According to a number of estimates, with accurate installation of the facility, it is possible to additionally free up more than 10% of the area of buildings currently occupied by utilities, i.e. in fact, increase the commissioning of construction capacities by 10% only due to the high-quality, formalized precise installation of structures and equipment.

Fundamentally, new opportunities open up at the stage of operation of the facility. This is not only environmental management technology (Smart Home technology), but also new approaches to solving engineering problems (including optimization) of real estate management.

9.4 Information interaction of participants in the life cycle of a construction project

Work in a shared data environment (CDE) significantly changes the order of interaction of the participants in the investment and construction project. In fig. 9.2 clearly shows what exactly the changes are. It is fundamentally important that there is a rejection of private exchanges of information, where when communicating "each with each other" significant distortions and loss of necessary data are possible.

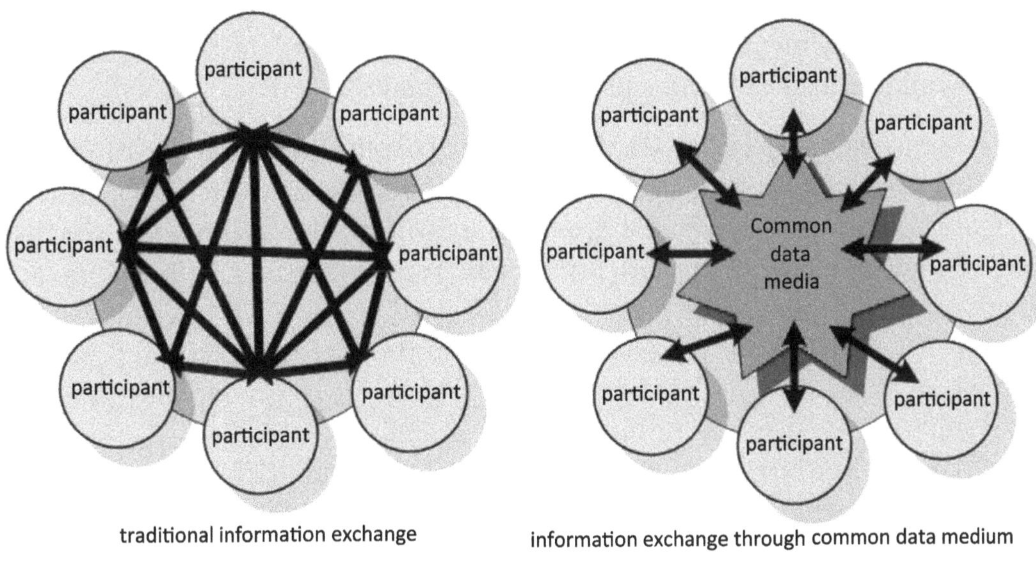

Figure 9.2: Organization of information exchange between the participants of the investment construction project.

Significant differences in the versions of the information circulating between the participants are also possible. In CDE, all participants' access the same data stored in a publicly accessible information space. Substantial divergence of materials in different parts of the project is simply impossible.

However, all the benefits have to "pay". In this case, it is necessary to provide a solution to a number of problems associated with the organization of effective, reliable and safe information interaction. In the general case, the problems are both technical and organizational in nature.

To solve organizational problems, as a rule, it is necessary to introduce new participants (BIM-managers, BIM-coordinators) or significantly change, supplement the competencies of traditional participants of the investment construction project. Organizations operating in the information environment adopt the so-called BIM standards of the organization that regulate a wide range of issues related to process management within the framework of information modeling technologies. Typically described:

- Requirements management (information requirements, requirements for processes, standards and project results);
- Planning management (implementation plan for a BIM project);
- Resource management (roles and functions of participants, BIM tools, component libraries, templates, hardware and network resources, etc.);
- Management of work processes (agreed standards, regulations, procedures);
- Quality management (model validation);
- change management (tracking and making changes, comparing models, 3D-communication between project participants).

For a specific project, **a BIM Project Implementation Plan** (*BEP-BIM Execution Plan)* is formed, reflecting the customer's requirements for information models, the tasks of applying information modeling, the required levels of development, roles and functional responsibilities of participants in the information modeling process.

Table 9.1 presents an approximate distribution of the roles and responsibilities of specialists in BIM-modeling, taking into account the functions implemented in the process of information modeling.

As part of the strategic function assigned to the BIM manager, it is provided:

- development of an organization strategy in the field of BIM;
- research and analysis of best practices;
- development of working BIM processes;

Table 9.1 Roles and responsibilities of specialists in the process of information modeling

Role	Strategic function						Managerial function				Production function	
	corporate goals	analytics	BIM – processes	Standards	introduction	training	*BIM Execution Plan*	model audit	model co-ordination	Content creation	modelling	documentation production
BIM Manager	Yes	Yes	Yes	Yes	Yes	Yes	Yes	Not	Not	Not	Not	Not
BIM coordinator	Not	Not	Not	Not	Not	Yes	Yes	Yes	Yes	Yes	Yes	Not
Model Developer / BIM Author	Not	Not	Not	Not	Not	Not	Not	Not	Not	Yes	Yes	Yes

- development and support of BIM standards and regulations; implementation of the process of information modeling;
- development of a staff training strategy.

As part of the management function assigned to the BIM manager and / or BIM coordinator, it is provided:

- development of a BIM project implementation plan;
- regular audit of project information and principles of model development used in the project;
- participation in interdisciplinary coordination meetings;
- management of the process of creating and distributing content and quality control.

Actually, the production function associated with the creation of information is assigned to the developer of the model (BIM-author). It should be borne in mind that in the production of the model, the main criterion is not experience with BIM, but professional experience in the construction industry. It is professional experience that determines the quality of the resulting model, and the quality of the final product.

In practice, for effective work it is necessary to ensure the coordination of a wide range of issues, such as:

- stages of work and control points for the issuance of information;
- requirements for the composition of information models and modeling volumes;
- requirements for levels of elaboration of model elements;
- requirements for the composition and formats for the issuance of project results.

- requirements for the quality of models;
- requirements for approval procedures, methods and formats of data exchange, shared network resources;
- requirements for file names, etc.

Each data exchange participant may have different views on these issues. Moreover, a number of differences can be quite objective. First of all, it is connected with various goals, interests and various tasks that the interacting parties face.

One of the most significant aspects for an agreement is the determination of the **Level of development of model elements — LOD** (Level *of Development).* LOD is a set of requirements that determines the completeness of the development of an element of the BIM model. The level of elaboration sets the minimum volume of geometric, spatial, quantitative, as well as any attributive information necessary for solving modeling problems at a particular stage in the life cycle of a construction object. Thus, LOD consists of two components: geometric — LOD (G) and attribute — LOD (I).

The practical basic LOD levels are presented in table 9.2.

Table 9.2 Basic LOD Levels

LOD Level	**Description**
LOD 100	A model element can be represented as volumetric forming elements with approximate dimensions, shape, spatial position and orientation, or as a 2D symbol
LOD 200	The model element is presented in the form of an object or assembly as a characteristic representative of the building system with preliminary dimensions, shape and spatial position, orientation and necessary attribute information
LOD 300	The model element is presented in the form of an object or assembly belonging to a specific building system, with exact dimensions, shape and spatial position, orientation, relationships and necessary attributive information
LOD 400	The model element is presented in the form of a specific assembly and with detailed dimensions, shape, spatial position, orientation, clear relationships, manufacturing and installation data, as well as other necessary attribute information
LOD 500	The model element is presented in the form of a specific assembly and with actual dimensions, shape, spatial position, orientation and attributive information sufficient to transfer the model into operation

The detailed elaboration of the model grows from level to level and increases with the transition from one stage of the life cycle of a construction object to another. However, in some cases, the division into LOD levels is conditional.

For example, when at the same stage elements of different levels are used for different parts of the model. In some cases, it is possible to decrease the level of LOD during the transition to the next stage of the life cycle. For example, if during the operation of this or that equipment whole blocks (modules) are serviced, the level of detail of the data on this equipment is required lower than during the initial assembly and installation.

A very important part of working in the information environment is validation. **Validation** is the process of checking the simulation results for compliance with the established requirements, which should be recorded in the Implementation Plan of the BIM project. The validation process determines whether the model meets the customer's information requirements, the requirements of the organization's standard, how accurately, optimally and fully it is developed, whether it is possible to identify and extract information from the elements of the BIM model without any conflicts, etc.

At different stages of working with the information model, different technical (hardware) and software can be used. In general, various developers can create the software and, accordingly, the presentation of data within each software package is carried out in different formats.

Interoperability — the ability to interact software applications, their interoperability is the key to the successful application of BIM technology. File protocols (data exchange rules) provide this compatibility. File protocols must be agreed upon by all participants in the BIM project and recorded in the Implementation Plan of the BIM project.

The most important aspect of information compatibility is the use of common data presentation formats. Currently, **the IFC** (*Industry Foundation Classes*) **format is** widely used as an international standard for exchanging information in the BIM environment. *Industry-* specific base classes are an open specification data format. The International Alliance originally developed the IFC format *for Interoperability,* created in 1995 by American and European architectural, engineering and design firms, together with manufacturers of building programs to implement better interaction between the various software in the industry. Since 2005, the IFC format specification has been developed and maintained by building SMART International. Currently, the Russian division of the company has been created.

The unification of data formats is not the only problem that needs to be addressed not at the level of a separate BIM project, but at the national level.

A prerequisite for the implementation of information modeling technologies in construction nationwide is the standardization of this area. So, in the UK, which already uses BIM, in preparation for the transfer of state orders in the construction industry to the mandatory use of information modeling technologies, a set of standards was developed that regulates the work of the customer and the executors, primarily for information management, introducing new roles and functions. The main UK standards in this area are currently being processed into international ISO standards.

The formation of the Russian system of regulatory technical documents that ensure the implementation of information modeling technologies in construction began in 2015. The development of sets of rules and standards continues and now within the framework of the roadmap developed by the Ministry of Construction of Russia for the implementation of BIM, which is officially called the "Plan of measures for the implementation of an assessment of the economic efficiency of investment justification and information modeling technology at all stages of the life cycle of a capital construction project. The Russian approach is based on the analysis of international experience: the standards of the international organization ISO, the European standardization body CEN and national standards of countries where there are positive results from the application of BIM technologies, as well as the practice of implementing these technologies by individual organizations in the Russian Federation.

The first national standards developed based on ISO standards are designed to provide digital interaction and data exchange based on open specifications. GOST R "Information modeling in construction. Industry Base Classes (IFC) for exchanging information at all stages of the life cycle. The main provisions" is intended to guarantee the full interaction of a wide range of domestic and foreign software products.

To date, a number of standards and sets of rules have been developed that define the conceptual framework and methodology for introducing information modeling into practice at certain stages of the life cycle — from the rationale for investments to the disposal and demolition of buildings and structures. Direct participants in the construction process can use these documents. In total, more than 50% of the standards and codes of rules of the national system of regulatory technical documents have been developed to ensure the implementation of information modeling technologies in construction.

All this work is in line with international developments and is largely based on international approaches. National documents account for more than 90% of current ISO standards. In the process of development, a number of ISO standards, which will be taken into account in national documents planned for development in 2019-2020, will form the basis of GOST R "Information modeling in construction. Key Points, Terms and Definitions."

As advanced foreign standards appear, as well as the results of approbation of domestic developments, the updating of domestic documents will be carried out.

The Russian Ministry of Construction believes that information modeling in construction, which means the industry's transition to digital processes, in addition to reducing labor costs, time and reducing the cost of project implementation, will increase the reliability of the assessment of construction processes. As a result, the state will receive an effective tool for managing public investment, planning and controlling the spending of budget funds.

9.5 Tasks solved with the help of information modeling at different stages of the life cycle of an investment construction project

As already noted, the composition of the information model is directly related to those tasks that are being solved, or will be solved at different stages of the life cycle of the investment construction project. It is very important in the early stages of the formation of the model to provide for the input of all the necessary information, including that which will be needed not now, but only in the future. Thus, the volume of the information model increases with the development of the project. Each participant supplements it with "their" data. Unfortunately, it is not always known exactly what will be required through the years of the object's existence.

At the same time, there is a danger of overloading ("weighting") the model by entering unnecessary information. For example, a number of developers of building products and equipment offer consumers already-formed data sets in the form of a ready-made element for use in the BIM model. The problem is that the LOD level of such an element is as high as possible, which often makes it inconvenient to use in the early stages of model formation, when almost all other elements are detailed no higher than LOD 200.

At the very beginning of the life cycle, **at the stage of deciding on the location of an object, justification of investments,** the following tasks are solved:

- project evaluation taking into account the financial, economic, social aspects of implementation;
- analysis of location, geotechnical, environmental situation;
- analysis of transport and pedestrian accessibility;
- analysis of the main human flows;
- analysis of air flows taking into account existing buildings;
- determination of technical and economic indicators for various space-planning decisions;
- development and comparison of options for concepts;

- analysis of the cost of the project by analogues and aggregated indicators and its
- optimization;
- preliminary calculation of operating costs and cost of ownership, etc.

The presence of a digital data model characterizing a construction object allows us to provide a variability analysis of all these indicators. The answer to the question: "What will happen if ..." Can be obtained in minutes. It is also important at an early stage in the life cycle to be able to visually present the appearance of the project to all interested parties.

A. At **the design stage, the** use of common libraries of typical units and structures significantly increases the variety of design solutions, their variability. At the same time, a high degree of automation of the development of individual parts of the project ensures high speed and accuracy of solving many optimization problems (determining the volume of work, the formation of sheets of the need for materials, labor, machines and mechanisms, calculation of estimates, etc.). Improving the accuracy of engineering calculations, the choice of rational solutions for energy and heat efficiency lay the foundation for reducing the cost of further ownership of the object. Model validation provides spatial coordination of engineering and other building subsystems and checks for possible conflicts, which allows you to shift the error correction process from the construction stage to the design stage. Ultimately, this provides an increase in the quality of project documentation, an increase in the accuracy of engineering and cost estimates, and a reduction in the duration of construction of facilities.

The implementation of information modeling at **the construction stage** is currently the most difficult. This is because the actual process of building an object, the process of construction and installation work is currently the least formalized and automated. Accordingly, the willingness to work in the information environment at the construction stage is the smallest. However, it is at this stage of the life cycle that very serious opportunities open up for achieving breakthrough solutions and reaching a qualitatively new level of tasks to be solved precisely within the framework of information technologies. Virtual and augmented reality systems that recreate an object that has not yet been erected based on an information model will allow, for example: an installer (and later a robot machine) to carry out construction and installation works with maximum accuracy. The use of modern monitoring systems (laser scanning, webcams, drones, etc.) allows us to ensure the absence of any deviations from the design documentation. The information model makes it possible to optimize the use of the actual construction site, improve logistics schemes, and provide effective spatial and temporal coordination of all work performed. Automation of planning, management and control of construction processes ensures their optimization and, as a result, improving the reliability and quality of the facility being built, reducing waste, reducing the cost of work, reducing the duration of construction. An important factor is the reduction of injuries, ensuring labor protection, safe working conditions at the construction site.

B. The stage of operation and management of the construction site is the stage at which the benefits of working with a single information model are revealed to the greatest extent. Augmented reality systems based on a digital model of the object allow you to control the location of hidden communications, nodes, equipment, which greatly facilitates their maintenance. The availability of comprehensive information about all the elements of the operating facility makes it possible to switch from the existing repair system "upon the accident" to the system of scheduled preventive maintenance of buildings and structures. Automated analysis of data on the service life of engineering and other systems of the facility, data on the dates of previously carried out routine and other works, allows, without waiting for accidents and malfunctions in the operation of serviced equipment, to carry out the necessary actions for its repair and replacement. In the future, it is possible to switch to servicing facilities based on operational monitoring of the objective parameters of all building systems. A set of sensors installed on communications, in critical nodes, structures, directly in the premises of the object, allows you to form and analyze an information picture of its current state. To date, there is no exhaustive list of models that allow not only effectively changing, but also sometimes even fully interpreting the generated informational "picture" of what is happening. Active research is being carried out in this direction; interesting practical developments are being implemented. Within the framework of the ideology of "Smart Home", efficient algorithms for controlling the parameters of the indoor microclimate and algorithms for economical resource consumption are proposed. Artificial intelligence systems allow you to adapt the object control algorithms to the individual requirements of its owner, to various conditions and situations, including emergency ones. The creation of the so-called cyber physical systems makes it possible to adapt to rapidly changing conditions not only the parameters of the internal environment of the object, but even its structural elements (the load, voltage, heat-conducting and heat-insulating characteristics, etc. can automatically vary).

Ultimately, information technology reduces operating costs, optimizes the use of space and other resources, reduces risks and improves the safety of the facility.

C. At the final stage of demolition and disposal of the facility, the availability of complete information about the real state of the facility, about the complex of structures, materials and products in its composition allows for the efficient dismantling and organization of reuse and recycling of waste.

Operational calculation of the volume and cost of work allows you to optimize the adoption of organizational decisions and, as a result, reduce the cost and duration of dismantling. Effective organization of work provides a high level of labor protection and safety at the construction site.

Summary: Speaking about BIM-technologies as a toolkit for creating an information model of the life cycle of an investment-building project, it is necessary to bear in mind that complex models are open information systems that can integrate data of different levels, i.e. data not directly related to the object, but directly affecting it.

Currently, widespread geographic information systems (GIS), used to process spatial-temporal data based on cartographic information. GIS are designed to provide decision-making on the effective management of land and resources, urban management, transport, etc. A wide range of graphical characterizes GIS and digital data collected using various methods and technologies processed by both analytical and expert methods. The information models of individual objects, of course, should be elements of a higher-level information system designed to integrate indicators characterizing complexes of objects, individual territories, regions, and regions as a whole.

In the general case, we can talk about a complex generalized information model of the living environment. This model is designed to solve the problems of urban planning and zoning, to be the basis for creating regional and sectoral development schemes up to the formation of regional and federal targeted programs for various purposes. The creation of a unified information model that comprehensively characterizes the human environment is an important step towards effective management of this environment, a serious basis and a tool for making informed, informed decisions based on a systematic analysis of a wide range of interrelated factors.

On the way to creating models of the living environment, it is necessary to solve a number of problems in creating models of a lower level. First of all, it is necessary to make adjustments at the level of the building complex. From the point of view of systems theory, a system that combines subsystems with conflicting interests simply cannot function efficiently. Thus, it is necessary to restructure the goals facing the system as a whole and the subsystems involved at different stages of the life cycle of the object in order to orient everyone towards effective achievement of the final result (formation of a comfortable living environment), and not at solving local multidirectional problems of numerous participants in the process.

By order of the Government of the Russian Federation of July 28, 2017 No. 1632-r, the program "Digital Economy of the Russian Federation" was approved, which implements the "Strategy for the Development of the Information Society in the Russian Federation for 2017-2030" (approved by Decree of the President of the Russian Federation of May 9, 2017 No. 203). Accordingly, in construction, approaches to solving the tasks are formulated. The strategy "Digital modernization of the industry will improve the quality of design, construction and operation of facilities, reduce the cost of construction and increase labor productivity, as well as ensure effective management at all stages of the life cycle of the facility."

Active implementation of information technologies in construction is an important step on the path of innovative development of the industry, a prerequisite for the transition to excellent technologies, the only opportunity for the effective formation of a comfortable and safe environment for human life.

9.6 Analysis of practical aspects of applying BIM technology (using Autodesk as an example)

The modern implementation of BIM-technologies is carried out in various computer programs, of which one can distinguish the most famous ones such as Autodesk Revit, ArchiCAD, Bentley, as well as the first Russian software system Renga Architecture, focused on architectural and construction design. Previously, in section 9.4, it was noted that the validation of information models is a very important part of working in an information environment that implements BIM technology. Recall that this term refers to the process of checking the simulation results for compliance with the established requirements, which should be recorded in the Implementation Plan of the BIM project. In other words, we can say that the validation process allows us to draw a conclusion regarding the adequacy of the model used in a specific BIM technology, with regard to those regulatory requirements that are imposed during design, in particular, in the Russian Federation.

Let us show the practical significance of the validation requirement by examples related to the line of software products, collectively called Autodesk Nevisworks, and the new version of Autodesk Revit-2018. Both of these products are the most universal in terms of the breadth of practical use, with the first product intended for the planning, control and management of construction, and the second for the field of building design. The Autodesk Revit-2018 program universally combines sections of architectural design, the design of internal engineering systems and building structures, as well as energy consumption calculations.

A distinctive feature of the Autodesk Nevisworks software complex is that it is implemented in the form of four functionally related programs, and each subsequent program "knows" everything that the "previous one" can and, in addition, implements additional functions that are presented in order of increasing functionality below.

The Autodesk Navisworks Freedom program is mainly focused on viewing three-dimensional models, and can directly work in a building site using wireless Internet (3G, SkyLink, WiFi, WiMAX). From the point of view of practical application, this program can be useful for the future owner of an immovable object, since it is at the design stage that it is important for him how the projected object will look in the future.

For the next three programs, it is possible to directly read the most popular file formats, which is achieved by creating a cache in the *.NWC format. This allows you to make changes to the build model, even if the source files have changed. You can make files in input formats (*.NWF), in which there will only be links to the source files. As a result, it becomes possible to create a "metafile" in which all the constituent files will be concatenated into a single whole (*.NWD format file).

The main task facing each chief engineer or architect of the project is to ensure the quality and consistency of the designed facility. Therefore, a program such as Autodesk Navisworks Review is precisely focused on the use of designers and representatives of architectural and technical supervision. Moreover, each individual specialist has his own individual file with a three-dimensional model of his section, made in any computer-aided design system that is compatible with the IFC standard, which was presented earlier in section 9.4. Thus, in the Autodesk Navisworks Review program, the chief engineer (architect) of the project can combine all the files created in different programs and see design errors when reading drawings. Along with this, to perform the functions of designer supervision and technical supervision of the customer, the program is equipped with a ruler for measuring dimensions and angles, areas of premises, and the program presents the opportunity to write your comments and suggestions anywhere in the project documentation.

Autodesk Navisworks Simulate is directly designed to accompany the construction phase and it is precisely in it that the 4th and 5th coordinates of BIM technology appear — time and finances, as was previously presented in the diagram shown in section 9.2. You can dock with project management programs such as Microsoft Project and Primavera, that is, set the correspondence between the dates of the planned work in the scheduling system and the three-dimensional model. Then on the computer screen in video mode, the building process can be visualized, from the beginning of the creation of the construction site and further along the technological chain of construction production until the end of construction. In this case, you can specify any date and see how the object under construction should look like at that moment. It is possible to make not only the planned dates of the work, but also the actual dates, as the construction progresses, revealing deviations of the fact from the plan, and while showing the customer who is to blame for the failure to meet the construction deadlines and cost overruns of the project. The program is equipped with a quality control tool, which makes it possible to measure and identify deviations of the real object from its design model.

From the point of view of critical analysis, it should be noted here that the validation of this program must necessarily be the object of research on the adequacy of the models used inside it. Therefore, it is necessary to establish those principles and algorithms of the considered program, which are incorporated in the calculations related, in particular, to the scheduling of the construction of the designed facility. This circumstance is especially significant in the case of the design and construction of unique facilities.

Autodesk Navisworks Manage integrates all previous information capabilities and adds new functionality to them. Obviously, after the immovable object was built, various imperfections and shortcomings or, in other words, collisions that determine deviations from design decisions are revealed. For example, in the program, you can simultaneously select elements of the ventilation system and supporting metal structures, indicate design tolerances for them and, based on an analysis of the identified deviations, make an appropriate management decision. Also in the program it is possible to carry out calculations related to the safety of the crane boom departure; it is possible to simulate a situation according to which it can be concluded that the crane arm does not touch any structure, and its length is enough to deliver the cargo to the desired point in the installation horizon. The program makes it possible to use a virtual guide that allows you to walk with him around the object. Using the animation method, you can set various spatio-temporal situations.

For example, a virtual guide went to the door, and she opened, left — she closed. It is possible to pass through the object taking into account the walls, which are spatial limiters of movement, or you can turn on the IDDQD option and go with a guide directly "through" the walls.

It is clear that the higher the functionality of a program that implements BIM technology, the more complex and expensive it is, this can become an obstacle to the performance of some functions. In particular, scheduling is only available in Autodesk Navisworks Simulate and Autodesk Navisworks Manage. However, as analysis of the entire Autodesk Neviswork **s** line of programs shows, part of the functions performed can be replaced by using the Revit-2018 program, which will make it possible to provide a qualitatively new technological level of construction organization in general and in particular with the smallest software resources.

Consider the possibility of simulating scheduling, potentially implemented in the Revit-2018 program.

To simulate scheduling in a program such as Revit-2018, when designing an immovable object, a parametric characteristic of a structural element such as a stage can be used. By definition, given in the help system of the Revit-2018 program, a stage is a time characteristic that is defined by the user in order to create some fixed time sequence. For example, if we take as a basis the stages of construction of residential buildings defined in the standards for the duration of construction, we can distinguish the following stages of construction: the implementation of preparatory work, the implementation of underground work, the performance of aboveground and finishing works. And, if we additionally take into account the specified number of storeys of the building, then the stage that determines the construction of the aboveground part can be divided into floors.

Each structural element in the Revit-2018 program can be characterized by a specific state (phase). Revit-2018 uses 4 phases that indicate that a feature can be considered existing, new, temporary, or deleted. As a result, using such a project parameter as a stage, and determining the phase of a structural element, in this program, you can simulate scheduling. By using the filters built into the program, multimedia systematic visualization of construction can be carried out. Moreover, the selected construction calendar dates can be modeled as a sequence of stages, and then the simulation of the calendar planning will become closer to the real schedule.

9.7 Validation of the energy model in Revit-2018

Consider the software organization of the energy consumption model created in the Revit-2018 program in terms of its adequacy to Russian standards related to calculations of the building's thermal safety. Geometrically purely, the energy consumption model created in Revit-2018 is defined by many analytical surfaces and analytical spaces, which represent a system of building envelopes and spaces through which heat transfer occurs between the building and the environment. The most detailed energy consumption model is created based on a previously created architectural model. After automated model generation, the Revit-2018 program presents three different forms.

- View of the 3D model of energy consumption.
- Specification of analytic spaces.
- Specification of analytical surfaces.

The 3D model of energy consumption (see Fig. 9.3) displays the analytical spaces that make up the building's internal environment and the analytical surfaces that separate the designed building from the environment external to the building.

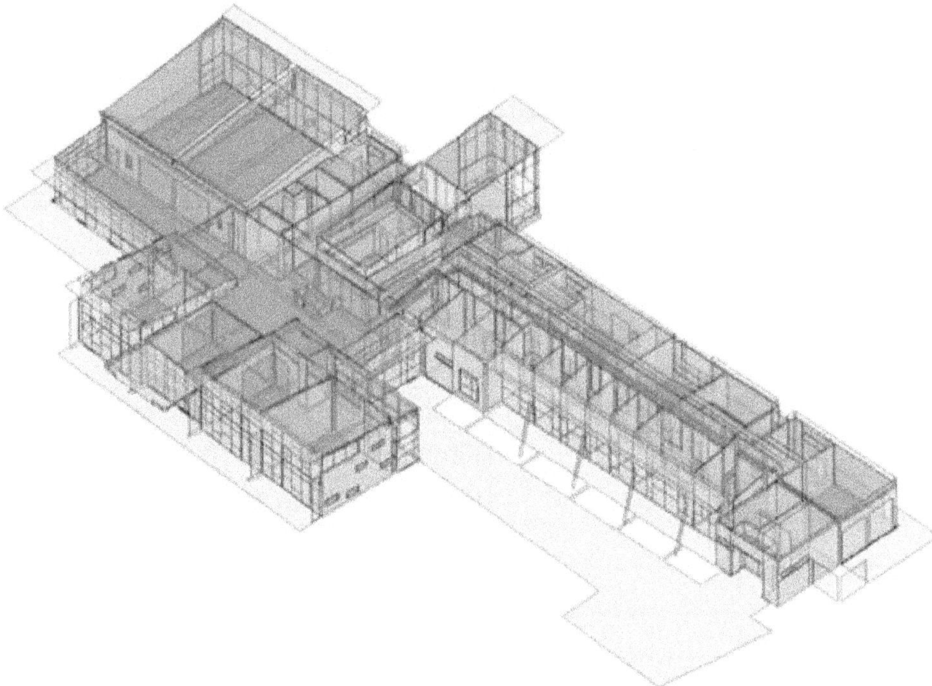

Figure 9.3: An example of a 3D form of an energy model

The specification of analytical spaces is presented in the form of a table (see table. 9.3), which reflects individual analytical spaces of the energy consumption model. These spaces are created for the model of energy consumption based on the explication of the premises of the building and various elements that limit the premises. The specification displays the areas and volumes of each space, as well as the area and volume of the entire model.

The specification of analytical surfaces is also presented in the form of a table (see table. 9.4), which reflects individual analytical surfaces of the energy consumption model. These surfaces are created for the model of energy consumption based on analytical spaces. The specification displays the area of each surface, the number of surfaces of a given size and the type of opening (e.g. doors and windows) or the type of surface (e.g. internal wall, external wall, roof, ceiling or slab).

When creating the architectural model, those elements that do not affect the energy consumption of the building are rejected, for example, reinforced concrete parapets arranged on the roof. Problems associated with structural rupture are also identified and eliminated, for which a technique such as surface tinting is used. Surface tinting is necessary when any of the architectural elements (or part of it) is located outside the main heat transfer surface of the building, for example, a wall cornice or a visor above the porch. To

Table 9.3 Example specification for analytic spaces

A	B	C	D
Area	Number	Room name	Volume
103 м²	1	Entry Hall 201	300.10 м³
6 м²	1	Laundry 104	14.02 м³
3 м²	1	Bath 103	8.09 м³
3 м²	1	Mech 102	5.76 м³
0 м²	1	Kitchen - Dining 10	0.93 м³
1 м²	1	Kitchen - Dining 10	0.62 м³
71 м²	1	Kitchen - Dining 10	185.78 м³
13 м²	1	Entry Hall 201	56.52 м³
14 м²	1	Bedroom 202	63.29 м³
25 м²	1	Master Bedroom 2	101.96 м³
6 м²	1	Bath 205	27.67 м³
13 м²	1	Bedroom 204	63.84 м³
4 м²	1		14.01 м³
5 м²	1	Master Bath 207	27.22 м³
4 м²	1	Bath 203	14.92 м³

create a power model from an architectural model, building elements must form an enclosed space. However, the model does not have to be completely impenetrable. Small clearances and tiling

The construction of each other is a natural part of real architectural models. Their presence is expected and permissible for creating a model of energy consumption. As a result, from a "geometric" point of view, the program allows you to create a accurate model of energy consumption.

In addition to the parameters of the individual structural elements of the building, the necessary characteristics are entered that describe the building as a whole. The corresponding initial data are presented in table 9.5.

An analysis of the source data presented in Table 9.5 and used in calculating energy consumption in Revit-2018 shows that the calculated winter outdoor temperature is used to calculate heat losses, but it is not known which and with what measure of security. The set of rules (SP) on the thermal protection of buildings gives specific values that are determined by the joint venture in building climatology. The type of building only integrally determines the internal temperature in the building, but in the joint venture for the

Table 9.4 Example specification for analytical surfaces

A	B	C	D
Area	Number	Room name	Volume
4 м^2	3	air	
161 м^2	49	Dull window	
27 м^2	13	Door	
60 м^2	8	Openable window	
2 м^2	2	Openable light	
92 м^2	17		Internal floor
240 м^2	54		Inner wall
214 м^2	16		roof
76 м^2	1		inclined floor
139 м^2	18		Outer wall
1 м^2	1		ceiling
960 м^2	56		shutter
101 м^2	7		Raised floor

thermal protection of buildings, it is required to use different temperatures for individual rooms. In the proposed source, data there is no duration of the heating period and its average temperature. An indication of the latitude and longitude of the location of the building determines its insolation, which, according to the joint venture for the thermal protection of buildings, is calculated differently.

As a result, the composition of the initial data used by the Revit-2018 program shows a significant difference in the calculation of heat losses regulated by the RF standards.

Table 9.6 shows the total power consumption characteristics.

An analysis of the results of the calculation of energy consumption shows that a greater number of calculated values are associated with a refrigeration load. In this regard, we note that for the mass systems of buildings designed in the Russian Federation, the two calculated characteristics are more relevant values — these are “Peak heating load” and “Peak air flow during heating”. However, to assess their usefulness, one must bear in mind that in the Russian Federation peak heating load is usually used to calculate heating devices, and then subject to the determination of the adopted heating system (water, underfloor heating, air, etc.). Of course, if you use additional information,

Table 9.5 Input data of the energy consumption model

Location and weather	
Project and address	Name and address of the project
Latitude and longitude	The latitude and longitude of the building
Air exchange parameters	For example, air exchange rate
The temperature in the summer for dry bulb	Summer air temperature
Temperature in summer with a wet thermometer	Summer temperature of adiabatic saturation during evaporation of water on a thermometer and its cooling effect.
The temperature in winter on dry bulb	Winter air temperature using a dry thermometer.
Average daily temperature range	The average temperature range determined by the location of the project.
Month and hour of peak refrigeration load	The date that is used to calculate peak loads.
Type of building	The type of building determines the indoor climate
Area and volume	The total analytical area and volume of the building's space, which are calculated from the clean surfaces of the bounding elements of the spaces.
Ground level	The value is necessary for a more accurate calculation of heat transfer.

then the value of the peak heating load can be converted into units of thermal energy spent during the heating season.

According to the joint venture on thermal protection of buildings for the main building envelopes, restrictions are introduced on the minimum possible thermal resistance. It is unlikely that these restrictions were used by default in the Revit-2018 program. It should also be noted that there is a difference in the terminology used. For example, in the Revit-2018 program, thermal resistance is called heat resistance. It is also necessary to refer to attention to the redundancy of the input information, for example, the heat transfer coefficient is the reciprocal of the thermal resistance. In addition, if at the same time the user incorrectly enters one of the two data, then there will be a contradiction, or, in the language adopted in the BIM technology, a conflict.

Summary: Because of the above analysis, the following conclusions can be made. The Revit-2018 program allows you to automatically generate quite adequate analytical surfaces and spaces that quite accurately determine the geometric characteristics of building envelopes. However, the parameters and methods of calculating the heat input and heat loss of the building incorporated into the program are not adequate to the standards for thermal protection of buildings adopted in the Russian Federation.

Table 9.6 Calculated energy consumption of the building

Energy Calculation Results	
Peak full refrigeration load	Total refrigeration load in all spaces in the building. This value includes heat gain from heat conduction, ventilation, pipes and ducts, and other explicit and latent loads.
Peak apparent heat load	The seasonal high point of the tangible cooling load in the building.
Peak latent load for latent heat	The seasonal top of the latent refrigeration load in the building.
Maximum cooling the ability	The maximum required cooling capacity, defined as the sum of peak refrigeration loads in the building zones. It is taken into account that peak loads can occur at different times depending on conditions, such as the location of zones in the building (for example, with access to the north or with access to the south).
The peak flow of air under cooling	The seasonal top point for cooling air flow throughout the building.
Peak Heating Load	Total heating load in all spaces in the building. This value includes heat gain from heat conduction, ventilation, pipes and ducts, as well as tangible and hidden loads.
The peak flow of air for heating	The seasonal upper point for heating air flow through the building.
Checksums	
Specific Refrigeration Load	The total refrigeration load in the building divided by the occupied analytical area of the building.
Cooling flow density	Cooling air flow divided by the occupied analytical area of the building.
Cooling flow / cooling load	Cooling air flow divided by the total refrigeration load in the building.
Cooling surface area / cooling load	The analytical area of the zone divided by the total refrigeration load in the building.
Specific heating load	The total heating load in the building divided by the occupied analytical area of the building.
Heating flow density	The consumption of heating air divided by the occupied analytical area of the building.

9.8 Energy calculation based on the synthesis of Revit-2018 and Excel programs

In BIM-design technology, quite often-used combined design, carried out in software products for various functional purposes. For example, we have previously shown a combined relationship between BIM technology programs and project management programs such as Microsoft Project and Primavera. Imagine a methodological scheme for calculating energy consumption, based on the use of interface communications between Revit and Excel. The scheme described below is described in detail in the work, and its usefulness lies in the fact that it can be used to expand the list of resources to be saved.

In the methodological scheme under consideration, it is possible to additionally take into account the possibility of calculating the catchment of precipitation from the roof of the building, which, for example, in St. Petersburg is 620 mm per 1 m^2 of horizontal surface per year. In this case, the volume of collected water will depend on the roof area, the geometric characteristics of which are included in the table of analytical surfaces formed in the Revit-2018 program. Also, as an additional energy resource, "pumping" of heat from under the base of the building with a heat pump can be designed, the heat removal of which will depend on the specific heat capacity of the pipeline laid in the ground, which is approximately 30–40 W/m^2. In this case, the additional thermal effect will depend either on the area of the land plot or on the base area of the building under which the primary circuit of the heat pump is laid. The insolation of individual building structures can also serve as an additional resource. The result of its calculation, carried out at the initial stage of design, should be interpreted as the maximum insolation potential. The traditional calculation of energy consumption is the calculation of the heat loss of a building, which also takes into account the heat loss due to the heating of the supply air.

To provide additional complex calculation in Excel, the specifications of analytical surfaces created earlier in Revit-2018 can be converted into text files using the sequence of commands "File" — "Export" — "Specification". As a result, the geometric characteristics of the enclosing surfaces will be placed in Excel. In this case, to ensure the automatic insertion of specifications, the corresponding macro written in Excel in a programming language such as Visual Basic for Application can be used.

Further calculation of technical and economic indicators in Excel can be implemented on a sheet selected for these purposes, on which a single settlement-dialog box can be created. At the same time, any additional data corresponding to the updated regulatory framework used in the Russian Federation and related to building resource calculations can be entered into the Excel program. Imagine an approximate list of calculated values.

1. The calculation of the coefficient of compactness of the building. This parameter is described in [ ] and it takes into account the approximation of the designed form of the building to its ideal value.

2. Heat losses of building envelopes.

3. Heat losses associated with the heating of the supply air.

4. Thermal gain associated with the insolation of the building.

5. Thermal gain associated with the presence of a heat pump in the ground.

6. Water supply associated with precipitation.

The presented methodology does not pretend to be universal in all situations related to calculations of energy consumption and consumption of other resources; it shows largely the possibilities of the proposed approach in order to expand the capabilities of the used software tools.

In this regard, we will analyze two, to some extent, alternative scenarios for calculating energy consumption. Consider the option of autonomous energy calculation performed in the Revit-2018 program. For the full implementation of such a calculation, it is necessary to link this program to an additional add-in that completely performs the calculation of energy consumption. This option has both advantages and disadvantages. The advantage should be the full immersion of the user in a universal software product that does not require the use of additional tools that go beyond the Autodesk product line. However, to implement this approach, an additional software resource is needed that performs the so-called "cloud" computing implemented through the following site: insight360.autodesk.com, which will require additional costs associated with a subscription to this resource and an increase in the traffic of information transfer through the network. On the other hand, there is a more significant circumstance, which is that when analyzing the solution, the question may arise, but will these calculations correspond to the current standard used in the Russian Federation?

A brief outline of the implementation of the second (alternative) approach comes down to the following procedures.

The building projected using BIM technology is used as input.

The initial data is supplemented by information from the joint venture in construction climatology.

In the Revit-2018 program, an analytical model of energy consumption is being formed.

The model formed by the Revit-2018 program is presented in the form of the specification for "Analytical Surfaces" and is supplemented by the necessary thermal characteristics of the structures that define the analytical surfaces. The specification is then exported to an Excel spreadsheet program.

The Excel table is supplemented with the necessary cells in which the calculation formulas are found that correspond to the code of rules for the thermal protection of buildings.

If necessary, using a programming language such as Visual Basic for Application, a macro can be written that allows you to fully automate the process of calculating energy consumption, based on a synthesis of Revit-2018 and Excel programs.

The main disadvantage of this development option is a certain contradiction to the modern marketing approach associated with the systematic integration of all functions in a single software package of one developer. The advantage of this approach is the saving on additional software resources and obtaining calculation results that correspond to the regulatory framework of heat engineering calculations used in the Russian Federation.

9.9 Modern methods for predicting the duration of construction

9.9.1 The random nature of the duration of the construction and the technical and economic significance of its prediction

A. Empirical facts showing the discrepancies between current and planned construction durations. Various models of the organization of construction, which are the basis for the variant formation of calendar schedules, can be divided into two classes, namely, the class of deterministic models and the class of stochastic models. At the same time, the basis of the class of deterministic models is the adoption of the hypothesis that the main characteristics of the work schedule are unchanged, which include both the duration of the construction as a whole and the timing of individual work. However, the practical implementation of deterministic construction work schedules is additionally associated with ensuring the invariability (invariance) of their technological sequence, which is defined as a topological scheme of work. Moreover, in the real practice of construction it is impossible to take into account all the numerous risks that affect the course of the actual implementation of the construction schedule. As a result, as an empirical fact, it should be recognized that in construction there is a random nature, both changes in the duration of work and a change in their topology. Taken together, both of these phenomena (phenomena) determine the deviations of the real (actual) terms of the work from their planned values. Therefore, in the scheduling of construction, carried out, as a rule, in the environment of project management programs, various methods for predicting the completion of construction are used to take into account the random nature of the change in the duration of work. For example, the forecast according to the PERT method is based on taking into account random durations of work, and the GERT method is used to take into account the random nature of changes in the topology of work.

The discrepancy between the planned and actual durations of the work is determined by their statistical data, obtained, as a rule, based on maintaining the executive calendar schedules of the work. Table 9.7 shows the results of the analysis of executive schedules, according to which the discrepancies of actually measured durations of various types of work and their planned values are determined [115].

Table 9.7 Practical data on the discrepancy between planned and actual durations

No. p.p	Type of work	Duration, planned, days	Actual duration, days	Excess of fact,%
	Territory fencing	8	12	fifty
	Territory preparation	23	thirty	thirty
	Zero cycle	135	150	eleven
	Frame assembly	fifty	60	20
	Internal walls and partitions	fifty	60	20
	Santehmontazh	thirty	40	33
	Electrical installation	thirty	45	fifty
	Facade decoration	thirty	45	fifty
	Interior decoration	10	fifteen	fifty
	Network Installation	fifteen	thirty	100
	Connecting utilities	7	10	43

As can be seen from the data presented in table 9.7, the maximum absolute deviation from the plan was 15 days, and the maximum relative excess of the actual duration exceeded the planned duration by 2 times (100%).

Analysis of the organization of construction in the United States shows that the facts of construction delays are unacceptable and are often considered as the subject of an economic dispute between the construction participants. However, this does not guarantee that the overall construction delay will be reduced to zero. Table 9.8 shows data on exceeding the construction time for facilities that were built under fixed-value contracts.

Table 9.8 Exceeding construction time relative to planned for fixed price contracts

Variation,%	0–20	21–40	41-60	61–80	81–100	More than 100
Shares,%	52	18	12.6	7.2	7.2	3

Table 109 shows the results of data processing taking into account their conversion to a uniform scale. The data presented show that the delay in completion of construction is a frequent occurrence. For example, the minimum delay, determined by the range of exceeding the actual duration of construction to 20%, is 52% of the number of investigated objects. In Russia, there are also quite a lot of cases of untimely implementation of construction projects.

Both of the above tables show the final data for separately performed work and for facilities in general. However, from the point of view of forecasting the final construction delay, the intermediate data obtained by monitoring the construction are no less important. Let us give an example of this kind of data obtained on the basis of monitoring the construction of the Clear Sky residential complex, the developer of which is the SetlCity construction organization (see table 9.9).

Table 9.9 Data from Three SetlCity Organization Monitoring

Monitoring	Start	the end	Mid	Time,%	Fact. volume%	Change forecast
No. 3	1/16/17	01/26/17	01/21/17	63.3	48.4	12/21/17
Number 4	01/27/17	02/09/17	02/04/17	66.2	49.7	12/31/17
Number 5	02/10/17	02/20/17	02/15/17	68.8	51.8	01/01/18

From the monitoring results presented in table 9.9, it can be seen that the forecast for the completion of construction is systematically shifting from the planned date (07.23.17) to a later date.

Thus, the above analysis of various data related to the deadlines for the execution of both individual works and the construction as a whole indicates objectively existing delays in fulfilling contractual obligations affecting the delay in the deadline for putting construction objects into operation.

B. Technical and economic importance of predicting the duration of construction. In world practice, the duration of construction is one of the main indicators determining the economic efficiency of the implementation of ISPs in Japan, the UK and the USA. In the construction industry, construction time is determined by labor productivity, which serves as the basis for evaluating contractors. In the UK construction sector, experience with claims related to time delays is constantly being compiled. The entire contract system in the United States is focused on minimizing the risks of late work. Therefore, the natural desire of many participants in the construction is the timely receipt of a forecast for the completion date of the facility as a whole, or a forecast for the timing of individual work. All this is necessary in order to further develop measures to counter therefore a negative phenomenon.

The occurrence of untimely performance of certain works and the construction of the facility as a whole is associated with numerous and diverse risks. The existing classification of methods for determining risks allows the use of a statistical apparatus for selecting the most significant risk factors. In some cases, the occurrence of untimeliness is associated with the category of failures.

In this case, risk is usually understood as the probability of something negative occurring, and failure means the probability of deviation from a certain regular regime.

Despite the fact that construction is carried out year-round, various analyzes of adverse weather conditions can be found in the scientific literature, which objectively lead to construction delays. The scientific literature describes both the causes of risk factors and the methods that quantify penalties for work delays. Since 2004, the Federal Law on shared construction has been in force in the Russian Federation, according to which the developer bears property liability to equity investors, for untimely commissioning of the facility.

Consider how the delay in completion of construction negatively affects the economic efficiency of the project, using the formula for calculating net present value (NPV).

$$NPV = \sum_{j=T^v}^{T^H} \frac{R_j}{(1+E)^{t_j}} - \sum_{i=1}^{T^v} \frac{C_i}{(1+E)^{t_i}}, \tag{9.1}$$

where E is the discount rate adopted for the calculation of economic efficiency;

i — ordinal index of the stage of the investment period, the total duration whose value is determined by the construction time T^v;

C_i, t_i — investment costs incurred at the t_i-th moment of time; j is the ordinal index of the stage of the operating period, the duration of it is determined by the difference between the accepted planning horizon T^H and the construction duration T^v;

R_i, t_j — operating income determined by the t_j-th moment of time.

From formula (9.1) it can be seen that the longer the construction takes place, for a given planning horizon, the lower the *NPV*. If we additionally consider indicators such as the internal rate of return and the discounted payback period, then taking into account the calculation of these indicators, we can come to the same conclusion that increasing the duration of construction worsens the planned estimates of the economic efficiency of ISPs.

From the foregoing, the following general conclusion can be drawn. An increase in the duration of construction almost always negatively affects the implementation of the project, while worsening the socio-economic indicators. Therefore, in order to effectively control the progress of construction production and in order to minimize the delay in putting the facility under construction into operation, a timely and, if possible, sufficiently accurate forecast of the duration of construction is required. However, it should be borne in mind that there is no ideal forecast, since its timeliness and accuracy depend on the quality of the information description of the building production system and on the methods used to predict the completion of construction.

9.9.2 Forecasting methods based on extrapolation of work performed

Consider modern methods for predicting completion of construction, based on measuring or evaluating the characteristics of the volume of work performed. It is necessary to make the following explanations. The scope of work can be determined during construction monitoring and directly measured in physical units. However, in many cases, and especially when performing work packages, their volumes are measured in cost terms. Another indirect unit of measurement of the volume of work can serve as the duration of its implementation. It should also be noted that sometimes an expert method based on a subjective assessment of construction could be used to determine the volume of work performed. And, finally, for the forecasting method based on the differential accounting of failures, which is presented below, the amount of work remains as if latent (hidden), since the delay in construction indirectly determines the direct measurement of the number of failures.

A. Index method for assessing the untimely construction.

To predict untimeliness, a concept such as a "point of no return" is introduced, the achievement of which with a high degree of probability should predict the fact of a future delay in the completion of construction, which can be interpreted as a global failure of the construction production system [143]. To establish the fact of the possible untimely completion of construction, an indicator has been developed, defined as an index of the timeliness of project execution (ITPE)

$$ITPE = \frac{T_{dir} - T_{prog}}{T_{dir} - T_{cur}}, \tag{9.2}$$

where T_{dir} is the date of the directive completion;

T_{prog} — the date of the projected completion of construction; T_{cur} — the current date monitoring of construction.

The ITPE calculated according to formula (9.2) is determined as the ratio of the forecast of the reserve for the time of completion of construction to the remaining (before the decision period) construction duration, while the negative reserve shows the forecast for the failure to meet the deadline for putting the facility into operation. It is necessary to divide the quantitative range of changes in the values of the ITPE into three gradations according to the so-called "semaphore" rule. Correction of the performance of work in the appropriate calendar schedule should be carried out when the value of the PSIS is less than –15%, and if the value of the ITPE is less than –30%, it is considered that a catastrophe is defined as the "red danger level". Thus, in the range of changes in the ITPE from –15 to –30%, the work schedule needs to be regulated, and the yellow color associated with the "warning traffic signal" is selected for this range. The drawback of the ITPE is that for its calculation, the date of the predicted completion of construction should be determined, which significantly reduces the practical value of the proposed approach.

Another index defines a "point of no return" on the basis of measuring the volume of work performed, and this index is defined as the index of project performance (IPP).

$$IPP = \frac{(N_{prod} - N_{plan})/N_{plan}}{(T_{dir} - T_{cur})/T_{dir}}, \tag{9.3}$$

where T_{dir} is the date of the directive completion;

T_{cur}— the current date monitoring of construction;

N_{plan} — the planned amount of work for the current date; N_{prod} — completed work on the current date.

"Physically" *IPP* shows the ratio of the index of the remaining work volume to the index of remaining time. In quantitative terms, it turns out that the smaller the *IPP* (taking into account the sign), the situation from the point of view of the occurrence of untimely implementation of the project becomes worse. For the practical interpretation of the values of the run-time indicators, the same "traffic light rules" can be applied. However, it happens that the "yellow zones", calculated in accordance with the *IPP*, do not coincide with the correspondingnyellow zones" established by the COI index. Obviously, this uncertainty requires the introduction of additional rules into the forecast algorithm, without which the proposed technique loses its practical meaning.

B. The method of differential accounting for failures.

In contrast to the integrated failure accounting, determined by the index method, it is possible to differentiate failures by their influence on the percentage of deviation from a given construction deadline. A description of the construction production system (CPS) is presented by highlighting five levels of construction duration exceeding: 0, 5, 20, 50 and 100%. The intensities of transitions from smaller delays to large delays are established empirically and are defined as factors that increase the duration of construction. The intensities of transitions from large untimely to lesser untimely are defined as factors that reduce the duration of construction. Combinatorial analysis showed that the set of intensities for both groups of factors is determined by the number of pair combinations for 5 selected levels, that is, the number 10. Using the empirical data described above, it is necessary to formalize the solution to the forecast problem by reducing it to the "death and reproduction" problem proposed in its time academician A.N. Kolmogorov. The result of the solution of this problem is reduced to calculating the probabilities of the CPS being in different states, which makes it possible to determine the average value of the outlook forecast and its error.

However, a more detailed analysis of the data showed that, despite taking into account various sources of delays in construction, their differentiation completely disappears, since when calculating the failure rates, their total number without any weighting factors is taken into account. Another observation that casts doubt on the result of the forecast is as follows. If for one and the same data set, which just should invariantly determine the general untimeliness, increase the number of CPS levels, then the calculation system of equations will significantly expand, since the number of variables and parameters in each equation will increase, and the number of equations will also increase. As a result, the solution of a new system of differential equations will lead to a different result. Thus, there is a paradoxical situation in which the initial data, which invariantly determine failures, lead to an ambiguous forecast result, since the result obtained will depend on the subjectively assigned number of SSP levels.

C. The method of linear and nonlinear extrapolation of the volume of work performed. This model allows you to quantify the end date of construction. We show its features on the example of monitoring carried out as part of an automated investment control system (ASIC), which is practically used at the facility, the developer of which is the construction organization SetlCity. The logic of this forecast method is based on the use of linear extrapolation of the planned work in time. However, considering the experience of organizing construction in the USA, it can be graphically shown that the planned construction progress is a nonlinear function of time. A similar non-linearity of the planned growth of capital investments over time is embedded in the Russian standards for the duration of construction. Table 9.10 shows an example of the planned distribution of capital investments during the construction of a residential brick building.

From the data in table 9.10 it follows that by the end of the 8th month of construction, 85% of the volume of all work should be completed.

Table 9.10 Options for the planned distribution of the implementation of the volume of work for 9-story brick building with an area of 6000 square meters

1 month	2 month	3 month	4 month	5 month	6 month	7 month	8 month	9 month	10 month
Prep.	Underground part		aboveground part					Finish	
Planned distribution of work on SNiP,%									
7	21	32	43	53	64	74	85	93	100
Planned uniform distribution of work,%									
10	20	30	40	50	60	70	80	90	100

If you do not take into account the real unevenness, then with a linear increase in the volume of work, the fulfillment of the volume of work by 80% will be considered normal. As a result, an additional increase in the pace of construction will not be planned for the next period of operational management of the construction progress, and this circumstance could potentially lead to the disruption of the planned completion date. An improved extrapolation method is presented in [60], taking into account the nonlinear nature of the growth in the volume of construction work over time.

The theoretical provisions of the nonlinear extrapolation method are illustrated in Figure 9.4.

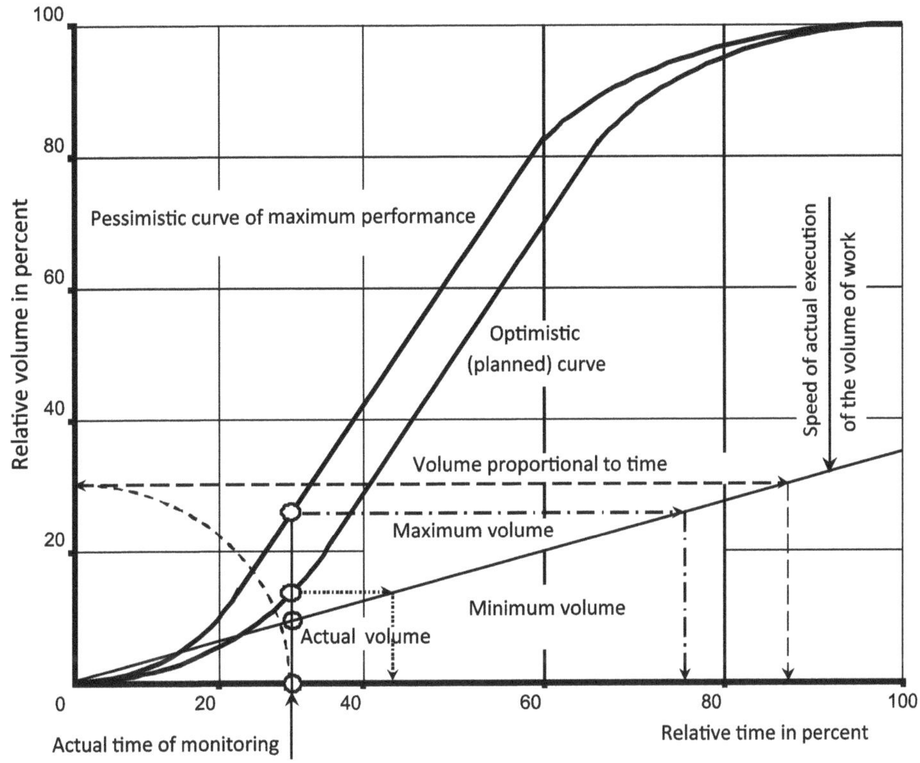

Figure 9.4: Outline sketch of the nonlinear extrapolation method

To display any option that differs in the absolute duration of the work package at the object in question, relative coordinates are introduced in terms of the volume and duration of the work. As a result, the growth of the actual and planned volume of work performed will vary from 0 to 100% in the corresponding coordinates of the relative time. As a result, for any embodiments, two points will remain unchanged. The beginning of the work corresponds to the origin, and the end of the work will correspond to 100% of the time and 100% of the volume completed. Figure 9.4 shows 2 sigma-shaped curves connecting these two points. The lower curve determines the deterministic nature of the work, and it corresponds to the planned progress of the work.

Consider the following example. Suppose that 30% of the time has passed since the start of construction, and then, according to the curve under consideration, the planned implementation should be equal to 15%, and the actual implementation amounted to 12% of the total volume. In this case, the forecast for the completion of construction is calculated as an extrapolation of the planned duration (T_{PL}) and taking into account these data, it turns out that the predicted duration should be increased in the following proportion $T_{prog}/T_{dir} = 15/12$, that is, 1.25 times.

The upper sigma-shaped curve characterizes the pessimistic performance of the volume of work, and this curve is formed through the use of statistical modeling, the main elements of which will be given below. In this case, the average index of untimely performance of completed work will be determined precisely by the ratio of the determined volume of execution to the volume actually performed. Suppose that the maximum amount of work according to statistical modeling was 25.9%. Consequently, the pessimistic forecast will be that thc plannod duration should be increased in the proportion of 25.9 / 12, that is, 2.16 times. Thus, unlike the linear extrapolation method, this method allows you to calculate the range of a possible forecast for the duration of the construction, ranging from optimistic to pessimistic.

D. Calculation of the forecast for completion of construction based on an estimate of the entropy of the current construction schedule. To understand the essence of the prediction model described below based on the entropy index, let us consider an example of the use of thermal energy in a thermodynamic system that implements the Carnot cycle. The source of thermal energy transfers energy to the working fluid in the amount of Q_1. Moreover, due to the isothermal expansion of the working fluid, part of this energy goes into useful mechanical work, then the working fluid is disconnected from the source of thermal energy, and it performs mechanical work without receiving heat. In order to return the working fluid to its original state, it is necessary to compress it, first due to isothermal heat transfer to the refrigerator Q_2, and then due to adiabatic compression. The useful work done by the working fluid and converted to mechanical work is calculated as the difference of energies received from the heater and given to the refrigerator $Q_1 Q_2$. As a result, it turns out that part of the thermal energy transferred to the refrigerator is irretrievably lost, since it, in fact, enters the environment, heating it uselessly. The loss of energy is because thermal energy is determined by the energy of the chaotic motion of atoms and molecules of matter. As a result, the law of not decreasing entropy determines the direction in which the heat flux acts. The increase in entropy is a property of the irreversibility of any processes of the macroscopic world and, therefore, extends to the system of construction production.

Using the above description of the operation of a heat engine, we present an analogy with the process of managing construction production. In the organization of construction production, one of the main results is the timely completion of construction work. In addition, if the actual terms of the work do not correspond to the planned dates, then it can be argued that the effectiveness of such general management functions as planning, organization and operational regulation of the construction of the production turned out to be low. There are many reasons for reducing management efficiency, some of them are classified by insufficient resource support, all sorts of risks determine others, others are various kinds of failures of technical systems, etc. etc. Important in this case is that part of management decisions cannot be implemented, and then the energy associated with their implementation will be uselessly dissipated into the environment.

Based on this, the following analogy can be substantiated. The flow of managerial energy (coming from the heater in thermodynamics) is directed to the direct performers of the work (working fluid in thermodynamics), while part of the managerial energy is unclaimed (in thermodynamics it is heat transferred to the refrigerator). As a result, it can be assumed that part of the managerial energy has the property of the same randomness as the heat flux energy. In this case, the measure of chaos is the untimely performance of work, and its integral estimate can be measured using the entropy indicator.

In the proposed model, the entropy calculation formula is used, which is adapted to the information obtained from the current construction schedule. As a result, the calculation of the average entropy (in bits) of the current construction schedule is carried out according to the formula

$$S\left(T^{m}\right)=\frac{\sum\limits_{i=1}^{n} c_i \ln \frac{t_i^{act}}{t_i^{plan}}}{(\ln 2)\cdot\sum\limits_{i=1}^{n} c_i}, \tag{9.4}$$

where $T^{\ m}$ is the time elapsed from the start of construction to monitoring the duration of the work performed;

n is the number of work performed at the time of monitoring;

c_i — the cost of the i- th work performed;

t_i^{plan} - the planned duration of the i-th work performed;

t_i^{act} — the actual duration of the i-th work performed.

We denote the planned duration of the construction of the facility as T^{plan}, and the corresponding projected duration as T^{for}. In order to build an object in a timely manner, the amount of work remaining after the monitoring date must be completed during the time $T^{plan}-T^{m}$. If the remaining amount of work will be completed during the time $T^{for} - T^m$, then the corresponding entropy (in bits) can be calculated by the formula:

$$S\left(T^{for}\right) = \frac{\ln\left(\frac{T^{for} - T^m}{T^{plan} - T^m}\right)}{\ln 2}. \tag{9.5}$$

If we assume that the quality of control determined by the entropy indicator in accordance with formula (9.4) does not change, then to find the forecast of construction duration that interests us, we can use the equality of the entropies calculated earlier.

$$T^{for} = T^m + \left(T^{plan} - T^m\right) \cdot Exp\left(\frac{\sum\limits_{i=1}^{n} c_i \ln \frac{t_i^{act}}{t_i^{plan}}}{\sum\limits_{i=1}^{n} c_i}\right). \tag{9.6}$$

Obviously, formula (9.6) is a special case, since it was derived on the assumption that the entropy remains unchanged after an intermediate assessment of the volume of work performed. In the general case, the analytical prediction formula for the duration of the construction can take a different form if, when processing the results of all previous monitoring, the actual trend of the entropy indicator is taken into account. Formula (9.6) can also be changed if, when measuring the entropy, we additionally take into account the changing values of the beginning of work, as presented in the paper.

Consider the following calculation example. It takes 15 months to build a two-section building. The planned duration of the preparatory work is 1 month. (cost 5%). The planned duration of foundation work in the first section is 2 months. (cost 12%), in the 2nd section is 1 month. (cost 8%). The planned duration of the construction of the box of the first section of the building is 7 months. (cost 30%), in the 2nd section is 5 months. (cost 25%). The planned duration of internal work in the first section is 4 months. (cost 10%), in the 2nd section is 3 months. (cost 10%). After 5 months from the start of construction, it was documented that the preparatory work was completed in 1 month, the foundation work in the first section was completed in 2.5 months, and the foundation work in the second section was completed in 1.5 months. Substitute the data in the formula (9.6) and get the following result:

$$T^{for} = 5 + (15 - 5) \cdot Exp\left(\frac{5\ln(1/1) + 12\ln(2.5/2) + 8\ln(1.5/1)}{5 + 12 + 8}\right) = 17.7c.$$

Thus, the monitoring result, based on documenting the execution of work, gives a forecast of a total construction delay of 2.7 months.

9.9.3 Statistical Description of Random Durations

A. Description of random work durations by distribution functions. During the monitoring of the volume of work performed, situations are possible where such detailed characteristics of construction work can be established that can form the basis for their statistical description. Then, using a statistical description of the duration of random jobs, you can generate many random calendar schedules. In this case, the total duration of each variant of the calendar schedule will be determined as a random variable. In aggregate, the described process is defined as the process of *statistical modeling* of construction schedules.

The first systematization of the methodological foundations of probabilistic scheduling was presented in [117]. In this paper, there are many functions of the distribution density that can be used to generate random work durations (GSPR). In the formal mathematical plane, any distribution functions can be represented in two forms — either in an integral form or in a differential form. However, to create a generator of random durations of work, it is more appropriate to use the differential form of the distribution function. The distribution density function of the random duration of work $f(t)$ determines the probability of finding the value of its duration in the range from t to $t + \Delta t$. Many functions of the distribution density of random work durations include: normal and uniform distribution, Poisson distribution, beta distribution, exponential distribution, etc.

Such a variety of distribution functions gives rise to the problem of choosing the most appropriate for the purposes associated with probabilistic scheduling of construction. For the purpose of planning and managing construction, beta distribution is recommended. The same distribution is widely used in such project management programs as *Microsoft Project, Open Plan, Primavera,* etc. Its temporal parameters have the following meaningful names: optimistic duration, most probable and pessimistic duration of work. However, in the scientific literature there is no convincing evidence of the adequacy of its use in the construction industry. It can also be noted that when using three parametric beta distribution, the following collision occurs. If the most probable value of the beta distribution is defined as the planned duration, then the deviation from the mode allows two risks at once — over fulfillment and under fulfillment of the plan. However, the practice of organizing construction production shows that over fulfillment of the plan on the one hand is unlikely and on the other hand (in some cases) is generally unacceptable.

For various applications, the normal distribution is most widely used, which is also referred to as the Gaussian or Laplace distribution. The differential form of the normal distribution has the following form:

$$f(t) = \frac{1}{\sigma\sqrt{2\pi}} \exp\left(\frac{-(t-m)^2}{2\sigma^2}\right). \tag{9.7}$$

where m and σ are the mean and standard deviation.

The well-known drawback of this distribution, when used to describe random work durations, is the infinite range, determined by the range from $-\infty$ to $+\infty$. However, if positive infinity can be interpreted as an infinite duration of work, then negative duration has no reasonable explanation at all. As a partial correction of this drawback, the so-called lognormal distribution is used, limited to the left by some positive parameter — a . As a result, the lognormal distribution formula is described by the following expression:

$$f(t) = \frac{1}{(t-a)\,\sigma\sqrt{2\pi}} \exp\left(\frac{-\left[\ln(t-a) - m^2\right]}{2\sigma^2}\right). \tag{9.8}$$

where a is a positive parameter limiting the minimum duration of work.

As can be seen from formula (9.8), this distribution includes three set parameters and, therefore, it is three parametric. However, it should be noted that for the purposes of statistical modeling of a random calendar, the number of parameters is quite significant. The fact is that for each parameter a certain justification is required, carried out either by processing a representative array of statistical data, or by constructing a specific theoretical model.

Let us consider specific examples of processing statistical data relating to the duration of construction of facilities in general and to the duration of individual work. Table 9.11 presents a statistical series of the intensity of the process of building partitions made of drywall where the ranges of changes in the intensity of the process are shown in the upper row and the number of days of work with this intensity in the lower row [120].

Table 9.11 A statistical series of the intensity of the process of installing drywall partitions

The intensity of the process, m^2/ shift	Duration of work, shifts
450–460	3
460–470	11
470–480	14
480-490	19
490–500	24
500–510	15
510–520	9
520–530	3
530–540	2

In accordance with the presented data, the average intensity of the process was calculated, and the random process itself was approximated by the normal distribution function. We draw attention to the fact that the normal distribution is symmetric with respect to the mode. However, in reality there is a certain asymmetry. Indeed, if all participants in the process under consideration are set a single norm, for example, 500 m^2/ day, then will the attitude to work not change? The laggards will strive to fulfill the norm, and those who exceeded the norm can reduce their results. Thus, the use of the derived standard will change the statistics by which this standard is calculated, and this change will shift the distribution mode to the left. This is confirmed by the fact that the number of failures corresponds to the Poisson distribution, which, as is known, has left asymmetry. If we assume that the number of failures is proportional to the delay, then the delay will also be determined by the distribution with left asymmetry.

The practical examples considered above (see tables 9.7–9.11) of determining the parameters of untimely performance of work indicate only the fundamental possibility of a statistical approach to this problem. In fact, no known scientific source has resolved issues related to the extrapolation of statistical data to other objects and other work performed by various organizations.

In practical situations of this kind, practical circumstances are quite objective, since even typical objects in construction have very specific features, and as for the construction organizations that perform work, the working conditions in them and resource equipment have always been and will be quite individual. To this should also be added that construction organizations have different experience in the production of various works, and may not have any experience at all, and its absence does not allow the formation of a representative statistical data array.

B. Determination of the distribution parameters of random work durations. An analysis of the previous material showed that when forming a generator of random durations of work (GSPR), one should strive to use low-parametric distribution functions. Moreover, for the minimum number of parameters, two main statistical characteristics should be taken that determine the magnitude of the random duration, namely its minimum value — a and its maximum value — b. From the point of view of the statistical modeling software, almost every computer application has a generator of uniformly distributed random numbers ranging from 0 to 1. And in this sense, the uniform distribution function, which is determined by the following, should be considered the most suitable distribution density function of random duration the formula:

$$f(t) = \frac{1}{b-a}. \tag{9.9}$$

At the same time, the planned duration of the corresponding work can be taken as the minimum duration. This is due to an empirically established psychological factor set forth in [113]: "... the work is performed during the time allotted to it. If the leader does not like people to sit idle, his subordinates will begin to create the appearance of work. Any work for one hour can be extended into two, rechecking something that you don't need to double-check, keeping additional records that no one needs — why not, if time allows! " From this statement, it follows that the performers have no constructive motivation to reduce the duration of work below the planned.

Either the planned duration of the construction is set normatively or directively, or in accordance with the construction organization project, or by agreement of the parties when concluding the contract; similarly, the planned duration of the individual work is set. As for determining the shape of the differential distribution curve of random work durations, an approach based on the following statements can be used to select it:

1. thc probability of reducing the planned duration is zero; 2. The maximum duration is determined by the limit value of the duration of the construction. For example, it is purely theoretically possible to determine such a duration at which the customer completes the construction with zero profitability;

3. the probability of a smaller deviation from the planned duration should be greater than the probability of a larger deviation from the same planned duration;

4. The rate of decrease in the probability of deviation from the planned value is either proportional to the change in the distribution density, or constant, or equal to zero.

The first statement determines the minimum (optimistic) duration of work — a. The second statement determines the maximum (pessimistic) duration of work — *in the* third statement determines a monotonic decrease in the distribution density function, and the fourth statement determines the specific form of an adequate distribution.

"Physically" the change in the speed of the distribution density means that there is some managerial effort, which is directed towards reducing the timeliness of the work [151]. In this case, the exponential law determines the distribution density function:

$$f(t) = \frac{1}{m-a} \exp \frac{-(t-a)}{m-a}. \tag{9.10}$$

where m is a parameter that determines the mathematical expectation of a random duration of work.

The resulting exponential distribution has one drawback, namely the lack of a clear upper limit on the possible duration of work, which can be overcome as follows. To do this, take the conditional boundary of the distribution, and take the value of one fourth of the conditional range as mathematical expectation, and then the formula describing the exponential distribution will be transformed into the following expression:

$$f\left(t\right)=\frac{4}{b-a}\,\exp\frac{-4\left(t-a\right)}{b-a}. \tag{9.11}$$

In this representation, the exponential distribution for a given range will ensure the generation of 98% of the "correct" values of random durations of work.

If we assume that the rate of change of the distribution density function is constant, then the corresponding distribution will be defined as a linearly decreasing triangular distribution, which is described by the following formula:

$$f\left(t\right)=\frac{2\left(b-t\right)}{\left(b-a\right)^{2}}. \tag{9.12}$$

If, at all, there is no force to counteract untimely performance of work, then this corresponds to a uniform distribution determined by formula (9.9).

Figure 105 shows all the types of distribution of random work durations described above.

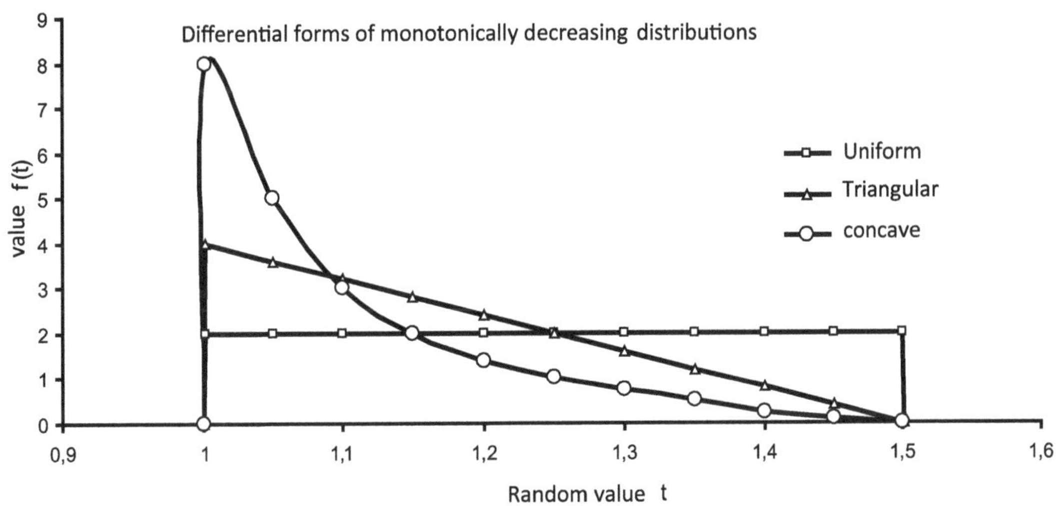

Figure 9.5: Possible monotonically decreasing probability density distribution curves of a random duration of work

Now let us point out a solution to the problem associated with the transition from the uniform distribution of a random variable to the distributions justified above. The transition from a uniform generator producing random numbers in the range from 0 to 1, to GSPR producing a triangular distribution of random work durations that vary in the range from a to b , is carried out according to the following formula:

$$t = a\left[1+\left(\frac{b}{a}-1\right)\left(1-\sqrt{Rnd}\right)\right], \tag{9.13}$$

where Rnd are the values of random numbers in the range from 0 to 1 evenly distributed generator; $b\ /\ a$ — the previously defined (without using statistics) index of the ratio of maximum untimeliness to the planned duration of the work.

For an exponential distribution, a similar formula will have the form

$$t = a - \frac{b-a}{4}\ln\left(Rnd\right). \tag{9.14}$$

Thus, one parameter, for all monotonically decreasing distributions, is determined without the use of statistical data, and the form of the distributions themselves is completely determined by the above statements. Now we turn to the logic of determining the parameter b, which can be interpreted as the pessimistic duration of the work. For its qualitative definition, we consider a model of the so-called spatial-temporal analogy [155].

In the scientific literature related to economic issues, the term "planning horizon" is often used. From a physical point of view, the concept of horizon is related to the distance to an imaginary line that defines the visual convergence of the sky and the surface of the earth. At the same time, the visible sizes of objects as they approach the horizon decrease linearly. A similar effect can be observed in organizational and economic planning, which directly or indirectly takes into account the fact that with increasing time, the degree of uncertainty in the description of the object increases, and its determinism decreases accordingly when approaching the planning horizon.

In economics, bringing future costs and revenues to date is called discounting, and discounting is often interpreted as reducing the value of money over time. However, if the cost of money decreases, then future investment costs also decrease. From this fact with necessity, the conclusion follows about a reduction in payment for the necessary resources. As a result, the less resources are used, the greater will be the increase in the planned duration of work. As a result, if some work determined by the planned duration a starts to be performed at time s, then its pessimistic duration b can be calculated using the following formula:

$$b = a\left(1+E\right)^{s}. \tag{9.15}$$

As can be seen from the presented formula, the pessimistic duration grows as the planned work is removed from the moment the construction begins. However, despite the apparent simplicity of the presented formula, its correct application in scheduling will depend on the topological structure of the calendar schedule, since any recount of it will entail a change in the beginning of work and, as a result, further recount of its pessimistic durations will be required. Thus, the procedure for calculating pessimistic durations will be iterative in nature, and its completion will be associated with the achievement of some predetermined divergence.

9.9.4 Forecast methods based on statistical modeling and a deterministic topology of work

A. Modeling a stochastic calendar chart using the PERT method. De facto, this method is the main method of probabilistic scheduling. It is based on statistical modeling, and as a function describing the distribution of random work durations, the previously described beta distribution is used. The application of this method makes it possible to present the predicted construction duration as a random function.

A feature of the PERT method lies in the possibility of taking into account the probabilistic nature of the durations of all or some of the work when calculating time parameters on a network model. This method allows you to determine the probabilities of the completion of the project in given periods of time and by given dates [148]. Instead of a single determinate duration, three duration estimates are given (usually by expert means) for the project: optimistic (work cannot be completed faster than for t_i^{opt}) ; pessimistic (work cannot be performed more slowly than for t_i^{pess}) and the most probable t_i^{ver}. Then, the probabilistic network model is transformed into a deterministic one by replacing three estimates of the durations of each of the works with one value, called the expected duration t_i^e and calculated as the arithmetic average of three expert estimates of the durations of this work. To characterize the degree of uncertainty in assessing the duration of an individual work, variance is used.

The timing of the work and the duration of the entire project can be calculated on a network model using deterministic methods. However, it becomes possible to determine the "extreme" duration of the project, namely:

1. *optimistic* T^{opt} — the total duration of the entire project under the most favorable conditions. To determine the optimistic duration of the project, it is necessary for all works to take their optimistic estimates as the duration of the work;

2. *pessimistic* T^{pess} — the value of the total duration of the project under the most adverse circumstances. To determine the pessimistic duration of the project, it is necessary for all the work to take their pessimistic estimates as the duration of the work.

The probabilities of completion of the project in terms determined by optimistic or pessimistic values tend to zero. If we substitute the expected durations of each work in a deterministic model, we can get the total duration of the project, the probability of completion of construction by the time determined by it is 50%, i.e. the so-called expected duration of the project.

Instead of a single value of the duration of the construction, the PERT method allows you to get a normal probability distribution of the duration, the mode of which corresponds to the expected duration of the project. To determine the probability of project implementation for a time other than expected, we consider the standard deviation (standard deviation) of the normal distribution curve, which reflects the degree of uncertainty in estimating the duration of the entire project.

B. The method of regression forecasting the completion of construction. The results of a statistical experiment make it possible to link the forecast of the total duration of the construction with indicators that evaluate the untimely performance of individual works. In this case, the processing of the results of a statistical experiment is carried out using the apparatus of multiple regression analysis. Thus, at first glance, it seems that using a combination of statistical test methods and multiple regression analysis, you can get a significant advantage over the integrated methods for predicting completion of construction, based on extrapolating the volume of work performed. However, upon closer examination, the application of the proposed combination may be limited by the presence of a nonlinear relationship between the total duration and duration of individual works, as well as the influence of dynamic changes in the structure of works that determine the composition of variables.

It is known that the method of multiple regression analysis is focused primarily on the regression description of linear models. If the model is non-linear, then the corresponding non-linear form must be known a priori (i.e. in advance) and then the regression model can be artificially reduced to a linear form, or a specific non-linear regression algorithm must be developed for it. In any case, to solve nonlinear problems, preliminary information on the form of the nonlinear connection of the desired function with its arguments is required. Due to its rather wide variety, scheduling does not have such information a priori. At the same time, the predictive efficiency of the multiple regression apparatus is that the regression equation is relevant only when it is transferred to a similar object that functions under similar conditions. Thus, a purely formal application of the combination of the method of statistical tests and multiple regression analysis allows us to obtain the desired forecast for the duration of the construction, but it is extremely difficult to determine the error of such a forecast.

C. Method of neural network modeling. Let us consider the possibility of solving the problem of predicting completion of construction based on the use of a neural network modeling apparatus, which makes it possible to form a nonlinear predictive model based on the training procedure [89]. Numerous neural networks are based on the mathematical image of a formal neuron, the scheme of which is shown in Figure 9.6.

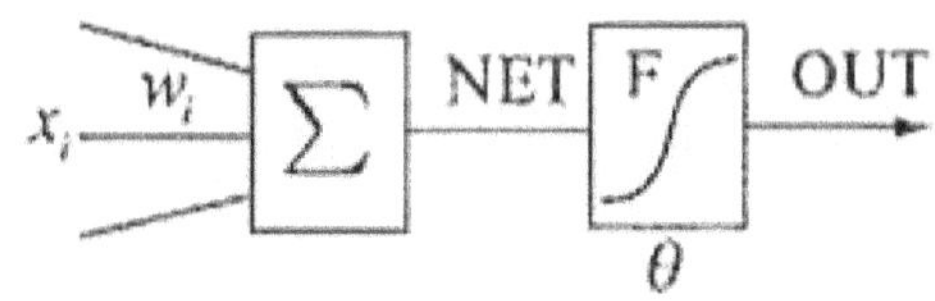

Figure 9.6: Scheme of the formal neuron.

The inputs of the formal neuron, which are called dendrites, are given signals x_i, which in the biological neural network come from adjacent axons (outputs of adjacent neurons). The contact points between adjacent axons and dendrites leading to the cell adder are called synapses in a biological neural network. The function of the synapses is to form the weight w_i for each input signal. Next in the diagram is the *NET* cell adder, which integrates the weighted signals according to the following formula:

$$NET = \sum w_i x_i. \tag{9.16}$$

The adder is followed by a nonlinear element that defines the nonlinear signal conversion function *Y (NET)* . Most often, the so-called sigmoid (Fermi function), which has the form:

$$Y = \frac{1}{1 + Exp\,(-NET)\,.} \tag{9.17}$$

Suppose that 4 values of the indices of untimely performance of work, measured on a certain date, and defined by the letters x_i, are supplied to the 4 inputs of the formal neuron. The weights of these inputs, denoted as w_i, are initially defined as random numbers uniformly distributed in the range from -0.5 to $+0.5$. The output of the system is connected with the input characteristics by the formula (9.17). Because of the adopted model, the functional relationship between the output and the inputs will have the following non-linear representation:

$$Y = \frac{1}{1 + Exp(-w_1x_1 - w_2x_2 - w_3x_3 - w_4x_4)}. \tag{9.18}$$

The solution to the problem of finding the set of weights w_i occurs in the training mode on a priori set sample size values that determine the delay in the completion of construction. An iterative procedure using a statistical image begins with the determination of an output error. The resulting error serves as the basis for the adjustment of weights, which is performed according to the inverse error distribution algorithm.

The presented method is implemented in the widely used computer program “Statistica”. However, to solve the problem of forecasting the duration of construction in this program, a certain adaptation is required. In particular, to obtain the forecast result, it will be necessary to determine the configuration of the neural network, the number of its layers, the number of neurons in each layer, the volume of the training sample, and the speed of adjustment of weights. Therefore, it can be argued that until the listed characteristics are reliably substantiated, the forecast value cannot be calculated. However, even if all specified characteristics are determined, it is also difficult to justify the forecast error for the neural network simulation method [59].

Thus, we can conclude that each of the considered methods for predicting completion of construction has its own advantages and disadvantages, as well as the field of optimal application, determined by the specifics of the information support of the problem being solved.

Questions for self-control

1. What is CALS technology? In connection with what did they arise?
2. What is BIM technology? What is the meaning of the concept of BIM?
3. What changes in the order of information exchange does the presence of a common data environment make?
4. What factors determine the composition of the information model of a construction project?
5. What are the levels of elaboration of the elements of the LOD model?
6. What is interoperability, what opportunities does it provide for information modeling?
7. What is information model validation?

8. Is it possible to accept the calculations of the supporting structures carried out in the Revit-2018 program as final design decisions?
9. Is it possible to accept the thermal engineering calculations of enclosing structures carried out in the Revit-2018 program as final design decisions?
10. By what means is the interface of programs that implement BIM technologies provided with other similar programs and with programs for other functional purposes?
11. Is it possible using the index method to quantify the delay time of completion of construction?
12. What is the main advantage of the method of non-linear extrapolation of the volume of work performed over its linear counterpart?
13. Describe the analogy of the process of transformation of thermal energy into mechanical work and the process of transformation of "managerial" energy into useful and timely work on the construction of the facility.
14. With the help of which apparatus can the influence of certain types of failures of the construction system on the timeliness of construction be established? 15. What are the statistical characteristics of the work used in the PERT method?
15. Explain the main advantage of using two-parameter density functions for the distribution of random work durations when comparing them with multiparameter analogs.
16. What is the limited use of regression analysis in predicting construction time?
17. What characteristics of a neural network do you need to know in order to use the Statistica program for appropriate simulation?
18. What is the technical and economic effect of timely and accurate prediction of completion of construction?

Questions for discussion

1. What is the difficulty of applying information technology in construction?
2. Are there any fundamental differences between BIM technology and ND design?
3. How does the technology for working with a building object change with a common information model?

4. To discuss the possibilities and prospects for the widespread implementation of the software potential of Russian developments in the field of BIM-technologies and CAD-technologies.
5. Discuss the possibility of implementing methods aimed at predicting the construction period, implemented in project management programs.
6. To assess the prospects and possibilities of introducing the methods of forecasting the terms in the practice of organizations that monitor the progress of construction.
7. What may be specific features when using various methods for predicting the timing of construction and in relation to the tasks of forecasting the timing of individual work.

Questions to solve the problem yourself

1. Formulate the tasks that can be solved on the basis of the information model of the life cycle of a construction object. Are there differences in solving these problems at different stages of the life cycle?
2. Suggest possible directions for organizing interaction between information models of individual buildings and structures.
3. Describe how you imagine the place of information technology in the construction industry in the overall system of the Digital Economy of Russia.
4. Conduct a study of scheduling principles embedded in Autodesk Navisworks Simulate and Autodesk Navisworks Manage.
5. To conduct a study of the principles of calculating energy consumption laid down in the Revit-2018 program and the cloud-based calculation program located at insight360.autodesk.com.
6. How to solve the problems of statistical modeling in the Open Plan project management program.
7. How the PERT method is implemented in the Microsoft project management program Project
8. What information tools are used to record the actual performance of work in the Microsoft Project project management program.
9. What information tools account for the actual performance of work in the Project Expert project management program.

Chapter 10

ORGANIZATION OF CONSTRUCTION OF UNIQUE OBJECTS. THE EFFECTIVENESS OF TERRITORIAL CONCENTRATION AND THE SPECIALIZATION OF INDUSTRIAL CONSTRUCTION

10.1 The main features of the organization of construction of unique objects

One of the most important areas of construction is the development of modern technologies and methods of construction of buildings and structures of increased complexity. These include such unique objects as high-rise and super-tall buildings, underground structures, large-span buildings and structures, as well as energy facilities, nuclear and thermal power plants and hydraulic structures. These structures, in their importance and complexity, relate to objects of a high degree of responsibility and risk.

Each type of unique structure has its own peculiarities in terms of design schemes, calculation methods, labor costs, volumes of financial resources and material and technical resources, organizational, technological and managerial decisions.

Unique buildings and structures, as a rule, have a long life cycle, they are characterized by common approaches to their design, construction, and subsequent operation of construction at all stages of the life cycle. Common to all facilities are the requirements for integrated security. The term "integrated security" means the state of the facility in which the prevention and elimination of all types of hazards that may arise during the construction and operation of a particularly complex facility is ensured.

This concept includes the provision of such types of safety as mechanical, explosion and fire safety, environmental safety, earthquake resistance, safety in emergencies. Besides, chemical and radiation safety, safety under combined effects are important.

High-rise (over 26 floors) and super-tall (over 100 meters high) buildings stand in a special place among unique objects. This is primarily because their functional purpose is directly related to human life. Whether it is residential, office or multi-purpose buildings, they must be even more stringent requirements in terms of creating a comfortable and safe environment inside the building and minimize negative impact on the external environment.

The formation of a comfortable and safe internal environment of a unique building is a complcx and multi-component task. This applies to systems such as:

- installation of the building frame and ensuring its stability and mechanical safety at all stages of construction and operation, which is achieved by appropriate calculation methods and installation technologies;
- engineering support systems (energy supply, water supply, drainage, heat supply, ventilation, air conditioning), which are based on the most modern engineering equipment;
- vertical transport systems, elevator facilities, which differ from the elevator equipment of buildings of standard number of storeys in view of the significant amplitudes of vibrations of the building frame under the influence of wind loads and self-oscillations;
- fire extinguishing systems, the peculiarity and complexity of which is that the fire cannot be eliminated using traditional equipment, but fundamentally different fire extinguishing methods (helicopters, airships, internal fire extinguishing systems) are required;
- waste disposal systems, windows and facades maintenance, internal security systems (zoning, access restriction, fencing, rescue equipment, etc.);
- systems providing a comfortable microclimate (sun protection, green areas, plants, interiors, etc.).

All these systems, arranged in one building, form a complex engineering infrastructure, which should organically fit into a single building structure, and be linked to the architectural concept and the organizational and technological process of its construction.

One of the main structural elements of the unique building is its *underground part*. The building itself is a complex geotechnical object, erected in urban areas. As a rule, the underground part is multi-tiered structures, at the base of which there is a monolithic slab that can absorb loads from the entire building. Not all soils can carry a huge load from a high-rise building, therefore, to establish the design parameters of the foundation, it is necessary to conduct high-quality engineering surveys, which is the most important condition for ensuring its comprehensive safety.

The choice of material for load-bearing structures is one of the most important tasks in the construction of unique buildings. In the USA, where, in particular, high-rise construction has a wide scope and a long history until the end of the seventies of the twentieth century, high-rise buildings mainly used steel supporting structures. However, over the past 30 years, concrete has begun to displace metal. The use of concrete in high-rise construction has several advantages, such as a better perception of wind loads, lower deformability of buildings with a reinforced concrete frame, a higher fire resistance, and the ability to give the building almost any architectural form.

With the development of the construction of unique buildings, more and more advanced concrete compositions and technologies for their preparation, modern types of formwork systems and mechanization equipment were required. All these requirements led in the seventies of the twentieth century to a revolutionary breakthrough in concrete technology. Starting from this period in high-rise construction, the time has come for modified concrete, which made it possible to control their technological properties, such as mobility, preservation of the normative requirements of concrete mix, elimination of shrinkage, and ensuring the necessary strength at a given time.

The construction and operation of a unique building requires a huge amount of energy capacity, so the topic of energy conservation and energy efficiency is very relevant here. In this regard, the concept of "green" buildings, "green" technologies, "green" standards in construction activities comes to the fore. Fears that the use of "green" standards greatly increases the cost of building a high-rise building are unfounded. So according to British experts who are the creators of the rating system (BREEAM), the cost is from 2 to 4% of the cost of the entire construction, and the return on green investments is achieved within 2-4 years. When calculating the entire life cycle of a building, these costs are not significant.

The birthplace of high-rise construction is considered the United States, where the first buildings of high floors began to be built at the end of the XIX century. A powerful impetus for the construction of high-rise buildings was the appearance of a passenger elevator, authored by engineer Elisha Graze Otis, who received a patent for the invention in 1857. Of great importance in the formation of methods of high-rise construction was the development of building materials, structures and technologies. The desire for the construction of high-rise buildings, with a height of 400 - 500 and more meters, stimulated the development of new architectural forms, structural, organizational, and technological solutions.

In the twentieth century, high-rise construction became widespread. Many countries considered it their duty to build such a building that would exceed its height erected earlier. Skyscrapers erected in countries such as: Dubai, Canada, Malaysia, China, South Korea and others are widely known. In essence, the construction of high-rise buildings has become a demonstration of the level of technological development of construction in a given period of time.

In Russia, the experience in building high-rise buildings and structures is relatively small. The most striking example is the construction of the Ostankino television tower in Moscow. This structure, with a height of 540 meters, was designed and built in 1964. An outstanding engineer Nikitin N.V. led the team of designers and constructors. The Ostankino tower underwent very serious tests during a fire in 2000, but withstood them flawlessly, confirming compliance with the requirements of integrated security.

For a long time, the palm of the championship was held by a complex of buildings (240 meters high) of Moscow State University named after M.V. Lomonosov on the Vorobiyevy Gory. However, in the early 2000s, a whole micro district of high-rise buildings, called Moscow City, began to be built in Moscow. To date, more than 10 buildings of bizarre architecture and a height of over 300 meters have been built. In total, more than 120 buildings with a height of more than 100 meters have been built and are under construction in Moscow. This is a very serious domestic experience in the construction of high-rise buildings, which indicates the demand for such objects. In recent years, construction has begun in several cities in Russia or projects are being developed for high-rise and super-tall buildings.

The requirements and approaches outlined above are also characteristic of other types of unique buildings and structures, primarily for large-span and special buildings and structures. Recently, a large number of unique objects have been built in Russia. In Moscow alone, more than 600 buildings with large-span structures and dozens of multifunctional high-rise complexes are operated.

Safety control of such buildings and structures is provided for by the Federal Law of the Russian Federation No. 384-FZ dated December 30, 2009, "Technical Regulation on the Safety of Buildings and Structures". These structures are characterized by spans of 100-150 meters, huge building volumes (up to 300 thousand meters), and at the same time accommodating a large number of people (up to 100 thousand people). The formation of a comprehensive security system for unique objects comes to the fore in connection with the collapse of load-bearing structures that have occurred in the last decade both in our country and abroad and resulting in fatalities.

Examples include: collapsing the dome cover of the Transvaal Park building (Moscow, 2004), covering the Dolphin pool (Chusovoy, Perm Territory, 2005), covering the terminal at Paris Roissy Charles de Gaulle Airport (2005), coverings of the Basmanny market (Moscow, 2006), coverings for the ice rink in Bad Reichenhall in Germany (2006), coverings for the sports complex in Blagoveshchensk (2009), coverings for the Metrodom stadium in Minneapolis USA (2010), coverage of a sports complex in the Vyborg district of St. Petersburg (2011), etc.

One of the important conditions for ensuring the integrated safety of the requirements for the construction of unique buildings and structures is the *formation of a monitoring system throughout the entire process of their construction and operation.* Monitoring includes the registration of stresses in the bearing elements of support structures, coating farms, foundation deposits, both the structure itself and neighboring buildings.

This system is based on a methodology for monitoring mechanical safety, which provides early diagnostics of load-bearing structures based on recording changes in their integral parameters; automation of structural condition monitoring with universal measuring systems.

The measuring elements of these complexes use various sensors (dynamic, fiber optic, string, temperature-humidity, acoustic, etc.) to obtain the necessary information. They are installed on thc supporting structure of the building in accordance with the features of its structural scheme and allow real-time recording of rolls, accelerations, natural vibration frequencies, deformations, material defects, spatial movement of the structure, etc.

When implementing projects for the construction of unique buildings and structures, according to experts, it is necessary to solve four problems, the so-called "four C" approach. These are four terms; clients, codes, consultants, contractors. That is, the project will then be *successful* if there are no problems with *customers* (customers), *codes* (rules and regulations), *consultants and contractors.*

Among these four problems, the issue of security with regulatory and technical documentation occupies a special place. Currently, in domestic construction issues of technical regulation, including for unique facilities, are very acute. Many positions of legal and regulatory support are closed by special technical conditions, which are often temporary. This problem requires constant attention and solution.

Another important direction in recent years in the construction of unique objects is the practice of the widespread use of information systems and modeling methods in the design of unique buildings and structures. The combination in a single system of databases and methods for the development and adoption of architectural, space planning, organizational and technological, design, managerial, resource and economic decisions led to the creation of a powerful software package, which was called "BIM-technology" (see chapter 9 part I).

This is facilitated by the rapid, one might say explosive, development of the information sphere, visualization methods, the speed of computer technology, computer modeling. Today they are talking not about 3D models, but about 5-6 D virtual objects.

In addition to three dimensions, the modeling process includes a wider range of parameters, factors, relationships, such as time parameters, cost parameters, construction time, construction site conditions and others, creating new virtual levels of models.

An important milestone in the development of the theory of modeling complex technical and building systems was the formation of an object's life cycle methodology, when not only the parameters related to the design and construction phase of an object, but also such an important stage as the period of operation of a building or structure are included in the model creation process. This approach allows you to see how the condition of the object changes over the entire service life, including periods of repair, modernization, up to its liquidation.

The presence of engineering personnel who own modern methods of designing, erecting, making organizational, technological and managerial decisions is the most important condition for the development of the theory and practice of construction, unique buildings and structures, ensuring their safety and effectiveness.

This textbook sets out the basics of building technology for the construction of unique structures.

The above features of the construction and operation of these buildings are also considered in other academic disciplines. A person who has mastered the design, construction and operation of unique buildings and structures is certainly a specialist in the construction of the highest qualifications.

10.2 Classification of industrial, civil and residential buildings by design solutions and features of the technology of construction and installation works

The gradation of buildings and structures by complexity classes is provided in order to determine the levels of complexity of work in the design and construction.

The basis for making decisions on assigning objects to complexity classes is their technical characteristics (height, volume, area, capacity, length, etc.).

Additional criteria may be the functional purpose of the main buildings and structures of the construction object, taking into account their technical and economic characteristics, the predicted economic, social and (or) environmental consequences in the event of an accident. *Classes of complexity of buildings and structures:*

1. *Objects of the first complexity class (K-1)*

- High-rise buildings (all buildings and structures above 75 m are considered high-rise, regardless of their purpose);
- Large-span buildings and structures with spans of 100 m or more;
- Industrial buildings and structures with an area of over 20,000 m^2 and their complexes (plants, factories, combines);
- Production facilities that use, store and transport explosive and explosive products, highly toxic and potent toxic substances;
- Monumental structures (monuments, obelisks, etc.) included in the established order in the State list of historical and cultural values of the Russian Federation;
- Objects included in the established order in the State list of historical and cultural values of the Russian Federation;
- Buildings and structures of nuclear energy and industry;
- Buildings and structures of thermal power with a capacity of 5 MW and above;
- Subways;
- Aerodromes and the main buildings and structures of airports;
- Railways and railway transport enterprises (stations, passenger pavilions, station structures) on lines of category I;
- Masts, towers, etc. height of 100 m or more;
- Chimneys with a height of more than 200 m;
- Permanent main hydraulic structures of I, II and III classes and their complexes (with the exception of reclamation hydraulic structures);
- Tanks of oil, oil products and liquefied gas with a capacity of 10,000 m or more;
- Underground storage of oil, oil products and gas;
- Main pipelines of oil, gas and oil products;
- High pressure pipelines;
- Large bridges (according to TKP 45-3.03-232);
- Power lines with voltage of 330 kV and higher;

- The main industrial buildings of substations with a voltage of 500 kV and higher;
- Supports and foundations of special crossings of overhead power lines with a height of 100 m and above through engineering structures and navigable rivers;
- Trunk engineering networks and underground utilities for various purposes.

2. *Objects of the second complexity class (K-2)*

- High-rise buildings (30 m or more high);
- Industrial buildings and structures ranging from 10,000 to 20,000 m;
- Enterprises, buildings and structures for the storage and processing of grain;
- Agricultural enterprises:
  - livestock complexes (for the production of milk for 800 or more cows, beef — for 6 thousand or more cattle places);
  - pig breeding — 54 thousand or more pigs per year;
  - poultry farming (according to the content of laying hens — 50 thousand or more heads; for meat production — 412.5 tons or more).
- Tunnels;
- Middle bridges;
- Chimneys with a height of 200 m or less;
- The main buildings and structures of substations with a voltage of 35-220 kV;
- Power lines with a voltage of 6-220 kV;
- Wind and solar power plants;
- Highways of category I and structures on them.

3. *Objects of the third complexity class (K-3)*

- Buildings and structures for various purposes with a height of up to 30 m (not related to classes K-1 and K-2);
- Agricultural enterprises:
  - livestock complexes (for the production of milk up to 800 cows; beef — up to 6 thousand cattle places);
  - pig breeding — up to 54 thousand pigs per year;
  - poultry farming (according to the content of laying hens — up to 50 thousand heads; for meat production — up to 412.5 tons);
  - greenhouse plants and greenhouses with an area of over 12 hectares;
- Distribution networks of underground communications for various purposes.

4. *Objects of the fourth complexity class (K-4)*

- Buildings and structures for various purposes with a height of up to 15 m (not related to the class K-1, K-2 and K-3);
- Greenhouse plants with an area of 1 ha or more;
- Open areas and parking for cars (in the amount of 100 cars or more).

5. *Objects of the fifth complexity class (K-5)*

- Buildings and structures for various purposes up to 7 m high (not related to the class K-1, K-2, K-3 and K-4);
- Temporary buildings and structures;
- Greenhouses up to 1 ha;
- Seasonal and auxiliary facilities (awnings, fences, etc.);
- Commercial seasonal and auxiliary facilities using pavilions, complete factory-made stalls with a trading area of up to 50 m^2;
- Mobile buildings (inventory) (in accordance with GOST 25957);
- Garden houses, farm buildings on household plots, gardens and summer cottages;
- Temporary power and communication lines (including pylons for power lines, communications and outdoor lighting);
- Objects of the agro-industrial complex — stand-alone facilities for utility and auxiliary purposes;
- One-story basement box-type garages with departures directly to the outside (in the amount of up to 100 cars);
- Open areas and parking for cars (in the amount of up to 100 cars);
- Warehouses without sorting and packaging processes up to 200 m^2
- Objects of agro ecotourism of 1 and 2 categories;

Note — The height of buildings is defined as the excess of the floor mark of the upper floor (with the exception of the technical one) over the passage closest to the building.

Engineering networks and systems are an integral part of the design documentation for the construction of buildings and structures specified in the recommendations.

All facilities under construction, regardless of their design features and purpose, by the complexity of the technology of their construction are divided into three groups: simple, complex and especially complex.

For *a simple* attribute objects, performed mainly of typical building structures and materials, built upon the simple technology, does not require them to build a large number of workers, a significant alignment in time of construction and installation works.

By the *complex* include objects made mainly of standard building materials and standard designs, but for large volumes, complex technology and organization of construction and commissioning, requires the involvement of a large number of workers of different specialties and hearty combination of the time of construction and installation works.

Particularly difficult are objects made mainly of atypical structures, complex in construction technology, requiring special equipment, and special materials, attracting a large number of workers, significant specialization and tight combination of construction and installation works in time.

According to their purpose, design features and technological methods of erecting buildings and structures of various nature can be classified as follows:

1. *Complex and especially complex objects,* including special structures and buildings for placement of the main technological process and equipment in them.

   Such complexes and buildings include blast furnace and steelmaking facilities, rolling mills, concentration and sintering plants, coke oven batteries, chemical synthesis plants, etc.

   The basis of their construction technology is the combined large-block installation of enlarged building structures and equipment, with the assembly of enlarged blocks at the picking bases, on-site enlargement sites and conveyor lines. The construction of complex facilities, as a rule, is organized by the nodal method.

2. *Ground facilities for the storage of products, raw materials, waste.* Engineering structures functionally related to the main technological process.

   To engineering structures of this kind, include pedestals, whatnots, galleries, bridges, etc.

   The most commonly used technological methods of their construction — combined tiered installation of load-bearing structures and large-sized equipment, whatnots; separate installation of columns and combined — bridge structures and equipment installed on them.

3. *Tanks, gas tanks, silos, bunker racks,* etc.

   The most often used are such technological methods of their construction as rolled of metal sheet structures, erection of reinforced concrete silos in a special (sliding, moving) formwork; combined large-block installation of enlarged structures (bunker racks).

4. *Buried in the ground structures.* These include pumping stations, reservoirs, treatment facilities, etc.

The most commonly used techniques are installation in an open foundation pit with natural, engineering-equipped steeply inclined or vertical slopes; construction by methods of a lowering well or "wall in the ground".

5. *Large-span single-story industrial and public buildings.* These include pavilion-type workshops (with large spans and column spacing), hangars, sports arenas, garages, markets, etc.

   The most commonly used technological methods for erecting building coatings are thrust, knurling of enlarged structural building blocks of the coating, assembly of coatings from enlarged sections, based on temporary supports; installation of fully assembled at zero level spatial blocks. Structural, membrane, hanging, cable-stayed, cable-stayed, domed and other spatial structures effective for large spans are used.

6. *High-rise engineering (metal and reinforced concrete) structures.* These include exhaust and chimneys, radio and television masts, cooling towers, etc.

   The most commonly used technological methods for the construction of monolithic reinforced concrete structures of this kind, such as concreting in a special (sliding, moving) formwork; installation of metal structures of masts by the method of building and growing. Use self-elevating cranes.

7. *High-rise prefabricated frame, frame-panel and panel residential and civil buildings* from metal, reinforced concrete and mixed structures.

   The most commonly used structural frame systems such as bond and frame-link with a different arrangement of vertical links — stiffness diaphragms. Girder-free overlap are used, including compressed ones by preliminary cross-tensioning of reinforcement.

   Installation of load-bearing and enclosing elements is carried out using reclining and self-elevating tower cranes.

8. *Monolithic panel and frame buildings with a wide step of bearing vertical elements, continuous beam and beam-free monolithic and precast-monolithic ceilings.*

   Most often, they use the technology of their construction using progressive types of collapsible small-panel and large-panel formwork, fixed formwork, and effective supporting structures. For floor supply of concrete, concrete pumps are used.

9. *Low-rise residential buildings of cottage type.*

   The most commonly used are prefabricated, precast-monolithic and monolithic solutions of supporting and enclosing structures using effective types of formwork. Apply fixed formwork made of expanded polystyrene of increased strength and heat resistance.

As you can see, the variety of structural solutions of buildings and structures creates the need for the development and use of a wide range of construction technologies. It is known that the leading element of any technology is the construction process. The basics of technology and practice of building processes are studied in the course "Technology of building processes."

The composition and structure of construction technologies used in the construction of simple objects are considered in the discipline "Technology of construction of buildings and structures." Both courses are based on knowledge of building materials and products, structural systems of buildings and structures, construction machinery, labor protection and safety. Inextricably linked with these courses, the courses "Organization of construction production" and "Organization of construction" are studied. For its successful study, knowledge of the fundamentals of the technology of construction processes, methods of building civil and industrial buildings is required.

10.3 Technological design

10.3.1 Organizational and technological documentation during construction unique objects

The composition of the construction and technological documentation for objects belonging to the 1st and 2nd category of complexity should include:

- a project for the organization of construction for the preparatory period;
- a project for the organization of construction for the main period;
- a project of work for the preparatory period as a whole for the facility;
- a project of work for the main period as a whole on the facility;
- a projects for the production of work for certain types of work, namely:
- a project for the production of works to reduce and remove atmospheric moisture;
- a project for the construction of temporary roads (during the construction of a complex of buildings);
- a project for the production of geodetic works;
- a project for the dismantling (relocation) of existing buildings;
- a project for the construction of temporary fencing of a construction site;
- a project for the installation of the security system of the construction site;
- a project for the construction of external water supply networks;
- a project for the construction of external heat supply networks;
- a project for the construction of external drainage networks;

- a project for the construction of an external telephone network;
- a project for the construction of external security networks;
- a project of works for laying external power supply networks;
- a project of works on the device and dismantling of the foundation pit fence;
- a project to strengthen the base (if this type is available) works);
- excavation project (including backfilling of the pit);
- a project for the production of piling works (with the installation of pile and pile foundation);
- a project for concreting foundation slabs (when installing slab and pile-slab foundations);
- a project for the construction of the underground part of the building;
- a project for the production of waterproofing works;
- a project for the installation of construction material handling equipment;
- a project for the construction of load-bearing structures of the aboveground part of the building;
- a project of works on the installation of building envelopes;
- a project for the construction and dismantling of scaffolding (in cases of scaffolding)
- a project for the installation of glazing structures;
- a project for the installation of elevators;
- a project for the installation of internal heating systems;
- a project for the installation of internal water supply systems;
- a project of works for the installation of internal drainage systems;
- a project for the installation of internal ventilation systems;
- a project for the installation of internal air conditioning systems; project for the installation of internal fire water supply systems;
- a project for the installation of internal power supply networks
- a project for the installation of internal fire safety systems
- a project for the installation of internal broadcasting systems;
- a project for the installation of internal telecommunication systems;
- a project for the installation of internal monitoring systems;
- a project of finishing work;
- a project for the installation of helipad structures;
- a project of works on the construction of permanent roads;
- a project for the production of storm sewer;

- a project for the construction of ground landing helipads;
- a project for the improvement of territories;
- sets of projects for the construction of related facilities (if any are provided for by design decisions).

Construction projects are being developed at the stage of a feasibility study (TEO), based on the materials of the preliminary design. Designing is carried out by a leading design organization, or a specialized organization certified for the right to develop PIC for unique objects (categories 1 and 2). The composition of the construction organization project is governed by the requirements of SP 48.13330.2011.

At the feasibility study stage, the following are being developed:

- general provisions justifying the possibility of building an object;
- complex integrated network or line schedule for the construction of plexus;
- basic organizational and technological schemes of construction;
- list of existing equipment for the performance of work;
- justification of the need to develop non-standard equipment and new methods of production.

In the future, during the development of the architectural and construction part of the project, it is necessary to coordinate the adopted space-planning and structural decisions with the requirements of the organization and technology of construction production.

The construction organization project for the main construction period includes:

- general provisions justifying the possibility of building an object;
- measures to ensure during the construction process the strength and stability of the constructed and existing buildings and structures;
- integrated enlarged network schedule or schedule;
- organizational and technological schemes of the construction of the facility;
- construction master plans for the main construction period, as well as, if necessary, a situational construction plan;
- statements of volumes of work and requirements for materials; a schedule of the need for workforce;
- decisions on labor protection, environmental and fire safety, as well as management organization;
- instructions on the procedure for constructing a geodetic layout basis for the construction and organization of a permanent geodetic group;

- programs of necessary research, testing and operational observations, including the organization of stations, polygons, measuring posts and (for complex and unique objects, such as high-rise buildings and complexes);
- a list of works and structures whose quality indicators affect the safety of the facility and during construction are subject to assessment of compliance with the requirements of regulatory documents and standards, which are the evidence base for compliance with technical regulations;
- decisions on the organization of transport, water supply, sewage, energy supply, communications, decisions on the erection of structures, the implementation of construction in difficult climatic conditions, as well as cramped conditions;
- measures to temporarily restrict traffic, change transport routes;
- the procedure and conditions for the use and restoration of territories located outside the land plot owned by the developer (customer);
- working drawings of specialized equipment and accessories, technological maps of their use;
- explanatory note.

The project of works (PW) is a further detailing of the organizational and technological solutions developed in the POC. The starting materials for the development of PW are a working draft, POC.

Given the complexity and uniqueness of high-rise construction objects, it is necessary to develop PW as a whole for the object, and for the construction of its individual nodes and for the execution of certain types of work.

The project of works (PW) for the construction of a high-rise building and complex should be drawn up by the contracting organization carrying out the construction, or by a specialized design organization with a certificate of conformity, design approval of the State Architectural and Construction Supervision Inspectorate (IGASN) and will be further agreed with the customer.

The project for the production of works at the facility is developed separately for the preparatory and main periods of construction.

The composition of the project work for the main period of construction:

- work schedule (integrated network schedule);
- construction master plans for the preparatory and main periods of construction;
- material demand schedules;
- a schedule of the need for workers and basic construction machines; technological maps;

- measures to control the quality of work (specified in the composition of the PPR for certain types of work);
- safety measures and environmental safety;
- decisions on the production of geodetic works; solutions for the deployment of temporary networks; explanatory note.

10.3.2 Organizational principles for the construction of high-rise buildings

Construction organization methods are determined depending on the type and degree of complexity of construction objects and complexes.

On complex objects and complexes, the question of construction organization methods is solved in each specific case depending on the quantity, uniformity and volume of work of specialized construction processes, technological interconnection of processes in the overall complex of works, the possibility of identifying captures that are the same or similar in volume of work and other organizational conditions. In this case, a combination of separate and continuous methods of organizing work is possible.

When assessing the organization of the process of erecting high-rise buildings, it is necessary to determine the area of rational decisions in terms of the sequence and methods of erecting buildings (complexes). Consideration of organizational principles includes:

- issues of spatial division of a building or complex into tiers, captures and sections;
- direction and sequence of deployment of works on the erection of buildings in tiers, grips and sections;
- characteristics of the basic methods of construction of objects.

The initial data for the development and selection of organization and construction schemes are:

- design solutions for the building (complex);
- analysis of the experience in implementing organizational decisions in the construction of domestic and foreign analogous facilities;
- information on the material and technical potential of organizations involved in the construction.

When developing organizational schemes, it is necessary to proceed from the possibility of using effective methods of building construction that ensure the required quality and safety of construction, as well as the possibility of realizing the set pace and timing of construction, which are most fully realized with the in-line construction method.

During the construction of high-rise buildings and complexes, a complex flow is organized, covering the whole range of construction and installation works: engineering communications of the hotel blocks of the building (complex) with their breakdown into the device of the foundations, underground and aboveground parts of the building, landscaping and landscaping.

When forming the structure of a complex flow for development, one should take into account the composition of the complex, the purpose of buildings and structures and their structural and space-planning decisions, the composition of the preparatory work and their characteristics, characteristics of the building implementing organizations (specialization, capacity, equipment) and other factors.

The number and list of object flows planned as part of the complex depends on the purpose, composition and size of the complex under construction, architectural and design characteristics of the objects included in its composition and other specific conditions. Technologically homogeneous objects are grouped into *object streams.* During the construction of housing and civil complexes, it is advisable to organize object streams for on-site and off-site communications separately by type; the construction of the main buildings; construction of auxiliary buildings; improvement and gardening.

With the aim of organizing the preparation of continuous construction, ensuring timely engineering training, commissioning of finished facilities for start-up complexes, and the correct sequence of construction, the time allotted for construction is divided into two periods: preparatory and main.

In the *preparatory period,* the following work:

- engineering preparation of the construction site with the development of the site — geodetic breakdown, drainage of the territory, demolition of buildings, liquidation or re-installation of existing communications, etc.;
- arrangement of access roads to the construction site, construction of construction facilities, including administrative and sanitary buildings, temporary warehouses, permanent structures used for temporary construction needs, temporary driveways and roads at the site, temporary water supply, energy supply and drainage networks (in cases when permanent networks cannot be laid);
- supply of the main lines of engineering networks and the laying of part of intra-quarter underground utilities and roads in order to use them for the needs of construction, minimizing the costs of temporary networks and roads and creating the necessary lead in these works in relation to the construction

of main buildings. At the same time, intra-quarter engineering structures should be erected: transformer substations, heating units, etc.

The work of the *main period* begins, as a rule, after the completion of preparatory work. In the main period of construction, underground and aboveground parts of the main and auxiliary buildings are being constructed, engineering equipment is being completed, landscaping and landscaping are being carried out, and ready-made facilities of the complex are being commissioned.

To *organize the construction flow, a* building (complex) is divided into vertical tiers and grips (sections) horizontally and vertically, which can be the same and different in size and scope of work.

The sizes and boundaries of the tiers and sections are established from the conditions of planning and constructive decisions, taking into account the requirements for ensuring spatial rigidity and stability of the erected parts of the structure (at individual sites), the possibility of temporary interruption and subsequent resumption of work at the boundaries of the sections, and the possibility of commissioning individual complex facilities.

The size and number of captures can (and will) vary depending on the type of work performed, while the location of the borders of the captures should allow stopping and resuming work without compromising the quality of both the structures and the work itself. When assigning sizes and number of grips, it should also be possible to perform various processes on adjacent grips.

Technical and economic indicators included in the explanatory note may include the following data: total construction duration, including the preparatory period and the installation period of the equipment; maximum number of employees; labor costs for construction and installation works.

Technical and economic indicators are determined by the integrated standards and they may contain the total complexity of the construction of the building; machine time costs; estimated cost.

10.3.3 The procedure for the development, coordination and approval of particularly complex work projects

The General Contractor is responsible for the development of the PW OC. In some cases, the Developer (or Technical Customer) may appoint the General Designer responsible for the development of some **particularly complex work projects** (OC PW) according to the list agreed upon with the General Contractor and the General Designer.

The person responsible for the development of the PW OC can conclude an agreement with a specialized organization for the development of the PW OC. In this case, the organization, the client of the PW is obliged to timely transfer to the developer of the OS of the PW the task with the necessary initial data and to ensure the consideration, coordination and approval of the OC of the PW. When developing OC PPR, incl. specialized organization, subcontracting construction and installation organizations are required to provide the information necessary for the development of OC PW at the request of the General Designer or General Contractor.

The procedures for the development, approval and approval of OC PW are specified in the contracts of construction participants. The general process of development, coordination and approval of OC PW.

10.4 Efficiency of concentration and specialization of single-industry industrial production

The more rapid development of Siberia and the eastern regions of the country needs scientific advice on the rational use of regional factors. The need for a comprehensive review of the influence of various factors on improving the efficiency of industrial production in the region is an urgent task to improve the economic mechanism in the field of combining industry and territorial planning and management, taking into account the application of the theory and practice of deepening the processes of concentration and specialization of industrial production in the regional aspect in relation to the functioning of special economic zones (SEZ) industrial orientation, areas of territorial development (ATD) and territories of leading social economic development (TLSED).

Below is table 10.1 of the differences between SEZ, ATD and TLSED.

10.4.1 Special Economic Zones (SEZs)

These are territories that the state gives a special legal status and economic benefits for attracting Russian and foreign investors to priority sectors for Russia (Federal Law of July 22, 2005 No. 116-FZ "On Special Economic Zones in the Russian Federation").

The purpose of creating special economic zones is to develop high-tech sectors of the economy, import-substituting industries, tourism and the spa sector, the development and production of new types of products, and the expansion of the transport-logistics system.

To create a SEZ, the highest executive body of state power of a constituent entity of the Federation submits an application to the executive body authorized by the Government of the Russian Federation for the creation of a SEZ with the rationale for the feasibility and effectiveness of its creation for solving tasks of federal, regional, local significance (clause 2 of article 6 of the Law on SEZ).

Conditions for the creation of the SEZ

According to Part 3 of Article 4 of the Law, SEZs may be located on the territory of one municipality or on the territories of several municipalities within the territory of one subject of the Russian Federation or the territories of several subjects of the Russian Federation. In addition, it is not allowed to create a SEZ in the territory of the municipality in which the zone of territorial development is created.

SEZs can be created on land plots that are in state or municipal ownership, including those provided for possession and (or) for use by citizens or legal entities, as well as on land plots owned by citizens or legal entities. In addition, it is allowed to include in the SEZ borders land plots on which buildings, structures located in state or municipal ownership are located, including those provided for possession and (or) for use by citizens or legal entities, as well as land plots on which buildings, structures owned by citizens or legal entities.

According to Art. 4 of the Law on SEZs on the territory of the Russian Federation, special economic zones can be created to host industrial production of the following types:

1. Industrial and production special economic zones;
2. Technical-innovative special economic zones;
3. Port special economic zones.

To date, special economic zones are actively developing on the territory of the Russian Federation and have more than ten existing SEZs of industrial production, technology and port type.

Benefits, preferences and services

There are general tax benefits for all types of special economic zones:

- Reduced rate of value added tax;
- Reduced income tax rate;
- Reduced property tax rate;
- Reduced rate on land tax;
- Reduced rate on transport tax.

Foreign goods imported into the territory of special economic zones are placed and used without payment of import customs duties, VAT, as well as without the application of non-tariff regulation measures.

Machines, components and equipment necessary for production are not subject to customs duties, which has a positive effect on the financial performance of residents of the SEZ.

When exporting goods / finished products of an organization from a free customs zone to the territory of the Russian Federation, customs authorities

Table 10.1 Classifier of distinctive features between SEZ, ATD and TLSED

Characteristic	Special economic zone	Territorial Development Zone	The territory of leading social economic development
Legislative framework	Federal Law of July 22, 2005 No. 116-FZ On Special Economic Zones in the Russian Federation	Federal Law dated 03.12.2011 No. 392-FZ "On Territorial Development Zones in the Russian Federation and on Amendments to Certain Legislative Acts of the Russian Federation"	Federal Law of December 29, 2014 No. 473- On Territories of Advancement of Socio-Economic Development in the Russian Federation
Purpose of creation	The development of manufacturing and high-tech industries, the development of tourism, the spa sector, port and transport infrastructure, the development of technologies and the commercialization of their results, the production of new products	Acceleration of socio-economic development of the subject of the Russian Federation	Creating favorable conditions for attracting investments, ensuring accelerated socio-economic development and creating comfortable conditions for ensuring the livelihoods of the population
Governing institutions	At the federal level: "Special economies zones "(founder — Government Russian Federation). At the zone level: management company (founder — OJSC "Special economic zones")	At the federal level: an authorized body of the Government of the Russian Federation. At the level of the zone — the executive body of state power of the subject of the Russian Federation; —administration of the zone	At the federal level: an authorized body of the Government of the Russian Federation; management company (founder, authorized body of the Government of the Russian Federation; at zone level: — supervisory board; — Management Company
Type of zone, specialization	Industrial production zones. Technological and innovative zones. Tourist and recreational areas. Port areas.	Restrictions are set on the application of benefits and preferences for residents representing certain types economic activity	The list of types of economic activity is established by Resolution Government of the Russian Federation
Limitations, special conditions	The area of the land: — For industrial production zones — up to 40 km^2; — For technology innovation zones — up to 4 km^2. It is not allowed to place living personal fund (except for tourist and recreation zones)	The term of operation is 12 years. Performance-socio-economic criteria.	The term of operation is 70 years with a possible extension. Installed: —Minimum amount of capital investments of residents of the territory; —Minimum level requirements technologies and production methods, equipment (if necessary)

levy customs duties and VAT. The duty is levied either on the components from which the finished product was produced, or on the finished product.

When organizations / goods are exported from the free customs zone outside the Russian Federation, export customs duties are payable in accordance with the export customs regime, with the exception of foreign goods imported into the territory of the SEZ from the territory of a foreign state.

Depending on the type of zone, investors are provided with additional benefits:

- Investors in industrial zones have the right to apply accelerated depreciation, setting a raising factor, not higher than 2, to fixed assets;
- For organizations that have the status of resident of a technology-innovative SEZ, it is envisaged to establish lower tariffs for insurance premiums (PFR, FSS, MHIF) for the transition period 2011–2019.

Residents of the SEZ are given the right to redeem the land, as well as preferential rates for the sale of real estate.

The amount of rent for a land plot is calculated on the basis of the order of the Ministry of Economic Development, Investments and Trade of the Russian Federation No. 190 of July 14, 2006.

"On approval of the methodology for calculating rent under lease agreements for state and (or) municipal real estate (buildings (their parts), structures) located on land within the territory of special economic zones of technology-innovative, port and tourist-recreational types, and the calculation method rent under land lease agreements located within the territories of special economic zones."

On the territory of the SEZ operates a system of "one window". The main objectives of the implementation of the principle of "one window" are:

- simplification of procedures for obtaining services and reducing the time for their provision;
- increasing the comfort of receiving various services;
- reduction in the number of documents submitted by applicants;
- exclusion of personal contacts of applicants with officials making decisions on the provision (refusal to provide) services;
- unification and automation of administrative procedures for the provision of services in the territory of the SEZ;
- increasing the satisfaction of service recipients with the quality of their provision.

Today in Russia, there are about 18 territories of advanced social and economic development (TLSED). In the period from 2016 to 2020, their number is planned to be increased to 45. For the effective functioning of the territories of priority social and economic development in Russia, Federal Law dated December 29, 2014 No. 473-FZ "On territories of advanced social and economic development in the Russian Federation" and a number of other by-laws. Industrial (industrial) parks and technology parks are being created at the TLSED.

10.4.2 Industrial park

— a complex of real estate objects managed by a specialized management company, consisting of a land plot (s) with industrial, administrative, warehouse and other buildings, structures and structures, provided with the engineering and transport infrastructure necessary for the creation of a new industrial production, and also having the necessary legal regime to carry out production activities. In Russia there are only about 146 industrial parks. Among them, 92 operating industrial parks, fully prepared for the placement of residents, and 54 — at the design and construction stage.

Information on all industrial parks, their status and main characteristics is published annually in the industry review "Industrial Parks of Russia" on the website www.indparks.ru, and is also available in the online version of the geographic information system "Industrial Parks of Russia".

A. Basic requirements for industrial parks:

- land and buildings of the industrial park are suitable for industrial production;
- the management company is entitled to provide infrastructure facilities to the ownership or lease of residents, and at least 80% of its revenue is generated from the management of an industrial park and the provision of services to residents;
- the territory of the park is more than 8 hectares, at least 50% of which is intended for industrial production;
- engineering infrastructure includes from 0.15 MW per 1 ha, but not less than 2 MW.

B. Services of the existing industrial park for investors:

- provision of production facilities (land or finished premises) for rent and / or property;
- connection to engineering networks, including sources of electricity, gas or heat supply, water supply and sanitation, treatment facilities;

- design and construction of production facilities in accordance with the requirements of the investor;
- operation and maintenance of utility networks, utilities and production infrastructure;
- additional services, which may include security and cleaning of the territory, administrative, transport, legal, consulting, personnel and other services.

C. Benefits for investors:

- ready-made engineering infrastructure and availability of connection points;
- administrative support from the management company and regional authorities;
- tax benefits (if provided for by the legislation of the subject of the Russian Federation);
- possible synergies with related enterprises (production chains).

D. Normative legal acts:

- Federal Law dated December 31, 2014 No. 488-FZ "On Industrial Policy in the Russian Federation";
- "GOST R 56301-2014. National standard of the Russian Federation. Industrial parks. Requirements" (approved and enforced by the Order of Rosstandart dated 12.12.2014 No.1982-st);
- Decree of the Government of the Russian Federation of 08/04/2015. No. 794 "On industrial (industrial) parks and management companies of industrial (industrial) parks."

Questions of theory and practice of the effectiveness of concentration and specialization processes should be considered together, i.e. these two tasks are interrelated and provide an opportunity to get a holistic picture in an integrated approach to improving the efficiency of implementation of innovative industrial production projects.

10.4.3 Concentration and specialization of industrial construction

The increase in the size of enterprises, the creation of industrial associations directly affect the growth of concentration of production. In addition, the consolidation of industrial enterprises has an indirect effect on increasing the degree of concentration on TOSED. This indirect effect is manifested in the strengthening of ties and interdependencies between the locations of individual enterprises within such territories. A large enterprise, as it were, attracts various related enterprises that supply it with raw materials, semi-finished products, fuel, and energy, consume its products and use waste from its production.

A large enterprise usually has a large number of employees. Given that many specialized enterprises primarily demand either female or male labor, the rational use of labor resources requires a combination of such enterprises in the territory. In addition, a significant number of employees in a large enterprise leads to territorial concentration of the population. This leads to the need to create appropriate infrastructure and implement a program to provide the working population with housing and social real estate. Thus, a large industrial enterprise plays the role of a kind of source of "raw materials" or "consumers" for a number of other business entities in the housing and construction sector. This ultimately contributes to the concentration of industrial production in the territory of priority development.

An important factor determining the process of territorial concentration of various enterprises is the development of production specialization. An ever-deeper division of the production process inevitably leads to the opposite process — a closer relationship between specialized enterprises.

The spatial division of a single production cycle causes the emergence of independent specialized industries, which, being separate links in a single process, require close mutual relations. Therefore, the specialization of enterprises naturally requires their cooperation, work on a single program to achieve a common goal. This implies the need for proper territorial arrangement of specialized enterprises in order to reduce transportation costs, as well as coordination of their actions.

The emergence of specialized territories of priority development is due to the development of productive forces and the deepening on this basis of the division of labor. The sectoral division of labor appears as the most progressive form of development of social production in the context of the formation of territorial production complexes.

As the territorial branch division of labor develops, certain branches of production are consolidated in the territory with favorable natural, labor and material and technical resources.

The accelerated development of scientific and technological progress, the premise of which is innovation, which leads to the restructuring of production along the lines of industry and territorial specialization.

A. The concentration of production is a natural process, due to the action of the whole system of economic laws. Concentration process creates the preconditions for improving the organization of labor, and production and implementation of innovations, advanced equipment and technology, revealing the law of concentration of production as the trend to ever greater concentration of industrial activity in the TLSED . A higher organizational, technical and managerial level of production, its highest efficiency — these are the main criteria for the process of concentration of modern enterprises on TLSED.

It is necessary to distinguish between absolute concentration and relative. Absolute concentration of production characterizes the size of the enterprise, relative — the distribution of the total volume of territorial production between enterprises of different sizes.

Absolute concentration underlies the relative concentration of production and is its indispensable prerequisite.

In production, concentration should develop based on a growing concentration of homogeneous products in specialized enterprises. Otherwise, the concentration of production by combining at one enterprise heterogeneous products of different industries that are not technologically related to each other can cause the enlargement of enterprises based on universal production.

Such an enlargement of enterprises in most cases does not lead to a substantial use of the advantages of concentration and does not provide further labor savings in production. Moreover, the concentration of technologically diverse products based on universalization hinders the possibility of using new technology, advanced technological processes and more complete use of high-performance equipment. This form of concentration on TLSED is undesirable.

The concentration of production is developing on the basis of technological progress and innovative equipment used, taking into account the growing demand for manufactured products. Technological progress leads to an increase in capacity. Concentration of production on the basis of new technology to certain limits increases labor productivity, reduces production costs and unit costs per unit of power, improves the use of fixed assets and working capital, leads to improved technical and economic indicators simulates computerization of labor and the use of smart technologies, i.e. is a prerequisite for them.

B. Specialized enterprises equipped with modern high-performance equipment create a higher concentration of production of homogeneous products than universal enterprises. However, it does not always cause an increase in the size of enterprises. Moreover, under the influence of deepening specialization and cooperation, the size of specialized production will grow, increase, and the size of an enterprise may even decrease compared to universal enterprises.

In the absence of a construction base for TLSED in Siberia and the Far East, the most effective is the detailed and technological specialization of the enterprises of the construction complex.

As you know, the level of specialization is significantly influenced by the development of standardization, unification and normalization. Moreover, standardization and unification lead not only to maintaining the achieved seriality, but also to increasing it in all divisions, as well as to the typification of technological processes. Deepening the specialization of construction industry creates the opportunity to introduce advanced equipment and technology.

The most effective combination of the deepening of specialization and the development of technological progress can be achieved through the construction of new enterprises, workshops and through the rearrangement of structurally technologically homogeneous products with their manufacture at existing production facilities. For this purpose, a structural and technological classification of parts and assemblies of various types of machines is necessary. The creation of such a classification should serve as a basis for accelerating technological preparation and organizing specialized production at TLSED.

In order to increase the efficiency of market production and increase labor productivity in the implemented COIs, it is necessary to envisage the production of new, highly efficient machines that, according to their technical and economic indicators, meet the best world standards.

Reserves of labor productivity growth are called objective opportunities to increase production per unit of time or reduce labor costs per unit of output. These reserves are used by eliminating production losses and improving the use of working time. The elimination of loss of working time is a large reserve of labor productivity. For example, one absenteeism per month by a worker not only reduces his monthly labor productivity, but also negatively affects the monthly labor productivity of workers performing subsequent operations, and the average values of the workshop.

Consequently, the concentration of both construction and industrial production in all cases should be based on their specializations. Only in such conditions can the greatest labor productivity and capital productivity be achieved.

The increasing importance of the territorial organization of production, territorial cost management is due primarily to the influence of scientific and technological progress, expressed in:

- consistent and intensive deepening of the division of labor;
- the continuous process of creating new highly efficient means of labor, automatic devices, systems and fully automated enterprises;
- differentiation of production associated with an increase in the number of technological redistributions of feedstock undergoing ever deeper processing;
- improving the structure of material production and the internal proportions of the main industry complexes in the direction of increasing the share of the most progressive industries and industries, contributing to an increase in the efficiency of competitive production;

- the formation of territorial-construction complexes, characterized by a complex structure of production and diverse specialization, leading to the strengthening of existing and the emergence of new economic ties;
- increasing the competitiveness of finished products based on the use of the achievements of science and technology of labor organization, production and management.

Within the region, it is possible to organize effective intersectoral relations. Firstly, the consumption of the bulk of products created in the region by enterprises of the same region, determines the establishment of stable intra-regional relations. Secondly, the unification of groups of interconnected industry productions into an integrated system provides the possibility of rational product movement through the stages of production and uniform control of this movement. Thirdly, the presence of inter-industry and intra-industry ties in the region is associated with the convergence of the interests of the economic units entering the region with the interests of the national economy as a whole.

Considering the forms of manifestation of the division of labor, we single out the main general ones: the territorial and sectoral division of labor. Like any category, the division of labor is due to the presence of space and time — the general conditions for the existence of any phenomenon. The space expresses the arrangement of simultaneously existing objects and reflects the territorial structure of the combination of elements of the division of labor. Time is the sequence of existence of successive objects; it represents the possibility of the existence of individual parts of the process of social production. Territorial and sectoral methods of division of labor cannot exist independently, since the movement of a product in time according to its individual types is at the same time a movement between separate territorial subsystems of the economy.

The territorial and sectoral division of labor is different, albeit interconnected, forms, which makes it possible to study them separately from each other. At present, it is possible to review the processes of combining the sectoral and territorial division of labor, analysis of new forms in which they appear.

The territories of advanced social and economic development that are forming in the region's economy are new forms of the territorial division of labor. Consideration of the territorial and sectoral division of labor at the regional level allows us to determine its influence on the formation of the region's specialization, its complexity and features of economic development. This provides the basis for using the laws of regional development in planned practice — a combination of the sectoral and territorial approach to development in it. For example, the East Siberian Economic Region is rich in a variety of raw materials. The reserves of hydropower, coal, and wood are such that they are enough to cover inter-district needs. Therefore, hydropower, non-ferrous metallurgy, and the forest industry are sectors of specialization in the regional division of labor. The importance of this problem has increased at the present stage, since the role of priority development areas is intensifying in ensuring the progressive development of the regional links of the single land and property complex.

Thus, the territorial division of labor, acting as a spatial expression of the social division of labor, is the *basis for the* specialization of economic regions and the establishment of rational ties, an integral part of which is the exchange of activities between different units of future competitive production.

10.4.4 Territorial reproduction forms of construction

On the territory of our country there are no identical regions similar in natural, climatic conditions, historical forms of development, and composition of the population. Therefore, all territorial links are different from each other. At the same time, according to the principle of similarity of the formation process, the scale of reproduction, and significance in the country's economy, all their diversity can be reduced to a limited number of forms of the territorial division of labor — regional organizational and economic clusters (large, medium, small), territorial organizational and economic clusters, territorial industrial complexes (TPK), territorial innovation centers (TIC), territorial multifunctional complexes (TMFC).

New territorial forms can be observed with a narrowing of the spatial framework of the division of labor. Within the boundaries of the macrodistrict, a distinctive feature of the division of labor will be the presence of separate middle areas (mesorrains) associated with the provision of the overall economic function of this macrodistrict (East Siberian, West Siberian and Far Eastern economic regions). In turn, the mesodistricts fall into smaller units of the territorial division of labor — micro-districts (Krasnoyarsk Territory — Irkutsk and Chita Regions, Buryat and Tuva ASSR); territorial production complexes (Sayansky, Kansk-Achinsky); industrial nodes, territorial innovation centers (Zarubinsky International Sea Port) and primary reproductive links are TMKK enterprises.

In different regions of the country, the production of the same product differs in material consumption, labor intensity, capital intensity, energy intensity, which ultimately affects efficiency.

The main tasks of increasing the efficiency of the territorial organization of production in the region are:

- *firstly* , in improving the territorial specialization of the industrial region, which can be achieved by linking the sectoral and territorial development of construction and industrial production and the formation of a complex of industries corresponding to the specialization of the region, the nature of its resources and its socio-economic tasks;

- *secondly*, in the further formation and development of organizational and economic clusters of territorial ZIK in the following areas:
  - improvement of the planning and management system within the region;
  - centralization of production, management and product planning of intersectoral application.
  - The variety of factors affecting the placement leads to the need for their classification. In an enlarged form, all factors can be divided into three groups:
  - internal production related to the organization of intersectoral production in the territorial organizational and economic cluster and territorial-diversified complexes;
  - non-production related to the technical and economic level and environmental conditions in the areas of intersectoral production;
  - industry specifics associated with the concentration of enterprises of one industry in large ASEZs.

Based on the above factors that influence the location of intersectoral production, it can be concluded that in Siberia and the Far East there are prerequisites for the organization of intersectoral production.

Their characteristic feature is their presence in other sectors of the economy: construction, transport, etc. Currently, in the structure of individual industrial units, auxiliary and servicing industries are absent or poorly developed. The sectors located in the nodes are oriented towards meeting the demand for products of interindustry use through departmental channels, i.e. organize "their" subsidiary, mostly low-power production or receive such products from outside the region. The same situation is with the organization for the creation of enterprises of the construction industry.

Thus, the formation of powerful territorial-multidisciplinary complexes (TMFK) leads to an increase in the consumption of products of intersectoral use. Significant volumes of consumption of this type of product create the necessary prerequisites for the organization of specialized production of products of intersectoral use at enterprises of optimal capacity, which significantly increases its efficiency,

Currently, the need has arisen for the formation of a unified management body for service industries. The advantage of a single governing body lies in its centralized management and development of processes of concentration and specialization of production.

The experience of a number of industrial regions in raising the level of specialization of intersectoral industries shows that in most cases this problem is solved by regional groups. This approach clearly does not correspond to the prevailing conditions and needs, does not meet the spirit of the times and the level of development of modern market production.

Specialization and concentration are hindered by the existing practice of expanding production and the associated financial difficulties. This refers to the desire to build new industries. Little attention is paid to the reconstruction and technical re-equipment of the existing base of the construction industry.

The problem of specialization and concentration of intersectoral production in the territory due to its versatility, complexity requires an integrated and systematic approach. Economic science to solve such problems has proposed a number of methods, the most promising of which are the program-targeted and systematic approach.

An important area of application of the program-target approach is the development of regional target comprehensive programs that determine the region's place in the social division of labor and aimed at solving complex intersectoral territorial problems of economic and social development.

The development of a comprehensive program to increase the efficiency of intersectoral production in the Far East and Eastern Siberia is currently an urgent task for the national economy. This confirms the economic analysis of the level of development of production and existing relations between enterprises.

The main areas of specialization are:

- exemption of enterprises from the manufacture of products unusual for their profile;
- increasing the concentration of production of structurally and technologically homogeneous products in economically feasible sizes;
- elimination of unjustified dispersal of homogeneous products at various enterprises by reducing or completely stopping their production at small non-specialized enterprises and sites;
- centralization of the overhaul of equipment for general industrial and interdisciplinary applications.

The development of a comprehensive program is planned in two stages.

At the *first stage,* an analysis of the existing level of concentration and specialization of production of products of intersectoral application in the industry of the region is carried out. At this stage, the actual volumes of production and the market demand for competitive products should be determined, the existing level of production development, cooperated ties and centralized deliveries of products of intersectoral use at enterprises in Eastern Siberia and the Far East should be analyzed. Information is collected to carry out this work with the help of questionnaires sent to enterprises, expert evaluations of specialists, and study of reporting data from statistical offices. Based on the data obtained as a result of the analysis of technical and economic indicators, the balances of production, consumption of products and services of intersectoral application should be compiled, the real need for competitive products capable of implementation in other countries of foundry, hardware production should be determined.

When developing proposals and activities, it is considered advisable to create zonal base enterprises in the territory of the economic region that service and provide products to the enterprises of the region, regardless of their departmental subordination. With the organization of specialized units, a gradual reduction in the unprofitability of production is planned.

At the end of the first stage, it is planned to prepare enlarged proposals on improving the efficiency of using import-substituting equipment based on the concentration and specialization of modern competitive industries.

At the *second stage,* in-depth development of proposals and measures based on the analysis of technical and economic indicators of inter-industry production in the region, their economic justification is expected. These proposals and activities should be developed at the level of development of innovative production. Activities should be aimed at:

- maximum use of the capabilities of large units of machine-building and metal-working enterprises of the region by increasing the level of concentration and specialization of production;
- reconstruction of technologically obsolete or unprofitable industries with the aim of creating highly specialized units with modern technology;
- re-profiling enterprises producing products not in demand in the region for the production of competitive products.

The second stage of work should end with the compilation of activities and the formation of the most comprehensive program. At this stage, the organization of managing the program and providing it with the necessary resources should be addressed.

To ensure higher growth rates of innovative products in comparison with the growth rates of fixed assets, it is necessary that the growth of labor productivity of workers outstrips the growth of their capital-labor ratio. The basis for the growth of labor productivity are energy and resource saving, environmental friendliness and increasing the level of mechanization and integrated automation. A significant gap in the ratio of the growth of labor productivity and capital-labor ratio, the slow growth of capital productivity (and even its decrease) while the growth of fixed assets prove their ineffective use.

Accelerating the development of the productive forces of Siberia and the Far East is impossible without further increasing the economic efficiency of industrial production, and in the first place engineering and electronics — industries that play a key role in the materialization of scientific and technological achievements. The development of modern industry in the eastern regions of the country is influenced by the features of the territorial organization of production, nature and climate, and the provision of labor resources. The most important conditions for increasing the development efficiency of a given region are: the integrated development of existing and emerging industrial and construction clusters of nodes, the creation of the necessary territorial industries in them, specialization and cooperation, and the concentration of total resources. The enterprises of Eastern Siberia and the Far East have large reserves of increasing labor productivity and reducing the number of employees. They consist in the modernization of the main production, the comprehensive mechanization of auxiliary processes, the improvement of the organization of production, including the development of in-depth specialization. It is advisable to create cluster enterprises for the production of innovative products to satisfy existing and under construction facilities through the introduction of territorial single-industry complexes.

10.4.5 Methods for determining the level of concentration of economic entities by their participation in the construction of multidisciplinary industrial complexes

There are various ways to measure market concentration. The first and easiest way is a method based on the so-called concentration curve. At any given time, a single market or industry will have such a curve. In the table. 10.3 shows the distribution of products between the largest firms in several hypothetical industries. In fig. 10.1 shows how the concentration curve is constructed for each industry based on the data presented.

Along the horizontal axis, we display five firms in the industry, *from among the largest.* The vertical axis measures the corresponding part of the products produced by each of these firms in the industry. For industry A, the largest firm has 60% of the market share. Since the second largest company accounts for 20% of the market, the total volume of production is in the hands of the two largest companies and amounts to 80%, etc. In our case, we have information

Table 10.2 Concentration levels for five hypothetical firms by industry

Industries	Share%					CR3 (concentration level for the three largest firms)
	Firm 1	Firm 2	Firm 3	Firm 4	Firm 5	
Branch A	60	20	10	5	5	90
Branch B	30	30	25	15	-	85
Branch C	80	5	5	5	5	90
Industry D	30	30	30	10	-	90
Branch E	30	30	15	15	10	75
Industry F	25	25	25	25	-	75
Branch G	70	10	10	10	-	90
Branch N	50	20	10	5	5	80

about all the companies in the industry A. We see that The five largest firms account for 100% of the market.

In fig. 10.1 In addition to the concentration curve of industry A, a concentration curve of industry D is also shown. In industry D there are three largest firms, each of which has 30% of the market share, with one leading company accounting for 30%. The concentration curve of industry D shows that together the first two firms have 60%, etc. Since there are only four firms in this industry, the concentration curve of industry D reaches 100% earlier than industry A. If there were more than five firms in the industry, the concentration curve would not reach the upper right corner of the chart, since in this example only the five largest firms are disassembled.

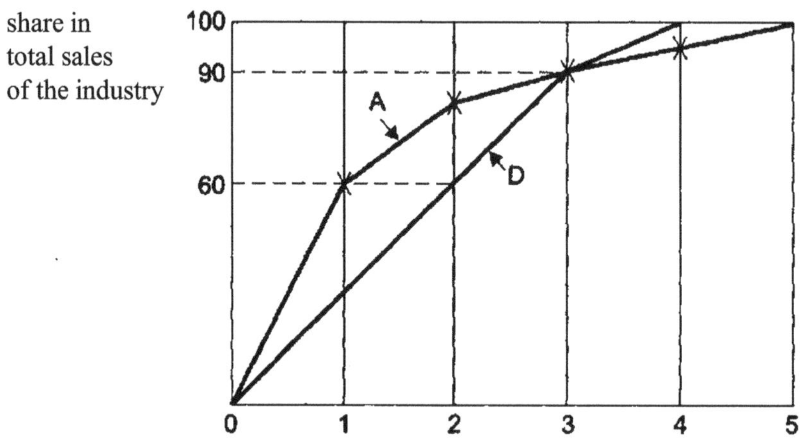

Figure 10.1: Explanatory concentration curves for the number of largest firms in the industry (n)

We can draw a concentration curve for any specific industry and at any time if we have the relevant information. Based on this concentration curve, the concentration level can be calculated. It is quite simple to measure. We select any arbitrary point on the concentration curve and ask the question: "What proportion of the total industry product is in the hands of the largest "n" firms?" For the UK, the normal value for "n" is three or five. In the American market, it's almost always four. Choosing an arbitrary point on the curve, we can see how industries are relatively concentrated.

In the table. 10.3 shows eight different industries, two of which — A and D - we plotted on the concentration curve. The last column of this table shows the concentration level for the three largest firms — CR3. For industry A — three leading firms account for 90% of the market, for industry B — leading firms have 85% of the market, etc. Thus, CR3 is useful because it gives a simple idea of the degree of concentration in the industry. Using the proportions of the volume of production, rather than the specific values of output, we can also make comparisons with other industries. Unfortunately, this simplicity makes practical use difficult. Such a simplification leads to the fact that we consider only one point on the curve, so that with the total measurement it is possible to miss very important information.

We can see this if we return to the concentration curves in Fig. 10.1. It is possible that the two concentration curves intersect. If they intersect, we can see how arbitrary the level of concentration is. Sectors A and D could be considered as industries with the same concentration, since both industries have a concentration level for the three largest firms — CR3 = 90%. However if we look at the concentration level of four firms, we will see that industry D will be more concentrated (CR4 = 100%) than industry A.

This problem does not occur if the concentration curves do not intersect. Consider, for example, industries A and N. We can say that industry A has a higher concentration level than industry H, since the concentration curve of industry A is completely above the curve of industry N. However if the curves intersect, it is difficult to say which industry has a greater concentration. So, if we want to consider, say, the relationship between the level of concentration and the profitability of an industry, the point on the concentration curve that we choose will be very important for determining the relative concentration of the industries we are considering. However, for all problems associated with this, this is a widely used measurement method, because it is simple, understandable, and contains information that is easy to obtain. Thus, in many studies examining the relationship between concentration and other variables, the concentration curve and its concentration level are used to measure market concentration.

Another problem associated with the concentration curve and concentration level may be apparent from the figure. Both market A and market D have the same concentration in the sense that they have 90% of the market share in the hands of three firms. However this does not tell us anything about the distribution of power *between* these three firms. For industry D, the distribution of power between the three firms is the same, since each firm has 30% of the market. However the distribution of power in industry A is significantly different, since the largest firm has 60% of the market. Pricing, advertising behavior in industry A may differ slightly when one firm dominates the market, compared to industry D, where all three firms are the same size.

Another way to measure concentration is to use a method known as the Lorentz curve, and based on the Lorentz curve we get what is called the Gini coefficient (index). Unlike the concentration curve, to build the Lorentz curve, we need information about all the firms in the industry. Let us consider fig. 10.2.

Horizontal, we set aside a percentage, starting with the largest firm. Vertically, we set aside the percentage of production / sales for the entire industry. It is clear that the beginning of the curve will lie in the lower left corner, since 0% of firms have 0% of output, and it always ends in the upper right corner, since 100% of firms will have 100% of output. If we consider an industry where all firms are the same size, then we have a line of absolute equality: 20% of firms will have 20% of output, 50% of firms will have 50% of output, etc. Now suppose that we have an industry where all firms are of different sizes, then we will have such a Lorenz curve that deviates from the line of absolute equality. For example, in fig. 10.2 presents industry G from table. 10.2. The larger the size of firms, the farther from the line of absolute equality the Lorentz curve deviates for this industry. In the most extreme case we will have a very small percentage of firms manufacturing all products in this industry.

Accounting for the different sizes of firms is the essence of the Lorentz curve. However, we can go further and work out a summary assessment of the branch market power. This is the Gini coefficient.

As we have seen, the further the Lorentz curve deviates from the line of absolute equality, the greater the variation in the size of firms. Thus if we look at the Lorentz curve for industry G, then region A represents the extent to which the Lorenz curve deviates from the line of absolute equality. Therefore, if we take the area of the figure A with respect to the area of the triangle (A + B), then we get an estimate of the degree of difference in the size of the firms. This we will call the Gini coefficient. If we have a monopoly industry, in which one company provides the entire industry output, then region A will occupy the entire region B. Thus the ratio of A to B will give 1.

If all firms are of the same size, then the area of area A is 0. Thus the Gini coefficient is always between 0 and 1. The more uneven the distribution of power in the industry is, the more the Gini coefficient approaches 1.

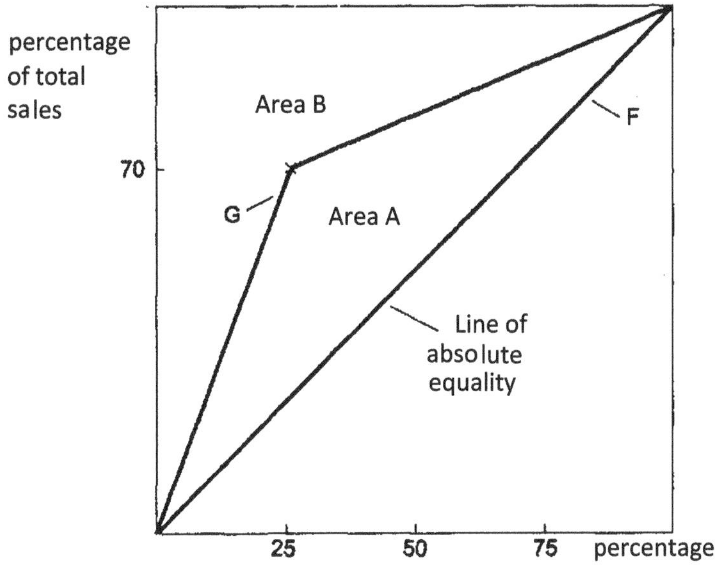

Figure 10.2: Figure Lorentz curve and Gini coefficient

There are various formulas for calculating the Gini coefficient. One of them:

$$G = 1/N \sum_{i=1}^{N} (N - 2i + l)Sj \ , \tag{10.1}$$

where N is the number of firms;

Sj is the share of the i-th company in the total sales of the industry.

We apply this formula for industry F, where we assume that all four firms each have 25% of the total market. Thus, based on what we talked about above, we must find that the Gini coefficient is 0. Suppose that in this case the market volume is 4 million pounds. Art., so that each company has 1 million pounds. Art.

We take the first company as the i-th one and let i = 1. We have 4 firms in the industry.

Then:

$$(4 - 2 + 1) \times 25 = 75$$

Now, take i = 2. This means that i is now the second company in the industry. For this company there are:

$$(4 - 4 + 1) \times 25 = 25.$$

Then we take i = 3. Then we get

$$(4 - 6 + 1) \times 25 = -25$$

and finally we take i = 4, therefore

$$(4 - 8 + 1) \times 25 = -75.$$

Thus, we got the indicators for each of the firms, and now we can summarize them. The result is 0. Finally, we multiply this by 1 / N, which equals 1/4 here. We get 0. In the case when all firms have the same size, the Gini coefficient is 0. We also note that the result does not depend on the size of each particular industry.

Thus the Gini coefficient is derived from the idea of the Lorentz curve. However remember that in order to be able to apply the Lorentz curve and thereby obtain the Gini coefficient, we need information about *all the* firms in the industry, and not just about the largest.

10.5 The effectiveness of the construction of launching territorial single-industry complexes in the industrial cluster

10.5.1 General

One of the ways to reduce the estimated construction cost at present is to place enterprises on TOSED as part of industrial clusters.

Studies have shown that the construction of enterprises as part of an industrial cluster reduces the size of built-up territories by 9–10%, the length of railways by 18–20%, highways by 9–11%, engineering networks by 10–15%, the number of individual buildings and structures by 25%, the number of sizes of reinforced concrete structures and other "factory-made products is 3-5 times.

Due to the creation of cluster-wide facilities and a unified communications infrastructure, as well as a reduction in the volume of construction and installation works, the duration of construction of facilities in industrial clusters can be reduced by about 10-12%. At the same time, there is a real opportunity to most fully and rationally use the capacities of construction organizations and provide them with the best working conditions.

Of particular note is the development and application of methods for selecting the most effective (optimal) solutions to problems of construction production based on their variability at all stages of the design, planning and implementation of the construction of a real estate property as part of territorial single-industry complexes (TMFK).

The optimal construction of facilities and complexes is cost management over the entire life cycle by organizing their construction in the optimal time taking into account energy and resource conservation and environmental friendliness using advanced technology, new materials with the most rational degree of combination of construction, installation and commissioning and testing of equipment. The main criterion of optimality in construction is the maximum commissioning of production capacities (facilities and complexes) at minimal cost. The early commissioning of production facilities and facilities should be considered only as part of the start-up TMFK to which they relate, taking into account the possibility of managing cost during operation.

Industrial clusters are created in order to make full use of the possibilities of cooperative construction of enterprises and facilities common to them, to increase economic efficiency (reduce the area allocated for industrial nodes, communications, reduce the number of buildings and structures, etc.), reduce operating costs compared with separate enterprises having their auxiliary production facilities and farms, as well as for the development of the most rational planning and development allotted territory, i.e., solving urban development problems.

Industrial clusters are formed both from new enterprises, and on the basis of existing ones. Despite the fact that industrial clusters are very diverse in composition, capacity of incoming enterprises, nomenclature of production, size of occupied territory, they can be divided into combined (diverse) and specialized. The construction of real estate by a single developer-developer as part of an industrial cluster can significantly reduce the number of standard sizes of structural elements due to general site unification. In accordance with the decrease in civil works for enterprises located in industrial clusters, capital investments are also reduced compared to similar facilities located separately. In addition, the use of generic auxiliary facilities leads to corresponding savings in operating costs, as the equivalent of all integral costs of real estate throughout the life cycle of its reproduction.

The master plan schemes for industrial clusters provide for the location of enterprises on one or adjacent sites on the basis of a clear planning organization of the territory with zoning by industry, with general facilities for auxiliary production and facilities, with unified schemes of transport, water and heat supply, sewage and other types of engineering support, which began to be linked by the Program for the implementation of projects as part of TLSED.

The construction of industrial clusters requires large expenditures for the development of the territory and the creation of auxiliary and service facilities and, in addition, significantly affects the development of the city and settlements. The planning of capital construction and the issuance of tasks for the design of industrial clusters and other facilities should be preceded by large economic work on drawing up interconnected long-term development schemes for individual industries and schemes for the development and deployment of productive forces in economic regions, as well as feasibility studies on the feasibility of constructing certain objects. It is only on the basis of these materials that regional planning schemes, TLSED master plans and industrial clusters should be developed. With this approach to the design of industrial construction, you can get significant budgetary and social effects, avoid miscalculations **in the** location of enterprises, and also rationally use the existing construction organizations and their base of the construction industry.

Foreign experience in the construction of industrial clusters confirms that all enterprises should be included in their composition, regardless of the nature of production and departmental subordination with auxiliary facilities, if this does not contradict sanitary requirements and ensures a reduction in construction time, as well as capital investments and operating costs. The construction of new enterprises outside the industrial unit is carried out only with the availability of appropriate feasibility studies.

Integrated architectural and planning solutions for the development of industrial and residential territories of public and cultural centers, as well as the compactness of development is ensured by the most appropriate connections of industrial enterprises with housing and communal services and other enterprises of the territory, reducing the delivery of labor resources to enterprises. This is crucial for the planned development of settlements, especially in the newly developed areas of the North and the Far East.

Planning for the construction of enterprises as part of industrial clusters is carried out on the basis of medium-term and strategic plans developed in accordance with the schemes for the development of economic regions of the country, schemes for the development and placement of enterprises as part of TOSED, which ensures:

- reasonable placement of industrial enterprises in separate parts of the country with a view to the rational use of natural and labor resources;
- the approximation of industry and services (seaports and harbors) to sources of raw materials and areas of consumption of finished industrial products with the elimination of irrational transport;
- comprehensive development of the economy in economic regions, taking into account the progressive principles of organizing industrial production.

To achieve the efficiency of building an industrial cluster, its design takes into account: competitiveness of products on the world market; information on local conditions (size of plots, their shape, bearing capacity of soils, the presence and condition of groundwater, topography, etc., about the labor force, about the enterprises of the construction industry and local building materials, about transport (with an indication of its types and routes of "capacity, the possibility of expanding roads and the conditions for connecting them), cargo turnover, places of storage of goods, taking into account the possibility of expanding storage areas and premises, local natural and meteorological conditions, types and quantities of industrial emissions and measures to eliminate their harmful effects.

The listed requirements for the location of industrial enterprises, developed taking into account the prospective growth of TLSED, are taken into account comprehensively, comparing with the possibilities of local conditions and various locations. Comparison of accommodation options carried out on the basis of refined technical and economic data allows us to determine the final optimal location of the enterprise.

The basis for planning the construction of industrial enterprises is the start-up TMPK, which may include industrial (industrial) parks, technology parks. The design of the technology and the organization of work on the construction of starting TMFK and their facilities is related to the specifics of production technology; architectural and construction features, space-planning and structural and technological solutions.

In order to make the most efficient use of capital investments, cluster-wide infrastructure facilities are designed taking into account anticipatory (compared to facilities for primary production) construction in the composition and volumes necessary to ensure their commissioning on time. In developing cluster-wide facilities, the state customer prepares proposals for placing a state order with a single contractor (Article 55 of Law No. 94-FZ). In accordance with this law, the customer proposes to conclude a contract with the winner of the tender by the developer-developer.

In some cases, when common objects are not common for the industrial cluster and TLSED, there may be several developers and developers.

The composition of the enterprises of the industrial cluster is established taking into account the specialization of production, their sanitary and hygienic characteristics of the order of construction, transport, energy consumption, water supply, the availability of free labor resources, etc. When designing these enterprises, excessive concentration of a large number of heterogeneous industries is not allowed, since this does not allow for the most effective cooperation and blocking. Thus, the composition of the industrial unit is formed on the basis of economic and industrial cooperation.

Economic cooperation in production is a prerequisite for the formation of an industrial cluster. It provides for cooperation on the creation of infrastructure (housing and communal services, transport, engineering networks and structures, social services, administrative management, construction base, housing).

Decisions on the creation of cluster-wide objects of the industrial cluster are made taking into account the planned needs of enterprises and their provision with electricity, heat, gas, water from existing sources, the availability of railways and roads, communications, warehouses and other types of auxiliary industries and farms based on proposals for cooperation and blocking general industries and farms, engineering structures and communications,

When designing general site facilities as part of TLSED, they strive to create the largest possible buildings and engineering support facilities based on their blocking. Since many common facilities have a specific shape with a certain architectural expressiveness (cooling towers, pipes, thermal power plants, water towers, etc.), this facilitates the design of the architectural appearance of industrial buildings. Thus, during the construction of industrial clusters, unified infrastructure facilities are created, while the number of buildings and structures is reduced, the area occupied by enterprises is reduced, the length of engineering networks and transport communications is reduced, which makes it possible to concentrate the volume of construction and installation work on the main objects of the industrial cluster.

10.5.2 The formation of factor space that affects the choice of decisions on creating an industrial cluster

The choice of territory for industrial clusters should be justified. For this, several variants of master plan schemes for industrial clusters with technical and economic indicators are developed, which are evaluated by urban planning, architectural planning, engineering, sanitary and hygienic characteristics. The geometrical shape and dimensions of the TOSED allocated for the construction of an industrial cluster must meet the conditions of the technological and architectural-planning layout of enterprises taking into account their expansion.

The sizes of industrial clusters are set depending on economic, transport and other conditions, taking into account environmental and urban requirements.

Depending on the nature of production, the number of industrial hazards emitted, the volume of cargo turnover and the type of transport links, industrial clusters as an integral part of an economic region can be located:

- outside the residential territory, if the enterprises of the industrial cluster emit a large number of production hazards, as well as if the enterprises have special production conditions (explosion and fire hazard, etc.);
- on the border of the residential territory or in the immediate vicinity of it, if enterprises emit a small amount of industrial hazards and have significant turnover, which requires the construction of railway access roads;
- within a residential territory, if the cluster enterprises do not emit industrial hazards and do not require access railway lines.

When placing industrial enterprises, specific architectural and planning, structural and technological features are also taken into account. Enterprises that require large areas with low building density and high cargo turnover occupy entire industrial areas. Their placement is possible inside or along the outskirts of the settlement, depending on the size of the territory of enterprises and the degree of their sanitary hazard.

Industrial enterprises, with average characteristics of the size of the territory and other indicators, usually approach residential areas and, depending on the size and degree of sanitary hazard of production, develop to the size of industrial or mixed areas within the city.

Enterprises that are part of the industrial cluster are located, if possible, on one common site, but they can also be located on small, nearby and rationally used sites, depending on the nature of the production of individual enterprises, sanitary requirements, the availability of sufficient territories needed to accommodate a group of enterprises and suitable for development, and other reasons.

The effectiveness of creating industrial clusters is due to the possibility of cooperation between individual enterprises. The cooperation of enterprises can be: production (main and auxiliary production enterprises), economic (serving enterprises), territorial (general master plan of the industrial unit) and construction (a single base for the construction of the industrial unit, which allows the use of unified building structures and parts). Determining the composition and location of an industrial cluster depends on a number of factors (table. 10.3).

Concentration of volumes of construction and installation works within the territory of the industrial cluster can significantly reduce the need for temporary buildings, and structures, clarify the time of use of construction machines and mechanisms, reduce their downtime, which reduces the cost of construction.

As a result of combining enterprises into industrial clusters, the area they occupy is reduced, which means that the amount of compensation for the land used is reduced. In addition, the reduction of the territory allows to reduce the volume of work on the planning, improvement, laying of intra-site communications; i.e. significantly reduce the total cost of work on the engineering preparation of construction sites.

When enterprises are combined into an industrial cluster, better conditions are created for observing the unity of building solutions of buildings and structures, which allows for additional unification of structures and parts, and this, in turn, ensures a reduction in the cost of its construction.

When solving the problems of territorial construction, taking into account modern requirements, it is advisable to more wide develop non-built "uncomfortable" lands.

A study of the planning and development status of the existing industrial areas and their fixed assets shows that the expansion and reconstruction of

Table 10.3 Factors affecting the cost-effectiveness of industrial cluster solutions

Factors	Change indicators
Creation of general site facilities for auxiliary industries and farms	Reducing the area and objects of buildings and structures, the length of transport and engineering communications, increasing the unit capacity of equipment at general facilities, reducing the number of workers, reducing the cost of fixed assets.
Blocking buildings and structures	Change in the area and volume of buildings and structures
Integrated placement of facilities in accordance with the master plan of the industrial cluster	Reduction of the territory (reduction of work on engineering preparation and improvement), change in the amount of compensation in connection with the occupation of agricultural land
Reducing the volume of construction and installation works and their concentration within a limited territory	Reducing the need for fixed and production assets of contracting construction organizations (construction machinery, mechanisms, temporary buildings and structures, etc.), reducing the cost of construction and installation works, reducing the number of workers in construction
Increased emissions	Change in treatment equipment requirements devices, volumes of construction of buildings and structures, cleaning, number
Temporary diversion of funds for the construction of general facilities	Commissioning, more than required for a certain period, of the capacity of common facilities
Creation of a joint directorate for the construction of industrial cluster enterprises	Decrease in the number of directorate staff and related maintenance costs
Decrease in housing and social construction	Decrease in the area and volume of buildings and structures, the length of transport and engineering communications
Uniform distribution of labor application points in cities and other settlements	Reducing capital investments and operating costs of public transport, reducing the time spent by workers and engineers on a trip to the place of work and back, "transport" fatigue and increasing labor productivity

a significant part of existing enterprises in large cities is carried out without due coordination with the general plan of the city, which, ultimately, leads to unsystematic construction of enterprises without urban planning requirements. Industrial facilities currently occupy from 25 to 50% of urban land, and the use of these "territories does not exceed 40%.

When updating the existing territory, the improvement of space-planning solutions is possible through the usage of new, more advanced production technologies, blocking buildings and combining technological installations, placing equipment and apparatus in open areas, building modernized enterprises with enlarged units, introducing large unit capacity units, and applying rational schemes of in-plant transport.

This allows you to reduce the area occupied by production facilities, and to obtain a significant economic effect.

When designing industrial clusters, design organizations use standard solutions and designs, achieving maximum unification, which allows you to freely choose planning and design solutions that are most appropriate and economical not only in terms of lump sum construction and operating costs, but also further modernization and development of technological processes.

In order to further cooperate, block and unify buildings and structures, it is necessary to use more widely in designing progressive methods for building buildings from standardized standard sections and spans, which allow the wide and effective implementation of large industrial buildings, which can accommodate not only several workshops, but also a whole enterprise, and in some cases even somewhat homogeneous, enterprises, industrial cluster. The master plan, developed with the use of such large buildings, is usually characterized by compactness and rationality of the use of the factory territory.

One of the directions for improving the master plans of industrial clusters is strict adherence to the principles of their layout, proper functional construction. The lack of clear planning principles for the solution of the master plan for transport and communications tracing leads to their excessive complexity and complicates the development.

Engineering networks on the territory of the industrial cluster, the underground production complex should be designed with mandatory and linking it with the general planning decisions of the general plan of the group of enterprises.

Further improvement in the design of master plans for industrial clusters should be based on a block layout scheme, clear zoning of the territory, prospective expansion of each zone, unification of the sizes of nodes and elements of the master plan, centralized laying of engineering networks in special communication corridors. At the same time, it is also important to take into account decisions of an economic and ecological urban planning nature, since it is more difficult to develop a good planning solution for industrial areas and to provide high-tech development with a large number of departments involved in the construction of many facilities at different times than to solve a similar problem in housing.

In order to ensure high labor productivity in the design of industrial clusters, attention should be paid not only to the issues of efficient location of industrial enterprises, their planning decisions and the most rational organization of production, but also to ensuring a favorable environment for workers, improving comfort in domestic services, solving industrial aesthetics, interiors, landscaping of built-up areas and especially landscaping (organization of places for recreation and sports). Landscaping of territories of enterprises and sanitary zones is a natural filter that absorbs a significant part of production hazards, so it should be taken into account when developing the master plan of the industrial cluster.

10.5.3 The choice of organizational methods of construction and options for the construction of facilities as part of industrial clusters

The unification of enterprises in industrial clusters is one of the most important areas for improving the regional economy and increasing its efficiency.

In order to increase the efficiency of capital investments, reduce construction in progress, accelerate the return on investment, the construction of large and medium-sized enterprises is planned in turn and in separate start-up complexes, which are put into operation before the complete completion of construction of all TMPK facilities.

To allocate the volume of work, construction objects can be concentrated, linearly extended and geographically dispersed.

According to the general construction and technological characteristics, objects are divided into two groups: homogeneous and heterogeneous.

In construction, the sub-node method of organizing and managing construction is widely used, the essence of which is the division of a complex or object into structurally separate and technologically interconnected parts — nodes, the technical readiness of which, after completion of construction and installation works, allows for the commissioning and testing of equipment, mechanisms, devices, as well as testing utility networks.

The sub-site method of organizing and managing construction allows you to:

- create a reliable, autonomous basis for planning the production of construction and installation works, staffing with material and technical and human resources, settlements with the customer and suppliers, operational management and supervisory control over the progress of construction;
- ensure maximum use of the front of work due to the organization of parallel flows at the nodes;
- identify the divisions of the general contracting and subcontracting organizations that throughout the entire construction period carry out their

functions of construction and installation work within strictly defined boundaries of the node;

- ensure clear organization and coordination of work within each node and the complex as a whole.

Development and experience in the implementation of computer-aided design in construction make it possible to open new reserves for increasing the efficiency of capital investments, reduce labor costs, the time and cost of erecting objects and complexes.

The design and construction of facilities and complexes are divided into several main stages associated with both the architectural and construction design of the facilities themselves, reflecting their features, the diversity and specificity of technological processes, and with the design of technology and the organization of their construction and the planning and management system for construction.

When designing such enterprises, it is necessary to determine the composition of the queues and launch complexes. Each stage and launch complex must correspond to a specific production cycle so that the constructed part of the enterprise can immediately produce products. The main component of the complex is a technological complex, which includes a group of industries united by one technological process, equipped with all necessary auxiliary and service systems and having an internal material balance.

Each technological complex is designed on the basis of the optimal combination of production within the industrial cluster, the internal material balance of production, the uniformity of its structure and relatively independent material and technical supply.

Depending on which product and in what quantity is planned, this or that technological complex is used. The production capacities included in the technological complex are mutually linked and subordinate to the internal material balance. So, for example, the structure of technological complexes of chemical enterprises is based on the following stages of processing: supply of raw materials, head production, production of intermediate products, production of finished products, and export of finished products.

In all technological complexes of these enterprises, not only the general structure is identical, but also the nature of the processes at each stage. Thus, the head production is present at each complex. Intermediate production has external relations with the railway for raw materials and internal transport with the production of finished products. All finished products are exported from the complex by rail.

Each complex is provided with an independent system of material and technical supply, which is also solved the same way. The composition of auxiliary facilities working directly for the technological complex is mostly constant, only the capacities of individual facilities can change, however, these changes are so insignificant that they do not affect the structure of the enterprise. The design of technological complexes is based on poor development of the enterprise, zoning of the territory, centralized laying of pipelines in the communication corridor, centralized placement of auxiliary facilities, etc.

An industrial enterprise is a complex of buildings and structures, the composition and architectural appearance of which depends on the production technology. The space-planning and structural solutions of industrial buildings are determined by their purpose — ensuring the normal functioning of the technological equipment placed in them and creating normal conditions for the production processes taking place in them, protecting staff and equipment from environmental influences (atmospheric influences).

Depending on the purpose of the building of an industrial enterprise, which is part of TMFK, they are divided into the following groups:

- production, designed to host the main production facilities of the enterprise;
- auxiliary, intended for placement of auxiliary production processes (repair, experimental, container and other workshops);
- energy, supplying enterprises with electricity, compressed air, steam and gas;
- transport, servicing means of transport at the disposal of the enterprise;
- warehouse;
- for plumbing purposes;
- factory-wide (office buildings, canteens, medical centers, fire station).

Depending on the purpose, capacity and specialization of the enterprise, it may include different groups of buildings.

The total number of varieties of buildings and structures used in the practice of industrial construction is very large.

Since in industrial construction, buildings and structures are different in type, purpose and volume, the technology of their construction is different. The main feature of the construction of industrial buildings and structures is the need to install technological equipment in them with the accompanying special construction work. As a rule, having a predominant share in the overall complexity of an object, these works determine the technology of building construction, the pace and nature of the coordination of work, as well as the general construction time. The construction of industrial enterprises also has a number of features peculiar only to this type of construction, which must be taken into account when choosing construction options, both for individual objects and their complexes. The main ones are:

- the complexity of the design and organization of preparatory work;
- the need to link construction work with the installation of technological equipment;
- implementation of construction by lines and launch complexes;
- adjustment, testing and commissioning of equipment; the implementation of the second and subsequent phases of construction simultaneously with the operation of previously completed production facilities, (phases).

Based on the technology of production under construction, an industrial enterprise determines, based on the technological cycle, the composition of the necessary equipment of buildings and structures and their structural and space-planning characteristics. Naturally, for different industries these characteristics will be different, which in turn also determines the specific features of the construction of industrial structures.

The preparation of construction production is carried out in order to ensure the necessary conditions for the deployment of construction of industrial facilities and start-up complexes and includes interrelated measures of an organizational, technical, technological and planned-economic nature, ensuring construction on schedule with a reduction in the cost of their construction. It includes pre-project preparation, preparation of design estimates, organizational preparatory measures and technological preparation for the construction of individual facilities and their complexes (on-site and off-site preparatory work).

Pre-project preparation includes the development of schemes and integrated programs for the development of the industry, as well as feasibility studies for the construction of industrial enterprises and their expansion, the necessary research and design assignments. Preparation of design estimates — this is the development of technical documentation, as well as its coordination on individual elements with the customer, general contractor, related design and other interested organizations.

During the implementation of organizational preparatory measures, the management apparatus is formed, issues of ensuring the construction of materials, structures, semi-finished products are solved and methods for their delivery are selected; construction and specialized and specialized organizations leading the construction are determined, design and estimate documentation is accepted for the first stages and launch complexes of construction; registration and acceptance in kind of construction sites are carried out; enterprises, residential buildings are transferred and organizations located on the territory of the construction site are relocated; issues of placing orders for materials, structures and equipment are being addressed; expand, if necessary, enterprises associated with their manufacture, and conclude a contract for construction.

During the construction of industrial enterprises in undeveloped territories, the duration of the construction includes the time for the construction of cultural facilities, production bases and enterprises providing construction with structures and products, as well as housing. In such cases, the duration of the construction of the enterprise increases, depending on the amount of work.

Off-site preparatory work includes the construction of trunk lines with a length of more than 3 km. These are railway tracks and highways with constructions on them, communication and power lines with transformer substations, water intake facilities, treatment facilities for domestic and drinking and industrial water supply, as well as sewage treatment facilities, main pipelines for sewage and water supply, shipping lanes with water moorings, etc. The duration of the off-site preparatory work for individual facilities should be determined according to existing standards for the duration of construction. The total duration of the construction of industrial enterprises is set by the standards depending on the development of the construction area and the volume of off-site preparatory work. Therefore, when determining it, the longest duration for the construction of one of the off-site preparatory period facilities or housing, cultural, domestic, industrial and service purposes, taking into account the combination factor in time, 0.5 should be added to the duration of the construction of the enterprise. Off-site and on-site preparatory work must be planned for the construction of the first complex in tandem, and for the subsequent ones, in parallel with the main construction and installation works on the construction of the previous complexes. They should be planned in volumes that ensure the implementation of the basic construction and installation works. On-site preparatory work includes work related to the development of a construction site and its engineering training. Their duration is established by the norms, is included in the total duration of the construction of the launch complex, line or enterprise and is 8–15%.

When considering possible combinations of preparatory and basic construction and installation works, one should take into account the reduction in the total duration of the launch complex construction both by combining on-site preparatory works with each other and by combining them with the main works.

On-site preparatory work can be of three types, depending on their relationship — work related technologically, i.e., one of the works opens the front to the other, organizationally, i.e. the transition of the appropriate teams of workers, machines and mechanisms, and work, not technologically and organizationally unrelated, which can be carried out in any sequence and combination.

The experience of organizing the production of on-site preparatory work and the technology of their production show that part of the work is carried out as a whole for the launch complex, while the other part is for individual objects and structures, as well as their groups.

The first should include inter-site communications, serving a number of start-up complexes, but necessary for starting up a new facility. Such communications are located along the contours of the blocks (blocks) occupied by the construction site of the launch complex. In addition, these include communications with structures on them located outside the territory of the construction site, up to 3 km long. During the construction of industrial enterprises, this group of works should also include the work as a whole on the construction site, which is in adverse conditions (draining it, setting up dykes, etc.). These works are carried out mainly during the construction of the first launch complex. Their implementation is not related to the production of on-site communications, the construction of temporary buildings and structures necessary for each individual facility or their groups. On-site preparatory work related to the laying of on-site communications and temporary buildings and structures necessary for individual objects and their groups are carried out in parallel with the first group of works.

Depending on the density of the building factor of the launch complex, specific features of the construction site and the sequence of its development, on-site preparatory work can be divided into two groups.

The demolition of buildings from the construction site, clearing the territory, water supply, and vertical planning with a building coefficient of $K_n > 0.25$ or using the construction area by more than 60% should be attributed to the first group of works, otherwise to the second.

The building density coefficient is determined by the ratio of the total area of enterprises, territories occupied by common facilities, auxiliary and auxiliary industries and farms, utilities, to the total territory alienated for the industrial unit. At the same time, the territory occupied by utilities is determined by their length and the standard width of the exclusion band using the formula

$$K_n = \frac{T_e' + T_{gs}' + T_k'}{T_{ny}'}\,, \tag{10.2}$$

where K_n — utilization of the territory; T_e — territory of enterprises, ha;

T_{gs} — the territory of general structures, auxiliary, utility industries, farms and dumps, ha;

T_k' — territory of communications, ha;

T_{ny}' is the total territory of the industrial unit, determined by the master plan scheme, ha.

Designing enterprises in industrial units is characterized by a high density (coefficient) of development.

The most rational method of production of these two groups of on-site preparatory work is their combined implementation. In the construction of facilities and facilities of the launch complex, the implementation of the second group of works allows you to combine preparatory and basic construction and installation work. At the same time, the intensity of their implementation according to regulatory recommendations is constant, and the combination with the basic construction and installation works is achieved without attracting additional resources, due to the improvement of the organization of work.

The beginning of the main works on the construction of the first of the considered facilities of the launch complex is determined by the formula:

$$t_1^P = t_1 + t_{II-I}^P, \tag{10.3}$$

where t_I^P— the total duration of the first group of preparatory work, sufficient to open the front to the work of the second group at the first facility, days; t_{II-I}^P — the duration of the second group of preparatory work at the first facility, days

Table 10.4 Density factor of the industrial cluster K_n

Energy and fuel industry	0.57
Ferrous and non-ferrous metallurgy	0.64
Chemical and petrochemical industry	0.50
Engineering and metalworking	0.57
Timber, woodworking and pulp and paper industry	0.5
Building materials industry	0.6
Light and food industry	0.62
Logistics, trade, transport	0.6
Diversified industrial units	0.6

The time of combining the preparatory and basic construction works of the launch complex is determined by the formula:

$$\Delta t_c = T^P - t_1^P = T - t_1^P - t_{II-1}^P. \tag{10.4}$$

where T^P— the total duration of the main construction works of the launch complex, days

The coefficient of combining preparatory and basic work during the construction of the complex can be determined by the formula:

$$K_c = \frac{\Delta t_c}{T^P}. \tag{10.5}$$

To solve the optimization problems of construction production, it is necessary, first of all, to formally describe the processes of erection of buildings, structures and complexes. This can be done using technological or organizational-technological models, in which a list of construction and installation works, the sequence of their implementation and the nature of the relationship between the works reflecting the specifics of space-planning and structural solutions, as well as the technology and organization of construction, rational use of resources and etc.

Modern construction as a system object is characterized by a high degree of complexity, a large number of constituent elements with complex functional relationships, dynamism, probabilistic nature and other features.

The organizational and technological model should be adequate to the object or complex under consideration, i.e. describe the object or complex and the requirements of the organization and construction technology with the degree of detail necessary to solve the problem. In addition, it must be stable, i.e. so that during operation, a minimum number of changes are introduced into it, caused by continuously occurring changes in the modeling object during construction.

At present, various models of technological processes have been developed, each of which describes certain organizational and technological schemes of production. The most widely used in the practice of planning construction projects are deterministic organizational and technological models that do not take into account the probabilistic nature of production.

The effectiveness of the facility construction option is due to a number of factors, the main of which are:

- work production methods (sequential, parallel or in-line), determined on the basis of the composition of the complex's structures, their mutual placement on the construction site, the composition and number of specialized organizations involved in the construction of the complex, the quantitative and qualitative composition of the available fleet of construction vehicles and mechanisms, the duration of construction, timing of supplies of materials, equipment products, etc.;
- methods of construction of facilities, adopted on the basis of structural, technological and space-planning characteristics of facilities, construction machines and mechanisms, taking into account local geological and hydrogeological conditions, production methods for the construction of the entire complex, conditions for the installation of technological equipment, etc.

The space-planning and structural characteristics of buildings and structures and the methods of their construction determine the possible options for the technological sequence of work. Aggregate accounting of work production methods determines possible typical technological models for the construction of facilities. Typical technological models for the construction of facilities in the form of integrated local network schedules for the production of the main types of work are shown in Fig. 10.3. They reflect the implementation of the main types of work on the construction of the pavilion type (Fig. 10.3, a–k), ordinary buildings (Fig. 10.3, l–s), as well as the installation of vertical apparatuses in open areas (Fig. 10.3, t).

The mass of mounting elements, installation methods of building structures and equipment, typical technological models for the construction of an object determine the possible means, schemes, and mechanization options for performing certain types of work.

Each version of mechanization and technology for performing a separate work corresponds to possible options for the implementation of this work ranging from the minimum possible to the maximum allowable duration of its implementation. The organization of their implementation is reflected in the technological model. All work is carried out in a clear sequence, determined by the topology of each model of the construction of the object. A continuous sequence of work and dependencies on the network: the construction of objects makes up the path. Options for the execution of individual works on the paths composed of these works have a different effect on the duration of the construction of the facility and the amount of reduced costs.

The total duration of work on an object is determined by the critical path — the full path that has the longest duration in this model. Each of the remaining full paths that are not critical requires less time to complete the work compared to parallel works of the critical path, and therefore has one or another reserve. time determined by the difference between the length of the critical path and any of the non-critical paths considered. The length of the path is determined by the sum of the duration of the individual work, its components, and the amount of reduced costs for its implementation is the sum of the reduced costs of the work that makes up this path. The combination of the accepted continuous sequence and dependencies of the performance of work on each of the paths forms a model for the production of work constituting these paths (Fig. 10.3).

These models can be divided into five types: models involving work along parallel tracks (Fig. 10.4, a);

- models, production work, in which one or more of the ways have common work (Fig. 10.4, *b, c);*
- models of the production of work having organizational ties (Fig. 10.4, d); models involving in-line production of works (Fig. 10.4, e).

When erecting the j-th object, m types of construction and installation works $x = 1, 2, 3, ..., m$ can be performed using various means of mechanization with serial numbers $i = l, 2, 3, ..., n$ for a number of different technological options building models $\gamma = 1, 2, 3, ..., n$ The cumulative consideration of all the above factors determines the set of possible options for building an object.

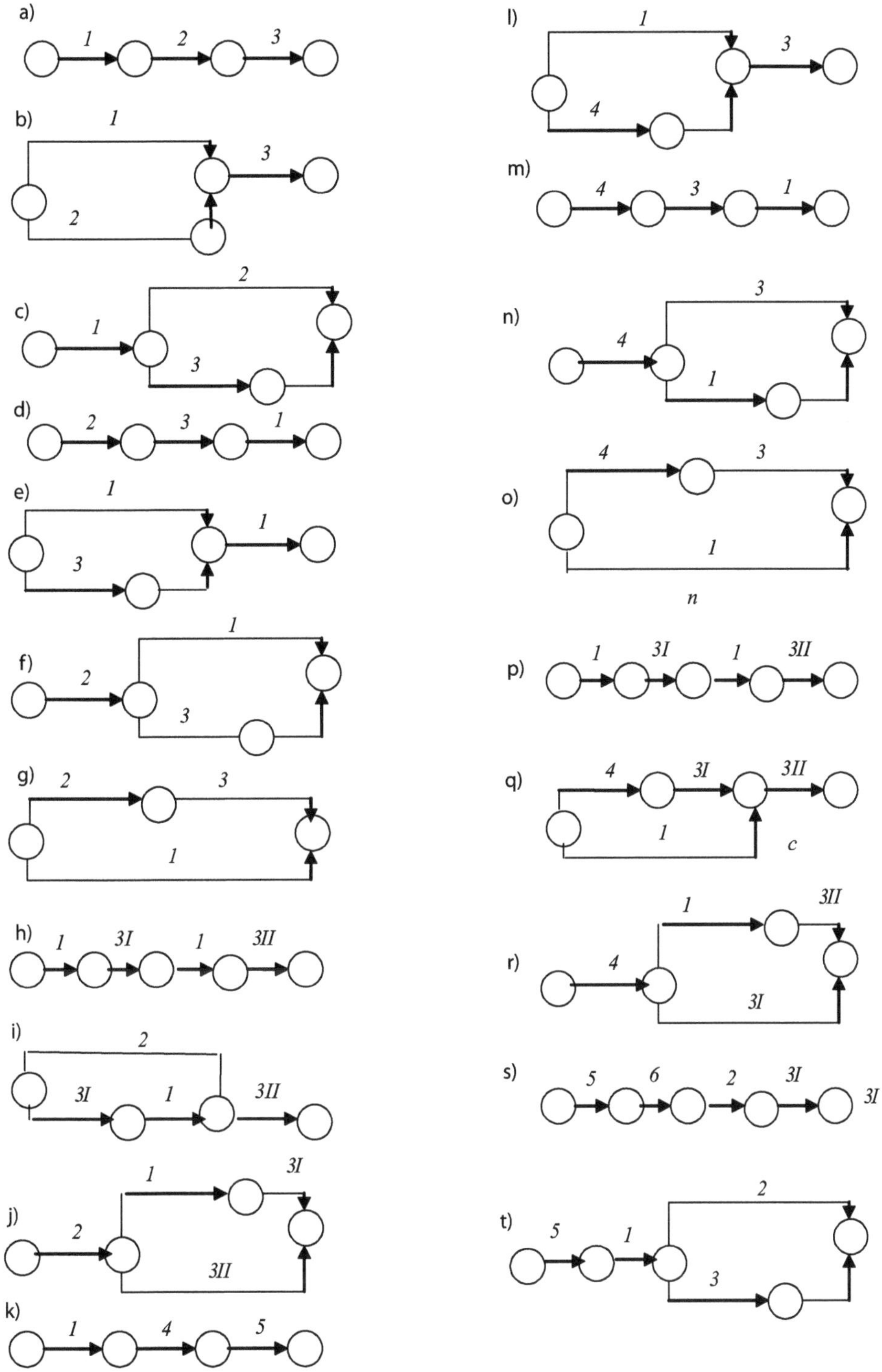

Figure 10.3: Typical technological models for the construction of facilities

a–k — pavilion type buildings; l–s — buildings of the usual type; t — platforms; I–II — sequentially executed work queues (capture of building structures); 2 — installation of shelving structures; 3 — installation of equipment and pipelines; 4 — installation foundations and installation foundations for vertical apparatus; 5 — installation foundations for vertical apparatus; 6 — installation of vertical apparatus

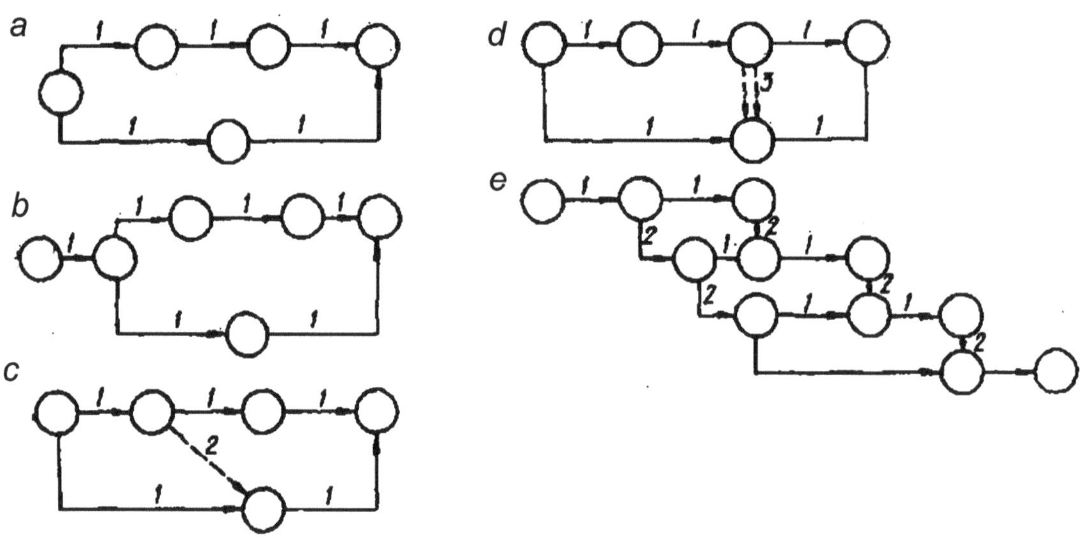

Figure 10.4: Work Models

a–b — providing for the execution of work, respectively, along parallel tracks and one or more paths that have common work; *c, d* — having technological and organizational ties between work; *e* — providing for continuous production of work; 1 — work; 2, 3 — respectively technological and organizational communication

The magnitude of the budget effect when evaluating options for the construction of a complex with different durations is determined from the expression

$$E = E_n + E_f + E_0 + E_d, \tag{10.6}$$

where E_n — the economic effect of reducing the conditionally constant part of overhead costs;

E_f — the economic effect achieved by reducing the period of functioning of fixed assets and working capital;

E_0 — effect (damage) from changing the size of abstract capital investments in the construction of the complex;

E_d — the economic effect of the early commissioning of the complex.

10.5.4 Modeling the work plan of a construction organization in the implementation of ISP at TOSER

The determination of local optimum must be performed for all possible models of construction and options, mechanization according to an algorithm that includes:

- array of source data;

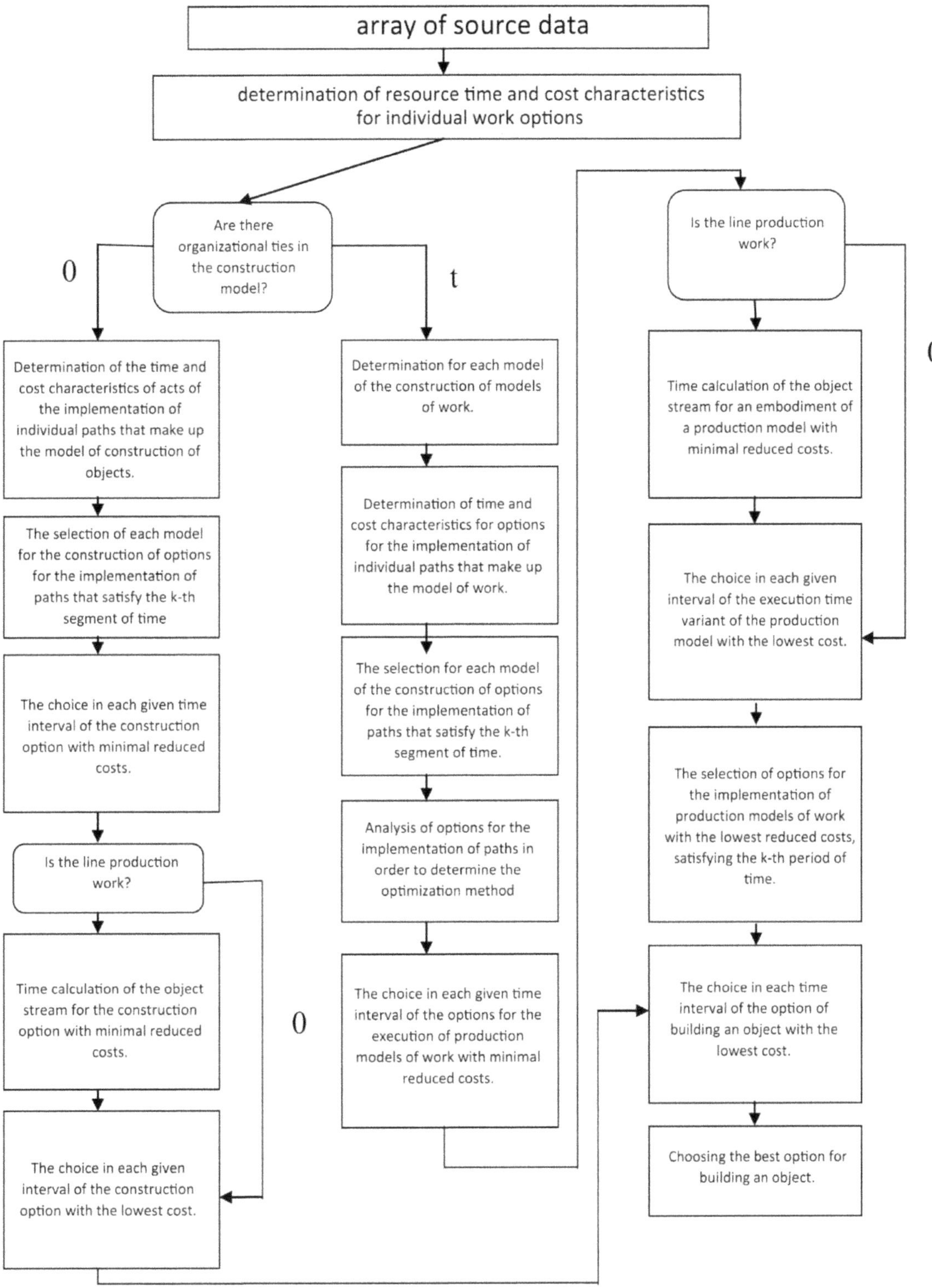

Figure 10.5: The block diagram of the simulation algorithm for the construction process of the object as part of TMPK

- determination of resource, time and cost characteristics for options for performing individual work in the group;
- determination of time and cost characteristics for options for the implementation of individual paths in a group of objects;
- selection for each group of objects of options for the implementation of paths that satisfy a given period of time;
- selection in a given range of options for the construction of each group of objects with minimal reduced costs;
- selection in a given time interval of the option of erecting the complex with minimal reduced costs;
- selection in a given time interval of the option of erecting the complex with the smallest reduced costs;
- selection of the best option for the construction of the complex.

Finding a global optimum is done by comparing among themselves options that have local optima.

When arbitrary values $\frac{P_{jx}}{I_{jx}}$ and Δt_{jx} are selected within the specified limits, the time moments of the beginning and end of each work performed during the construction of an independent object are determined using the following equations:

$$K_{jx} = H_{jx} + \frac{P_{jx}}{\Delta t_{jx}} \tag{10.7}$$

$$H_{jx} = H_{jx-1} + \Delta t_{jx} \; . \tag{10.8}$$

Practical calculations using these equations have their own characteristics for each of the groups of objects under consideration.

The objects of the *first* group ($\eta = 1$). In the calculation, it is assumed that $H_{j1} = 0$, since the object is being built from the very beginning of the period under review for the construction organization. Then, K_{j1} is determined from the given values of the volume of work not yet completed of the first type P_{j1} and their intensity I_{j1}. Similar calculations are performed for other types of work begun, but not yet completed in the previous period, if any.

For other types of work that begin and end in the period under review, the values of H_{jx} and K_{jx} are successively determined by their volumes and arbitrarily selected (within specified limits) Δt_{jx} and I_{j1} values.

An exception is the latter type of work *(x = t),* for which K_{jx} cannot be determined by formula (10.8), since the time for putting the object into operation K_j is given and $K_{jm} = K_j$. This condition strictly determines the value of the intensity of the last type of work I_{j1}, which is easy to obtain from the equation

$$I_{jm} = \frac{P_{jm}}{K_{jm} - H_{im}} \,. \tag{10.9}$$

If the value of I_{jm} is within the established limits ($I'_{jm} \leq I_{jm} \leq I''_{jm}$), then the formation of the moments of the beginning and end of all types of work on the j-th object can be considered complete. The obtained values of H $_{jm}$ and K_{jm}, as well as the values of the adjustable parameters I_{jm} and Δt_{jm} adopted in the calculation, are memorized. If the obtained values of I_{jm} are outside the set limits, it is necessary to set other values of the adjustable parameters I_{jx} and Δt_{jx} so that I_{jm} turns out to be in a given interval.

Objects of the second group (η = 2). For them, in addition to I_{jx} and Δt_{jx}, one more adjustable parameter is introduced — the beginning of the construction of the j-th object H_j. The moments of the beginning and end of each type of work are determined as follows. The time moment of the start of the first type of work on the object $H_{j1}= H_j$ is set. Then, setting arbitrary (within the established limits) values of Δt_{jx}, x = 2, 3, ..., t and $I_{jx} = 1, 2, 3, ..., m$, we subsequently determine K_{j1}, H $_{j1}$, K_{j2}, H_{j2}, etc. up to the definition of H_{jm}. As for the first group of objects, $K_{jm}= K_j$ is given. The value corresponding to this condition is determined I_{jm} in order to track whether it goes beyond the limits of Permissible changes. In the case under consideration, in addition to the obtained values of H_{jx}, K_{jx} and adjustable parameters I_{jx} and $\Delta t_{jx,the}$ value of the adjustable parameter (for this group of objects) of H_j is also set.

Objects of the *third* group (η = 3). The times of the beginning and end of each type of work are determined in the same way as for the objects of the first group, without exception, accepted for the last type of work, because the objects of the third group are not starting ones. Consistent calculation according to the formulas is carried out until the values of K_t are obtained, which should exceed the directive deadline for performing work on all the objects under consideration ($K_{jm} \leq T_d$). If this condition is met, I_{jx}, K_{jx}, I_{jx}, t_{jx} are memorized ; otherwise, a transition to another possible option is carried out.

Objects of the *fourth* group (η = 4). The time of the beginning and end of each type of work is determined in the same way as for the objects of the second group, but with the restriction ($T < K_{jx} < T_D$) adopted for the third group of objects. This restriction for some reason (conditions for the supply of materials, technological equipment, etc.) may apply not only to the last, but also to some other type of work ($T <\ T_{jx}< T'_D$) performed during the construction of facilities of the third and fourth groups. For objects of the fourth group, the values of H_{jx}, K_{jx} and adjustable parameters H_{jx}, $I\ _{jx}$ and Δt_{jx} are remembered.

As a result of calculations for all four groups of objects and binding to the calendar of the most effective options for the construction plan of individual launch complexes, one of the acceptable options for the plan is obtained.

A plan refers to a combination of the following parameters: the time of the start of work H_{jx}, the time of the end of work $K\ _{jx}$ and the intensity I_{jx} for each x- th operation of each j- th object.

When drawing up the reference plan (the reference plan in this case is a set of independent plans for all construction projects), it is necessary to arrange the time of operation of each object so that the approximation between two adjacent works is not less than Δt_{min} and not more than Δt_{max} i.e. $H_{jx} + \Delta t_{min} \leq H_{jx} - 1 \leq \Delta t_{maxix}$, and the end of the work preceding in time should not come before the end of the work, followed by the next one, i.e. $K_{jx} \leq K_{jx}$-1.

In the reference plan, the initial intensity is taken equal to I_{max}.

$$
\begin{gathered}
H_{jx} = H_{jx-1} + \Delta t_{\min\ jx}; \\
K_{jx} \begin{cases} H_{jx} + \frac{P_{jx}}{I_{jx}}, & \text{if } K_{jx} \geqslant K_{jx-1} \\ H_{jx} + \frac{P_{jx}}{I_{\min\ jx}} + \Delta t_{jx}, & \text{if } \Delta t_{jx} \leqslant \Delta t_{\max\ jx} \end{cases} \\
I_{\min\ jx} \leqslant I_{jx} \leqslant I_{\max\ jx}
\end{gathered} \tag{10.10}
$$

Thus, an object is excluded from the plan if at least one of the object's activities does not satisfy the condition $K_{jx} \geq K_{jx} - 1$, or if the construction completion time, calculated by calculation, is longer than the specified one, which may occur in case of incorrectly specified initial data.

A support plan, i.e., a set of independent plans for all construction projects, is the starting point for finding the optimal plan. Under ΔT_P we will take the time interval from a certain fixed moment, time T_f during which none of the work in question begins and ends. At the beginning of the work $T_f = 0$. All works that fall in the interval ΔT_P receive the sign — "to the plan". For the plan under consideration, the total construction intensity for this type of work is determined for those of them that have the characteristic P, and the inequality is checked

$$
N_x \leqslant \sum_{\pi} I_{ix}^{\pi};\ x = (1,\ m)_0 \tag{10.11}
$$

If $\sum_{\pi} I_{jx}^{\pi} \leq N_x$, then the following type of work is considered, i.e. $x = x + 1$.

If the inequality is true for all $x = 1\ ,\ 2\ ,\ ...,\ m$, then $T_f' = T_f + \Delta T_p$ and a new ΔT_P is found. This is done until $T_f < T$. The optimal plan is built, when $T_p = T$.

If $\sum_{\pi} I^{\pi}_{jx} > N_x$, then there are works for which $H_{jx}= T_f$ and among them the work that is conducted with the lowest intensity I_{jx} is selected, and the object to which it belongs has the largest margin of time until completion. If such a job x_0 exists, then the beginning of all jobs whose number $x \geq x_{\ 0}$ is shifted by $\Delta\ T_{\ P}$, i.e.

$$H'_{jx} = H_{jx} + \Delta T \quad x \geqslant x_0. \tag{10.12}$$

Otherwise, among the works having the attribute P, those that are conducted with an intensity of $I_{jx} \geq I_{\min\ jx}$ are selected. Of these, one is chosen so that the object to which it belongs has the largest margin of time until the end, and the intensity of this work is reduced.

The intensity is reduced with a given step and with subsequent verification of inequality (2.21). If no work is found that satisfies these conditions, then the object to be excluded from the plan is determined and the total intensity is recalculated until inequality is achieved.

$$\sum_{\pi} I^{\pi}_{jx} \leq N_x, \tag{10.13}$$

Based on the simulation results, the following key performance indicators of the construction organization for the planning period are determined:

- the volume of work performed by the construction organization for the period under review,

$$P_x = P_{ex} + I_{ex}(T - T_e); \tag{10.14}$$

- coefficients of capacity utilization of a construction organization by type of work

$$K_c = \frac{P_e}{N_x T}; \tag{10.15}$$

- total amount of work performed by the construction organization in monetary terms for the period under review

$$C = \sum_{x=1}^{m} P_x C_x, \tag{10.16}$$

where $C, \ = 1,\ 2,\ ...,\ m$ is the cost of performing a physical unit of volume construction and installation work for each type; overall capacity utilization factor of a construction organization

$$K_x = \frac{C}{T \sum\limits_{x=1}^{m} N_x C_x}. \tag{10.17}$$

The coefficients K_x and K serve as an assessment of the obtained version of the plan. The best is the one at which the coefficient values are maximum, i.e. close to one.

Taking into account the complexity of the corresponding calculations, as well as the fact that during optimization they have to be repeated many times, compiling, evaluating and comparing various versions of the plan, such calculations must be performed using a computer (Fig. 10.6).

Each account operator in fig. 10.6 is indicated by a rectangle, on the left side of which a definable value is affixed. Logical operators are indicated by circles. If the condition indicated in the circle is fulfilled, then the arrow denoting the transfer of the command is provided with a "1" sign, otherwise — with an "O" sign.

The block diagram of the algorithm is a mathematical model for modeling the work plan of the enterprises of the ISK of the work of the construction organization, which allows to determine for each version of the plan the total amount of work of the construction organization, which can serve as a criterion for the optimality of this option. When drawing up one version of the plan, one has to set arbitrary values of the adjustable parameters H_{jx}, M_{ix}, I_{jx}. By changing these parameters, all other things being equal, given conditions, one can obtain different values of the optimality criterion.

In other words, there is a functional relationship

$$\mathrm{P} = \mathrm{P}(H_{jx},\ I_{jx},\ \Delta t_{jx}) \tag{10.18}$$

Optimization of the plan comes down to finding the maximum of the objective function. However, the analytical expression and the nature of this function are not known. It is only possible to determine its values depending on the accepted values of the controlled parameters by simulation. Under these conditions, optimization should be performed by one of the known methods for optimizing multi-parameter systems, for example, by the steepest descent method or the random search method.

Having determined P_{max}, we unequivocally find the optimal version of the plan. Indeed, P_{max} corresponds to well-defined values of H_{jx}, I_{jx}, Δt_{jx}, as well as the values of the beginning and end of each type of work at each object H_{jx} and K_{jx}, which can be transferred to the calendar schedule.

The solution of this problem opens the practical possibility of increasing the volume of work due to the most complete, even use of the available capacities of the construction organization and compliance with the basic principles of flow, and also makes it possible to establish scientifically sound optimal volumes of work of the construction organization of a given capacity for a given deadline for commissioning of launch facilities.

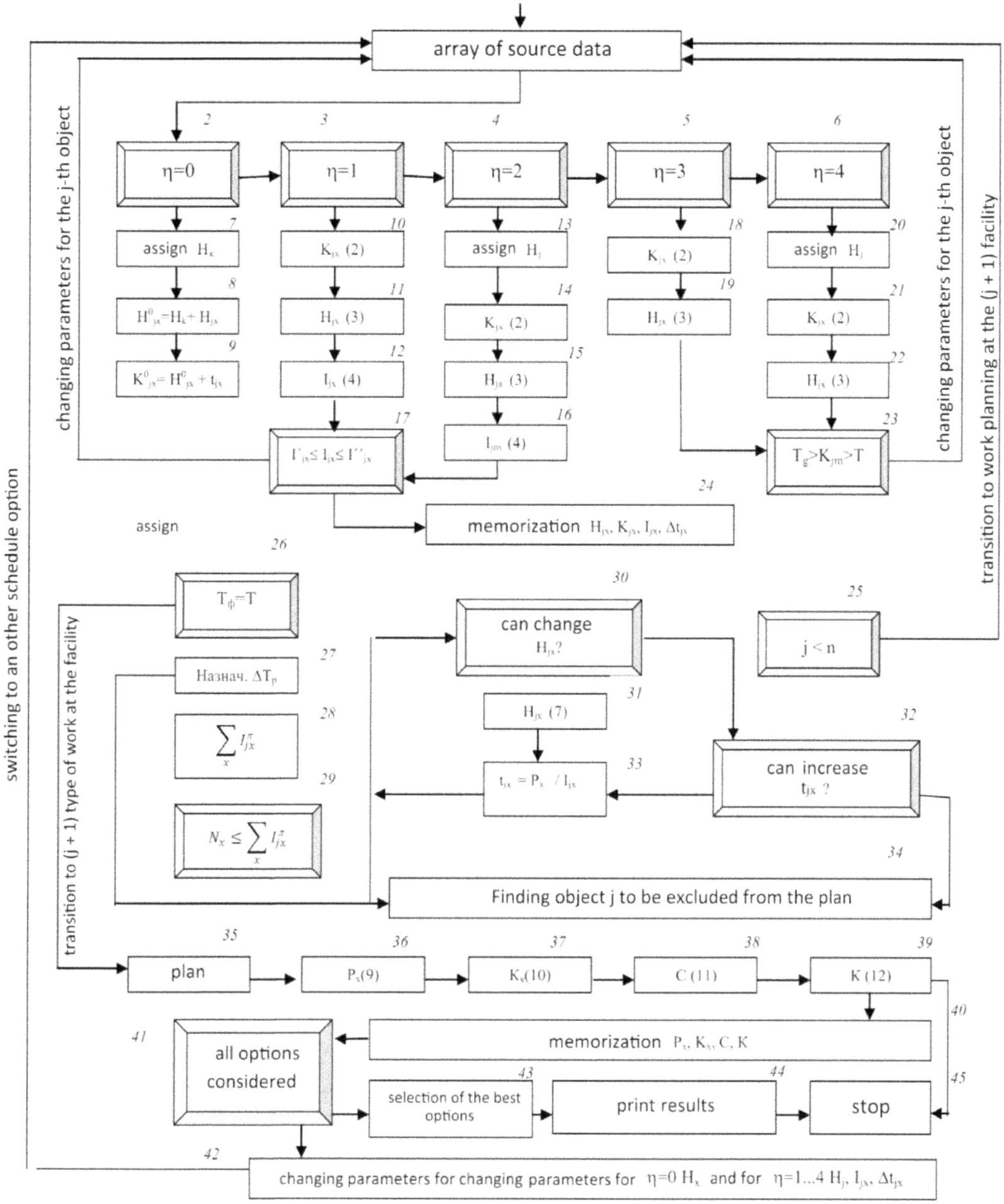

Figure 10.6: Block diagram of the simulation algorithm for the work plan of the construction organization as part of TLSED

If the construction organization has a predetermined planned one, the amount of work is less than the optimal one obtained as a result of the calculation, then by formula (99) it can be found by what types of work there are excess capacities in order to reduce them; otherwise, what capacities are not enough to increase or reduce the planned task.

An optimized production group construction plan is the basis for developing integrated network schedules for the construction of individual launch complexes and local network schedules for the construction of individual facilities.

Based on these schedules, applications are compiled and schedules for the supply of necessary materials, products, structures and equipment are developed and delivered to construction sites; work schedules of machines and crews of workers, taking into account their transition from facility to facility, as well as weekly schedules through which control and operational planning and construction management are carried out through the dispatch service.

Until now, the site option for the industrial cluster or enterprise and its layout, ceteris paribus, have been chosen on the basis of minimizing the cost of developing the territory. At the same time, due to the lack of a methodology for determining the value of agricultural lands, the problem of their economy did not find a fairly objective solution. In addition, over many years of industrial design, there was an opinion that it is impossible to effectively use territories with adverse natural factors. Under these conditions, much attention needs to be paid to the development of architectural and planning solutions for industrial units located in areas with difficult terrain, which, as a rule, are unsuitable for agricultural use. In some cases, such territories can be used as defense zones, for example, in explosive petrochemical industries.

The efficiency of the use of the territory can be improved due to the wider use of multi-storey industrial buildings, whose share in the total volume of industrial construction is still small (about 20%). For these purposes, it would be necessary to expand relevant studies and clarify the scope of multi-storey buildings based on their objective comparison of the most important technical and economic indicators with single-storey buildings.

When developing schemes of industrial units, one of the main conditions is to provide opportunities for their subsequent development. The importance of this task is so great that in some cases it is to its solution that the entire planning structure should be subordinated.

When developing industrial clusters in order to create the most favorable environment, ensure normal working conditions of enterprises and reduce capital investments, the conditions for optimizing their master plans and architectural and planning decisions of industrial buildings that were in line with the climatic features of the zones were determined.

The experience of building industrial clusters in these areas allows us to distinguish the following four periods of their development.

First, a pioneer base is created, which usually includes a plant for ready-mixed concrete and mortar, an work supply department base and logistics, in some cases a sawmill and carpentry workshop, as well as temporary indoor or outdoor storage areas for building structures and products. In the second period, construction of the construction industry base is carried out, the composition of which depends on the characteristics of the district, in the third — objects of basic production purpose, mining and processing enterprises, and in the fourth, further development and improvement of the structure of industrial construction and expansion of production ties within the economic region are provided.

The experience in the design and construction of start-up complexes as part of industrial clusters testifies to their feasibility and effectiveness in comparison with separate placement of industrial enterprises. When enterprises are located in the industrial cluster, the area under construction is significantly reduced and, accordingly, the amount of compensation for the alienation of agricultural land by creating common facilities for auxiliary production facilities, blocking buildings and structures, more complete placement of facilities, etc. In addition, construction volumes are significantly reduced -installation work, as well as the volume of housing and social construction, the organization of construction is improving, since the volume of work is concentrated within a limited area.

The placement of industrial clusters in the city limits leads to streamlining of development, improvement of architectural and spatial planning solutions.

Thus, the construction of start-up complexes as part of an industrial cluster is an important area for improving capital construction and increasing its efficiency.

Questions for self-control

1. What is a "unique object"?
2. What buildings and structures are unique objects?
3. What are the main structural elements of a unique building and why?
4. What federal law controls the safety of unique objects?
5. What is the complexity of buildings and structures and what classes of complexity do you know?
6. What initial data are necessary for the selection of construction and installation management schemes for the construction of high-rise buildings?
7. What is single industry and what is its relationship with industrial construction?
8. What are the differences between the SEZ, ZTR and TOSER in terms of specialization in industrial production?
9. What is an industrial park in ZTR?

10. What is the relationship between the concentration of production and industrial construction?
11. What is an industrial cluster?
12. What is the relationship between the specialization of industrial production and production cooperation?
13. What methods of measuring market concentration do you know?
14. What factors influence the economic efficiency of decisions on creating industrial clusters?
15. What is a building density coefficient?

Questions for discussion

1. Why is the formation of a comprehensive security system for unique objects comes to the fore during their operation?
2. Why is the basis of the technology for the construction of complex and especially complex real estate objects a combined large-block installation of enlarged building structures and equipment?
3. How does the concentration and specialization of multifunctional industrial production influence the territorial concentration of the location of construction objects and the specialization of construction organizations?
4. In what cases is it necessary to apply the nodal method of construction and parallel flow of the organization of construction?
5. How do industrial innovations affect the duration, cost and quality of construction?

Questions to solve the problem yourself

1. How are safety and uniqueness interconnected with the so-called "four 'C' approach?"
2. In the preparatory period for the construction of unique facilities, in-house engineering networks must be on a critical path, why?
3. Find the advantages and disadvantages for the work of construction organizations in the SEZ, ATD and TLSED.
4. How can one use typical technological models for the construction of facilities during the construction of industrial (industrial) parks?
5. How can one increase the efficiency of using the territory of an industrial park?

Chapter 11

GREEN BUILDING

11.1 General Provisions

The term "Green Building" appeared back in the 70s of the twentieth century in America, when the US was going through a period of construction of chic skyscrapers, energy consumption of which required a huge amount of resources, and the oil crisis, which caused a sharp increase in fuel prices. As a result of these events, the movement of ecologists in favor of saving the environment intensified, and at the same time a group of "environmentally-minded" architects emerged offering innovative ideas for improving the energy efficiency of buildings and structures and their rational use. The merger of ecologists and architects formed a movement for environmentally friendly — "green" construction or as it is also called environmental construction.

Green building is a comprehensive knowledge that is structured by design and construction standards, aimed at reducing the overall impact of development on the environment and human health, which is achieved through the efficient use of energy, water and other resources, as well as reducing waste, emissions and other effects on environment.

The level of its development directly depends on the achievements of science and technology, on the activity of industrial engineers and on society's awareness of environmental principles.

Green standards are designed to accelerate the transition from traditional design and construction of buildings and structures to sustainable, which preaches the following principles:

- safety and favorable healthy living conditions;
- limitation of negative environmental impact;
- taking into account the interests of future generations.

Green standards are designed to regulate a sustainable approach in construction and assess the degree to which buildings comply with the original principles.

The development and implementation of green building standards stimulates the development of business, innovative technologies and the economy, improves the quality of society and the environment. They are an instrument of a rational economy — they save money at all stages and facilitate integration into the global movement, they are the key to foreign investment and international recognition.

Today, the entire world community is interested in sustainable development and rational use of natural resources.

Green building directly contributes to sustainable development and is one of the ways to rationally use resources, energy, reduce waste, reduce the human impact on the environment and improve people's living conditions.

The goal is to reduce the level of consumption of energy and material resources throughout the entire life cycle of the building: selecting a site for design, construction, operation, repair and destruction.

Preservation or improvement of the quality of buildings and the comfort of their internal environment. This practice extends and complements classical building design with the concepts of economy, usefulness, durability and comfort.

New technologies are constantly being improved for use in the current practice of creating green buildings, the main objective of this approach is to reduce the overall impact of buildings on the environment and human health, which is achieved by:

- efficient use of energy, water and other resources;
- attention to supporting the health of inhabitants and increasing the productivity of employees;
- reduction of waste, emissions and other environmental impacts.

Throughout the world, BREEAM and LEED assessment systems are the most common evidence of building compliance with environmental standards. These certificates can be obtained at any stage of the building construction. BREEAM and LEED differ from each other in technical parameters and are regularly updated and improved based on existing market trends.

The main advantages of green certification are the demand from tenant companies that impose certain environmental requirements for the leased space, improving the brand recognition of the company, reducing operating costs and the impact on rental levels. Among the main problems hindering the active spread of environmental development in Russia are considered the slow processes of improving legislation in the field of energy efficiency and the environment, as well as the general lack of understanding of the importance and necessity of "green" standards both for business and among government representatives. From a financial point of view, environmental development is characterized by a long payback period, which carries additional risks, given the current unstable macroeconomic situation in Russia.

Progress and rapidly developing industry will inevitably affect the global environmental situation. This is characteristic of each country, no matter how modern and highly organized its industrial sphere would be, which is one of the components of this problem. And the second important aspect is the urbanization of the population and the gradual development of territories for the construction of housing, residential complexes and the construction of industrial facilities. The solution to this problem lies in the "green" construction.

Green construction is one of the types of construction and operation of buildings that minimize environmental impact.

Such construction is being implemented using such measures and technologies as:

- LED lighting
- Mechanical ventilation with heat recovery
- Green roofs
- Air and underground heat pumps
- Presence sensors
- Water-saving plumbing equipment and other types of energy-saving technologies.

Along with the American, British, and German green building rating systems in Russia, the first comprehensive national green building standard was created. It is a voluntary certification of real estate "Green Standards". Basic documents must be agreed with the Ministry of Nature of the Russian Federation. This system was registered by the Federal Agency for Technical Regulation and Metrology in 2010. Its main task is the introduction of resource-saving energy-efficient technologies, the use of environmentally friendly materials that reduce the negative impact of real estate on people's livelihoods and the environment, and the interest of developers, builders, architects and designers and buyers in the latest environmentally friendly technologies. The national standard STO NOSTROY 2.35.4–2011 "Green Building" is also significant for the market. Residential and public buildings. Rating system for assessing the sustainability of the environment. "On March 1, 2013, the new GOST R 54964-2012 "Conformity assessment. Environmental requirements for real estate." The criteria specified by GOST provide for a large-scale reduction in the consumption of energy resources, the creation of artificially created ponds, bicycle parking lots and stations for charging hybrid cars and electric vehicles near construction sites.

In Russia, as in other countries where green construction projects are being implemented, all aspects of the construction process benefit: developers, construction investors, manufacturers of building materials and equipment, designers, contractors and end users of buildings. Residents and tenants are given the opportunity to create a more favorable environment, increase labor productivity, comfort levels, as well as save on operating costs by 25-30% by reducing energy consumption, strengthening the reputation in the market and the implementation of corporate social responsibility towards consumers. Cities, in turn, are a market mechanism for saving energy resources and improving the environment, a lever for introducing innovative environmental technologies and implementing support for environmental legislation. Developers receive marketing advantages in the market that contribute to the quick delivery and sale of buildings (increase in rental costs by 2-16%, cost of sales by 6-35%), increase in the capitalization rate, attraction of additional funds, provision of permanent and solvent tenants to buildings. Justification of the characteristics of objects is the basis of an advertising company. Investors, in turn, receive a reduction in the risk of obsolescence of the asset, an increase in energy prices and an increase in corporate image. Architects and designers search for new architectural forms and solutions based on the use of modern high technologies, which allows them to realize their talent and increase their popularity. As a result, manufacturers of equipment and materials have a market advantage in taking the best positions in the implementation of innovative, highly environmentally friendly and energy-saving materials and equipment.

Thus, a number of tasks necessary for the development of "green" construction set in Russia can be distinguished:

- creating a favorable human environment;
- solving tasks of national importance related to the implementation of energy conservation policies;
- stimulating the development of highly environmentally friendly production of materials and equipment in Russia;
- raising the qualification level of specialists involved in the construction process;
- development of the scientific base of "green" construction;
- introduction of green building methods into the educational process.

11.2 Promotion of green building abroad

Description of energy efficiency of buildings is at different levels of rigor and detail in different countries, and this affects the efficiency and rigor of voluntary standards for environmental construction. Germany is the leader in the development of the regulatory framework for environmental construction. The first standards for thermal protection of buildings were issued here back in 1977, over the past 33 years, these standards have been regularly tightened.

The Energy Efficiency Act strengthened the requirements of the European Directive on the energy performance of buildings in 2007. Among other things, within the framework of this law, a unified generalized system for calculating energy efficiency was introduced, the Energy Performance Certificates were modernized, and a regular inspection of air conditioners was introduced.

The latest amendment to the Law on Energy Efficiency was introduced in 2009; it tightened the requirements by 30%. In addition, it has become mandatory for new construction projects to use renewable energy sources for heating the premises (part of the energy spent on heating must be provided by renewable energy sources). A new tightening of the law on energy efficiency occurred in 2012.

Work on the implementation of standards for zero-energy homes is ongoing at the national level. The energy efficiency requirements of buildings and structures, first introduced in 1977, included the requirements for thermal insulation of buildings, as well as the energy efficiency requirements of the main engineering systems — hot water supply, ventilation, and air conditioning. In addition, utility costs were normalized.

All US building codes are the responsibility of the states or local authorities, and therefore vary significantly across different regions of the United States due to different needs and climatic conditions in those regions. States in which local authorities are involved in building codes require local codes to be stricter than state minimum standards.

In California, for example, per capita energy consumption in buildings has remained surprisingly stable over the past 30 years, following state-level building and equipment standards in the 1970s. Most states have adopted standards based on standards set forth in the International Code of Energy Conservation and developed by the American Society of Heating, Refrigeration, and Air-Conditioning Engineers. The strictness of the standards adopted depends on the state climate and legal environment, as well as the strengths and interests of stakeholders at the local level.

The US federal government does not have direct control over building codes, although since 1977 the government has been involved in the development of standard codes and requires states to consider adopting them. The federal government also provides states with technical support in the adoption, implementation, and monitoring of building codes.

UK building codes and standards are changing in both energy efficiency and climate change. Regulation No. 1 of the Planning Policy: Implementing the principles of sustainable development 25 (PPS1) requires adaptation to climate change, including the Key Principle, according to which "regional and local planning bodies must ensure that urban planning plans comply with global principles of sustainable development, eliminating the causes and possible consequences of climate change through a policy that ... takes into account the effects of climate change in the place and project of this development. " The Office of the Deputy Prime Minister of the country has issued a climate change planning guide that contains recommendations for regional and local planning authorities on adaptation to climate change.

The United States stands out among all countries in terms of growth and volume of the green building market (as evidenced by the number of certified buildings, as well as the number of members recruited by the U.S. Green Building Council), the main incentive for green building is the financial and tax support of the state. In Germany, where, on the contrary, the number of certified buildings is not so large, the general level of energy efficiency of construction is striking, associated with initially high energy efficiency standards established by the regulatory framework for construction (table 11.1).

11.3 International certification system of "green building"

The following international certification systems are used in Russia: LEED (Leadership in Energy and Environmental Design, "Guide to Energy and Environmental Design, USA)

BREEAM (Building Research Establishment Environmental Assessment Method, "Environmental Performance Assessment Method from the Building Research Institute", UK). In addition, known is DGNB (Deutsche Gesellschaft fur Nachhaltiges Bauen, German Sustainable Construction Council).

Several Russian systems have been developed, including GOST R 54964-2012, "Conformity assessment. Environmental requirements for real estate", recognized by the state as a national standard for green building.

Of great importance for the market is the national standard STO NOSTROY 2.35.4–2011 "Green Building". Residential and public buildings. Rating system for assessing the sustainability of the environment."

The international standard "Passive House" developed in Germany is developing and has a great future.

11.3.1 LEED Standard

The LEED standard was founded in 1998 by the American Green Building Council (USGBC). More than 10,000 buildings with a total area of 608 million m2 in 135 countries are certified.

It is based on American ASHRAE standards (NP "ABOK" has been an associate member of ASHRAE since 1991).

In the LEED2009 (v3) system, indicators are grouped into six sections:

- A construction site (building site) that takes into account future needs (sustainable sites, SS).
- Water efficiency (WE).
- Energy consumption and atmosphere parameters (energy and atmosphere, EA).
- Consumption of materials and resources (materials and resources, MR).
- Indoor environmental quality (IEQ).
- Innovation in design (innovation in design, ID).

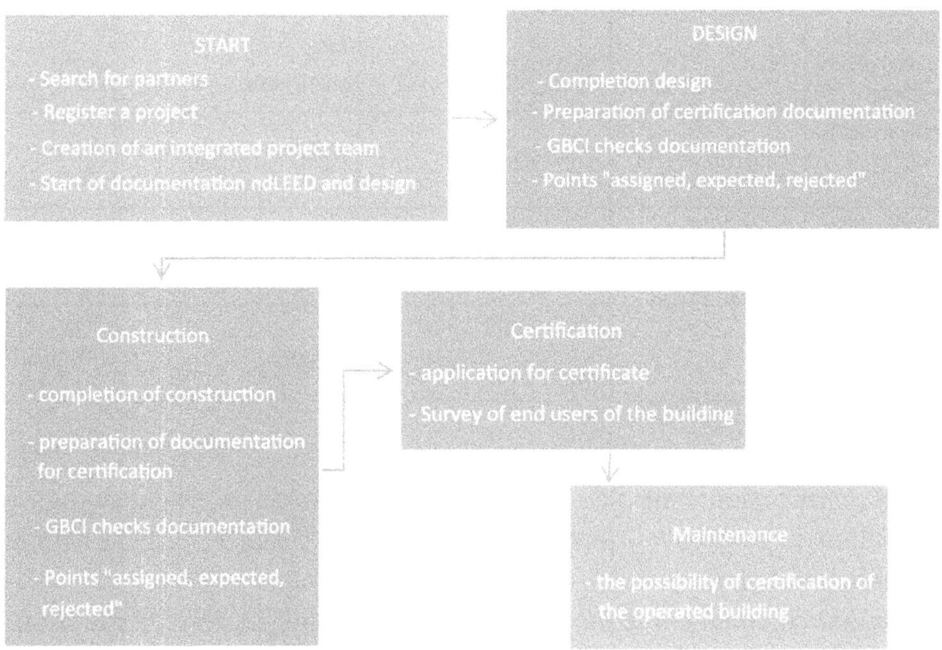

Figure 11.1: LEED certification scheme

There is also a difference in how LEED scores are calculated. Many criteria are tied to the US dollar (for example, criteria for energy efficiency — energy conservation), therefore, with unfavorable fluctuations in the exchange rate, the overall rating of buildings may suffer (30).

Table 11.1 Comparison of measures to stimulate environmental construction in different countries of the world

	USA	United Kingdom	Germany	Russia
State policy - goals to reduce CO_2	By 2020, 15% compared with 2009	By 2020, 34% compared with 1990	40% by 2012 compared with 1990	By 2020, 40% compared with 2007
The legal base of construction	State- specific; ASHRAE standard accepted in most cases	A unified method for calculating energy efficiency has been developed and approved.	Energy Efficiency Standards were developed in 1977 and have been continuously developed	There is no single method for counting Energy efficiency
Certification of energy efficiency	Energy Star , is required for the new system stances	EPC (Energy Performance certificate), mandatory for new construction DEC (the Display Energy Certificate)	EPC (Energy the Performance Certificate), required for the new system stances	Energy passports are required for the new construction
National environmental standard	LEED	BREEAM	DGNB	Green standard
Financial initiatives	Set on tax concessions, compensation costs for the mid -identification	Having resumed on the budget begin from scratch SOURCE energy nicks on bark at market mechanisms	stimulation of renewable energy	No
Share of countries in the global photovoltaic market (12)	5%	n/a green rates	44% green rates	2,3%
Corporative social responsibility of business	Highly developed	Highly developed	Highly developed	Weak effect - mostly on paper
National Council environmental construction	The U SGBC, 13213 members (2008)	UKGBC, 200 Members (2008)	DGNB, 300 Members, (2010)	RuGBC, 175 members (2011)
Pilotprojects		BedZed, BRE Innovation Park, Eden, London 2012	Freiburg	Active House, Sochi 2014, Skolkovo

LEED certification will also require the conversion of all drawings to the American metric system — feet instead of meters, which can be difficult, as well as additional costs.

The LEED certification process is automated and allows certification to be made without leaving the country where the project is located. The online system has electronic samples of documents that need to be filled out for each criterion. The LEED online system also contains points interpretation rules that provide answers to technical questions asked by other users. It is important to note that to get points on certain parameters, it is necessary that the building is populated for a certain time after the construction is completed. When all documentation is collected and construction is completed, the report

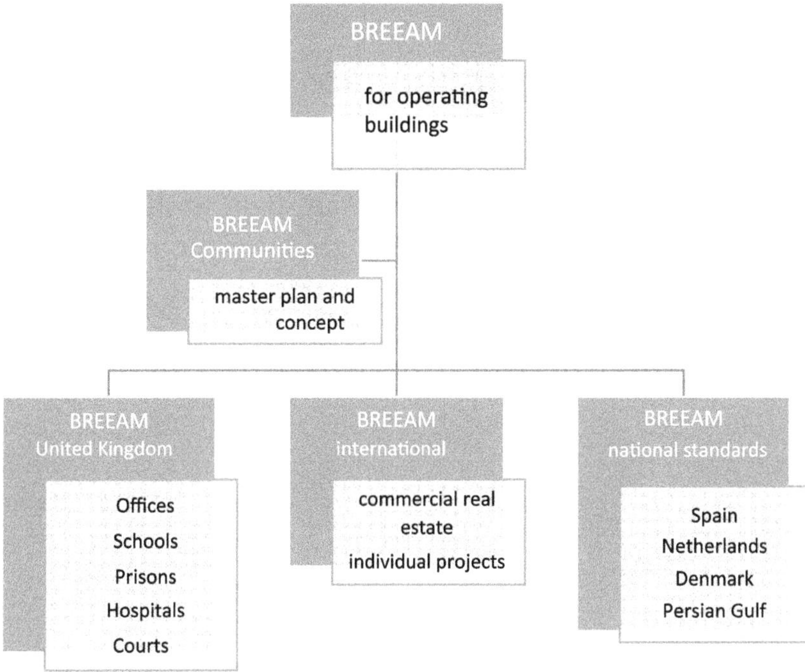

Figure 11.2: BREEAM family of standards

is submitted to the Institute for verification and certification. The entire LEED certification process usually takes from one year to five years, depending on the type and requirements of the desired certification level.

Table 11.2 LEED Family

LEED Design and Construction	LEED NC New Construction
	LEED FOR SHELL & CORE Commercial buildings without decoration
	LEED SCHOOLS Schools
	LEED HEALTHCARE Healthcare Facilities
	LEED RETAIL Trading buildings and premises
LEED For finishing work	LEED FOR COMMERCIAL INTERIORS Office Interiors
	LEED FOR RETAIL INTERIOR Trading interiors
LEED For operating buildings	LEED EB Operation and Maintenance
LEED For the residential sector	LEED for HOMES
LEED For mass development	LEED for Neighborhood Development

11.3.2 BREEAM

The BREEAM standard was founded in 1990 by the British company BRE Global.

More than 200,000 buildings certified. 90% of properties are located in the UK. It is based on EU norms (many are translated into Russian).

In the BREEAM system, indicators are grouped into nine sections:

- Management.
- Health.
- Energy.
- Transport.
- Water.
- Materials.
- Recycling.
- Use of land.
- Pollution.

The BREEAM system serves as an example of a successful concept that effectively implements the protection of the environment from human activity by satisfying the interests of all market participants without involving international or local law as a punitive tool. Depending on the number of points scored during certification, a rating is assigned in the BREEAM green building rating system.

11.3.3 BREEAM In-Use Standard

Within the framework of the BREEAM standards group, the BREEAM In-Use standard is gaining popularity in Russia, which involves the certification of buildings built without first taking into account the requirements of the standard and operated for at least two years at the time of initiation of the certification procedure. This standard is quite flexible, but already has international recognition. To achieve a level higher than Pass ("Certified"), most likely, it will be necessary to reconstruct the engineering systems of the building, as well as introduce new activities and programs related to the management and maintenance of the building.

BREEAM In-Use is an environmental impact assessment scheme for non-residential buildings. The assessment is carried out according to three criteria:

- Technical characteristics of the building: quality of architectural solutions and engineering systems. The level of consumption of basic resources (energy, water, materials, equipment), the level of waste generation are estimated.

- Performance indicators of the management company: assessment of the degree to which environmental aspects are taken into account when formulating policies, procedures, and when implementing building maintenance practices.
- Organizational effectiveness: assessing user activity in implementing environmental management practices.

All objects certified according to BREEAM and BREEAM In-Use, as well as their rating, are listed on the international website www.greenbooklive.com and can serve as a guide for future tenants who care about the environmental friendliness of their offices.

11.3.4 Russian standard GOST R 54964-2012

GOST R 54964-2012 "Conformity assessment. Environmental requirements for real estate "was developed jointly by the NP" Center for Environmental Certification — Green Standards ", FSBI "Central Bureau of Information of the Ministry of Natural Resources of Russia", the National Association of Builders (NOSTROY) and NP "ABOK". Approved in 2012 by Rosstandart, it began to operate on March 1, 2013.

Table 11.3 Basic environmental criteria of the standard for GOST R 54964-2012

Base category	Criterion
1. Environmental management	1.1 Organization of environmental management and monitoring 1.2 Optimization of design decisions 1.3 Qualification Requirements
2. Infrastructure and environmental quality	2.1 the selection of land for construction 2.2 Accessibility of public transport 2.3 Availability of social infrastructure facilities 2.4 the security of the local area with sports and fitness, sports and playgrounds 2.5 greening of the territory 2.6 Landscape irrigation 2.7 Proximity to the aquatic environment and visual comfort 2.8 Insolation of the adjacent area 2.9 Protection of the local area from noise, vibration and infrasound 2.10 Illumination of the territory and the protection of the territory from light pollution 2.11 Immunity to ionizing and electromagnetic radiation 2.12 Accessibility of ecological transport 2.13 Accessibility of buildings for people with limited mobility

3.Quality of architecture and layout of the facility	3.1 Quality of the architectural appearance of the building 3.2 Provision of premises with natural light and insolation 3.3 Gardening of the building 3.4 Availability of floor space 3.5 Comfort of space-planning decisions 3.6 Placement of social facilities in the building 3.7 Parking spaces 3.8 Optimality of the shape and orientation of the building 3.9 Protecting rooms from excessive ionization
4. Comfort and ecology of the internal environment	4.1 Air-thermal comfort 4.2 Light comfort 4.3 Acoustic comfort 4.4 Protecting the premises from the accumulation of radon 4.5 Monitoring and control of building engineering systems 4.6 Air monitoring and control
5. Quality of sanitary protection and waste disposal	5.1 Quality of sanitary protection 5.2 The quality of the organization of waste collection and disposal 5.3 Organization of storage facilities for flammable materials and hazardous household chemicals
6. Rational water use and stormwater regulation	6.1 Building water supply 6.2 Disposal 6.3 Water-saving fittings 6.4 Prevention of surface and groundwater pollution 6.5 Violations of natural hydrological conditions
7. Energy Saving and Energy Efficiency	7.1 Reducing heat energy consumption for heating and ventilation of a building 7.2 Reducing the consumption of thermal energy for hot water supply 7.3 Reduced power consumption 7.4 Specific total primary energy consumption for engineering support systems 7.5 Use of secondary energy resources 7.6 Use of renewable energy resources 7.7 Improving the efficiency of energy infrastructure
8. Environmental protection during construction, operation and disposal of the facility	8.1 Minimizing the environmental impact of materials used in construction 8.2 Minimization of waste during construction 8.3 Measures to protect and restore the environment during the construction process 8.4 Minimization of environmental impact during the construction, operation and disposal of a building
9. Ensuring life safety the activities	9.1 Providing backup power 9.2 Providing backup heat supply 9.3 Providing backup water supply

STO NOSTROY 2.35.4–2011 "Green Building". Residential and public buildings. The rating system for assessing the sustainability of the environment "was developed by NP "AVOK", OJSC "TsNIIPromzdaniy" and LLC "NPO TERMEK"on the instructions and with the participation of NOSTROY and was put into effect on November 11, 2011.

It complies with international ISO standards, takes into account the requirements of national standards, construction and sanitary norms, rules and methodological documents, as well as the main provisions of the rating systems LEED, BREEAM, DGNB and HQE (France).

The standard defines principles, categories, evaluation criteria, indicators of environmental sustainability, as well as weighted indicators for the purpose of rating an object.

It contains a system of basic indicators (indicators), which, if necessary, is adjusted by coefficients or supplemented by parameters reflecting regional or local climatic, energy, economic, social and object features.

Establishes habitat sustainability classes for built, reconstructed or overhauled residential and public buildings, as well as for their design documentation.

The requirements of GOST R 54964-2012 are based on the norms of the Russian Federation (GOSTs and SNiPs), as well as the standards of BREEAM and LEED systems.

Standard STO NOSTROY 2.35.68–2012 "Green Building". Residential and public buildings. The inclusion of regional features in the rating system for assessing the sustainability of the environment "provides for the procedure for taking into account the characteristics of the regions of the Russian Federation that differ in climate, resource potential (water and energy), alternative energy potential and economic potential from the conditions accepted as basic in STO NOSTROY 2.35.4 2011.

Regional features are taken into account by applying the coefficients to the results obtained when conducting a rating assessment (certification) of the sustainability of the living environment of residential and public buildings.

The purpose of taking into account regional characteristics is determined by the need to reduce the consumption of energy resources, the use of non-traditional, renewable and secondary energy resources, rational water use in those regions where there is a significant shortage of energy and water resources.

The basis of regional characteristics is the formula

$$S = \sum S_{red} + S_{unchanged} \tag{11.1}$$

Here S is the total S factor;

$\sum S_{red}$ — the given total of points by categories and criteria taking into account regional peculiarities;

$S_{unchanged}$ — the sum of points for categories and criteria that do not take into account regional characteristics, according to STO NOSTROY 2.35.4–2011.

Regional features are taken into account through corrective regional factors.

11.3.5 Benefits of certification

Certification for compliance with green building standards allows not only to obtain an independent assessment of the construction site, but also to increase the investment attractiveness of the project.

In general, investors can expect a 5.9% increase in net operating income.

Factors to increase the investment attractiveness of green construction projects:

- increase in rental costs (rental rates) by 2–16%;
- occupancy rates increased by 2–18%;
- 25–30% reduction in operating expenses due to reduced energy consumption;
- increase in value upon sale by 5.8–35%;
- 1% increase in employee productivity for LEED Certified and Silver and 1.5% for Gold and Platinum certificates;
- attraction and retention of the most solvent and long-term tenants.

Marketing advantages of the certification object:

- novelty and uniqueness of the offer; substantiation of the quality of the object, which will be believed by the international community and tenants;
- attracting tenants whose corporate culture includes environmental responsibility, including wealthy and prestigious global brands;
- certification results can be used as the basis for advertising campaigns.

Reaching the basic levels of standards leads to an increase in the cost of the building by 2-3% compared with a conventional building. Achieving the highest levels of standards requires additional costs of 5-7.5%.

The average time for receiving a certificate from the moment of registration for new construction is 8–32 months.

11.4 Technical reliability of LEED and BREAM standards. Comparison of technical characteristics

Voluntary standards are determined by a set of mandatory and selectable criteria that exist in both LEED and BREEAM. In BREEAM, the number of requirements that must be fulfilled is necessarily growing with the increase in the desired rating.

11.4.1 Mandatory LEED requirements for all projects:

- SSP1 — Reducing pollution from construction activities
- WE1 — Reduced Water Consumption
- EAP1 — Commissioning of energy-saving systems in a building
- EAP2 — Minimum Energy Efficiency Requirements
- EAP3 — Air Conditioning Management
- MRP1 — Collection and storage of secondary resources
- EQP1 — Microclimate Quality
- EQP2 — Prohibition of smoking (or automation of the ventilation system)

In addition, it is necessary to ensure full compliance with building codes and the obligation to provide data on energy and water consumption during the operation of the building.

11.4.2 Comparison of LEED and BREEAM selection criteria

Energy efficiency

• The EAP2 criterion requires building design according to the American ASHRAE 90.1 standard. This standard is more stringent than European and British standards. Both LEED and BREEAM are focused on energy efficiency indicators rather than specific engineering solutions.

• The EAP3 criterion is related to the design of air conditioning, this requirement is mandatory according to the rules and regulations of the European Union, therefore it is not included in BREEAM.

• EA1 Criterion Energy efficiency follows the same principles as Ene 1 in BREEAM. Nevertheless, there is a significant difference — unlike BREEAM, it is expressed as a percentage of energy consumption compared to average indicators, and not in reducing greenhouse gas emissions, in addition, it is expressed in terms of the cost of energy consumed. The same effect is observed in the Ene 5 criterion, which describes the use of renewable energy sources.

• A total of 11.85% of the total points are available for a building with zero greenhouse gas emissions in BREEAM. In LEED, the maximum number of points available is 48% for increasing energy efficiency by 48%, the improvement should be calculated according to the ASHRAE methodology 90.1-2007. Thus, according to LEED, for a low-energy building, you can get up to 17% points, which of course is less effective than BREEAM.

• In LEED and BREEAM, additional points are awarded for purchasing electricity from green suppliers.

Land use and spatial planning

• The SS1 criterion prohibits the use of agricultural systems, wetlands, as well as the water protection zone, the equivalent in BREEAM is the point awarded for reuse of land.

• The SS2 criterion is aimed at calculating building density, while BREEAM does not conduct such calculations. However, the criteria are similar in terms of infrastructure requirements within walking distance — a store, bank, post office, etc.

• Criterion SS3 — re- use of the site — correlated with LE2 in BREEAM, although it's much easier to achieve on LEED.

• Criteria related to ensuring transport accessibility and reducing the use of private transport are less stringent than BREEAM. For example, 30,000 square meters. a foot building on BREEAM will have to provide up to 95 bicycle parking spaces, while on LEED this figure is less than 36.

• The SS5.2 criterion is aimed at increasing green areas and increasing biodiversity, according to BREEAM, up to 5 points can be obtained according to this criterion and methods for achieving the criterion are much more stringent compared to LEED.

• Criteria SS7.1 and 7.2 reward the reduction of the "thermal island" effect, which is not directly mentioned in BREEAM, although some elements of this problem are reflected in the criteria LE 4, LE 5, LE 6 and Pol 5.

Water consumption

• Criterion WEP1 does not establish clear criteria for reducing water consumption compared to BREEAM

• Criteria WE1 Irrigation and WE 2 Water reuse — similar to BREEAM's Wat 6 and Wat 5 counterparts, although not fully consistent.

• In addition, BREEAM is awarded up to 3 points for the use of solutions aimed at reducing water consumption (metering devices, water shut-off by presence sensors and leakage control).

Materials and waste

• Criterion MRP1 Storage of secondary raw materials according to LEED is similar to the criterion Wst3 according to BREEAM, although the area of the space for waste storage is almost 1.5 times larger than according to BREEAM.

• Additional LEED points can be obtained for the use of rapidly renewable resources, local materials and the reuse of interior elements, which is not available in BREEAM.

• BREEAM uses eco-labels assigned by independent certification organizations in determining the environmental friendliness of materials, while LEED relies on the experience and knowledge of the evaluator and the project team.

• BREEAM encourages the reuse of materials and the introduction of measures to increase their service life, while LEED focuses on recycling.

Climate quality

• IEQP1 criterion Microclimate quality is based on ASHRAE 62.1, while BREEAM refers to national standards.

• The criteria of IEQ1, IEQ2, IEQ3, and IEQ5 are consistent with BREEAM's ventilation quality requirements, although they present stricter assessment parameters.

• IEQ7.1 criterion Thermal comfort is similar to Hea 10 in BREEAM, the difference is only in the choice of mathematical modeling systems.

11.4.3 Comparison of technical features in an international context

Both schemes have much in common and there is every reason to believe that a building that has received a high BREEAM rating will receive a good LEED rating. The minimum building requirements in LEED are stricter, which allows BREEAM, in turn, to be a more flexible system. Both standards are result oriented — i.e. they do not prescribe technologies or materials, but I propose an indicator that should be achieved by the project team in the process of project development.

LEED's strengths — control of internal pollution, the effect of a thermal island, its use in climatic zones where ventilation with mechanical induction and conditioning are actively used, will bring better results (30).

BREEAM's strengths are reduced use of personal vehicles, the formation of a comfortable outdoor environment, noise pollution and reduced water consumption. In addition, BREEAM pays a lot of attention to the process of control and construction management, which, undoubtedly, is a great advantage in countries with transitional economies.

11.4.4 Comparison of environmental performance indicators

Comparing the environmental performance of two international standards (LEED, BREEAM), it can be noted that they have different approaches to solving the same environmental problems (Table 11.4). For example, on the criterion of "energy efficiency" in LEED, you can score more points than in BREEAM. However, this does not mean that buildings built according

Table 11.4 The main environmental problems and criteria of international standards BREEAM and LEED

Environmental problem	Criteria for BREEAM Europe Commercial 2009	Coefficient ratings *, (%)	LEED NC 2009 Criteria	Coefficient ratings *, (%)
Increase energy efficiency	Energy efficiency, energy metering, lighting, renewable energy sources, equipment, reducing the use of mechanical ventilation, design taking into account the maximum use of daylight, creating lighting and thermal comfort zones in the room, analyzing the full life cycle of the building, the rules for putting the building into operation	32.3	Reducing the effect of heat islands— roof and paving of the territory, the procedure for acceptance of the building into operation, reduction of energy consumption, management of refrigeration equipment, energy metering and optimization, renewable energy sources, banning smoking in the building, zoning lighting and thermal comfort, maximizing the use of daylight	38
Air pollution (including road transport and quality microclimate)	Site selection, taking into account the transport accessibility, promotion of use alternative modes of transport, lower the number of parking spaces in the building, pollution reduction from construction site (reduced number of trips due to the choice of local materials)	18.4	Encouraging the use of alternative modes of transport and public transport, reducing the number of parking spaces	23
Reduced water pollution	Reducing and accounting for water use, reduction of emergency and current water consumption, reducing the use of drinking water for irrigation, reducing the load on urban water treatment systems	8.68	Reducing water consumption for irrigation, ecological drainage systems, accounting for foliage of drainage water, innovative water purification systems; extra consumption	10
Groundwater pollution	Reduction of groundwater pollution, environmental drainage systems, reducing water pollution from the construction process	2.83	Innovative Water Treatment Technologies	2
Waste Management – Reduction landfill	Reducing the level of waste from the construction site, creating conditions for the separate collection of garbage in the building, composting, reusing structures and facade elements of buildings, respect for finishing materials, encouraging the use of materials from recycled materials, analyzing the full life cycle of the building	13.36	Warehousing and removal of secondary resources, reuse of parts of a building, management of construction waste, reuse of materials, promotion of the use of materials from recycled materials, use of rapidly renewable materials	10
Spatial planning	Reuse of the site for construction, land reclamation, increase in green areas	2	Site selection, building density, site reuse	1
Biodiversity reduction	Increased biodiversity on the site, landscaping, protection of rare species	8	Protecting and restoring ecosystems, maximization of green areas	2
Other	Management Measures — Environmental management standards, life cycle assessment, noise pollution, environmental comfort		Social inclusion, comfortable environment	

*The rating coefficient is expressed as a percentage (%) of the total number of points assigned for fulfilling all the criteria. This assessment does not determine the effectiveness of a solution proposed by the standards. First, it describes the difference in approach to ecology between LEED and BREEAM.

to LEED will be more energy efficient than those constructed according to BREEAM. Therefore, to earn 15 points on the criterion of "energy efficiency" according to BREEAM, you need to build a practically autonomous building with zero power consumption from the network. To earn 19 points in the same category, guided by LEED standards, you just need to increase energy efficiency by 50%. Therefore, the task of comparing the environmental performance of standards is not as simple as it seems at first glance.

The environmental effectiveness of certain measures prescribed by the standards will also directly depend on the supporting infrastructure, such as, for example, enterprises for the separate collection and processing of recyclables or the availability of a bicycle lane system. In this regard, the application of environmental standards at selected advanced commercial real estate objects can be a good incentive for city authorities and entrepreneurs to develop programs for introducing centralized measures to improve the environmental performance of the city as a whole.

11.5 Green construction in Russia

11.5.1 On the role of green building

The very concepts of "green technologies", "green standards", "green city", "green construction", "green architecture", "green products" and others, bearing the same semantic load, began to take shape relatively recently in society and in professional circles. The very paradigm of the "green" environment is formed on the basis of the vital interests of a person, the development of his understanding and knowledge of the world in which he exists, what we call the living environment.

Until 2016, the concept of "green" construction was absent in Russia, there were no national standards with a comprehensive approach to the relationship of energy efficiency, resource conservation, environmental safety and comfortable environmental conditions of human life. Little attention was paid to the disposal and reuse of materials and products; some issues of the comfort of the living environment were not taken into account at all [64]. All this was expressed as a lag behind European countries in the regulatory and technical requirements for organizing, designing and conducting construction, operation of buildings and structures, and therefore there was an urgent need to develop a Russian system of national standards for green building [121].

At the same time, a lot of speculation has appeared on the "green" topic in the construction market and there is a misunderstanding in the professional community regarding the definition of "green" technologies,

The beginning of international cooperation in the field of environmental protection was laid in 1972 at the Stockholm Conference on the Environment. In 1987, the UN General Assembly adopted a resolution on a program of environmental measures, where the term "sustainable development" was officially introduced [54]. This material will be presented in more detail in Chapter 1, part two of the textbook.

The path from the first scientific research and theoretical generalizations in this field, to legislative and legal acts, normative-technical and methodological documents, has been enormous over the years. In essence, this is a movement from general provisions and principles of "sustainable development" to specific documents in the field of technical regulation, the formation of a system of quantitative and qualitative assessments, requirements, norms, standards. One of the important results of this movement was the emergence of "green" technologies in various areas of human activity.

The content of the concept of "green" technology is very broad and is characterized by the following provisions:

- "Green" technologies — a system concept that should be described in a system setting with the identification of subsystems and categories, elements, relationships, the establishment of quantitative and qualitative characteristics and parameters, criteria, restrictions, manuals and functions.
- "Green" technologies are a set of measures, methods, regulatory documents, design decisions of a managerial, organizational, technological and economic nature, based on legislative acts in the field of environmental protection, principles of resource and energy conservation, waste management, nature conservation, positive human experience in product manufacturing activities.
- "Green" technologies, as a direction in scientific and educational activities in the field of technology, organization and construction, training of professional and scientific personnel.
- "Green" technologies ensure the implementation of regulatory formal procedures in the process of conducting various levels of environmental impact assessment, environmental impact assessment, environmental risk insurance, environmental control, the application of an appropriate system of administrative and legal responsibility of persons for decisions.
- "Green" technologies are formed for all stages of the product life cycle, therefore, the effectiveness of their application should be considered as a whole for the object or its individual components.
- "Green" technologies have an information basis, rely on databases obtained in the course of practical implementation around the world, long-term observations, environmental monitoring using global information systems and computer technologies.

Green technologies (ST) are widely developed in various manufacturing sectors: construction, transport, energy, agriculture, and processing industries. The process of widespread development and application of ST is constrained, in many respects, by the lack of specific documents relating to a particular industry, of techniques aimed at the correct application of these documents.

The main factors that impede the development of ST are:

- undeveloped system of technical regulation;
- insufficient level of understanding in society, including in professional circles, of the principles of managing the life cycles of final products, on which, among other things, the approach of green technologies is based;
- lack of competitive offers on the market from Russian companies, approved methods, software products, expert methods, regulatory and technical documents.

This state of affairs restrains the development of production sectors and negatively affects import substitution, especially of high-tech products.

Currently, there is a widespread opinion about the high cost of all kinds of innovations, when the calculation is carried out only on the basis of one-time costs, without taking into account the fact that the final product will serve for many decades, because it is throughout the entire product life cycle that visible efficiency will be achieved from the introduction of green technologies.

At the same time, many modern approaches and concepts based on the philosophy of the life cycle have already firmly entered into the practice of managing various types of production activities and, it is especially important, formalize them to the level of norms, codes of rules, standards.

One of the main levers contributing to giving these processes concrete and targeted development is the development and promotion of standards in the manufacturing sector, which are called green standards in the terminology of ST.

We can say that the environmental requirements of the regulations and the "green" standards perform three critical functions:

1. "Green" standards should become a set of standards for limit emissions, norms for maximum emissions, norms for maximum discharges and norms for maximum permissible concentrations, as well as environmental safety rules, for example, in construction, ensuring the operation of industry in terms of observing uniform environmental safety requirements for technology and technology.
2. "Green" standards establish in technical regulations the environmental requirements for product safety and environmental quality standards, ensuring primarily its environmental safety and functional suitability. This

direction in standardization turned out to be the most problematic for us, since the state found itself without environmentally oriented technical regulations and standards, and practically does not provide effective protection of the consumer market from environmentally poor products.

3. "Green" standards perform the functions of environmental safety management; establish the rules for the construction and operation of production process control systems in society. This is a rapidly developing standardization function, which opens up new perspectives for the state, since standards of this type can and should be used by them to carry out certain environmental policies.

The development and implementation of green technologies in various areas of urban structures is especially relevant for large cities and megacities. So, for example, in modern Moscow, road and housing construction is being actively carried out, subway stations and social facilities are being built, improvement works are being carried out, which helps to improve the standard of living of citizens. At the same time, experts are increasingly talking about the need to comply with the environmental safety of construction and the transition to new construction technologies.

Examples of modernization of the urban environment with the introduction of "green" technologies can be considered from three levels:

1. Administration:

- sustainable development of the city through the creation of a comfortable and environmentally friendly urban environment;
- The international image of the city and the management policy of the administration, as a leader in the field of innovative approaches to the development of the city;
- positive attitude of residents, public organizations and mass environmental movements, in connection with the implementation of specific measures aimed at real improvement of the urban environment.

2. Residents:

- improvement of the urban environment, including domestic territories, micro districts;
- improving the quality of housing and communal services, modern equipment of common areas in homes, installation of modern equipment and engineering systems;
- gradual reduction of utility bills (up to 30-50%), costs of major and current repairs of houses through the use of resource and energy-saving systems, equipment and technologies.

3. Business:

- tax, financial preferences and privileges of production enterprises, in terms of receiving a city order;
- a significant reduction in the cost of operating facilities per life cycle;
- high public image, increasing competitiveness, increasing market value of commercial real estate, increasing rental costs.

11.5.2 Standardization of "Green" environmental technologies

STI and "green" innovative products"

NRU MGSU has taken the initiative to create at the Federal Agency for Technical Regulation and Metrology (Rosstandart) a technical committee for standardization "Green technologies for the living environment". By the order No. 1315 of September 15, 2016, Rosstandart decided to create the Technical Committee for Standardization No. 366 "Green" technologies for the life environment and "green" innovative products "(hereinafter referred to as TC 366). The created TC 366 opens up new directions for the development of research in science and technology, provides an improvement of the known results and normative and technical documentation, ensuring at all stages of the life cycle of a product (facility) its maximum compliance with the conditions and parameters of the natural and techno genic environment in order to improve the quality of the environment human life.

In addition to the main ones, TC 366 is also called upon to solve the following tasks:

- Search and implementation of best practices in the field of maintaining sustainable development and ensuring environmental safety, using green technologies;
- Analysis of foreign documents in the field of standardization in the application of green technologies to maintain sustainable development and ensure environmental safety;
- Scientific activities in the field of maintaining sustainable development and ensuring environmental safety based on "green" technologies;
- Regular verification of national and interstate standards in force in the Russian Federation in order to identify the need for updating or canceling them;
- Consideration of proposals for the development of international standards, including based on national and interstate standards.

11.6 Terms and definitions of "green" technologies of the life environment

"Green" environment ("green habitat") — a set of objects and environmental factors that ensure safe and favorable conditions for human life, as well as the conservation and restoration of the natural environment, the rational use and reproduction of natural resources, and the prevention of negative impacts economic and other activities on the environment and the elimination of its consequences.

Note — The objects of a "green" living environment include buildings, structures, structures and the adjacent territory.

The factors of the "green" living environment include rational planning zoning, design solutions, engineering systems and equipment of buildings, structures, structures, premises.

"Green" innovative products — products with new or significantly improved properties, combining the beneficial effect of its functional purpose with ensuring safe and favorable conditions for human life, as well as preserving and restoring the natural environment, rational use and reproduction of natural resources, preventing the negative impact of economic and other activities on the environment and the elimination of its consequences throughout its life cycle.

"Green" standard — a **standardization** document that establishes the requirements, norms and rules for a "green" environment, "green" innovative products, "green" technologies, approved in the established manner.

"Green" construction (Green Building) — the construction of real estate, minimizing the negative impact of real estate on the environment, improving quality indicators of environmental safety for users of real estate, improving the quality of life of the population, improving energy efficiency of objects, reducing resource costs and harmful emissions.

"Green" technology — a set of methods, tools and knowledge used to produce products and provide services that provide safe and favorable conditions for human life, as well as the conservation and restoration of the natural environment, the rational use and reproduction of natural resources, and the prevention of the negative impact of economic and other activities on the environment and the elimination of its consequences.

"Green" technologies of the living environment — a set of methods, tools and knowledge used in the construction and operation of buildings and structures that provide safe and favorable conditions for human life, as well as the conservation and restoration of the natural environment, the rational use and reproduction of natural resources, and the prevention of the negative impact of economic and other activities on the environment and the elimination of its consequences.

"Green" products — products that combine the beneficial effect of its functional purpose with ensuring safe and favorable conditions for human life, as well as preserving and restoring the natural environment, rational use and reproduction of natural resources, preventing the negative impact of economic and other activities on the environment and eliminating it consequences throughout its life cycle.

11.7 Classification of green technologies

TC 366 has developed a standard for classifying "green" technologies by various types of economic activity in order to assess and reduce the negative impact of the life cycle of a particular technology on the environment, while creating a comfortable living environment for humans. The need to develop a standard was to create a system of categories and related requirements for all subsequent standards for green technologies.

This standard is designed to raise awareness among citizens and professionals about the benefits and value of green technologies.

The classification of green technologies is based on the following principles:

- Using a scientific approach to quantify and calibrate the criteria for green technologies.
- Cost-effectiveness and explicit parameters for determining environmental quality.
- Use international best practices, including legislation, climate and nature of use.
- Association of specialists of various types of manufacturing industries to ensure widespread understanding and accessibility.
- Use existing industry tools, practices, and standards, where possible, to minimize costs.

The classification method of "green" technology in various types of economic activity is based on a system for evaluating the performance indicators of certain criteria, using reliable environmental and cost-effective approaches. This approach allows you to identify the criteria for "green" technology at various stages of the life cycle. For this, it will be necessary to carry out certain measurements, evaluate and determine specific characteristics of the effectiveness of the technology under consideration in comparison with other non-green ones on an independent and reliable basis.

All criteria for the effectiveness of "green" technology are reduced to a quantitative assessment of individual measures and indicators, distributed in the following categories:

I. Management
II. Comfort
III. Energy efficiency
IV. Transport
V. Water
VI. Materials
VII. Waste
VIII. Land use
IX. Security
X. Innovation

It is important to understand that these categories mainly reflect the overall effectiveness of the green technology in question, and not just the opportunities or limitations for specific stakeholders.

To develop standards for green technologies, the following sequence must be observed:

- To determine the type of economic activity in the framework of which the "green" technology is implemented.
- To develop the main criteria for the categories indicated above, the considered "green" technology.
- Identify the minimum requirements for green technology that are mandatory.
- Set weight values for the developed criteria based on the system.

Standards in the system of "green" technologies are developed by groups of types of economic activity based on the sections and classes presented. In general, a standard is developed for a class of a type of economic activity, and if necessary, subclasses of a type of economic activity can be used. The developed standards for groupings of types of economic activity should meet the following requirements:

- The developer (developers) of the standard for "green" technologies for any specific type of economic activity should use the performance criteria distributed in the categories indicated above.
- Weighted values for assessing the criteria for the effectiveness of "green" technology are set depending on the specific type of economic activity of the organization.
- Development of a standard for "green" technologies requires a preliminary determination of the weight value of the criteria for each category based on research on individual types of economic activity. The value of weighting factors is determined for each market segment separately from other segments.

Research should be carried out by research organizations independent of the developers of the standard, with appropriate competence. Research should be objective and representative.

Ultimately, the study should establish weighted values for a specific set of criteria characterizing the considered "green" technology for a specific type of economic activity.

Complex technologies, consisting of several separate technologies of various functional types, performing many different functions, require separate consideration. Since the weighted values of the evaluation criteria in such a situation may differ depending on the functional purpose of the considered "green" technology. If the technology in question is not represented in existing types of economic activity, then the development of standards for "green" technology will still be possible. Such types of "green" technologies will require the development of an individual set of criteria for use in combination with the previously approved criteria for classifying "green" technologies.

The process of identifying "green" technologies of the living environment can be carried out in two stages:

A) The stage of designing "green" technology (EP) , which consists in the compliance of the created set of documentation with certain criteria, distributed according to established categories.

Evaluation on electronic information is an intermediate confirmation of the estimated effectiveness of the developed "green" technology with strict adherence to its implementation.

B) The stage of implementation of "green" technology (ER) , which consists in meeting certain criteria during startup, operation and, if appropriate, disposal of the technology in question.

When evaluating "green" technology according to a system of criteria, a balanced approach should be used. This means that when assessing the compliance of the considered "green" technology, some criteria established in the standard may not be used, i.e. a mismatch in one category may be replaced by a match in another. However, to preserve the fundamental environmental and economic criteria in each standard for green technologies, minimum requirements must be established for a specific set of criteria from each category.

Maintaining innovation in various types of economic activity of the Russian Federation is one of the most important tasks of green technologies. In the system of standards criteria for "green" technologies, this is achieved in category X. "Innovation". It establishes additional criteria that correspond to the principles of sustainable development, which are the modern achievements of science and technology, know-how and utility models. This accelerates the process of their implementation in certain types of economic activity.

There are two ways to recognize innovation in a particular "green" technology. The first method is the achievement of exemplary indicators outlined in the existing criteria for green technologies, that is, going beyond the standard evaluation criteria and, accordingly, best practices. However, not all evaluation criteria contain exemplary indicators. The second way: when the developer of the standard for "green" technology has a set of supporting documents with scientific justification and testing of a new criterion that has not been previously used, then it can be considered "innovative". In the case of developing an innovative criterion for the existing standard for "green" technology, within 5 (five) years, this standard should be revised.

11.7.1 Green Technology Criteria

In TC 366, a methodology is developed in a separate standard for determining the criteria for classifying the environment as "green" technologies for their benefits to humans and the environment. The standard is designed to ensure the implementation of best practices at all stages of the life cycle of the technology in question, and will also allow the identification of cost-effective technologies and innovative solutions that minimize environmental impact and have a beneficial effect on humans; will help the customer to formulate the terms of reference taking into account the principles of sustainable development and environmental safety.

Each green criterion should consist of the following sections:

1. Information about the criterion — reference information about the criterion, name, number of points available and whether the criterion contains an indication of the mandatory minimum requirements.
2. Goal — indicates the general objectives of the criterion and the source of the impact, which it measures or reduces.
3. Evaluation Criteria — Set out acceptable and best levels of best practice benchmarks and assessment requirements. If the technology in question meets the evaluation criteria, according to the decision of the expert, then the corresponding number of points is awarded. Some criteria contain questions of the "innovative" level; if the technology corresponds to the innovative level, an additional point for innovation is awarded.
4. Lists and tables — this section contains lists and tables referenced in the Evaluation Criteria section. These may include benchmarks or specific performance indicators for various types of technologies.
5. Compliance notes — Contain additional information regarding the application and interpretation of the main assessment criteria, including informa-

tion on how to conduct conformity assessment in a particular technology or in a particular place.

6. Methodology — this section contains a description of the methodology, according to which the number of points that can be achieved for a certain level is determined. It includes, for example, calculation procedures or an indication of how the standards or qualifications of specialists specified in the assessment criteria relate to these requirements.

7. Basic confirmations — this section describes various types of project information that should be submitted by the client / project team to an expert in order to establish the conformity of the technology indicators to the evaluation criteria, and thus confirmation of the fact of the award of the corresponding number of points.

8. Additional information — this section contains any additional information regarding the application of the evaluation criteria, including any definitions used in the evaluation criteria, or sources of additional information that may be useful in relation to this issue.

Some "green" criteria may contain mandatory minimum requirements, which means that in order to achieve a certain level of certification, it is necessary to achieve points according to certain criteria. Most of the "green" criteria are mutually interchangeable, i.e. the customer and the project team can choose the target certification level, build a certification strategy and achieve the desired certification level.

All classification criteria are divided into 10 categories presented in the previous section, a brief summary of which is presented below, and an example is given in table 11.4.

I. *Management* — this category encourages the use of "green" management methods in connection with the design, implementation, independent acceptance, transfer to operation and subsequent operation of the technology in question. In this category, the focus is on the implementation of measures to ensure organizational quality, the launch of technology at key stages of design, procurement and supply, initial operation, from the initial stage of the technical assignment and the start of design to proper after-project maintenance.

The main content of the "Management" category:

- Consultations with interested project participants regarding the implementation of projects and relevant third parties.
- Recognizing and encouraging the use of life cycle costing and technology life cycle planning, as well as data exchange to increase awareness and understanding.

- The general contractor demonstrates sound environmental management practices, taking into account the principle of sustainable development as part of the implementation of the technology.
- The environmental impact of technology related to energy, water and transport use is monitored and taken into account to ensure compliance at the stages of implementation, transfer and launch of the technology, as well as to increase awareness and understanding for future projects.
- Schedule of independent acceptance of the implemented technology, including the optimal period and appropriate testing and commissioning of all engineering systems and structures, in accordance with the principles of best practices.
- Verification, testing, identification and elimination of defects using the appropriate method. Providing a user guide for technologies that are not technical experts, staff training or operator training in the appropriate time frame for the stages of transfer of green technology and its operation.
- Providing the necessary infrastructure and resources to provide follow-up assistance to users or staff of launched green technology.

II. *Comfort* — this category encourages an increased level of comfort, health and safety of users, visitors and others who are in the immediate vicinity of green technology. Questions in this category are aimed at improving the quality of human life, recognizing activities that contribute to the creation of a healthy and comfortable and external environment for all users of green technology.

The main content of the Comfort category:

- The likelihood of blinding by light was excluded in all relevant stages of the implementation of the green technology.
- Levels of daylight achieved in accordance with best practices.
- Indoor and outdoor lighting systems are designed to avoid flickering and provide adequate levels of illumination.
- Lighting is probed for individual control.
- Minimize sources of air pollution through careful design, specifications, and planning.
- A ventilation strategy has been developed that allows flexibility and adaptation to the potential needs of users and staff, and climate scenarios.
- Thermal modeling conducted in accordance with relevant standards.
- Scenarios of projected climate change are considered as part of the thermal model.
- Analysis of thermal modeling allowed us to determine a temperature management strategy for each user of "green" technology.

- The technology meets the requirements for acoustics (sound insulation, noise level of the internal environment, damping time).
- Reducing the risk of water pollution and providing users with clean water.

III. *Energy Efficiency* — this category encourages the selection and design of energy-saving solutions, systems and equipment to support the principles of environmentally sustainable use of energy in green technology. The questions in this section evaluate measures to improve the technology's energy efficiency, encourage carbon reduction, and support effective management approaches throughout the green technology operation phase.

The main content of the Energy Efficiency category:

- Recognize the improvement in the energy performance of the green technology compared to the traditional approach to its implementation, in relation to the energy needs for heating and cooling, primary energy consumption and carbon dioxide emissions.
- Encourage measures to reduce energy demand through design decisions and the selection of engineering equipment.
- Energy metering systems are installed to identify the share of end-user consumption.
- Additional meters are installed for equipment with high energy loads.
- Installation of devices for visual display of energy consumption.
- Selection of energy-efficient lighting and controls to prevent their use during the day or after school hours.
- Conducting a feasibility study to establish the most suitable, low- or carbon-neutral alternative energy sources installed at or near the implementation of green technology.
- Refrigeration systems, its controls and components have been developed in accordance with the standards and demonstrate the saving of indirect greenhouse gases (CO_2) throughout the life of the green technology.
- An analysis of the structure of demand and use of transport is carried out to determine the optimal number and size of elevators, escalators or moving walkways. Energy efficient transportation systems.
- Selection of energy-efficient equipment of best practices and related activities for their operation.
- Identify unregulated energy loads that have a significant impact on overall energy demand.
- Demonstrate a significant reduction in energy requirements at all stages of the green technology life cycle.

IV. *Transport* — this category encourages greater access to environmentally sustainable modes of transport for users of this technology. The questions in this section relate to the accessibility of public transport and other alternative transport options (cyclists, local infrastructure) that help reduce car travel and therefore CO_2 emissions over the life of the green technology.

The main content of the Transport category:

- Promoting technology in close proximity to developed public transport networks, which helps reduce pollution and congestion.
- Providing funds to encourage the use of low-carbon modes of transport and reduce individual travel.
- To contribute to the sustainable reduction of transport costs by conducting an assessment or a statement about the assessment of a specific site and developing a travel plan based on the needs of the technology being implemented.
- Provide the necessary space and services to enable work at home and reduce the need for travel to work.

V. *Water* — this category promotes sustainable water use in the operation of the technology under consideration. This section focuses on identifying methods to reduce the consumption of (internal and external) drinking water throughout the life of the green technology and to minimize leakage losses.

The main content of the category "Water":

- Reducing the need for drinking water through the selection of efficient sanitary equipment, rainwater collection and recycling systems.
- Installation of water meters on the water supply network to encourage the management and control of water consumption, aimed at reducing inefficiencies in consumption and leakage.
- Installation of leak detection systems capable of detecting large water leaks in the mains water supply.
- Flow control devices that control the flow of water to each plumbing area or installation to reduce water loss.
- Shut-off valves with easy access to them, which allow stopping and quickly eliminating leaks with minimal water loss.
- Determine the needs of water for technology for purposes other than household, food and sanitary in order to both reduce and reduce its consumption.

VI. *Materials* — this category encourages measures aimed at reducing the environmental impact of the materials used in the design, implementation, maintenance and repair of the technology in question. In matters of this section, the focus is on the supply of materials that are of appropriate origin and low impact throughout the life of the product, including mining, processing, and production and processing.

The main content of the category "Materials":

- Reducing the environmental impact of a technology's life cycle by evaluating its basic elements.
- Materials are delivered in accordance with an environmentally sustainable procurement plan.
- Basic materials are delivered in a responsible manner to reduce environmental and socio-economic impacts.
- The technology uses measures to reduce the effects of material damage and wear.
- Appropriate design and technical measures have been applied for the relevant elements in order to limit the decline in material quality due to environmental factors.
- Opportunities were identified and measures taken to optimize the use of materials.

VII. *Waste* — this category encourages the environmentally sustainable management (and reuse, if possible) of production and operational waste, as well as waste from the maintenance and repair of the technology in question. Encouraging good design and implementation practices, the questions in this section are aimed at reducing waste arising from the production and operation of green technology, and reducing the amount of waste disposed of in landfills.

The main content of the category "Waste":

- Development of a waste management plan at the design stage of the technology.
- Reducing the flow of garbage in the territory where technology or manufacturing is implemented.
- Reduction in the volume of non-hazardous waste sent to a landfill for disposal (on the territory of sale and on the territory of production), demolition waste and earthwork (if applicable) generated during the implementation of the project.
- The amount of recycled waste from reuse expressed as a percentage and indicated in accordance with the target level.
- Provision of suitable facilities and equipment to ensure separate collection and storage of volumes of operational waste to be recycled generated from the technology or unit under consideration, people and their operational activities.

- The selection of certain types of materials for technology that contribute to the reduction of possible waste.
- Facilitate consideration and implementation of mitigation measures for more extreme weather conditions caused by climate change throughout the life of the technology.
- Facilitate the consideration and implementation of measures for future changes in the functional purpose of the technology and its systems throughout the entire service life.

VIII. *Land use* — this category encourages sustainable land use, the creation and protection of places of residence, and in the long term, the improvement of the biodiversity of the site where the technology is located. The issues in this section are related to the use of previously used territory or objects with low environmental value, mitigation and improvement of the ecology of the site and long-term biodiversity management.

The main content of the Land Use category:

- Encourage the use of previously exploited or contaminated land.
- Encourage the implementation of technology on those lands that already have limited value for wildlife and protect existing environmental facilities from significant damage in preparing the site for the development and implementation of any work.
- Encourage actions taken during the implementation of technology aimed at increasing the ecological value of the site.
- Minimize long-term impacts on land and environmental biodiversity.

IX. *Safety* — this category considers measures to prevent and control hazardous effects on humans, their property and the environment associated with the location and implementation of the technology in question. The questions in this section are aimed at reducing the impact arising from hazards of anthropogenic and natural character.

The main content of the Security category:

- Providing effective measures to ensure safe passage to and from the technology being implemented. Safety requirements are studied and taken into account in the design and specifications.
- Risk assessment of natural hazards that may affect the technology being implemented and the implementation of measures to mitigate any risks.
- Providing an open space that gives a sense of privacy and well-being for the person.
- Prevention or reduction of exposure to refrigerants through specification and prevention of leakage or its detection.

- Reduction of NOx emissions associated with the use of water heating systems.
- Implementation of technology in areas with a low probability of flooding, where design decisions minimize the effects of flooding.
- The organization of surface runoff should not become worse compared to the scenario on the site before the implementation of the technology. Water pollution prevention systems have been installed.
- External light pollution is eliminated due to an efficient design or eliminating the need for unnecessary outdoor lighting.
- Measures to reduce the likelihood of discomfort due to noise from stationary engineering installations.

X. *Innovation* — this category provides an opportunity for benchmarks and innovations to be recognized in the evaluation of "green" technology, which for some reason were not included in the requirements of the nine previous categories or go beyond them. The category includes innovative points if the technology meets the criteria of an exemplary level on a specific assessment issue. This also includes innovative products and processes that may qualify for an innovative score, provided they are scientifically sound. In this category, there is a stimulation of the development and application of innovative technological solutions with evidence-based economic, social or environmental benefits for their accelerated market promotion and implementation.

11.7.2 Conformity assessment according to the requirements of "green" standards

To assess the level of compliance of the technology under consideration, the point method was used with rating values of the degree of compliance with the criteria of "green" standards.

The standard presents the basic principles of assessment and the qualification requirements of the experts conducting the assessment, as well as the requirements for evidence necessary to set off the criteria.

Conformity assessment according to the requirements of "green" standards is organized and carried out while ensuring the necessary level of objectivity and reliability of the assessment results. Conducting activities to assess compliance with "green" standards is based on the following basic principles:

- voluntariness;
- openness;
- non-discriminatory access to applicants when assessed according to "green" standards;

- objectivity and reliability of the assessment and reproducibility of its results;
- confidentiality of information;
- protecting the interests of applicants;
- the availability of information on the results of the assessment to interested parties;
- competence of experts.

The presented principles are the basis for the development of requirements for assessing green technologies in various types of economic activity of business entities.

Conformity assessment according to the requirements of "green" standards is carried out at the initiative of a business entity (hereinafter — the organization). Compliance assessment according to the requirements of "green" standards is carried out by expert (quality) method. The expert method is used in order to:

- determine the supplier (contractor, contractor) of green technology in order to meet state and municipal needs in accordance with;
- selection of the contractor of services (works) as the general contractor, contractor, subcontractor, contractor, supplier of goods to launch the "green" technology;
- obtaining by the organization's management an objective assessment of compliance with the requirements of "green" standards used in the production of technologies.

When conducting a conformity assessment according to the requirements of green standards, a third party should use document forms (application, application form, certificate of conformity, appendices to the certificate of conformity, permission to use the conformity mark) and the conformity mark established by documents of voluntary certification systems in which certification bodies are authorized to conduct certification.

In order to conduct an expert assessment by a third party, the applicant, a business entity (hereinafter referred to as the applicant), sends an application and a questionnaire to the certification body.

The certification body assesses the requirements of green standards on a contractual basis with the applicant. Entrepreneurship entities declare specific types of economic activity by grouping in order to assess business reputation in accordance with the all-Russian classifiers of types of economic activity. Assessment of compliance with the requirements of green standards by an expert method is carried out by experts of the certification body, appointed in the manner prescribed by the rules of the System in accordance with the legislation of the Russian Federation. To conduct the assessment, the certification body forms a group of experts who analyze the applicant's questionnaire and assess compliance with the requirements of the "green" standards using points to determine the rating.

In the event experts identify knowingly inaccurate information specified in the questionnaire, the process of evaluating the organization may be suspended or terminated. Experts have the right to request from the applicant additional information, in addition to that indicated in the questionnaire. To verify the accuracy of the source data, experts must travel to the place (to the company's office, to the production base, to the place of the actual provision of services or work) within the time agreed by the parties. Based on the results of the expert review, the experts generate a report with the necessary set of supporting documents on compliance with the requirements of the "green" standards of the considered technology.

Based on the results of the assessment, the expert group draws up a report indicating the result of the assessment of compliance with the requirements of "green" standards. Based on the expert opinion, the certification body issues a certificate of conformity. Certification bodies should conduct an assessment according to the "green" standards of business entities taking into account legislation in the field of personal data protection.

In order to ensure stable trust in evaluations by third parties, Voluntary Certification Systems recognize a public body under the technical committee for standardization, whose area of activity is standardization in the field of "green" technologies of the living environment of business entities, as a commission on appeals of these Systems. The task of such a public body under the technical committee is to ensure confidence in the assessments and increase the responsibility of third parties evaluating according to "green" standards.

Certification bodies authorized to carry out certification work in the field of assessment of green technologies of business entities in the relevant voluntary certification systems must meet the requirements established by the legislation of the Russian Federation in the field of accreditation and the requirements for certification bodies established in the corresponding system. The competence of the certification body should be ensured by the availability of experts to assess compliance with the requirements of the "green" standards of business entities.

Experts to assess compliance with the requirements of standards for green technologies of business entities must meet the following requirements:

- have a higher education and an academic degree;
- undergo additional education and training according to the programs established by the requirements of the corresponding voluntary certification

systems in the field of assessment according to the standards of "green" technologies;

- have the skills to perform work in the field of assessment according to "green" standards.

Note — Skills should be confirmed by practical experience or training in the field of assessment according to the standards of "green" technologies in various types of economic activity in the amount of at least three internships.

Information about experts involved in certification in the field of assessment according to the standards of "green" technologies should be available on the Internet site of the certification body and include the following information: surname, name, patronymic of the expert; number of the document confirming the status of the expert; name of the organization that issued the document, its validity.

The methodology for determining the rating of compliance with the requirements of standards for "green" technologies is based on the percentage of the points scored to their total number and is distributed according to the following principle (table 11.5):

Table 11.5 Rating values of the degree of compliance with the requirements of "green" standards expressed in a point ratio.

Rating	Outstanding	Excellent	Good	Satisfactory	Unsatisfactory
% points	≥ 70	≥ 55	≥ 40	≥ 30	< 30

The rating value of the assessment of compliance with the "green" standard allows the customer and other interested parties to compare "green" technologies from one type of economic activity with each other through the percentage ratio of the points scored. An unsatisfactory rating is a type of economic activity with technology that does not meet the minimum requirements and / or does not meet sufficiently assessed criteria.

To assign the technology in question the status of "green", it must meet the minimum requirements and score more than 30% of all categories for a specific type of economic activity.

Consider, as an example, "green" technologies with an **outstanding** certification level, which should act as a model for this type of economic activity. To set off the highest rating, scientific research of these technologies must be carried out so that other project groups and organizations can use them in order to disseminate best practices and achieve the best results. Therefore, prior to final certification, a project team or organization whose technology claims to be Outstanding, submit a case study or information allowing the experts of the technical committee to conduct a study on their own for consideration by the technical committee.

The Technical Committee publishes all case studies on green technologies with a rating of **Outstanding** on the secretariat website of the Technical Committee.

The rating values of the degree of compliance with the requirements of the "green" standards specified in table 11.3 are applicable both for the design stage of the "green" technology and for the stage of the already implemented "green" technology.

The process of determining the degree of technology compliance by rating value is carried out in the following sequence:

1. The scope of the economic activity of the technology being evaluated is determined.
2. Then, the system expert will determine the number of points awarded for each of the ten categories.
3. The percentage of points achieved is calculated for each category separately.
4. The percentage achieved for each category of points is then multiplied by the corresponding section significance factor.
5. The results by category are added together and an overall score is obtained.
6. The overall assessment score is then compared with the reference indicators of the certification level from table 11.1 and, subject to all other requirements, an appropriate rating is achieved.
7. Additional points to the calculated rating can be added for each achieved innovative criterion, but not more than 10% of the total weight value of all categories.

The main document confirming compliance with the requirements of the standard for "green" technologies is the expert report. In order to preserve the reliability of the data, all certification decisions should be based on verified and reliable information about the technology under consideration, which is easily traceable, i.e., based on the evidence presented. Based on the report, the expert determines the rating value on the compliance of the technology under consideration with the established indicators in table 11.3.

The role of the expert is to collect information about the technology, to use it competently and impartially to evaluate the criteria for a suitable standard. When scoring points for achieving the criteria, the expert must be convinced that all the evidence collected demonstrates a clear compliance with all relevant criteria specified in the "green" standard. All evidence in the expert report should be with appropriate links.

Evidence does not have to be specially prepared for evaluation purposes. In many cases, the expert must have available and already prepared information about the technology in order to confirm compliance with the standard set of documentation. For this reason, the process of assessing compliance with the requirements of "green" standards does not aim to prescribe any type of evidence, but at the same time, each criterion may contain a certain set of specific documents necessary to set off one criterion.

When evaluating "green" technology at the design stage, it is permissible to use officially registered letters to demonstrate intentions to achieve compliance with clauses of the criteria for "green" standards. Such evidence should also clearly explain the anticipated actions that will be taken at the final stage of the assessment when implementing green technology. However, letters of commitment that were counted during the conformity assessment at the design stage will not be a substitute for confirming compliance at the green technology implementation stage. The expert should not assign points for which there is reason to doubt the reliability of the data or there is intent only written obligations. Evidence at the green technology implementation phase should reflect the characteristics that arc alrcady bcing implemented. Appropriate evidence may be an expert report based on a technology inspection with supporting photos and / or executive drawings.

Reliability of evidence provides confirmation that the assessment was carried out correctly and the technology meets the criteria points provided in the "green" standard. Below is an indicative list of information that an expert should rely on to set off some types of evidence:

- Records of communications of communications: any record of communications of officials that is used as evidence should provide clear evidence of the technology in question, identify the author and his role, date and identity of the recipient.
- Letters of official correspondence: must be on the letterhead of the company with a signature (allowed with electronic signature), registered in the prescribed manner.
- Minutes of meetings: must contain the date, place and information about the participants (names and positions in the organization), as well as the agenda being discussed and decisions made.
- Drawings: all drawings must contain the name of the technology being evaluated, the stage of its implementation, the name of the drawing, date, version number and scale.
- Specification: The specification should give a clear idea of what is relevant to the technology in question as part of the assessment and should have a date and number.

- Report of the visit being implemented: the report should contain the name of the technology being evaluated, the date, the name of the expert and a short text of what has been witnessed. Photographic evidence may be used to confirm the text in the report.

Table 11.6 Example of calculating points and determining the final rating by weight

Rating Categories	Points earned	Maximum score	% of points scored	Weighted section values	Section Summary
Control	7	10	70%	0.12	8.40%
Comfort	11	14	79%	0.15	11.79%
Energy efficiency	10	21	48%	0.19	9.05%
Transport	5	10	50%	0.08	4.00%
Water	4	6	67%	0.06	4.00%
Materials	6	12	50%	0.125	6.25%
Waste	3	7	43%	0.075	3.21%
Land use	4	10	40%	0.10	4.00%
Security	5	12	42%	0.10	4.17%
Innovation	2	10	20%	0.10	2.00%
			Overall value	**56.87%**	
			Rating	**A GREAT**	

Questions for self-control

1. When did the first green building standards appear?
2. What regulatory framework governs the green construction of Russia.
3. In which countries are BREAM, LEED standards used 4. What is the point assessment of buildings and structures
4. What types of buildings are rated by BREEAM?
5. How to choose an appraiser?
6. How to become a BREEAM accredited appraiser?
7. What type of certification is applicable in Russia?
8. When is the building evaluated according to the BREAM standard?
9. Waste classification.
10. Recycling of construction waste
11. How is energy efficiency of buildings achieved?

12. When the paradigm of “green” construction was created, with what directions is it connected?
13. What is included in the concept of “green” construction?
14. What are the obstacles to the introduction of “green” technologies in construction and what may be the mechanisms for their development?
15. What structure in Russia is developing national “green” standards, when, by whom and where was it created?
16. What is meant by the term “green” standard, disclose its requirements that they establish?
17. What sequence must be followed to develop a green building standard?
18. What can be the steps for identifying green” environmental technologies that they include?
19. What sections should each “green” criteria consist of?
20. What are the rating values for the degree of compliance with the requirements of “green” standards?
21. What functions does the expert perform in assessing the degree of compliance of the construction project with “green” standards?

Questions for discussion

1. The place of green spaces in the architectural space.
2. Types of modern environmentally friendly materials for the formation of the surrounding space, exterior and interior of energy-saving buildings.
3. Three examples of ecological settlements that meet international environmental standards.
4. Describe the types of residential buildings from the standpoint of energy conservation.
5. Three examples of environmental areas consistent with international environmental standards.
6. Three examples of eco-cities that meet international environmental standards.
7. The principles of organizing eco-sustainable space.
8. Measures to stimulate legislation in the field of environmental construction in European countries.
9. What other areas of human activity is associated with the “green” theme?

10. What can be the benefits for different categories of citizens when using "green" technologies in construction?
11. What categories of green technologies can be added to those already identified?
12. Why does the "green" standards need a category on innovation, what criteria can it be used for?
13. What principles should be based on the assessment of "green" standards and who can be its member?

Questions to solve the problem yourself

1. Assessment of the ecosystem potential of construction projects.
2. Environmental factors in eco-certification systems.
3. The impact of eco-certified construction projects on sustainable development of cities and territories.
4. The multi-comfort environment as part of eco-certification of construction projects.
5. Classification of solar buildings according to the heat supply system.
6. Problems of wind energy.
7. The principles of building design using hydrothermal energy. Town-planning techniques.
8. Using the example of modern buildings, determine the technologies used for green building.
9. Identify related technical standardization committees that develop national standards in the construction field.
10. Prepare a description of several "green" criteria for the designated ten categories.
11. Calculate the points and determine the final rating according to the "green" standards on your example.
12. Consider examples of assessments conducted on the territory of the Russian Federation according to the international "green" BREEAM or LEED standards.

Chapter 12

LOW-RISE COTTAGE CONSTRUCTION

12.1 A common part

The global all-Russian modern trend in housing construction is its reorientation to the low-rise housing market. Restructuring of supply and demand in the market has led to the fact that the relative share of low-rise housing has increased over the last 20 years by more than four times. In 2016, this figure was 25.3%, while in 1990, it was only 6.2%, and in the first half of 2017, it was 50.8%. According to the forecasts of the Government of the Russian Federation, the share of low-rise construction in the total commissioning of housing in 2018 should be at least 60%, and in 2020 — 70%. Despite the positive dynamics, the share of low-rise housing construction in Russia lags significantly behind climatic conditions such as Canada (79%), the USA (92%), and European countries — 80%.

At present, a crisis transformation is taking place in the input structure and the restructuring of the construction complex of the Russian Federation for priority housing construction of low-rise housing. This feature of the priority of housing construction forms a new image of the country as a "one-story Russia" and reflects world development trends in the reproduction of housing, focused on the formation of a more comfortable and ecological population environment.

The idea of "one-story Russia" is increasingly supported at the state level. This confirms both the adoption by the State Duma of the Russian Federation of the program for the development of low-rise housing construction "Home" in 2009, and a significant number of similar programs in the regions of Russia. The current FTP "Housing" emphasizes low-priority construction priority and outlines specific program and targeted measures to support it in the areas of supply and demand development. Federal, regional and corporate **programs for low-rise construction should be an alternative to the construction of residential panel and monolithic skyscrapers.**

12.2 The modern structure of building materials and structures of low-rise housing

At the present stage of development of low-rise construction in the Russian Federation, brick and stone housing construction (53% and 15%, respectively) occupy a significant place in materials and structures, wooden housing construction — 22%, 10% of houses are built from other materials, including polystyrene foam (see fig. 12.1).

The most commonly used construction technologies are at the same time the most expensive. In particular, brick and stone house building has the highest cost of construction, and their total share in the structure of low-rise construction takes 68%. Data on the cost are presented in table 12.1.

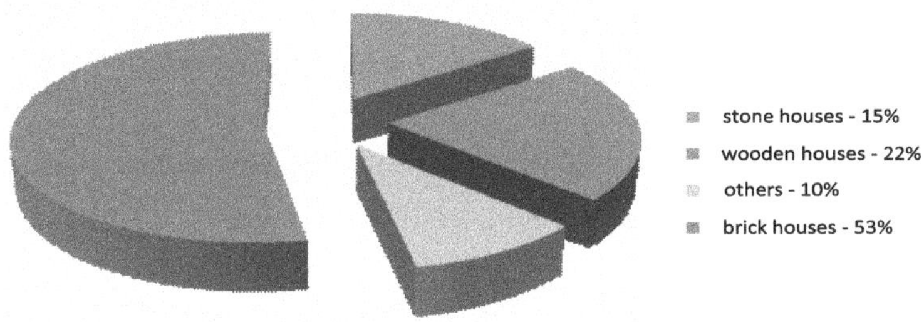

Figure 12.1: The structure of building materials of low-rise housing in the Russian Federation

Table 12.1 Cost of 1 square. m living space

No.	Construction material	The average cost of 1 square. m of living space (house kit without decoration and external networks)
1	Brick	20 000 rub.
2	Tree	16 000 rub.
3	Building materials from deep wood	10 000 rub.
4	Expanded polystyrene	9 000 rub.
5	Cellular concrete	8 500 rub.

Thus, the most promising in terms of reducing the cost of construction is the use of wood and materials for its processing.

The application of new technologies (erection of low-rise buildings based on materials from cellular concrete, modernized technologies of large-panel housing construction based on elements of permanent formwork made of expanded polystyrene, technology of thermos structural panels) that allows you to work at any time of the year remains relevant. At the same time, the production, transportation, installation of bearing and self-supporting structures, as well as the subsequent operation of the building, require much lower costs than construction technologies associated with traditional materials.

We can distinguish the following classification of technology groups of low-rise construction and the range of their cost:

I. *Stone houses:* brick; foam block; gas block; ceramic block; 5 fixed formwork; monolithic-modular designs. In this group, the cost price range is sq.m. frame house: the *maximum value* is *21,000 rubles / sq.m.* and the *minimum — 15 000 rub./sq.m .;*

II. Frame houses: wooden frame; metal carcass; bulk modular houses; SIP panels. Range of prime cost sq.m. frame house. *The maximum value* is *25,000 rubles / sq.m.* and the *average minimum value is 14,000 rubles/sq.m.;*

III. Wooden houses: glued beams; profiled timber; rounded log. *The maximum value* is *22,000 rubles / sq.m.* and the *average minimum value is 10,000 rubles / sq.m. ;*

Comparative characteristics of the construction of various types of low-rise residential buildings according to the project "Russian House of the Future" are given in Table 12.2

The most optimal should be recognized as the type of low-rise houses with a base of wood and its combinations

12.3 Classification of the main organizational and technological schemes of wooden low-rise housing construction

The analysis shows that the structure of low-rise construction as a whole is currently ineffective. Dominated by the construction of the most expensive materials, inferior to other materials, not only in cost but also in quality characteristics.

Cost of 1 square. m of a wooden house is at least 10-20% lower than in houses built from other materials. At the same time, wood is an affordable, renewable, local and cheap building material. For the mass construction of low-rise wooden housing using industrial technology, its cost is about 2 times lower than the traditional Russian multi-storey monolithic-concrete housing.

The cost of one square meter of the total area of a residential building made of modern wooden structures ensures the availability of housing for all working citizens of the country. That is why it is important to significantly increase the achieved share of the construction of wooden houses in low-rise construction by 24%, which is unacceptably small for a forest power that has 25% of the world's timber reserves.

The main organizational and technological types of wooden low-rise housing construction are:

1. Construction of wooden houses from chopped logs. The structural basis of a chopped wooden house is a log cabin, consisting of logs horizontally stacked on top of each other — "crowns". The log house is made up of hand-cut logs, their thickness varies from one end to the other. Traditionally, wooden houses were built from raw wood, which was necessarily accompanied by shrinkage of the structure. Under natural conditions, the tree dries up to a year and a half. Due to this feature of wood, the construction of the house was long, since the log house had to "stand". Modern technology pos.

Table 12.2 Comparative organizational characteristics of different types of low-rise residential buildings with a total area of 200 square meters

House type	Footing Type	labor input on factory / construction site	Instalation duration at presence of footing	Time of year for construc-tion	shrinkage of the walls	home decoration deadlines	Comfortable accommodation since the start of construction
Brick	strip Mono-lithic	0/100%	3-4 months	Spring-fall	2 years	6 months	1 -2 i ode
Log	Columnar Monolithic strip	60% / 40%	1-2 months	Roundyear	2 years	3 months	1 year
Glued beam	Columnar Monolithic strip	70% / 30%	2-3 weeks	Roundyear	No	1 month	2-3 months
aerated concrete	strip Monolithic	0/100%	2-3 months	Spring-fall	1 year	6 months	1-2 years
Wooden Panel frame	Columnar Monolithic strip (lightweight)	80% / 20%	1 week	roundyear	No	1 month	1-1 , 5 months
Wooden modular	Columnar Monolithic strip (lightweight)	95% / 5%	2 days	Roundyear	No	Factory finish	1-2 weeks

They want to eliminate this drawback thanks to new technologies for the production and assembly of houses.

2. Construction of wooden houses from logs. To combat the uneven shrinkage of the house, special vertical studs are used — "ties", which not only add rigidity to the wall, but also allow you to control the process of shrinkage at home.

3. Construction of wooden houses from glued beams. The difficulty of using wood as a building material is associated with the processes of drying and processing, as well as the shrinkage of the built house. At present, industrial technologies have appeared in wooden housing construction, which make it possible to build wooden houses with guaranteed high quality, which is the technology of building houses from glued beams. Glued beam technology allows you to mount houses all year round, while the installation of house structures on a finished foundation does not exceed 3-4 weeks. Glued beams are much warmer than usual, since the glue layers are good heat insulators, and the spiked connection of the beam to each other creates several sealing loops and makes it impossible for cold air to enter the room. Glued beam in terms of breathability and tightness exceeds the parameters of a conventional round log. The advantages of glued beam houses are the absence of deformation of the house structures, resistance to decay and insect damage, and high fire resistance.

4. Construction of wooden houses from profiled timber. In addition to round logs, chopped logs and glued beams, profiled timber is widely used for the construction of wooden houses. In its manufacture, a conventional beam is given a strictly defined standard shape (profile), its surfaces are planed according to the first class of cleanliness, that is, to the level of euro lining. The advantage of a profiled beam is that houses are quickly and easily assembled from it, since all products are manufactured in the factory on machines with high accuracy. A wooden house from a profiled beam is built much faster and after the construction has a neat and attractive appearance.

5. Construction of wooden houses from frame-panel panels. The technologies of frame and frame-panel housing construction are today one of the most promising and rapidly developing areas of suburban construction in Russia. The Soviet experience of frame housing construction can not be considered sufficient, it was limited to the design, construction and operation of temporary workers' settlements and military settlements. In Russia, the intensive use of technologies related to the wooden frame began in the last 5–7 years.

At the same time, today frame housing construction can be considered one of the dominant technologies in the global market for the construction of individual houses. The share of frame houses in the world is 70%, and in the USA and Canada, it reaches 90%. The frame and frame-panel technologies may become dominant in the near future in the low-rise construction market Of Russia.

The basis of these technologies is the use of the wooden frame of the building. The lumber frame is assembled according to the principle of a honeycomb building structure and is a rigid and durable structure with a long service life (up to 150 years).

The main advantages of frame and frame-panel housing construction are the short construction time (the box of the building can be erected in three to four days, and the whole house "turnkey" — in two months) and the excellent thermal insulation properties of the panels. A wall panel with mineral wool insulation with a thickness of 80 mm provides thermal resistance that is not inferior to a wall made of aerated concrete with a thickness of 400 mm, or a brick wall with a thickness of 490 mm. Such houses do not require massive foundations, and the absence of shrinkage allows finishing work immediately after the installation of the supporting frame, which allows you to build an environmentally friendly, warm and comfortable house in the shortest possible time. In addition, there is the opportunity to build in the winter season.

In frame houses, the external walls consist of a multi-layer "pie" mounted on the construction site: OSP moisture-resistant oriented particleboards, insulation between them and layers of hydro-, wind- and vapor barrier. Oriented particleboards consist of 90% of wood obtained from sanitary logging; synthetic resins and paraffin emulsion are used as bonding elements. Cement chipboards and other materials may also be used.

In frame-panel (or, otherwise, "sandwich") houses, the walls of the building are sandwich panels (two enclosing plates and insulation between them), made at the factory and "hung" on the frame. One of the undoubted advantages of sandwich panels is their manufacturability: the supply of all necessary components for the installation of panels (corners, fasteners, sealants) practically reduces the work on the construction site to assembly according to the principle of the designer. A team of two qualified installers and one lifting device in one shift can cover up to 200 square meters. m surface. Sandwich panels can be made immediately with a facade solution, and then the house does not need additional decoration.

One of the varieties of frame-panel housing construction is Canadian technology using the Ecopan sandwich panels, which is actively promoted today in Russia. In this embodiment, the wall and floor panels are a multilayer monolith in which three layers are glued under high pressure: the external OSB boards and the internal insulation — expanded polystyrene foam. Such a panel is obtained by the carrier, walls and floors from these panels withstand loads up to 150 kg per cubic meter. m. The house, built on the Ecopan technology, does not have "cold bridges" and drafts, because the panels are hermetically fitted to each other due to factory production.

The differences between frame and frame-panel technologies are very significant. The manufacture of wall panels in the factory allows for faster construction, good quality control and cost savings. At the same time, the use of such technology requires good access roads and the use of mechanization. The advantages of frame-panel housing construction can be most fully disclosed in projects with the construction of a large number of houses. For the construction of individual residential buildings in small areas and with difficult access conditions, the use of frame technology may be more appropriate.

Such low-rise residential buildings have already become widespread in Russia (Moscow region, Tatarstan, etc.). They are economical in construction and can provide a high level of architectural design. In Europe, the last 15 years there is a constant demand for frame houses. The main advantages of such houses are environmental friendliness, low heat loss, fire safety, resistance to the spread of mold and fungi, the possibility of individual design, quick installation and relatively low price. Due to the constant increase in energy prices, the demand for these houses is growing inexorably. Therefore, fuel consumption for heating such a house is from 3 to 5 liters (in terms of fuel oil) per square meter. square meter per year. This is three times less than the cost of heating a brick house. Today, the share of such houses in Germany is already 16%. Their feature is that the supporting support is the frame, and inside the structure there is a heater that perfectly saves heat. The main positive factors in the production of frame-panel houses are: low cost; minimum level of competition; modern technology; high speed of construction and commissioning of houses (up to one month); flexible production. The ability of the technology to produce houses of any configuration and type, as well as various buildings for industrial and other purposes; short start-up time of the plant (8-10 months) and quick return on investment; reduced need for highly qualified personnel due to the short term of their training; a real opportunity to place such plants in each regional center; An ideal opportunity to use this technology to add additional floors and "townhouses" on previously constructed buildings.

6. Modular wooden housing construction. Modular this type of houses is called because they are built in the form of sections or modules. For example, a house with an area of 105 square meters consists of two modules, and the house has an area of 209 square meters of 4 modules. The main advantage of this technology is that high-quality houses are built at the factory, and not at the construction site. Modules of a wooden house are assembled in the factory, which distinguishes this technology from the assembly of components on a construction site.

7. Wooden house-building: glued-beam technologies The urban development system that prevailed in the Soviet Union virtually eliminated wood as a building material, largely due to existing fire safety rules and reliance on pre-fabricated, multi-storey large-panel housing. The result of the 20th century was the fact that in Russia the culture of working with wood was almost completely lost.

Wood is a wonderful building material — environmentally friendly, durable, fireproof and easy to recycle. The most important factor is that the tree is a renewable resource. Wooden houses are not inferior to stone or brick in any parameter: for example, the fire safety of a building is easily achieved thanks to special processing of wood. It is important to note that the tree burns for a long time in the event of a fire and provides valuable time for taking various measures against fire, and the metal literally five minutes after the start of the fire loses its load-bearing capacity.

An important feature of a tree is its inertness. It does not rust, is not susceptible to corrosion, has enormous chemical resistance and is the best material in an aggressive environment. The service life of a tree with proper processing (primarily stripping), protection and supervision is almost unlimited.

In a wooden house, a peculiar microclimate is always maintained due to the ability of wood to absorb odors, excess moisture, or give it away when the room is over dried. A housing made of wood aromatized with essential oils and antiseptic resins inherent in this type of tree. Microorganisms that are useful for people and animals that impede the development of pathogenic bacteria live in the tree.

The difficulties of using wood as a building material are associated with the difficulties of drying, processing and shrinkage of the built house. However, today in the wooden housing industry there are industrial technologies that allow you to build wooden houses with guaranteed quality. One of these technologies is the construction of houses from glued beams.

Glued beams are produced at a factory equipped with modern equipment. As a material for its production, a conifer board is used. Schematically, the technological process of its production is as follows: a high-quality log with a natural moisture content is sawn into boards of a small cross section, which are easily dried to a level of 10–12% humidity. Dried boards are planed on four sides for precise geometry. Then these boards are glued (under a press) using a special environmentally friendly glue that does not affect the breathability of wood. Glue penetrates under pressure deep into the pores of the tree, which ensures a strong connection.

When gluing in a single beam, the direction of the wood fibers in the lamellas is set in opposite directions from each other. Due to this, glued beams are more durable than ordinary ones, and when humidity changes, it does not change its shape. After the lamellas are glued into a single and indivisible beam, it is profiled on four-sided machines. The quality of the entire glued beam and, ultimately, the quality of the future home depends on the accuracy of the manufacture of the tongue-and-groove joint. After giving the glued beam a profile, it cuts to size — it is cut into elements of the required size with high accuracy. Well, the final step in the production of glued beams is "killing" in it on special cup-cutting machines for crown cups and drilling holes for pins.

Glued beam technology allows you to mount houses all year round; installation of house structures on a finished foundation does not exceed 3–4 weeks. Glued beams are much warmer than usual, since the glue layers are good heat insulators, and the spiked connection of the beam to each other creates several sealing loops and makes it impossible for cold air to enter the room. In addition, ordinary timber gives cracks when it dries (bursts) and these cracks significantly reduce the working thickness of the timber. Glued beam in terms of breathability and tightness exceeds the best parameters of a round log. Profiled parts are tightly connected during assembly, so there is no need to put a tow or heater in the grooves between the parts.

The surface of the glued beam, made in compliance with all technological requirements, is even and smooth; the wall assembled from glued beams looks monolithic, which gives houses from glued beams one more advantage: they do not need external and internal decoration. Due to the lack of costs for interior and exterior decoration, the cost of building a house from glued beams is reduced by 50 percent or more compared, for example, with a brick house. Glued timber houses, like all wooden ones, are much lighter than stone or brick (weight 600–900 kg / cubic meter), and therefore do not require deep and heavy foundations.

The main advantages of glued beams:

- does not change its shape during operation;
- has greater strength compared to conventional wood and lower thermal conductivity;
- has minimal shrinkage in height;
- does not crack;
- has high quality of front surfaces;
- the grooves and ridges of the glued beam along the length of the wall beam are rigidly fixed bar in the wall and do not let moisture in;
- the wall of glued beams looks monolithic and does not require additional decoration.

In creating a modern industry of wooden housing construction, Russia has huge reserves of economic growth. Today, Russia sells at least 80% of its timber in the form of a round timber and at extremely low prices. One of the priority tasks of the government aimed at reviving wooden housing construction in Russia is the transition from export of round timber to deep wood processing in Russia.

8. New technologies of low-rise housing construction from porous ceramic stones Of the total amount of thermal energy consumed by builders and maintenance workers, 90% is spent on heating. New standards for heat protection of buildings provide for an increase of 1.5-3.5 times the resistance to heat transfer of wall structures and reduction of heat loss. When using ordinary brick, to achieve the desired result, it would be necessary to erect walls with a thickness of more than 1 m, therefore, enterprises are forced to complicate their design due to the use of various heaters.

Porized ceramic stone makes it possible to erect walls of traditional thickness in two and a half bricks, while new stringent requirements for thermal protection are fully respected. Porous stone is made by introducing sawdust into the charge, which burns out during firing and leaves pores in the stone. With the help of automation, it is possible to achieve high precision dosing of components and a uniform distribution of voids in the products. The degree of physical uniformity of the stone is high. The result of this process is a sharp decrease in bulk density. For ordinary solid bricks this figure is 1350–1600 kg/m^3, for porous stone — 900 kg/m^3. The volumetric weight of porous stone is lower than the volumetric weight of water of 1000 kg/m^3.

The use of porous ceramic stone simplifies the process: solution consumption is reduced, the time of erection of walls is reduced, and labor costs are reduced. These factors lead to cheaper construction as a whole. Another advantage of porous stone is its low calculated coefficient of thermal conductivity, equal to 0.29 W/m°C (for ordinary brick — 0.39–0.42 W/m°C). This allows you to make walls with a thickness of 64 cm, the inner part of which consists of porous stone, and the outer — of a layer of facing brick. Such a sharp decrease in the coefficient of thermal conductivity of the porous stone is due to the following factors: the chemical nature of the crock changes and, as a result, bonds between the atomic groups of crystals decrease; abrupt changes in the heat flux density occur due to changes in the cross-sectional area perpendicular to the direction of its cross-section and great resistance to the movement of heat fluxes in places of their high concentration; the pores formed as a result of the burnout of the additives have mainly a fused surface and a closed volume, which sharply reduces the radiant and convective components of heat transfer.

9. Teploskor high-speed housing construction technology One of the interesting Russian low-rise construction technologies is the Teploskor high-speed housing construction system. The system was developed by Russian scientists under the guidance of Doctor of Technical Sciences, Honored Engineer of Russia Valery Leshchikov, head of the NII Teplosten company. The composition of this system includes a new generation dwelling creation technique, high-speed housing construction technology and a new building material — a heat-efficient block, as well as equipment for automated production of heat-efficient wall blocks.

The Teplosten system provides the erection of a building box up to three floors in one to two months at a relatively low cost price and with improved building performance: architectural expressiveness, heat engineering properties, fire resistance and durability.

The basis of the technology is a new building material — three-layer heat-efficient wall blocks "Teplosten". The three-layer construction consists of a supporting layer (porous expanded clay concrete of class B7.5-B10 with a density of 1200-1400 kg / cubic meter), an inner layer (effective expanded polystyrene with a density of 25 kg / cubic meter) and a facade (concrete of class B10 – B12.5 density of 1500-1700 kg / cubic m). The external, protective and decorative layer is made of dense concrete, can have any texture and is subsequently painted in any color with facade paints.

The main raw materials for the production of heat-efficient multilayer wall blocks are Portland cement, expanded clay gravel, sand, hardening accelerator, foaming agent, polystyrene foam and water. For the manufacture of blocks can also be used a variety of local bulk materials, in particular, ashes, waste from ferrous metallurgy, slag. When using local raw materials, the cost of the resulting product — a heat-efficient unit — is significantly reduced, without reducing its consumer qualities.

The blocks are light and relatively large — 400x300x200 mm. They are attached to each other with glue, which is laid in a thickness of not more than 2–4 mm. The use of glue makes it possible at the end of the construction of even one first floor to proceed to the interior decoration with plasterboard or plaster mixes, that is, the technology of erecting walls from Teplosten blocks provides for an almost complete absence of "wet" processes. The use of a heat-efficient unit saves builders from such labor-consuming and expensive operations as wall insulation and its decorative design.

The low weight of the blocks reduces transport costs and eliminates the need for construction sites to have lifting devices. The use of glue, rather than cement mortar, eliminates the delivery of large amounts of water, cement and sand to the site, provides constantly high quality masonry, and minimizes heavy, unproductive manual labor. The clear geometric dimensions of the unit and its well-thought-out nomenclature allow the use of lower-skilled personnel.

The developed system of high-speed construction of low-rise buildings "Teplosten" includes 6 subsystems:

- finely buried insulated monolithic reinforced concrete foundations, combined with the base, on a sand cushion (piles on weakly bearing soils are possible);
- walls of buildings made of heat-efficient blocks with an external protective and decorative layer;
- monolithic spatial reinforced concrete frames;
- precast-monolithic reinforced concrete floors from prestressed beams of T-section;
- roof made of polymer-sand tiles;
- small architectural forms for decorating the facade.

10. The technology of fixed polystyrene foam formwork. The technology of fixed polystyrene foam formwork, which appeared in Europe more than 30 years ago, has been developing in Russia for 10 years. In recent years, the volume of construction using this technology has grown significantly.

The essence of the technology is that as a permanent formwork for monolithic walls, blocks from an effective insulation — polystyrene foam — are used. Thus, the issue of building heat efficiency is solved and time savings during construction are achieved: when using conventional formwork, considerable time is spent on its installation, dismantling, cleaning, etc. 2.5-3 months are usually spent on building a building using fixed formwork technology.

Fixed formwork is manufactured in the factory in the form of blocks, which are two plates of special building polystyrene foam, connected by jumpers from the same material or PVC. Blocks have a very low weight, which is very convenient during construction. Blocks have cavities that are reinforced and filled with concrete during the construction process.

The upper and lower planes of the system elements are equipped with special locks of complex shape. Their design allows you to abandon the use of temporary retaining elements and maintain the geometric dimensions of the walls, ensuring tight joints and blocking the flow of concrete. On the inner surfaces of all the blocks have grooves, which ensures the reliability of adhesion of concrete to the walls of the block. Blocks can be cut with a hand saw according to the size of the project.

Formwork is at the same time a perfectly flat surface, ready for finishing with any materials. The finish is fixed either by glue connection with polystyrene, or by mechanical fastening in the concrete body. Thus, in one technological operation, a monolithic reinforced concrete wall is erected, having a heat and sound insulating shell on the inside and outside, which completely eliminates the formation of cold bridges. The outer layer of the insulation protects and protects the monolithic structure from external environmental factors, in particular, from freezing, and the inner layer serves as a barrier to heat exchange between the heated air and the walls. The range of blocks allows you to choose modules with the thickness of the external insulation corresponding to the climatic zone of the building.

The advantages of the technology include the speed of construction of buildings (on average 2.5–3 months), savings on the foundation due to the relatively low weight of the building and on the cost of walls (the cost per square meter is about one and a half times lower than the cost of a brick wall), high strength and thermal qualities of the building, as well as sufficient ease of construction.

11. Technology of fixed reinforced concrete formwork. The sequence of work on this technology is as follows. After marking the axles and developing the soil on the construction site, formwork, fittings and waterproofing are installed, wiring is made for heating and underfloor heating. Then the concrete is slab. EUROBAU's modern fixed formwork is a progressive home building technology created in Germany. The reliability of the technology is confirmed by many design institutes and has been used for many years in the construction of houses in European countries.

This technology can significantly reduce construction time, since houses from fixed formwork require less labor-intensive processes. All elements of the building are manufactured. The uniqueness of fixed formwork is that it has excellently proven itself in the construction of objects for various purposes. Work can be carried out at any time of the year, and they will not depend on the weather. In addition, the EUROBAU system provides one hundred percent waterproofing. Fixed formwork allows you to build the basement of the house in just a few days, significantly reduce labor costs by performing most of the operations in the factory, does not require complex construction technical support. The construction of structures based on fixed formwork makes it possible to combine EUROBAU technology with other building technologies.

Prefabricated monolithic technology immediately involves the construction of perfectly even walls, ready for decoration. Such structures withstand high loads and are resistant to various physical influences. Since the construction cycle is carried out all year round, fixed formwork reduces the time for erection of buildings by three times.

12.4 Optimal conditions for assessing the choice of site for construction

A. Development of the general plan of a low-rise village

Low-rise villages begin with the development of a general plan. The quality of the general plan is significantly influenced by the presence of the following main factors: highways, engineering networks (power lines, treatment facilities, gas pipeline, and water supply), water bodies (lake, pond, and river), and forest. The infrastructure of the general plan depends on the number of residential buildings and residents. Therefore, in villages with a number of cottages of 150 or more, the following buildings of social and cultural life are planned: a shop, a kindergarten-nursery, sports and playgrounds, a recreation area. The planning decision of the streets is diverse in nature, depending on the terrain, the presence of a reservoir and forest planting.

The area of the plots is affected by the source of financing: commercial construction or individual.

Commercial construction is carried out through loans granted, for example, by banks or investors. In this case, architects develop several standard designs.

For example, 10–15 options that have variously decorated facades, floor plans, shapes of roofs, windows, doors, etc., with the same dimensions of the building in plan. In this case, the area of the house on the first floor should not exceed 1/10 of the area of the site.

This ratio of the areas of the house and the plot allows you to make the layout of the entire village more spacious, and cottages of approximately equal size contribute to the creation of moral comfort for those living, like — I look from the window of my house and see my house.

The creation of a "spacious" layout of the village is significantly affected by the refusal to build all kinds of small buildings on the sites (commercial buildings for various functional purposes). The fencing of the sections along the facade and the boundary is carried out in the form of transparent fences. An exception is the fence of the village on the outer perimeter, performed by the "deaf", of metal or wood.

The design of the landscape on each site, although it is individual in nature, necessarily contains a certain percentage of the area under the lawn, trees, flower beds.

Public roads and sidewalks are paved with household stone, on a hard or soft foundation.

In the gap between the road and the sidewalk, external networks and communications (gas, sewage, water supply, electric cable, as well as a hidden drainage system) are laid. A lawn is placed on top of the communications system.

Street lighting is provided by electric decorative lamps on metal poles — uprights, up to 3 meters high, located on both sides of the road.

Fire-fighting measures consist of fire hydrants distributed through the streets of the village, with a pitch of 200 m, powered through a technical water supply system, with a reservoir located near the village.

B. Choosing a site for the construction of a low-rise village

The choice of a site for the construction of the village is one of the key points in the successful implementation of the project. It is known that to sell or rent a bad building in a good place is easier than a good building in a bad place. The famous aphorism of American developers says: "Cost is determined by three factors: location, location and, finally, location."

In fig. 12.2, 12.3 a situational plan and spatial diagram of the Oksky Bereg residential complex of the Nizhny Novgorod Region, the Bogorodsky District, the village of Novinki (Applicant: EcoGrad LLC) with an area of 650 ha are presented.

A. Project Overview

The project involves the implementation of 1,500,000 sq.m. residential premises (about 30,000 households and apartments) with a potential population of 75,000 people on an area of 650 hectares. Okskiy Bank is one of the largest devoloper projects in Russia.

"Oksky Bereg" — a project for integrated development of the territory, providing for:

- multi-format residential development of mainly low floors (up to 3 floors): apartment buildings, townhouses, duplexes, cottages;
- objects of social infrastructure (10 kindergartens, 5 schools, medical center);
- objects of sports infrastructure (fitness center, ski school, stadium, sports camps and playgrounds);
- recreation areas: eco park and boulevards with a total area of 120 hectares;
- shopping and entertainment centers, convenience stores;
- consumer services enterprises;
- engineering infrastructure and service companies.

The market segment is an environmentally friendly suburb of economy and comfort class. The project became the creator of a new market niche for the Nizhny Novgorod region.

Positioning — "First Ecograd", which emphasizes leadership, uniqueness, environmental friendliness and complexity ("turnkey city").

Figure 12.2: Appearance of the residential complex "Oksky coast"

B. Architectural and planning decisions

Being the largest in the region, the project most successfully combines suburban comfort and the usual urban lifestyle. Low-rise residential development

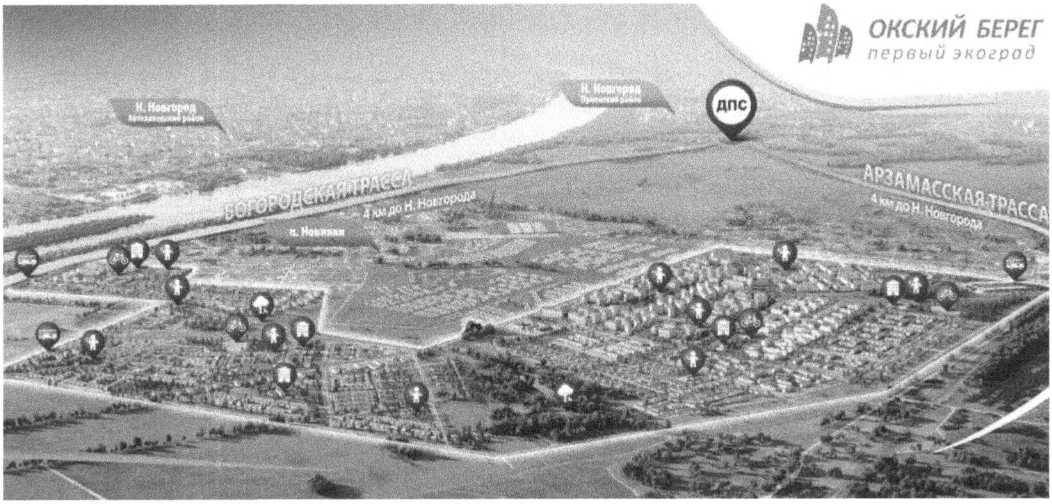

Figure 12.3: Spatial diagram of the residential complex “Oksky Bereg”

is surrounded by picturesque meadows and forests, away from industrial urban enterprises. The terrain — semi-flat, semi-hilly — “dictated” the features of architectural solutions of residential buildings and neighborhoods. This is mainly a small number of storeys (up to 3 floors). The houses are located with the greatest possible distance from each other. Main features LCD — natural space and clean air.

The Okskiy Bereg project consists of four sections, one of which (204 Ha) is almost completely covered by forest. In the middle of it is a natural reservoir. To preserve the natural landscape, this plot was not allocated for apartment buildings, but for individual houses and townhouses.

In the remaining three areas (185Ga, 145Ga, 115Ga), with the location of residential areas and utilities, all natural forest belts are preserved. Therefore, to date, residential development is located not in a “clean” field, but surrounded by mature trees and shrubs.

In terms of flatography in the residential complex, more than 50 planning solutions are used. When making planning decisions, the opinions of the customers of the first phases of the completed houses, as well as market trends, are taken into account. Practically for each residential quarter, its own apartmentography is used: the ratio of 1-2-3-room apartments, their area, as well as the types of layouts: euro and classic. The apartments are offered with a turnkey finish.

C. Courtyards, safe living, barrier environment

Residential quarters in Okskiy Bereg are designed in such a way that the courtyards are located in a closed zone, that is, parking spaces are located on the outer perimeter of residential buildings. This ensures the safety of the courtyards. The indicator of the availability of parking spaces = 1. The residential complex has its own security company, which, in addition to providing commercial services to the population, serves as a "public squad", plying the entire housing estate, observing order and preventing possible violations.

All residential buildings in the Okskiy Bereg are made in compliance with the norms and requirements for barrier-free access for people with limited mobility: disabled people, mothers with strollers, etc., namely, some of the entrances are made in ramps, and some are using electric lifts.

D. Energy Efficiency

Energy efficiency of residential buildings in the Okskiy Bereg is provided in several areas:

Individual heating — 95% of the housing is rented with individual 2-circuit gas boilers, which provide savings on heating / hot water, and allow you to adjust the temperature in the apartment at any time of the day. On average, savings are up to 50% of utility bills compared with city payments;

Energy consumption — in the residential complex has built its own step-down substation with a capacity of 110/10 kV 24 MW. The launch of this substation ensures the energy security of the population not only of the Oka Coast, but also of nearby settlements, and also allows saving on losses in power lines, minimizes the number of emergencies;

Reinforced concrete plant — in the residential complex operates its own factory for the manufacture of finished products from three-layer reinforced concrete panels. Three-layer panels are a "pie" of reinforced concrete and mineral wool insulation. Future residential areas are made of new modern materials that combine strength and heat capacity.

The choice of a site for the construction of a cottage village should take into account several key factors — the location of transport routes, the overall image of a suburban area or countryside, the presence of water bodies (river, lake, pond) and forest, the prospects for the sale or lease of cottage buildings built on this site, purpose and quality of development of adjacent plots, dimensions, topography, site configuration, existing architectural and urban restrictions, difficulties in conducting communications, zoning e, soil options, ecology.

12.4.1 Features of the organization of construction

A comparative analysis of the operating costs of various types of houses, according to the costs of heating and hot water supply are presented in table 12.3.

From table 12.3 it is seen that the cost of heating and hot water in terms of 1 m^2 in timber-frame houses is 9 times lower than the standard cost in multi-storey stone houses that practically heat the environment.

Table 12.3 Consumption for heating, hot water (DHW)

Type of housing	Area, m^2	Cost, rub.		Cost rub/m^2
		normative	preferential	
Wood — frame cottage	144.9	62.72	62.72	0.43
1 bedroom apartment in a brick 5-storey building	32.8	126.40	18.99	3.85 / 0.58
2 rooms apartment in a panel 9-storey building	47.7	216.20	25.02	4.53 / 0.53

For each village, a work production project (PPR) is being developed, which reflects all the stages and sequence of work, including data on the needs of labor, technical, building materials and products.

The development of the territory, as a rule, begins with the arrangement of a residential town for work and office premises — for engineers and technicians. For employees living far from the construction site, a "hotel" is being built, in which the private security company is located. These temporary buildings are mounted from warm inventory trailers with a different set of functional purposes: — sleeping, showers, plumbing, laundry, public, household. Temporary buildings are provided with all necessary amenities — cold and hot water, heating, electricity, gas. The area of temporary buildings depends on the volume of one-time work. With large volumes of work, a working camp is being erected. For small ones, several wagons are mounted, and as the volume of work increases, the town is being completed. The choice of location for the working camp is determined taking into account the territory free of development or development in the last turn; minimum distance to workplaces near existing communications and other data that contribute to lower operating costs.

Construction equipment, storage and utility workshops are usually located compactly with a working camp. A temporary fence surrounds the territory of the working village and the farm.

After the resettlement of workers, general construction work begins:

- erection of a "deaf" permanent fence around the village;
- construction of a checkpoint;
- erection of a "transparent" permanent fence around the plots for cottages;
- construction of permanent roads (without "clean" pavement and sidewalks);
- installation of engineering networks and communications: water supply, sewerage, gas, underground cable networks, hidden storm sewers;
- installation of office and hotel buildings;
- installation of electrical transformer substations;
- well drilling and construction of water towers.

Branches to the future structure are laid from external networks and communications, along corridors planned on the general plan to each site. After laying the communications, sidewalks with a "clean" coating are arranged. Along the roads, luminaires are mounted on both sides to illuminate the roadway and sidewalks. Along the streets, on plots of land free of hard surfaces, lawns and flower beds are arranged, trees are planted. At this stage, the general construction work is being completed, and the **second stage is** unfolding , which is divided, depending on the funding source into two areas:

A) The first direction is the commercial construction of cottages, which is the most promising and profitable. Its financing is carried out through bank loans. This direction allows you to create a stream method for the construction of cottages according to the standard designs developed in several versions. With the same area and dimensions, the layout and facades of cottages vary significantly due to the architectural and artistic design and tinting. Stream construction is divided into the following stages of capture carried out by specialized teams:

1. planning, binding and breakdown of the building plan on the ground;
2. earthwork — mechanized development for slab, strip or bored pile foundations;
3. reinforcing works — manufacturing and installation of reinforcing frames for reinforced concrete foundations of specified types;
4. formwork — the formwork device from inventory elements;
5. Concrete work — laying concrete mixture by means of a concrete pump into the formwork, followed by vibration.
6. Technical support for hardening concrete in the formwork and after it has been removed within 28 days, with recording in the logbook of work, observations of the technologist, including laboratory tests of concrete samples

Some captures can be combined and performed by one unit of the team. The narrow specialization of workers' links will give excellent quality and high economic efficiency in this area.

To conduct a professional level of production units, lectures and practical exercises are constantly held directly on the line of willows of specially equipped rooms. As a rule, classes are held before the start of large volumes of work in any direction. Classes are required for linear engineering (foremen, foremen, foremen, team leaders). Ordinary performers receive instruction at the workplace. Lectures are delivered by highly qualified specialists from among the employees of the company, as well as those from outside, including those from MSUCE.

Quality control is monitored daily by an experienced technical supervision engineer. All observations are recorded in the log. Observation data is analyzed in order to eliminate the marriage, improve the technology of work, improve tools. Based on the results of serious violations, a analysis is made of the causes and ways to eliminate them and prevent them in the next stages.

The built-in system allows minimizing rejects and technological failures, thereby ensuring high quality construction products. This system covers in the **first direction** all parts of the building, from foundations to the roof ridge, including finishing work at the first level (clean facade and first puttying of internal walls and ceilings).

B) The second direction — non-profit construction, refers to individual orders. It is financed by a specific "customer" and is completely subordinate to his will and wishes. This direction, although it makes a profit, especially during the economic crisis, is unprofitable, because poorly amenable to the organization of the flow method. The main reasons for the failure are changes in the project during construction (deviation from the project), up to the construction of additional volumes of the building. Despite the higher cost of work on an individual order, relative to commercial construction, the final income in this case is much lower.

Regardless of the type of direction, construction, installation and finishing work is carried out at the highest level. Some of the reasons have been indicated above, but one of the important components of high-quality work production is that the construction company becomes the managing organization and independently operates the constructed villages. In addition, cottage owners are given a guarantee for all types of buildings for a period of 3 years. Given the large volume of buildings erected, the cost of their operation should be minimal. In other words, building poor-quality, unprofitable. This explains the formation of the professional composition of all construction divisions. For such a direction, in the construction industry, the future.

12.4.2 Production planning under construction

A. General

According to the periods of its implementation, the construction object can be divided into various stages, which are, for example, earthwork, foundations, the construction of basic structures and finishing work. As you know, at large construction sites (for example, during the construction of industrial enterprises), such traditional stages of construction often overlap to a large extent and at such construction sites, planning is carried out for periods of, for example, three months, which include work related to various stages construction.

Production planning for each of the so-called traditional stages of construction consists of the following parts:

- preparation or refinement of the construction site plan;
- preparation and maintenance of a schedule at the construction stage; organization of work by weeks (weekly planning); preparation of numerous special plans and clarification of previously made in accordance with actual conditions;
- control over the implementation of plans, coordination of issues at production meetings and adjustment of plans.

B. Construction site plans

A new construction site plan is drawn up at each stage of construction. The plan shows the placement of installations and equipment, buildings, roads, storage areas, rest rooms and other premises for workers at the construction stages (Fig. 12.4).

The first plan of the construction site is drawn up at the stage of general planning of the facility before construction begins. As a rule, for each stage of construction, a separate plan for the construction site is not developed, and the initial plan is specified as necessary when planning this stage.

C. Schedules

Schedules under construction, or the so-called Periodic calendar plans are drawn up in more detail than the general calendar plan, on its basis and, based on other previously made plans.

D. Weekly planning

Weekly plans are drawn up by clarifying the schedule for the construction phase, usually for a period of two weeks. The weekly plan is used as a practical tool in organizing work for every day.

12.4.3 Construction site plans

The initial construction site plan is being developed at the general planning stage of the facility, before construction begins. As a rule, for each stage of construction, a separate plan for the construction site is not developed, and the initial plan is necessary to be specified in the planning of this stage.

Users

Masters, subcontractors and representatives of external third-party organizations, labor protection personnel.

Appointment

Provide information on the organization of the construction site territory (on traffic routes, equipment placement, as well as storage and domestic premises, etc.).

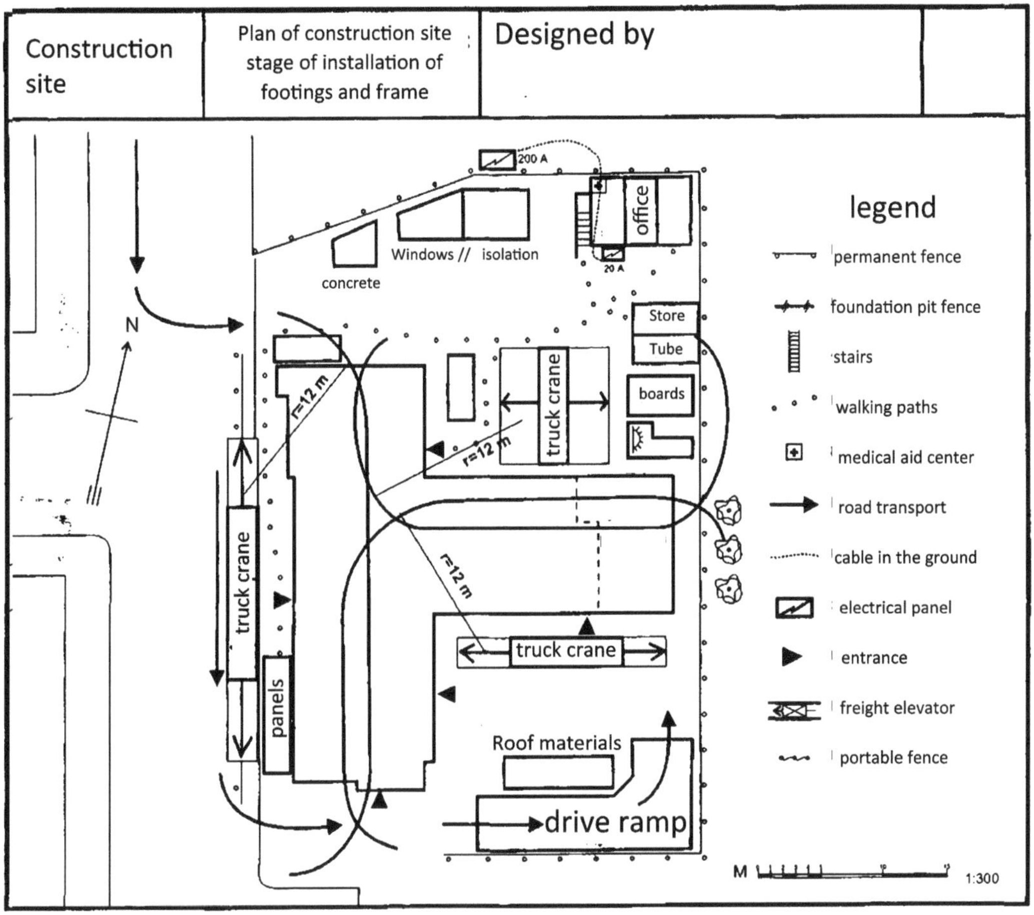

Figure 12.4: Site plan at the stage of work on foundations and main structures

Content

A drawing made on a scale that shows facts that are significant in terms of the organization of the construction site at each stage of construction. Of the information provided, for example, the following can be mentioned:

- buildings, structures, trees, etc.
- dumps,
- working and storage areas
- site boundaries, fences, gates, signs
- first aid items
- places of connection of electricity, heat
- pedestrian and transport routes
- office, household and storage facilities
- other material equipment

- placement of lifting equipment and its working area
- power supply
- boundaries of the excavation zone

Compilers
Chief project engineer, site engineer, supervisor
Compilation moment
Before starting a specific construction stage
Principles of Compilation
The needs of various contractors in transport, storage and work areas are being clarified. Rational from the point of view of the functioning of the construction site is determined by the placement of various temporary structures, machinery and equipment. The organization of the construction site is presented in the form of a drawing, which also shows the necessary additional information (for example, data on the current strength of electrical panels).
Authorizing and responsible person
Supervisor
The control
Construction site plans are adjusted if the organization of work changes significantly
Interaction with other plans
Initial data: preliminary construction site plan, general schedule. It serves as a source of information in the preparation of the calendar plan at the construction stage and the labor protection plan.

12.4.4 Schedules under construction

Users
Production manager, supervisors, supply personnel, subcontractors and third parties.
Appointment
Serve as a model for the implementation of the facility at the construction stage and provide an economical way to implement it with the uniform use of resources, detailing the overall schedule. It serves as a source of information and sets goals for weekly planning and for the preparation of special plans at the construction stage.
Content
A temporary linear diagram, in which depending on the object, from 20 to 200 items (see page 20 Drawing up a list of works and sections), the most important works at a certain stage of construction and transfer of resources from one work on another.

Compilers

Specialist in work planning, supervisor, civil engineer on site.

Compilation moment

Before starting work at this particular stage.

Principles of Compilation

Names are selected using the general calendar plan and a statement of work and sections of the construction site. The interdependencies of the work are clarified, the order of their implementation is planned, and their durations are calculated based on the time of work shifts of the main labor resources (TK) and volumes by type of work, taking into account the goals established in the general calendar plan, the resources available, the ways of performing work and other production plans. In winter, the influence of frosty days off should also be foreseen.

Authorizing and responsible person

Supervisor

The control

It is monitored after 1..2 weeks, is considered at meetings according to the schedule. It is corrected in the form of new dated versions if the discrepancies (planned / implemented) are significant (at least 15–20% of the total duration of the construction stage).

Interaction with other plans

Initial data: general schedule, statement of volumes, target estimates, explanatory notes, drawings, contract documents, production statistics, data on available resources, special plans. It is used as a source of information for weekly planning and other calendar plans at the construction stage.

12.4.5 Weekly daily plan

Masters, subcontractors, third-party organizations, supervisors.

Appointment

Serve as a guide for short-term planning of the use of equipment, supply lines and the daily organization of work in accordance with the goals set in the schedule of the construction stage, doing all this in such a way as to maximize the efficient use of available resources

Content

A plan drawn up most often for a two-week period, from which you can see the initial amount of work, resources involved, capacity or labor costs, the amount of work scheduled for the week, as well as, as a rule, a time chart drawn up to 1/2 work shift.

Compilers

Supervisor, foreman, engineer at a construction site.

Compilation moment

It is usually compiled on Fridays in such a way that the next (1) week is displayed accurately and the next (2) week before it.

Principles of Compilation

The goals for the week are determined on the basis of the calendar plan of the construction stage and previously made weekly plans. After that, the rationality of the organization of work and its overlay is checked, taking into account the possible overlay of resources, the supply schedule and their compliance with the work of subcontractors and third-party organizations working on the site. In the end, the need for labor is calculated by the type of work in accordance with the goals set, compared with the available labor resources accurate to the employee or team (carpenter Lehtonen, Oyaly brigade), if necessary, varying in each case either resources or weekly goals.

Weekly plans can also be drawn up in such a way that each master responsible for a particular type of work or site draws up his own weekly plan, and all of them are then reduced by a supervisor, covering the entire construction site.

Authorizing and responsible person

Supervisor

The control

Each week (often on Thursday or Friday), the degree of readiness of key works is fixed (ready, in progress, not started) and the volumes remaining for implementation are changed, as well as, if necessary, labor costs, for drawing up the next weekly plan.

Interaction with other plans

Initial data: schedule under construction, previous weekly plan, production statistics, supply plan.

12.4.6 Monitoring the implementation of plans

Schedule Monitoring

Resource Usage Control

Cost control

Quality control

The purpose of the production planning of a construction project is to describe the proposed method for the sale of the property and to ensure that the property is ready on time using the available resources. With the help of cost planning, goals are set for the object, the achievement of which provides a good economic result.

However, good plans do not in themselves guarantee a good result, without monitoring carried out at the construction stage, detecting and eliminating deviations and analysis. Achievement of the goals is also ensured by the refinement of plans and the implementation of necessary management activities.

It is carried out for each type of plan (general, under construction, weekly, blueprint for execution of drawings and other calendar plans) with the frequency expected by each plan (see Control, in the sections on each type of plan). When performing control it is especially important to fix the realized part on the plan, while the discrepancies are clearly visible and it becomes possible to concentrate on eliminating them (changing resources, ways of performing work, etc.). The realized part can be noted using a situation-fixing strip placed at the bottom of the time chart, or a vertical line dividing the calendar plan through points reached for each type of work on one common date.

On the plan for the use of labor, special plans for other resources and in the target estimates), the completed part is recorded, which is compared with the planned one. The control object is, as a rule, the hours worked, but depending on the construction site, the realized volume (m^2), for example, planking, can also be additionally controlled. During control, a drawing is often used, in which time is marked on the horizontal axis, and the total demand (for example, person-hour, concrete m^3, boards — m^2) is marked on the vertical axis. The drawing separately indicates the planned and actual use of resources, so that the general situation with the type of resource being checked at a particular point in time is clearly visible.

Cost control is done using targeted estimates for their coded groups. From the target budget, you can also select the leading groups of indicators, which, due to their significant influence on the overall situation, are monitored especially carefully. The costs are controlled separately for the costs of work, materials, subcontractors and our own services, from which it is determined the unit and total costs realized by groups in the budget (FIM / hour, FIM / unit, FIM).

With the help of quality control, it is ensured that the result complies with the drawings, explanatory notes and general guidelines for the quality of construction work. The control, therefore, focuses on the materials used, the work (methods of work and technology) and the quality of the work of subcontractors. An important part of the control is the acceptance of work performed. The rule for her is the principle of "readiness the first time." To date, quality control has not been systematic, varying significantly depending on the personality of the director of the enterprise or the superintendent.

12.4.7 Production meetings and meetings

During the construction, various meetings are held, the need for part of which is determined by the contract, while the part is carried out voluntarily, while the practice of holding meetings varies greatly, depending on the facility and the persons responsible for resolving issues.

The purpose of production meetings is to coordinate and resolve unclear issues regarding the various parties involved. The way in which questions are addressed, however, varies depending on the type of meeting. For example, at general meetings of the construction site, questions are posed and resolved in a very concise way, while in weekly meetings an attempt is made to analyze the problems as detailed as possible before deciding on them. The most typical meetings held at almost any construction site are: a meeting at the construction site, meetings of the contractor, a weekly meeting and a meeting under construction.

Construction site meeting

Purpose: Solving issues related to contractual obligations and coordination of work between the developer, general contractor, subcontractors and involved organizations.

Participants: the developer, contractors and designers, and if necessary, for example, subcontractors and other required persons.

Issues under **consideration:** for example, coordination of the general schedule and completed work, missing plans and activities that are caused by a delay in the execution of work, invoicing of phased payments, ext. work and work not covered by the contract, changes in projects and schedules, moments of inspections and inspections.

The moment of carrying out: as necessary, usually in 2-4 weeks.

Contractor Meeting

Purpose: to plan and coordinate the implementation of work by different contractors.

Participants: representatives of contractors (and technical supervision).

Issues under **consideration:** for example, the situation according to the schedule and the goals of the next stage, the need for project documentation, the interdependence of the work of different contractors and their required joint work, as well as ongoing inspections and checks.

The moment of carrying out: in 2-3 weeks, at small objects along with a weekly meeting. Once a week, if the facility is seriously late.

Weekly meeting

Purpose: To agree on goals for the next 1-2-week period of work.

Participants: an engineer at a construction site, artisans.

Issues under **consideration:** implementation of the previous weekly plan, work being completed and started, and the situation with the workforce, materials, and many other issues related to the implementation of the facility.
Event: on Thursdays or Fridays.

Meeting under construction

Purpose: to agree on targets for time and costs, as well as the area of responsibility of the artisans, for the beginning stage of construction.

Participants: Construction manager, engineer at the construction site, work planning specialist, foremen.

Issues to be considered: construction site plan, general schedule, supply schedules, drawings, machinery and equipment, construction schedule, tasks and responsibilities of the supervisors, the need for project documentation and control.

Moment: before the start of the construction phase.

12.4.8 Inspections and checks

Inspections and inspections carried out at the construction site are divided into two groups:

- mutual checks of contractual parties (e.g. contractor / developer or general contractor / subcontractor)
- conducted by representatives of the authorities.

A. Mutual verification of contractual parties

The purpose of mutual checks between the parties involved in the contract is to fix:

- situations caused by a strike or other force majeure
- execution of work in accordance with the contract for the achievement of intermediate stages of the situation with the schedule.

Most often, the following inspections are carried out at the construction site with the participation of contractual parties:

- acceptance
- spot verification of contract execution
- inspection of the sample room
- warranty check
- verification after completion of work.

Various kinds of inspections are carried out as necessary to clarify the situation at the construction site, depending on the specifics of the facility. Of the mutual inspections of the contracting parties, the inspection of suspended ceilings and facades should be mentioned. In connection with the execution of contracts for engineering systems, various tests and trial operation are carried out.

Based on the results of inspections and inspections, a protocol is drawn up which indicates:

- time of
- object of inspection or inspection
- present
- contractual parties
- party requiring an inspection or inspection
- requirements put forward by the parties to each other
- result of inspection or inspection

B. Official checks

The purpose of official inspections is to make sure that work is done using materials and methods in accordance with approved drawings and building codes.

Of the official inspections and checks, the following shall be noted:

- construction site inspection — plumbing inspection
- inspection of soil and sewage
- foundation inspection — electrical system inspection
- inspection of basic structures — antenna test
- ventilation shaft inspection — shelter check
- final inspection — elevator inspection
- heat supply check.

The construction work includes many inspections, for example, the condition of machinery and equipment, as well as other factors related to safety.

12.4.9 Closing the construction site

The closure of the construction site is carried out in three separate stages: commissioning of the object; dismantling of the construction site; assessment of the implementation of the object (discussion of the result)

Commissioning facility

The concept of commissioning an object includes the following activities: a final inspection carried out by representatives of the authorities an acceptance check conducted by the developer with subsequent checks:

- clarification of economic issues between contractors and the developer (the so-called final disassembly);

- transfer of documents;
- training in the operation of the facility (in connection with the end of the warranty period, a warranty inspection is carried out, as well as inspection and verification related to the warranty work).

If an object is handed over and accepted for operation in many parts, the final inspection and acceptance is carried out separately for each part (for example, inspection of internal and external works).

Site dismantling

When dismantling the construction site, temporary structures are disassembled, as well as cars, plants and trailers are removed from the site. In addition, orders for the supply of electricity and telephone communications are canceled and the necessary ones related to the closure of the construction site are notified to the authorities.

Assessment of the implementation of the facility

Upon completion of the facility, the contractor organizes, as a rule, an internal meeting at which factors that affect the economic result during the implementation of the facility are considered. The meeting considers the progress of work at the facility in time (adherence to the schedule), the difference between the targets of target estimates and real costs, various kinds of costs for the main groups of work (goal / implementation), as well as ultimately looking for reasons that caused a significant increase in costs or their savings. The meeting is attended by the production manager, the budget chief, the cost estimator and the supervisor, as well as, possibly, the manager responsible for this activity in the company.

In order to get the maximum benefit from the meeting based on the results of the work, it is necessary to accurately preserve information on the implementation of the facility (construction site plans, calendar plans, supply documents, protocols, etc.). In addition to the final meeting, these documents are required for negotiations on warranty work and when planning new facilities.

12.4.10 Using flow forms and shift organization methods low-rise housing

The implementation of these technologies is based on the implementation of flow-based forms of organization, increased mobility, the use of complete block and expeditionary-shift forms of labor organization, and a high degree of factory readiness.

A. Complete block construction of low-rise residential real estate

The main principle of the block-and-block construction of facilities is to transfer construction, installation and commissioning works to the sphere of industrial production. To solve this problem, the implementation of interconnected technical and organizational measures is required.

Technical activities include:

- designing enterprises, buildings and structures in a complete block design;
- technological and construction design of blocks with their unification and typification;
- transportation of blocks to a construction site using various modes of transport and their combinations;
- arrangement of foundations and external communications;
- installation of blocks, as well as additional structures and elements in the design position, their connecting installation and the creation, thus, of fully finished objects in a complete block design;
- completing factory production of blocks with necessary materials, products, building structures and technological equipment;
- development of means for the manufacture, delivery and installation of blocks in the design position.

Economic activities include:

- justification of the feasibility of constructing an object (a group of objects in the region) by the block-block method and, if necessary, the creation of a regional assembly and assembly plant for the manufacture of blocks;
- planning of material and technical resources of construction production in connection with an increase in the share of industrial enterprises in the structure of construction and installation works (suppliers of technological equipment or enterprises of the construction industry).

Organizational activities include:

- organization of production of blocks and their delivery;
- completion of facilities with blocks of various types and purposes, as well as additional structures and elements, appropriate nomenclature, high factory readiness and installation adaptability;
- preparation of building production for the implementation of the complete block method;
- formation of the organizational structure of management of assembly-and-assembly enterprises and construction and installation divisions during the construction of facilities by the block-and-block method;

- organization of installation of blocks in the design position, installation of communications, commissioning and integrated testing.

The implementation of the complete block method is aimed at increasing the efficiency of capital investments by increasing the industrialization of construction by turning industrial complexes into sets of blocks and transferring the main labor costs (especially unproductive ones) from the construction site to the scope of industrial factory production. At the same time, the construction time is significantly reduced, the cost of work per unit of power is reduced, the number of contractors, subcontractors, and the total number of employees are reduced.

B. Expeditionary-shift forms of labor organization in low-rise housing

The specifics of mobile low-rise housing construction correspond to such forms of labor organization as expeditionary, shift, expeditionary-shift methods of production. Having a lot in common, these methods differ among themselves in a number of elements: the management structure, the regime of work and rest, the organization of social infrastructure, etc.

The expeditionary method involves the movement of labor collectives without families to significant distances from places of residence for a period until the completion of work or for a time limited by the capabilities of a person with placement in expeditionary mobile villages (or settlements) as close as possible to the place of work. At the end of the work, the village is relocated to a new place, and the workers return to the place of family residence. The cycles of trips to the place of work and homecoming are repeated in the planned order. The method is characterized by undeveloped infrastructure at the place of work and the related need to ensure the living conditions of workers in an autonomous environment.

The shift method proceeds from the fact that when the objects are significantly removed from the places of deployment of construction organizations and the permanent residence of builders, work on them is carried out by shift (shift) personnel living without a family in special shift villages and periodically returning home for rest. The regular alternation of periods of work and rest in places of residence is a characteristic feature of this method, used in the development of new territories, with the dispersal of objects, for example, in rural construction.

The expeditionary rotational method is a combination of the previous methods and involves moving workers without members of their families to a significant distance to base villages or cities for the duration of the expedition with their further work on a rotational basis.

Expeditionary and rotational construction is characterized by a special regime of work and rest, based on summarized accounting of working time, accumulation of processing (over an 8-hour working day) and a systematic return to the place of permanent residence. When assigning a specific mode of work and rest, climatic and seasonal influences, remoteness from the base and delivery conditions are taken into account.

An important element of the social preparation of mobile construction is a developed infrastructure, including field towns (shift camps), consisting of residential, warehouse and auxiliary zones. The residential area includes residential buildings and buildings for social and cultural services.

Further development of low-rise housing construction should be based on the implementation of the following areas:

1. Evaluation and accounting of risk factors and uncertainties at the phases of the construction cycle in the activities of enterprises of the construction complex. For this purpose, it is necessary to develop the main organizational and economic decisions aimed at reducing losses in production processes due to: creation, rational functioning and development of the production and social sphere of the construction complex;

transition to rational organizational forms of enterprise functioning taking into account various organizational schemes;

2. Increasing the degree of mobility of enterprises in the investment construction complex. For this purpose, it is necessary to create normal conditions for the technical, material, information, financial support of enterprises and firms by:

- rational development of production processes in stages and phases;
- transition to new space-planning and structural solutions of residential buildings;

3. Development of the marketing service at enterprises of organizational and economic redistribution and the construction complex as a whole in all directions to create normal conditions for the use of rational forms of organization and management through marketing research aimed at:

- creation of new final products;
- creating a system of new consumers of final products and investors both within the construction complex and beyond;
- creation of a system of constant reliable suppliers of raw materials, semi-finished products both within the investment and construction complex, and beyond;
- pursuing a new pricing policy by enterprises when creating new end products;

- determination of rational locations of production and social bases and dispersed construction projects within the investment construction complex and beyond;
- determination of the total costs (investments) associated with the development of production processes in the construction of construction projects and their sale on the housing market;
- the creation of highly qualified personnel, services at enterprises to perform complex types of work in various conditions of organizational and economic situations;
- creating the necessary organizational, economic and investment conditions for maximizing the use of the potential of enterprises within the construction complex and beyond;
- rational development of all types of production processes in the construction of dispersed construction projects and the sale of final products at all stages of the development of the construction complex;
- creating the necessary conditions for entering new housing markets and areas activities.

4. Transition of construction to new space-planning (SPD) and constructive (SCD) solutions. For this purpose, a set of measures of an economic, organizational and social nature should be carried out due to:

transition to new planning decisions;

transition to new design solutions;

5. The use of rational forms of organization, management and technology for the construction of objects in streams. The implementation of a set of relevant measures and decisions should be carried out by:

- transition to mobile schemes of functioning of redistribution enterprises (shift, expeditionary, expeditionary and rotational shift);
- use of progressive forms of organization of production (stand, aggregate-flow, conveyor, complete-block);
- Creation within the regional building complexes and beyond, of a system of mobile production and social bases and their infrastructures;
- ensuring a rhythmic and reliable system of financing the activities of enterprises.

6. Creating investment attractiveness of the enterprises of the construction complex of the region. This should be done by:

- creating a system of regular investors both within the region and beyond;
- creation of a system of tourist, cultural, historical, health centers and routes;

- creation of a system of investment companies, centers, banks to provide financial support for the construction complex and the implementation of housing programs, reforms in the housing and communal services;
- Creation of a system of mobile construction units, enterprises capable of erecting various groups of construction objects in all regions of Russia and abroad by creating powerful potential and a high level of their use in them;
- creating conditions for the construction of cheap housing based on the transition to new SPD and SCD and the implementation of resource-saving policies.

Each of these areas of low-rise housing construction, based on the implementation of a wide range of tasks, requires the development of appropriate programs, actions, regulatory, legal documents, financial and investment frameworks for their implementation. The implementation of these tasks should be carried out in stages, taking into account the prospects for the development of thc cntire construction complex.

12.5 Mobility of construction production with low housing construction

The effectiveness of low-rise housing construction largely depends on the mobility of construction production. The mobility of the construction system for the use of labor resources means the ability of its units to move in certain directions, concentrate in the required quantity and combination in the construction area in the form of capacities and specialized units and function rationally in specific conditions when constructing or updating facilities and capacities with the aim of putting them into operation on time with minimal labor.

Based on the probabilistic and regional nature of construction production and the features of its manifestation in low-rise housing construction, the construction system can be in two positions:

- the movement and concentration of its labor, material and technical resources in a certain combination, which is established within the framework of the created production and social bases and ensures their given capacity;
- their direct functioning within the construction site in the given parameters. At the same time, the first position characterizes the process of formation of the building system potential, and the second — its use.

The influence of various organizational and technological factors on the use of the labor potential of enterprises leads to its transformation in the direction of its reduction and removes the efficiency of using units in various organizational and technological situations that occur during the construction of low-rise housing projects.

Based on this, when organizing flows, it is necessary: to consider and analyze the main organizational and technological situations and the state of development of the construction system; to identify and determine the most significant factors that, in the conditions of mobility and uncertainty of construction production, affect the process of accumulation and use of the potential of construction enterprises at technological stages of processes. Their accounting allows you to more accurately determine the criteria, parameters for evaluating the options for organizing the work of specialized units in the specific conditions of the construction of low-rise housing projects.

In order to quantitatively take into account the influence of mobility conditions and construction production uncertainty factors, taking into account all three conditions of the construction system development on the activities of specialized units when organizing flows on the main construction and installation processes, it is necessary to calculate the degree of mobility of construction units on technological stages of installation processes, which can be calculated as :

$$K_{M_i}^{(G_i)} = \frac{\sum\limits_{\gamma=1}^{k}\sum\limits_{i=1}^{n}\sum\limits_{j=1}^{m} K_i^{(P_1;P_2;P_3)} \times K_i^{(P_1;P_2;P_3)} \times V_{ij\gamma}}{K_i^{(P_1;P_2;P_3)} \times K_i^{(P_1;P_2;P_3)} \times \sum\limits_{\gamma=1}^{k}\sum\limits_{i=1}^{n}\sum\limits_{j=1}^{m} V_{ij\gamma}} \qquad (12.1)$$

where:

$K_{M_i}^{(G_i)}$ — the degree of mobility of the construction unit in the i- th process for a specific organizational and technological situation $G\ _i$;

$\overline{i, n}$ — labor collectives of the construction division;

$\overline{i, m}$ — estimated period of time of their functioning in the process (month, quarter, year);

$\overline{\gamma, k}$ — is the number of construction objects;

V_{ijk} — the volume of construction and installation work performed by the construction division for all construction projects, rubles;

$K_i^{(P_1;P_2;P_3)}$; $K_i^{(P_1;P_2;P_3)}$ — mobility and reliability of the building system, its labor, technical and material resources;

$K_i^{(P_1;P_2;P_3)}$; $K_i^{(P_1;P_2;P_3)}$ — the same for normal operating conditions of the enterprise (0.90...0.95).

The degree of mobility of the construction enterprise and the dependence on the specific conditions of the construction of the object ranges from "zero" to "unity", i.e. $K_{M_i}^{(G_i)} = (0 \ldots 1)$. The influence of various factors of mobility and uncertainty on the activity of construction enterprises during these periods leads to a change in the degree of their mobility (downward), which, in turn, leads to a change in the parameters of the potential of enterprises, for example, the time of their functioning at the redistribution of their process (in side of its increase). This leads to a decrease in the level of utilization of the accumulated potential of enterprises, which, in turn, leads to a disruption in the normal course of the development of the construction process by technological stages and contributes to the formation of time losses both at their stages and between them at the junctions.

In addition, the development of various forms of labor organization in process redistribution units provides a certain reduction in time losses at each of the stages separately, but does not solve the problem as a whole throughout the process, since this increases the time loss at the joints between them.

Therefore, in order to reduce the total loss of time in the construction and installation processes when organizing flows in the conditions of transition periods mobility, it is necessary to providc for the development of such forms of labor organization at enterprises as in-line brigade-precinct consecutive at each of the processes with the establishment of rational boundaries, the union of units of enterprises of technological periods, and also a collective contract for all construction systems, their construction divisions for all construction and installation processes, I have its place at the low-rise residential construction.

12.6 Formation of rational forms of organization, management of the process of construction of low-rise residential real estate

When providing all types of processes in real construction conditions, it is necessary to compare all possible options for their support. As a result of the analysis of the external and internal environment for the future functioning and development of enterprises, the most rational option is selected (table. 12.4).

The development of the main, auxiliary and servicing production processes by enterprises is based on the rationality of combinations of available resources and the maximum use of the accumulated potential of the complex enterprises.

To this end, the construction system uses one of the possible options for their development on the basis of providing one of the possible forms of their organization (W_1, W_2, W_3) (Table 12.5).

Providing principles of rational choice embodiment should provide a mix between the different forms of real production. Each of these forms, with their positive and negative sides, at the same time should provide rational combination of resource industries.

Table 12.4 Characterization of production processes

The name of the production process	Characteristics of the production proces	Types of job
Attendan	The conditions are created for the normal development and functioning of the main and auxiliary processe	Warehousing and transportation of raw materials, materials and products, implementation of technical control. Creation of production infrastructure (transport communications, engineering networks)
Auxiliar	Final product is created that is not characteristic of the main process, but contributes to the production of main product	Repair of construction vehicles, quality control of the subject of work, manufacture of tools for own needs, repair of fixed assets, etc
Main	A part of the final product is created, objects of labor are transformed into finished products	Underground work, overhead work, from finishing work, construction and installation work, special work

The effectiveness of using each of these options should be based on taking into account the situations in which the enterprise may be, developing its production processes according to the organizational and economic redistribution of the construction complex. Each of these situations is characterized by the following main parameters:

1. P — spatial parameters of the activity.
2. T — time parameters of activity.
3. R_i — resource parameters of activity. These parameters can be in various combinations among themselves, which determines the nature of the situations themselves and the size of the total cost of their provision, i.e. S total i .

The main situations of firms' activities in the processes $(Q_1 - Q_8)$, within which rational options are used (B_3, B_4), can be presented in the form of a table (see table. 12.6).

The creation of production and social spheres within the framework of one or several forms of material production depends on the use of the following concepts.

"V_1" is a **single — branch circuit** . In a single-branch scheme, the construction units B_i are located in the zone of the head stationary complex residential and production base. The construction and commissioning of facilities and facilities is carried out in the area of daily transport accessibility l_i.

This scheme is better from the point of view of investment, but worse in terms of implementing a rational option for providing parameters, since not all characteristic situations are evaluated.

Table 12.5 Characteristic of the forms of construction production of construction organization at implementation of investment project of cottage building

	Scheme	Symbols	Criteria	Advantages and disadvantages
1	2	3	4	5
W_1	**1. bench form** 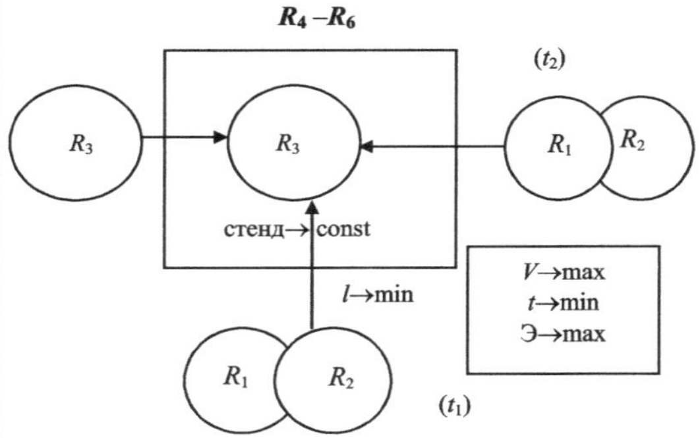 	V is the volume of the final product t is the time of creation of the final product at the special economic zone R — SEZ production resources l — moving resources E — the effectiveness of the use of options	$V \to$max, $t \to$min, $R_3 \to$min $l \to$min	**Advantages of the bench form:** 1. versatility 2. multi-purpose booth 3. there are opportunities and prerequisites for the use of a large number of machines, equipment and qualified personnel 4. requires minimal time for production preparation **Disadvantages of the poster form:** 1. Significantly long production cycle, because all work is performed sequentially 2. low level of specialization, as few jobs are done by one person 3. low level of mechanization 4. low level of labor productivity

Table 12.5 continuation

	Scheme	Symbols	Criteria	Advantages and disadvantages
1	2	3	4	5
W_2	**2. aggregate-flow form** 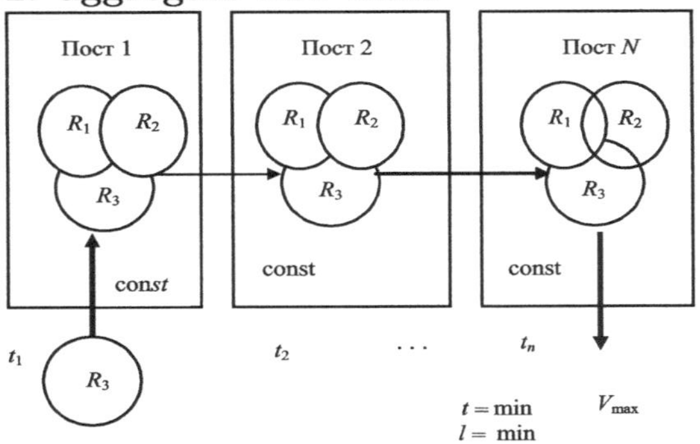	V is the volume of the final product t is the time of creation of the final product at the special economic zone R — SEZ production resources I — moving resources E — the effectiveness of the use of options	$V \to \max$, $t \to \min$, $R_3 \to \min$ $l \to \min$	**Advantages of the aggregate-flow form:** 1. created the necessary conditions for specialization and concentration of production 2. Labor productivity has sharply increased since high performance equipment 3. high level of mechanization 4. increases the rhythm of production **The disadvantages of the aggregate-flow form:** 1. loss of versatility in production and processes 2. no free region
W_3	**3. conveyor mold** 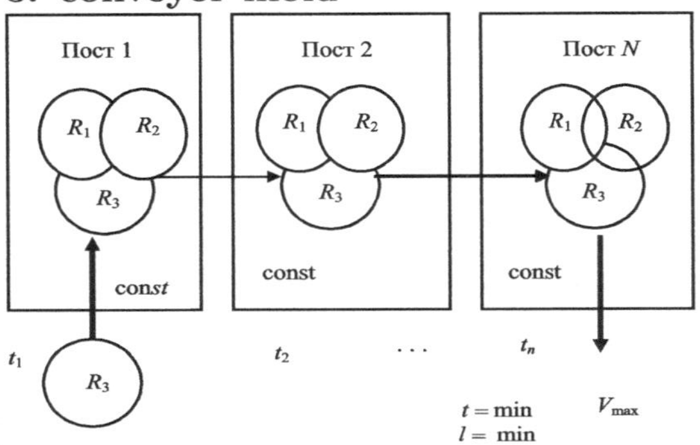	V is the volume of the final product t is the time of creation of the final product at the special economic zone R — SEZ production resources I — moving resources E — the effectiveness of the use of options	$V \to \max$, $t \to \min$, $R_3 \to \min$ $l \to \min$	**Advantages of the conveyor form:** 1. high arbitrariness of the line (flow) 2. high degree of mechanization 3. high rhythm of production **Disadvantages of the conveyor form:** 1. low versatility of the line (one or two types of products) 2. large specific capital investments that require a lot of investment 3. great complexity and time to prepare production

Table 12.6 The main organizational and economic situations of production processes in the organizational and economic redistribution

Options	Characterization of situation parameters	Possible process development options	Performance criteria for RISK enterprises
Q_1	P = const, $W_1 - W_3$	T, R_i = Var	T, $R_i \to$ min
Q_2	T = const, $W_1 - W_3$	P, R_i = Var	P, $R_i \to$ min
Q_3	R_i = const, $W_1 - W_3$	P, T = Var	T, $P \to$ min
Q_4	P, T = const, $W_1 - W_3$	R_i = Var	$R_i \to$ min
Q_5	P, R_i = const W_1-W_3	T = Var	$T \to$ min
Q_6	T, R_i = const $W_1 - W_3$	P = Var	$u \to$ min
Q_7	P, T, R_i = const $W_1 - W_3$	Var = 0	$S \to$ max
Q_8	P, T, $R_i \neq$ const $W_1 - W_3$	P, T, R_i =Var Var $\to \infty$	P, T, $R_i \to$ min $S \to$ min

"V_2" — a **two — branch scheme with the creation of an intermediate shift base.** The provision of resources is carried out by creating a shift base D_i, since the distance $\bar{l}_j$ greater than the daily transport accessibility ($\bar{l}_j > \bar{l}_i$).

"V_3" is a **two — branch scheme with the creation of an intermediate (expeditionary) base**. The provision of resources is carried out by creating the main (B_i) and expeditionary base (E_i) so that the distance between them is within the limits of daily transport accessibility. The expeditionary base is more powerful, comfortable. With its help, it is possible to concentrate resources for a period of 6 months or more.

"V_4" — a **three — branch scheme with shift and expeditionary bases.** Providing organizations with resources at the point of construction of the property (C_i) is carried out by moving them from the parent (B_i) to the regional residential and production base, then from it to a mobile base. After that, at the last stage, resources are transferred to the temporary construction infrastructure at the facility. The expeditionary form of organization provides a transition to a higher degree of mobility, since it is based on the interregional use of labor resources.

"V_5" — a **combined circuit.** Construction divisions are located in the zones of the head, auxiliary shift and expeditionary residential and production bases with reference to objects within the limits of daily transport accessibility in the presence of local bases.

The choice of the best option is carried out by comparing among themselves the various schemes for ensuring the production and social bases for specific production conditions (Table 12.7).

In the framework of the functioning of enterprises and the development of the building complex, it is necessary to use the following basic development schemes when forming options for how to move the concentration of each type of resource. The main ones are:

V_1' — all resources are supplied from one (head) base (B_i) in a certain quantity and combination;

V_2' — part of the resources is supplied from the main (head) base (B_i), part — from the regional (T) in various proportions. This method is more reliable;

V_3' — part of the resources is supplied from the main (head) base (B_i), part — from the local (mobile) (M) in various combinations;

V_4' — resources in a rational combination are delivered from the main (B_i), regional (T) and local bases (M).

Table 12.7. The main options for the functioning and development of enterprises of the construction complex at the phases of the construction cycle

option number	scheme	option description
1	2	3
phase "F1" Creation of production and social bases		
V_1	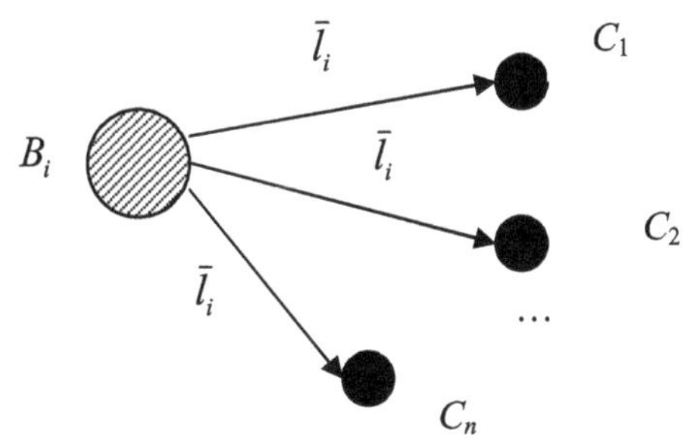	single branch circuit
1	2	3
V_2	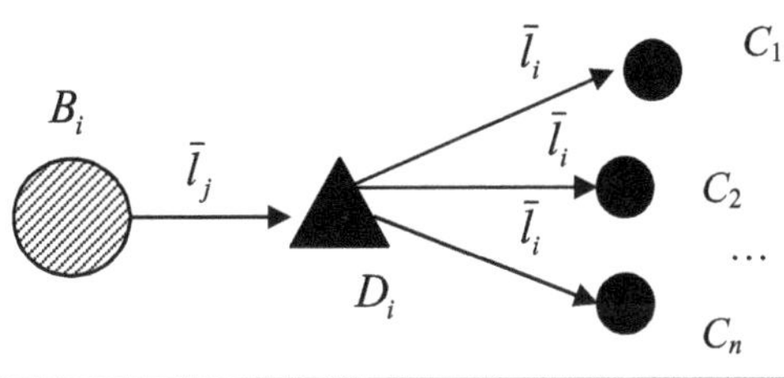	two-branch scheme (shift)
V_3	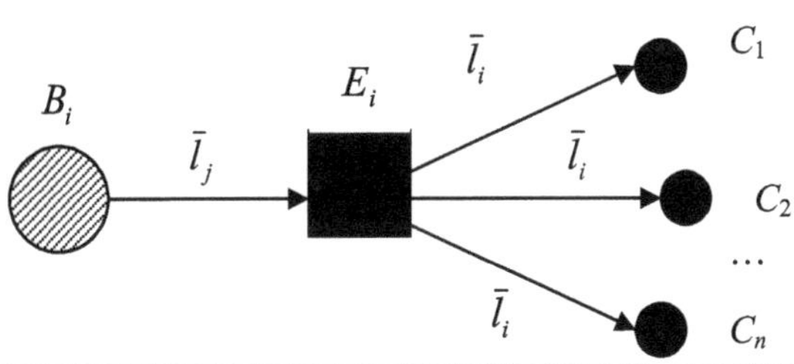	two-branch with the creation of an intermediate (expeditionary) base

V_4	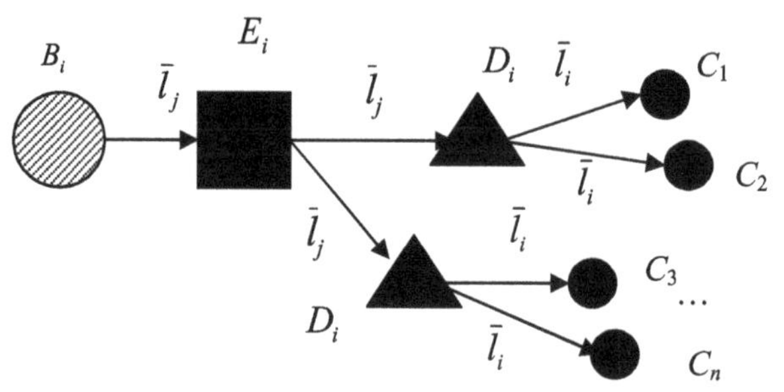	three-branch
	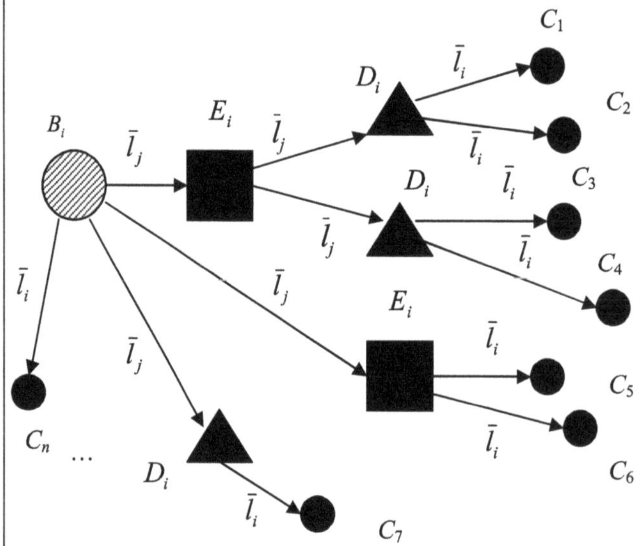	combined
phase "F2" The movement and concentration of resources of building		
V'_1	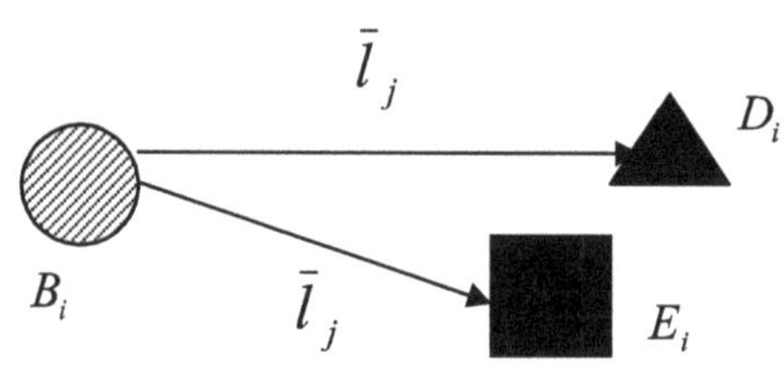	All resources are supplied from one (head) base of Bi in a certain quantity and combination
V'_2	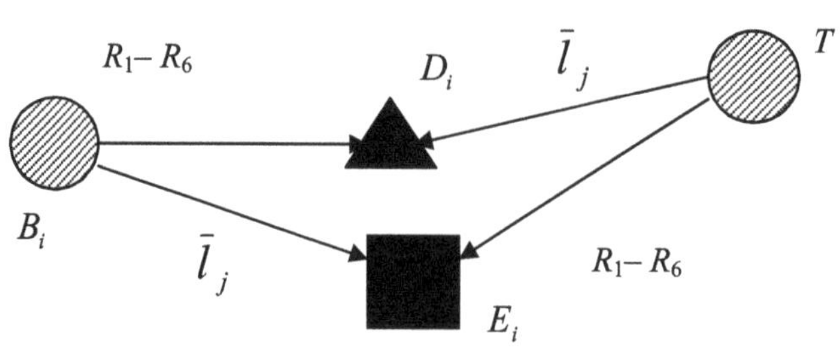	part of the resources is supplied with the base (head) base of Bı, part - from the regional (T)

V'_3	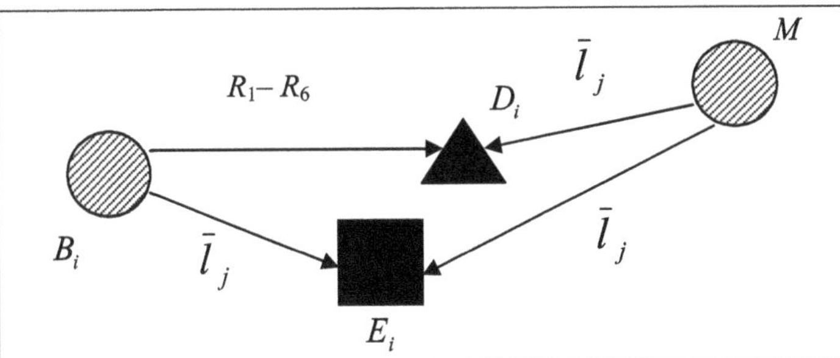	part of the resources is supplied with the base (head) base of BI, part - from the local (mobile) (M)
V'_4	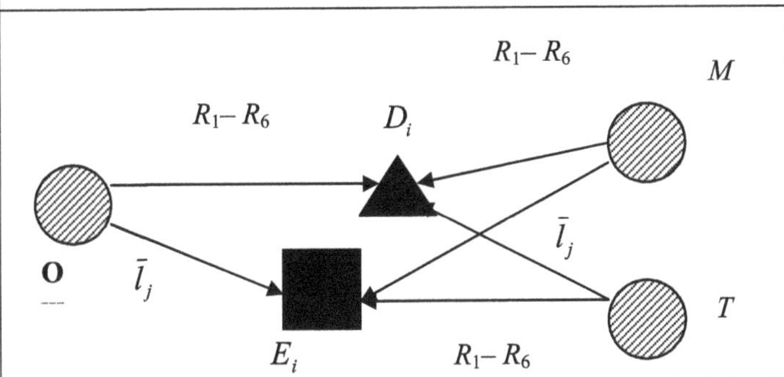	part of the resources in a rational combination comes from the main (Bi), regional (T) and local bases (M) $S \rightarrow$ min (cost)

A search of possible organizational (logistic) schemes for the functioning and development of enterprises forms a set of different organizational and economic situations in the complex, each of which is characterized by the basic parameters of the activities of all enterprises of the complex and has a large degree of dynamics and changes. Among these parameters, depending on the redistribution are:

$$B_i = f \left| \begin{array}{c} \sum S_i \rightarrow \min; \\ \sum R_i \rightarrow \min; \\ \sum t_i \rightarrow \min; \\ \sum_i \rightarrow \max; \\ \sum V_i \rightarrow \max; \\ \sum l_j \sum l_i \rightarrow \min\,. \end{array} \right| \rightarrow \text{opt.} \qquad (12.2)$$

At the same time, the assessment of the performance of both enterprises and the entire construction complex as a whole should be based on taking into account all organizational, economic, and social aspects, which determines the stage-by-stage process of their assessment, taking into account various theoretical and methodological scientific and practical principles and approaches.

12.7 The main features of the scientific organization of construction low-rise residential real estate

For the speedy commissioning of low-rise residential real estate into operation, there is a transition to stream construction. At the same time, the previously created production and social sphere of the built-up territories and their infrastructure will be used to the maximum in the construction of subsequent individual objects and cottage villages.

A system of house-building plants is being created in the places of construction of cottage villages, which contribute to the allocation of work at the main technological stages of production processes for the manufacture of special structures, their transportation to the construction site, assembly and installation.

The initial periods of the construction of cottage-type suburban villages, despite the economic development of the regions of the European part of the country, are characterized by the integrated development of the territory, due to the insufficient development of transport links, main engineering networks, fuel and energy base, material and technical base for construction, residential and household services, as well as lack of labor resources, high cost and low efficiency of living labor.

Cottage-type suburban villages are considered as dispersed objects, the construction of which occurs under conditions when the distances between them exclude the possibility of workers shifts from the main base of the construction organization to the construction objects on a shift basis, and the conditions in the places of their construction sharply differ from each other.

At the same time, the transition of labor resources from one site to another can be carried out in two ways:

- "demographic mobility" (the transition is carried out by using the organizational set to create the required number of construction units in new places of construction);
- "industrial mobility" (the transition is carried out with stable mobile specialized construction units of organizations).

The movement of people with demographic mobility plays a dual role: firstly, it accelerates the process of overpopulation of people from one region of the country to another and is one of the existing methods of developing new regions; secondly, it does not always lead to the proper effect if this process is poorly prepared. This method is characterized by huge costs for creating a socio-spatial infrastructure near construction sites. Demographic mobility of labor resources, on the one hand, helps to ensure the maximum value of the actual fund of time for workers, since it does not require the cost of their movement more than the distance of daily transport accessibility, but, on the other hand, the costs of this type of mobility reach significant values.

Another method ("industrial mobility") compared with the first method, especially when it is necessary to ensure the concentration of specialized units for a certain period, has a number of significant advantages, which makes it highly efficient under these conditions. For example, significant costs are reduced for the creation and development of the social sphere near construction sites, the level of qualifications of workers in specialized mobile units is much higher than for workers in organizational recruitment, people live with families in normal conditions in places of permanent residence; in the building production system, specialized units (as its element) have their own specifics, which is as follows:

- firstly, a frequent change of work and constantly changing social infrastructure leads to the fact that the adaptation of a person to new conditions requires a longer time than for means of production;
- secondly, the development of the social sphere affects only a person, since it is typical for him to satisfy non-future ("postponed for later") needs, in everyday, that is, current, that determine his daily performance;
- thirdly, in the conditions of mobility of construction of low-rise housing construction objects, the movement of material and technical resources is largely determined by the organization of their distribution among the objects. They can be quickly moved and concentrated in any region of the country, gaining a foothold for the entire period of existence. For the movement and concentration of construction units in the construction sites of low-rise housing, it is necessary to create certain incentives based on a large number of measures that require additional capital investments and time for their implementation, therefore, the consolidation of mobile construction enterprises in new places and the effective use of their labor potential is probabilistic nature.

Thus, during the construction of suburban cottage-type villages, there are features that determine the working conditions of construction enterprises and organizations and characterize:

- a transitional period during the construction of each village due to the need to organize the transfer of stable or the creation of new specialized units;
- the presence of complex work requiring the use of highly qualified specialized construction personnel, especially during transitional periods;
- the presence of organizational difficulties in the transfer of stable or the creation of new specialized units of construction enterprises in places of construction of low-rise housing.

An important condition for the introduction of new options for the organization of construction is the use of new technologies in the construction of low-rise residential real estate, the main of which is wooden low-rise housing construction.

12.8 The main trends in the commissioning of low-rise residential development by the example of a development company

A) Non-public joint-stock company "Development Corporation "Antei" was established in 2005 to implement investment and construction projects of low-rise residential complexes. The corporation's team has been professionally engaged in the implementation of low-rise housing projects using energy-saving technologies since 1992. During this time, Antey DK JSC has built many residential and industrial facilities, the best of which, in terms of the quality of living conditions, is Polyanka residential complex in Pushkin district of the Moscow region, where more than a thousand people live on an area of 50 hectares.

Since 2007, Kazan residents have been discovering the European lifestyle in the **Svetly Residential Complex**.

The territory of the unique residential district "Svetly" is located just a few minutes drive from the heart of a large boiling city. The highlight of the location of the complex is not only proximity to Kazan, however ecology, which is one of the best in the Republic of Tatarstan. In the immediate vicinity of the residential complex there are a birch grove and local clean lakes, which prevents the appearance of polluted air and creates an ideal resting place for lovers of peace, comfort and coziness.

The stylistics of all buildings in the Svetly residential area is subordinated to a single composition, which together with the developing infrastructure exquisitely emphasizes the ease and modernity of the new lifestyle. Twelve, eighteen and twenty-apartment single-entry houses were built using innovative construction technologies and engineering solutions.

B) Energy-efficient technologies of low-rise housing construction

In the Svetly residential complex, houses were built using the energy-efficient technology of low-rise housing construction LSTK (light steel thin-walled structures). According to the results of an independent non-state examination No. 77-2-1-2-0192-16 of November 14, 2016, the model frame-panel 18-apartment building was assigned energy efficiency class B.

A pile foundation with a grillage with a cross section of 30 × 90 cm was designed. — The economic benefit of using this foundation is up to 40% compared to the block one (labor-saving — no earthwork). The use of the pile foundation in the Svetly residential complex is due to the geology of local soils (wet-porous soils, clay lenses). Piles pass through the upper soil layers and plunge into mainland soil. This technology allows you to perform work at any time of the year.

Figure 12.5: Svetly Residential Complex.

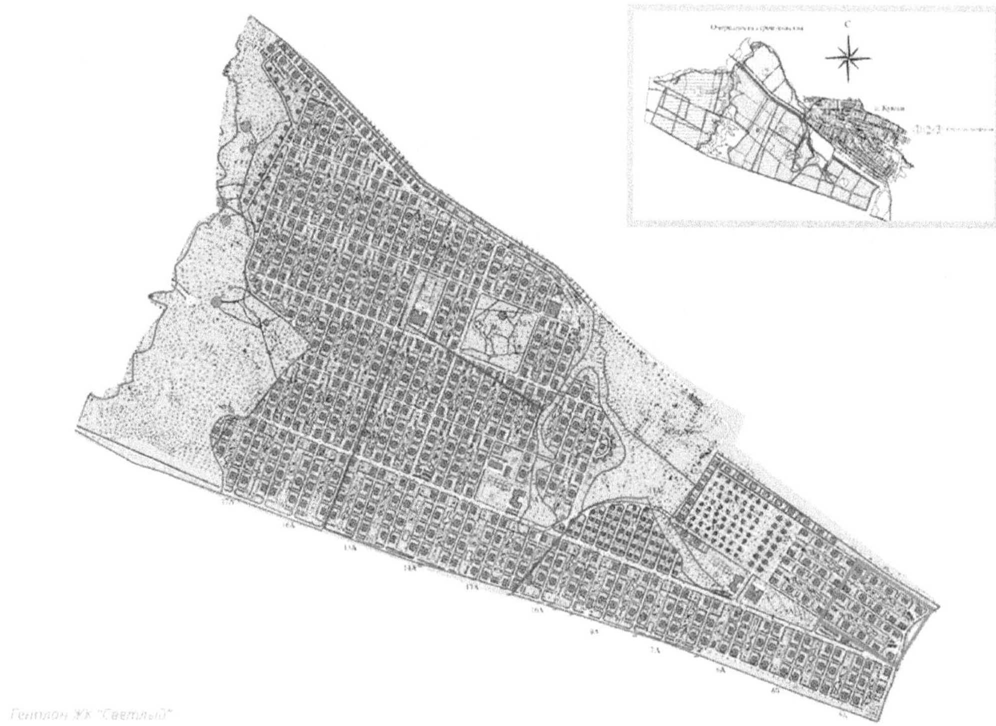

Figure 12.6: General plan of Svetly Residential Complex.

Piles are immersed by the indentation method by the SVU-V-6 installation (due to the installation weight of 74 tons). The pile installation process consists of the following operations:

- pulling and lifting piles;
- installation of piles in the place of immersion;
- a headband is fixed on the pile head, which transfers pressure from the base machine to the pile, which, thanks to this pressure, gradually sinks into the ground. After reaching the design mark and bearing capacity, the dive is stopped, the headband is dismantled, the unit moves to a new position. In cases of shortage of bearing capacity at a distance of 400–500 mm, a duplicate pile is immersed.

Next, the aboveground part of the pile (tip) is crushed, while maintaining the supporting reinforcement for release into the grillage (at least 400 mm). Then the reinforcement of the belt connecting the piles is carried out and concreted. This design serves to transfer the load of the wall weight to the pile base.

After concrete pouring is completed, brickwork of the grillage is completed to the design level and reinforced with 100x100 mm masonry mesh.

Overlapping of 1,2,3 floors is carried out according to the technology of fixed formwork from profiled sheet H114–750 mm, or H114–600 mm 150 mm thick with fastening of a bent galvanized profile 150 mm around the perimeter of the floors. Reinforcement is performed by fittings f12 mm, f14 mm and f18 mm along the stiffeners of the profiled sheet with additional reinforcement by masonry mesh with a mesh size of 150x150 mm in the concrete body. Stacked concrete grade M400.

The panels of walls and partitions are made of galvanized profile 150 mm, 100 mm and 80 mm with a thickness of 1.0 mm, 1.2 mm, and 1.5 mm according to the design documentation. External wall panels are fastened with anchors to the concrete floor, internal — with the help of special screws along the entire height of the extreme profile to the adjacent panel.

Rafter trusses and roof overhang panels are made of 100 mm galvanized profile with a thickness of 1.0 mm and 1.2 mm. When installing truss trusses along the perimeter of the outer walls, as well as in places adjacent to the inner walls and partitions, a board of 150×50 mm and 100×50 mm is installed using insulating materials. During the installation of truss trusses, the verticality of their installation is strictly checked (vertical tolerance +/–5 mm).

Particular attention when installing overhang panels should be given to the additional fastening of the perforated corner 100×100 mm to the roof trusses.

After the installation of the truss trusses, the roof battens are fixed along the trusses. It is performed using boards of 100×25 mm. The waterproofing of the roof of the Izospan D type is fastened using 100×25 mm boards along the crate of 100x25 mm boards along the truss trusses. After completion of the waterproofing, a counter-lattice of a roof made of 100×50 mm timber is arranged.

After completing work on the device of the counter-lattice, the metal tiles are laid with the device of the drainage system.

The cells in the walls are filled with basalt insulation with a thickness of 15–20 cm and a density of 35 kg/m^3 with a vapor barrier on the inside of the premises. Applied energy-saving modern technology using effective heaters can reduce energy costs.

On average, savings in the heating season are 40–50% of the costs for heating similar houses built using traditional technologies.

The inner walls are sheathed with drywall in 2 layers (12.5 mm each). In public places, the lining is made in 3 layers. The walls in the bathrooms are sheathed with 2 layers of moisture-proof drywall. The pitch of the self-tapping screws of the 1st layer of plating should be no more than 600 mm, the pitch of the self-tapping screws when plating with the 2nd layer of drywall is not more than 250 mm.

The stairwell is laid out of solid brick with reinforcement with masonry mesh mesh size 100×100 mm.

The internal walls of the mine are plastered with lime mortar, followed by the application of the finishing layer and painting with water-dispersion paint in 2 layers. The device of staircases is made according to the brackets from channel 18, installed on reinforced concrete lintels according to design marks, fixed formwork from profiled sheet H60, with reinforcement device from bar reinforcement 12 mm and laying concrete M350. After the concrete laying works, the installation of reinforced concrete stair steps of the LS-11 brand is carried out with grouting of the joints with cement-sand mortar M100.

The final exterior finish of the Senargi brand is a combined building thermal protection system consisting of a heat-insulating material on which a reinforcing layer is applied, and then a finishing layer. This system is quick and easy to install, environmentally friendly, does not respond to temperature changes, does not crack, is steam-pipe.

1. The base of the OSB wall (oriented particle board);
2. Thermal insulation layer (basalt insulation — fire cuts, polystyrene foam);
3. Fixture for heat-insulating plates;
4. Reinforcing plaster composition (adhesive);
5. Glass mesh reinforcing reinforcement;
6. Finishing plaster layers with painting.

After the construction of the house is completed, roads, parking lots, soil leveling with the subsequent laying of black soil, landscaping with a lawn and tree planting are underway.

At the moment, more than 130 houses have been built in the Svetly Residential Complex, with about 5,000 inhabitants.

Despite the expressed priorities of supply and demand in the direction of low-rise housing construction, the current economic mechanism for the development of territorial low-rise housing markets (MLS) is still not quite effective. It is not focused on priority urban planning for the development of urban areas in the direction of the formation of suburban ecological low-rise areas of population. As you know, the cluster of multistory building companies is very competitive. Land plots of comparable size are more profitable and attractive for investors, which makes low-rise developers less competitive than traditionally operating companies.

Another problem for the development of MZHS is the high cost of land for the construction of low-rise housing, which can be up to half the cost of construction. Land markets preceding the construction process in low-rise housing construction currently do not sufficiently reflect the priority of low-rise construction. The land plots currently being offered for development for complex low-rise buildings, as well as individual housing construction, are mostly not attractive due to the high cost of technical conditions, the connection of external engineering networks, and the high cost of connection fees.

The scientific aspects include the need to significantly increase the level of cost, energy efficiency, energy saving and environmental friendliness of all low-rise construction projects, as a prerequisite for the formation of competitive advantages of MZHS over multi-story buildings.

The above-mentioned main modern key problematic factors of efficiency, like many others, require innovative changes in the economic mechanism of functioning both in corporate development systems for customer developers and in state-municipal program-targeted regulation of development priorities for this segment of the housing market.

Questions for self-control

1. What are the main organizational and technological schemes of wooden low-rise housing construction.
2. List the main steps to create optimal conditions when assessing the choice of site for construction.
3. Formulate the main features of the organization of construction.
4. Expand the features of commercial and non-commercial areas of construction of cottages.
5. List and disclose the main stages of production planning at the construction stage of low-rise housing construction.
6. Expand the order and essence of holding production meetings and meetings during the construction of low-rise residential real estate.
7. Expand the essence and advantages of the block construction of low-rise residential real estate.
8. Expand the essence and advantages of expeditionary-shift forms of labor organization in the construction of low-rise residential real estate.
9. Expand the features and benefits of increasing the mobility of construction in low-rise housing.
10. List the main forms of material production, organization, management of the process of construction of construction objects. What are the advantages and disadvantages of the "bench" form of material production?

11. What are the main organizational and economic situations of production processes.
12. List and disclose the main options for the functioning and development of enterprises in the phases of the construction cycle.
13. What are the main features of the scientific organization of the construction of low-rise residential real estate.

Questions for discussion

1. Consider the basic organizational and technological schemes of wooden low-rise housing construction. Give a description of each of them and how you can take into account their degree of influence when choosing effective options for wooden low-rise housing construction.
2. Describe the role and place of each form of material production in the construction and reconstruction of real estate.
3. Describe the role of modern methods of organizing the construction of low-rise residential real estate and their impact on improving the efficiency of construction production.
4. Outline the main steps to create optimal conditions when assessing the choice of site for construction. Describe their features of their use.
5. What is meant by the features of the scientific organization of the construction of low-rise residential real estate objects. Describe the content of each of them during the construction of low-rise residential real estate.

Questions to solve the problem yourself

1. Formulate the requirements for the use of the main organizational and technological schemes of wooden low-rise housing construction.
2. Name and research the main reasons for the inefficient use of the aggregate-flow and conveyor forms of material production in the conditions of the modern real estate market.
3. Expand the basic principles of the flow form of organization and management of production during the development of production processes in low-rise construction of residential real estate, requiring their permission.
4. Consider the main criteria for assessing organizational and economic situations when choosing rational options for the development of processes used in construction, give them an assessment of the role of their influence on the efficiency of using various forms of material production

5. Expand the provisions and approaches, the implementation of which will increase the efficiency of using flow forms of organization of production and various types of models.
6. Consider the main options for the phases of the construction cycle; give them an assessment of the role of their influence on the efficiency of using in-line forms of material production.

CONSTRUCTION MANAGEMENT
and
REAL ESTATE DEVELOPMENT

The textbook in two parts

Under the general scientific editorship of Professor P.G. Graboviy

PART I

ASV Construction, Sweden,
Mårdvägen 16 131 50 Saltsjö-Duvnäs e-mail: iasv@iasv.ru

Milton Keynes UK
Ingram Content Group UK Ltd.
UKHW031809161123
432711UK00009B/607

9 789198 222388